# Thomas Jefferson's
# Garden Book

THOMAS JEFFERSON

*From the painting by Thomas Sully*

# THOMAS JEFFERSON'S
# GARDEN BOOK
## 1766–1824

*With relevant extracts from*
*his other writings*

ANNOTATED BY

## EDWIN MORRIS BETTS

*Assistant Professor of Biology, Miller School of Biology*
*University of Virginia*

### WITH INTRODUCTION BY PETER J. HATCH

*Director of Gardens and Grounds*
*Monticello*

PUBLISHED BY
THOMAS JEFFERSON MEMORIAL FOUNDATION, INC.
1999

For assistance with the 1999 printing of this volume, the
Thomas Jefferson Memorial Foundation wishes to thank the
Massachusetts Historical Society and the American
Philosophical Society, as well as to acknowledge access to the
Edwin M. Betts Papers (#5980), Special Collections
Department, at the University of Virginia Library.

The 1999 printing of *Thomas Jefferson's Garden Book* was
made possible by a gift from Mrs. W. L. Lyons Brown, Sr.

Jacket illustration: *Jeffersonia diphylla*, or Twinleaf

Book production and coordination by Laing Communications,
Redmond, Washington

ISBN 1-882886-11-9

Printed in the United States of America

# PREFACE

WHEN Thomas Jefferson died on July 4, 1826, he left behind one of the richest treasures of personal and public documents in America. He named his oldest grandson, Thomas Jefferson Randolph, the executor of his estate, and stated in his will: "My papers of business going of course to him as my executor, all others of a literary or other character I give to him as of his own property." Since *Edgehill* later became the home of Thomas Jefferson Randolph, the bulk of Jefferson's papers were moved there from *Monticello*.

In 1848 a collection of Jefferson's public papers was purchased by the United States Government and deposited in the Library of the State Department, to be transferred later to the Division of Manuscripts of the Library of Congress. The private papers remained in possession of the Randolph family until 1898, when Jefferson's great-grandson, Thomas Jefferson Coolidge, of Boston, the son of Ellen Randolph and Joseph Coolidge, purchased about seven thousand pieces and gave them on June 9, of the same year, to the Massachusetts Historical Society. Among these items was the original *Garden Book*.

This *Garden Book* contains the most varied entries of all of Jefferson's memorandum books. The book that began as a diary of the garden became a written repository for numerous interests of Jefferson. The entries range from contracts with overseers, plans for building roads and fish ponds, and observations on the greatest flood in Albemarle, to comments on Mrs. Wythe's wine and figures on the number of strawberries in a pint measure. Here is revealed what was probably the most absorbing of all the interests of one who was the foremost philosopher of his time, Governor of Virginia, Secretary of State in President Washington's cabinet, Vice President and President of the United States, President of the American Philosophical Society for eighteen years, and founder of the University of Virginia. He was possessed of a love of nature so intense that his observant eye caught almost every

passing change in it.   And whatever he saw rarely escaped
being recorded.   So we know when the first purple hyacinth
blooms in the spring, when peas are up, when they blossom
and pod, and when they are ready for the table.   We are further informed that *Lunaria* and Eastern Mallow are indifferent flowers, that *Mirabilis* is very clever, that peaches and
almonds blossom on certain days, and that according to old
Sharpe a bushel of lime will weigh one hundred and fourteen
pounds.   One wonders how a man with so many other interests and with the multitudinous duties of his offices could have
found the time to record all these observations.

The varied entries in the *Garden Book* not only show us
what Jefferson was doing and planting at *Monticello, Poplar
Forest,* and his other estates, but also give us a clue as to his
interests in introducing new plants and in improving farming,
horticulture, viticulture, and many other aspects of the rural
life of his time.   The gardens and groves at *Monticello* became experimental plots where new plants were introduced
and nurtured, and if they were found suitable for use or ornament, they were passed on to interested neighbors and friends
in various parts of the country.

That these interests at *Monticello* were also tied up with
the agricultural and horticultural needs of the United States,
is shown in part by Jefferson's attempt to introduce the cultivation of olive trees and dry rice into South Carolina and
Georgia, mainly for the purpose of improving the living conditions of the slaves and saving them from the ravages of
disease that swept the low countries.   He was equally interested in cultivating a grape that would produce a wine comparable to those of Europe.   Further he invented a "mould-
board of least resistance" and kept improving it over a period
of years so that plowing could be done more scientifically.
Then with the aid of his son-in-law, Thomas Mann Randolph,
he introduced contour plowing at *Monticello,* an innovation
which soon spread rapidly over the nation.   His practice of
sending plants from Europe to America when he was living in
France was a forerunner of what our Division of Plant Exploration and Introduction has since done with mounting success.   Even the Lewis and Clark Expedition had as one of its
fundamental purposes the collection of native Western plants
for the purpose of experimental cultivation in the East.   Some

of these plants were grown in Jefferson's gardens at *Monti-cello* and in the gardens of Bernard McMahon and William Hamilton, of Philadelphia.    Certain of them, such as *Lewisia, Clarkia, Mahonia, Maclura,* and a species of *Symphoricarpos,* now hold a recognized place in ornamental horticulture.

In summarizing what he considered his most important serv-ices to man, Jefferson mentions the introduction of the olive tree and dry rice into South Carolina.    He ranks these along with the writing of the Declaration of Independence, his advo-cating freedom of religion, abolishing the law of entails, and striving to diffuse knowledge more widely.    He concludes the note on his effort to introduce dry rice into South Carolina by saying: "The greatest service which can be rendered any coun-try is, to add an useful plant to its culture; especially, a bread grain; next in value is oil."    In a letter to M. Giroud, after thanking him for the seeds of the bread tree he had sent, Jef-ferson writes: "One service of this kind rendered to a nation, is worth more to them than all the victories of the most splen-did pages of their history, and becomes a source of exalted pleasure to those who have been instrumental in it."    That introducing new plants into cultivation was a passion with him will be noted throughout the *Garden Book*.

Jefferson began the *Garden Book* in 1766 and continued it until the autumn of 1824, two years before his death.    There were necessarily many lapses in it, caused in part by Jefferson's frequent and lengthy absences from *Monticello*.    The most extensive absence occurred from 1784 to 1789, when he served as Minister Plenipotentiary to France.    Even in the years in which he spent much of his time at *Monticello,* the entries are often irregular.    Also, Jefferson used memorandum books other than the *Garden Book* in which to record his planting activities.    For instance, the notes on gardening for 1795 and 1796 were jotted down in the *Farm Book,* while those of 1807 and 1808 were written in the *Weather Memorandum Book 1776–1820*.    Then, too, he often wrote down impor-tant garden matters on odd sheets of paper.    Occasionally Jefferson took pains to copy into his *Garden Book* observations recorded originally in these other memoranda.

In order to get a complete picture of Jefferson's gardening and agricultural interests, one must also continually consult his correspondence.    In his letters Jefferson expressed his theories

on agriculture and gardening, told what he was planting, inquired after the gardens and farms of friends and neighbors,
requested plants from them, and ordered plants and seeds from
nurseries and seedsmen.   His correspondents often reciprocated with valuable information and on numerous occasions
they sent plants and seeds.

In annotating the *Garden Book,* I have therefore felt it
necessary to add copious notes.   Relevant material has been
taken from the *Farm Book,* the *Weather Memorandum Book
1776–1820,* account books, stray memoranda, and letters.
Since the *Garden Book* is in chronological order, each year is
treated separately, with a brief outline of Jefferson's principal
activities, followed by notes and letters.   An effort has also
been made to fill the gaps in the *Garden Book* by presenting
all related material from other sources.   Additional pertinent information has been given in the form of appendices.
Throughout, I have adhered faithfully to Jefferson's orthography.   In only a few instances have the annotations been
extended beyond the *Garden Book* to Jefferson's other writings.   No attempt has been made to compare the currency
values of Jefferson's time with those of to-day because of the
constant fluctuation of monetary standards in the Jeffersonian
era.   The reader should keep this in mind when he considers
the prices that Jefferson paid for plants and services of various
kinds.

In April, 1939, the American Philosophical Society awarded
the late Rodney H. True, of the University of Pennsylvania,
a grant from the Penrose Fund to edit for publication Jefferson's *Garden Book.*   Dr. True had long been a student of
Jefferson and was, through his botanical knowledge, especially
fitted to edit the *Garden Book.*   Unfortunately, however,
after securing a careful transcription of the text, he lived long
enough to write only the first draft of an introduction, the
principal ideas of which have been incorporated into this
preface.   The grant was later transferred to me, with the
request that I prepare a "definitive" edition of the *Garden
Book,* taking into account Jefferson's deep interest in general
agriculture as well as in gardening—an interest that appears
constantly not only in his *Farm Book* but also in his account
books and letters.

Although a large amount of material has been introduced here, much of it published for the first time, there still remains related material not available for publication. Not until this material is released can there be a strictly definitive account of Jefferson's agricultural and horticultural pursuits. Princeton University is undertaking to publish the complete correspondence, writings, addresses, drawings, and miscellaneous documents of Thomas Jefferson. The project is under the general direction of a committee with Dr. Douglas S. Freeman as chairman, and with Dr. Julian P. Boyd as editor.

It is a pleasure to thank the following institutions for permission to publish Jefferson manuscripts: the Massachusetts Historical Society, for the *Garden Book*, the *Farm Book*, the *Account Books 1771, 1772, 1774, 1776–1778, 1783–1790, 1804–1808, 1809–1820,* and *1821–1826,* and many of Jefferson's drawings and letters; the Library of Congress, for letters, the *Weather Memorandum Book 1776–1820,* and *Account Books 1767–1770, 1773,* and *1779–1782;* the Henry E. Huntington Library and Art Gallery, for drawings, letters, and the *Account Book 1775;* the New York Public Library, for the *Account Book 1791–1803;* the Yale University Library, for letters; the Maryland Historical Society, for letters; the Missouri Historical Society, for letters; the Rosenbach Company, of Philadelphia, for letters and memoranda; the Thomas Jefferson Memorial Foundation, for letters; the United States Department of Agriculture, for letters; and the Alderman Memorial Library, University of Virginia, for letters and memoranda.

It is also a pleasure to thank Brigadier General Jefferson R. Kean for permission to quote from the *Account Book 1767–1770,* which is at present deposited in the Library of Congress.

I wish further to express my appreciation to the following publishers and individuals who have given permission to quote excerpts from their published works: Charles Scribner's Sons, Dr. Gilbert Chinard, Miss Norma B. Cuthbert, Dr. Cecil Garlick, Dr. Fiske Kimball, Missouri Historical Society, Miss Mary Rawlings, Dr. E. G. Swem for Miss Marjorie Warner, and Mrs. Lyon G. Tyler.

My especial thanks are due the following persons: the staff of the Rare Book and Manuscript Division of the University of Virginia Library, for their assistance in securing manuscripts and books, and for helpful suggestions; Miss Norma B. Cuthbert, of the Huntington Library and Art Gallery, for aid in securing photostats and for other courtesies; Dr. Fiske Kimball, for valuable assistance; Mrs. Helen Bullock, for suggestions from her wide knowledge of Jefferson manuscripts; my colleagues, Dr. Bernard Mayo and Dr. C. William Miller, for a critical reading of the manuscript; Mrs. Ida D. Swindler, for typing and checking the manuscript; and my wife, Mary Hall Betts, for designing and drawing the paper jacket of the *Garden Book* and assisting me in innumerable ways.

Finally I wish to express my deep gratitude to the American Philosophical Society which made this publication possible. It was this Society that welcomed Jefferson to membership in 1780. During the following forty-six years he was respectively a Councilor of the society, its Vice President, and from 1797 to 1815 its President. In 1818 he was again elected a Councilor and served in that capacity until his death in 1826. While a member of the Society Jefferson took an active part in its meetings. He contributed papers to the *Transactions,* gave fossils and other objects of natural history to the cabinet, and books to the library. Since he contributed so generously to the life of the society and served it so selflessly for many years, it is fitting that in the bicentennial year of his birth the society should honor him by publishing the *Garden Book* in its *Memoirs.*

E. M. B.

UNIVERSITY OF VIRGINIA
CHARLOTTESVILLE, VIRGINIA
*September 20, 1943* [1]

---

[1] Because of government restrictions on the use of paper, publication of this work has been deferred of necessity until 1944.

# CONTENTS

# ILLUSTRATIONS

Thomas Jefferson, from the Painting by Thomas Sully

*Frontispiece*

# INTRODUCTION

THE EDWIN MORRIS BETTS edition of *Thomas Jefferson's Garden Book* reprinted here is much more than the transcription of the horticultural diary of the sage of Monticello. The Garden Book itself, which resides in the Massachusetts Historical Society, consists of sporadic and rather mundane horticultural notations, culminating in the detailed *Kalendar* Jefferson kept for his kitchen garden between 1809 and 1824. Although an enduring testament to the horticultural imagination of Mr. Jefferson, the Garden Book itself makes up only fifteen percent of Betts's classic volume, first published by the American Philosophical Society in 1944. The remaining eighty-five percent of *Thomas Jefferson's Garden Book*—the compelling letters, extensive annotation, various unpublished memoranda, and selections from the Farm, Account, and Weather Memorandum Books—is the work of Mr. Betts, a traditional scholar of the first rank who, according to former Monticello Director and Curator James A. Bear, Jr., "read more Jefferson manuscripts than anyone else on earth."

Edwin Morris Betts [1892–1958] was professor of biology at the University of Virginia for thirty-one years. He first became interested in Jefferson's gardening and farming pursuits while studying the trees Jefferson imported from abroad for planting on the grounds of the University. His scholarly legacy also includes his editing of *Thomas Jefferson's Farm Book* (American Philosophical Society, 1953) and, with James A. Bear, *The Family Letters of Thomas Jefferson* (Missouri, 1956). He also co-authored *Thomas Jefferson's Flower Garden at Monticello* (Virginia, 1941). With his botanical knowledge and unrelenting devotion to detail, Edwin Betts was a perfect match for editing and interpreting the garden world of Thomas Jefferson.

Thomas Jefferson gardened during the infancy of American horticulture, and while the documentary record about gardens in the colonial and early republic has swelled with the resurgence of interest in garden history, *Thomas Jefferson's Garden Book* is a singular resource to plant introduction, landscape design, early American agriculture, and fruit, vegetable, and ornamental gardening. Perhaps more importantly, I often argue that few topics reveal the human or personal Thomas Jefferson as well as gardening, and that *Thomas Jefferson's Garden Book* is the emphatic expression of the intellectual and emotional sensibility of the sage of Monticello. It tells us some important lessons about Jefferson.

First of all, I think Jefferson's interest in gardening arose from a wide-eyed sense of wonder about the natural world. When he said, "There is not a shoot of grass that springs uninteresting to me," or in the Garden Book on July 18 of 1767, when he said of the common prickly poppy flower, "this is the 4th of the year," his enthusiasm reflected an almost childlike appreciation of the natural world around him. He wrote, "How sublime to look upon the workhouse of nature—to see her clouds, hail, snow, rain, thunder, all fabricated at our feet." Surely, for Jefferson, the landscape was a workhouse, the gardens of Monticello became an experimental laboratory, and Jefferson himself was very much the scientist as he observed and defined seemingly all the natural phenomena around him—whether the wind direction or the blooming dates of the wildflowers in the spring. At the same time, the *Garden Book* is a testament to Jefferson as a garden scientist. Jefferson was forever measuring, always meticulous, maddeningly methodical—counting, for example, the number of Carolina beans which would fill a quart jar, which would in turn plant so many feet of rows.

We also see Jefferson's love of botany, "the most valuable of the sciences." The botanical historian Joseph Ewan has remarked how Jefferson looked at botany not through the magnifying lens of the field taxonomist, but rather with a market basket in hand. Not a botanical theoretician, Jefferson was a "horto-botanist" whose paramount passion was the practical or horticultural uses of plants. Through his sponsorship of the Lewis and Clark expedition, and his active participation in the American Philosophical Society and the Albemarle Agricultural Society, Jefferson set a standard for the advancement of natural history and science that, perhaps with the exception of Theodore Roosevelt, has never been equaled by a leading American public servant.

Like all scientists Jefferson's horticultural efforts were essentially experimental, and Monticello became a botanic garden, an experimental station of new and unusual introductions from around the world. The variety of sources for the plants grown at Monticello testifies to the range of his horticultural interests—whether the Quarantine corn brought back by the Lewis and Clark expedition, the numerous peach and grape varieties sent from Italy by friend Philip Mazzei, or the Texas bird pepper sent by Samuel Brown from San Antonio in 1814. Monticello was an Ellis Island of immigrant crops. Plants were a vehicle for social change, a means of transforming the social and economic culture of the young republic.

Another theme evident in the *Garden Book* is Jefferson's unflinching attention to non-germinating seeds and crop failure. Few gardeners failed as often as Jefferson, or else few confessed to failure as often as he did. The *Garden Book* reveals a holistic view of the gardening process. As the Hessian fly was devouring the Monticello wheat harvest, Jefferson seemed more concerned with the life cycle of this destructive pest than the demise of his money crop. Weeds were a source of green manure rather than thieves of soil fertility. When he wrote that in gardening, "The failure of one thing is repaired by the success of another," he was expressing confidence in the wholesome balance of unhindered nature and the cultivated garden.

The *Garden Book* also reveals Jefferson as a nativist, a strong proponent of the natural products of the New World. As Minister to France Jefferson aggressively imported seeds of American trees and shrubs, and he cultivated Indian corn outside his French hôtel. His *Notes on the State of Virginia* was a patriotic treatise, composed in part to refute the European theories of continental degeneracy in the Western Hemisphere. The ornamental plantings around the house at Monticello include a pleasing complement of American native plants—from the tulip trees, the "Juno of our Groves," he planted at the corners or "angles," of the house, to the cardinal flower and sweet four o'clock planted in the flower borders. Twenty-five percent of the herbaceous ornamentals and fifty percent of the trees planted by Jefferson were North American natives. The Monticello Grove, an ornamental forest of eighteen acres on the northwest slope of Monticello mountain, was also an expression of Jefferson's love of native landscape. In America, he said, "gardens may be made without expense. We have only to cut out the superabundant plants."

The letters in the *Garden Book* also reveal how gardening for Jefferson was a way of relating to people: garden commentary was a common thread in his friendships, his family relationships, even his political collaborations. The gardens at Monticello hardly existed in a horticultural vacuum, but were nourished generously by a society of local, national, and international gardeners. The famous spring pea contests, where Jefferson and his neighbors competed for the first spring dish, illustrated how gardening was a vehicle for social intercourse. Similarly, the garden gossip between Jefferson and his granddaughters, and his moving correspondence with friends like Margaret Bayard Smith and Madame de Tessé, reveal the union of gardening and sociability.

Biographers have consistently defined Jefferson as a man of contradictions; they depict a mind in perennial oscillation between conflicting ideologies. Jefferson's ideas on the organization of the landscape evolved dramatically over a lifetime of garden design. His early plans for the grounds at Monticello demonstrate a geometric rigor, a strong adherence to regularity and mathematical precision. However, after his 1786 English garden tour he wrote, "The gardening in that country is the article in which it surpasses all the earth. I mean their pleasure gardening." Jefferson was smitten by the English gardening movement, where garden designers consciously imitated the picturesque style of eighteenth-century landscape painters. Jefferson's Monticello landscape eventually included English-style serpentine walkways, clumps of trees, open lawns with shrubberies, and an ornamental, naturalistic Grove. Nevertheless, after 1812, Jefferson returned to formal plantings at his summer retreat, Poplar Forest, where he deliberately designed a landscape in which the organization of the gardens was a clear reflection of the geometric architecture of the house.

Gardening was also the source for a fountain of literary expression by Thomas Jefferson. On May 26, 1811, he wrote Anne Cary Bankhead, his granddaughter:

> Nothing new has happened in our neighborhood . . . the houses and the trees stand where they did. The flowers come forth like the belles of the day, have their short reign of beauty and splendor, and retire, like them, to the more interesting offices of reproducing their like. The Hyacinths and Tulips are off the stage, the Irises are giving place to the Belladonnas, as these will the Tuberoses—as your mama has done to you, my dear Anne, as you will do to the sisters of little John, and as I shall soon and cheerfully do to you all in wishing you a long, long good night.

Not only do the letters in the Betts edition of the *Garden Book* contain passages of soaring poetry, but Jefferson's prose style is elevated when gardens and landscape are the subject. His prose exhibits a playful eloquence, an exaggerated use of metaphor and imagery, an elemental passion for the physical world. A prime example occurred in his famous letter to Charles Willson Peale in 1811, when he concluded with a stirring ode to an alternative life as a market gardener with the echoing phrase, "But though an old man, I am but a young gardener."

PETER J. HATCH
Director of Gardens and Grounds

*Monticello*
*January 1999*

# MONTICELLO

I remember you told me when we parted, you would come to see me at Monticello. and tho' I believe this to be impossible, I have been planning what I would shew you: a flower here, a tree there; yonder a grove, near it a fountain; on this side a hill, on that a river. indeed madam, I know nothing so charming as our own country. the learned say it is a new creation; and I believe them; not for their reasons, but because it is made on an improved plan. Europe is a first idea, a crude production, before the maker knew his trade, or had made up his mind as to what he wanted.

JEFFERSON TO MRS. ANGELICA CHURCH
*Paris, February 17, 1788*

# GARDENING

I have often thought that if heaven had given me choice of my position and calling, it should have been on a rich spot of earth, well watered, and near a good market for the productions of the garden. No occupation is so delightful to me as the culture of the earth, and no culture comparable to that of the garden. Such a variety of subjects, some one always comming to perfection, the failure of one thing repaired by the success of another, and instead of one harvest a continued one through the year. Under a total want of demand except for our family table, I am still devoted to the garden. But though an old man, I am but a young gardener.

JEFFERSON TO CHARLES WILLSON PEALE
*Poplar Forest, August 20, 1811*

# AGRICULTURE

Those who labour in the earth are the chosen people of God, if ever he had a chosen people, whose breasts he has made his peculiar deposit for substantial and genuine virtue. It is the focus in which he keeps alive that sacred fire, which otherwise might escape from the face of the earth. Corruption of morals in the mass of cultivators is a phaenomenon of which no age nor nation has furnished an example.

JEFFERSON
*Notes on the State of Virginia, 1787*

# 1766

SHADWELL [2]

Mar. 30.   Purple hyacinth [3] begins to bloom.

Apr.  6.   Narcissus [4] and Puckoon [5] open.

    13.   Puckoon flowers fallen.

    16.   a bluish colored, funnel-formed flower [6] in low-grounds in bloom.

    30.   purple flag [7] blooms.   Hyacinth & Narcissus gone.

May.  4.   Wild honeysuckle [8] in our woods open.—also the Dwarf flag [9] & Violets. [10]

     7.   blue flower in low grounds vanished. [11]

    11.   the purple flag, Dwarf flag, Violet & wild Honeysuckle still in bloom.  went journey to Maryland, Pennsylvā, New York.  so observations cease [12]

---

[1] *1766.* Jefferson reached his twenty-third birthday on April 13, 1766.  He had already passed through many experiences, some of which were to have a profound influence on his future life.  When he was two years old, his family moved to *Tuckahoe,* on the north bank of the James River a few miles above Richmond, the home of his father's late friend, Colonel William Randolph, where at five he was placed in an English School.  On the return of the family to *Shadwell,* he attended

the school of Mr. William Douglas, a Scotch clergyman, remaining there until his father's death, four years later. During the following years he was a pupil in the school of the Reverend James Maury, located in Louisa County, fourteen miles from *Shadwell*. The greater part of the next seven years, 1760–1767, Jefferson spent in Williamsburg, attending the College of William and Mary during the first two, and spending the next five in the study of law under his friend, George Wythe.

He became of age in 1764. In the autumn of 1765 he lost his favorite sister, Jane. They had often roamed together over the fields and hills of *Shadwell,* observing and gathering the spring flowers. So this spring of 1766 was a poignant one for Jefferson as he recorded the blooming and the disappearing of the flowers in his garden and the fields about him. Little is known of his life during 1766, except as recorded in his *Garden Book* and in his letters to John Page.

[2] *Shadwell* is located in Albemarle County, Virginia, near the city of Charlottesville. It was the home of Peter Jefferson and his wife, Jane Randolph, and was named *Shadwell* after the London parish where Jane was born. Ten children were born to Peter and Jane Jefferson. The six daughters were Jane, Mary, Elizabeth, Martha, Lucy, and Anna Scott; the four sons, Thomas, Peter Field, a son still-born, and Randolph. Thomas, the eldest son, was born at *Shadwell* on April 2, 1743, old style, or April 13, 1743, by the present calendar.

*Shadwell,* a weather-boarded house, was Jefferson's home until it burned on February 1, 1770. The following November he moved to *Monticello,* his home for the remainder of his life. All that is known about the flower garden at *Shadwell* is that there were flower beds numbered from *I* to *VI-c.*

[3] *Hyacinthus orientalis* L.

[4] Probably *Narcissus jonquilla* L.

[5] *Sanguinaria canadensis* L. Now commonly called blood-root.

[6] Probably *Mertensia virginica* DC., Virginia bluebells. This plant grows in the alluvial soil of the Rivanna River, which flows through the *Shadwell* estate.

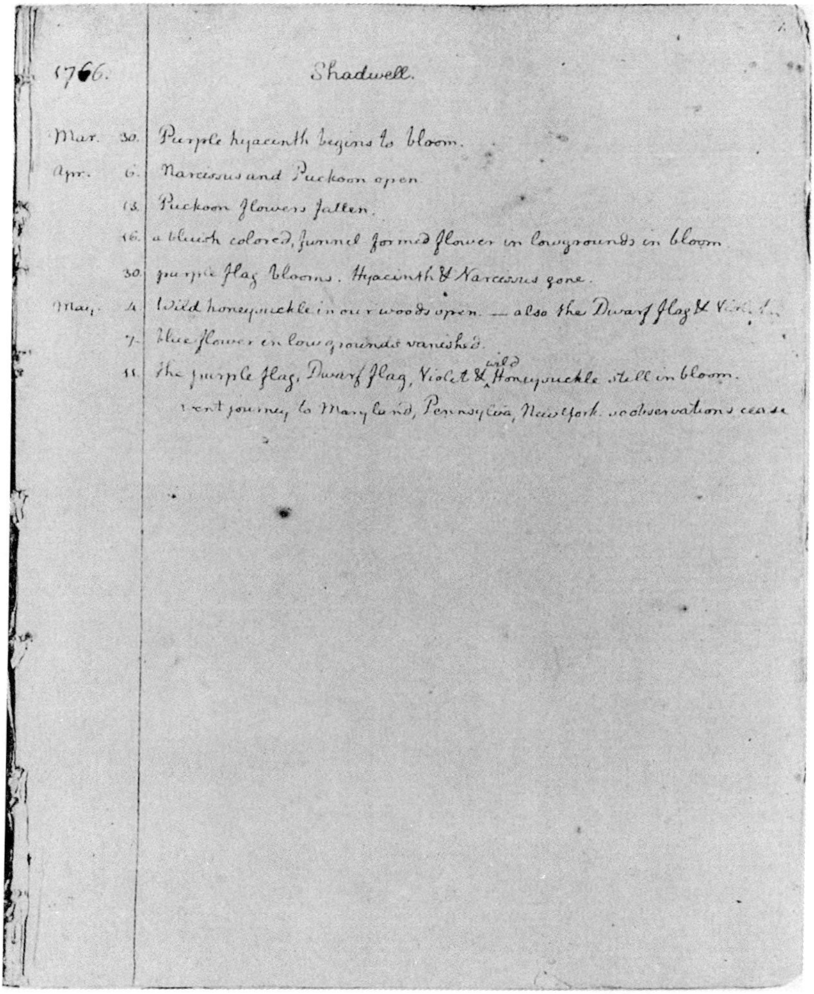

1766.                   Shadwell.

Mar. 30. | Purple hyacinth begins to bloom.
Apr.   6. | Narcissus and Puckoon open
      13. | Puckoon flowers fallen.
      16. | a bluish colored, funnel formed flower in lowgrounds in bloom
      30. | purple flag blooms. Hyacinth & Narcissus gone.
May.   4. | Wild honeysuckle in our woods open — also the Dwarf flag & Violet.
       7. | blue flower in lowgrounds vanished.
      11. | the purple flag, Dwarf flag, Violet & wild Honeysuckle still in bloom.
          | went journey to Maryland, Pennsylva, New York. so observations cease

PLATE I.—Page 1 of the original *Garden Book*.

PLATE II.—Jefferson's original *Garden Book*, 1766–1824, now in possession of the Massachusetts Historical Society.

The *Garden Book* is a memorandum book with leather-strip board covers, 20.3 cm. by 16.2 cm. It contains 158 leaves, of which 33 are filled with Jefferson's notes and 125 are blank. The pages are not numbered after 49. Pages 33, 34, 37, and 38 are missing.

[7] *Iris* sp.

[8] *Rhododendron nudiflorum* (L.) Torr. This shrub grows in abundance in the woods around *Shadwell*.

[9] *Iris cristata* Ait. The dwarf iris grows in large patches near *Shadwell* and makes a lovely carpet on the forest floor of *Monticello* Mountain.

[10] *Viola* L. The following species of *Viola* grow around *Shadwell* and *Monticello*: *Viola cucullata* Ait., *V. scabriuscula* Schwein., *V. striata* Ait., *V. palmata* L., *V. pedata* L., *V. canadensis* L., *V. hastata* Michx., *V. rafinesquii* Greene.

[11] Twenty-two days, the blooming period of the blue flower in the low grounds. This kind of observation was of considerable interest to Jefferson. It will be noticed many times in the *Garden Book*.

[12] This was Jefferson's first visit to Maryland, Pennsylvania, and New York. He was in Annapolis when the people were celebrating the repeal of the Stamp Act. Here also, he observed the houses and gardens and wrote to his friend, John Page: "The situation of the place is extremely beautiful, and very commodious. . . . The houses are in general better than those at Williamsburg, but the gardens are more indifferent." In Philadelphia he stopped to be inoculated for the smallpox. At New York he lodged at the same boarding-house with Elbridge Gerry from Massachusetts, who, with Jefferson, was to play a leading role in the new Republic. He seems to have made most of the journey in his one-horse chair.

# 1767

Feb. 20.   sowed a bed of forwardest and a bed of midling peas.[2]

          *500. of these peas weighed $3^{oz}-18^{dwt}$.[3] about 2500. fill a pint.[4]

Mar. 9.   both beds of peas up.

    15.   planted asparagus seed [5] in 5. beds of 4.f. width. 4. rows in each.[6]

    17.   sowed a bed of forwardest peas, and a bed of the latest of all.[7]

    23.   Purple Hyacinth & Narcissus bloom.[8]

          sowed 2. rows of Celery 9.I. apart.[9]

          sowed 2 rows of Spanish onions [10] & 2.d°. of Lettuce.[11]

Apr. 1.   peas of Mar. 17. just appearing.

    2.   sowed Carnations,[12] Indian pink,[13] Marygold,[14] Globe amaranth,[15] Auricula,[16] Double balsam,[17] Tricolor,[18] Dutch violet,[19] Sensitive plant,[20] Cockscomb, a flower like the Prince's feather,[21] Lathyrus.[22]

          planted Lilac,[23] Spanish broom,[24] Umbrella,[25] Laurel.[26] Almonds,[27] Muscle plumbs,[28] Cayenne pepper.[29] 12. cuttings of Goosberries.[30]

4

4.    planted suckers of Roses, seeds of Althaea [31] & Prince's feather.[32]

6.    planted lillies & wild honeysuckles.[33]

7.    planted strawberry roots.[34]

9.    sowed 3. rows of Celery, 2 d°. of Lettuce—2 d°. of Radish.[35]

Lunaria [36] in full bloom.

16.   Sweet Williams [37] begin to open.

24.   forwardest peas of Feb. 20. come to table [38]

25.   Asparagus 3. inches high, and branched.[39]

Feathered hyacinth [40] in bloom.   also Sweet Williams.

a pink in bed VI.c.[41] blooming.

Lunaria still in bloom.   an indifferent flower.[42]

May. 27.  sowed Lettuce, Radish, Broccoli,[43] & Cauliflower.[44]

28.   Flower-de luces just opening.[45]

*strawberries come to table.  note this is the first year of their bearing having been planted in the spring of 1766. and on an average the plants bear 20. strawberries each.  100 fill half a pint.[46]

forwardest peas of March 17. come to table.[47]

latest peas of Feb. 20. will come to table within about 4. days.[48]

Snap-dragon [49] blooming.

June. 4.   Larkspur[50] & Lychnis[51]
           bloom & Poppies[52]

     10.   Pinks[53] & Hollyhocks[54]
           bloom.                        } by information of
                                            m͞rs Carr.[57]
     12.   Carnations bloom.[55]

     18.   Argemone[56] put out one
           flower.

July. 5.   larger Poppy has vanished—Dwarf poppy still
           in bloom but on the decline.  pinks V.c. just
           disappear.—pinks in VI.c.[58] still shew a few.

           Carnations in full life—Larkspur, Lychnis in
           bloom.—a few hollyhocks remaining—Eastern
           mallow almost vanished. an indifferent flower.[59]

           *Colō Moore[60] tells me a hill of artichokes[61]
           generally bears 8. of a year, and they continue
           in season about 6. weeks.

     18.   Lesser poppy still blooming—pinks V.c. a few.
           —pinks VI.c. a few.—a few Carnations.—
           Larkspur in bloom.—Eastern mallow & Lych-
           nis in bloom.—Mirabilis[62] just opened.  very
           clever.—Argemone, one flower out.  this is yᵉ
           4ᵗʰ yˢ year

     31.   Cucumbers[63] come to table.

Aug.  1.   inoculated May cherry[64] buds into 4. stocks of
           unknown kind.

      2.   inoculated English walnut[65] buds into stocks of
           the Black walnut.

      3.   inoculated common cherry buds into stocks of
           large kind at Monticello.[66]

Nov. 22.    *8 or 10. bundles of fodder are as much as a horse will generally eat thro' the night. 9 bundles × 130. days = 1170. for the winter.[67]

———————————————————

[1] *1767.* Jefferson was introduced to the practice of law at the bar of the General Court of Virginia in 1767 by George Wythe. According to his *Account Book 1767–1770,* in which he registered his law cases, he was employed during the year in 68 cases, taking him in the fall quarter alone to Staunton, Orange Court House, Culpeper Court House, Winchester, Fauquier Court House, and Richmond. Yet, despite these frequent absences from home, he took an increasingly active interest in his flower and vegetable gardens.

[2] Many varieties of the pea, *Pisum sativum* L., are mentioned in the *Garden Book.* Forwardest and Middling were the earliest varieties of this species and were probably variations of the Charlton Hotspur. (See *Garden Book,* February 24, 1768.) Peas were Jefferson's favorite vegetable.

[3]    Table of Troy Weight

24 grains (gr.) = 1 pennyweight (dwt.)
20 pennyweights = 1 ounce (oz. t.) = 480 grains
12 ounces = 1 pound (lb. t.) = 240 pennyweights = 5,760 grains.

[4] Another kind of detailed observation which delighted Jefferson. It is noted in all of his memorandum books, account books, and *Farm Book,* as well as in letters and the *Garden Book.* Observations of this kind in the last two centuries reveal to us today just how much has been accomplished in improving fruits, seeds, and vegetables.

[5] *Asparagus officinalis* L.

[6] Like the flower garden at *Shadwell,* there is no plan known for the vegetable garden. This entry indicates that the garden was divided into beds of a definite size and also that the beds were planted in rows.

[7] Another variety of *Pisum sativum* L.

[8] Compared with the blooming record of 1766, purple hyacinth and narcissus bloomed seven days earlier. One of Jefferson's objects in keeping a record of the garden activities

was to make a comparative study of the blooming, the fruiting, the time the different articles came to the table, and their disappearance.   These discrete observations were summarized many years later, so that he had an accurate tabulation of the vegetables, fruits, and flowers at *Shadwell* and *Monticello*.

[9] *Apium graveolens* L. var. *dulce* DC.   On account of the hot summers very little celery is raised in Albemarle County today.

[10] *Allium cepa* L.   Spanish onion, any of several varieties of large-bulbed, mild-flavored onions; in the United States originally applied only to imported stock but now used more broadly.

[11] *Lactuca sativa* L.

[12] *Dianthus caryophyllus* L.   Although the records do not show where Jefferson got these seeds, most of them were probably given to him by neighbors and acquaintances on his many trips.

[13] A species of either *Dianthus* L. or *Silene* L.

[14] *Tagetes* sp.

[15] *Gomphrena globosa* L.

[16] *Primula auricula* L., yellow-flowered primrose.

[17] *Impatiens balsamina* L.

[18] Probably *Viola tricolor* L., pansy.

[19] Dutch violet.   Unidentified.

[20] *Mimosa pudica* L.

[21] *Celosia argentea* L.   No doubt one lacking fasciation.

[22] Either *Lathyrus odoratus* L., sweet pea, or *L. latifolius* L., everlasting pea.

[23] *Syringa vulgaris* L.

[24] *Spartium junceum* Lam.

[25] *Magnolia tripetala* L.   A native deciduous magnolia.

[26] May be either *Rhododendron maximum* L., great laurel, or *Kalmia latifolia* L., mountain laurel.   The native mountain folk often call rhododendron "laurel."

[27] *Prunus communis* Fritsch.

[28] Muscle plumbs.   Unidentified.

[29] *Capsicum frutescens* L. var. *longum* Bailey.

[30] Probably *Ribes grossularia* L., English gooseberry.

[31] *Hibiscus syriacus* L.   Rose-of-Sharon.

[32] *Amaranthus hybridus* L. var. *hypochondriacus* Bailey.

[33] *Rhododendron nudiflorum* Torr.

[34] *Fragaria* sp. and var.

[35] *Raphanus sativus* L.

[36] *Lunaria annua* L.

[37] *Dianthus barbatus* L.

[38] Forwardest peas, planted on February 20, came up on March 9; they were ready for the table on April 24, a total of 64 days from planting to eating.

[39] This asparagus was planted on March 15. Asparagus seeds are rarely planted today by gardeners. New beds are made by planting roots.

[40] *Muscari comosum* var. *monstrosum* L. When Jefferson moved to *Monticello,* he carried plants of feathered hyacinths with him. The descendants of these plants are still growing in the fields on top of the mountain.

[41] The first indication that the flower beds at *Shadwell* were numbered in a definite way.

[42] Jefferson often gave expression to his personal taste in flowers.

[43] *Brassica oleracea* var. *botrytis* L.

[44] Identified with no. 43.

[45] *Fleur-de-lis,* flag. A general name for several species of *Iris* L. Since the blooming period of this flower is nearly a month later than that mentioned in the spring of 1766, it is probably a different species or variety of *Iris.*

[46] So greatly have strawberries increased in size since this observation was made that today 15 strawberries often fill one half-pint.

[47] Peas of March 17 appeared above ground on April 1. They came to the table on May 28, a total of 73 days from time of planting to eating.

[48] February 20 to June 2, 103 days for this variety of pea to come to table.

[49] *Antirrhinum majus* L.

[50] *Delphinium* sp.

[51] *Lychnis* sp., catchfly.

[52] *Papaver* sp.

[53] *Dianthus* L. Probably *Dianthus plumarius* L.

[54] *Althaea rosea* Cav.

[55] The carnation seeds were sown on April 2, a total of 72 days from sowing to blooming.

[56] *Argemone* L.   Probably *Argemone grandiflora* Sweet, often called prickly poppy.

[57] Mrs. Carr, whose maiden name was Martha, was the fourth sister of Jefferson.   She was married to Dabney Carr, Jefferson's inseparable friend, on July 20, 1765.   He died on May 16, 1773, leaving a widow, three sons, and three daughters.   Jefferson took the entire family into his home and reared and educated the children as his own.   (See Henry S. Randall, *The Life of Thomas Jefferson* (3 v., New York, 1858), 1: 82–84.   Hereafter cited as Randall, *Jefferson.*)

[58] *VI-c,* refers to the number of one of the flower beds.

[59] Probably one of the mallows (*Hibiscus* sp.) grown from seed collected at Williamsburg.   Mallows are abundant in the swamps around Williamsburg.

[60] Bernard Moore, born in 1720, was a son of Colonel Augustine Moore, of *Chelsea,* King William County, and Elizabeth Todd, his wife.   He was a justice and a colonel of the militia in King William County and served as burgess for the county from 1744 to 1758 and from 1761 to 1772.   He married Anna Catherine Spotswood, daughter of Governor Alexander Spotswood.   (See Lyon G. Tyler, *Encyclopedia of Virginia Biography* (3 v., New York, 1915), 1: 294.   Hereafter cited as Tyler, *Virginia Biography.*)   Jefferson often visited his friend, Colonel Moore, on his trips to Williamsburg.

[61] *Cynara scolymus* L.   Since only a few gardeners grow artichokes in Albemarle County today, one has difficulty determining the number of artichokes a hill bears.

[62] *Mirabilis jalapa* L.   Often called four-o'clocks or marvel-of-Peru.

[63] *Cucumis sativus* L.   No mention is made of the planting date.

[64] May cherry.   In A. J. Downing's *The Fruits and Fruit Trees of America* (New York and Boston, 1846), the May cherry is placed under the *Morello* variety of cherries.   He describes it as one of the smallest, as well as the earliest, of cherries.   The tree is very small and dwarfish, growing scarcely more than 8 feet high.   The fruit is small, round, slightly flattened, the stalk an inch long, rather slender, and pretty deeply set.   The skin is pale red, or, at maturity, a rather lively red, with the flesh soft, juicy, and quite acid.

⁶⁵ English walnut, *Juglans regia* L.; black walnut, *Juglans nigra* L.   Jefferson rarely recorded the results of this kind of experiment.   In the Eastern States, where the English walnut is not grown commercially, the *Paradox,* a hybrid between the black walnut and the English walnut, is used for the stock of the English walnut today.   (See *Farmers' Bulletin* 1501, August, 1926.)   Michaux wrote: "By grafting the European upon the American species at the height of 8 or 10 feet, their advantages, with respect to the quality of wood and of fruit, might be united."   (See Cuthbert W. Johnson, *The Farmer's and Planter's Encyclopedia* (New York, 1855): 1103.)

⁶⁶ This is the earliest mention of *Monticello* in all the writings of Jefferson.   Just when he decided to name his new home *Monticello* is not known.

⁶⁷ If Jefferson, in his conversations with others, found they displayed sound judgment and knowledge of the subject, he entered the information in one or more of his memorandum books for future reference.   This entry, which appears to be an original observation, reveals his interest in farming operations and management.

# 1768

Feb. 24.   sowed a patch of early peas, having first soaked them.   Charlton Hotspur.[2]   *500. of these peas weighed 3$^{oz}$–7$^{dwt}$   2000 filled a pint accurately.

Mar. 5.   sowed a patch of Spanish Marotto peas.[3]

  14.   peas of Feb. 24. just appearing.[4]

  28.   peas of Mar. 5. just appearing.[5]

---

[1] *1768.*   Jefferson continued the practice of law during 1768.   He was employed in 115 cases, with a total profit of £304 8s. 5d.   (See *Account Book 1767–1770;* also Randall, *Jefferson* 1: 47–48.)

Jefferson was absent from *Shadwell* a considerable part of the year.   He went to Williamsburg for several visits, attended to law cases at Staunton, and paid social visits to *Rosewell,* Colonel Moore's *Chelsea,* Duncastle, *Greenspring,* and Gloucester.   While at Williamsburg he not only attended to his law duties, but also enjoyed the playhouse, musicals, and other gayeties of the capital.

The *Garden Book* has only four entries for the year, all of them made in early spring.   Although Jefferson had little time to record the garden activities at *Shadwell,* his mind was constantly on his new home, *Monticello.*   He made specifications for his new house (*Account Book 1767–1770:* 26–27) and made a contract for leveling the top of his mountain:

May 15, Agreed with mr Moore that he shall level 250 f. square on the top of the mountain at the N. E. end by Christmas, for which I am to give 180 bushels of wheat, and 24 bushels of corn, 12 of which are not to be paid till corn comes in.  if there should be any solid rock to dig we will leave to indifferent men to settle that part between us.

He also bought quarts of seeds to be planted at *Shadwell* and *Monticello*.  The following entries from the *Account Book 1767–1770* indicate the large number of seeds purchased during the year:

June 15.   p<sup>d</sup>. F. Foxcroft [of Williamsburg] 46/ to purchase white clover seed in Philadelphia.

June 30.   purchased of Sandy 13½ q<sup>ts</sup>. goose-grass seed for 27/.

July  11.   purchased at Myrtilla 2 q<sup>ts</sup>. of G.[oose] Grass seeds for 4/.

July  12.   bought of N. Meriwether's Anthony 5. q<sup>ts</sup>. & ½ pint d<sup>o</sup>. for 10/6.

Aug.   4.   bo<sup>t</sup>. of N. Meriwether's Anthony 2 q<sup>ts</sup>. white clover seed for 4/.

Aug.   7.   bo<sup>t</sup>. of Harry 5½ q<sup>ts</sup>. G. grass seed, and 1½ pints clover seed 12/6.

"     ".   bo<sup>t</sup>. of Phill 3 q<sup>ts</sup>. G. grass seed 6/.

"     ".   bo<sup>t</sup>. of N. Meriwether's Patrick 2 q<sup>ts</sup>. clover seed. 4/

"     "...........................  2 d<sup>o</sup>. G. grass seeds. 4/.

"     "..................... Anthony 2 d<sup>o</sup>. clover 4/.

"     "..................... Thom 3½ pints G. grass 3/6.

Aug. 24.   bo<sup>t</sup>. of N. Meriwether's Anthony 5 pints clover 5/.

"    28.   bo<sup>t</sup>. of N. M.'s Patrick 17 pints clover 17/.

Sept. 13.   mem. I have now of clover seeds 23 q<sup>ts</sup>, ½ p<sup>t</sup>. + 11.9 q<sup>ts</sup> = 34 q<sup>ts</sup>. 1 pt.

Nov. 21.   p<sup>d</sup>. Sandy in full for seed 20/.

[2] The Messrs. Lawson say that Hotspur dates back to 1670; and the name in some of its modifications continued for at least a century.  Some of the Hotspurs or "Hots" headed the list of earlier peas during most of the century, but about 1750 the variety, or the name, "Early Charlton," from the "Charlton Hotspur," became common, and remained popular until displaced by Early Frame about 1770.  (U. P. Hedrick, *Peas of New York* (Albany, pt. I, 1928): 22.  Hereafter cited as Hedrick, *Peas*.)

There are the Charlton hotspur, Reading hotspur, and Master hotspur, but are very little different from one another.  These are the earliest, and are reckoned much preferable in flavor to any other kind. . . . The Charlton and Marrowfats may be sown at the same time: some people soak their Peas before sowing, but this often turns out unsuccessfully, for in a wet season they are apt to rot.  (John Randolph, Jr., *A Treatise on Gardening* (Marjorie F. Warner ed.) (Richmond, 3d ed., 1924): 39–40.  Hereafter cited as Randolph, *Gardening*.  Randolph's book was probably published about 1765.  There was a copy of it in Jefferson's library.)

[3] Spanish Morotto peas.   These were advertised for sale by "William Wills, Chirurgeon in Richmond Town, and John Donlevy in Petersburg in the *Virginia Gazette* in March, 1767 & 1768."   (Randolph, *Gardening:* 54.)   Jefferson probably bought his seeds from one of them.

[4] The Charlton Hotspur requires 19 days to appear above ground.

[5] The Spanish Morotto requires 24 days to appear above ground.

# 1769

MONTICELLO.[2]

Mar. 14.  planted on the S.E. side[3] of the hill as follows.

On the Ridge beginning at the bottom.

1. row of Pears.[4]  25.f. apart 12 in a row. left vacant.

1. row of d°. ingrafted.

2. rows of cherries intended for stocks to inoculation.

2. of New York apples[5] ingrafted.

1. of Peach[6] stocks for inoculating almonds.[7]

1. of d°. . . . for d°. . . . apricots[8]

$\frac{1}{2}$ row of d°. for Nectarines.[9]—$\frac{1}{2}$ row of quinces.[10]

In the Hollow.

1. row of Pomegranates[11] 12$\frac{1}{2}$ f. apart 12 in a row.

2. d°. of figs.[12]

1. d°. Peach stocks for inoculating Apricots.

1. d°. Walnuts.[13]

July. 27.  *a bed of mortar which makes 2000. bricks takes 6. hhd̄s̄. of water.[14]

*Nich⁸. Meriwether[15] sais that 30. hills of Cucumbers 4.f. apart will supply a middling family plentifully.

*Nich. Lewis[16] thinks 40.f. square of watermelons[17] will supply a family that is not very large.

*Millar's Gard's dict.[18] sais that 50. hills of Cucumbers will yeild 400. cucumbers a week during the time they are in season, which he sais is 5 weeks. so that 50 hills will yeild 2000, or 1. hill yeild 40. cucumbers.

---

[1] *1769.* Jefferson increased his law practice during 1769. He was employed in 198 cases and received £370 11s. in fees. (Randall, *Jefferson* 1: 47–48.) In this year also he was elected to the House of Burgesses, convening at Williamsburg, where he was soon to become an influential member. While in Williamsburg attending to his duties, he had time for the playhouse, paid Pelham 2/6 for playing on the organ, "pᵈ. for seeing a hog weighing more than 1050 lbs," saw a Puppet Show, and "pᵈ. for seeing a tyger 1/3."

In spite of the months away from home which Jefferson's new office required, work at *Monticello* moved forward rapidly. The year before, John Moore had leveled the top of the mountain. This year the actual work of building the new house began. The northeast end of the clearing became the site of the house. Jefferson recorded in the *Account Book 1767–1770:*

four good fellows, a lad and two girls of abᵗ. 16. each in 8½ hours dug in my cellar of mountain clay a place 3 f. deep, 8f. wide and 16½ f. long = 14⅔ cubical yds. under these disadvantages, to wit; a very cold snowy day which obliged them to be very often warming; under a cover of planks, so low, that in about half the work their stroke was not more than ⅔ of a good one; they eat their breakfast in the time which one of them went to cook; they were obliged to keep one or two constantly hauling away the earth to prevent it's rolling in again.   from

[this] I think a midling hand in 12. hours (including his breakfast) could dig & haul away the earth of 4 cubical yds, in the same soil.

This cellar became the basement for the South Pavilion, the first building completed at *Monticello*.

While the South Pavilion was being completed, work on the grounds was moving forward. By September 20, 1769, Jefferson had cleared a park on the north side of his mountain, 1850 yards in circumference, and had contracted with R. Sorrels to mawl 8000 rails for him by Christmas, for which he was to pay him 20/ the thousand. They were all to be chestnut, and W. Hickman was to judge if any of them were bad. They were not to be counted until put up. (*Account Book 1767–1770.*)

The well was also begun this year. The same *Account Book* tells us:

in digging my dry well, at the depth of 14 f. I observe one digger, one filler, one drawer at the windlace with a basket at each end of his rope very accurately gave one another full emploiment, but note it was yellow rotten stone with a great many hard stones as large as a man's head and some larger, or else the digger would have had time to spare. they dug and drew out 8. cubical yds in a day.

And on "Oct. 3, W. Beck has worked in the well 46 days. We are to settle the price." The well was located a little southeast of the South Pavilion. (See appendix II.)

During the late summer and early fall of the year Jefferson bought over 85 quarts of clover seed from his neighbors and others. His own crops of clover and grass were successful, for he records: "Sept. 7, gathered for myself this year 8 q$^{ts}$. cloverseed, also $52 + 18 = 70$ q$\overline{ts}$ goose grass seed" (*Account Book 1767–1770*).

$^2$ *Monticello* is an Italian word which means Little Mountain. Its origin as used by Jefferson is not known. As mentioned above, the first use of it in all of his surviving manuscripts was in the *Garden Book* in 1767. In the *Account Book 1767–1770*, at the end of July, 1769, he used a shortened form of the word, *Moncello*, as if not quite sure what form he wished to use.

July 31, tob°. made at Moncello in 1768 ................. 9787
W. Hickman's part (2¼ shares out of 12¾) .............. 1727

My part 10½ shares. ................................... 8060 lb.
Note, I think another year I shall allow him but 2. shares.

In his third attempt to name Little Mountain, he hit upon the word *Hermitage;* but he had no sooner written that word than he crossed it out and made the final decision to call his estate *Monticello.* (*Account Book 1767–1770.*) See last paragraph, 1770.

[3] This is the first planting plan for *Monticello.* The southeastern exposure was an ideal one for fruit trees. The fact that he planted the trees 25 feet apart showed his knowledge of the proper spacing of fruit trees. (See plate VII for location of these trees.)

[4] *Pyrus communis* L.

[5] *Malus pumila* Mill.

[6] *Prunus persica* Batsch.

[7] *Prunus communis* Arcang.

[8] *Prunus armeniaca* L.

[9] *Prunus persica* var. *nucipersica* Schneid.

[10] *Cydonia oblonga* Mill.

[11] *Punica granatum* L. Pomegranates are rarely grown in Albemarle today.

[12] *Ficus carica* L.

[13] Probably *Juglans nigra* L. for inoculating the English walnut.

[14] Jefferson's mountaintop was a busy place in the summer of 1769. An orchard had been started, a garden was in preparation, and bricks were being made by the thousands. Water was scarce. The only source of it was the springs on the sides of the mountain. The well was probably not yet supplying water. It was therefore important for Jefferson to figure accurately the amount of water needed for making brick, since it had to be carried a considerable distance. In the *Account Book 1767–1770,* we find: "July 16, Mem. George Dudley began on Friday 14th inst. about my bricks. I am to give him 3/·p$^r$ 1000 for mould$^g$ and burning, and 4/ a week for diet."

[15] Nicholas Meriwether, a neighbor and friend of Jefferson, was the eldest son of Thomas Meriwether and Elizabeth Thornton, his wife. He married Margaret Douglas, the daughter of the Reverend William Douglas, a native of Scotland, then rector of the parish of St. James, Northam, Goochland. This Mr. Douglas was an early teacher of Jefferson. (See Edgar Woods, *History of Albemarle County in Virginia*

(1901): 272–274. Hereafter cited as Woods, *Albemarle County*.)

[16] Nicholas Lewis was a son of Robert Lewis, who married Jane, the daughter of Nicholas Meriwether.

Nicholas lived at the Farm, adjoining Charlottesville on the east, a gift from his grandfather, Nicholas Meriwether. He was a public spirited man, a captain in the Revolution, a magistrate, Surveyor and Sheriff of the county, possessed of a sound judgment and kindly spirit, appealed to on all occasions to compose the strifes of the neighborhood, the trusted friend of Mr. Jefferson, and the advisor of his family during his long absences from home. He married Mary, the eldest daughter of Dr. Thomas Walker, and died in 1808. (Woods, *Albemarle County*: 252.)

[17] *Citrullus vulgaris* Schrad.

[18] Philip Miller (Jefferson used the spelling *Millar,* instead of Miller, also in the catalogue of his books, 1783) was born at either Deptford or Greenwich, England, in 1691. He died near Chelsea Churchyard, December 18, 1771. He was head gardener at Chelsea Gardens for many years and probably had more influence on gardens and gardening than any man of his time. His greatest work was *The Gardener's Dictionary,* published in 1731, in London. It went through eight editions during Miller's life. It was not until the seventh edition, published in 1759, that Miller used the Linnaean system. Another popular book by Miller was *The Gardener's Kalendar* (London, 1732). This volume ran through twelve editions. (*Dict. Nat. Biog.* (63 v., New York, 1885–1900), 37: 420–422.)

At least three of Miller's works were in Jefferson's library: *Dictionnaire des Jardiniers,* tr. de l'anglois par M. DeChazelles, avec notes, etc., par M. Hollandre, 5 v. 4°, Paris, 1785; *Gardener's Dictionary,* folio, London, 1768; *Gardener's Calendar,* 8°, London, 1765.

# 1770

*1770.** Jefferson made no entries in the *Garden Book* during 1770. The memorandum book for the year, too, is almost silent on the activities going on at *Monticello*. His law practice continued to absorb much of his time; he was employed in 121 cases and received fees amounting to £421 5s. 10½d. (Randall, *Jefferson*: 47–48.) During the sessions of the House of Burgesses he was in Williamsburg. Trips were made also to *Tuckahoe, Chelsea, The Forest,* in Charles City County, the home of his future wife, and Staunton.

Two important events occurred this year: *Shadwell* was burned, and Jefferson moved to *Monticello*. In the burning of *Shadwell* he lost most of his possessions. The most cherished of them were his books. Fortunately the *Garden Book* and some of the memorandum books were saved. The *Garden Book* was probably at his unfinished house at *Monticello,* where his garden activities were being recorded. In moving to *Monticello* on November 26, 1770, he established a home which was to be among his chief joys for the remainder of his life. Although he was destined to be absent from his beloved mountaintop for many years, it was a place where he always longed to be and where he was happier than at any other place.

In the early part of the spring of 1770, Jefferson sent William Beck to Williamsburg to bring back Bantam pomegranates and nectarines from George Wythe (*Account Book 1767–1770*). Mr. Wythe, in sending them on March 9, wrote:

I send you some nectarines and apricot graffs and grape vines, the best I had; and have directed your messenger to call upon Major Taliaferro [he lived near Williamsburg] for some of his. You will also receive two of Toulis's catalogues. Mrs. Wythe will send you some garden peas.

You bear your misfortune [burning of *Shadwell*] so becomingly, that, as I am convinced you will surmount the difficulties it has plunged you into, so I foresee you will hereafter reap advantages from it several ways. *Durate, et vosmet servate secundis.* (*Jefferson Papers,* Massachusetts Historical Society. Hereafter cited as *Jefferson Papers,* M. H. S.)

* This year not represented in the *Garden Book.*

A few days later Jefferson wrote: "Work to be done at the ~~Hermitage~~ Monticello.   plant raspberries, gooseberries—currans—strawberries—asparagus—artichokes—fill up trees—sow grass—henhouse—cherry tree—Lucerne—road—waggoning wood and sand—lop cherry trees." (*Account Book 1767–1770.*)   We are not told whether this program was carried out during the spring.   Jefferson was away from home a good part of the summer.   On September 9, he "bo$^t$. of neg. of D$^r$. Walker's 4 q$^{ts}$ grass seed & p$^d$ 5/" and also "bo$^t$ of N. M's [Meriwether's] Anthony 3 q$^{ts}$." (*Account Book 1767–1770.*)

# 1771

Mar.  6.  sowed a patch of peas after steeping them in in water 24. hours. (note the seed came from J. Bolling's [2])

7.  rain snow & hail with an Easterly wind for 4. days.[3]

11.  cleared up cold with a North West wind.

25.  replanted all the pomegranates [4] in their proper row.   also planted 4. others on S.E. edge of garden.[5]   also a Medlar Russetin.[6]

in the row of Peach trees for Apricots planted 4. apricot trees, viz. the 1st. 2d. 4th. & 5th. counting from S.W. end.[7]

peas up.[8]

28.  planted 5. grapes from N. Lewis's on S.E. edge of garden.

29.  sowed peas. (from T. Morgan's [9])

planted 2. beds of Asparagus seed.

30.  cold easterly wind, rain & hail.

May.  8.  eat peas at Barclay [10] in Charles-City.

15.  eat strawberries at Doctr. Rickman's [11]

26.  the greatest flood [12] ever known in Virginia.

30.  peas of Mar. 6. come to table.[13]

Sep.  7.  *Cart. H. Harrison [14] tells me it is generally allowed that 250 lb green pork makes 220. lb pickled.  he weighed a ham & shoulder when green.  the one weighed 24. lb. the other 17. lb. after they were made into bacon each had lost exactly a fourth.  they were of corn-fed hogs.[15]

11.  *Stephen Willis [16] sais it takes 15. bushels of lime to lay 1000. bricks.

*Old Sharpe [17] sais a bushel of Lime-stone will weigh 114 lb and if well burnt will make 2. bushels of slacked lime.

30.  *John Moore's [18] ford over the Rivanna [19] cost 28.£ on accurate estimate.

Shrubs [20] not exceeding 10.f. in height. Alder [21]—Bastard indigo. flowering. Amorpha [22]—Barberry [23]—Cassioberry. Cassine.[24]—Chinquapin.[25]—Jersey tea. Flowering. Ceanothus.[26]—Dwarf cherry. F.—Cerasus.[27] 5.—Clethra [28]—Cock-spur hawthorn, or haw. Crataegus.[29] 4.—Laurel [30]—Scorpion—Sena. Emerus.[31]—Hazel.[32]—Althaea.[33] F.—Callicarpa.[34]—Rose.[35]— Wild-Honey-suckle.[36] — Sweet-briar.[37] — Ivy.[38]

Trees. Lilac.[39]—wild Cherry.[40]—Dog-wood.[41]—Red-bud.[42]—Horse-chestnut.[43]—Catalpa.[44]—Magnolia.[45]—Mulberry.[46]—Locust.[47]—Honeysuckle.—Jessamine.[48]—Elder.[49]—Poison oak.[50]—Haw.[51]

Climbing shrubby plants. Trumpet flower.[52]—Jasmine [53]—Honey-suckle.[54]

Evergreens. Holly.[55]—Juniper.[56]—Laurel [57]—
Magnolia [58]—Yew.[59]

Hardy perennial flowers. Snapdragon —
Daisy [60] — Larkspur. — Gilliflower [61] — Sun-
flower.[62]—Lilly [63]—Mallow—Flower de luce.
— Everlasting pea [64] — Piony.[65] — Poppy. —
Pasque flower.[66] — Goldy-lock. Trollius.[67] —
Anemone—Lilly of the valley.[68]—Primrose.[69]
—Periwinkle [70]—violet—Flag.

———————————

[1] *1771.* Jefferson's reputation as a lawyer increased to such
an extent that he was employed by many of the distinguished
citizens of the colony. His profits also increased. The law
cases, as before, took him to many sections of the colony. He
continued to spend much time at Williamsburg, where he met
old friends, attended the playhouse, and enjoyed the other opportunities of the capital. Also Mrs. Martha Skelton's home,
*The Forest,* was near by. The *Account Book 1771* relates
that he was a frequent guest there during the year.

Work at *Monticello* continued with alacrity. There was a
reason—he was to marry Mrs. Skelton the first day of the
next year. The *Garden Book* records a few of the spring
plantings but tells nothing of what was done during the summer and fall. Jefferson talked to different men on the subject of farming, building, and the like, and jotted down what
might be of use later. It made no difference to him whether
the information came from a Harrison or Old Sharpe. His
only criterion was whether or not it would be of value later.

Sometime during the year, the date not given, he ordered
seeds of peas, celery, spinach, asparagus, artichokes, and cabbages from N. Campbell. On August 4 he bought of Nicholas
Meriwether's Patrick 5 quarts of grass seeds, and 7 quarts of
timothy seeds. On the 17th following he bought from Meriwether's Abraham 23 quarts of goose grass seeds. (*Account
Book 1771.*)

On September 7 Jefferson "wrote to Alex M°Caul, Glasgow to send me a gardener from 10 to 15£ a year, indentured for five years" (*Account Book 1771*). He did not state whether Mr. McCaul complied with his request.

At the end of the *Account Book 1771*, Jefferson set down elaborate plans for the development of the grounds at *Monticello*. Some of these plans were fanciful and never carried out; others were gradually incorporated into his working plans. They are interesting in showing how deeply his Little Mountain had gripped his imagination. They also show his talent for landscape planning and planting. Why he wrote the plans in his *Account Book 1771*, instead of in the *Garden Book*, is not known. Randall suggests that they were probably written away from home and were cogitations of unfilled hours on circuit, perhaps to wear off a dull evening at a country tavern. However, it is difficult to believe that Jefferson ever spent a dull evening, certainly not at this time of his life. The only part of the plans that he transferred to the *Garden Book* was that entitled, "The Open Ground on the West—A Shrubbery."

Here are Jefferson's plans as they appear in the *Account Book:*

choose out for a Burying place some unfrequented vale in the park, where is, 'no sound to break the stillness but a brook, that bubbling winds among the weeds; no mark of any human shape that had been there, unless the skeleton of some poor wretch, Who sought that place out to despair and die in.' let it be among antient and venerable oaks; intersperse some gloomy evergreens. the area circular, abᵗ. 60 f. diameter, encircled with an untrimmed hedge of cedar, or of stone wall with a holly hedge on it in the form below. [He makes a drawing of a spiral on the margin to illustrate this.] in the center of it erect a small Gothic temple of antique appearance. appropriate one half to the use of my own family, the other of strangers, servants, etc. erect pedestals with urns, etc., and proper inscriptions. the passage between the walls, 4 f. wide. on the grave of a favorite and faithful servant might be a pyramid erected of the rough rock-stone; the pedestal made plain to receive an inscription. let the exit of the spiral at (a) [this *a* refers to spiral diagram] look on a small and distant part of the blue mountains. in the middle of the temple an altar, the sides of turf, the top of plain stone. very little light, perhaps none at all, save only the feeble ray of an half extinguished lamp.

Jane Jefferson

*'Ah! Joanna, puellarum optima!*
*Ah! aevi virentis flore praerepta!*
*Sit tibi terra laevis!*
*Longe, longeque valeto!'*

at the spring on the North side of the park.

a few feet below the spring level the ground 40 or 50 f. sq. let the water fall from the spring in the upper level over a terrace in the form of a cascade. then conduct it along the foot of the terrace to the Western side of the level, where it may fall into a cistern under a temple, from which it may go off by the western border till it falls over another terrace at the Northern or lower side. let the temple be raised 2. f. for the first floor of stone. under this is the cistern, which may be a bath or anything else. the 1^st story arches on three sides; the back or western side being close because the hill there comes down, and also to carry up stairs on the outside. the 2^d story to have a door on one side, a spacious window in each of the other sides, the rooms each 8. f. cube; with a small table and a couple of chairs. the roof may be Chinese, Grecian, or in the taste of the Lantern of Demosthenes at Athens.

the ground just about the spring smoothed and turfed; close to the spring a sleeping figure reclined on a plain marble slab, surrounded with turf; on the slab this inscription:

*Hujus nympha loci, sacri custodia fontis*
*Dormio, dum blandae sentio murmur aquae*
*Parce meum, quisquis tangis cava marmora, sommum*
*Rumpere; si bibas, sive lavere, tace.*

near the spring also inscribe on stone, or a metal plate fastened to a tree, these lines: *'Beatus ille qui procul negotiis, Ut prisca gens mortalium, Paterna rura bobus exercet suis, solutus omni foenore; Forumque vitat et superba civium Potentiorum limina. Liget jacere modo sub antiqua ilice, modo in tenaci gramine: Labuntur altis interim ripis aquae; Queruntur in silvis aves; Fontesque lymphis obstrepunt manantibus, somnos quod invitet leves.'* plant trees of Beech and Aspen about it. open a vista to the millpond, river, road, etc. qu, if a view to the neighboring town would have a good effect? intersperse in this and every other part of the ground (except the environs of the Burying ground) abundance of Jesamine, Honeysuckle, sweet briar, etc. under the temple, an Aeolian harp, where it may be concealed as well as covered from the weather.

This would be better.

the ground above the spring being very steep, dig into the hill and form a cave or grotto. build up the sides and arch with stiff clay. cover this with moss. spangle it with translucent pebbles from Hanovertown, and beautiful shells from the shore at Burwell's ferry. pave the floor with pebbles. let the spring enter at a corner of the grotto, pretty high up the side, and trickle down, or fall by a spout into a basin, from which it may pass off through the grotto.  the figure will be better placed in this.  form a couch of moss.  the English inscription will then be proper.

> *Nymph of the grot, these sacred springs I keep,*
> *And to the murmur of these waters sleep;*
> *Ah! spare my slumbers! gently tread the cave!*
> *And drink in silence, or in silence lave!*

### The ground in General

thin the trees.  cut out stumps and undergrowth.  remove old trees and other rubbish, except where they may look well.  cover the whole with grass.  intersperse Jessamine, honeysuckle, sweetbriar, and even hardy flowers which may not require attention.  keep in it deer, rabbits, Peacocks, Guinea poultry, pigeons, etc.  let it be an asylum for hares, squirrels, pheasants, partridges, and every other wild animal (except those of prey).  court them to it, by laying food for them in proper places.  procure a buck-elk, to be, as it were, monarch of the wood; but keep him shy, that his appearance may not lose its effect by too much familiarity.  a buffalo might be confined also.  inscriptions in various places, on the bark of trees or metal plates, suited to the character or expression of the particular spot.

benches or seats of rock or turf.

### The Open Ground on the West—a shrubbery

Shrubs—(Not exceeding a growth of 10. f.).  Alder—Bastard indigo. flowering Amorpha—Barberry—Cassioberry. Cassine.—Chinquapin— Jersey-tea. F. Ceanothus—Dwarf Cherry. F. Cerasus. 5. Clethra— Cockspur hawthorn, or haw. Crataegus. 4. Laurel—Scorpion Sena. Emerus—Hazel.—Althea F.—Callicarpa—Rose—Wild honeysuckle —Sweet-briar—Ivy.

Trees.—Lilac—Wild Cherry—Dogwood—Redbud—Horse chestnut— Catalpa—Magnolia—Mulberry—Locust—Honeysuckle—Jessamine —Elder—Poison oak—Haw—Fig.

Climbing shrubby plants.—Trumpet flower—Jasmine—Honeysuckle.

Evergreens.—Holly—Juniper—Laurel—Magnolia—Yew.

Hardy perennial flowers.—Snapdragon—Daisy—Larkspur—Gilliflower —Sunflower—Lily—Mallow—Flower de luce—Everlasting pea— Piony—Poppy—Pasque flower—Goldy-lock, Trollius ═ Anemone— Lilly of the Valley—Primrose—Periwinkle—Violet—Flag.—(*Account Book 1771.*)

² John Bolling was a son of Colonel John Bolling, of *Cobbs*. He lived first in Goochland County, from which he was a delegate in the House of Burgesses in 1766–1768.  Afterwards, in 1778, he was a member of the House of Delegates from

Chesterfield County. He married Mary, a sister of Thomas Jefferson. He was born June 24, 1737, and died in 179–. (Tyler, *Virginia Biography* 1: 189.) Jefferson was at Mr. Bolling's home several times during 1771.

³ Weather conditions were of the first importance to Jefferson tending a garden on top of a mountain. He began his systematic record of the weather in the year 1776, while in Philadelphia to attend the Continental Congress. From this year through 1816, he kept an almost continuous weather record. This record was taken not only at *Monticello* but wherever he was located.

⁴ These pomegranates were probably the ones sent by George Wythe the year before. (See letter of George Wythe to Jefferson, March 9, 1770.)

⁵ This is the first mention of the garden. Where it was located is not known. It was not until March 31, 1774, that Jefferson mentioned laying off ground for a permanent garden.

⁶ *Mespilus germanica* L.

⁷ See plate VII.

⁸ Twenty days for peas to come up. They were planted March 6.

⁹ T. Morgan was hired by Jefferson to work at *Monticello*. Just what kind of work he did is not clear. In the *Account Book* for the year there are several references to paying him, similar to this one: "July 31, settled with T. Morgan, and I owe him of the wages of 1770 £4.10. I am to continue his wages £8. this year, and afterwards he is to maintain himself till the mill is ready for him."

¹⁰ *Barclay* (= Berkeley), the home of Benjamin Harrison, the Revolutionary statesman, Governor of Virginia, and signer of the Declaration of Independence. He was born in 1726(?) and died on April 24, 1791. Jefferson here intends by his reference to peas to compare the time that peas came to the table at Charles City with the time of their appearance on the table at *Monticello*. Jefferson's peas came to the table on May 30. There was a difference of 22 days.

¹¹ Probably Doctor William Rickman, a surgeon, who was appointed by Benjamin Harrison, or through his influence in Congress, as Physician and Director General to the Continental Hospital in the colony. (John Daly Burk, *The History of Virginia* (4 v., Petersburg, 1804–1816) 4: 155.)

[12] The flood of May 26, 1771, evidently did tremendous damage in Virginia. Jefferson referred to it many times.

[13] The peas of March 6 were up on March 25 and came to the table on May 30. Eighty-six days elapsed from the time of planting to eating.

[14] Carter Henry Harrison (1727–1793 or 1794) was a son of Benjamin Harrison, of *Berkeley*, and a brother of Benjamin Harrison, the signer of the Declaration of Independence. He attended William and Mary College, resided at *Clifton*, Cumberland County, was chairman of the county committee of safety, and on April 22, 1776, drafted and submitted to the people assembled at Cumberland Court House the first explicit instructions in favor of independence adopted by a public meeting in any of the colonies. He was later a member of the House of Delegates under the new constitution of Virginia. (Tyler, *Virginia Biography* 2: 11–12.)

[15] Jefferson often wrote information of this kind in several different places. One would expect to find this type of information in the *Farm Book,* but instead it occurs in the *Garden Book* and the *Account Book 1771.* The statement in the *Account Book* differs slightly from that in the *Garden Book:*

Sept. 7, Carter H. Harrison tells me that it is generally allowed that 250 lb. green pork makes 220 lb. pickled pork. he made a trial on a ham and shoulder, the one weighing 24 lb. and the other 17 lb. green. When made into bacon they had lost nearly one fourth. they were cornfed.

[16] Stephen Willis began to work for Jefferson on August 4, 1771 (*Account Book 1771,* September 11).

[17] Probably Robert Sharpe from whom, on March 29, Jefferson purchased

one acre of limestone land on Plumb tree branch other ways called Scale's creek to be laid off as I please. under these restrictions. I am not to enter his fence on the Southside of the road, nor to include his spring on the N. side of the road. I give him 40/3 for it. Watt Mousley present at making the bargain. (*Account Book 1771.*)

[18] John Moore was evidently a man of means and fine business capacity. At different times he owned more than 5,000 acres in the county. From the fact that it was through his land east of the town that the road to the river was made,

it is surmised that the name of Moore's was given to the ford, which crossed just below· the site of the Free Bridge. (Woods, *Albemarle County:* 283–284.)

   [19] Rivanna River.

Rivanna was in use from the first, according to the fashion then in vogue, of honoring Queen Anne with the names of rivers recently discovered.   In the earliest patents and deeds it was more frequently called the north fork of the James, as the James above the Rivanna passed under the name of the South Fork, or more euphuistically, the Fluvanna. In some instances the Rivanna was simply termed the North River, and the Fluvanna the South.   The crossing of the Rivanna at the Free Bridge was known as Moore's Ford, or Lewis' Ferry, according to the stage of water.   (Woods, *Albemarle County:* 20.)

   It is interesting to compare Jefferson's use of words in describing the same information recorded in different account books.   In this case, in the *Garden Book,* he speaks of an "accurate estimate," while in the *Account Book 1771* he writes: "Mr. Moore's ford on a nice estimate cost £28."

   [20] For a comparison of this with the *Account Book 1771,* see above, "The Open Ground on the West—a shrubbery."

   [21] Probably *Alnus rugosa* Spreng.   This is the common alder in Albemarle County.

   [22] *Amorpha fruticosa* L.

   [23] Either *Berberis canadensis* Mill. or *Berberis vulgaris* L.

   [24] *Ilex vomitoria* Ait.

   [25] *Castanea pumila* Mill.

   [26] *Ceanothus americanus* L.

   [27] *Prunus cerasus* L.

   [28] *Clethra alnifolia* L.

   [29] *Crataegus crus-galli* L.

   [30] Either *Rhododendron maximum* L. or *Kalmia latifolia* L.

   [31] *Coronilla emerus* L.

   [32] *Corylus americana* Marsh.

   [33] *Hibiscus syriacus* L.

   [34] *Callicarpa americana* L.

   [35] *Rosa* spp.

   [36] *Rhododendron nudiflorum* Torr.

   [37] *Rosa rubiginosa* L. or *Rosa eglanteria* L.

   [38] Native mountain people often call *Kalmia latifolia* L. "ivy."

[39] Either *Syringa vulgaris* L. or *S. persica* L.    Persian lilac.

[40] Either *Prunus serotina* Ehrh. or *P. virginiana* L.    Jefferson called the latter *wild cherry*, in his *Notes on the State of Virginia*.

[41] *Cornus florida* L.

[42] *Cercis canadensis* L.

[43] *Aesculus hippocastanum* L.

[44] *Catalpa bignonioides* Walt.

[45] *Magnolia tripetala* L.    Umbrella tree.    Probably this deciduous magnolia, since he mentions magnolia again under evergreens.

[46] Either *Morus alba* L., *M. nigra* L., or *M. rubra* L.

[47] *Robinia pseudoacacia* L.

[48] *Gelsemium sempervirens* Ait. f.    This is called jessamine in the Southern United States.    However, it is a vine.    We do not know why Jefferson included this and poison oak under trees.    It may have been because these two plants often climb to the tops of tall trees.

[49] Either *Sambucus canadensis* L. or *S. racemosa* L.

[50] *Rhus toxicodendron* L.

[51] *Viburnum prunifolium* L.

[52] Either *Tecoma radicans* (L.) Juss. or *Bignonia capreolata* L.

[53] In Jefferson's *Notes on the State of Virginia*, yellow jasmine is called *Bignonia sempervirens;* it is called today *Gelsemium sempervirens* Ait. f.

[54] In Jefferson's *Notes on the State of Virginia*, trumpet honeysuckle goes by the name of *Lonicera sempervirens* L.

[55] Either *Ilex opaca* Ait., American holly, or *I. aquifolium* L., English holly.

[56] *Juniperus virginiana* L., red cedar.

[57] See note 30, above.

[58] *Magnolia grandiflora* L.

[59] *Taxus baccata* L., English yew, or *Taxus canadensis* Marsh., American yew.

[60] *Bellis perennis* L.

[61] *Mathiola incana* R. Br.    It is also called stock.

[62] *Helianthus annuus* L.

[63] Lily, *Lilium* (various species).

[64] *Lathyrus latifolius* L.

[65] Probably *Paeonia albiflora* Pallas.
[66] *Anemone pulsatilla* L.
[67] Probably *Trollius asiaticus* L.
[68] *Convallaria majalis* L.
[69] *Primula vulgaris* Huds.
[70] *Vinca minor* L.

# 1772

1772.[1]

Jan. 26. the deepest snow we have ever seen.  in Albemarle it was about 3.f. deep.[2]

Mar. 30. sowed a patch of latter peas.[3]

other patches were sowed afterwards.

July. 15. Cucumbers came to table.[4]

planted out Celery.[5]

sowed patch of peas for the Fall.[6]

planted snap-beans.[7]

22. had the last dish of our spring peas.[8]

31. had Irish potatoes [9] from the garden.

*Julius Shard [10] fills the two-wheeled barrow in 3. minutes and carries it 30. y$\bar{\text{d}}$s. in $1\frac{1}{2}$ minutes more.  now this is four loads of the common barrow with one wheel.  so that suppose the 4. loads put in in the same time viz. 3. minutes, 4. trips will take $4 \times 1\frac{1}{2}$ minutes $= 6'$ which added to 3' filling is $= 9'$ to fill and carry the same earth which was filled & carried in the two-wheeled barrow in $4\frac{1}{2}'$.  from a trial I made with the same two-wheeled barrow I found that a man would dig & carry to the distance of 50. y$\bar{\text{d}}$s 5. cubical y$\bar{\text{d}}$s of earth in a day of 12. hours length.  Ford's Phill [11] did

*33*

it; not overlooked, and having to mount his loaded barrow up a bank 2.f. high & tolerably steep.[12]

Aug. 20.   *the waggon with 4. horses & the driver without any assistant brought about 300 yds wood which measured 4, 8, & 19½ f. i.e. nearly 5. cords calling a cord 4, 4, & 8. in one day.   it took 10. loads.[13]

*the waggon brings 28. rails at a load up a steep part of the mountain.[14]

*Ry. Randolph's mason cuts stone @ 8ᵈ. the superficial foot, the blocks being furnished to his hand.   provision found, but no attendance.[15]

*park-paling,[16] every other pale high, the tall pales to have 5 nails. the low one 4. nails is worth but 30/ the 100. yds, out and out.   calculated by Skip Harris.[17]

*a coach & six will turn in 80. feet.

Octob. 8.   gathered 2. plumb-peaches at Monticello.[18]

Nov. 12.   *William Gillum [19] sais it will take a bushel of Lime-stone (which he sais is equal to 2. bushels of slacked lime.) to a perch of stonework 18.I. thick.[20]—but Anderson [21] sais 3. bushels of Lime.

*in making the Round-about walk,[22] 3 hands would make 80. yds in a day in the old feild, but in the woods where they had stumps to clear, not more than 40. & sometimes 25. yds.

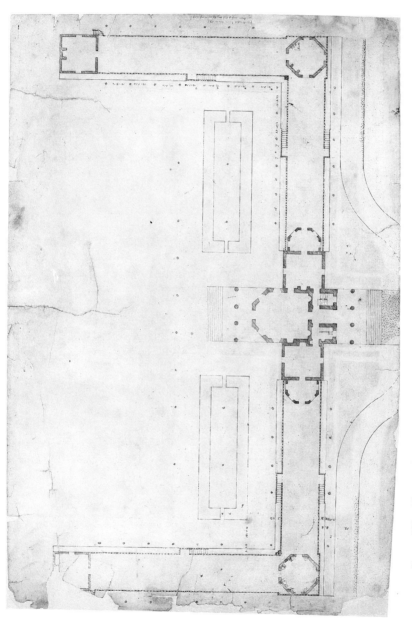

PLATE III.—Plan of the *Monticello* house and rectangular flower beds, prior to 1772. So far as known, the flower beds were never laid out and planted. (*Jefferson Papers*, M. H. S.)

¹ *1772.*   In the *Account Book 1771,* Jefferson wrote: "Dec. 30, inclosed to M. [Mordecai] Debnam for marriage license 40/."   On the first day of January, 1772, he was married to Mrs. Martha Skelton, widow of Mr. Bathurst Skelton, and daughter of John Wayles, of *The Forest,* in Charles City County.   Jefferson's marriage was for him the supreme event of the year and, one might say, for all years.   It profoundly affected every phase of his life then and thereafter. The wedding was celebrated with happy festivities.   The couple made a leisurely journey to *Monticello,* visiting friends along the way, arriving finally on January 25.   Mrs. Randolph, Jefferson's eldest daughter, wrote years later an account of Mr. and Mrs. Jefferson's trip to *Monticello:*

They left the *Forest* after a fall of snow, light then, but increasing in depth as they advanced up the country.   They were finally obliged to quit the carriage and proceed on horseback.   Having stopped for a short time at Blenheim, where an overseer resided, they left it at sunset to pursue their way through a mountain track rather than a road, in which the snow lay from eighteen inches to two feet deep, having eight miles to go before reaching *Monticello.*   They arrived late at night, the fires all out and the servants retired to their own houses for the night.   The horrible dreariness of such a house, at the end of such a journey, I have often heard both relate.   (Randall, *Jefferson* 1: 64.)

On January 26 Jefferson recorded in the *Garden Book:* "the deepest snow we have ever seen.   in Albermale it was about 3. f. deep."

Jefferson's law cases continued to take him from home.   He was in Williamsburg several times during the year, attending the meetings of the General Court and looking after other affairs.   He did not neglect his cultural interests.   He was often at the playhouse and on May 14 paid 2/6 for hearing musical glasses.   On another visit to Williamsburg he "pᵈ. revᵈ. mr̄ Gwatkin for 10 months schooling Rand[olph] Jefferson [his only brother] £10.   pᵈ. dº. for revᵈ. mr̄ Johnson entrance money for dº. in Grammar school 20/."   (*Account Book 1772.*)

However, things were happening at *Monticello.*   From computations of various kinds made in the *Garden Book,* and in the *Account Book* for the year, there was much building, clearing and leveling of new ground, and making of new roads. On March 28, a few days before leaving for Williamsburg,

Jefferson got an estimate for cleaning and burning the fruitery; "James Lackey on view of the ground in my fruitery sais it is worth 18/ an acre & an acre may be done by one man in a week, to be grubbed cleaned & burnt. p<sup>d</sup> Rich<sup>d</sup> Sorrels 40/ which is his wages till Apri. 4. and settles all our account. He agrees then immediately to grub, clean & burn my fruitery @ 18/ the acre." And on August 23 he wrote: "Old Sharpe tells me a bushel of limestone will weigh 114 lb. and if well burned will make 2 bushels of lime" (*Account Book 1772*).

In the latter part of the year a daughter, Martha Wayles, was born to Mr. and Mrs. Jefferson. She was destined to play a conspicuous part in Jefferson's life.

The *Account Book* mentions only a few seeds bought this year:

Aug. 16.   p<sup>d</sup>. Gill for potato seed 2/.
Aug. 23.   p<sup>d</sup>. N. M's Tom for 5½ q<sup>ts</sup>. clover seed.   6/10½.
Sept. 20.   bo<sup>t</sup> of N. M's. Abram. 5 p<sup>ts</sup>. clover seed.
Sept. 20.   gave m̄rs Wills's Sam, ord. on m̄r Anderson for 11/3 for 18 p<sup>ts</sup>. clover seed.
Nov.   2.   p<sup>d</sup> a gardener for seeds 17/6.

² This snow, like the flood of 1771, was often referred to by Jefferson. It is interesting to note that in recording this event he used the pronoun *we* instead of *I*. On July 22 Jefferson speaks of *our* peas.

³ A later variety of *Pisum sativum* L. Randolph (*Gardening: 39*) lists rouncivals, the Spanish morotto, and the marrowfat or Dutch admiral as the later kind. He writes: "These . . . are intended to come in succession, when the forward kind are gone. You should sow your Peas every fortnight, and as the hot weather comes on the latter sort should be in a sheltered situation, otherwise they will burn up."

⁴ Entries of this kind, and there are many of them in the *Garden Book*, indicate that Jefferson planted seeds without entering the date of planting.

⁵ July was the proper time to plant out into trenches the crop of celery for autumn and winter use.

⁶ See note 3.

⁷ A variety of *Phaseolus vulgaris* L.

⁸ The spring peas were planted around March 30. This was a long bearing time for peas.

[9] *Solanum tuberosum* L.   This is the first mention of the Irish potato in the *Garden Book*.

[10] Julius Shard, one of Jefferson's workmen at *Monticello*. He is mentioned several times in the account books.

[11] Phill, another one of Jefferson's workmen.   He was evidently owned by Bartlet Ford, of Albemarle.

[12] The relative efficiency of the two-wheeled barrow over the one-wheeled barrow was of considerable interest to Jefferson. This was rightly so, for there were great quantities of earth to be moved in leveling and building cellars and roads.   The entry about Julius Shard is found also in the *Account Book 1772* and in the *Farm Book* (1774–1822).   The entry in the *Account Book* was made on July 23 and is somewhat fuller in expression, but the same in content.   The one in the *Farm Book* is synoptic but includes some data not found in the other two entries.   Here is the entry from the *Farm Book:*

### Wheel Barrows

the two-wheeled barrow carries 4. loads of the single one at once. it is loaded & carried 30 yards in $3' + 1\frac{1}{2}' = 4\frac{1}{2}'$.

it will do then exactly double the work in the same time, loading being equal.

a man digs & carries 50 yds. 5 cubical yards of earth in a day of 12 hours.

a man carries 75. brick with the old lime sticking to them, say 500. lb. in the two wheeled barrow on level ground.   24 cubic yards of very solid earth made 122. loads which is $3\frac{1}{2}$ cub. feet to a load.

[13] This entry appears in the *Account Book* as follows:

Aug. 20, 1772.   The wagon with 4. horses and only the driver (Phil) brought from that part of the cleared ground next the Thoroughfare in one day wood which measured 4, 8, & 19½ feet, that is nearly 5. cords calling a cord 4, 4, & 8.   it took 10. loads.

[14] In the same *Account Book* this entry reads: "he [Phil] brings 28 rails at a load up a part of the ground somewhat steeper."

[15] Ryland Randolph was the third son of Colonel Richard Randolph and Jane Bolling, of *Curls,* Henrico County.   He inherited lands in the fork of the Appomattox in Goochland and Amelia Counties, and at Bush River and Falling Creek, Amelia County, also stocks thereon.   (See *Virginia Mag.*

*Hist. and Biography* 22: 441–443, 1914.)  This entry occurs in the *Account Book 1772,* also, under August 20.

[16] The park, which these palings were to inclose, was laid
out on the north side of the mountain in 1769.  (See note 1,
under 1769, and plate XIII.)  The entry in the *Account
Book 1772* is as follows:

July 23, park paling, every other pale high, the tall pales to have 5
nails, the low ones 4. nails is worth, but 30/ the 100 yds, taking every
individual thing into consideration.  assisted by Skip Harris in making
the calculations.

[17] Skip Harris, a workman at *Monticello.*
[18] This is the first fruit, of which there is a record, gathered
at *Monticello.*  The tree was probably planted in 1769, when
a large number of fruit trees was set out.  We have been unable to identify a plumb-peach.  This entry in the *Account
Book 1772* reads: "Oct. 8, this day gather[d] 2. plumb peaches
at Monticello."

[19] William Gillum, spelled Gillam in the *Account Book,* was
a workman at *Monticello.*  He is mentioned several times in
the acount books.

[20] This entry also occurs in the *Account Book 1772.*  Jefferson does not there mention Anderson.

[21] There were many Andersons in Albemarle County.  Jefferson had business dealings with several of them.  It is not
known which one he refers to here.  ("Sept. 14. 1775. p[d].
old Anderson (Mason) 6/" (*Account Book 1775*).)

[22] There were four *Round-about* roads, which completely
encircled the mountain at different levels.  These roads were
connected by oblique roads.  This is the first mention of
*Round-abouts.*  This entry is found in the *Account Book 1772*
and in the *Farm Book.*  In the former it is the same, in the
latter it is fuller.  From the *Farm Book:*

1772. Nov.  in making the Upper Roundabout, 3 hands made 80. yds
a day in the old field = 26 yds a day, but in the woods where they had
stumps to take away, not more than 40 & sometimes 25 yds. = 13, or 8.
this walk is 926. yds = .5261 mile in circumference.

(See plates XXI, XXII, and XXX.)

# 1773

*Gordon, the Mill-wright, sais where the workman is found & every thing brought into place, he should make a double armed water-wheel for 12/ the foot, & the cog-wheel for 15/ the foot in diameter, and the shaft and Gudgeon supporters into the bargain. and a single-armed water wheel for 20/ the foot.[2]

*mr̄s Wythe [3] puts $\frac{1}{10}$ very rich superfine Malmesey to a dry Madeira and makes a fine wine.[4]

Mar. 12.   sowed a patch of Early peas,[5] & another of Marrow fats.[6]

   31.   grafted 5. French chesnuts [7] into two stocks of Common chesnut.[8]

sent Patrick Morton [9] the following slips of fruits from Sandy point.[10]

    N°. 1.   Green Gage plumb.[11]

       2.   Almonds.

       3.   Carnation cherry.[12]

       4.   Duke cherry.[13]

       5.   forward pear.[14]

       6.   late d°.

       7.   fine late large pear.

8.   New-town pippins.[15]

9.   French chesnut.

10.   English Mulberry.[16]

11.   Broadnax's cherry.[17]

12.   very fine late cherry.

Apr.  1.   both patches of peas up.

set out strawberries.

2.   planted 50. vines of various kinds from the Forest.

3.   sowed a patch of Early peas & another of Marrow-fats.

May. 22.   first patch of peas come to table. note this spring is remarkeably forward.

May. 22.   *2. hands grubbed the Grave yard [18] 80.f.sq. = $\frac{1}{7}$ of an acre in $3\frac{1}{2}$ hours so that one would have done it in 7. hours, and would grub an acre in 49. hours = 4. days.

*Ry. Randolph's fencing chain weighs $\frac{1}{2}$ lb per foot, and is 3 f. 3 I. from the ground.

*articles for contracts with overseers.[19]

he shall let his emploier have his share of grain if he chuses it at a fixed price.

he shall not have his share till enough is taken out to sow.

and then only of what is sold or eaten by measure.

allow ½ a share for every horse, & the same for a plough-boy.

to have at the rate of a share for every 8. hands, but never to have more than 2. shares if there be ever so many hands.

provision 400. lb pork if single. 500 lb if married.

to be turned off at any time of year if employer disapproves of his conduct, on paying a proportion of what shall be made, according to the time he has staid.

to pay for carrying his share of the crop to market.

to pay for carriage of all refused tobō.

to pay his own levies.

to pay his share of liquor & hiring at harvest.

and never to bleed a negro.

―――――

¹ *1773.* Two sad events happened in 1773, which affected the personal life of Jefferson. On May 16 Dabney Carr died. He had been Jefferson's most intimate friend since boyhood. He married Jefferson's sister, Martha. After Carr's death, Jefferson cared for her and their six children at *Monticello.* Jefferson was at Williamsburg when his friend died. On account of a mutual promise made when they were students together, to the effect that the one who survived should see that the body of the other was buried at the foot of a favorite oak tree on *Monticello* mountain, Jefferson had Carr's body removed from *Shadwell,* where he was buried, to the graveyard at *Monticello.* The preparation of the graveyard was begun

on May 22, the day after Jefferson returned from Williamsburg. (See entry in *Garden Book,* May 22, 1773.) The body of Carr was probably moved soon after and was the first to be interred in the graveyard at *Monticello.*

The second event was the death, on May 28, of Mrs. Jefferson's father, John Wayles, of *The Forest.* By his death Mrs. Jefferson inherited about 40,000 acres of land and 135 slaves. The land included *Poplar Forest,* in Bedford County, a favorite estate of Jefferson. (Randall, *Jefferson* 1: 66.) He later built a house there, which he loved almost as well as *Monticello.*

Politically, the year was important for the part Jefferson played in the House of Burgesses on the Committee of Correspondence and Inquiry. (Randall, *Jefferson* 1: 78–82.)

Jefferson recorded little about the garden for this year. He was away from *Monticello* for long periods of time, returning long enough to plant and eat his favorite pea. He attended the meetings of the House of Burgesses and was employed in law cases as in previous years. He was not idle, however, on his mountaintop. In 1772 he had contracted with George Dudley to make in the next two years 100,000 workable bricks, some of them stock brick and the others place brick. He was to make "50. M. bricks in 1773." (*Account Book 1773.*) He planted fruit trees from Sandy Point and 50 vines from *The Forest.* On one of his trips to *The Forest* he "pᵈ Jamey for two Mockᵍ birds 11/6" (*ibid.*). The mocking bird was Jefferson's favorite among birds. He considered it far superior to the nightingale of Europe. On September 8 he made his first trip to *Poplar Forest* to look after his lands in Bedford County.

² Jefferson owned two mills on the Rivanna. One he inherited from his father, and the other he built during his presidency. Gordon, the millwright, probably built the mills, or set up the machinery for them, along the watercourses in Albemarle County.

³ Mrs. Wythe, the wife of George Wythe of Williamsburg. She was Elizabeth Taliaferro, daughter of Colonel Richard and Eliza Taliaferro, of *Powhatan,* James City County, and married George Wythe about 1755. (*Dict. Am. Biog.* 20: 586–589.)

⁴ Jefferson was in Williamsburg and its environs during most of January and February, so he no doubt drank of this new wine made from Madeira and Malmesey.

⁵ An early variety of *Pisum sativum* L.   Probably one of the Charlton Hotspur.   They were up on April 1 and came to the table on May 22.

⁶ Marrowfats belong to the later varieties of peas.   Jefferson did not record the first planting of Marrowfats.   They appeared above ground on April 1.

⁷ *Castanea sativa* Mill.   This is more commonly called Spanish chestnut.

⁸ *Castanea dentata* Borkh., American chestnut.   It was a common practice to graft the European chestnut onto the American one.   Johnson (*Farmers Encyclopedia:* 321) says: "It may be budded on the common chestnut, but is apt to overgrow the stock."

⁹ Patrick Morton worked for Jefferson at *Monticello*.   In the *Account Book 1767–1770* is found this entry: "July 23, pᵈ Patrick Morton for 5 days work 12/6."   Jefferson wrote on the Plan for Orchard, 1778 (pl. VII) : "Newtown pippins, from Sandy Point, Medlar Russeting, Golden Wildings, ingrafted by Patrick Morton in 1773. & planted out in 1778." (See *Garden Book*, March 9, 1778.)

¹⁰ Sandy Point, Charles City County.   It was near *The Forest.*

¹¹ A variety of *Prunus domestica* L.

The Green Gage is universally admitted to hold the first rank in flavor among all plums, and is everywhere highly esteemed.   During the last century, an English family by the name of Gage, obtained a number of fruit trees from the monks of Chartreuse, near Paris.   Among them was a tree of this plum, which, having lost its name, was called by the gardener Green Gage.   (Downing, *Fruits:* 276.)

¹² A variety of *Prunus cerasus* L.   Downing divides the varieties of cherries into four classes: Heart Cherries, Bigarreau Cherries, Duke Cherries, and Morello Cherries.   He places Carnation Cherries under the last group.   He describes it as "a very handsome, light red, large cherry, highly esteemed here for brandying and preserving" (Downing, *Fruits:* 194).   See plate VII for location of Carnation Cherries.   This was Jefferson's favorite cherry.   (See letter, Jefferson to James Barbour, March 15, 1816.)

[18] Downing lists six Duke Cherries. It is impossible to tell which one of them Jefferson planted here.

[14] Probably belonging to the summer pears. See plate VII for location of these pears.

[15] Newton Pippin, a variety of *Malus pumila* Mill.,

stands at the head of all apples, and is, when in perfection, acknowledged to be unrivalled in all the qualities which constitute a high flavoured dessert apple, to which it combines the quality of long keeping without the least shrivelling, retaining its high flavour to the last. . . . This variety is a native of Newtown, Long Island. (Downing, *Fruits:* 118.)

[16] The English mulberry, *Morus nigra* L.

[17] Broadnax's Cherry. (See plate VII.)

[18] As mentioned above, the graveyard was prepared to receive the body of Dabney Carr, who had died on May 16 of this year. Since then it has been the resting place of all of Jefferson's immediate family and many of his descendants. It has been increased many times since the original 80 feet square were grubbed. Jefferson died July 4, 1826. Soon after his death there was found among his papers the following inscription which he had written for his tombstone:

Here was buried

Thomas Jefferson,

Author of the Declaration of American Independence,
Of the Statute of Virginia for Religious Freedom,
And Father of the University of Virginia.

Born April 2, 1743, O. S.

Died

The original graveyard was surrounded by weeping willows. In a memorandum, about 1808, to Edmund Bacon, his overseer, Jefferson told him to plant a hedge of weeping willows around the graveyard. The original tomb of Jefferson was so mutilated by vandals and souvenir-hunters that the Government of the United States erected the present obelisk and surrounded the graveyard with a tall iron fence. Although the *Monticello* estate has passed through several hands, the graveyard belongs to Jefferson's descendants. They have organized the Monticello Graveyard Association, which looks after its upkeep. They meet annually at *Monticello* during the month of May. (See plate XXI for location of graveyard.)

In the *Farm Book,* under the heading *Hoes,* Jefferson wrote the following about grubbing:

a laborer will grub from half an acre to an acre a week of common bushy land in winter.

2. hands grubbed the grave yard 80 f. sq. = ¼ acre in 3½ hours. 1 dº. will grub 1¼ acre a week in summer of the worst woodlands. inclosed lands in thicket are worse.

the price of grubbing is 24/ pʳ. acre in Augusta, & cutting down & cutting up the large timber ready for burning is 16/.

[19] In addition to the articles for contracts with overseers, in the *Garden Book,* Jefferson wrote similar articles for contracts in the *Farm Book* and in the *Account Book 1773.* They are given here because of their importance in showing his attitude toward contracts with laborers. All of them vary in certain minor ways.

From the *Account Book 1773:*

### Hints for contracts with *Overseers.*

—— pay part of harvest expenses, liquor & reaping
—— he shall let his employer have his share of grain at a fixed price.
—— he shall not have his share till enough is taken out to sow.
—— allow a share for every plough boy & horse, or for every two horses where no boy.
—— to have at the rate of a share for every 2 hands til it gets 2. shares, and never to have more.
—— allowances 400 lb. pork if single, 500 lb. if marrᵈ.
—— to be turned off at any time of year if misbehaves, on paying 30/ per month for the time past.
—— to pay for carrying own tobº. to market.
—— to pay for carriage of all refused tobacco.

From the *Farm Book:*

### *Overseers*

Articles for contracts with them.

*the* employer to have his share of grain at a fixed price at the end of the year if he chuses it.
*not* to share till seed-grain is taken out, & then of what is sold or eaten by measure only.
*allow* ½ a share for every horse, & the same for a plough boy.
*a* share for every 8. hands as far as 16. but never more than 2. shares.
*provision* 400 lb. pork if single, 500 lb. if married.
*to* be turned off at any time of the year if his employer disapproves of

his conduct on paying a proportion of what shall be made according to
the time he has staid.
*to* pay for carrying his share of the crop to market.
*to* pay the carriage of all refused tob°.
*to* pay his own taxes & levies.
*to* pay his share of liquor & hiring at harvest.
*to* exchange clear profits with his employer at the end of the year, if the
employer chuses it.
*not* allowed to keep a horse or goose, or keep a woman out of the crop
for waiting on them.

# 1774

Mar. 10. sowed a bed of Early & a bed of Marrow-fat peas.[2]

12. planted in the S.W. border of the garden[3] the following stones.

N°. 1. a Virginian Almond.—N°. 2—to 13. Almonds[4] from the Streights[5]

N°. 14. 15. 16. Apricots.—N°. 16. a Filbert.[6]

15. sowed the following seeds[7] & distinguished them by sticking numbered sticks in the beds. Aglio di Toscania. Garlic.[8]

N°. 15. Radicchio di Pistoia. Succory, or Wild Endive.[9]

26. Cipolle bianche di Tuckahoe,[10] the Spanish Onion of Miller.[11]

31. Savoys.[12]

33. Salsafia.[13]

34. Cabbage.[14]

35. Lettuce.[15]

36. Lettuce (different)

38. Radishes.[16]

39. Pepper grass.[17]

47

40.  [Cancelled.]

41.  Salvastrella [18] di Pisa.

42.  Sorrel. Acetosa di Pisa.[19]

18.  ......46.  Coclearia di Pisa.  (Scurvy grass or perhaps Horse-radish.[20])

47.  Cavol  Capuccio  Spagnola  di Pisa.[21]

56.  Prezzemolo. parsley.[22]

58.  d⁰.

21.  Peas of Mar. 10. are up.[23]

23.  sowed the following seeds distinguished by numbered sticks.

N°. 12.  Cluster peas. or Bunch peas.[24]

13.  Windsor beans.[25]

14.  Green beans [26] from Colō Bland.[27]

16.  Vetch.[28]

37.  Spinaci. Spinach.[29]

45.  Carote di Pisa.[30] Carrots.

48.  Cavol broccolo Francese di Pisa.[31] Broccoli.

49.  Carote. Carrots.

51.  Beans. Dʳ. Bland.[32]

54.  Lattuga. Lettuce.

55.  Cipolle. Col. Cary.[33] Onions.

57.  Parsnips.[34] Col. Cary.

59.  Parsnips. m͞r Eppes.[35]

60.  Salmon radishes.[36]

61.  Carrots.

72.  Siberian wheat.[37]

24.  sowed the following things distinguished by numbered sticks

N°. 8.⎫
        ⎬ early & later peas from Col. Cary.
9.⎭

28.  small Lentils.[38]

25.  ...N°. 29.  green Lentils

32.  Italian Cresses.

73.  Garden Cresses.  m͞r Webb.

4.  Black eyed peas [39] which yeild two crops. Colō R. Randolph [40]

26.  .....seven rows of Grano Estivo [41] from Tuscany.

N°. 50.  Nasturcium[42] in 35. little hills.

29.  Cresses

23.  Celery

Radichio. the same as N°. 15. . . .

⎱in the meadow.[43]

28.  ....Solid Celery.[44]  in the Meadow.

29.   ....Nº. 18.  Asparagus.

5.  Beans Dʳ. Clayton.⁴⁵

Peach trees at Monticello in general bloom

Mar. 31.  laid off ground to be levelled for a future gar-
den.⁴⁶   the upper side is 44.f. below the upper
edge of the Round-about and parallel thereto.
it is 668. feet long, 80 f. wide, and at each end
forms a triangle, rectangular & isosceles, of
which the legs are 80.f. & the hypothenuse 113.
feet. ~~it will be better to add 2.f. in width on
the upper side, which will permit bed under
upper wall to be 8.f.~~

planted the following seeds, trees, etc.

twenty four apple trees. ⎤ from the Mountain
                        ⎥ plains ⁴⁷
nineteen cherry trees . .⎦

Nº. 3.   a doz. sweet almonds ⁴⁸ with smooth
rinds, 8 of which were cracked, the
others not.

5.   a doz. dº. with hairy rinds. 8. cracked.
the others not.

7.   a doz. dº. with hard shells. 8 cracked.

10.   32. bitter almonds. 20. cracked.

13.   20. Meliache e Albicocche ⁴⁹ (2 diffᵗ.
kinds of apricots) 12 of them cracked,
the others not.

8.   4. Ciriege corniole.⁵⁰ (a particular
kind of cherry.) 2 of them cracked.

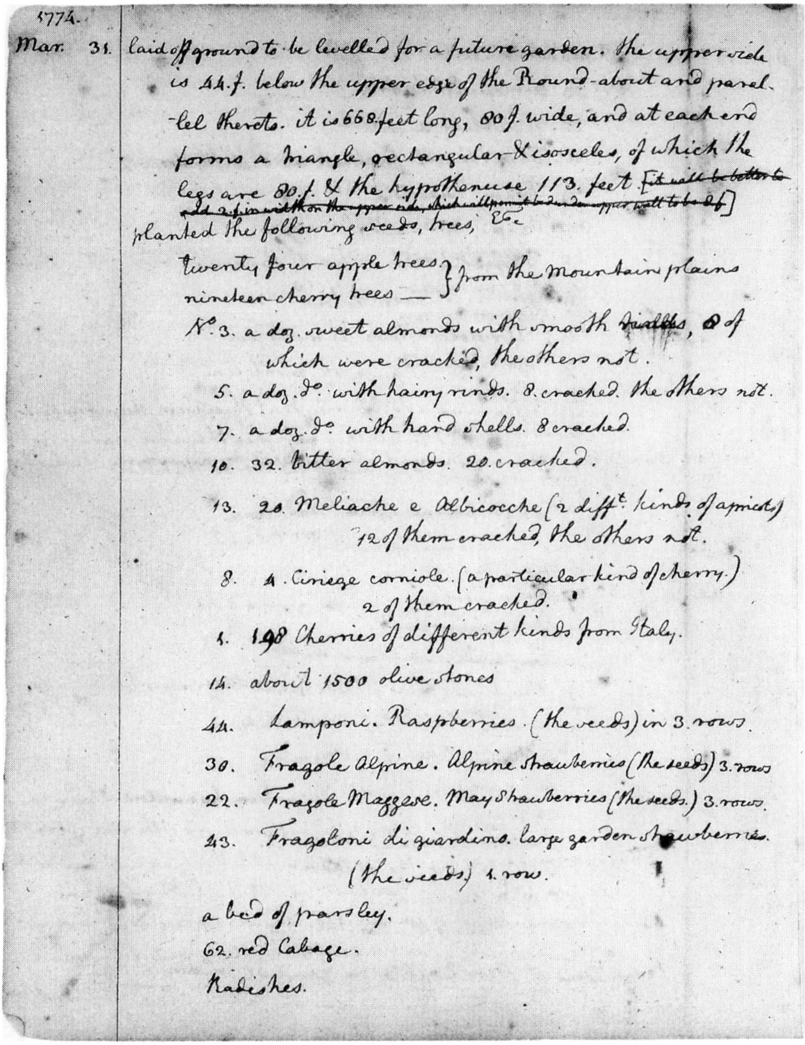

1774.

Mar. 31. laid off ground to be levelled for a future garden. the upper side
is 44.f. below the upper edge of the Round-about and parel-
-lel thereto. it is 668.feet long, 80.f. wide, and at each end
forms a triangle, rectangular & isosceles, of which the
legs are 80.f. & the hypothenuse 113. feet. [it will be better to
add a [...] from the upper [...] which will permit [...] [...] upper wall to be left]
planted the following seeds, trees, &c.

    twenty four apple trees  } from the mountain plains
    nineteen cherry trees ——

    N°.3. a doz. sweet almonds with smooth shells, 8 of
          which were cracked, the others not.
    5. a doz. d°. with hairy rinds. 8.cracked. the others not.
    7. a doz. d°. with hard shells. 8 cracked.
    10. 32. bitter almonds. 20.cracked.

    13. 20. Meliache e Albicocche (2 diff.t kinds of apricots)
          12 of them cracked, the others not.

    8. 4. Ciriege corniole. (a particular kind of cherry.)
          2 of them cracked.

    1. 198 Cherries of different kinds from Italy.

    14. about 1500 olive stones

    44. Lamponi. Raspberries. (the seeds) in 3.rows.

    30. Fragole Alpine. Alpine strawberries (the seeds) 3.rows

    22. Fragole Maggese. May strawberries (the seeds.) 3.rows.

    43. Fragoloni di giardino. large garden strawberries.
          (the seeds) 1.row.

    a bed of parsley.
    62. red Cabage.
    Radishes.

PLATE IV.—Page 14 of the original *Garden Book*.  Note the first mention of
laying off a garden, and also the use of Italian names for vegetables.

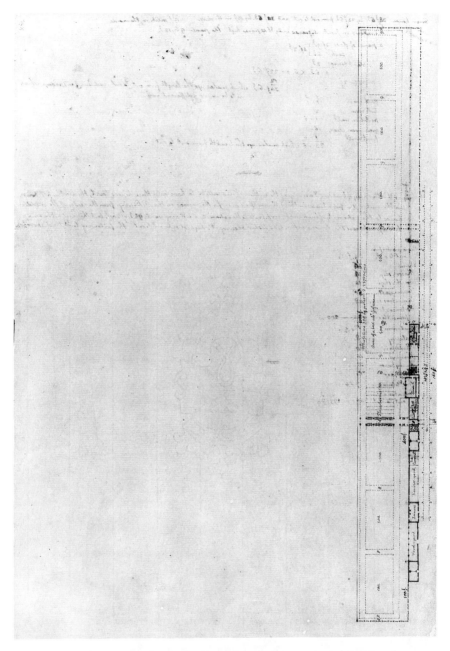

PLATE V.—Jefferson's earliest plan of the vegetable garden. He probably drew
the plan about 1774, at the time he laid off the ground for a garden. The garden was
later regraded and leveled, and the number of squares was increased to 24. Note the
outhouses above the garden. (*Jefferson Papers*, M. H. S.)

1.   198 Cherries of different kinds from Italy.[51]

14.   about 1500 olive stones [52]

44.   Lamponi. Raspberries. (the seeds) in 3. rows.

30.   Fragole Alpine. Alpine strawberries (the seeds) 3. rows.

22.   Fragole Mazzese. May Strawberries (the seeds.) 3. rows.

43.   Fragoloni di giardino. large garden strawberries. (the seeds.) 1. row.

a bed of parsley.

62.   red Cabage.[53]

Radishes.

Apr.   1.   sowed & planted as follows.

N°. 53.   turneps.[54] D'. Bland.

25.   Fagiuoli d'Augusta.[55]

19.   d°. verdi coll' occhio bianco.[56] D. Hylton.[57]

71.   Bonny-Bess.[58] Colō Bland.

70.   Snap-beans. Colō Bland.

2.   Fagiuoli coll' occhio di Provenza.[59]

7.   d°.   bianchi di Parigi [60]

6.   Cetriuoli.[61] Webb.[62] 9. monticini.[63]

5.   d°.   Eppes.[64] 12. monticini.

4. the peas of Mar. 24. come up.

5. Cucumbers. the same as N°. 6. only that these were steeped in water from Mar. 31. till this day when they were sprouted.[65] 10. hill

d°. same as N°. 5. only soaked as before. 17. hills.

N°. 63.    Piperone.[66] John Wood.[67]

52.    Cayenne Pepper. D^r. Bland.

24.    Purple beans.[68] Ja^s. Donald.[69]

17.    White & purple d°. d°.

21.    Sugar beans.[70]

1.    Fagiuoli bianchi di Toscana.[71]

6. N°. 65.    Hotspur peas.   Monticello.[72]

66.    Marrow fat d°. d°.

Planted 30. vines just below where the new garden wall [73] will run, towards the Westermost end.   8 of them at the Westermost end of the row were Spanish Raisins [74] from Colō Bland's, next to them were 16. native vines from Winslow's in New Kent,[75] and at the Eastermost end were 6. native vines of Monticello. they were planted by some Tuscan Vignerons [76] who came over with m̄r Mazzei.[77] the manner was as follows.

Apr. 6. A trench 4.f. deep and 4.f. wide was dug.   at the bottom were put small green bushes, and on them a thin coat of dung and earth mixed, which raised the bed to within 2½ feet of the

surface.   the cuttings which were from $3\frac{1}{2}$ to
6.f. long, and which had been hitherto buried
in the earth, were then produced, about 18.I.
of their butts were dipt into a thick paste made
of cowdung and water and then planted in the
bottom, the Raisins 3.f. apart the rest about
2.f. having a stick stuck by each to which it was
bound with bear grass in order to support it
while the earth should be drawn in.   the earth
was then thrown in, the mould first, and afterwards the other earth in the same order in
which it was dug, leaving the bottom clay for
the last.   the earth was thrown in very loose &
care was taken to avoid trampling in it.   the
trench was not quite filled, but left somewhat
hollowing to receive & retain the water, & the
superfluous earth was left on each side without
the trench.   then the supporting sticks were
drawn out and would have served for the other
rows had the plantation been to be continued.
in such a case, the rows are to be 4 f. apart, so
that in fact the whole surface is taken up to the
depth of 4.f.   the best way of doing it is to dig
every other trench, and leave the earth which is
thrown out exposed for a twelve month.   then
the vines may be planted at any time from the
middle of November to the first week in April.
afterwards dig the other alternate trenches, and
leave the earth of these also exposed for a
twelvemonth.   when the latter trenches are
planted, leave the superfluous earth in ridges
between the rows of vines till by the subsidence
of the earth it becomes necessary to pull it into
the trenches.   if any of your grapes turn out
illy, cut off the vine & ingraft another on the

stock.   an acre in vines where they are $2\frac{1}{2}$ f apart in the row will admit 4316. in all.

7.   sowed, planted etc as follows.

N°. 1.   Cocomere di Pistoia.[78] Watermelons. 34. hills.

2.   Cocomore di seme Neapolitane.[79] 37. hills.

12.   Zatte di Massa.[80] Canteloupe melons. 18. hills.

18.   Popone Arancini di Pistoia.[81] Musk melons. 11. hills

64.   in the Meadow. Rice [82]

8.   ....

Meadow
{
7.   Zucche bianche. white pumpkins. 22. monticini

8.   Zucche nere.  black d°.[83]  42. hills.

9.   d°.  di Monacho.  8. monticini.

10.  d°.  Lauri.[84] 9. monticini

11.  d°.  da Pescatori.[85] 3. d°.
}

11.   *in making a stone wall [86] in my garden I find by an accurate calculation that $7\frac{1}{2}$ cubical feet may be done in a day by one hand who brings his own stone into place and does every thing.

25.   sowed 4. rows of forward peas.

2. d°. of [87]

30.   sowed N°. 67.   white beet [88]
68.   red beet.
} from England.

69.  Scarlet radishes.[89]  Tuckahoe.

May. 2.  sowed N°.  3.  Carrots.

6.  Spinach.

10.  Curled Parsley.[90]

11.  Peas.

20.  Rape.[91]     } from D[r] Brown's [94]

32.  Savoys

73.  Coleworts [92]

75.  Broccoli

40.  Ice Lettuce [93]

May. 4.  the blue ridge [95] of mountains covered with snow.

5.  a frost which destroyed almost every thing. it killed the wheat, rye, corn, many tobacco plants, and even large saplings.  the leaves of the trees were entirely killed.  all the shoots of vines.  at Monticello near half the fruit of every kind was killed; and before this no instance had ever occurred of any fruit killed here by the frost.  in all other places in the neighborhood the destruction of fruit was total. this frost was general & equally destructive thro the whole country and the neighboring colonies.[96]

14.  cherries ripe.

16.  first dish of pease from earliest patch.[97]

26.  a second patch of peas come to table.[98]

June. 4.  Windsor beans come to table.[99]

    5.  a third & fourth patch of peas come to table.[100]

  13.  a fifth patch of peas come in.

July. 13.  last dish of peas.

  18.  last lettuce from Gehee's/[101]

  23.  Cucumbers from our garden.

  31.  Watermelons from our patch.[102]

Aug. 3.  Indian corn comes to table.[103]

      black eyed peas come to table [104]

Nov. 16.  this morning the Northern part of the Blue ridge is white with snow.

  17.  the first frost sufficient to kill any thing.[105]

---

[1] *1774.* Jefferson was at *Monticello* during the months of March and April of this year, so that he was able to make the most complete record of the spring plantings since the *Garden Book* was begun. The record was made more interesting by the fact that a large number of the plant names were written in Italian. This interest in Italian plant names came from the association of Jefferson with Philip Mazzei, an Italian who came to Virginia in the latter part of 1773, to raise grapes and other plants. He brought with him many seeds and plants from Europe, some of which he gave to Jefferson in time for the spring planting. Mazzei, while searching for a tract of land to carry on his agricultural schemes, stopped off at *Monticello* to see Jefferson. Since Jefferson had an intense interest in agriculture, he persuaded Mazzei to settle on a tract of land adjoining *Monticello* on the east, of about 2,000 acres, which Jefferson gave him. Mazzei named his place *Colle,* and while

the house was being built, he lived with Jefferson at *Monticello*. It was during his sojourn there that the Italian names were used in the *Garden Book*. (See Richard Cecil Garlick, Jr., *Philip Mazzei, Friend of Jefferson* (Baltimore, 1933): 41. Hereafter cited as Garlick, *Philip Mazzei*.)

Meanwhile events other than gardening were taking place at *Monticello*. On "Feb. 21, at 2:11 P. M. felt a shock of an earthquake at *Monticello*. it shook the houses so sensibly that everybody ran out doors." (*Account Book 1774*.) This quake was felt over a large part of Virginia, for John Blair, of Williamsburg, wrote to Jefferson on March 2: "The 21st. ult. about 2 in the afternoon (some say ½ Hour later) we had a very moderate trembling of the Earth, so moderate that not many perceived it, but Dr. Gilmer informed me it was a pretty smart shook with you; & by all accts. it was more severe as you advance to the West" (*Jefferson Papers, M. H. S.*) And on "Mar. 6. a flood in the Rivanna 18 I. higher than the one which carried N. Lewis's bridge away & that was the highest ever known except the great fresh in May 1771" (*Account Book 1774*).

Mr. and Mrs. Jefferson's second daughter, Jane Randolph, was born on April 3. This approaching event was probably the cause for Jefferson remaining home much of the early spring.

We do not know how much of the main house at *Monticello* was completed by this year. Workman continued to burn brick. On June 2, Jefferson "agreed with William Pond to make brick for me this summer. he is to have 2/6 a thousand for making & burning the place brick. the price of the stock bricks is to be fixt by Stephen Willis." (*Account Book 1774*.)

The Revolutionary Period was approaching. Jefferson was playing an important part in shaping its policies. This year he and other patriotic leaders had the House of Burgesses proclaim a "Fast Day," as Virginia's reply to the Boston Port Bill. He also wrote the draft of "Resolution of Albemarle County."

² "Mar. 10. pd m͞r Cole's Ned for a galln of peas 5/" (*Account Book 1774*).

³ The location of this garden is not known. The permanent garden, located on the southeastern slope, was not laid off until March 31 of this year.

[4] A variety of *Prunus communis* L.

[5] Probably the Strait of Gibraltar or the Strait of Messina. Around these areas the almond is grown extensively and exported to all parts of the globe. These almond stones as well as the stones of apricots and the filberts were given to Jefferson by Mazzei.

[6] *Corylus avellana* L.

[7] Most of the plants, written with Italian names, were given to Jefferson by Mazzei, but occasionally Jefferson supplied the Italian name to plants he had already.

[8] Translated, garlic from Tuscany, Italy. *Allium sativum* L.

[9] Translated, succory from Pistoia, Italy. *Cichorium intybus* L.

[10] Translated, white onion from *Tuckahoe*. Mazzei had probably given this onion to Mr. Randolph, at *Tuckahoe*, and he in turn had given it to Jefferson. *Tuckahoe*, in Goochland County, was the home of the late Colonel William Randolph. Jefferson spent several years of his early childhood there.

[11] This white onion was called Spanish Onion by Philip Miller, in *The Gardener's Dictionary* (London, 1759).

[12] A kind of blistered and puckered cabbage, *Brassica oleracea* var. *capitata* L., from Savoy.

[13] *Tragopogon porrifolius* L. Called also salsify and oyster plant.

[14] *Brassica oleracea* var. *capitata* L.

[15] *Lactuca sativa* L.

[16] *Raphanus sativus* L.

[17] *Lepidium sativum* L.

[18] Pimpernel, used as a salad by man and as a forage for animals.

[19] *Rumex acetosa* L. Translated, sorrel from Pisa, Italy.

[20] Translated, scurvy-grass from Pisa. *Cochlearia officinalis* L., scurvy-grass. (*Armoracia rusticana* Gaertn., horseradish.)

[21] Translated, Spanish cabbage heads from Pisa.

[22] *Petroselinum hortense* Hoffm.

[23] Twelve days for peas planted March 10 to germinate and come above ground.

[24] A variety of *Pisum sativum* L. Probably the same as Bush Pea and akin to the Tom Thumb group of peas.

[25] The Windsor Bean is a variety of the English Bean, *Vicia faba* L.

[26] Probably the Green Windsor Bean, a longer bearer than the Windsor.

[27] Colonel Richard Bland (1710–1776), born in Williamsburg, Virginia, was the son of Richard Bland and Elizabeth (Randolph) Bland, of *Jordans Point,* Prince George County. He was educated at William and Mary College and at the University of Edinburgh. After 1748 he was for many years a leading member of the House of Burgesses. He was a distinguished Revolutionary patriot, holding continued public office until his death. (Tyler, *Virginia Biography* 2: 4–5.)

[28] *Vicia* sp.

[29] *Spinacia oleracea* L.

[30] Translated, carrot from Pisa, Italy.

[31] Translated, French broccoli from Pisa.

[32] Doctor Theodorick Bland (1751–1790) was a son of Colonel Theodorick Bland of *Cawsons,* Prince George County. At the age of eleven he was sent to England and studied at Wakefield, in Yorkshire, afterwards pursuing a medical course at the University of Edinburgh, and in 1764 he returned to America. He was among the first in Virginia who opposed the practice of medicine without a license. He continued his profession until the outbreak of the Revolutionary War, when he volunteered for service. He was appointed first a captain, later a lieutenant-colonel, and afterwards a colonel. In 1779–1780 he was in command of the troops stationed at Albemarle barracks, in Virginia. He was later a member of Congress and served his country conspicuously in many ways. (Tyler, *Virginia Biography* 2: 5.)

[33] Colonel Archibald Cary (1721–1787) was the son of Henry Cary of *Ampthill,* Chesterfield County, and Anne Edwards, his wife. He was educated at William and Mary College, and later was a member of all the assemblies from 1756 to 1776, and of the Revolutionary conventions of 1774, 1775, and 1776. He was the first speaker of the Senate in 1776 and remained its presiding officer until his death. (Tyler, *Virginia Biography* 2: 8.)

[34] *Pastinaca sativa* L.

[35] Francis Eppes (1747–1808) married Elizabeth Wayles, daughter of John Wayles, of *The Forest*. He lived at *Eppington*, Chesterfield County. His son, John Wayles Eppes, married Jefferson's daughter Maria, who was his cousin. Jefferson and Francis Eppes were close friends and correspondents for many years.

[36] Salmon radish, a variety of *Raphanus sativus* L.

[37] *Triticum aestivum* L. Siberian wheat is a variety of this.

[38] *Lens esculenta* Moench. The small and green lentils are varieties of *Lens esculenta*. They resemble each other, particularly in the habit of growth. The principal distinction is in the color of the seeds. Lentils are used as food for man and cattle.

[39] A variety of *Vigna sinensis* Endl. This pea is mainly a field pea and is grown extensively in the South, where it is considered one of the choice peas. It is cooked when green or dry.

[40] Probably Colonel Richard Randolph, of Henrico County, who

owned land in Albemarle. . . . To Dr. Thomas Walker, as trustee of the county, he sold a thousand acres . . . on which in 1762, Charlottesville, the new court house, was established. (Woods, *Albemarle County*: 302–303.)

[41] Translated, summer wheat.

[42] *Tropaeolum majus* L.

[43] The location of this meadow has not been determined.

[44] The celery, *Apium graveolens* var. *dulce* L., is divided into those with hollow stems and those with solid stems. The solid celery is either red or white.

[45] The beans here mentioned probably came from the home of John Clayton, the botanist, who had died in December of the previous year. John Clayton lived at *Windsor*, his home in Gloucester County. "He was an eminent botanist; member of some of the most learned societies of Europe; president of the Virginia Society for Promoting Useful Knowledge, 1773; and author of *Flora Virginica*. He was for fifty years clerk of Gloucester County, and had a botanical garden at his estate, *Windsor*." (Tyler, *Virginia Biography* 1: 212.)

[46] The vegetable garden was located on the southeastern slope of the mountain, just below the first *Round-about*. This

is the first mention of laying out a garden on *Monticello* mountain.    It was not completed until after Jefferson's retirement from the Presidency in 1809.    (See plates V, VI, XXI, XXII, and XXX for the location of the garden.)

[47] *Mountain Plains* was the plantation of Michael Woods on Mechum's River and Lickinghole, Albemarle County.

[48] The sweet almond and those mentioned in Numbers 5, 7, 10, are varieties of the almond, *Prunus communis* L.    The classification is based mainly on the sweetness or bitterness of the kernel.    It is interesting to note, in each case, the larger proportion of cracked shells planted over those not cracked. Jefferson did not indicate which method gave the better results.

[49] Translated, applelike apricots.

[50] *Ciriege* is the Italian word for cherry.    *Corniole* is a special variety of Italian cherry.

[51] These were given to Jefferson by Mazzei.

[52] *Olea europaea* L.    This was the beginning of Jefferson's intense interest in growing the olive tree in the United States. He wished and tried to make it one of the important crops of the South.    The climate was too severe for its successful culture at *Monticello*.

[53] A red-leaved form of *Brassica oleracea* var. *capitata* L.

[54] *Brassica rapa* L.

[55] Jefferson is here translating the phrase "beans from Augusta County, Virginia" into Italian.    These beans were probably given to Thomas Adams, Mazzei's adviser, who was at this time building a house in Augusta County.    Mr. Adams gave them to Jefferson.

[56] Translated, green beans with white eyes.

[57] Daniel L. Hylton was a prominent merchant in Richmond, Virginia.    Jefferson corresponded with him, and referred to him frequently in his account books.

[58] Probably a variety of bean or pea.

[59] Translated, beans with the eye from Provence.

[60] Translated, white beans from Paris.

[61] Translated, cucumber.

[62] Probably George Webb, of Charles City, Virginia, who in 1737 patented upwards of 7,000 acres of land, near a mountain north of Earlysville, Albemarle County, still called by his name.    (Woods, *Albemarle County:* 7.)

[63] Translated, 9 little hills.

[64] Francis Eppes.    See note 35 for this year.

[65] Another one of Jefferson's experiments with soaking seeds. Farmers in Albemarle County today rarely soak cucumber seeds, certainly not for 6 days.

[66] Translated, pepper.

[67] Probably John Wood of Albemarle County. Woods (*Albemarle County*) lists several people by the name of John Wood.

[68] A variety of the English bean, *Vicia faba* L.

[69] William and James Donald were merchants and shipowners, of Greenocks, Scotland. They carried on an extensive trade with Virginians.

[70] Probably *Pisum sativum* L. var. *macrocarpon* Ser.

[71] Translated, white beans from Tuscany.

[72] These Hotspur peas came from Jefferson's plants grown at *Monticello*.

[73] This garden wall separated the vegetable garden from the terraced orchard below.    (See plate VII.)

[74] A variety of the grape, *Vitis vinifera* L.    "A large and showy grape, ripening late, but requiring a good deal of heat. . . . Bunches large; berries very large, oval; skin thick, dark red, flavour tolerably sweet and rich."    (Downing, *Fruits:* 238.)

[75] Winslow's, New Kent County.    Unidentified.

[76] Philip Mazzei brought over with him from Italy ten vignerons. They landed in Virginia late in 1773. In the summer of 1774 six others arrived from Luca, Italy.    (Garlick, *Philip Mazzei:* 39–43.)

The *Triumph,* captain Rogers, arrived in James river near 3 weeks ago, from Leghorn, addressed to Mr. Mazzei: By this vessel, we understand, Mr. Mazzei has received sundry seeds, vine cuttings, plants, &c. together with several Italian emigrants, consisting of husbandmen and mechanics; and by her we also learn that the presents of birds, seeds, and plants, sent by Mr. Mazzei, to the grand duke of Tuscany, were graciously received, and that his highness was pleased to order his thanks to be given Mr. Mazzei for his attention and kindness, and to assure him of his royal favour and protection, on all occasions, that may contribute to his advantage and success. (*Virginia Gazette* (Rind), Thurs., July 28, 1774.)    (Courtesy of Dr. Cecil Garlick, Jr.)

[77] Philip Mazzei was born on December 25, 1730, in Tuscany. He died on March 19, 1816, at Pisa.

He was successively physician, merchant, horticulturalist, Virginia's Agent in Europe during the last years of the American Revolution, author of the first accurate history of America in French, Intelligencer in Paris to the King of Poland for the first three and a half years of the French Revolution, and Private Adviser to the King of Poland just prior to the Second Division of that unfortunate State. Although he was a native of Tuscany, he lived for a number of years in Smyrna, London, and Paris, and for a shorter length of time in twenty odd other cities of importance in both the Old and New Worlds, was a naturalized citizen of Virginia, and later a naturalized Pole. Though a bourgeois by birth, he became the personal friend of six rulers, and was aquainted with six more. He had the distinction, not to say misfortune, of being present at the three great national upheavals of the late eighteenth century: the American Revolution, the French Revolution, and the Second Division of Poland. (Garlick, *Philip Mazzei: 7.*)

On January 25, 1793, Jefferson wrote to Albert Gallatin the following concerning Mr. Mazzei:

Mr. Legaux called on me this morning to ask a statement of the ex- periment which was made in Virginia by a Mr. Mazzei, for the raising vines and making wines, and desired I would address it to you. Mr. Mazzei was an Italian, and brought over with him about a dozen laborers of his own country, bound to serve him four or five years. . . . We made up a subscription for him of 2000 pounds sterling, and he began his experiment on a piece of land adjoining to mine. His inten- tion was before the time of his people should expire, to import more from Italy. He planted a considerable vineyard, and attended to it with great diligence for three years. The war then came on, the time of his people soon expired, some of them enlisted, others chose to settle on other lands and labor for themselves; some were taken away by the gentlemen of the country for gardeners, so that there did not remain a single one with him, and the interruption of navigation prevented his importing others. In this state of things he was himself employed by the State of Virginia to go to Europe as their agent to do some par- ticular business. He rented his place to General Riedesel, whose horses in one week destroyed the whole labor of three or four years; and thus ended an experiment which, from every appearance, would in a year or two more have established the practicability of that branch of culture in America. This is the sum of the experiment as exactly as I am able to state it from memory, after such an interval of time. (Lipscomb and Bergh, *Jefferson* 9: 14–15.)

[78] Translated, watermelons from Pistoia, Italy. *Citrullus vulgaris* Schrad.

[79] Translated, watermelon seeds from Naples.

[80] Translated, cantaloupe melons from Massa. *Cucumis melo* var. *cantalupensis* Naud.

⁸¹ Translated, muskmelons from Pistoia.   *Cucumis melo* L.

⁸² A variety of *Oryza sativa* L.

⁸³ *Cucurbita pepo* L.   The black and white pumpkins were varieties of this species.   No. 9, translated, black pumpkin from Monaco.

⁸⁴ Translated, black pumpkin from Lauri.

⁸⁵ Translated, black pumpkin used by fishermen in Italy.

⁸⁶ Probably the stone wall below the garden terrace.   This is the first mention of building the garden wall.

⁸⁷ Jefferson failed to mention what he planted in these two rows.

⁸⁸ White and red beets are varieties of *Beta vulgaris* L.

⁸⁹ Varieties of *Raphanus sativus* L.

⁹⁰ A variety of parsley, *Petroselinum hortense* var. *crispum* Bailey.

⁹¹ *Brassica napus* L.

⁹² *Brassica oleracea* var. *acephala* DC.   In the South these are called collards.

⁹³ Jefferson was probably planting either Ice Cos lettuce or Ice Cabbage lettuce.

⁹⁴ Probably Dr. William Brown, of Alexandria, Virginia, a friend of Jefferson.   He was born in 1752 in Haddington-shire, Scotland, where his father was studying for the ministry. He received his medical education in the University of Edinburgh, where he received his M.D. degree in 1770.   After graduation he returned to America and settled in Alexandria, Virginia, where he soon established a reputation as a physician. He was appointed a surgeon in the Revolutionary War, and while serving brought out the first pharmacopeia published in the United States.   He died on January 11, 1792, and was buried in the Old Pohick Churchyard, near Alexandria. (*Dict. Am. Biog.* 3: 157.)

⁹⁵ The Blue Ridge Mountains present a magnificent pano-rama from *Monticello,* and at no time during the year are they more impressive than when covered with snow.   Jefferson often recorded this fact.

⁹⁶ The frost that killed almost every plant that had come into leaf at *Monticello,* also killed all of Mazzei's plants lately set out at *Colle.*   It was so severe at Williamsburg that it killed all of the grapes in the public vineyard.   (See Garlick, *Philip Mazzei:* 43.)

[97] These peas were sown March 10, were up by March 21, and came to the table May 26, making 78 days from time of planting to eating.

[98] Probably the cluster peas sown on March 23.

[99] The Windsor beans were sown on March 23, making a total of 74 days.

[100] On June 5 the third and fourth patch of peas came to the table; on June 13, a fifth patch; and on July 13 the last dish of peas came to the table.  By planting the peas in succession, Jefferson was able to have fresh peas on the table from May 16 to July 13.

[101] Jefferson is evidently writing of William McGehee, who, in 1768, patented nearly 200 acres on Henderson's Branch, and near Secretary's Ford.  Jefferson bought from McGehee 193 acres near *Colle,* in 1774.  (Memorandum April 4, 1774, *Jefferson Papers,* M. H. S.)  This lettuce was probably some that Gehee (McGehee) had planted.

[102] Today watermelons in Albemarle County do not ripen at so early a date.

[103] *Zea mays* L.  Jefferson did not indicate when it was planted.

[104] The black-eyed peas were sown on March 25, a period of 132 days from planting to serving at the table.

[105] In Albemarle County the average first killing frost comes on November 5.

# 1775

Feb. 25.   sowed a bed of Early and a bed of Marrowfat peas.

Mar. 10.   the peach trees at Monticello in blossom.

we have had the most favorable winter ever known in the memory of man.  not more than three or four snows to cover the ground, of which two might lie about two days and the others not one.  the only weather which could be called any thing cold was for about a week following the frost before noted Nov. 17.

some time in this month (the particular time I omitted to note) there came very cold weather & frosts every night for a week, which killed every peach at Monticello.  they were generally killed in—(tho' not universally) in the neighborhood also.  apples & cherries were also killed.  this was the first instance since Monticello was seated of the fruit being totally killed; as the frost of May. 5. 1774. was the first of a partial loss.[2]

Sep. 21.   this morning the Northern part of the blue ridge (to wit from opposite to Monticello Northwardly as far as we can see) is white with snow.[3]

---

66

PLATE VI.—The location of Jefferson's vegetable garden and orchard as it appears today (ca. 1944). The vegetables were planted in 24 squares on the leveled part, while the orchard occupied the sloping hill to the left. The trees and the foundation of an outhouse are on the side of "Mulberry Row." The house in the right background is the South Pavilion, the first house completed at *Monticello*.

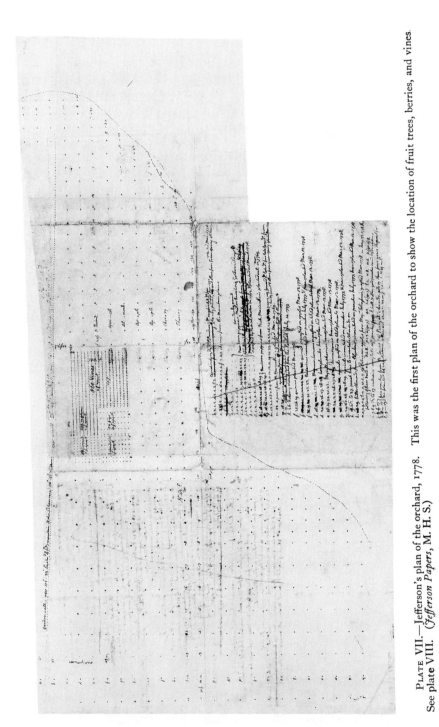

PLATE VII.—Jefferson's plan of the orchard, 1778. This was the first plan of the orchard to show the location of fruit trees, berries, and vines. See plate VIII. (*Jefferson Papers*, M. H. S.)

¹ *1775.* Jefferson recorded only one planting for the garden in 1775. This was his favorite pea, which was planted 14 days earlier than in 1774. Although no records were kept, there were evidently many seeds of vegetables planted to take care of the ever-increasing family. Randall says that Jefferson's family in 1775 consisted of 34 free persons and 83 slaves.

This was a very busy year for Jefferson. Early in the spring he was in Richmond attending the convention at which he was elected to the Continental Congress. He was twice in Williamsburg for the meetings of the House of Burgesses, and in Philadelphia in June and October for the Continental Congress. He was a member of many of the important committees. In spite of these meetings his mind was constantly at *Monticello.* He was busy making additions to the house and improving the grounds and roads.

Although Jefferson's *Account Book 1775* does not mention any seeds or plants bought during the year, it does show that he was reading books and talking to people about garden matters. The following are some of the observations on gardening and farming that he wrote down at the beginning of the *Account Book 1775:*

27 head of cattle convert 65 loads of straw & haulm (besides what they eat of it) into about 300. loads of dung. horses well littered yeild from 12. to 17. loads of dung per horse. 88. fat hogs converted 5. loads of straw & 4 of stubble into 90 loads of very rotten dung. but they had not litter enough. they would have made 12. or 15. loads into manure. this is much the best of dungs. the above from Young's *rural* aeconomy.

A pint of cotton seed contains of good seed . . . . . . . . . . . . . . . . .   900
consequently a bushel will contain . . . . . . . . . . . . . . . . . . . . . . .   57600
put 4. in a hill, and it will plant hills . . . . . . . . . . . . . . . . . . . . .   14400
if hills are 2.f. apart, an acre will contain abᵗ. . . . . . . . . . . . . . .   11025
so that a bushel of seed will plant 1⅓ acres.

Feb. 8. a large plough with 4. oxen ploughed 24. furrows half a mile long 10. I. broad & 6. I. deep in a day, which is about 1¼ acres.

Feb. 8. calves which fall after the 1ˢᵗ. June should be killed. Wᵐ. Fitzhugh. lambs that fall after the first of May. a lamb whether ewe or ram should not be permitted to breed till the season after it is two years old. the ram not run with the ewes till the rutting season comes on.

Feb. 8. Wheat in high land should be sown as early as August. (note corn is laid by about the last of July generally or first of August) Wheat in low grounds should be sown about the middle of September. W. F., T. M. R.

Dr. Walker sais he remembers that the years 1724 & 1741 were great locust years. we all remember that 1758. was and now they are come again this year 1775. it appears then that they come periodically once in 17 years. they come out of the ground from a prodigious depth. it is thought that they eat nothing while in this state, laying their eggs in the small twigs of trees seems to be their only business. The females make a noise well known. The males are silent.

two waggons bringing stone from the quarry to Monticello went from
the house to the quarry in ......................................... 15'
loaded both of them in .................................. 25'
came up in ......................................... 30'
unloaded both in ......................................... 10'

so that to fetch 2 loads takes in the whole              80'

[2] At Charlottesville, where a continuous weather record has been kept for the past 40 years, the killing frost average-dates are April 6, the last in the spring, and November 5, the first in the fall. (See 1941 *Yearbook of Agriculture, Climate and Man:* 1159.)

[3] This was an early date for the Blue Ridge Mountains to be covered with snow.

# 1776

*1776.** Jefferson seems to have been too busy to make any recordings in the *Garden Book* for 1776. This was unusual, for he was at *Monticello* most of the spring, and the *Account Book* was filled with the usual detail. His mother died on March 31. He had the responsibility of settling her estate. He left for Philadelphia on May 7, and remained there until September 3. The important event of the year was the adoption of the Declaration of Independence on July 4. It is interesting to note from the *Account Book 1776–1778* some of his minor interests preceding this eventful day.

May 24. p$^d$ Hillegas for fiddlestrings 27/.
May 28. p$^d$ for a Doll 2/.
June  1. p$^d$ for seeing a monkey 1/.
July  4. p$^d$ for 7 p$^r$. women's gloves, 27/.

Also on July 4, he "p$^d$ Sparhawk for a thermometer £3–15," and recorded the temperature four times. At 6 A. M. the temperature was 68°, at 9 A. M. 72$\frac{1}{4}$°, at 1 P. M. 76°, and at 9 P. M. 73$\frac{1}{2}$°. From July 1, of this year, until the end of 1816, Jefferson kept an almost continuous record of the weather. This record was made not only at *Monticello,* but wherever he was located. On July 8, he paid Sparhawk £4–10 for a barometer and on September 15, after his return to *Monticello,* he made several barometrical observations on the top of *Monticello* and in the surrounding country. (See *Account Book 1776–1778.*) During a part of the fall he was in Williamsburg attending the Assembly.

Building continued at *Monticello.* On September 13 he "agreed with Randolph Johnson, a bricklayer, to work @ £4. a month.  he begins tomorrow" (*Account Book 1776–1778*). On February 8 he bought a deer from a man named Reynolds for 20/, and on September 19 he bought a fawn from the same for 12/6. This was the beginning of stocking his park with deer. (See plate XIII for location of park.)

* This year not represented in the *Garden Book.*

# 1777

the fall of the last year was fine.[2]  the first snow fell the 20th. of December, but did not lay a day.  the day before Christmas the weather set in cold.   Christmas night a snow fell 22 I. deep. and from that time till the 7th. of March was the coldest weather & upon the whole the severest winter remembered. from the 20th. Dec. to the 6th. of March fell ten snows to cover the ground, and some of them deep.  the 9th. of March I think was the first rain in this year.  the rivers all that time so low that there could be no water transportation above the falls.[3]  the 10th. of March is the first day we can do any thing in the garden.  scarce any appearance of vegetation yet.  ~~except in some daffodils~~

March. 10.  sowed a patch of forward & a patch of latter peas.

11.  sowed Cavolo Romano Paonazzo[4] (purple cabbage) in lower division of the uppermost triangular bed.[5]

sowed Neapolitan cabbage[6] in the division next above.

& Cavolo Romano a broccolini[7] (Cabbage) in the next above that.

sowed also lettuce & radishes.

70

12.  planted 2 beds of strawberries.

sowed in an upper long bed Cavolo nero (Coleworts) in the one next below it Russia curled greens.[8]

13.  planted another bed of strawberries.

21.  peas up.[9]

26.  sowed patch of peas. qu.[10] whether forward or latter. in N.Westermost beds.

April.  1.  Peach trees & Cherry trees at Monticello begin to blossom.[11]

sowed a square of peas, of one kind only. qu. what ?

7.  sowed a bed of peas.

8.  peas of March 26. up.[12]

9.  sowed radishes, lettuce, endive, & red mustard.

14.  sowed bed of peas.

19.  planted Cucumbers, Lima beans, Irish potatoes

June.  4.  forward peas of March 10. come to table.

July.  6.  cucumbers come to table.

July.  24.  sowed Spinach, endive,[13] lettuce, cresses[14] & peas.

*T. G.[15] (who was allowed to kill what he chose) killed only 9 hogs for his own family & H. Gaines,[16] for whom he allowed 3 of the

9.   four of them were the smallest we had.
he also had a beef.[17]

*fauns are cut from 3 to 6 weeks old.

*kids are fit for the table from 3 weeks to 3
months old.

*it takes 11 lb $\overline{db}$le ref$^d$.[18] sugar to 1 lb good
Congo tea.

*$\frac{1}{2}$ $\overline{dwt}$[19] good Congo makes a dish, i.e. 640
dishes to the pound.

*veals are best from 6. to 8. weeks old, but
may do from 5. to 9. weeks.

---

[1] *1777.* Jefferson's continued absence from *Monticello*
made noticeable gaps in the *Garden Book* for the year. The
record is partially complete for March and April; after July
24 it is blank. He was in Williamsburg at three different
times attending the Assembly, and each time he stayed there
for many weeks. As at previous Assemblies, he was placed
on many important committees, and upon him fell the weight
of preparing the reports. In addition to his trips to Williamsburg, he was at Fredericksburg, Richmond, Bedford,
Cumberland Court House, *The Forest,* and several other
places.

The birth of his only son on May 28, and his death on June
14, must have affected Jefferson profoundly. He recorded it,
however, with the same detail.

The *Account Book* for this year throws little light on the
progress of building and other activities taking place on the
mountaintop. On February 13 he "engaged Beckley to saw
me as much plank as will yeild me 1200 f. fine flooring plank
in lengths of 19. & 25 f. I am to take good & bad & shall
allow him as before." On February 26 he paid Zacharia
Rowland for freight on mahogany, and on April 26 John

Brewer began to make bricks.   In August he added a buck to his deer park.   (*Account Book 1776–1778.*)

² For a record of the temperature for 1777, see the *Account Book* for this year.   Jefferson wrote from Williamsburg on June 8, 1778, to John Fabroni, a friend in France, describing his method of keeping a record of the weather and requesting particulars about the climate there, in order to make a comparative estimate of the climates of the two countries.   Since Jefferson often mentioned the weather in the *Garden Book,* it will be of value to quote a portion of this letter here.

It might not be unacceptable to you to be informed for instance of the true power of our climate as discoverable from the thermometer, from the force and direction of the winds, the quantity of rain, the plants which grow without shelter in the winter etc.   On the other hand we should be much pleased with the contemporary observations on the same particulars in your country, which will give us a comparative view of the two climates.   Farenheit's thermometer is the only one in use with us, I make my daily observations as early as possible in the morning & again about 4 o'clock in the afternoon, these generally showing the maxima of cold & heat in the course of 24 hours.   (Paul Leicester Ford, ed., *The Works of Thomas Jefferson* (12 v., New York, 1904) 2: 340. Hereafter cited as Ford, *Jefferson.*)

³ Jefferson referred here to the falls of the James River, which are situated at Richmond, Virginia.

⁴ Translated, Roman purple cabbage.

⁵ At each end of Jefferson's new vegetable garden on the southeastern side of the mountain was a triangular bed. These triangular beds were later discarded.

⁶ A cabbage from Naples given him by Mazzei.

⁷ Translated, a Roman cabbage in the form of small broccoli.

⁸ Greens are either young plants raised in the fall, and wintered expressly for early cutting, as spinach, German kale, &c., or they are similar young plants raised in the spring for the same purpose, as spinach, cabbage, mustard, &c., or they are the first young spring growth of roots or stems wintered for the purpose of producing them, as kale, cabbage, dock, &c.   (Alexander Watson, *The American Home Garden* (New York, 1865): 143.   Hereafter cited as Watson, *Garden.*)

The seeds of the *greens* mentioned here were probably given to Jefferson by Mr. Mazzei.

⁹ The peas planted on March 10 required 11 days to come up.

[10] *qu.* is the abbreviation for *query* or *question.*

[11] In 1774 the peach trees bloomed on March 29. In 1775 they were in bloom as early as March 10, while this year they bloomed as late as April 1.

[12] The peas planted on March 26 required 14 days to come up.

[13] *Cichorium endivia* L.

[14] Probably *Lepidium sativum* L.   Garden cress.

[15] Thomas Garth.

The first of the Garth family in Albemarle was Thomas. . . . The next three or four years [after 1770] he was employed by Mr. Jefferson to buy the Lego estate from William and James Hickman. . . . He owned all the land stretching from near the Staunton Road . . . to the forks of Mechum's and Moorman's Rivers. . . . He was appointed a magistrate in 1791, and served as Sheriff in 1807. He died in 1812. (Woods, *Albemarle County:* 203.)

There are many references to Thomas Garth in Jefferson's account books. When Jefferson was in France, Garth was second to Nicholas Lewis in attending to his affairs.

[16] Humphrey Gaines. He worked for Jefferson at *Monticello.* There were several other workmen by the name of Gaines. In the *Account Book* for the year, Jefferson wrote: "July 5. p^d Humphrey Gaines £19 4. balance due him for 3. last years as by settlement £34 17 4. Note y^e year ended June 12. agreed in writing to give him £35. for the current year, & he takes my word that I will give him £5. more."

[17] In the *Account Book 1776–1778* Jefferson wrote a fuller statement of this entry, "Jan. 29, Note T. Garth last year killed 9 hogs for himself & Humphr. Gaines (for whom he allowed 3. of the 9) four of them were the smallest we had. Brock has killed 12 this year."

[18] Double refined sugar.   Congo tea, a kind of black tea.

[19] ½ pennyweight equals $\frac{1}{10}$ of an ounce, Troy weight.

# 1778

Feb. 26.   sowed a patch of Hotspur peas [2]

    28.   planted carrots & Salsafy

Mar. 2.   sowed lettuce & Madeira onions. [3]

Mar. 7.   planted 19 Bubby flower shrubs, calycanthus. [4] from the Green mountain, [5] the only place in this country I have ever heard of them.   they are said to be very common in Sᵒ. Carolina. [6]

   9–14.   ingrafted, or planted etc.   Cherries, viz *Carnation, *Duke, *Broadnax's, *very fine late, Myrilla. [7]   Apples, viz. *Newtown pippins, †Medlar Russetins †Golden wildings, Robinson, Codlin, White. [8] Pears, viz *Forward, *Late, *fine late large, Sugar dᵒ., 3 kinds of English dᵒ., 2 other kinds. [9]

Quinces,

Nectarines, plumb

Plumbs, viz Magnum bonum, Damascene, horse, [10]

Apricots

Almonds bitter.

for the places see plan of the orchard. [11]

75

\* these were sent me from Sandy point by
Mordecai Debnam, in slips, March 1773. &
then ingrafted by P. Morton.[12]

† these were from Greenspring [13]

14.  planted in a nursery [14] the following stones &
seeds

Nº.  1.  choice peaches

Nº.  2.  an Almond

Nº.  3.  English Walnuts

Nº.  4.  a French dº.[15]

Nº.  5.  Mogul plumbs [16]

Nº.  6.  Prunes [17]

Nº.  7.  small green plumbs [18]

Nº.  8.  Pride of China.[19]

Nº.  9.  Strawberry tree [20]

Nº.  10.  Apples.

13.  sowed Radish seed & Burnet [21]

14.  sowed Charlton & Early pearl peas.[22]   the former are in the 4. lower rows.

planted out Raspberries, goose berries & currans.[23]

Peach-trees begin to blossom.[24]

peas of . . Feb. 26. just appearing.[25]

Mar. 13.  sowed radishes & burnet

14. sowed a bed of Early Charlton, and another of Early pearl peas.

sowed Mazzei's beans,[26] snap beans & parsley.

lettuce of Mar. 2. come up.[27]

May.  bought two Aegyptian Acacias (Mimosa Nilotica[28]) from the Gardner[29] at Greenspring. they are from seeds planted March 1777.

Sep. 12.  one of the Acacias 23 I. high the other 18 I.

Oct. 12.  their heights   $28\frac{1}{2}$ I.   and   23.I.[30]

Oct. 12.  brought an olive tree from Colle.[31] it is a shoot from an old root, being one of many brought from Italy in 1773. they stood the winter of that year and the remarkeable frost of May 5. 1774. also the winters of 1774 & 1775.[32] planted in the open feild & without any cover. in Decemb. 1775 & Jan. 1776. there was a frost of four or five weeks duration, the earth being frozen like a rock the whole time. this killed all the olives; the others totally, this one alone sprung up from the old root. it's height now is $21\frac{3}{4}$ I. took a cutting from it & planted it. when an olive tree is killed in Italy and a new shoot puts out, it is ten years before it bears.

17.  brought from Colle four sour Orange trees, being new shoots from old roots brought from Italy in 1775.[33] which have been killed to the root. these are all remaining out of some hundreds the rest being killed totally. they were planted there in the earth, and sheltered to the North by a plank wall, and on the top & to the

South by matts. two of them indeed were planted at the ends of houses, one to the South, the other to the East, and protected by matts. they are now put into boxes of good Virgin mould. their heights are $6\frac{1}{4}$ I. $6\frac{1}{2}$ I. 16 I. and $18\frac{1}{2}$ I. in S. Carolina the Orange trees [34] were killed generally by frost in 1771. the shoots which put out from the old roots begin to bear this year.

23.  the Roundabout walk [35] is in circumference 926 yds. by a survey of 1806 Aug. 3. with a chain very exact it is 169.16 po. = .529 mile. from Monticello door [36] to the stone gate ..........    198. yds = .1125  [mile = .5216]

    thence to the second gate by the orchard ........    231        = .1312

    thence to the Overseer's house ..............    473        = .2687

    thence to the stone flood mark of 1778. by the river ...............    $\dfrac{1760}{2662}$    $\begin{array}{l} = 1.0000 \\ = 1.5124 \end{array}$

from head of the Canal along my private road into public road by Shadwell 1175.        = .6676

    thence down public road to where the mill road will come in .........    $\dfrac{660}{1835}$    $\begin{array}{l} = .3750 \\ = 1.0426 \end{array}$

from head of the Canal
down the same to Walnut
where mill house will
stand. .................  1225      = .6960

  thence down the mill
  road along river side to
  Chapel branch .......  819       = .4653

  thence up Chapel branch
  as the mill road is to go
  into the public road ...  616     = .3500
                          2660    = 1.5113

Oct. 27.  planted 59. Aspens.[37] (Populus tremula.)

   31.  planted 32 Umbrellas.[38]

Nov. 5.  planted 27. wild crabs.[39]  11.[40] transplanted.
       14. Pride of China trees.[41] from seed sown in
       Nursery.

   To inclose all my lands on the S.W. side of the
   Thoroughfare road[42] following the meanders
   of the road and in other places following the
   line would take in about 400 acres of land, &
   require a fence about 1323 poles[43] long.  suppose this to be a dry stone fence 23.I thick
   at bottom, 19 I. thick at top & 4 f. 3 I.
   high.  every perch[44] length of such a fence
   is very nearly 5. perch of work.  of course
   there will be 6615 perch.  I think a hand
   will lay 10 perch of brick work a day having
   his stone brought into place.  one hand then
   would lay the whole in $661\frac{1}{2}$ days = $110\frac{1}{2}$ weeks
   Years  Month  Weeks[45]
   = 2———1———2

Nov. 12.    placing the Theodolite[46] on the top of the house, the Eastern spur of the High mountain[47] intersects the Horizon 19°. Westward of Willis's mountain.[48] note the observation was made on the intersection of the ground (not the trees) with the horizon.

―――――――――――――〜∽∙∽〜―――――――――――――

[1] *1778.* Jefferson was principally occupied in 1778 with the law revision of Virginia, along with George Wythe and Edmund Pendleton, the other members of the Committee of Law Revisers.   He was in Williamsburg three times during the year, and visited *Tuckahoe, Cowles,* and *Greenspring.*   While in Williamsburg, in early January, he "p$^d$ rev$^d$ m$\bar{r}$ Andrews for Theodolite £45," which he often used at *Monticello* for measuring horizontal and vertical angles.   On June 2 he "p$^d$ for hearing organ at church 12/"—an enjoyment he almost always indulged in when in Williamsburg, and on June 5 he "p$^d$ Robert Nicholson for a flower. 5/6." (*Account Book 1776–1778.*)

On August 1 the Jeffersons' third daughter, Maria, was born.   Martha and Maria, affectionately called *Polly,* were the only children to survive childhood.

Building on the mountaintop continued with unusual speed this year.   Early in February Jefferson "agreed with W$^m$. Rice that he shall make 3 stone columns, to find himself provisions, and assist in quarrying.   I am to allow him the caps and bases which are done, the labor on my two stone-cutters and give him £10 a column."   On the same day he credited "John Brewer ninety thousand workable bricks made & burnt @ 5/ the thousand.   the kiln had 36 eyes, & he estimated it to contain 103,000 bricks, which is 2861 to the eye.   he deducted 13,000 for soft outside bricks unfit for use." (*Account Book 1776–1778.*)   In the middle of July "two of Stephen Willis's people begin to work."   They laid brick until August 14, when "Willis's people left off work having laid 14,120 bricks." (*Account Book 1776–1778.*)

During the year Jefferson hired several other men to work for him, the most important of whom was Anthony Giannini, a vigneron, brought over from Italy by Mazzei to work at *Colle*. The following agreement was made with Giannini on November 2:

agreed with Anthony Giannini that he shall serve me one year from the 27th Inst. I am to give him £50. & find him 15 bushels of wheat & 480 lb. meat. i.e. bacon when we have it. if Mazzei undertakes in writing to pay the expenses of his passage to Italy hereafter, I am to stand security for it so long as he is in my service. (*Account Book 1776–1778*.)

A buck fawn was added to Jefferson's park on October 9.

bought of Charles Goodman a buck faun. it is to be brought home between Christmas & blossoming time. if I fetch it soon after Christmas I am to pay 40/. if not till near blossoming time 50/. if he brings it I pay £3.

On December 8 he "p[d] B. Harrison (Brandon) in part for an elk £7.–10" (*Account Book 1776–1778*).

Jefferson's planting this year was chiefly in the orchard and nursery, although the usual peas and a few other vegetables were planted in the garden. On September 28 he "p[d] F. Eppes for seeds from Mazzei's 30/," and on October 10 he "p[d] Doct[r]. Walker's Scipio for Will for 35 pints of greensword seed 43/9" (*Account Book 1776–1778*).

In November Jefferson drew a plan of the orchard, showing the location of the fruit trees and berries, and wrote a memorandum on "the state of fruit trees, 1778," to accompany it. (See plates VII and VIII.) The plan and memorandum reveal the abundance of fruit trees planted from 1769 to 1778. This was an unusual accomplishment, in view of the many other activities with which Jefferson was associated.

[2] See note 2 under 1768.

[3] A variety of *Allium cepa* L. "The variety is much prized for its extraordinary size, and for its mild, sugary flavor. . . . It requires a long, warm season for its greatest perfection." (Burr, *Vegetables*: 135.)

[4] *Calycanthus floridus* L. goes by several common names: bubby flower, strawberry bush, sweet-shrub, and sweet Betsy.

[5] A range of low mountains in the southwestern part of Albemarle County. The range is separated from Carter's Mountain by the Hardware River.

⁶ So far as I have been able to ascertain, *Calycanthus* is not native to the Green Mountain today. It is, however, indigenous to certain parts of the mountains of Virginia.

⁷ The cherries mentioned here are varieties of *Prunus cerasus* L. Comment has already been made on the Carnation, Duke, and Broadnax. The *Myrilla* is probably Jefferson's spelling for *Morello,* which Downing says is a fine fruit.

⁸ All of these apples are varieties of *Malus pumila.* Comment has been made on the Newtown pippins. *Mespilus germanica* L., the medlar russetin, is not included in the apple group today. The Goldenwilding originated in North Carolina. It was of medium size, yellow color, and a sweet acid flavor. There are over one dozen Robinson Apples noted in Ragan's *Nomenclature of the Apple* (1905). The codlin, also spelled codling, "is a favorite apple in England for pies and stewing; is fit for this use in August, and lasts till October" (T. G. Fessenden, *The New American Gardener* (Boston, 1839): 129. Hereafter cited as Fessenden, *Gardener*). Downing says that the fruit of the White apples has a "flesh white, crisp, tender, sometimes almost melting, and of a mild agreeable flavor." He also wrote that it was carried from eastern to western Virginia by Neisley, a nurseryman, on the banks of the Ohio, about the beginning of the nineteenth century. The White Apple was sent to Jefferson in 1773 from eastern Virginia.

⁹ All of these pears are varieties of *Pyrus communis* L.

¹⁰ Varieties of *Prunus domestica* L. The Magnum bonum

is a very popular fruit, chiefly on account of its large and splendid appearance, and a slight acidity, which renders it admirably suited for making showy sweetmeats or preserves. When it is raised in a fine warm situation, and is fully matured, it is pretty well flavoured, but ordinarily, it is considered coarse, and as belonging to the kitchen, and not to the dessert. (Downing, *Fruits:* 286.)

The horse plum is "a very common and inferior fruit. . . . The seedlings make good stocks for the nursery." (Downing, *Fruits:* 301.)

¹¹ See plate VII.

¹² On March 14 Jefferson wrote in the *Account Book 1776–1778:* "pᵈ Patrick Morton 15/6 which balances our accᵗˢ to this day." Mordecai Debnam was Clerk of Court for Charles City County, Virginia.

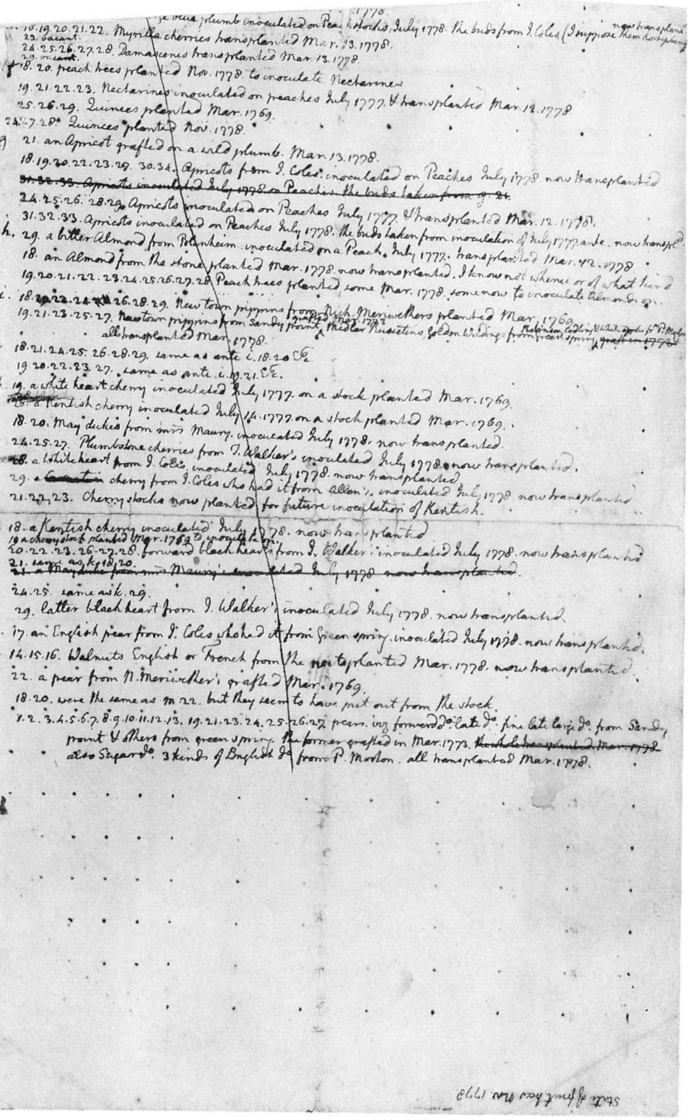
18.19.20.21.22. Myrilla cherries transplanted Mar. 13. 1778.
23. vacant.
24.25.26.27.28. Damascenes transplanted Mar 13. 1778.
29. vacant.
f. 18. 20. peach trees planted Nov. 1778. to inoculate Nectarines
19. 21. 22. 23. Nectarines inoculated on peaches July 1777. & transplanted Mar. 12. 1778
25. 26. 29. Quinces planted Mar. 1769.
24. 27. 28. Quinces planted Nov. 1778.
g. 21. an Apricot grafted on a wild plumb. Mar. 13. 1778.
18. 19. 20. 22. 23. 29. 30. 34. Apricots from J. Coles inoculated on Peaches July 1778 now transplanted
24. 25. 26. 28. 29. Apricots inoculated on Peaches July 1777 & transplanted Mar. 12. 1778.
31. 32. 33. Apricots inoculated on Peaches July 1778. the buds taken from inoculation of July 1777. &c. now transpl.
h. 29. a bitter Almond from Blenheim. inoculated on a Peach. July 1777. transplanted Mar. 12. 1778
18. an Almond from the stone planted Mar. 1778. now transplanted. I know not whence or of what kind
19. 20. 21. 22. 23. 24. 25. 26. 27. 28 Peach trees planted some Mar. 1778. some now to inoculate Almonds on.
i. 18. 26. 28. 29. New town pippins from Nich. Meriwethers planted Mar. 1769.
19. 21. 23. 25. 27. Newtown pippins from Sandy point, Medlar Russetins, Golden Wildings from Green spring, grafted Mar. 1773
all transplanted Mar. 1778.
l. 18. 21. 24. 25. 26. 28. 29. same as ante i. 18. 20 &c.
19. 20. 22. 23. 27. same as ante i. 19. 21. &c.
k. 19. a white heart cherry inoculated July 1777. on a stock planted Mar. 1769.
20. a Kentish cherry inoculated July 14. 1777. on a stock planted Mar. 1769.
18. 20. May dukes from mrs Maury. inoculated July 1778. now transplanted.
24. 25. 27. Plumbstone cherries from J. Walker's inoculated July 1778. now transplanted.
28. a white heart from J. Coles. inoculated July 1778. now transplanted.
29. a cherry from J. Coles who had it from Allen's, inoculated July 1778. now transplanted
21. 22, 23. Cherry stocks now planted for future inoculation of Kentish.
l. 18. a Kentish cherry inoculated July 1778. now transplanted
19. a cherry stock planted Mar. 1769 to inoculate on.
20. 22. 23. 26. 27. 28. forward black hearts from J. Walker's inoculated July 1778. now transplanted
21. same as k. 18. 20.
24. 25. same as k. 29.
29. latter black heart from J. Walker's inoculated July 1778. now transplanted.
m. 17. an English pear from J. Coles who had it from Green spring. inoculated July 1778. now transplanted.
m. 14. 15. 16. Walnuts English or French from the nuts planted Mar. 1778. now transplanted.
22. a pear from N. Meriwether's grafted Mar. 1769.
18. 20. were the same as m 22. but they seem to have put out from the stock.
1. 2. 3. 4. 5. 6. 7. 8. 9. 10. 11. 12. 13. 19. 21. 23. 24. 25. 26. 27 pears. viz forward do. late do. fine late large do. from Sandy point & others from green spring. the former grafted in Mar. 1773.
also Segar do. 3 kinds of English do from P. Morton. all transplanted Mar. 1778.

State of fruit trees 1778

PLATE VIII.—Jefferson's memorandum of the state of the fruit trees, 1778. See plate VII. (*Jefferson Papers*, M. H. S.)

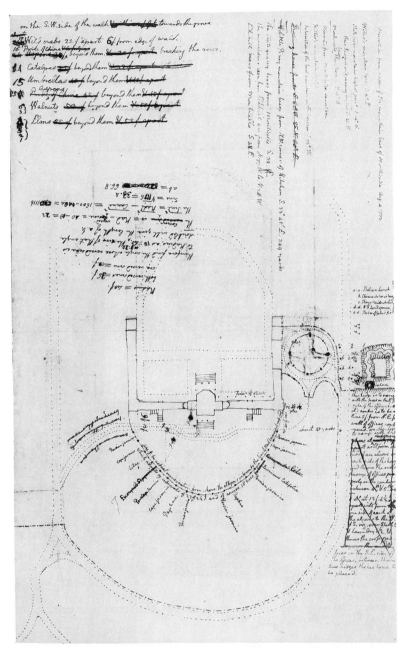

PLATE IX.—General plan of Monticello. The plan of the house was drawn prior to 1772. The addition of shrubs and willows in the semicircle in front of the house was made about 1808 or 1809. (*Jefferson Papers*, M. H. S.)

[13] *Greenspring,* near Williamsburg, was the ancient residence of Governor Sir William Berkeley, of three Philips Ludwells, and of William Lee, at one time Minister of the United States to Holland.   It was burned by Federal troops in 1862.   Jefferson often visited *Greenspring* when he was in the Williamsburg area and bought plants from the gardener.   The estate was celebrated for its three extensive orchards, its vegetable garden, orangery, and field of indigo.

[14] The location of this nursery not known.

[15] French walnut.   Probably another name for English walnut.

[16] Mogul.   Unidentified.

[17] A variety of *Prunus domestica* L.

[18] Probably a greengage plum.

[19] *Melia azedarach* L.   Often called chinaberry tree in the Southern United States.

[20] *Arbutus unedo* L.

[21] *Sanguisorba minor* Scop.   The young leaves are used as a salad and also for sheep forage.

[22] An early variety of *Pisum sativum.*   The pearl pea was also known as the Nonesuch Pea.

[23] Either the black raspberry, *Rubus occidentalis* L., or the red raspberry, *Rubus idaeus* L.   The gooseberry, *Ribes grossularia* L.   The currant, either *Ribes nigrum* L., the black currant, or *Ribes rubrum* L., the red currant.

[24] This year the peach trees bloomed earlier than in the preceding years.

[25] It took 17 days for the Hotspur peas, planted on February 26, to appear above ground.

[26] Probably some kind of Italian bean given to Jefferson by Mazzei.

[27] Thirteen days were required for lettuce to appear above ground.

[28] *Mimosa nilotica.*   Now called *Acacia farnesiana* Willd.

[29] "May 24. p^d a gardener at Greenspring for two Acacias & a pretended debt of m͞r Wayles's 36/." (*Account Book 1776–1778.*)

[30] The *Mimosa nilotica* was a favorite flower of Jefferson. Jefferson shows again his keen interest in detail by taking the measurements of these acacias.

[31] See notes about *Colle* and Mazzei under the year 1774.

[32] See *Garden Book* for the years 1774 and 1775.

[33] These orange trees were probably brought back to Virginia in the ship under Captain Woodford, which Mazzei had sent to Leghorn to bring back plants and vignerons.

[34] The sour orange, *Citrus aurantium* L. It is grown extensively in Southern Europe for the making of marmalade and perfumery. It is more hardy than the sweet orange and is often used as a stock for it.

[35] This *Round-about* was completed in 1772. See note 22 under that year.

[36] See plates XXI, XXII, and XXX.

[37] This was the beginning of the Aspen Thicket which Jefferson mentioned several times later. No mention was made of its location. *Populus tremula* L.

[38] *Magnolia tripetala* L. Umbrella tree.

[39] *Pyrus coronaria* L. Wild crab apple.

[40] This figure refers to November 11.

[41] The seeds of the Pride of China trees were sown on March 14 of this year.

[42] The Thoroughfare Road ran through *Monticello* Gap and is the main road today leading to the entrance of *Monticello*. For many years the Thoroughfare Road was the only road by which people of Fluvanna County, south of the Rivanna River, could reach Charlottesville.

[43] A pole is one rod.

[44] In measuring masonwork or stone, a perch is usually $24\frac{3}{4}$ cubic feet ($5\frac{1}{2}$ yards by 1 foot by $1\frac{1}{2}$ feet).

[45] There is no evidence that Jefferson built a dry stone wall to enclose the lands on the southwest side of the Thoroughfare. The lands were enclosed by a fence.

[46] This is the first time that Jefferson mentioned the use of his theodolite. He bought it in January of this year. See note 1, 1778.

[47] High Mountain, now called Patterson Mountain, was on the south side of the Thoroughfare Road. *Monticello* Gap is between High Mountain and *Monticello* Mountain.

[48] Willis Mountain, which has a height of 1,159 feet, is situated 40 miles southeast of *Monticello* in Buckingham County. Because Willis Mountain is an isolated one, easily seen from *Monticello* on a clear day, Jefferson used it as the focal point in calculating the latitude and longitude of various

surrounding places.    Willis Mountain also fascinated him because of the optical phenomenon called *looming,* which he
could observe from *Monticello*.    He wrote:

Having had occasion to mention the particular situation of Monticello
for other purposes, I will just take notice that its elevation affords an
opportunity of seeing a phenomenon which is rare at land, though frequent at sea.    The seamen call it *looming*.    Philosophy is as yet in the
rear of the seamen, for so far from having accounted for it, she has not
given it a name.    Its principal effect is to make distant objects appear
larger, in opposition to the general law of vision, by which they are
diminished.    I knew an instance, at York-town, from whence the water
prospect eastwardly is without termination, wherein a canoe with three
men, at a great distance was taken for a ship with its three masts.    I am
little acquainted with the phaenomenon as it shews itself at sea; but at
Monticello it is familiar.    There is a solitary mountain [Willis Mountain] about forty miles off, in the South, whose natural shape, as presented to view there, is a regular cone; but, by the effect of looming, it
sometimes subsides almost totally into the horizon; sometimes it rises
more acute and more elevated; sometimes it is hemispherical; and sometimes its sides are perpendicular, its top flat, and as broad as its base.    In
short it assumes at times the most whimsical shapes, and all these perhaps successively in the same morning.    (Thomas Jefferson, *Notes on
the State of Virginia* (London, 1787): 135–136.)

# 1779

March. 10.    from where the park[2] fence crosses the branch at the upper side of the park to where a point of land makes in so as to separate the upper & lower meadow in the park, & forms a good place for stopping the water with a short dam the water falls 44 f. 2. I.

C. H. Harrison[3] sais fauns may be cut the spring after fauned, or at almost any age.

Ry. Randolph's[4] park pales are 8.f. & 11.f. high.

brought another Aegyptian Acacia[5] from Greenspring.    it is in blossom.

about the 8th. of Feb. this spring the weather set in remarkeably mild & indeed hot & so continued till the middle of March, which had brought forward the vegetation more than was ever remembered at so early a period.    then it set in cold; the blue ridge covered with snow, and the thermometer below freezing.    this killed all the fruits which had blossomed forward.    the very few blossoms which were backward escaped. Monticello seemed to suffer as much as it's neighborhood.    the weather then again became mild till a thunder storm on the 17th. April.    and wind at N.W. brought on several severe frosts. the fruit was too forward to be hurt by them; but the garden suffered extremely, every thing young & tender being killed. at Monticello nothing was hurt except the leaves of the trees which had put out late.[6] but the forest except near the tops of the mountains was totally blasted so as to put on the appearance of autumn, every leaf being killed on the hardiest trees. dogwoods & other early budding trees escaped. all the flax [7] was killed. all the Indian corn which was up.

Apr.  17. in opening the road from a little above the Thoroughfare to mr̄ Lewis's mill [8] six hands did about 120. yards a day.

---

[1] *1779.* The two events which most vitally affected life at *Monticello* during this year were the coming of the Convention Troops to Albemarle County in early January, and the election of Jefferson as Governor of Virginia on June 1.

The Convention Troops were British and German soldiers who had been taken prisoners at Saratoga on the surrender of Burgoyne in October, 1777. They were first sent to Boston and then in the early part of 1779 to Charlottesville, Virginia. Their camp was located on the northern bank of Ivy Creek. The place has since been known as *The Barracks.*

The troops were preparing their camp and gardens during the severe cold spell which Jefferson mentioned in the *Garden Book* for this year. Their gardens, along with other gardens of the county, were almost totally destroyed by the severe frost which followed the thunderstorm and wind of April 17. This loss and other unusual hardships caused much suffering to them and were the reasons for remonstrances and requests to Governor Patrick Henry to remove the camp to some other place. Jefferson did not agree with the officers and men that the camp should be moved and wrote a letter to Governor Henry opposing the suggestion. One paragraph from his letter describes the garden and rural activities carried on at the camp:

The environs of the barracks are delightful, the ground cleared, laid off in hundreds of gardens, each enclosed in its separate paling; these are well prepared, and exhibiting a fine appearance. General Riedesel alone laid out upwards of two hundred pounds in garden seeds for the German troops only. Judge what an extent of ground these seeds would cover. There is little doubt that their own gardens will furnish them a great abundance of vegetables through the year. Their poultry, pigeons and other preparations of that kind present to the mind the idea of a company of farmers, rather than a camp of soldiers. In addition to the barracks built for them by the public, and now very comfortable, they have built great numbers for themselves in such messes as fancied each other; and the whole corps, both officers and men, seem now happy and satisfied with their situation. (Woods, *Albemarle County:* 33.)

Baron and Madame Riedesel, one of the German officers and his wife, established themselves at *Colle,* Philip Mazzei's home, and a warm friendship grew up between them and the Jefferson household. On April 29, 1779, Jefferson recorded in his account book: "Sold my Pianoforte to Gen¹ Riedesel, he is to give me £100."

Friendships were also made between Jefferson and other soldiers of the camp, especially those with musical talents. Jefferson, having an intense passion for music, often invited the men with their instruments to *Monticello* for a musical evening. The troops remained in Albemarle County until October, 1780. (See Randall, *Jefferson* 1: 232–237, and Woods, *Albemarle County:* 31–34, for interesting accounts of the encampment of the Convention Troops in Albemarle County.)

The election of Jefferson to the Governorship made it imperative for him to be in Williamsburg, the capital. Mrs. Jefferson and their children went with him to Williamsburg, leaving at *Monticello* only Thomas Garth (the overseer), the workmen, and the slaves.

Sept. 3. on settlement of all accts with T. Garth this day the balance in my favor was 338£–4s–3d whereon he gave me up my note paiable Jan. 14. 1775 & my bond paiable Dec. 25, 1777. which turned the balance against me £40–7–9. but in the account no allowance was made him for his services as steward for 1778, which we have agreed to have settled by Nichˢ. Lewis, James Garland, & James Kerr whose

award must be added to the preceding balance & will make up my whole
debit to him.   moreover to save the trouble of a second reference we
agreed the same gentlemen should at the same time settle his wages as
steward for this current year 1779.   (*Account Book 1779–1782.*)

Jefferson made no entry in the *Garden Book* about plants in
the garden for the year.   But the fact that his garden escaped
the severe frost following the thunderstorm of April 17, indicates that the usual plants were growing in it.

He made a few purchases of trees and shrubs during the
year.   From the *Account Book 1779–1782:*

Jan. 28.   p^d Tho^s Potter for three trees £3.
Aug. 9.   p^d Tho^s Potter for a tree £3.   (extravag^t.)
Oct. 1.   p^d gardener at Greenspring for trees £11–8.

In the same account book he also mentioned hiring a gardener
from Mr. Prentis, and lending the gardener, Thompson, £50.
Since Jefferson was in Williamsburg at the time these two items
were recorded, they may both concern the gardeners at the
Governor's Palace.

  [2] See plate XIII for location of park.   Jefferson is again
making plans for beautifying the grounds at *Monticello*.   This
kind of landscaping linked up with his grandiose plans of 1771.

  [3] Carter H. Harrison.   See note 14, 1771.

  [4] Ryland Randolph.   See note 15, 1772.

  [5] "Feb. 27. p^d for an Acacia £3–6" (*Account Book 1779–
1782*).

  [6] The southeastern exposure of Jefferson's garden and its
height above the valley often saved his fruits and vegetables
from the late frosts.

  [7] *Linum usitatissimum* L.   This was the first mention that
flax was planted at *Monticello*.   On February 3 of this year
Jefferson wrote: "P^d W. D. Fitz. mend^g 2 Spinn^g wheels 48/"
(*Account Book 1779–1782*).

  [8] Nicholas Lewis's mill was on the Rivanna River.

# 1780

*1780.** Jefferson was almost continuously in Williamsburg during the first three months of the year. On April 1 the seat of the state government was moved to Richmond, and since that date the capital of the Commonwealth of Virginia has been located there. The change of the capital from Williamsburg to Richmond was a convenience for Jefferson because it brought him nearer to Monticello. On June 1 he was re-elected Governor of Virginia and he remained in office until he resigned the following year. A fourth daughter was born to the Jeffersons in Richmond on November 3. They now had three daughters living, having lost one daughter and one son. The fourth daughter died the following April.

The year was a difficult one for Jefferson. Mrs. Jefferson's health was precarious. The increasing tempo of the war brought new problems for him to solve. There is little wonder that no time was left for jottings in the *Garden Book*. His visits to *Monticello* were short, with little time to record the various happenings on his busy mountaintop. The house was probably almost completed.

He wrote in the *Account Book* for 1780 the following entries:

Mar.  4.   pᵈ. Patrick Morton for stocks & grafting £39.
Mar. 26.   pᵈ Abel 24/.  pᵈ. for 1 quart seed peas £6.
Mar. 27.   pᵈ. Gardener at Greenspring for seeds £39.

Jefferson was in Williamsburg when these entries were made, but since he moved to Richmond on April 1, the seeds were probably carried to *Monticello*.

A portion of a letter from George Mason, of *Gunston Hall,* Fairfax County, written on October 6, shows that his agricultural friends continued to send him plants.

* This year not represented in the *Garden Book*.

October 6, 1780
Fairfax County, Gunston Hall

Dear Sir,

As my very ill Health, at present, makes my attendance at the next Session of the Assembly rather uncertain, I take this opportunity, by my son, of sending you a pint of the Portugal, and best kind of rare-ripe peach stones. Almost all my Portugal peaches were stolen this year, before they were ripe; but I have saved the few stones I send you myself, & know they are the true sort. I have observed this kind of peach requires more care than most others, & if the trees are not tended, & the Ground cultivated, the fruit is apt to be coarse & harsh; with due culture the peaches are the finest I ever tasted. . . . The sooner the peach stones are planted the better; if it is deferred 'til late in the winter, very few will come up next spring; they should be secured from the moles. by slabs, or some such thing, let into the ground. (*Jefferson Papers, Library of Congress.*)

# 1781

Aug. 7. in making the terrasses which run off level from
the 22ᵈ terras, they effected at the rate of 20. feet
in length a day to each hand, the terrasses [2] being
from 8. to 10 f. wide.

―――――――――――――――――――――――――――――――

[1] *1781.* Jefferson continued as Governor of Virginia until
June 3. The war was converging on Virginia from all sides.
The state was not prepared to repel the enemy, since she had
contributed more than her share to the welfare of the colonies.
The early part of this year was one of the most trying periods
in all of Jefferson's public career.

He was in Richmond, except for short visits to Westham,
Manchester, and *Tuckahoe,* until May 14, when he left for
Charlottesville and *Monticello.* While at *Monticello* on June
4, he escaped capture by Tarleton and his troops. Although
the British did practically no damage to *Monticello,* they almost completely demolished *Elk Hill,* his estate on the James
River.

Late in June, at *Poplar Forest,* Jefferson fell from a horse
he was riding, and although the injuries were not serious, they
kept him confined to the house for several weeks. It was during this confinement that he wrote the greater part of his book,
*Notes on the State of Virginia.*

This was another year in which only one entry was made in
the *Garden Book,* despite the fact that Jefferson was at *Monticello* most of the summer and until early November. This
entry was about the terraces of the orchard.

The *Account Book 1779–1782* shows that on March 31 he
"sent Brown gardener at Tuckahoe for garden seeds £150."

He also bought a mockingbird from some one named Jame for £18, and on November 30 he made a contract with Richard Gaines to act as overseer over all of his plantations on the north side of the Rivanna River.   *Monticello* is on the south side of the river.

² The terraces mentioned here were those of the orchard.

# 1782

1782.[1]

Feb. 12.[2] sent to Poplar For.[3] 6 Apricot trees, 2 large Morellas,[4] 2 Kentish cherries [5] 2. May Dukes.[6] 2 Carnations, 2 Black hearts,[7] 2 White hearts,[8] 2 Newtown pippings, 2 Russetins, 2 Golden Wildings, & some white strawberries.[9]

Feb. 28. a flock of wild geese flying to N.W.

Mar. 30. the Farm second-round-about,[10] taking in the Mulberry-row [11] is 4444.4 feet = 269.36 po.[12] = .84 of a mile.

Mar. 17. Almonds & peaches blossom.[13]

May. 6. Aur. Bor.[14] at 9. P.M. a quart of Currant juice makes 2. blue teacups of Jelly, 1 quart of juice to 4. of puree [15]

June 10. Raspberries come & last a month.

| a Calendar [16] of the bloom of flowers in 1782. Note they were planted this spring, and the season was very backward. | | | | | | | |
|---|---|---|---|---|---|---|---|
| March. | April | May. | June. | July | Aug. | Sep. | Octob. |
| 17 | 1 / 20 23 27 29 | 8 12 14 / 20 22 | 18 22 25 | | | | |

Narcissus      Feath.

Hyacinth [17]

Jonquil [18]

Hyacinth [19] Anem.[20]

Ranunc.[21]

M. Iris Iris bicolor [22]  Nasturtium.[23]

Tulips [24]    Peony.[27]

Fiery Lil.[25]

White Lilly.[26]

Pink

Sw.Wm.[28]  Holly hock [29]

Calicanthus [30]

Crims.Dw.Rose [31]

94

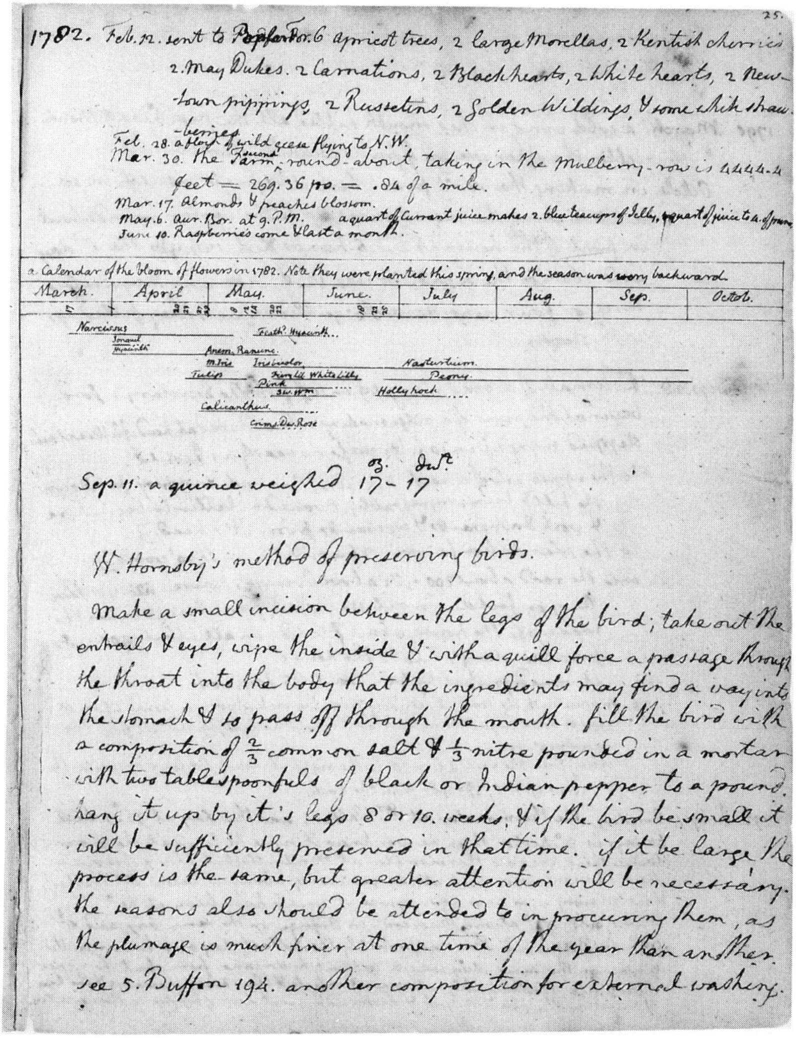

1782. Feb. 12. sent to Poplar Forest. 6 apricot trees, 2 large Morellas, 2 Kentish cherries
2. May Dukes. 2 Carnations, 2 Blackhearts, 2 White hearts, 2 New-
town pippings, 2 Russetins, 2 Golden Wildings, & some thick shells.

Feb. 28. a flight of wild geese flying to N.W.
Mar. 30. the Farm round-about, taking in the Mulberry-row is 4.4.4.4.4.
          feet = 269. 36 f10. = .84 of a mile.
Mar. 17. Almonds & peaches blossom.
May 6. Aur. Bor. at 9. P.M.   a quart of currant juice makes 2 blue teacups of jelly, a quart of juice to a pound
June 10. Raspberries come & last a month.

a Calendar of the bloom of flowers in 1782. Note they were planted this spring, and the season was very backward.

| March. | April. | May. | June. | July. | Aug. | Sep. | Octob. |
|---|---|---|---|---|---|---|---|
| 5 | | | | | | | |

Narcissus
  Jonquil
  Hyacinth
                        Gldth. Hyacinth...
            Anem. Ranunc.
          m.tric   Iridivolor
          Tulips      Nasturtium
                    Narrold White Lily    Peony
                    Pink          Holly hock
                    Iris Wm ....
          Calicanthus
              Crimson Dw. Rose

Sep. 11. a quince weighed  03/17 – Dwt/17

W. Hornsby's method of preserving birds.

make a small incision between the legs of the bird; take out the
entrails & eyes, wipe the inside & with a quill force a passage through
the throat into the body that the ingredients may find a way into
the stomach & so pass off through the mouth. fill the bird with
a composition of ⅔ common salt & ⅓ nitre pounded in a mortar
with two tablespoonfuls of black or Indian pepper to a pound.
hang it up by it's legs 8 or 10. weeks, & if the bird be small it
will be sufficiently preserved in that time. if it be large the
process is the same, but greater attention will be necessary.
the seasons also should be attended to in procuring them, as
the plumage is much finer at one time of the year than another
see 5. Buffon 194. another composition for external washing.

PLATE X.—Page 25 of the original *Garden Book.* Of special interest is Jefferson's
chart for noting the time and duration of bloom of certain flowers.

Sep. 11.   a quince [32] weighed $17^{oz}.-17^{dwt}.$ [33]

W. Hornsby's [34] method of preserving birds.

Make a small incision between the legs of the bird; take out the entrails & eyes, wipe the inside & with a quill force a passage through the throat into the body that the ingredients may find a way into the stomach & so pass off through the mouth.   fill the bird with a composition of $\frac{2}{3}$ common salt & $\frac{1}{3}$ nitre pounded in a mortar with two tablespoonfuls of black or Indian pepper to a pound.   hang it up by it's legs 8 or 10. weeks, & if the bird be small it will be sufficiently preserved in that time.   if it be large, the process is the same, but greater attention will be necessary.   the seasons also should be attended to in procuring them, as the plumage is much finer at one time of the year than another.   see 5. Buffon [35] 194. another composition for external washing.

Oct. 22.   seventeen bushels of winter grapes [36] (the stems first excluded) made 40 gallons of vinegar of the first running, & pouring water on, yeilded gallons [37] of a weaker kind

20 bushels of peaches will make 75 gall[s]. of mobby [38] i.e. $\frac{5}{12}$ of it's bulk.

---

[1] *1782.* Jefferson appears to have been at *Monticello* from the first of January through the first of November except for a short trip to *Poplar Forest* in July, where he agreed to have Bennet continue in Bedford County as his overseer for the following year.

The delicate condition of Mrs. Jefferson's health in the spring had caused Jefferson such concern that he abandoned practically all of his activities except that of watching after her comforts.

Their sixth child, and their fifth daughter, was born on May 8.   She was the second daughter to bear the name of Lucy Elizabeth.   After the child's birth, Mrs. Jefferson's health rapidly declined.   She died on September 6, leaving her husband with three daughters, the youngest four months old. Mrs. Jefferson's death was the tragedy of Jefferson's life, one from which he never fully recovered.

On November 6 Jefferson was in Richmond attending the Assembly, and on November 12 he was appointed Peace Commissioner to Europe.   He left *Monticello* for Philadelphia in December, preparatory to undertaking this mission.

There were several varied entries in the *Garden Book* for the year, the most interesting being the "Calendar of bloom of flowers in 1782."   This was the first time in several years that he had mentioned the garden flowers planted and their blooming period.   The only purchase of seeds, according to the *Account Book 1782,* was on August 4, when he "p⁴ Dr. Walker's Trim for 6½ qᵗˢ. clover seed 6/8."

The Marquis de Chastellux visited *Monticello* in the spring of 1782, and sketched in his *Travels in North America* (2: 48) a charming description of *Monticello* and the Jefferson family.   We quote only one paragraph from the book, to show that Jefferson had carried out at least one phase of his landscaping plans of 1771, namely his deer park.

Mr. Jefferson amused himself by raising a score of these animals [deer] in his park; they are become very familiar, which happens to all the animals of America; for they are in general much easier to tame than those of Europe.   He amuses himself by feeding them with Indian corn, of which they are very fond, and which they eat out of his hand.   I followed him one evening into a deep valley, where they are accustomed to assemble towards the close of the day, and saw them walk, run, and bound; but the more I examined their paces, the less I was inclined to annex them to any particular species in Europe.   Mr. Jefferson being no sportsman, and not having crossed the sea could have no decided opinion on this part of natural history; but he has not neglected the other branches.

² Jefferson sent the fruit trees to *Poplar Forest* by Jupiter, one of his slaves. In order to get to *Poplar Forest* he had to pass over the James River by ferry. Jefferson wrote in the *Account Book 1779–1782:* "Feb. 12. gave Jup. for ferr͞ge to Pop. For. 3/."

³ *Poplar Forest,* Jefferson's other home, is in Bedford County, Virginia. The land on which the house was built was left to Mrs. Jefferson by her father at his death. The house, which is still in a fine state of preservation, was begun in 1806, but not completed until several years after Jefferson retired from the Presidency in 1809. A portion of a letter, written to Mr. Randall in 1856 by one of the granddaughters, gives a charming description of the house and the life there during Jefferson's visits.

The house at Poplar Forest was very pretty and pleasant. It was of brick, one story in front, and, owing to the falling of the ground, two in the rear. It was an exact octagon, with a centre-hall twenty feet square, lighted from above. This was a beautiful room, and served as a dining-room. Round it were grouped a bright drawing-room, looking south, my grandfather's own chamber, three other bedrooms, and a pantry. A terrace extended from one side of the house; there was a portico in front connected by a vestibule with the center room, and in the rear a verandah, on which the drawing-room opened, with its windows to the floor. . . . Mr. Jefferson, from the time of his return home in 1809, was in the habit of visiting this Bedford plantation, but it was some years before the house was ready for the reception of his family. It was furnished in the simplest manner, but had a very tasty air; there was nothing common or second-rate about any part of the establishment, although there was no appearance of expense. As soon as the house was habitable, my grandfather began to take the ladies of his family, generally two at a time, with him, whenever he went. His first visit of a fortnight or three weeks was in the spring—the second, of about six weeks, in the early or late autumn. We have staid as much as two months at a time. My Mother went occasionally—not very often—for she had too much to do at home. I . . . generally accompanied him with one of my younger sisters. Mr. Jefferson greatly enjoyed these visits. The crowd at Monticello of friends and strangers, of stationary or ever-varying guests, the coming and going, the incessant calls upon his own time and attention, the want of leisure that such a state of things entailed as a necessary consequence, the bustle and hurry of an almost perpetual round of company, wearied and harassed him in the end, whatever pleasure he may have taken, and it was sometimes great, in the society and conversation of his guests. At Poplar Forest he found in a pleasant home, rest, leisure, power to carry on his favorite pursuits—to think, to study, to read—whilst the presence of part of his family took away all character of solitude from his retreat.  (Randall, *Jefferson* 3: 342–343.)

See plate XXXVI.

[4] A variety of the sour cherry, *Prunus cerasus* L.   Downing says that it is a fine fruit and that its name is said to be derived from the dark purple color of its juice, which resembles that of the *Morus* or mulberry.

[5] A variety of the sour cherry, *Prunus cerasus* L.   This is probably what Downing calls the Late Kentish, or the Pie Cherry.

[6] A variety of the sour cherry, *Prunus cerasus* L.   Downing says (*Fruits:* 191): "This invaluable early cherry is one of the most popular sorts in all countries, thriving almost equally well in cold or warm climates.   This, the Black Heart, and the Bigarreau, are the most extensively diffused of all the finer varieties in the United States."

[7] "The Black Heart, an old variety, is better known than almost any other cherry in this country, and its great fruitfulness and good flavour, together with the hardiness and the large size to which the tree grows, render it everywhere esteemed" (Downing, *Fruits:* 169).

[8] The White Heart also belongs to the sweet cherry group. Downing writes (*Fruits:* 173): "An old variety, long cultivated in this country, and one of the earliest, ripening before the Mayduke."

[9] A variety of *Fragaria vesca* L.   The white strawberries are the white-fruited forms of the Alpine strawberries, which came from *Fragaria vesca* L.

[10] This is the first mention of the second *Round-about*.   It is not known when it was begun or completed.   (See plate XXII.)

[11] The Mulberry Row was also a part of the First *Round-about*.   It was just above the terraced garden and ran in front of the Nailery and other outhouses.   Its name came from the mulberries planted along the side.   (See plate XXI.)

[12] *Po.* is the abbreviation for poles.

[13] This was the last time Jefferson mentioned the blossoming of the peach trees before his departure for France.

[14] Aurora borealis.   This was a phenomenon which fascinated Jefferson.   He recorded it often in his weather records.

[15] *Puree* here means pulp, *i. e.,* four quarts of pulp to make one quart of juice.

[16] This *Calendar of Bloom* is important because it shows the length of the blooming period of certain flowers.   While Jefferson was President, he kept a similar memorandum of the Vegetable Market of Washington.   (See appendix III.)

[17] *Muscari comosum* var. *monstrosum* L.

[18] *Narcissus jonquilla* L.

[19] *Hyacinthus orientalis* L.

[20] Probably *Anemone pulsatilla* L.   This species was grown at *Monticello.*

[21] Probably *Ranunculus repens* L. var. *pleniflorus* Fernald. This variety of double buttercup was later planted at *Monticello.*

[22] *Iris bicolor,* a trade-name of uncertain application (L. H. Bailey, *Hortus* (New York, 1930) : 328).

[23] *Tropaeolum majus* L.

[24] *Tulipa* spp.

[25] Probably *Lilium chalcedonicum* L.   Scarlet lily.

[26] *Lilium candidum* L.   Now commonly called Madonna Lily.

[27] *Paeonia* sp.

[28] *Dianthus barbatus* L.

[29] *Althaea rosea* Cav.

[30] *Calycanthus floridus* L.

[31] Crimson Dwarf Rose, *Rosa* sp.

[32] *Cydonia oblonga* Mill.

[33] See note 3, under 1767, for *Table of Troy Weight.*

[34] W. Hornsby lived in Albemarle County.

[35] Georges Louis Leclerc de Buffon was born at Montbard, in Burgundy, in 1707.   After studying law, he devoted himself wholly to science.   He was later admitted to the Academy and in 1739 was appointed director of the *Jardin du Roi.* His greatest contribution to science was his *Histoire Naturelle* in 15 volumes.   He was a friend of Jefferson and carried on a correspondence with him.   Buffon died in 1788.   (Funk and Wagnalls, *Standard Encyclopedia* (New York, 1912) 5: 171–172.)

[36] It is difficult to tell here whether Jefferson is writing of his own winter grapes or setting down some information he had obtained from a book or conversation.

[37] Jefferson failed to write the number of gallons.

[38] In the West Indies *mobby* is a spirituous liquor made from batatas or sweet potato.   In America it is the expressed juice of apples and peaches, used in the distillation of apple and peach brandy; also the brandy itself.   (*Oxford English Dictionary* 6: 560.)

# 1783

1783.[1]

2ᵈ. & 3ᵈ September.  White frosts which killed vines in
this neighborhood, killed tobō in the N. Garden,[2] fodder & latter corn in Augusta,[3] & forward corn in Greenbriar[4]

---

[1] *1783.*  Jefferson was at Philadelphia, Baltimore, Richmond, and *Tuckahoe* during the early months of the year.
He returned to *Monticello* on May 15.

In November of the preceding year he had been appointed
Peace Commissioner to Europe.  Soon after, rumors of peace
reached him, so that he spent most of the winter waiting for a
confirmation of it.  In the spring of this year a provisional
treaty was signed, and since there was no further need for
Jefferson to go to France, he returned to *Monticello* and spent
most of the summer there with his children and the Carr
family, who were still making their home with him.

He was elected to Congress on June 6, and on October 16
left *Monticello* to take his seat in the Congress then meeting
in Trenton, N. J.  On November 4 the Congress adjourned
to Annapolis, to meet again on the 26th.  He was in Philadelphia and Annapolis for the remainder of the year.

Before leaving for Congress, Jefferson had left his two
younger daughters with Mr. and Mrs. Francis Eppes, of
*Eppington* in Virginia.  He took Martha, his oldest daughter,
with him and placed her in a boarding school in Philadelphia.
*Monticello* was closed until his return to Virginia in December, 1789.

Although Jefferson was at *Monticello* most of the summer
and fall, there is but a solitary entry in the *Garden Book* for

the year, and this dealt with the frosts of September 2 and 3. The garden apparently was planted as usual, and the first peas and other vegetables came to the table as in former years, for there was the usual large number of persons to feed. The account books, which often supplemented the *Garden Book,* have practically nothing in them to indicate what was happening on the mountain.

Three entries in the *Account Book 1783–1790* indicate that men were still being hired to carry on the work. On "May 16. W^m. Orr begins to work," and on September 20 he "agreed with Joseph Price to serve me a year as carpenter. I give him £30. 500 lb. pork & fodder for a horse & cow." Four days later he "agreed with John Key to serve me as steward another year for £80."

² North Garden, a small village about 12 miles south of Charlottesville.

³ Augusta County, Virginia, is west from *Monticello,* across the Blue Ridge Mountains.

⁴ Greenbriar County, Virginia. This county is now a part of West Virginia.

# 1784

*1784.** Jefferson was still at Annapolis when the year opened. On May 7 he was appointed Minister Plenipotentiary to France to act in conjunction with Benjamin Franklin and John Adams. He accepted this mission and made preparations to leave Annapolis on May 11 for Boston, in order to sail from that port to France. Martha, his oldest daughter, was to accompany him.

Jefferson did not return to *Monticello* before his departure for Europe. The house remained closed until his return in 1789. Early in the year he made an agreement with Nicholas Lewis, of Albemarle County, to manage his entire estates with the aid of Mr. Francis Eppes, of Chesterfield County, while he was absent. They were to apply all of the profits to the payment of his debts. (See letter, Jefferson to Alexander McCaul, London, April 19, 1786. Ford, *Jefferson's Writings* 5: 90. Also "Agreement with Nicholas Lewis," *Jefferson Papers,* M. H. S.)

There were no entries in the *Garden Book* for this year and the succeeding ones until 1790. We know very little about what happened at *Monticello* during Jefferson's absence.

In the spring of 1784 Jefferson received an interesting letter from Mr. Ralph Izard, his friend, which reveals in part Jefferson's reputation as an agriculturist and farmer.

The Elms, South Carolina
27ᵗʰ April, 1784

Dear Sir,

. . . I am settled upon an agreeable spot, about 18 miles from Charles Town. A Plantation long neglected, but pleasantly situated, & capable of great improvement. This I am attempting; & my inclination would lead me never to enter again into public life. I have sown Ten Acres of Lucerne in Drills, at the distance of 40 Inches from each other. This was done about the 10th March, & it is come up very well. I have lately had a very troublesome piece of work. A quantity of grass, & weeds got so intimately connected, & combined with the Plants, that the

* This year not represented in the *Garden Book.*

Hoe was of little, or no service, & I was obliged to have the whole hand-picked, which employed 20 working hands six days. The ground had lain fallow three or four years; & I was so backward in other parts of my Farm, that I ploughed & harrowed it only once, which I believe is the reason of my having so much trouble with it. If it would not be deemed too selfish, and too injurious to our friends in Virginia, I could express a wish, which I sincerely feel, that you were settled within a Mile, or Two of me, that I might have recourse to you for advice on this, & other occasions.

Ra. Izard

Is there a possibility of having three, or four Hundred young Grafted Crab apple Trees sent me here from Virginia?

(Jefferson Papers, L. C.)

Jefferson, with his daughter Martha, sailed from Boston on July 5, on the ship *Ceres*. His records of the temperature and observations of the birds and marine life seen each day on the voyage show his keen interest in nature. They were in Paris on August 6. By August 26 Martha, or Patsy, as he lovingly called her, was in school at the *Abbaie de Panthemont*. On September 15 he went to see the gardens at *Versailles*, a beauty spot he frequented during his stay in Paris. For the remainder of the year he attended to his official duties and enjoyed the intellectual and artistic life of Paris.

# 1785

*1785.** By the beginning of this year Jefferson, who had been in France nearly six months, had become fully acquainted with the varied life of Paris. His interests and sympathies were so broad that he was quick to avail himself of all the cultural phases of French life. In the early years of his stay music especially attracted him, and he was a constant attendant at the concerts. On September 30 he wrote to Carlo Bellini, professor of modern languages at the College of William and Mary:

Were I to proceed to tell you how much I enjoy their architecture, sculpture, painting, music, I should want words. It is in these arts they shine. The last of them, particularly, is an enjoyment, the deprivation of which, with us, cannot be calculated. I am almost ready to say, it is the only thing which from my heart I envy them, and which, in spite of all the authority of the Decalogue, I do covet. (Randall, *Jefferson* 1: 433–434.)

Early in January Jefferson received word from Virginia that his youngest daughter, Lucy Elizabeth, who had been left in Virginia with Mr. and Mrs. Francis Eppes, had died in November of the preceding year. Jefferson had only two surviving children, Maria in Virginia, and Martha with him in Paris.

In the spring of the year Dr. Franklin returned to America, and Mr. Adams went to England as Minister Plenipotentiary to the British Court. Jefferson was appointed to succeed Franklin in the same capacity in the Court of France.

There are several entries from the *Account Book 1783–1790* relative to Jefferson's interest in gardens and gardening:

Jan 29. p$^d$. for a dial. 12 f.
May 22. Petit comes into my service. [Petit was a favorite steward of Jefferson's. He later followed Jefferson to Philadelphia and served him in various capacities.]
June 27. p$^d$ ferrage, breakfast, & coach hire King's gardens 3 f 16.
July 19. p$^d$ chair hire at Versailles 1 f 4.

* This year not represented in the *Garden Book*.

Aug. 8.    p<sup>d</sup> seeing the windlass plough, 3 f.
Sept. 1.    p<sup>d</sup> for seeds 27–8.
Sept. 9.    p<sup>d</sup> Noseda for a thermometer, 12 f.

On October 25 Jefferson went to Fontainebleau (*Account
Book 1791–1803*).   While there he wrote to the Reverend
James Madison, President of the College of William and
Mary, at Williamsburg, Virginia, an illuminating letter on
fruits and fruit trees of France.   How many of the trees col-
lected for him were brought back to Virginia is not known.

Fontainebleau, Oct. 28, 1785.

To Reverend James Madison,

   . . . After descending the hill again I saw a man cutting fern.   I
went to him under pretence of asking the shortest road to town, and
afterwards asked for what use he was cutting fern.   He told me that
this part of the country furnished a great deal of fruit to Paris.   That
when packed in straw it acquired an ill taste, but that dry fern preserved
it perfectly without communicating any taste at all.
   I treasured this observation for the preservation of my apples on my
return to my own country.   They have no apples here to compare with
our *Redtown* pippin.   They have nothing which deserves the name of
a peach; there being not sun enough to ripen the plum-peach and the
best of their soft peaches being like our autumn peaches.   Their cherries
and strawberries are fair, but I think lack flavor.   Their plums I think
are better; so also their gooseberries, and the pears infinitely beyond any
thing we possess.   They have nothing better than our sweet-water; but
they have a succession of as good from early in the summer till frost.
   I am tomorrow to get (to) M. Malsherbes (an uncle of the Chevalier
Luzerne's) about seven leagues from hence, who is the most curious man
in France as to his trees.   He is making for me a collection of the vines
from which the Burgundy, Champagne, Bordeaux, Frontignac, and other
of the most valuable wines of this country are made.   Another gentleman is collecting for me the best eating grapes, including what we call
the raisin.   I propose also to endeavor to colonize their hare, rabbit, red
and gray partridge, pheasants of different kinds, and some other birds.
. . . (Lipscomb and Bergh, *Jefferson* **19**: 19–20.)

Toward the close of the year Jefferson was elected an
honorary member of the South Carolina Society for Promoting Agriculture, an honor which he prized highly.   This honor
opened a correspondence between him and members of the society, which resulted in Jefferson's sending great quantities of
olive trees and rice to the society in order to test the possibility
of their culture in the South.

Charleston, South Carolina
November 23ᵈ 1785

Sir,

As chairman of the Committee of the South Carolina Society for promoting & improving Agriculture & other rural Concerns, I am directed
to inform your Excellency, that you are unanimously elected an honorary
member of that Society; and I herewith transmit to your Excellency a
copy of an Address & their Rules, published at their Institution.

I have the Honour to be with great Respect
Your Excellency's most obedient & most humble
Servant.

Wm. Drayton
(*Jefferson Papers, L. C.*)

# 1786

*1786.*\* During January and February, 1786, Jefferson spent a considerable part of his time replying to a series of questions on America asked him by the editor of the *Encyclopédie Méthodique*. However, he found time early in January to write to his friend, David Ramsay, physician and historian of Charleston, South Carolina, requesting Dr. Ramsay to send to him plants of *Magnolia* and *Dionaea*.

Paris, Jan. 1786

Dear Sir,

Since writing my letter of yesterday a person whom I am very desirous of obliging, has asked me to procure from South Carolina some plants of the Magnolia grandiflora, sometimes called altissima, and some seeds of the Dionaea muscipula. if you can be instrumental in procuring them you will gratify me much. I have heard that there is one Watson at Charleston who furnishes these articles well. I am of the opinion they had better come to N. York, and from thence to be sent here in the packet, for I think there is scarcely any direct communication between Charleston & France. the proper season for sending the plants of Magnolia must of course be awaited; but the seeds of the Dionaea I suppose may come at any time. (*Jefferson Papers,* L. C.)

In order to introduce native plants to the gardens of France, Jefferson often wrote home to his friends to send him certain plants that he thought would be of interest and value to his friends in France. Among the first of these requests was one to his friend, Francis Hopkinson, of Philadelphia, to send him some nuts of the paccan (pecan) tree. He had described this tree in his *Notes on Virginia,* and this no doubt created an interest among his French friends to see it. The tree seemed to fascinate Jefferson, for he constantly wrote to other friends for its nuts. When he returned to *Monticello,* he planted several hundred of them there.

\* This year not represented in the *Garden Book.*

Paris January 3. 1786

Dear Sir,

. . . the third commission is more distant. it is to procure me two or three hundred Paccan nuts from the Western country. I expect they can always be got at Pittsburg, and am in hopes that by yourself or your friends some attentive person there may be engaged to send them to you. they should come as fresh as possible, and come best I believe in a box of sand. of this Bartram could best advise you. I imagine vessels are always coming from Philadelphia to France. if there be a choice of ports, Havre would be best. (*Jefferson Papers,* L. C.)

The following letter, with a long list of plants inclosed, was written by Jefferson to John Bartram, Jr., the botanist of Philadelphia:

Paris Jan. 17. 1786.

By mᵣ Bingham who left Paris about a fortnight ago I took the liberty of asking your acceptance of a copy of Linnaeus's *Systema vegetabilium* translated into English and enlarged with many new plants furnished by Linnaeus, the son, and which have never before been published.

Inclosed is a list of plants and seeds which I should be very glad to obtain from America for a friend here whom I wish much to oblige. I have stated the Linnaean name to every one except those which are mentioned otherwise. I will pray you to send me these plants and seeds, packed in that careful manner which you are so perfectly acquainted. for the time of the year proper to send them, I leave it to yourself, only hoping it will be as soon as the proper season will admit. mᵣ F. Hopkinson will have the goodness to pay your demand for these things, & the expense attending them. mᵣ Rob. Morris will have occasion to send many vessels to France. some of these will probably come to Havre. this would be the best port to send them to, because they would come from thence by water. but if no opportunity occurs to that port, let them come to Nantes or l'Orient. in every case address them to the care of the American Consul at the port. Your favor herein will greatly oblige Sir your most obedient humble servant.

| Plants. | Andromeda arborea. | Laurus Sassafras. |
|---|---|---|
| | Clethra. | Lilium Canadense. |
| | Geranium maculatum. | Magnolia grandiflora. |
| | Geranium gibbosum. | "    glauca. |
| | Itea. | "    acuminata. |
| | Kalmia latifolia. | "    tripetala. |
| | Kalmia angustifolia. | Nyssa. |
| | Laurus Benzoin. | Quercus phellos. |
| | | Rhododendron maximum. |

Seeds.   Annona.
         Azalea nudiflora.
         Acer negundo.
             rubrum.
             Pensylvanicum
         Cornus florida.
         Chionanthus Virginica.
         Ceanothus Americana.
         Cupressus disticha.
         Cupressus thyoides.
         Crataegus tomentosa.
         Campanula perfoliata.
         Campanula Americana of
         Millar.
         Diospyros Virginiana.
         Fraxinus Americana.
         Guilandina Bonduc.
         Gleditsia triacanthos.
         Halesia tetraptera.
         Juglans nigra.

Juglans cinerea.
Juglans alba.
Juglans alba, fructu minori cortice
glabro.  not described by Linneus.
Juglans cortice squamosa. Clayton.
Juniperus Virginica.
Liriodendron tulipifera.  in quan-
tity.
Liquidambar styraciflua.
Prunus Virginiana.
Pinus Balsamea.
Ptelea trifoliata.
Ptelea pinnata.
Phytolacca decandra.
Populus heterophylla.
Quercus Virginiana.  of Millar.
Rhus glabrum.
Rhus Coppallinum.
Robinia Pseudo-acacia.
Viburnum acerifolium.
Viburnum nudum.

Padus foliis lanceolatis, acute denticulatis, sempervirentibus, called in
America Bastard Mahogany.  this description is not Linnaean.  per-
haps mr̄ Bartram may know what plant it belongs to.  (*Jefferson
Papers*, M. H. S.)

Towards the close of February Jefferson was urged by John
Adams to come to London to aid in negotiating a treaty with
Portugal and to attend to other important state affairs.   This
official visit to London afforded him the opportunity to see the
gardens of England and to observe the English methods of
gardening.
Jefferson used for his guide through the gardens Thomas
Whately's *Observations on Modern Gardening* (London,
1770), which he either owned before he came to France or
bought soon after his arrival.   His complementary notes on
the gardens described by Whately show that he had studied
the book and was ready to compare his own observations of
them with Whately's.   This tour of English gardens had a
considerable influence on Jefferson in landscaping his grounds
at *Monticello*.   Although he admired France and her civiliza-
tion, he considered England far superior to all other countries
in gardening.   Her naturalistic gardens were to him more desirable for America than the formal gardens of Paris.   He

wrote to his early friend, John Page, of Virginia, soon after his return from England to Paris: "The gardening in that country is the article in which it surpasses all the earth. I mean their pleasure gardening. This, indeed, went far beyond my ideas." (Randall, *Jefferson* 1: 447.)

Jefferson left Paris on March 5. He was in London on the 11th. For the remainder of the month he busied himself with state duties. The first of April he started on the tour of historical places and gardens mentioned above. The following are his comments on the gardens he visited.

A Tour to Some of the Gardens of England

(Memorandum made on a tour to some of the gardens in England, described by Whateley in his book on Gardening.)

While his descriptions, in point of style, are models of perfect elegance and classical correctness, they are as remarkable for their exactness. I always walked over the gardens with his book in my hand, examined with attention the particular spots he described, found them so justly characterized by him as to be easily recognized, and saw with wonder, that his fine imagination had never been able to seduce him from the truth. My inquiries were directed chiefly to such practical things as might enable me to estimate the expense of making and maintaining a garden in that style. My journey was in the months of March and April, 1786.

*Chiswick.*—Belongs to Duke of Devonshire. A garden about six acres;—the octagonal dome has an ill effect, both within and without: the garden shows still too much of art. An obelisk of very ill effect; another in the middle of a pond useless. ["April 2, gave servants at Chiswick (D. of Devonshire's) 4/6" (*Account Book 1783–1790*).]

*Hampton-Court.*—Old fashioned. Clipt yews grown wild. ["April 2, gave servants at Hampton Court 4/6" (*ibid.*).]

*Twickenham.*—Pope's original garden, three and a half acres. Sir. Wm. Stanhope added one and a half acres. This is a long narrow slip, grass and trees in the middle, walk all around. Now Sir Wellbore Ellis's. Obelisk at bottom of Pope's garden, as monument to his mother. Inscription, "Ah! Editha, matrum optima, mulierum amantissima, Vale." The house about thirty yards from the Thames: the ground shelves gently to the water side; on the back of the house passes the street, and beyond that the garden. The grotto is under the street, and goes out level to the water. In the centre of the garden a mound with a spiral walk round it. A rookery. ["April 2, gave servants at Twickenham, Pope's garden, 2/" (*ibid.*).]

*Esher-Place.*—The house in a bottom near the river; on the other side the ground rises pretty much. The road by which we come to the house forms a dividing line in the middle of the front; on the right are heights, rising one beyond and above another, with clumps of trees; on the farthest a temple. A hollow filled up with a clump of trees, the tallest in the bottom, so that the top is quite flat. On the left the ground descends. Clumps of trees, the clumps on each hand balance finely—a most lovely mixture of concave and convex. The garden is of about forty-five acres, besides the park which joins. Belongs to Lady Frances Pelham. ["April 2, gave servants at Esherplace 6/" (*ibid.*).]

*Claremont.*—Lord Clive's. Nothing remarkable.

*Paynshill.*—Mr. Hopkins. Three hundred and twenty-three acres, garden and park all in one. Well described by Whately. Grotto said to have cost £7,000. Whately says one of the bridges is of stone, but both now are of wood, the lower sixty feet high: there is too much evergreen. The dwelling-house built by Hopkins, ill-situated: he has not been there in five years. He lived there four years while building the present house. It is not finished; its architecture is incorrect. A Doric temple, beautiful. ["April 2, gave servants at *Paynshill* 7/" (*ibid.*).]

*Woburn.*—Belongs to Lord Peters. Lord Loughborough is the present tenant for two lives. Four people to the farm, four to the pleasure garden, four to the kitchen garden. All are intermixed, the pleasure garden being merely a highly-ornamented walk through and round the divisions of the farm and kitchen garden. ["April 3, gave servants at Woburn's farm 6/6" (*ibid.*).]

*Caversham.*—Sold by Lord Cadogan to Major Marsac. Twenty-five acres of garden, four hundred acres of park, six acres of kitchen garden. A large lawn, separated by a sunk fence from the garden, appears to be part of it. A straight, broad gravel walk passes before the front and parallel to it, terminated on the right by a Doric temple, and opening at the other end on a fine prospect. This straight walk has an ill effect. The lawn in front, which is pasture, well disposed with clumps of trees. ["April 4, Caversham, gave servants 3/6" (*ibid.*).]

*Wotton.*—Now belongs to the Marquis of Buckingham, son of George Grenville. The lake covers fifty acres, the river five acres, the basin fifteen acres, the little river two acres—equal to seventy-two acres of water. The lake and great river are on a level; they fall into the basin five feet below, and that again into the little river five feet lower. These waters lie in the form of ⌐·: the house is in middle of the open side, fronting the angle. A walk goes round the whole, three miles in circumference, and containing within it about three hundred acres: sometimes it passes close to the water, sometimes so far off as to leave large pasture grounds between it and the water. But two hands to keep the pleasure grounds in order; much neglected. The water affords two thousand brace of carp a year. There is a Palladian bridge, of which, I think, Whatley does not speak. ["April 5, Wotton (Marquis of Buckingham's) servants 3/" (*ibid.*).]

*Stowe.*—Belongs to the Marquis of Buckingham, son of George Grenville, and who takes it from Lord Temple. Fifteen men and eighteen boys employed in keeping pleasure grounds. Within the walk are considerable portions separated by enclosures and used for pasture. The Egyptian pyramid is almost entirely taken down by the late Lord

Temple, to erect a building there, in commemoration of Mr. Pitt, but he died before beginning it, and nothing is done to it yet. The grotto and two rotundas are taken away. There are four levels of water, receiving it one from the other. The basin contains seven acres, the lake below that ten acres. Kent's building is called the temple of Venus. The enclosure is entirely by ha-ha. At each end of the front line there is a recess like the bastion of a fort. In one of these is the temple of Friendship, in the other the temple of Venus. They are seen the one from the other, the line of sight passing, not through the garden, but through the country parallel to the line of the garden. This has a good effect. In the approach to Stowe, you are brought a mile through a straight avenue, pointing to the Corinthian arch and to the house, till you get to the arch, then you turn short to the right. The straight approach is very ill. The Corinthian arch has a very useless appearance, inasmuch as it has no pretension to any destination. Instead of being an object from the house, it is an obstacle to a very pleasing distant prospect. The Grecian valley being clear of trees, while the hill on each side is covered with them, is much deepened to appearance. ["April 6, Stowe (Marquis of Buckingham's) servants 8/" (*ibid.*).]

*Leasowes, in Shropshire.*—Now the property of Mr. Horne by purchase. One hundred and fifty acres within the walk. The waters small. This is not even an ornamented farm—it is only a grazing farm with a path round it, here and there a seat of board, rarely anything better. Architecture has contributed nothing. The obelisk is of brick. Shenstone had but three hundred pounds a year, and ruined himself by what he did to this farm. It is said that he died of the heart-aches which his debts occasioned him. The part next to the road is of red earth, that on the further part grey. The first and second cascades are beautiful. The landscape at number eighteen, and prospect at thirty-two, are fine. The walk through the wood is umbrageous and pleasing. The whole arch of prospect may be of ninety degrees. Many of the inscriptions are lost. ["Apr. 7, Leasowes (Shenstone's. now Horne's) serv^ts 5/" (*ibid.*).]

*Hagley, now Lord Wescot's.*—One thousand acres: no distinction between park and garden—both blended, but more of the character of garden. Eight or nine laborers keep it in order. Between two and three hundred deer in it, some of them red deer. They breed sometimes with the fallow. This garden occupying a descending hollow between the Clent and Witchbury hills, with the spurs from those hills, there is no level in it for a spacious water. There are, therefore, only some small ponds. From one of these there is a fine cascade; but it can only be occasionally, by opening the sluice. This is in a small, dark, deep hollow, with recesses of stone in the banks on every side. In one of these is a Venus predique, turned half round as if inviting you with her into the recess. There is another cascade seen from the portico on the bridge. The castle is triangular, with a round tower at each angle, one only entire; it seems to be between forty and fifty feet high. The ponds yield a great deal of trout.   The walks are scarcely gravelled.   ["April 8, Hagley (L^d Wescott's) serv^ts 5/.—ent^t. in the village 2/6" (*ibid.*).]

*Blenheim.*—Twenty-five hundred acres, of which two hundred is garden, one hundred and fifty water, twelve kitchen garden, and the rest park.   Two hundred people employed to keep it in order, and to make alterations and additions.   About fifty of these employed in pleasure grounds.   The turf is mowed once in ten days.   In summer, about two thousand fallow deer in the park, and two or three thousand sheep.   The palace of Henry II. was remaining till taken down by Sarah, widow of the first Duke of Marlborough.   It was on a round spot levelled by art, near what is now water, and but a little above it.   The island was a part of the high road leading to the palace.   Rosamond's bower was near where is now a little grove, about two hundred yards from the palace.   The well is near where the bower was.   The water here is very beautiful, and very grand.   The cascade from the lake, a fine one; except this the garden has no great beauties.   It is not laid out in fine lawns and woods, but the trees are scattered thinly over the ground, and every here and there small thickets of shrubs, in oval raised beds, cultivated, and flowers among the shrubs.   The gravelled walks are broad— art appears too much.   There are but a few seats in it, and nothing of architecture more dignified.   There is no one striking position in it. There has been a great addition to the length of the river since Whateley wrote.   ["April 9, Blenheim (D. of Marlborough's) serv^ts 7/" (*ibid.*).]

*Enfield Chase.*—One of the four lodges.   Garden about sixty acres. Originally by Lord Chatham, now in the tenure of Dr. Beaver, who married the daughter of Mr. Sharpe.   The lease lately renewed—not in good repair.   The water very fine; would admit of great improvement by extending walks, etc., to the principal water at the bottom of the lawn.

*Moor Park.*—The lawn about thirty acres.   A piece of ground up the hill of six acres.   A small lake.   Clumps of spruce firs.   Surrounded by walk—separately inclosed—destroys unity.   The property of Mr. Rous, who bought of Sir Thomas Dundas.   The building superb; the principal front a Corinthian portico of four columns; in front of the wings a colonnade, Ionic, subordinate.   Back front a terrace, four Corinthian pilasters.   Pulling down wings of building; removing deer; wants water.

*Kew.*—Archimedes' screw for raising water.   [He draws a diagram of this screw and describes it.]   ["Apr. 14, gave serv^ts at Kew 5/.— lemonade 6 ^d." (*ibid.*).]   (Lipscomb and Bergh, *Jefferson* 17: 236–244.)

Before leaving London for Paris on April 26, Jefferson "left with Col^o. Smith for James Lee. Hammersmith for plants 4£–15."   These plants, of which a list follows, were to be sent to Tours, probably for a friend.

M^r. Jefferson Bought of James Lee & Co.

1786   24 April

| number tied on each sort | Quantity of each sort | | £ | s | C |
|---|---|---|---|---|---|
| N° 1............ | 3 | Cornus florida ............ | | .4. | 6 |
| 2............ | 3 | Cupressus thyoides ........ | | .4. | 6 |
| 3............ | 6 | Gleditsia triacanthus ...... | | .3 | ... |
| 4............ | 3 | Itea Virginica ............ | | .4. | 6 |
| 5............ | 3 | Juglans alba ............ | | .3 | ... |
| 6............ | 3 | ———— cinerea .......... | | .4. | 6 |
| 7............ | 3 | ———— nigra ............ | | .3 | ... |
| 8............ | 3 | Laurus benzoin .......... | | .4. | 6 |
| 9............ | 3 | Liquidambar Styraciflua ... | | .4. | 6 |
| 10............ | 3 | Magnolia grandiflora ...... | | .15 | ... |
| 11............ | 6 | Pinus Balsamea .......... | | 1. | 6 |
| 12............ | 3 | Populus heterophylla ...... | | .4. | 6 |
| 13............ | 6 | Ptelea trifoliata .......... | | .3 | ... |
| 14............ | 6 | Robinia pseudo Acacia ..... | | .3 | ... |
| 15............ | 3 | Viburnum nudum ........ | | .3 | ... |
| 16............12 | | Vaccinium Occycoccos ..... | | .18 | ... |
| 17............ | 3 | Lilium Canadense ........ | | .6 | ... |
| | | Box package etc. .......... | | .4 | |
| | | Carriage to Tours ........ | | .1 | |
| | | | | £4.15.... | |

(*Jefferson Papers,* United States Department of Agriculture.)

Jefferson arrived in Paris on May 1, beginning soon after correspondence with friends in America about the exchange of plants between the two countries. The first of these letters was to Richard Cary, his kinsman and friend in Virginia.

Paris May 4. 1786.

Dear Sir,

Knowing your fondness for Botany, and meeting with a new edition of Linnaeus's *systema vegetabilium* in English, with many additions furnished the editors by young Linneaus which have never yet been in print, I procurred one for you, and now avail myself of the return of *Mon* de la Croix to Williamsburg to convey it to you and ask your acceptance of it. I saw in the hands of m^r Mazzei a list of flower roots & seeds which you had desired him to send you. I have taken a copy of it, and will endeavor to find an opportunity of sending them when the season shall be proper, which you know will not be till fall. should you hereafter have any other wishes in this line you cannot oblige me more than by communicating them to me, and I will do my best to execute them. the only difficulty will be an opportunity by a careful hand in the proper season, but this chance may be in our favor as well as it may be against us. (*Jefferson Papers,* L. C.)

On May 6 he wrote to William Drayton, chairman of the South Carolina Society for Promoting Agriculture, accepting membership in that society, to which he had been elected the preceding year.   In his letter of acceptance he wrote:

I send at present by mr McQueen some seeds of a grass found very useful in the Southern parts of Europe, & particularly & almost solely cultivated in Malta.   it is called by the names of Sulla, and Spanish St. foin, and is the *Hedysarum coronarium* of Linnaeus.   it is usually sown early in autumn.   (*Jefferson Papers,* L. C.)

He also sent Drayton acorns of the cork oak, a species he thought should be experimented with in order to find out if it could be grown profitably in the South.   Jefferson attempted to grow it at *Monticello* but without success.

In August Jefferson again wrote Richard Cary, sending him a long list of native plants which he asked to be sent to him. He wrote detailed instructions about packing them.   At the same time Jefferson reciprocated with some choice plants from the Continent.   This list of plants and the list sent to Bartram are especially interesting because they reveal Jefferson's wide knowledge of native plants.

Paris, Aug. 12. 1786

To R. Cary

. . . . . . . . . . . . . . . .

*Andromeda arborea
*Azalea nudiflora
 Azalea viscosa
*Acer Pensylvanicum
 Cornus florida
 Ceanothus americana
 Cupressus disticha
 Cupressus thyoides
 Juglans cinerea
 the Gloster hiccory
 Laurus Benzoin
*Magnolia glauca
*Kalmia latifolia
 Nyssa
 Ptelea trifoliata
 Kalmia angustifolia
 Ptelea pinnata

Clethra
Campanula perfoliata
Campanula americana
Geranium maculatum
Geranium gibbosum
Guilandina Bonduc
Halesia tetraptera
Itea
Populus heterophylla
*Quercus phellos
Quercus virginiana of Millar
*Rhododendron maximum
Rhus copallinum
Viburnum acerifolium
Viburnum nudum
*Bignonia sempervirens (yellow jasmine)

Those marked * are desired in greater quantities & particularly in plants.   The others to be in plants where the plant succeeds tolerably, and seeds of the whole or as many as can be got will be desirable.   The reason of desiring plants is that they may be the sooner enjoyed.

. . . I send you seeds of Ranunculus, Broccoli & Cauliflower, bulbs of the tulip. having thought it best to put off getting the articles till the bearer of this was near setting out, they have disappointed me of Carnations, Auriculas, Tuberoses, Hyacinths, & Belladonna lillies which I had ordered. the *Arno* pink seed can of course only be sent you by Mazzei from Florence if he should ever go there. the Alpine strawberry I expect you have got from m͞r Eppes. Mushmelons, such as are here, are worse than the worst in Virginia. there is not sun enough to ripen them, & give them flavor. the caper bush would require a better opportunity than the present, therefore I have not enquired whether it can be got here. I do not know what the Nutberry pine is. I have no Miller's Dictionary here. You must therefore always give the Linnaean names.

### Method of packing the Plants

Take the plants up by the roots, leaving good roots. Trim off all the boughs & cut the stems to the length of your box. Near the tip end of every plant cut a number of notches which will serve as labels, giving the same number to all plants of the same species. Where the plant is too small to be notched, notch a separate stick & tye it to the plant. Make a list on paper of the plants by their names & number of notches.

Take fresh moss just gathered, lay a layer of it at the bottom of the box 2 inches thick, then a layer of plants & again moss alternately, finishing with a layer of moss 2 inches thick, or more if more be necessary to fill the box. large roots must be separately wrapped in moss. (*Jefferson Papers,* L. C.)

On August 13 a letter went to Mr. Benjamin Hawkins, of North Carolina, requesting him to send seeds of *Dionaea,* a plant Jefferson would have delighted in showing his Paris friends.

Paris August 13, 1786.

To Mr. Hawkins,

. . . Your attention to one burthen I laid on you, encourages me to remind you of another, which is the sending me some of the seeds of the Dionaea Muscipula, or Venus fly-trap, called also with you, I believe, the Sensitive Plant. This can come folded in a letter. . . . (Lipscomb and Bergh, *Jefferson* 5: 390.)

Jefferson, always interested in encouraging trade between America and Europe, wrote to Dr. Ramsay in October, seeking the reason why so little rice came to France from South Carolina and Georgia, despite the fact that the people in France consumed large quantities of it and that the rice from the South was superior to that they imported from other countries.

Paris Oct. 27. 1786.

To Dr. Ramsey,

. . . Having observed the immence consumption of rice in this country, it became matter of wonder to me why so few ships come here with that article from S. Carolina & Georgia.   the information I received on my first inquiry was that little Carolina rice came here, because it was less clean & less good than what is brought them from the Levant.   further enquiry however has satisfied me of the inexactitude of this information.   the case is as follows.   about one half the rice consumed in France is from Carolina, the other half is chiefly from Piedmont.   the Piedmont rice is thought by connoisseurs to be best *au gras,* the Carolina rice best *au lait.*   yet the superior whiteness of the latter is so much more pleasing to the eye as to compensate with every purchase it's deficiency in quality.   Carolina rice sells at Havre by wholesale at 22, 23, 24, livres the French quintal, the livre being 10<sup>d</sup> sterling & the French quintal 10 g the English.   at the approach of lent it rises to 27 livres.   it is retailed in Paris 6 to 10 sous the French pound according to it's quality being sorted.   Piedmont rice sells always at 10 sous (5<sup>d</sup> sterling the pound.   in the wholesale it is 3 or 4 times the quintal dearer than Carolina rice.   it would supplant that of Piedmont rice if brought in sufficient quantity, & to France directly.   but it is first carried & deposited in England, & it is the merchant of that country who sends it here [making] a great profit himself, while the commodity is moreover [also] subjected of double voiage.   (*Jefferson Papers,* L. C.)

Although letters passed frequently between Jefferson and Mr. Nicholas Lewis, his manager in Albemarle, little was written about gardening and plants.   When farm affairs were mentioned, the discussion dealt mainly with the financial outlook.   Jefferson did, however, write to Mr. Lewis about plants in a letter dated December 19, in which he said:

I am much obliged to you for your attention to my trees & grass the latter is one of the principal pillows on which I shall rely for subsistance when I shall be at liberty to try projects without injury to any body. . . . I shall endeavor to send with this a packet of the seeds of trees which I wish Anthony to sow in a large nursery noting well their names. There will be a little Spanish S<sup>t</sup>. foin, represented to me as a very precious grass in a hot country.   I would have it sowed in one of the vacant lots of my grass ground.

He also sent Spanish broom, yellow-flowered locust, bladder senna, and *Thuja.*   (*Jefferson Papers,* L. C.)

Earlier in the year Jefferson had requested Francis Hopkinson to send him some paccan nuts.   Hopkinson, not knowing which species Jefferson desired, wrote him concerning them. Jefferson in his reply wrote: "The Paccan nut is, as you conjecture the Illinois nut, the former is the vulgar name South of the Potomac as also with the Indians & Spaniards, and enters also into the Botanical name which is Juglans Paccan" (*Jefferson Papers*, L. C.)

In a reply to Ferdinand Grand about plants to send Benjamin Franklin, written late in December, Jefferson gave him a valuable comparison between the plants grown in Europe and America.

Paris Dec. 28. 1786.

(Jefferson to Ferdinand Grand.)

. . . I did not answer in the instant the letter you favored me with yesterday, because I wished to reflect on the article of seeds for Dr. Franklin, on which you were pleased to ask my opinion. we import annually from England to every part of America garden seeds of all sorts. you may judge therefore that these & what we raise from them furnish garden vegetables in good perfection. the only garden vegetable I find here better than ours, is the turnep.

Of fruits, the pears, & apricots alone are better than ours, and we have not the Apricot-peche at all. but the stones of good apricots & of the peach-apricot would answer well. the fruits of the peach-class do not degenerate from the stone so much as is imagined here. we have so much experience of this in America that tho' we graft all other kinds of fruits, we rarely graft the peach, the nectarine, the apricot or the almond. the tree proceeding from the stone yields a faithful copy of its fruit, & the tree is always healthier. . . .

P. S.   I must add that tho' we have some grapes as good as in France, yet we have by no means such a variety, nor so perfect a succession of them. (*Jefferson Papers*, L. C.)

The *Account Book 1783–1791* gives a few entries concerning Jefferson's interest in gardens and gardening in France.

June   7.   p$^d$ Marc. garden utensils 64–3.
June 28.   p$^d$ seeing Hermitage. 4 f 4. d°. Audinot's garden 2 f 8.
July 10.   p$^d$ Petit—garden—1–4.

# 1787

*1787.*\* Two events occurred this year which gave Jefferson unlimited pleasure. One was the arrival of Maria, his younger daughter, come from Virginia to join Martha and him in France; the other was a tour through southern France and northern Italy.

During the journey, which incidentally Jefferson took alone in his carriage and post horses, he kept a journal of what he saw and did. This record, supplemented by pertinent details from the ever faithfully kept account books, presents a full description of his movements and interests. Concerning the journal Randall remarks:

> Like his journal in England, it is chiefly occupied with practical descriptions; but in this case agriculture and wine-making, instead of gardening, receive the principal share of his attention. In regard to these, his information is extensive, and oftentimes almost exact enough for the directions of those about to engage, without previous practice, in the culture of vineyards and the production of the different varieties of wine. Spirited sketches of scenery occur in the journal, but they are brief, and are only intended to show what kind of a country, topographically speaking, is adapted to this or that kind of culture. (Randall, *Jefferson* 1: 467.)

Jefferson took notes on almost every phase of agriculture as he passed through the rural sections of France and Italy—soils, fruits, vegetables, flowers, and even the living conditions of the farmers. Rice and olives received his closest attention. He was interested first of all in finding a dry rice to supplement or supplant the wet rice of the Carolinas and Georgia, because he thought wet rice "a plant which sows life and death with almost equal hand." Secondly, he considered the olive the worthiest plant to be introduced into America. He remarks of the olive:

> Of all the gifts of heaven to man, it is next to the most precious, if it be not the most precious. Perhaps it may claim a preference even to

\* This year not represented in the *Garden Book*.

bread, because there is such an infinitude of vegetables, which it renders a proper and comfortable nourishment.

Jefferson sent rice, olive trees, and seeds to South Carolina and Georgia for experimental culture. The rice flourished, but the olive-growing experiments were failures. In 1813 Jefferson wrote from Monticello to his friend, Mr. James Ronaldson:

It is now twenty-five years since I sent them [his southern fellow citizens] two shipments (about 500 plants) of the Olive tree of Aix, the finest Olives in the world. If any of them still exist, it is merely as a curiosity in their gardens, not a single orchard of them has been planted. (Ford, *Jefferson* 11: 272.)

On February 7 Jefferson sent a list of plants, similar to the ones he had sent the previous year to Mr. Bartram and to Mr. Cary, to Mr. John Banister, Jr. The list of plants was accompanied by detailed instructions on packing and sending them. (Letter and list of plants, *Jefferson Papers*, L. C.)

Shipping plants from America to Europe in Jefferson's day involved great difficulties. Usually more plants died in transport than survived, either because the shipments were allowed to stand for months on the wharves awaiting adequate shipping space, or because they were unable to weather the lengthy sea voyage, often of several weeks or months. On account of this uncertainty Jefferson usually preferred his friends sending him seeds rather than plants. A letter from Jefferson to Andrew Limozin, his agent in Havre, France, shows the difficulties involved in sending plants.

Paris Feb. 11, 1787.

Sir,

A friend in S. Carolina sent a letter & a box of plants for me to mr. Otto, *chargé des affaires* of France at New York. the letter came by the packet the Courier de l'Europe, and was sent to me from l'Orient. I presume Mr. Otto sent the box of plants by the same conveiance, but as the packet received orders on her arrival at l'Orient to repair immediately to Havre, she landed only her passengers and letters, and proceeded to Havre, where I suppose she is now and that she has there the box of plants for me. I leave Paris the 16th. instant, and it is very interesting for me to receive that box before I go. you will oblige me extremely if you can have it sought out in the instant of receiving this, & forwarded by the first Diligence to me here. I beg your pardon for troubling you so much: but these plants are precious, & have already come from S. Carolina to N. York, from N. York to Lorient, & from Lorient to

Havre. There is danger therefore of their losing their vegetative power by delay, and my departure renders that delay still more interesting. I am with very much esteem & respect Sir your most obedient & most humble serv^t. (*Jefferson Papers*, M. H. S.)

For biographical information on Madame de Tessé, whose name appears frequently in the correspondence from this point on, see page 398, note 26.

## LETTERS AND EXTRACTS OF LETTERS, 1787

(Jefferson to William Drayton.)

Paris Feb. 6. 1787

Sir—

I had the honour of addressing you on the 6^th. of May last by m̃r Mc Quin, and of sending you by the same gentleman some seed of the Sulla, or Spanish S^t foin. I hope it has succeeded, as some seeds of the same parcel which I sowed in my garden here vegetated well and gave me an opportunity of seeing that it is a most luxuriant grass. it's success in the climate of Malta seems to ensure it with you. the present serves to inform you that I send with it, to the care of your delegates in Congress, some acorns of the Cork oak. I am told that they must not be covered above two inches deep. their being pierced by the worm will not affect their power of vegetating. I am just setting out on a journey to the South of France. should any objects present themselves in the course of my journey which may promise to forward the views of the society, I shall with great pleasure avail you of them. . . . (*Jefferson Papers*, L. C.)

(Jefferson to Madame de Tessé.)

Paris Feb. 22. 1787

. . . I have had the pleasure to learn from Mr. Berard of Lorient that he has our box of Magnolia & Dionaea safe; that he will send it by the first Diligence. . . . My servant will carry them to you the moment they arrive, as well as any other parcels of seeds or plants, should any other escape thru all the dangers & difficulties which beset them. . . . (*Jefferson Papers*, Missouri Historical Society.)

(Jefferson to William Short.)

Nice, April 12, 1787.

. . . At Marseilles, they told me I should encounter the rice fields of Piedmont soon after crossing the Alps. Here they tell me there are none nearer than Vercelli and Novarra, which is carrying me almost to Milan. I fear that this circumstance will occasion me a greater delay than I had calculated on. However I am embarked in the project, and shall go through with it. . . . (Lipscomb and Bergh, *Jefferson* 6: 110.)

(Jefferson to John Jay.)

Marseilles, May 4, 1787.

. . . Among other objects of inquiry, this was the place to learn something more certain on the subject of rice, as it is a great emporium for that of the Levant and of Italy.　I wished particularly to know whether it was the use of a different machine for cleaning, which brought European rice to market less broken than ours, as has been represented to me by those who deal in that article in Paris.　I found several persons who had passed through the rice country of Italy, but not one who could explain to me the nature of the machine.　But I was given to believe that I might see it myself immediately on entering Piedmont.　As this would require but about three weeks, I determined to go and ascertain this point, as the chance only of placing our rice above all rivalship in quality, as it is in color, by the introduction of a better machine, if a better existed, seemed to justify the application of that much time to it. I found the rice country to be in truth Lombardy, one hundred miles further than had been represented, and that though called Piedmont rice, not a grain is made in the country of Piedmont.　I passed through the rice fields of the Venellese [= Vercellese?] and Milanese, about sixty miles, and returned from thence last night, having found that the machine is absolutely the same as ours, and of course, that we need not listen more to that suggestion.　It is a difference in the species of grain, of which the government of Turin is so sensible, that, as I was informed, they prohibit the exportation of rough rice on pain of death.　I have taken measures, however, which I think will not fail for obtaining a quantity of it, and I bought on the spot a small parcel, which I have with me.　As further details on this subject to Congress would be misplaced, I propose, on my return to Paris, to communicate them, and send the rice to the society at Charleston for promoting agriculture, supposing that they will be best able to try the experiment of cultivating the rice of this quality, and to communicate the species to the two States of South Carolina and Georgia, if they find it answer.　I thought the staple of these two States was entitled to this attention, and that it must be desirable to them to be able to furnish rice of the two qualities demanded in Europe, especially, as the greater consumption is in the forms for which the Lombardy quality is preferred. . . . (Lipscomb and Bergh, *Jefferson* 6: 112–113.)

(Jefferson to John Adams.)

Paris July 1. 1787.

. . . I had expected to satisfy myself, at Marseilles, of the causes of the difference of quality between the rice of Carolina, and that of Piedmont, which is brought in quantities to Marseilles.　not being able to do it, I made an excursion of three weeks into the rice country beyond the Alps, going through it from Vercelli to Pavia, about sixty miles.　I found the difference to be, not in the management, as had been supposed both here and in Carolina, but in the species of rice; and I hope to enable them in Carolina, to begin the cultivation of the Piedmont Rice, and carry it on, hand in hand, with their own, that they may supply both qualities; which is absolutely necessary at this market. . . . (*Jefferson Papers*, L. C.)

### (Jefferson to E. Rutledge.)

Paris. July 14. 1787.

. . . I found their machine exactly such a one as you had described to me in Congress in the year 1783. there was but one conclusion then to draw, to wit, that the rice was of a different species, and I determined to take enough to put you in seed; they informed me, however, that its exportation in the husk was prohibited, so I could only bring off as much as my coat and surtout pockets would hold. I took measures with a muleteer to run a couple of sacks across the Apennines to Genoa, but have not great dependence on its success. the little, therefore, which I brought myself, must be relied on for fear we should get no more; and because, also, it is genuine from Vercelli, where the best is made of all the Sardinian Lombardy, the whole of which is considered as producing a better rice than the Milanese. (*Jefferson Papers*, L. C.)

### (Jefferson to Nicholas Lewis.)

Paris July 29. 1787.

. . . I will put into this letter some more seeds of the Spanish Sainfoin lest those formerly sent should have miscarried. . . . (*Jefferson Papers,* L. C.)

### (Jefferson to William Drayton.)

Paris, July 30, 1787.

Sir,—Having observed that the consumption of rice in this country, and particularly in this capital, was very great, I thought it my duty to inform myself from what markets they draw their supplies, in what proportion from ours, and whether it might not be practicable to increase that proportion. This city being little concerned in foreign commerce, it is difficult to obtain information on particular branches of it in the detail. I addressed myself to the retailers of rice, and from them received a mixture of truth and error, which I was unable to sift apart in the first moment. Continuing, however, my inquiries, they produced at length this result: that the dealers here were in the habit of selling two qualities of rice, that of Carolina, with which they were supplied chiefly from England, and that of Piedmont; that the Carolina rice was long, slender, white and transparent, answers well when prepared with milk, sugar, &c., but not so well when prepared *au gras;* that that of Piedmont was shorter, thicker, and less white, but that it presented its form better when dressed *au gras,* was better tasted, and, therefore, preferred by good judges for those purposes; that the consumption of rice, in this form, was much the most considerable, but that the superior beauty of the Carolina rice, seducing the eye of those purchasers who are attached to appearances, the demand for it was upon the whole as great as for that of Piedmont. They supposed this difference of quality to proceed from a difference of management; that the Carolina rice was husked with an instrument that broke it more, and that less pains were taken to separate the broken from the unbroken grains, imagining that it was the broken grains which dissolved in oily preparations; that the Carolina rice costs somewhat less than that of Piedmont; but that being obliged to sort the whole grains from the broken, in order to satisfy the tastes of their customers, they asked and receive as much for the first quality of Carolina, when sorted, as for the rice of Piedmont; but the second and third qualities, obtained by sorting, are sold much cheaper. The objection to the Carolina rice then, being, that it crumbles in certain forms of preparation, and this supposed to be the effect of a less perfect machine for husking, I flattered myself I should be able to learn what might be the machines of Piedmont, when I should arrive at Marseilles, to which place I was to go in the course of a tour through the seaport towns of this country. At Marseilles, however, they differed as much in account of the machines, as at Paris they had differed about other circumstances. Some said it was husked between mill-stones, others between rubbers of wood in the form of mill-stones, others of cork. They concurred in one fact, however, that the machine might be seen by me, immediately on crossing the Alps. This would be an affair of three weeks. I crossed them and went through the rice country from Vercelli to Pavia, about sixty miles. I found the machine to be absolutely the same with that used in Carolina, as well as I could recollect a description which Mr. E. Rutledge had given me of it. It is on the plan of a powder mill. In some of them, indeed, they arm each pestle with an iron tooth, consisting of nine spikes hooked together, which I do not remember in the description of Mr. Rutledge. I therefore had a tooth made which I have the honor of forwarding you with this letter; observing, at the same time, that as many of their machines are without teeth as with them, and of course, that the advantage is not very palpable. It seems to follow, then, that the rice of Lombardy (for though called Piedmont rice, it does not grow in that county but in Lombardy) is of a different species from that of Carolina; different in form, in color and in quality. We know that in Asia they have several distinct species of this grain. Monsieur Poivre, a former Governor of the Isle of France, in travelling through several countries of Asia, observed with particular attention the objects of their agriculture, and he tells us, that in Cochin-China they cultivate six several kinds of rice, which he describes, three of them requiring water, and three growing on highlands. The rice of Carolina is said to have come from Madagascar, and De Poivre tells us, it is the white rice which is cultivated there. This favors the probability of its being of a different species originally, from that of Piedmont; and time, culture and climate may have made it still more different. Under this idea, I thought it would be well to furnish you with some of the Piedmont rice, unhusked, but was told it was contrary to the laws to export it in that form. I took such measures as I could, however, to have a quantity brought out, and lest these should fail, I brought, myself, a few pounds. A part of this I have addressed to you by the way of London; a part comes with this letter; and I shall send another parcel by some other conveyance, to prevent the danger of miscarriage. Any one of them arriving safe, may serve to put in seed, should the society think it an object. This seed too, coming from Vercelli, where the best rice is supposed to grow, is more to be depended on than what may be sent me hereafter. There is a rice from the Levant, which is considered as of a quality still different, and some think it superior to that of Piedmont. The troubles which have existed in that country for several years back, have intercepted it from the European market, so that it is become almost unknown. I procured a bag of it, however, at Marseilles, and another of the best rice of Lombardy, which are on their way to this place, and when arrived, I will forward you a quantity of each, sufficient to enable you to judge of their qualities when prepared for the table. I have also taken measures to have a quantity of it brought from the Levant, unhusked. If I succeed, it shall be forwarded in like manner. I should think it certainly advantageous to cultivate, in Carolina and Georgia, the two qualities demanded at market; because the progress of culture, with us, may soon get beyond the demand for the white rice; and because too, there is often a brisk demand for the one quality, when the market is glutted with the other. I should hope there would be no danger of losing the species of white rice, by a confusion with the other. This would be a real misfortune, as I should not hesitate to pronounce the white, upon the whole, the most precious of the two, for us. The dry rice of Cochin-China has the reputation of being the whitest to the eye, best flavored to the taste, and most productive. It seems then to unite the good qualities of both the others known to us. Could it supplant them, it would be a great happiness, as it would enable us to get rid of those ponds of stagnant water, so fatal to human health and life. But such is the force of habit, and caprice of taste, that we could not be sure before hand it would produce this effect. The experiment, however, is worth trying, should it only end in producing a third quality, and increasing the demand. I will endeavor to procure some to be brought from Cochin-China. The event, however, will be uncertain and distant.

I was induced, in the course of my journey through the south of France, to pay very particular attention to the objects of their culture, because the resemblance of their climate to that of the southern parts of the United States, authorizes us to presume we may adopt any of their articles of culture, which we would wish for. We should not wish for their wines, though they are good and abundant. The culture of the vine is not desirable in lands capable of producing anything else. It is a species of gambling, and of desperate gambling too, wherein, whether you make much or nothing, you are equally ruined. The middling crop alone is the saving point, and that the seasons seldom hit. Accordingly, we see much wretchedness among this class of cultivators. Wine, too, is so cheap in these countries, that a laborer with us, employed in the culture of any other article, may exchange it for wine, more and better than he could raise himself. It is a resource for a country, the whole of whose good soil is otherwise employed, and which still has some barren spots, and surplus of population to employ on them. There the vine is good, because it is something in the place of nothing. It may become a resource to us at a still earlier period; when the increase of population shall increase our productions beyond the demand for them, both at home and abroad. Instead of going on to make an useless surplus of them, we may employ our supernumerary hands on the vine. But that period is not yet arrived.

The almond tree is also so precarious, that none can depend for subsistence on its produce, but persons of capital.

The caper, though a more tender plant, is more certain in its produce, because a mound of earth of the size of a cucumber hill, thrown over the plant in the fall, protects it effectually against the cold of winter. When the danger of frost is over in the spring, they uncover it, and begin its culture. There is a great deal of this in the neighborhood of Toulon. The plants are set about eight feet apart, and yield, one year with another, about two pounds of caper each, worth on the spot sixpence sterling per pound. They require little culture, and this may be performed either with the plough or hoe. The principal work is the gathering of the fruit as it forms. Every plant must be picked every other day, from the last of June till the middle of October. But this is the work of women and children. This plant does well in any kind of soil which is dry, or even in walls where there is no soil, and it lasts the life of man. Toulon would be the proper port to apply for them. I must observe, that the preceding details cannot be relied on with the fullest certainty, because, in the canton where this plant is cultivated, the inhabitants speak no written language, but a medley, which I could understand but very imperfectly.

The fig and mulberry are so well known in America, that nothing need be said of them. Their culture, too, is by women and children, and, therefore, earnestly to be desired in countries where there are slaves. In these, the women and children are often employed in labors disproportioned to their sex and age. By presenting to the master objects of culture, easier and equally beneficial, all temptation to misemploy them would be removed, and the lot of this tender part of our species be much softened. By varying, too, the articles of culture, we multiply the chances for making something, and disarm the seasons in a proportionable degree, of their calamitous effects.

The olive is a tree the least known in America, and yet the most worthy of being known. Of all the gifts of heaven to man, it is next to the most precious, if it be not the most precious. Perhaps it may claim a preference even to bread, because there is such an infinitude of vegetables, which it renders a proper and comfortable nourishment. In passing the Alps at the Col de Tende, where they are mere masses of rock, wherever there happens to be a little soil, there are a number of olive trees, and a village supported by them. Take away these trees, and the same ground in corn would not support a single family. A pound of oil, which can be bought for three or four pence sterling, is equivalent to many pounds of flesh, by the quantity of vegetables it will prepare, and render fit and comfortable food. Without this tree, the country of Provence and territory of Genoa would not support one-half, perhaps not one-third, their present inhabitants. The nature of the soil is of little consequence if it be dry. The trees are planted from fifteen to twenty feet apart, and when tolerably good, will yield fifteen or twenty pounds of oil yearly, one with another. There are trees which yield much more. They begin to render good crops at twenty years old, and last till killed by cold, which happens at some time or other, even in their best positions in France. But they put out again from their roots. In Italy, I am told, they have trees two hundred years old. They afford an easy but constant employment through the year, and require so little nourishment, that if the soil be fit for any other production, it may be cultivated among the olive trees without injuring them. The northern limits of this tree are the mountains of Cevennes, from about the meridian of Carcassonne to the Rhone, and from thence, the Alps and the Apennines as far as Genoa, I know, and how much farther I am not informed. The shelter of these mountains may be considered as equivalent to a degree and a half of latitude, at least, because westward of the commencement of the Cevennes, there are no olive trees in $43\frac{1}{2}°$ or even $43°$ of latitude, whereas, we find them *now* on the Rhone at Pierrelatte, in $44\frac{1}{2}°$, and *formerly* they were at Tains, above the mouth of the Isere, in $45°$, sheltered by the near approach of the Cevennes and Alps, which only leave there a passage for the Rhone. Whether such a shelter exists or not in the States of South Carolina and Georgia, I know not. But this we may say, either that it exists or that it is not necessary there, because we know that they produce the orange in open air; and wherever the orange will stand at all, experience shows that the olive will stand well, being a hardier tree. Notwithstanding the great quantities of oil made in France, they have not enough for their own consumption, and, therefore import from other countries. This is an article, the consumption of which will always keep pace with its production. Raise it, and it begets its own demand. Little is carried to America, because Europe has it not to spare. We, therefore, have not learned the use of it. But cover the southern States with it, and every man will become a consumer of oil, within whose reach it can be bought in point of price. If the memory of those persons is held in great respect in South Carolina who introduced there the culture of rice, a plant which sows life and death with almost equal hand, what obligations would be due to him who should introduce the olive tree, and set the example of its culture! Were the owner of slaves to view it only as a means of bettering their condition, how much would he better that by planting one of those trees for every slave he possessed! Having been myself an eye witness to the blessings which this tree sheds on the poor, I never had my wishes so kindled for the introduction of any article of new culture into our own country. South Carolina and Georgia appear to me to be the States, wherein its success, in favorable positions at least, could not be doubted, and I flattered myself it would come within the views of the society for agriculture to begin the experiments which are to prove its practicability. Carcassonne is the place from which the plants may be most certainly and cheaply obtained. They can be sent from thence by water to Bordeaux, where they may be embarked on vessels bound for Charleston. There is too little intercourse between Charleston and Marseilles to propose this as the port of exportation. I offer my services to the society for the obtaining and forwarding any number of plants which may be desired.

Before I quit the subject of climates, and the plants adapted to them, I will add, as a matter of curiosity, and of some utility, too, that my journey through the southern parts of France, and the territory of Genoa, but still more the crossing of the Alps, enabled me to form a scale of the tenderer plants, and to arrange them according to their different powers of resisting cold. In passing the Alps at the Col de Tende, we cross three very high moutains successively. In ascending, we lose these plants, one after another, as we rise, and find them again in the contrary order as we descend on the other side; and this is repeated three times. Their order, proceeding from the tenderest to the hardiest, is as follows: caper, orange, palm, aloe, olive, pomegranate, walnut, fig, almond. But this must be understood of the plant only; for as to the fruit, the order is somewhat different. The caper, for example, is the tenderest plant, yet, being so easily protected, it is among the most certain in its fruit. The almond, the hardiest, loses its fruit the oftenest, on account of its forwardness. The palm, hardier than the caper and orange, never produces perfect fruit here.

I had the honor of sending you, the last year, some seeds of the sulla of Malta, or Spanish St. Foin. Lest they should have miscarried, I now pack with the rice a cannister of the same kind of seed, raised by myself. By Colonel Franks, in the month of February last, I sent a parcel of acorns of the cork oak, which I desired him to ask the favor of the Delegates of South Carolina in Congress to forward to you. . . . (Lipscomb and Bergh, *Jefferson* 6: 193–204.)

(Jefferson to Benjamin Hawkins.)

Paris, August 4, 1787.

I have to acknowledge the receipt of your favors of March the 8th and June the 9th, and to give you many thanks for the trouble you have taken with the dionaea muscipula. I have not yet heard anything of them, which makes me fear they have perished by the way. I believe the most effectual means of conveying them hither, will be by the seed. . . . (Lipscomb and Bergh, *Jefferson* 6: 231.)

(Jefferson to Richard Cary.)

Paris Aug. 13. 1787.

. . . I shall be sending a box of books directed to mr̄ Wythe. in this I will put the seeds & bulbs which I was disappointed in sending you last year, as well as a repetition of those I sent. . . . I will send you also some plants of the melon apricot, a variety of fruit obtained in France only 8. or 10. years ago & as yet known no where else.  it is an Apricot with the high flavor of a mushmelon, & is certainly the best fruit in this country.  you have never yet told me what seeds etc. you wish for most, so I am obliged still to go on the old edition in Mazzei's hands. . . . (*Jefferson Papers*, L. C.)

(Jefferson to Andrew Limozin.)

Paris Sep. 2. 1787.

By the inclosed paper I presume there are arrived for me on board the packet three small boxes of seeds or plants, and a large box, the contents of which I know not.  I will beg the favor of you to pay for me the freight & other expenses, and to send the three small boxes by the Diligence.  as to the large one, I conjecture it may contain bones & other objects of Natural history which should come by water, as the motion of a carriage would destroy them.  I will therefore pray you to send the large box up here by water, taking such precautions as are necessary to prevent their being stopped at Rouen.  perhaps the plumbing the box may be necessary; in which case I will take particular care to return any Acquit á caution you may be so kind as to enter into for me. . . . (*Jefferson Papers*, M. H. S.)

(Jefferson to Nicholas Lewis.)

Paris Sept. 17. 1787.

. . . I cultivate in my garden here Indian corn for the use of my own table to eat green in our manner.  but the species I am able to get here for seed, is hard with a thick skin, & dry.  I had at Monticello a species of small white rare ripe corn which we call Homony-corn, and of which we used to make about 20 barrels a year for table use, green, in homony, & in bread.  great George will know well what kind I mean. I wish it were possible for me to receive an ear of this in time for the next year.  I think it too might be done if you would be so good as to find an opportunity of sending one to mr̄ Madison at New York, and another to mr̄ A. Donald at Richmond.  more at your leisure I would ask you to send me also an ear or two of the drying corn from the Cherokee country, some best watermelon seeds, some fine canteloupe melon seeds, seeds of the common sweet potato (I mean the real seeds & not the roots, which cannot be brought here without rotting,) an hundred or two acorns of the willow oak and about a peck of acorns of the ground oak or dwarf oak, of the kind that George gathered for me one year upon the barrens of buck island creek.  as these will be of some bulk, I will ask the favor of you to send them to mr̄ Donald of Richmond who will find a conveiance for them to Havre. (*Jefferson Papers*, L. C.)

(Jefferson to the Delegates of South Carolina.)

Paris Sept. 18. 1787.

I take the liberty of sending to your care the third and last parcel of Piedmont rice, addressed to mr Drayton, and will beg favor of you to have it forwarded. I divided it into three separate parcels that the chances of some one of them getting safely to hand might be multiplied. . . . (*Jefferson Papers*, L. C.)

(Jefferson to Madame la Comtesse de Tessé.)

Paris Octob. 17, 1787

The last parcel of seeds which I had the honor of sending you, Madam, overburthened you in quantity, and stinted you in variety. I now enclose you a list which has exactly the contrary faults, the variety is great, the quantities small, in some instances there is not more than one, two, or three grains. Your goodness will pardon this, as you know the difficulties which attend the obtaining supplies of seeds from America. These have been very long detained on their passage. . . . The packages are all numbered in correspondence with the list inclosed. The second order of numbers from 1 to 39 are distinguished on the packages by the letter H meaning the Herbaceous plants. . . . (*Jefferson Papers*, Missouri Historical Society.)

(Ralph Izard to Jefferson.)

South Bay, Charleston, Nov. 10th, 1787

Your letter of 1st August came to my hands several weeks before Mr. Drayton received his on the subject of Rice, olives, & etc, to which I was refered. We are much obliged to you for the trouble you have taken, & for the information you have given. When I was in Italy, the Rice of that Country appeared inferior to ours. I had been several years absent from America, & the difference did not then appear to me so great as it does now. The Seed which you have sent, & which you say is of the best kind, will bear no comparison with ours; & I am surprised to learn that the price is nearly equal. You say that our Rice dissolves when dressed with Meat: this must be owing to some mismanagement in dressing it. I have examined my cook on the subject, & find that as meat requires to be longer on the fire than Rice, they must be dressed separately, until each is nearly done, & then the combination is to be made. The water must boil before the Rice is put into it, or the grains will not be distinct from each other. The rice you have sent will be planted. I hope great care will be taken to keep it at a distance from the other Rice Fields; for if the Farina should blow on them, it may be the means of propagating an inferior species among us. For that reason I should be glad that you would not send any more of it. As the quality of our rice is infinitely superior to that of Italy, I am persuaded it will annually gain ground in France, & finally exclude the other entirely. This is a considerable object to us, & will likewise be of service to the manufacturers of France.   I believe Italy receives money from France in return for her Rice.   We should want Negroes, Cloth, Blank & implements of Husbandry as articles of absolute necessity; besides many others of convenience, & some of Luxury. . . .  (*Jefferson Papers,* L. C.)

(Jefferson to Stephen Cathalan.)

Paris Dec. 28. 1787.

I have this day received your favor of the 19th instant and avail myself of the first post to pray you to send the second couffe of rice of Egypt by the American brig Nancy, Capt. Shewell, consigned to mr̄ Wm. Drayton Chairman of the society for Agriculture at Charleston in South Carolina, writing a line to him at the same time to inform him of it, & that it comes from me.  (*Jefferson Papers,* L. C.)

The following entries from Jefferson's *Account Book 1783–1790* supplement his letters about agricultural, gardening, and botanical pursuits during the year:

Jan.  10.   pᵈ Petit for garden seeds—10–10.
Feb.   5.   pᵈ l'Abbé Arnoud portage of cork acorns 12 f 10.
Apr.   8.   Hieres.  seeing gardens 2 f 8.
Apr.  10.   Nice.  seeing King's garden 1 f 4.
Apr.  20.   Vercelli.  rough rice 3 f.
Apr.  23.   Casino.  see rice mill 1 f.  teeth for Rice pestil 5 f 10.
Apr.  23.   Pavia.  seeing botanical garden etc. 3 f.
May 11.   Sᵗ. foin seed 8 f.
July 19.   pᵈ Sʳ. John Lamb for Cathalan, for rice 85 f 5.
Sept. 30.   pᵈ at King's garden 18ˢ.
Oct.   1.   pᵈ Mr. Short 1200 f. charge him also 86.35 dollars pᵈ by C. Thomson for plants for Mᵈᵉ de Tessé and 23 H–12 s–6 d. pᵈ for their freight = 476 H–18 s–6 d.
Oct.  20.   pᵈ portage of boxes of plants & bones from Havre 18 f.
Nov.   1.   pᵈ Limozin's bill for freight of plants & bones 160 H–7.

# 1788

*1788.** On March 4 Jefferson left Paris for a trip to Amsterdam intent on official duties. On the return journey to the French capital he took a tour of the Rhine as far as Strasburg. He related his observations in a journal ("Memorandum on a Tour from Paris to Amsterdam, Strasburg, and back to Paris." Lipscomb and Bergh, *Jefferson* 17: 244–290) and in his *Account Book 1783–1790*. Randall says of this journal:

> It is as dry and utilitarian in its tone and topics as his previous productions of the same class. It gives precise and oftentimes minute details in regard to the topography, agriculture, population, architecture, mechanical arts, etc., of the country passed through. (Randall, *Jefferson* 1: 500.)

Jefferson discussed rice and olives in his letters to friends, and again sent to them seeds and plants, as in 1787. In return he received more seeds and plants from America. Early in January Jefferson made the following disbursements to M. Limozin, his agent, for seeds and fruits:

1788, Jan. 11, Disbursements on a barrel of rice 36–17–6.
Jan. 27, Disbursements on 2 boxes of seeds sent by J. Madison 12–18.
Disbursements on 4 barrels of fruit & 1 caisse of trees recᵈ. by the Packet 59–1–3.

(*Jefferson Papers*, M. H. S.)

### LETTERS AND EXTRACTS OF LETTERS, 1788

(Jefferson to Andrew Limozin.)

Paris Jan 13. 1788.

By the Carrossa which goes from hence to Havre I have forwarded a package of rough rice addressed to you. I am in hopes it may arrive in time to go with the inclosed letter by the *Juno* Capt. Jenkins. I will beg the favour of you to put on it this address 'For Mr. William Drayton, Charleston: to the care of the Delegates of S. Carolina in Congress,'

* This year not represented in the *Garden Book*.

and to pay the freight for me. . . . I have had the rice brought from Egypt, to furnish S. Carolina with a species of that grain which it does not possess. I wish the captain of the vessel therefore would so place it as that it may not be exposed neither to heat or moisture, which would destroy it's vegetative power. . . . (*Jefferson Papers, L. C.*)

### (Jefferson to the Delegates of South Carolina.)

Paris Jan. 13. 1788.

In hopes that a *Couffe* of rough rice which I have just received from Egypt may reach Havre in time to go by the *Juno* Capt. Jenkins, I have sent it off for that port. it is addressed to mr̄ Drayton at Charleston & I take the liberty of recommending it to your care, to be forwarded so as that it may arrive in time for the season of sowing, if possible. (*Jefferson Papers, L. C.*)

### (Jefferson to William Drayton.)

Paris Jan. 13. 1788.

By Capt. Shewell, who is sailing about this time from Marseilles for Charleston I directed to be forwarded to you one of two Couffes of rough rice which I had had brought from Egypt. the other came to me here, and will be carried from Havre to New York addressed to you to the care of the delegates of S. Carolina in Congress. I wish both may arrive in time for the approaching seed time, and that the trials with this, & the Piedmont rice may furnish new advantages to your agriculture. I have considerable hopes of receiving some dry rice from Cochin-China, the young prince of that country lately gone from hence, having undertaken that it shall come to me. but it will be some time first. these are all but experiments; the precept however is wise which directs us to 'try all things, & hold fast that which is good.' (*Jefferson Papers, L. C.*)

### (Jefferson to John Rutledge, Jr.)

Paris, January 19, 1788.

. . . I must press on you, my dear Sir, a very particular attention to the climate and culture of the olive tree. This is the most interesting plant in existence for South Carolina and Georgia. You will see in various places that it gives being to whole villages in places where there is not soil enough to subsist a family by the means of any other culture. But consider it as the means of bettering the condition of your slaves in South Carolina. See in the poorer parts of France and Italy what a number of vegetables are rendered eatable by the aid of a little oil, which would otherwise be useless. Remark very particularly the northern limits of this tree, and whether it exists by the help of shelter from the mountains, etc. I know this is the case in France. I wish to know where the northern limit of this plant crosses the Apennines; where it crosses the Adriatic and the Archipelago, and if possible what course it takes through Asia.   The fig, the dried raisin, the pistache, the date, the caper, are all very interesting objects for your study.   Should you not in your passage through countries where they are cultivated inform yourself of their hardiness, their culture, the manner of transporting, etc., you might hereafter much repent it.   Both then and now I hope you will excuse me for suggesting them to your attention; not omitting the article of rice also, of which you will see species different from your own. . . . (Lipscomb and Bergh, *Jefferson* 7: 51–52.)

### (Jefferson to Andrew Limozin.)

Paris Jan 22. 1788.

I am much obliged to you for your care of the rice, & hope will arrive in time for the sowing season. . . . by the packet lately arrived he [Mr. James Madison] has sent me

> a box of plants
> 2. barrels of apples.
> 2. barrels of cranberries.

be so good as to send the box of plants by the Diligence or by a Roulier as you shall see best.   I had rather by the Diligence unless it be very heavy indeed & of course too expensive for the object.   the barrels of Apples & Cranberries can come by water only, as the motion of land carriage would reduce them to mummy.*   (*Jefferson Papers, L. C.*)

### (Stephen Cathalan to Jefferson.)

Marseilles, 25 Jan. 1788

Invoice of Sundries-Provisions sent as follows p. order & For acct. of his excellency Thos. Jefferson Esq. of Paris.

T. J.   2 Couffes Egyptian Rice, unshielded, and sent to his address by land at Paris.
W D   1 loaded on the vessel Nancy Capt. Rob<sup>t</sup>. Shewell, to the ad-
E C   dress of William Drayton Esq. president of the Society of Agri-
culture at Charleston.   Amounting as to Invoice . . . . . . . . . .
£ 108.14
(*Jefferson Papers, L. C.*)

### (Jefferson to James Madison.)

Paris Feb. 6. 1788.

I wrote you last on the 20<sup>th</sup>. of December since which yours of the same day and of the 9<sup>th</sup>. have come to hand.   the apples and cranberries you were so kind as to send at the same time were all spoiled when they arrived at Havre, so that probably those articles will not keep during the passage.   the box of plants is arrived at the Custom house here, but I shall probably not receive them till after I shall have sealed my letter.

* The apples and cranberries had spoiled when Jefferson received them.—Ed.

they are well chosen, as to the species, for this country. I wish there had been some willow oaks (Quercus Phellos Linnaeus) among them, either the plants or acorns, as that tree is much desired here, & absolutely unknown. as the red-birds & opossums are not to be had at New York, I will release you from the trouble of procuring them elsewhere. this trouble, with the incertainty of their coming safe, is more than the importance of the object will justify. you omitted to inclose Princes's catalogue of plants which your letter mentions to have been inclosed. I send herewith two small boxes, one addressed to mr̄ Drayton to the care of the S. Carolina delegates, with a letter. will you be so good as to ask those gentlemen to forward the letter & box without delay. the box contains cork acorns, & Sulla, which should arrive at their destination as quick as possible. the other box is addressed to you, & contains, cork acorns, Sulla, and peas, the two first articles to be forwarded to Monticello to Colᵒ. Nicholas Lewis, taking thereout what proportion of them you please for yourself. the peas are brought me from the South of France and are said to be valuable. considering the season of the year I think it would be best to sow them at New York, and to send the produce on next winter to such persons as you please in Virginia, in order to try whether they are any of them better than what we already have. the Sulla is a species of Sᵗ. foin which comes from Malta, and is proof against any degree of drought. I have raised it in my garden here, and find it a luxuriant & precious plant. . . .

I will beg the favor of you to send me a copy of the American philosophical transactions, both the 1ˢᵗ. & 2ᵈ. volumes, by the first packet. . . . (*Jefferson Papers,* L. C.)

### (Jefferson to Andrew Limozin.)

Paris Feb. 6. 1788.

The box of plants you were so kind as to forward me arrived at the Douane. I shall send for them tomorrow morning. [See letter January 22.] (*Jefferson Papers,* L. C.)

### (Jefferson to William Drayton.)

Paris Feb. 6. 1788.

. . . I now send a small box containing cork acorns of the last year, a small paper of Sulla-seed from Malta, and a larger one of the same species of seeds from plants growing in my own garden. I am persuaded from what I see and have heard of this plant that it will be precious for your climate. . . . (*Jefferson Papers,* L. C.)

### (Jefferson to Monsieur de Bertroux.)

Paris Feb. 21, 1788.

I am now to acknowledge the receipt of the letter you did me the honor to write me on the 21st. of January, together with the book on the culture of the olive tree. This is a precious present to me, and I pray you to accept my thanks for it. I am just gratified by letters from

South Carolina, which inform me that in consequence of the information I had given them on the subject of the olive tree, and the probability of its succeeding with them, several rich individuals propose to begin its culture there. This will not interfere with the commerce of France, because she imports much more oil than she exports, and because the consumption of oil in the United States at present, is so inconsiderable, that should their demand be totally withdrawn at the European market, and supplied at home, it will produce no sensible effect in Europe. We can never produce that article in very great quantity, because it happens that in our two southernmost States, where only the climate is adapted to the olive, the soil is so generally rich as to be unfit for that tree, and proper for other productions of more immediate profit. I am to thank you, also, for the raisins of Smyrna, without seed, which I received from you through Mr. Grand. (Lipscomb and Bergh, *Jefferson* 6: 431.)

(Jefferson to William Short.)

Amsterdam Mar. 29. 1788.

My friend Bannister must have been negligent if his plants are not arriving by this time. I have written from hence to Limozin to send them on by the *roulier* or Diligence the moment they arrive. you will be so good as to mention this to Madame de Tessé, with my respects to her & Made de Tott. some few of the plants & seeds I intended for another friend but it is impossible for me to direct any partition from hence. (*Jefferson Papers*, L. C.)

(Jefferson to Francis Coffyn.)

Paris April 28. 1788.

Your favor of March 22. arrived during my absence on a journey to Amsterdam from which I am but lately returned. I thank you for your attention to the 4. boxes of plants and have to ask the favor of you to send them by the first conveiance by sea to Havre to the care of M. Limozin. I have reason to believe there are some seeds also. if these are packed in a separate box I will beg of you to send them (that is, the seeds) by the Diligence immediately, or indeed if they are in the same boxes with the plants, if you can get at them readily without disturbing the plants I will thank you to pack them in a box and send them by the Diligence, because there is not a moment to lose for putting them into the ground. be so good as to write me the amount of the expences these things may cost you, & tell me if you have any correspondent at Paris to whom I may pay it. if not, I can send it to you by Mr. Rotch who is here from Dunkirk. . . . (*Jefferson Papers*, M. H. S.)

(Jefferson to Nicholas Lewis.)

Paris July 11, 1788.

. . . I thank Mrs. Lewis kindly for the ears of corn & the seeds accompanying them which are safely come to hand. The homony corn is

a precious present.   The corn of this country and of Italy, as far as I
have seen it, cannot be eaten, either in the form of corn or of bread, by
any person who has eaten that of America.   I have planted some grains
which may perhaps come to maturity as we have still 3 months & a half
to frost. . . .  (Ford, *Jefferson* 5: 417.)

(Jefferson to William Drayton.)

Paris July 17. 1787 [= 1788].

My letters of Jan. 13. & Feb. 6. informed you that I had sent to your
address 1. a couffe of Egyptian rough rice by capt Shaw—all bound from
Marseilles to Charleston.  2. another d°. by the Juno capt. Jenkins
bound from Havre to N. York.  3. a box with cork acorns & Sulla
seed by the Packet from Havre to N. York.  a letter from the delegates
of S. Carolina dated New York Apr. 25. announced to me the safe arrival there of the 2ᵈ. couffe, and their hopes of getting it to you before
the seed time would be over.
I am now to acknolege the receipt of your favor of Nov. 25. 1787
which did not get to my hands till April 24. 1788. in consequence
thereof I wrote to a mr̄. Cathalan at Marseilles to engage a gardener
to prepare a large number of olive plants, of those which yeild the
best Provence oil, & to have them in readiness to be sent by any vessels
which may occur, bound to Charleston: & besides this, to send a great
quantity of olives to be sown in order to raise stocks.   these stocks would
yeild a wilding fruit, & worthless: they are only to serve therefore to engraft on from the plants which will go, & which will yeild cuttings.   this
is the quickest way of procuring extensive plantations, & it is the best also.
mr̄. Cathalan writes me word he will charge a gardener to do this, but
that as the objects cannot be sent from Marseilles till the last of January,
it will be March or April before you can receive them.   Messʳˢ. Brailsford & Morris have remitted to me 726. livre tournois for this object
which have been duly paid.   Mʳ. Rutledge, the son of Governor Rutledge, having lately set out from this place on a tour which will take in
Italy & the South of France, I recommended to him to pay very particular attention to the character & culture of this tree, as also to the
caper, dates, fig, raisin, pistache and also to the article of rice.   I am in
hopes he will be able to enrich you with much more particular details
than it has been in my power to do.—I shall be happy to be further instrumental in promoting the views of the Agricultural society, and of
executing their commands at all times. . . .  (*Jefferson Papers,* L. C.)

(Madame de Tessé to Jefferson.)

A Chaville, le 8 août [1788].

Monsieur Jefferson aiant eu la bonté de faire connaître à Mde de
Tessé que ce moment cy etoit convenable pour demander des plans et
des graines de Virginie, elle prend la liberté de lui adresser une petite
notte de ce qu'elle désire plus particulièrement et plus abondamment.

Elle y ajoute quelque chose pour la Caroline dans le cas où Monsieur
Jefferson se trouveroit devoir écrire à Charles-Town, et souhaiterait bien
qu'il s'adresse aux correspondens de Mr. Short, bien préférable à ceux
qu'il emploie en ce qu'on reçoit leurs mémoires. . . .

PLANTS DE VIRGINIE *

Quercus rubra maxima.
Quercus rubra ramosissima.
Quercus rubra nana.
Quercus Phellos of all sorts.
Fagus castanea, pumelo dit chinquepin.
Stewartia Malacodendron.   Cet arbuste d'une grande beauté ne croît
    qu'en Virginie et dans le Maryland.   Il est très rare même en Angle-
    terre, et les marchands de Philadelphie n'en mettent qu'une graine ou
    deux dans leurs assortimens.

GRAINES DE VIRGINIE

Pinus palustris.
Cupressus Disticha.
Liriodendrum Tulipifera.
Diospyros.

PLANTS DE CAROLINE

Populus cordifolia.  *Populus heterophylla. Linn.*
Pinus Palustris.  *Pinus picea.*
Annona glabra.  *Papaw of Virginia.*
Andromeda arborea.
Andromeda plumata 9.
Laurus nova 9.
Laurus estivalis.
Callicarpa Americana.
Syderoxilon.  *Not in Virginia.   qu [aere] if in America.*
*Gardenia or Tothergille [= Fothergilla], this grows in Florida only.*

(Gilbert Chinard, *Trois Amitiés françaises de Jefferson* (Paris, 1927):
104–106.)

(Jefferson to J. Banister, Jr.)

Paris Aug. 9. 1788.

I am to return you many thanks for the trouble you gave yourself in
collecting & sending me the plants.   a concurrence of unlucky circumstances has in a considerable degree defeated the effect of your goodness.
the ship on arriving at Havre in Feb. or Mar. was obliged to go instantly
to Dunkirk.   my correspondent at Dunkirk immediately wrote to me
for orders.   I had just set out on a journey to Holland & Germany &
did not return till April, & then they had to come here by land, which

* Les mots en italique sont de la main de Jefferson.

circumstance with the lateness of the season had destroyed a great part of them.   I must trouble you once more for the same lady, who asks me to procure her what is contained in the inclosed list.   be so good as to collect & pack them as soon as the season will admit, & being thus held in readiness they can be put on board the first vessel from Appomattox or James river for Havre addressed to Mons$^r$. Limozin merchant at that place for me, & 'in case of my absence for Madame la Comtesse de Tessé à Paris.'   the latter precaution is necessary lest I should be absent. . . .
(*Jefferson Papers, L. C.*)

### (List inclosed in letter to J. Banister, Jr., Aug. 9, 1788.)

Plants
{
Quercus rubra maxima.   large red oak.
Quercus rubra ramosissima.   Branchy red oak.
Quercus rubra nana.   Dwarf red oak.
   do we know these kinds of red oak in Virginia?
   is the last of the three what we call Ground oak?
Quercus Phellos, willow oak.   the several varieties.
Chinquapin.
Stewartia melacodendron.   Soft wood.   See Millar's diction-ary & Catesby's Carolina Appendix 13.
Populus heterophylla.   a kind of Poplar described in Catesby's [illegible] 34. & in Millar's dict. Populus. 5.
Populus [illegible] it is called Black poplar. [illegible].   see Millar. Pinus. 14.
Annona glabra.   the Common Papaw of Virginia.
Andromeda arborea.   Catesby Appendix. 17.   calls this the Sorrel tree.
Andromeda plumata.   I do not know what this is.
Laurus nova 9.   I do not know what this is.
Laurus estivalis.   Summer bay. 2. Catesby 28. Millar. Laurus. 8.
Callicarpa Americana.   2. Catesby 47.
Gardenia or Fothergilla.

Cones
{
Pinus picea.   Black pine or Pitch pine.
Cupressus disticha.   Cypress.
Liriodendron tulipifera.   Common Poplar.

Diospyros.   Persimmon.   send the seeds.   I think they will come best in the fruit.

### (Jefferson to Stephen Cathalan.)

Paris Aug. 13. 1788.

. . . when the nurseryman to whom you have been so good as to employ to prepare the olives & olive plants to be sent to Charleston, shall be executing that Commission, I shall be glad if he will at the same time prepare a few plants only of the following kinds:

Figs.  the best kind for drying.  a few plants,
Raisins.  d°.
Cork Trees, a few plants.
Pistaches} a few plants.
Capers   }

(*Jefferson Manuscript,* L. C.)

(Jefferson to Francis Hopkinson.)

Paris, December 21, 1788.

. . . I received letters from Marseilles this morning informing me the winter is more severe there than it was in 1709, when they lost all their olive trees.  They apprehend the same calamity now; and it will take twenty years to replace them. . . . (Lipscomb and Bergh, *Jefferson* 19: 51–52.)

## From the *Account Book 1783–1790:*

Jan.  7.  p^d portage from Marseilles, viz. of rice etc. 84^H.
July 12.  rec^d. from M. Petrie 726^H on a bill of Brailsford and Morris sent to me on account of the Agricultural society of S. Carolina to be employed in sending them olive trees.

# 1789

*1789.** This year marked the end of Jefferson's stay in Europe. The preceding year Jefferson had asked Congress for a leave of absence, but when he did not receive a favorable reply, he wrote directly to General Washington, urging him to grant his leave. This General Washington did in June, but Jefferson did not receive confirmation of it until the end of August. He left Paris on September 26, for Havre, arriving there on the 28th. He was detained in Havre until October 8, when he went by packet to Cowes, where he and his two daughters boarded the *Clermont* for Norfolk, Virginia. They arrived in Virginia on November 23, and after a leisurely visit with relatives and friends along the route, reached *Monticello* on December 24.

While stopping a few days at *Eppington,* the home of Mr. and Mrs. Francis Eppes, he wrote the following to a friend: "Tomorrow I go on with Mr. Skipwith to his house, and then plunge into the Forests of Albemarle." (Letter written to William Short, December 14, 1789, from *Eppington. Jefferson Papers,* L. C.)

Jefferson and his daughters had been absent from *Monticello* for almost seven years. Jefferson returned to it with mingled feelings of joy and sadness, for he had lived at *Monticello* only a few months since Mrs. Jefferson's death. Still, to see his mountaintop again, brought a new light into his life.

This year, as in other years of Jefferson's stay in Paris, he continued his correspondence with friends and agents about plants, especially about rice and olives. One of his chief interests during the last months of his stay in France was to secure the seeds of a dry rice, a variety of rice that would grow on the uplands, where a constant supply of water was not available.

* This year not represented in the *Garden Book.*

LETTERS AND EXTRACTS OF LETTERS, 1789

(Jefferson to James Madison.)

Paris, January 12, 1789.

. . . I have just received the Flora Caroliniana of Walter, a very learned and good work. . . . (Lipscomb and Bergh, *Jefferson* 7: 270.)

(Jefferson to Monsieur de Malesherbes.)

Paris March 11. 1789.

Your zeal to promote the general good of mankind by an interchange of useful things, and particularly in the line of agriculture, and the weight which your rank and station would give to your interposition, induce me to ask it for the purpose of obtaining one of the species of rice which grows in Cochin-China on high lands, and which needs no other watering than the ordinary rains. the sun and soil of Carolina are sufficiently powerful to ensure success of this plant, and Monsieur de Poivre gives such an account of it's quality as might induce the Carolinians to introduce it instead of the kind they now possess, which requiring the whole country to be laid under water during a certain season of the year, sweeps off numbers of the inhabitants annually with pestilential fevers. If you would be so good as to interest yourself in the procuring for me some seeds of the dry-rice of Cochin-China you would render the most precious service to my countrymen on whose behalf I take the liberty of asking your interposition. . . . (*Jefferson Papers*, L. C.)

(Benjamin Vaughan to Jefferson.)

London, Mar. 26, 1789.

I have the honor to send you by this conveyance three sorts of dry rice seed.

1. Padee Coccos ballam; the finest sort. ⎫
2. Padee Laye; the best for a crop ⎬ from Sumatra
3. Padee Undallan; the ordinary sort. . . . ⎭

(*Jefferson Papers*, L. C.)

(Jefferson to William Drayton.)

Paris May 7. 1789.

. . . I own to you that I have exceedingly at heart the introduction of this tree [olive tree] into Carolina & Georgia being convinced it is one of the most precious productions of nature and contributes the most to the happiness of mankind. . . . Plants sent by Mr. Cathalan:

> 44 figuiers, de 3. especes. (The Marseilles-fig is admitted to be the best in the world)

43  pieces de vigne (I ordered the Muscat of which the *dried raisens* are made.)

16. prunieres (I ordered the plumb called Brugnol for drying. I presume this is it.)

12. poirieres ⎫
12. pecheres  ⎬ Some of these may prove agreeable additions
10. pommiers  ⎥ to the species you possess.
12. abriestiers ⎭

4. Meuriers feuillie à la seine (the best kind for the silk worm)

3. pistachieres.  Ordered merely for experiment.

*(Jefferson Papers, L. C.)*

## (Jefferson to Benjamin Vaughan.)

Paris May 17. 1789.

I . . . return you abundant thanks for your attention to the article of Dry rice, and the parcel of seeds you sent me.  this is interesting, because even should it not take place of the wet rice in S. Carolina, it will enable us to cultivate this grain in Virginia, where we have not lands disposed for the wet rice. . . . *(Jefferson Papers, L. C.)*

## (Jefferson to Stephen Cathalan.)

Paris July 27. 1789.

. . . I have not seen the gardener who you said you should employ to complete the Commission from South Carolina, and who was to come to Paris.  I must interest your friendly & exact attention to the sending of the articles to Charleston this fall, and let the olive plants, & olive seeds be considered as the important object, sending but little of the other articles before noted to you.  I could wish one half to be sent from Marseilles by sea for Charleston directly, the other half thro' the canal of Languedoc to Bordeaux to the care of m̄r John Bondfield there; unless there should happen two vessels bound from Marseilles to Charleston, which would give an equal opportunity of dividing the risk between two different conveyances, & would be preferable to the sending any part through the canal. . . . *(Jefferson Papers, L. C.)*

## (Jefferson to Benjamin Vaughan.)

Paris Sept. 13. 1789.

I am still to thank you for the grains of dry rice, the copy of the corn report, and N̄s of the repository.  the latter I gave to m̄r Stuart according to your desire, as I had one before.  should the age of the rice have destroyed it's vegetative principle, I shall still hope, from the other resources you have been so good as to apply to, as well as the measures I have taken & shall still take myself that I may get the seed somewhere. . . . *(Jefferson Papers, L. C.)*

(Jefferson to Mr. Ralph Izard.)

Paris Sept. 18, 1789.

. . . I wish the cargo of olives spoken of in the inclosed letter, & which went to Baltimore, may have got on safe to Carolina, & that the one he is about to send may also arrive safe. This my dear friend should be the object of the Carolina patriot. After bread, I know no blessing to the poor, in this world, equal to that of oil. But there should be an annual sum steadily applied to that object: because a first and second essay may fail. The plants cost little; the transportation little. It is unremitting attention which is requisite. A common country labourer whose business it should be to prepare and pack his plants at Marseilles & to go with them through the canal of Languedoc to Bordeaux and there stay with them till put on board a ship to Charleston, & to send at the same time great quantities of the berries to sow for stocks, would require but a moderate annual sum. He would make the journey every fall only, till you should have such a stock of plants taken in the country, as to render you sure of success. But of this too we will talk on meeting. . . . (Ford, *Jefferson* 6: 15–16.)

(Jefferson to E. Rutledge.)

Paris, September 18, 1789.

. . . I have obtained from different quarters seeds of the dry rice; but having had time to try them, I find they will not vegetate, having been too long kept. I have still several other expectations from the East Indies. If this rice be as good, the object of health will render it worth experiment with you. Cotton is a precious resource, and which cannot fail with you. I wish the cargo of olive plants sent by the way of Baltimore, and that which you will perceive my correspondent is preparing now to send, may arrive to you in good order. This is the object for the patriots of your country; for that tree once established there, will be the source of the greatest wealth and happiness. But to insure success, perseverance may be necessary. An essay or two may fail. I think, therefore, that an annual sum should be subscribed, and it need not be a great one. A common country laborer should be engaged to make it his sole occupation, to prepare and pack plants and berries at Marseilles, and in the autumn to go with them himself through the canal of Languedoc to Bordeaux, and there to stay with them till he can put them on board a vessel bound directly for Charleston; and this repeated annually, till you have a sufficient stock insured, to propagate from without further importation. I should guess that fifty guineas a year would do this, and if you think proper to set such a subscription afoot, write me down for ten guineas of money, yearly, during my stay in France, and offer my superintendence of the business on this side the water, if no better can be had. . . . (Lipscomb and Bergh, *Jefferson* 7: 465–466.)

(Benjamin Hawkins to Jefferson.)

Warrenton, N. C., Oct. 6, 1789.

I have never had it in my power, until now, to procure for you the seed of the *Dionaea muscipula*. The gentlemen who had promised to get some for me had been too late both years in their endeavors. This year on my return from Wilmington, I discovered it was in bloom on the 6th of June, pointed it out to a farmer who knew it well and at my request he some days past sent the seed which I enclose. I could not discover any of the plants farther north than about Lat. 35.30. They grow in piny moist lands, and appeared to grow best when somewhat shaded. I have some plants which I brought with me in a box having carefully taken up the dirt with the roots; I put them in a part of my garden exposed to the sun all day and buried the box level with the surface of the earth, after a drought of near four weeks they appeared quite dead, the box was then taken up and accidently left under a pear tree. The weather being seasonable one third of them put forth leaves, and there they remain ever since.

I am to have some more of the seed sent to me in November. I will then enclose you a further supply. . . . (*Jefferson Papers,* M. H. S.)

The following list of plants was requested of Jefferson on the eve of his departure for America (1789) by la comtesse d'Houdetot. The names in italic written on both margins are in Jefferson's hand.

Liste des arbres et arbustes d'Amerique
que demande M^me la C^tsse d'Houdetot.

| | |
|---|---|
| *Gladitsia* | Accacia triacantos ou [ . . . . . ] d'Amerique. |
| *Androm. polufolia* | Amandier d'Amerique. |
| | Andromeda Polifolia. |
| *Myrica cerifera* | Arbre de cire. |
| *Bignonia semperv.* | Bignognia ou jasmin de Virginie. |
| *Azalea pudiss.* | Chevrefeuille de Virginie      *Loricera* [= *Lonicera*] *Py.* |
| | Chevrefeuille du nord de l'Amerique. |
| | Cletra major                *Not in America.* |
| | Epine a bouquet           *Astragalus tragacantha.* |
| *Acer rubra* | Erable de Virginie a fleurs rouge. |
| | Framboisier de Canada      *Rubus Canadensis.* |
| | Glauca |
| *Magn. grandifl.* | Laurier tulipier ou Magnolia granda flora. |
| *Populus balsamifera* | Peuplier beaumier de Virginie ou de la Caroline. |
| *Platanus occidentalis* | Platane de Virginie. |
| *Calyc. fl.* | Pompadoura Calycanthus floridus. |
| *Pt. trifoliata* | Ptéléa. |
| | Arbre d'or du Canada *Rhododendron. Maz 4.* |

*Laur. sassafr.*        Sassafras.
*Liriod*        Tulipier de Virginie ou Loriendendron.
*Tulipif.*        Tuliper fera.
*Mde d'Houdetot.*

(Gilbert Chinard, *Les Amitiés américaines de Madame d'Houdetot* (Paris, 1924): 49–50.)

From the *Account Book 1783–1790:*

May 11.   p^d Petit for Abbema & co. by order of Cathalan 152^H. Note this paiment to Abbema is for m̄r Drayton of S. Carolina for trees to be credited against the 726^H rec^d. by me July 12. 1789. for the Agricultural society of S. Carolina.

July 1.   p^d Fraser for 2. quarts grass seed 96^H.

# 1790

March.　a cold wind in this month killed all the peaches at Monticello. the other species of fruits escaped tolerably well.

Octob.　in making the road from where it begins to rise 1.f. in 10. a little above the negro houses, up to the upper roundabout in front of the house (N.E.) 5. hands did 127. yds the 1ˢᵗ. day and 165. yds the second. it was 12.f. wide, and they crossed three or four considerable gullies which they filled up with stone.²

---

¹ *1790.* Soon after Jefferson arrived in America from France, he was invited by President Washington to become Secretary of State in his new Cabinet. After much deliberation he accepted. He left *Monticello* on March 1, for New York, the seat of the government at that time, and was there until September 1; he was back at home by September 19. His stay at *Monticello* was a busy one because he had to attend to his long neglected private affairs and set his mountain-top in order. He left *Monticello* again on November 8, for Philadelphia, now the new seat of the federal government.

The most important event to affect Jefferson's life at *Monticello* during the year, other than that of becoming Secretary of State, was the marriage of his daughter, Martha, to her second cousin, Thomas Mann Randolph, of *Tuckahoe*. (For biographical data, see p. 398, note 23.)

There is no record in the *Account Book* for the year or in the *Garden Book* about garden activities at *Monticello* during 1790. The two entries in the *Garden Book* are about other matters.    Jefferson continued to write to friends about rice and olives, and continued to exchange plants with them at home and across the ocean.    It is in these letters that we get additional glimpses of Jefferson's interest in plants and learn what plants he sent to *Monticello*.

While in Richmond in March, on his way to New York, he drew up the following agreement with Nicholas Lewis to serve as his attorney during his absence from Albemarle:

Know all men by these presents that I Thomas Jefferson of Monticello in the county of Albemarle & Commonwealth of Virginia do . . . constitute & appoint Col° Nicholas Lewis of Albemarle my attorney during my absence from s^d Commonwealth.    Mar. 7. 1790.

And on the same day he wrote to Thomas Garth, also of Albemarle, that in case of Mr. Lewis' death he was to take charge. (Letter and agreement in *Jefferson Papers*, M. H. S.)

Mr. and Mrs. Randolph stayed at *Monticello* during the spring, but whether Mr. Randolph acted as his agent is not clear.    Probably Mr. Lewis attended to all matters of the estate.

² Jefferson also recorded this entry in another form in the *Farm Book:*

1790. Oct.    in making the road from where it begins to rise 1. f. in 10. a little above the Antient field to the upper Roundabout, 5 hands did 127. yds. the first day, & 165. yds the second, = 25 to 33 yds. a day.    it was 12. f. wide & they crossed 3. or 4. considerable gullies which they filled with stone.    [See plate XXII.]

### LETTERS AND EXTRACTS OF LETTERS, 1790

(Jefferson to his brother Randolph Jefferson.)

Monticello Feb. 28. 1790

. . . I will give the orders you desire to George, relative to peach stones. I send you by Orange some very fine Apricot & Plumb stones to be planted immediately & to be cracked before they are planted. . . . (*Jefferson Papers*, M. H. S.)

(Jefferson to Countess de Tessé.)

Alexandria. March 11. 1790

Being here on my way from Monticello to New York and learning that there is a vessel here bound to France, I cannot omit the opportunity of informing you of my proceedings in the execution of your botanical commission.    I arrived at home about the end of the old year.    the first days of the new were taken up in receiving visits from my neighbors &

friends, so that before I could possibly attend either to your business or my own there came on a frost which rendered it impossible to take a plant out of the earth till the middle of February. from the first moment of the thaw till the last day of February I had persons employed in collecting the plants you had desired; & on that day I attended myself to the packing of them. they are as follows:

No. 1. Nyssa aquatica.
    2. Magnolia tripetala.
    3. Liriodendron.
    4. Kalmia latifolia.
    5. Juniperus Virginiana.
    6. Gleditsia triacanthos.
    7. Laurus Sassafras.
    8. Prunus Coronaria.
    9. Diospyros Virginiana.
    10. Cornus florida.
    11. Juglans nigra.
    12. Quercus Phellos, both plants & acorns.
    13. Quercus pumila.
    14. Magnolia glauca.
    15. Acer rubrum.
    16. Calycanthus floridus.

the plants were young, in most perfect condition, & well packed in fresh moss, and over every layer of plants is a stick numbered as above, going across the plants and indicating what those are which are next under the stick. you will find the highest numbers uppermost, because we begun with N°. 1. at the bottom. I carried the box with me to Richmond & there desired a friend to send it to Norfolk to his correspondent with orders to ship it by the first ship sailing to Havre or Dunkirk. I now write to Monsʳ. Lamotte of Havre & mr̄ Coffin of Dunkirk to receive & forward the box to you at Paris by a waggon. after all I lament that this commission could not have been sooner executed and that it is still liable to further delay should there be no vessel going immediately to France. but it shall be followed by another containing the same things in the fall. I should have observed that I had ordered a dozen of each kind of plant but as they got more of some of them in order to chuse the best, I thought the best was to put them all in. so you will find from 12 to 20 of every kind. . . . (*Jefferson Papers,* L. C.)

(Jefferson to Francis Coffyn.)

Virginia March 11. 1790.

I have sent to Norfolk to be forwarded by the first vessel to Havre or Ostend a box of plants addressed to 'Madame la Comtesse de Tessé á Paris.' should they come to your port, I beg you to receive & forward them to their address by some of the Tourgons which go from thence to Paris. . . . (*Jefferson Papers,* L. C.)

(Jefferson to Thomas Mann Randolph.)

New York, May 30, 1790.

. . . I have, therefore, to answer your two favors of April 23 and May 3, and in the first place to thank you for your attention to the Paccan, Gloucester and European walnuts, which will be great acquisitions at Monticello. . . . (Lipscomb and Bergh, *Jefferson* 8: 29.)

(Jefferson to George Wythe.)

New York June 13. 1790.

. . . I enclose a few seeds of high-land rice which was gathered last autumn in the East Indies. if well attended to, it may not be too late to sow & mature it after you shall receive it. I have sowed a few seeds in earthen pots. it is a most precious thing if we can save it. . . . (*Jefferson Papers*, L. C.)

(Jefferson to Nicholas Lewis.)

New York June 13. 1790.

. . . I enclose a few grains of high-land rice which I received yesterday from England, & was gathered in the East Indies last fall. it may perhaps yet ripen in Virginia tho' very late. . . . (*Jefferson Papers*, L. C.)

(Jefferson to Maria Jefferson.)

New York, June 13th, 1790.

. . . We had not peas nor strawberries here till the 8th day of this month. On the same day I heard the first whip-poor-will whistle. Swallows and martins appeared here on the 21st of April. When did they appear with you? and when had you peas, strawberries, and whip-poor-wills in Virginia? Take notice hereafter whether the whip-poor-wills always come with the strawberries and peas. . . . (Sarah N. Randolph, *The Domestic Life of Thomas Jefferson* (New York, 1871): 185. Hereafter cited as Randolph, *Jefferson*.)

(Maria Jefferson to Jefferson.)

Eppington, ——————, 1790.

. . . We had peas the 10th of May, and strawberries the 17th of the same month, though not in that abundance we are accustomed to, in consequence of a frost this spring. As for the martins, swallows, and whip-poor-wills, I was so taken up with my chickens that I never attended to them, and therefore cannot tell you when they came, though I was so unfortunate as to lose half of them (the chickens), for my cousin Bolling and myself have raised but thirteen between us. . . . (Randolph, *Jefferson*, 186–187.)

(Jefferson to Benjamin Vaughan.)

New York June 27. 1790.

Your favor of March 27. came duly to hand on the 12th inst. as did your very valuable present of the dry rice brought from the Moluccas by Lieut. Bligh. I immediately sent a few seeds to Virginia where I am in hopes there would still be force of summer sufficient to mature it. I reserve a little for next spring besides sowing some in pots, from which

I have now 23. young plants just come up.   I fear however there is not summer enough remaining here to ripen them without the uncertain aid of a hot-house.   upon your encouragement I think I shall venture to write to Mr. Hinton Este of Jamaica on the subject.

Though large countries within our union are covered with the Sugar maple as heavily as can be conceived, and that this tree yields a sugar equal to the best from cane, yields it in great quantity, with no other labor than what the women & girls can bestow, who attend to the drawing off & boiling the liquor, & the trees when skillfully tapped will last a great number of years, yet the ease with which we had formerly got cane sugar, had prevented our attending to this resource.   late difficulties in the sugar trade have excited attention to our sugar trees, and it seems fully believed by judicious persons, that we can not only supply our own demand, but make for exportation.   I will send you a sample of it if I can find a conveyance without possessing it through the expensive one of the post.   what a blessing to substitute a sugar which requires only the labour of children, for that which it is said renders the slavery of the blacks necessary. . . . (*Jefferson Papers,* L. C.)

(Jefferson to Nicholas Lewis.)

New York July 4, 1790.

. . . I cannot, therefore, my dear Sir, omit to press, for myself, the going into that culture [of wheat] as much as you think practicable.   In Albemarle, I presume we may lay aside tobacco entirely; and in Bedford, the more we can lay it aside the happier I shall be. . . . It is vastly desirable to be getting under way with our domestic cultivation & manufacture of hemp, flax, cotton & Wool for the negroes.   (Lipscomb and Bergh, *Jefferson* 8: 58–59.)

(Jefferson to Maria Jefferson.)

New York, July 4th, 1790.

. . . How many chickens have you raised this summer? . . . Tell me what sort of weather you have had, what sort of crops are likely to be made. . . . (Randolph, *Jefferson,* 185–186.)

(Jefferson to A. Donald.)

New York Aug. 29. 1790.

. . . Our crops of wheat are good in quantity & quality, & those of corn very promising.   so far also this (I hope our last) crop of tobacco looks well.   little will be done in that way the next year, & less and less every year after. . . . (*Jefferson Papers* L. C.)

(Jefferson to Stephen Cathalan.)

Philadelphia Sept. 7. 1790.

. . . The object of the present is merely to enquire into the execution of the commission for sending olives & olive trees to Charleston.   of this

I have heard nothing from you since I left France; nor anything very particular from Charleston, the gentlemen from that state only saying to me in general that they have not heard that any were arrived.  if they be not already sent to the amount formerly desired, I must beg of you my dear Sir, to have it done in such season, and by such conveyance as will promise the best success.  the money for the purpose will be furnished by Mr. Short at Paris, & I feel myself bound in point of honour to have this object effectually fulfilled for the persons who have confided it's execution to me.  be so good as to inform me by a line (sent through Mr. Short) what is done, and what shall be done. . . . (*Jefferson Papers,* L. C.)

## (Samuel Vaughan, Jr., to Jefferson.)

St. James's Jamaica 4 Oct^r. 1790.

Sir, My father lately sent me a Note of your's requesting some seeds of the Mountain Rice.  I am sorry I cannot accommodate you as you would wish, but I do what I can by sending you 40 Seeds by two different opportunities.  Inclosed is 20 of them.  In the Middle Parts of Hispaniola it is in great plenty, and I had a promise of 2 Barrels.  A scarcity of Provisions first, and then the Disturbances have disappointed me in my Expectations.  If ever they are sent I shall amply supply you.

The seeds I have at present came from the Island of Timor in the East Indies, brought by the unfortunate Capt. Bligh.  I had near 200 of them thro my Brother from Sir Joseph Banks: I have given them in small Parcels to the Mountain settlers and have the pleasure to find it succeeds both with them and myself remarkably well. . . .

[Enclosure]

Directions to be observed with the Mountain Rice

It is to be sown like Indian Corn, three Seeds in a Hole.  In the East they do not cover the Holes with Earth but leave them exposed.  If they are covered it should be very lightly.  They should be sown in spring as they do not bear the winter—or in a Hothouse.  The Plants may be transplanted & separated & planted at greater distances when young. Great Care must be taken to prevent Fowls getting at it when ripe. New Land is the best for it, but it succeeds here in Jamaica on Ridges and in Glades.  It will not live under Water.  (Worthington Chauncey Ford, ed., *Thomas Jefferson Correspondence* (Boston, 1916): 44–45. Hereafter cited as Ford, *Jefferson Correspondence.*)

## (Jefferson to Thomas Mann Randolph.)

Georgetown, Nov. 12. 1790.

I inclose you some wheat which the President assures me from many years experience to be the best kind he has ever seen.  he spread it through the Eastern shore of Maryland several years ago, and it has ever been considered as the best of the white wheat of that state so much

celebrated.  it is said to weigh 62. 63. 64 ᵗᵇ to the bushel.  the grain,
tho' small, is always plump.  the President is so excellent a farmer that
I place full confidence in his recommendation.  will you be so good as
to make George (under your directions & eye) set it out in distinct holes
at proper distances so as to make the most seed from it possible?  the
richest ground in the garden will be best, and the partition fence they
are to make will guard it.  after harvest we will divide the produce.
I imagine the rows should be far enough apart to admit them to go between them with the hoes for the purpose of weeding.  (*Jefferson
Papers,* L. C.)

(Jefferson to Thomas Mann Randolph.)

Philadelphia Nov. 23. 1790.

. . . I believe I asked your attention to the upland rice.  I have re-
ceived a few more grains of that of the Moluccas from mͬ Samuel
Vaughan of Jamaica, with a note of which the enclosed is a copy. . . .
(*Jefferson Papers,* L. C.)

(Jefferson to J. B. Cutting.)

Philadelphia Nov. 26. 1790.

. . . The cask of mountain rice came also safely, for which precious
present accept my grateful thanks.  I have already distributed it into so
many hands as to ensure a fair experiment whether it may not be raised
in the lands and climates of the middle states and so render it useless to
poison the air with those inundations which sweep off annually so many
of our fellow-creatures. . . . (*Jefferson Papers,* L. C.)

(Jefferson to Samuel Vaughan, Jr.)

Philadelphia Nov. 27. 1790.

We have lately had introduced a plant of the melon species which
from it's external resemblance to the pumpkin, we have called a pumpkin,
distinguishing it specifically as the potatoe-pumpkin, on account of the
extreme resemblance of its taste to that of the sweet-potatoe.  it is as
yet but little known, is well esteemed at our tables, and particularly
valued by our negroes.  coming much earlier than the real potatoe, we
are so much the sooner furnished with a substitute for that root.  I
know not from whence it came; so that perhaps it may be originally
from your islands.  in that case you will only have the trouble of
throwing away the few seeds I enclose you herewith.  on the other hand,
if unknown to you, I think it will probably succeed in the islands, and
may add to the catalogue of plants which will do as substitutes for bread.
I have always thought that if in the experiments to introduce or to communicate new plants, one species in a hundred is found useful and succeeds, the ninety nine found otherwise are more than paid for.

My present situation and occupations are not friendly to Agricultural experiments, however strongly I am led to them by inclination. but whenever I shall be more free to indulge that inclination I will ask permission to address your quarter, freely offering you reciprocal services in the same or any other line in which you will be so good as to command them. . . . (*Jefferson Papers,* L. C.)

## (Jefferson to Thomas Mann Randolph.)

Philadelphia Dec. 16. 1790.

. . . I send herewith some seeds which I must trouble you with the care of. they are the seeds of the Sugar maple and the Paccan nuts. be so good as to make George prepare a nursery in a proper place and to plant in it the Paccan nuts immediately, and the maple seeds at a proper season. mr̄. Lewis must be so good as to have it so inclosed as to keep the horses out. there is also in the same tin box some seeds of the Cypress vine for Patsy. (*Jefferson Papers,* L. C.)

## (Jefferson to Martha (Jefferson) Randolph.)

Philadelphia, Dec. 23d, 1790

. . . Perhaps you think you have nothing to say to me. It is a great deal to say you are all well; or that one has a cold, another a fever, etc.: besides that, there is not a sprig of grass that shoots uninteresting to me. . . . (Randolph, *Jefferson:* 192.)

## From the *Account Book 1783–1790:*

June  8.   heard the first whip-poor-will.  [New York.]
June  12.   pᵈ 2 flower pots 2/6.
June  23.   pᵈ subscription for Bartram's travels 16/.  [New York]
July  23.   the first kildees I have seen this year.  [New York]

# 1791

Sep. 28. Estimate of a road rising 1.f. in 10.f. from the Secretary's ford.[2]

begun at the point of a ridge making into old road at head of little wet meadow

stepped rising 1.f. in 10.f. by guess as nearly as I could.

to the upper end of a rock 414 y$\overline{\text{ds}}$. [this rock dropping far down the hill & being impassible, it would be better to begin here & work downwards & upwards from it's head.]

to the plantation fence 264. y$\overline{\text{ds}}$ [so far thro' woods.]

into the road about 200 yds above Overseer's house 426. yds thro' the open feild. in all 1104 yds. & from where it enters the road up to the house about 700 yds. in all about 1900. yds from Secretary's ford to the house.

it would probably be about 85 days work[3]

30. on trial with the level, descending from the rock above mentioned 1.f. in 10

would have crossed the antient country road half way up the hill from the Secretary's ford.

156

rising from the rock 1.f. in 10. to the right, it struck the fence opposite the stone spring,⁴ 376 yds from the rock.

————————————⟨᳁⟩————————————

¹ *1791.* Jefferson continued in office as Secretary of State in Washington's Cabinet during the year. On May 17 Jefferson and Mr. James Madison set out on a month's excursion to the North. They visited, among other places, Albany, Ticonderoga, Springfield, Hartford, and New York. In Bennington, Vermont, Jefferson gave close study to the sugar maple industry. One of their most enjoyable experiences was a boat trip on Lake George. In the following letters to his son-in-law and to his daughter, Martha, Jefferson gave glowing descriptions of the lake and the plant life surrounding it.

(Jefferson to Martha (Jefferson) Randolph.)

Lake Champlain, May 31st, 1791.

My dear Martha:

I wrote to Maria yesterday while sailing on Lake George, and the same kind of leisure is afforded me to-day to write to you. Lake George is, without comparison, the most beautiful water I ever saw; formed by a contour of mountains into a basin thirty-five miles long, and from two to four miles broad, finely interspersed with islands, its water limpid as crystal, and the mountain sides covered with rich groves of thuja, silver fir, white pine, aspen and paper birch down to the water-edge; here and there precipices of rock to checker the scene and save it from monotony. An abundance of speckled trout, salmon trout, bass, and other fish, with which it is stored, have added to our other amusements, the sport of taking them. . . . Our journey has hitherto been prosperous and pleasant, except as to the weather, which has been sultry hot through the whole as could be found in Carolina or Georgia. I suspect, indeed, that the heats of northern climates may be more powerful than those of southern ones in proportion as they are shorter. Perhaps vegetation requires this. . . . Strawberries here are in the blossom or just formed. With you I suppose the season is over. On the whole, I find nothing anywhere else, in point of climate, which Virginia need envy to any part of the world. Here they are locked up in ice and snow for six months. Spring and autumn, which make a paradise of our country, are rigorous winter with them. And a tropical summer breaks on them all at once. When we consider how much climate contributes to the happiness of our conditions, by the fine sensations it excites, and the productions it is parent of, we have reason to value highly the accident of birth in such a one as that of Virginia. (Randall, *Jefferson* 2: 20–21.)

(Jefferson to Thomas Mann Randolph.)

Bennington, in Vermont, June 5, 1791.

. . . We were more pleased, however, with the botanical objects which continually presented themselves. Those either unknown or rare in Virginia, were the sugar maple in vast abundance. The silver fir, white pine, pitch pine, spruce pine, a shrub with decumbent stems, which they call juniper, an azalea, very different from the nudiflora, with very large clusters of flowers, more thickly set on the branches, of a deeper red, and high pink-fragrance. It is the richest shrub I have ever seen. The honey-suckle of the gardens growing wild on the banks of Lake George, the paper-birch, an aspen with a velvet leaf, a shrub-willow with downy catkins, a wild goose berry, the wild cherry with single fruit, (not the bunch cherry,) strawberries in abundance. . . . I think I asked the favor of you to send for Anthony in the season for inoculation, as well as to do what is necessary in the orchard, as to pursue the object of inoculating all the spontaneous cherry trees in the fields with good fruit. (Lipscomb and Bergh, *Jefferson* 8: 204–206.)

Jefferson remained in Philadelphia during the summer, being unable to leave for *Monticello* until September 2. He had been away from *Monticello* for almost a year. On the day he left for Virginia he "p^d Leslie for an odometer 10. D." This odometer he attached to the wheel of his carriage, and kept a tabular record of the distance from Philadelphia to *Monticello*. He arrived home on September 12, and observed the following details about the accuracy of the odometer:

These measures were on the belief that the wheel of the Phaeton made exactly 360. revolutions in a mile. but on measuring it accurately at the end of the journey it's circumference was 14 ft. 10½ I. and consequently made 354.95 revol^ns in a mile. these numbers should be greater then in the proportion of 71 : 72 or a mile added to every 71.

(See *Account Book 1791–1803* for the record of the trip.)

Petit, Jefferson's faithful steward in France, arrived in Philadelphia on July 19. He no doubt accompanied Jefferson to *Monticello* in September. During the following years he was to play a conspicuous part in Jefferson's comfort and to serve him in various ways.

Jefferson's interest in olive trees and rice continued unabated during the year, as letters quoted below will show. He sent rice and olives to South Carolina with the same zeal.

Since Jefferson was absent from *Monticello* during the spring and summer, there were no entries in the *Garden Book* about plants and gardening. He was, however, by no means idle. He placed orders with William Prince, of Long Island, New York, for a large shipment of plants to be sent to *Monticello*. They were received at *Monticello* and planted by Mr. Randolph.

Jefferson's new interest this year was the attempt to establish sugar maples at *Monticello*. He hoped and believed that sugar maples would be grown as profitably at *Monticello* as in Vermont. In order to try the experiment at *Monticello,* he bought over one hundred maple trees from William Prince, and also bought many maple buds for inoculation from a man named Elsworth. His maple trees never flourished. He was doomed to failure with this experiment as he was with his other two plant experiments, rice and olives, in South Carolina and Georgia.

[2] The great highway for stage travel from Richmond to Charlottesville followed the Rivanna River, and passed through *Shadwell,* and crossed the river at Secretary's Ford, just below what is now the Charlottesville Woolen Mills. *The Weekly Chronicle* of Charlottesville for February 19, 1870, under the heading of "Old Records of Albemarle County," gives the following interesting account of the origin of the name:

The ford is situated below Piraeus, and an opinion has prevailed to some extent that it was named in honor of Thomas Jefferson, when Secretary of State under President George Washington, as well as the Secretary road along which he is said to have travelled. But this is an error; here is the record which is to be found on the County Court Record:

At a court held for this county of Albemarle on the fourth Thursday and 28th day of March, 1745: Present Joshua Fry, Peter Jefferson, William Cabell, and Thomas Bellew, gentlemen Justices. Charles Lynch, gentleman, is appointed surveyor of the highway from the late Secretary's ford to number 12, and likewise of the road to the said Lynch's Ferry, and the same male citizens, that formerly worked under the said Lynch are ordered to clean both roads.

Mr. Jefferson at the time of this entry was not quite two years old. In the years 1744 and 1745 there are several entries which speak of Secretary Ford, Secretary Mountain, Secretary Mill, etc., and one of these says of the *late* Secretary. The gentleman for whom the Secretary's Ford, mill, Road, etc., were named was Charles Carter, some-

times called King Carter, His Majesty's Colonial Secretary.   He owned
a vast body of land in this section of country, and had here large plantations settled with negro slaves.   His line tree is now standing.   The
land from Fluvanna, along both sides of Carter's Mountain, and south
side of the county and in Nelson and Amherst was his.   (*The Weekly
Chronicle,* Charlottesville, Va., **5** (23): 1, Feb. 19, 1870.)

See plates XIV and XXII for location of Secretary's Ford.
³ See plate XXII.
⁴ One of the springs on the north side of *Monticello* mountain.   See plate XXII for location of this spring.

### LETTERS AND EXTRACTS OF LETTERS, 1791

(Jefferson to Stephen Cathalan le fils.)

Phila. Jan. 25. 1791.

. . . He [Cathalan le fils' father] desires me to say whether I still wish
to have the commission executed as to the olives.   I wish it, Sir, extremely.   my honour is somewhat compromitted in that matter with the
State of South Carolina, as it was on my earnest sollicitations they undertook it, and sent me about 30. Louis for that purpose; the balance of
which (after paying the parcel you sent) has laid at Paris ever since.
I must entreat you then at the Commencement of the proper season to
send one half the adventure of olive berries & olive plants to Bordeaux
to mr̄ Fenwick American consul there to be forwarded directly to
Charlestown, and to endeavor to find for the other half a vessel coming
from Marseilles to Charlestown direct.   let the two adventures make
up thirty Louis with what you have furnished before, & draw for the
balance on mr̄ Short.   (*Jefferson Papers,* L. C.)

(Jefferson to Martha (Jefferson) Randolph.)

Philadelphia, Feb. 9th, 1791.

. . . You will be out in time to begin your garden, and that will
tempt you to be out a great deal, than which nothing will tend more to
give you health and strength. . . . (Randall, *Jefferson* 2: 15.)

(Jefferson to Maria Jefferson.)

Philadelphia, Mar. 9th, 1791.

. . . On the 27th of February I saw blackbirds and robin-redbreasts,
and on the 7th of this month I heard frogs for the first time this year.
Have you noted the first appearance of these things at Monticello?   I
hope you have, and will continue to note every appearance, animal and
vegetable, which indicates the approach of spring, and will communicate
them to me.   By these means we shall be able to compare the climates
of Philadelphia and Monticello.   Tell me when you shall have peas, etc.,

up; when everything comes to table; when you shall have the first chickens hatched; when every kind of tree blossoms, or puts forth leaves; when each kind of flower blooms. . . . (Randall, *Jefferson* 2: 16.)

### (Martha (Jefferson) Randolph to Jefferson.)

Monticello March 22. 1791.

. . . Polly and myself have planted the cypress vine in boxes in the window and also date seeds and some other flowers. I hope you have not forgot the collection of garden seed you promised me. . . . (*Jefferson Papers,* M. H. S.)

### (Jefferson to Martha (Jefferson) Randolph.)

Philadelphia, Mar. 24, 1791.

. . . I suppose you are busily engaged in your garden. I expect full details on that subject as well as from Poll, that I may judge what sort of a gardener you make. . . . (Randall, *Jefferson* 2: 17.)

### (Jefferson to Maria Jefferson.)

Philadelphia, Mar. 31st, 1791.

. . . I wrote you in my last that the frogs had begun their songs on the 7th; since that the blue-birds saluted us on the 17th; the weeping-willow began to leaf on the 18th; the lilac and gooseberry on the 25th, and the goldenwillow on the 26. I enclose for your sister three kinds of flowering beans, very beautiful and very rare. She must plant and nourish them with her own hand this year in order to save enough seeds for herself and me. . . . (Randall, *Jefferson* 2: 17–18.)

### (Jefferson to Thomas Mann Randolph.)

Philadelphia Apr. 6. 1791.

. . . I have received my daughter's letter, and will execute her wish for the calash for herself, & seeds for her friend. . . . (*Jefferson Papers,* L. C.)

### (Jefferson to Martha (Jefferson) Randolph.)

Philadelphia, April 17, 1791.

. . . I hope your garden is flourishing. . . . (Randall, *Jefferson* 2: 18).

### (Maria Jefferson to Jefferson.)

Monticello, April 18th, 1791.

. . . The garden is backward, the inclosure having but lately been finished. . . . (Randolph, *Jefferson:* 199.)

(Jefferson to Maria Jefferson.)

Philadelphia, April 24, 1791.

I have received, my dear Maria, your letter of March 26; I find I have counted too much on you as a Botanical and Zoological correspondent, for I undertook to affirm here that the fruit was not killed in Virginia, because I had a young daughter there who was in that kind of correspondence with me, and who, I was sure would have mentioned it, if it had been so.    However, I shall go on communicating to you whatever may contribute to a comparative estimate of the two climates, in hopes that it will induce you to do the same to me. . . .

> April 5.  Apricots in bloom.
>          Cherry leafing.
>      9.  Peach in blossom.
>          Apple leafing.
>     11.  Cherry in blossom. . . .

(Randall, Jefferson 2: 18–19.)

Thomas Mann Randolph, in a letter to Jefferson, written from *Monticello* on April 30, gave him a detailed account of the weather for the month and listed the blooming time for the following plants:

April 1, Violae 1, 2, 3.
      2, Leontodon taraxacum.
      4, Silene, Fragaria vesca.
     30, Chionanthus virg[inica.] Cypripedium Calc[eolus], Crataegus crus ga[lli], Morus Rubra, Aquilegia canad[ensis,] Prunus virg[iniana], Magnolia 3 sp. Hyacin[thus] com[osus].

(Jefferson Papers, M. H. S.)

(Jefferson to Messrs. Robert Gilmore & Co.)

Phila. May 1. 1791.

I am just informed that there is arrived at Baltimore addressed to you by mr Cathalan of Marseilles 6. barrels containing olive trees, and a chest containing olives to sow, for me.    I must beg the favor of you to send them by the first vessel to Charleston (S. C.) addressed 'to Messieurs Brailsford & Morris for mr Wm. Drayton.'    as the success of this endeavor to introduce the culture of the olive into the U. S. depends on the plants arriving at their destination in due season, & that is now passing fast away, I must beg your attention to send them by, the very first vessel bound from your port.    (*Jefferson Papers*, L. C.)

(Jefferson to Thomas Mann Randolph.)

Philadelphia May 1. 1791.

. . . We are still sitting before fires here. The fruit in this country is untouched. I thank you for having replaced my dead trees. It is exactly what I would have wished. I shall be glad to hear how the white wheat, mountain rice, Paccan & Sugar Maples have succeeded. Evidence grows upon us that the U. S. may not only supply themselves sugar for their own consumption but be great exporters. I have received a cargo of olive trees from Marseilles, which I am ordering on to Charleston, so that the U. S. have a certain prospect that sugar and oil will be added to their productions, no mean addition. I shall be glad to have a pair of puppies of the Shepherd's dog selected for the President. A committee of the Philosophical Society is charged with collecting materials for the natural history of the Hessian fly. I do not think that of the weavil of Virginia has been yet sufficiently detailed. What do you think of beginning to turn your attention to this insect, in order to give its history to the Phil. society? It would require some summer's observations.—Bartram here tells me that it is one & the same insect which by depositing it's egg in the young plumbs, apricots, nectarines & peaches renders them gummy & good for nothing. He promises to shew me the insect this summer. I long to be free for pursuits of this kind instead of the detestable ones in which I am now labouring without pleasure to myself, or profit to others. In short I long to be with you at Monticello. (Ford, *Jefferson* 6: 250–251.)

(Jefferson to William Drayton.)

Philadelphia May 1. 1791.

my Mortification has been extreme at the delays which have attended the procuring the olive plants so long ago recommended by myself, so long ago agreed to by the agricultural society, & for which their money has been so long lying in the hands of a banker at Paris. I assure you Sir that my endeavors have been unremitting. in addition to the first small parcel which were sent soon after the receipt of your orders, I have now the pleasure to inform you that a second cargo is arrived at Baltimore consisting of 6. barrels which contain 40. young olive trees of the best species, to afford grafts, and a box of olives to sow for stocks. this I order on immediately to Charleston to the care of Mess^rs. Brailsford & Morris for you, and I inclose herewith a copy of the directions given for the manner of treating them. a third cargo is on it's way from Bordeaux, but for what port I have not learned. this consists of 2. barrels containing 44. olive trees of which 24 are very young.—I shall immediately write to my correspondent at Marseilles to send another cargo the ensuing winter.—I delivered to m^r Izard a barrel of Mountain rice of last year's growth, which I received from the island of Bananas on the coast of Africa & which I desired him to share with you for the use of the society. the attention now paying to the sugar-maple tree promises us an abundant supply of sugar at home: and I confess I look with infinite gratification to the addition to the products of the U. S. of three such articles as oil, sugar, & upland rice.  the last I value, in the hopes it may be a complete substitute for the pestiferous culture of the wet rice. . . .

### Memorandum for the Olive Trees

If the olive trees arrive safely on the ground where they are intended to be planted, before the end of the month of May next, they may yet be planted one foot depth in the earth above the root & from 15 to 18 feet distance one from the other in a Square.  If on the contrary they arrive after the month of May, they will open a trench in the earth of the depth of the barrels in which they will place the barrels near each other, taking out the hoops and 3 or 4 staves and filling the hole all round with earth.  They will water 3 or 4 times in summer all the trench 'till the water penetrates below the bottoms of the barrels.  They will shade them from the sun during the great heats & in convenient season they will be planted as above.

As for the chest of olives for sowing.  They will make a hole of 3 feet depth in the earth put the chest in it, as it is, cover it over with the same earth and water it well afterwards.  They will then leave the whole so 'till next February, when they will uncover the chest without deranging it & take some of the Olives which they will break to see if the almond has germinated; if it has not yet swelled they will cover it again & leave it for one year more.  If they have swelled they will sow them at an inch depth in the earth cover them again with earth & put on them horse dung one inch watering them with a watering pot then they will sprout out in 2 or 3 months or perhaps not till the ensuing year. (*Jefferson Papers*, L. C.)

### (Jefferson to George Washington.)
Philadelphia May 1. 1791.

. . . A Mr. Noble has been here, from the country where they are busied with the Sugar maple tree.  He thinks Mr. Cooper will bring 3000 £'s worth to market this season, and gives the most flattering calculations of what may be done in that way.  He informs me of another very satisfactory fact, that less profit is made by converting the juice into a spirit than into sugar.  He gave me specimens of the spirit, which is exactly whiskey.

I have arrived at Baltimore from Marseilles 40 olive trees of the best kind from Marseilles, & a box of the seed.  The latter to raise stocks, & the former cuttings to engraft on the stocks.  I am ordering them instantly to Charleston, where if they arrive in the course of this month they will be in time.  Another cargo is on it's way from Bordeaux, so that I hope to secure the commencement of this culture, and from the best species.  Sugar & oil will be no mean addition to the articles of our culture. . . .  (Ford, *Jefferson* **6**: 253.)

(Benjamin Hawkins to Jefferson.)

Warren in N. C. 3ʳᵈ. of May 1791.

I had the pleasure to receive the letter you did me the honor to write to me of the 1ˢᵗ. of April enclosing some of the scarlet blossom beans . . . for which I request you to accept my thanks.   I wish you and Mʳˢ. Trist may have been as fortunate with your beans as I am with mine, the largest and middle sized are up and promising; I imagine the largest to be the Caracalla. . . . (*Jefferson Papers, M. H. S.*)

(Jefferson to Maria Jefferson.)

Philadelphia, May 8ᵗʰ, 1791.

. . . April 30th the lilac blossomed.   May 4th the gelder-rose, dogwood, redbud, azalea were in blossom.   We have still pretty constant fires here. . . . (Randall, *Jefferson* 2: 19.)

(Jefferson to David Rittenhouse.)

Philadelphia, May 8. 1791.

. . . The diary of the flowering plants and appearance of birds may amuse you a minute.   I observe the martin appeared there the 14ᵗʰ of April.   here it was the 21ˢᵗ. this year, & exactly on the same day at New York the last year.   the object of this diary is to show what birds disappear in winter & when, & also to enable us to form a comparative view of the climates of that & this place, for I was to have kept a similar diary here; but a town situation does not admit it. . . . (*Jefferson Papers, L. C.*)

(Jefferson to Benjamin Vaughan.)

Philadelphia May 11. 1791.

. . . The parcels of mountain rice from Timor came to hand too late in the last season to produce seed.   I have sowed this spring some of the same, but it has not yet come up.   I was fortunate in receiving from the coast of Africa last fall a cask of mountain rice of the last year's growth. This I have dispersed into many hands, having sent the mass of it to S. Carolina.   The information which accompanied this cask was that they have there (on the coast of Africa) 3. kinds of Mountain rice, which sowed at the same time, comes to harvest a month distant from each other.   They did not say of which kind that is which was sent to me. The kind which ripens quickest will surely find sun enough to ripen in our middle states.   (Ford, *Jefferson* 6: 259–260.)

(Jefferson to James Madison.)

Philadelphia, June 21. 1791.

. . . I am sorry we did not bring with us some leaves of the different plants which struck our attention [on their northern trip], as it is the

leaf which principally decides *specific* differences.  You may still have
it in your power to repair the omission in some degree.  The Balsam
tree at Govr. Robinson's is the Balsam poplar, *Populus Balsamifera* of
Linnaeus.  The *Arolea* [*Azalea*] I can only suspect to be the *viscosa,*
because I find but two kinds the *nudiflora* [and] *viscosa* acknoledged
to grow with us.  I am sure it is not the *nudiflora.*  The white pine is
the *Pinus Strobus.* . . . (Ford, *Jefferson* 6: 272.)

### (Jefferson to James Madison.)

Philadelphia, July 6. 1791.

. . . I received safely the packet by cap$^t$. Sims.  The Guinea corn is
new to me, & shall be taken care of.  My African upland rice is
flourishing. . . .

P. S.  If you leave N. York, will you leave directions with Mr. Elsworth
to forward to me the two parcels of Maple buds, & that of the Birch
bark respectively as they arrive.  The last I think had better come by
water.  (Ford, *Jefferson* 6: 277–278.)

### (Thomas Mann Randolph to Jefferson.)

Monticello, July 7, 1791.

. . . In a late letter you desire us to let you know our success with
the seeds you sent from Philadelphia.  The sugar maple has failed entirely, a few plants only having appeared which perished almost immediately.  The yellow rice failed allso from the badness of the seed, but
the dark colored came up tolerably well & the plants are thriving.  The
first kind was transmitted to Colo. Lewis on your account by a Gentleman in Jamaica, the 2$^d$. you left in one of the niches in the parlour here.
For both of these & the maple we preferred the flat ground below the
park on the little stream which passes thro' it, being the natural situation of the latter, & more suitable to the former than the garden.  The
Pacans have not appeared as yet.  Thinking that they would not bear
transplantation I took the liberty to place them partly on each side of the
new way leading from the gate to the house & partly in the garden.
Several of those in the garden were destroyed unluckily by the hogs before it was enclosed.  The white wheat did poorly. . . . (*Jefferson
Papers,* M. H. S.)

### (Jefferson to Wm. Prince.)

Philadelphia July 6. 1791.

When I was at your house in June I left with you a note to furnish
me with the following trees, to wit:

Sugar maples.  all you have
bush cranberries.  all you have
3. balsam poplars.
6. Venetian sumachs.
12. Bursé pears.

To these I must now desire you to add the following; the names of which I take from your catalogue, to wit

6. Brignole plumbs.
12. apricots.  I leave to you to fix on three or four of the best kinds, making in the whole 12 trees.
6. red Roman nectarines.
6. yellow Roman nectarines.
6. green nutmeg peaches.
6. large yellow clingstone peaches ripening Oct. 15.
12. Spitzenberg apples.  I leave to you to decide on the best kind, as I would chuse to have only one kind.
6. of the very earliest apples you have.
   Roses Moss Provence.  yellow. rosa mundi: large Provence. the monthly. the white damask. the primrose. musk rose. cinnamon rose. thornless rose.  3 of each, making in all 30.
3. Hemlock spruce firs.
3. large silver firs.
3. balm of Gilead firs.
6. monthly honeysuckles.
3. Carolina kidney bean trees with purple flowers.
3. balsam of Peru.
6. yellow willows
6. Rhododendrons.
12. Madeira nuts.
(12?) fill-buds.

according to your estimate & the prices in your catalogue these will be covered by 30. dollars * which sum you will receive herewith.  I must trouble you to send them yourself to Richmond, addressed to the care of m$^r$ James Brown merch$^t$. of that place, who will receive them & pay freight &c.  Send them to no other port of that country, for I shall never get them, and there are vessels going from New York to Richmond frequently.  be so good as to forward them as soon as the season will admit.  I am, Sir. . . . (*Jefferson Papers,* M. H. S.)  (Published in Fiske Kimball, *Jefferson's Grounds and Gardens at Monticello,* n.d.)

* "July 6, [1791], gave order on bank for Prince for trees, also for 100 lb. Maple sugar, etc. on acc$^t$. making 60.D & inclos$^d$ to him." (*Account Book 1791–1803.*)

(Joseph Fay to Jefferson.)

Bennington [Vermont] 9$^{th}$ August 1791.

I have this day had the honor to receive your letter of the 16$^{th}$. of June, respecting the sugar maple seed, by what means the letter has been so long detained I cannot account.  I had determined to furnish you had you not written, but the seed does not come to maturity until the Month of October, when the frost kills the stem of the leaf & seed, & causes them to fall from the tree, this circumstance will prevent my furnishing you so early as you mention, but no time shall be lost in doing it in the proper season & forwarding them to you.

I have examined my young groves since you left this, & find the young maple very thrifty & numerous, by calculation nearly one thousand to the acre.  I intend to plant an orchard in regular form next Spring, in hopes to encourage others in the same laudable undertaking in case I succeed. . . . (*Jefferson Papers,* M. H. S.)

Mr. Prince completed Jefferson's order of July 6, in November, and on the eighth of that month sent him the following itemized statement, adding that the shipment of trees and shrubs was being sent to his agent, Mr. James Brown of Richmond.  It reached Richmond on December 3, and was soon after sent to *Monticello.*

Nov. 8, 1791.
Flushing

Thomas Jefferson, Esq.                      Bot. of W^m prince

The following trees—

| | |
|---|---|
| No. 1.—60 Sugar Maple trees | at 1/:–3–0–0 |
| 2.— 6 Cranberry trees | 2/:–0–12–0 |
| 3.— 3 Balsam Poplar | 1/6–0–4–6 |
| 4.— 6 Venetian Sumach | 1/6–0–9–0 |
| 5.— 8 Burré Pears | 1/6–0–12–0 |
| 6.— 4 Brignole Plumbs | 0–6–0 |
| 7.— 4 Red Roman Nectarines | 1/6–0–6–0 |
| 8.— 4 Large early Apricots | |
| 9.— 4 Brussels do. | |
| 10.— 4 Roman (Moor park) do. | |
| 11.— 4 Yellow Roman Nectarines | 40 trees |
| 12.— 4 Green Nutmeg Peach | at      1/6–3–0–0 |
| 13.— 4 Yellow October Cling^ne. | |
| 14.—12 Esopus Spitzenburgh apple | |
| 15.— 4 Large early harvest apples | |
| 16.— 2. Moss rose | 0–6–0 |
| 17.— 2. Rosa mundi | 2/:–0–4–0 |
| 18.— 2. Monthly rose | 2/:–0–4–0 |
| 19.— 2. Large Provence rose | 2/  0–4–0 |
| 20.— 2. Musk rose | 2/  0–4–0 |
| 21.— 2 Prim roses | 1/: 0–2–0 |
| 22.— 2 White rose | 1/: 0–2–0 |
| 23.— 2 Thornless rose | 4 —0–2–0 |
| 24.— 2 Cinnamon rose | 1/. 0–2–0 |
| 25.— 2 Yellow rose | 1/6–0–4–6 |
| 27.— 3 Hemlock spruce | 1/6–0–4–6 |
| 28.— 3 Silver fir | 1/6–0–4–6 |
| 29.— 6 Monthly (honey suckle) | 0/6–0–3–0 |

| | |
|---|---|
| 30.— 3 Balsam of Peru | 1/6–0–4–6 |
| 31.— 6 Rhododendron | 1/6–0–9–0 |
| 32.—12 Filbud trees | 1/6–0–18–0 |
| Matts the trees are packed in | 0–6–0 |
| Cartiage | 00–1.0 |

£   12–12–0

Gures [?] in No. 33—Lemon Clingstone the largest & best of peaches. The above trees are in four bundles. some cuttings of Yellow Willow tyed to one of the Bundles of trees.
                                    (*Jefferson Papers*, L. C.)

(Jefferson to Thomas Mann Randolph.)

Philadelphia Nov. 27. 1791.

By a letter from Prince, I find that he has forwarded to the care of mr̄ Brown in Richmond 4. bundles of trees for me, numbered as on the next leaf. I have written to mr̄ Brown to forward them, & wish this may get in time for you to understand the numbers before you plant them. . . . (*Jefferson Papers*, L. C.)

The list of trees referred to in the letter is the same as the list sent to Jefferson by Prince, except in this list the price is left off.

(Jefferson to James Brown.)

Philadelphia Nov. 28. 1791.

By a letter just received from Prince, the nurseryman of Long Island, I learn he has forwarded 4. bundles of trees for me to Richmond addressed to your care. . . . (*Jefferson Papers*, M. H. S.)

Jefferson asked Mr. Brown to send them to *Monticello* or Nicholas Lewis, and not to let them freeze.

(James Brown to Jefferson.)

Richmond December 4, 1791.

. . . Yesterday your four bundles of Trees came to hand from New York. They shall be taken care of and forwarded as you point out. . . . (*Jefferson Papers*, M. H. S.)

(Jefferson to Thomas Mann Randolph.)

Philadelphia Dec. 11. 1791.

. . . mr. Brown writes me word that the 4. bundles of trees from Prince are safe arrived there, so that I am in hopes you have received them. . . . (*Jefferson Papers*, L. C.)

From the *Account Book 1791–1803:*

April   9.   p<sup>d</sup> Bartram the 6. Louis M<sup>de</sup> de Tessé had given me [for
             plants] for him = 27 D.
April 14.   four flower-pots 6/.
April 15.   2 flower-pots .2
April 18.   7 flower-pots 5/9.
May  17.   heard the first whip-poor-will.
June   8.   East Springfield.   saw *2 elms* 6f. 8 I. & 7 f. 7 I. diam.
Dec.  20.   p<sup>d</sup> for seeing a lion 21 Months old 11½ c.

# 1792

July 1. Sunday. the thermometer at D$^r$. Walker's[2] was this day at 96°. which he says is 3°. higher than he ever knew it since he lived at the mountains. there was no thermometer at Monticello: but I have observed when I had one here, that it was generally about 2°. below D$^r$. Walker's & m͞r Maury's.[3] so we may suppose it would have been at 94°. it was at 97°. at m͞r Madison's in Orange[4] on the same day, and at 99°. in Richmond. this was probably the hottest day ever known in Virginia. on the same day was a violent hurricane from about the capes of Virginia[5] Northwardly. it overset vessels & blew down chimneys & the tops of houses in Philadā & N. York, & destroyed a great deal of timber in the country.[6]

Aug. 31. *G. Divers[7] thinks feilds of 50. acres of wheat the best size.

*he estimates 2. bushels of wheat for every cubic yard of wheat in the straw when stacked.

Sep. 18. the lower Round-about[8] measured by the Odometer[9] to my Phaeton[10] is 4420 feet = 1473$\frac{1}{3}$ $\overset{\text{yds.}}{}$

mile[11]
= .837.

¹ *1792.* Jefferson continued as Secretary of State with great reluctance during 1792, only to oblige and support his friend, President Washington, during a very critical period. As early as May 23, Jefferson wrote to Washington from Philadelphia, urging him to accept another term in office, but at the same time making it quite clear that he did not wish to serve another term as Secretary of State.

I have, therefore, no motive to consult but my own inclination, which is bent irresistibly on the tranquil enjoyment of my family, my farm, and my books. I should repose among them, it is true in far greater security if I were to know that you remained at the watch; and I hope it will be so. (Randall, *Jefferson* 2: 64.)

Jefferson was in Philadelphia most of the year, except for a single visit to *Monticello,* which lasted from July 22 to September 27. Maria, who was with him in Philadelphia, added much to his enjoyment and relieved him of some of the loneliness which completely engulfed him when he was away from his family.

On May 18, a paper by Benjamin Smith Barton was read before the American Philosophical Society, assembled in Philadelphia, naming that plant *Jeffersonia* (pl. XI) which previously had been called *Podophyllum diphyllum.* After describing the plant in detail, Barton continues:

From the account which I have given of this plant, I have little doubt that you will agree with me in considering it as a genus, distinct from the *Sanguinaria* and the *Podophyllum,* to both which, however, it must be confessed, it bears considerable relation. As I have not found it described by any authors, except Linnaeus and Clayton, neither of whom had seen the flowers, and as it is, certainly, a new family, I take the liberty of making it known to the botanist by the name of

### JEFFERSONIA,

in honour of Thomas Jefferson, Esq. Secretary of State to the United-States.

I beg leave to observe to you, in this place, that in imposing upon this genus the name of Mr. Jefferson, I have had no reference to his political character, or to his reputation for general science, and for literature. My business was with his knowledge of natural history. In the various departments of this science, but especially in botany and in zoology, the information of this gentleman is equalled by that of few persons in the United-States.

Of the genus which I have been describing, we, as yet, know but one species, which I call

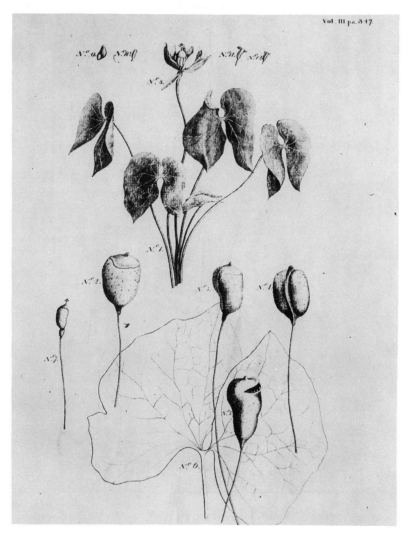

PLATE XI.—The drawing of *Jeffersonia diphylla* by Benjamin Smith **Barton,** who named the plant in honor of Jefferson in 1792 (*Trans. Am. Philos. Soc.*).

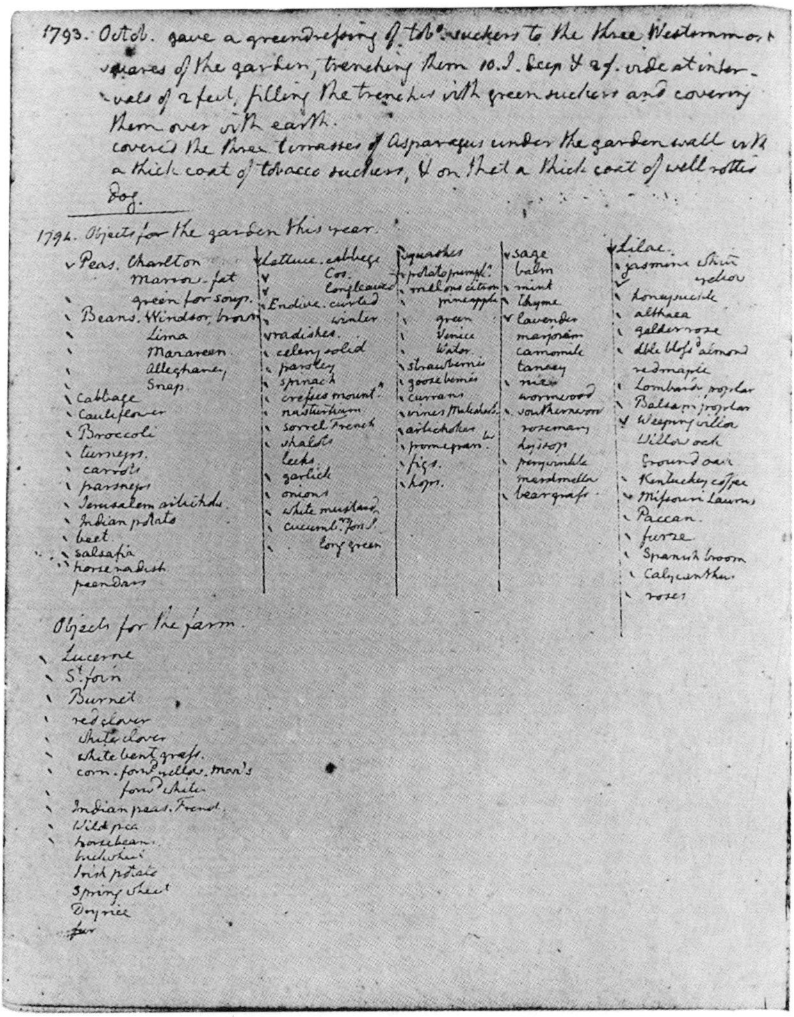

1793. Octob. gave a green dressing of tob° suckers to the three Westernmost
squares of the garden, trenching them 10.I. deep & 2.f. wide at intervals of 2 feet, filling the trenches with green suckers and covering
them over with earth.
 covered the three terrasses of Asparagus under the garden wall with
a thick coat of tobacco suckers, & on that a thick coat of well rotted
dung.

1794. Objects for the garden this year.

| | | | | |
|---|---|---|---|---|
| Pears. Charlton | Lettuce. cabbage | squashes | sage | Lilac. |
| Marrow-fat | Cos. | potato pumpk. | balm | jasmine white |
| green for soup. | Longleaves | melons citron | mint | yellow |
| Beans. Windsor, brown | Endive. curled | pineapple | thyme | honeysuckle |
| Lima | winter | green | Lavender | althaea |
| Mazarean | radishes. | Venice | marjoram | gelder rose |
| Alleghaney, | celery solid | water. | camomile | dble bloss. almond |
| Snap. | parsley | strawberies | tansey | redmaple |
| Cabbage | spinach | gooseberies | nice | Lombardy poplar |
| Cauliflower | cresses mount° | currans | wormwood | Balsam poplar |
| Broccoli | nasturtium | vines Muldach. | southernwood | Weeping willow |
| turneps. | sorrel french | artichokes | rosemary | Willow oak |
| carrots | shalots | pomegran. | hyssop | Ground oak |
| parsneps | leeks | figs. | pervinkle | Kentucky coffee |
| Jerusalem artichokes. | garlick | hops. | meadmelilla | Missouri laurus |
| Indian potato | onions | | beargrass | Paccan |
| beet | white mustard | | | furze |
| salsafia | cucumbr. for d. | | | Spanish broom |
| horse radish | long green | | | Calycanthus |
| pseudacus | | | | roses |

Objects for the farm.

Lucerne
St foin
Burnet
red clover
white clover
white bent grass.
corn. for d. yellow. mon's for d. white.
Indian peas. French,
wild pea
horsebean.
huckshur
Irish potato
spring wheat
Doynee
fur

PLATE. XII.—Page 28 of the original *Garden Book*.

JEFFERSONIA BINATA.

Barton's paper was printed the following year in the *Transactions of the American Philosophical Society* (3: 334–347, 1793).

Since Jefferson was in Philadelphia during the month of May, he was probably an attendant at the meeting when this honor was conferred upon him. In the spring of 1807 he planted *Jeffersonia* in one of the oval beds in front of his house at *Monticello*. *Jeffersonia binata* Bart. is now called *Jeffersonia diphylla* (L.) Pers.

This was another year in which Jefferson failed to make any entries in the *Garden Book* about the activities in the garden. From letters and the account book for the year, his continued interest in olives, rice, and sugar maples is apparent.

*Monticello* had suffered greatly during Jefferson's almost continuous absence of ten years. The house was unfinished, and there were many changes to be made both indoors and outdoors. He began his plans for a complete change in the house this year. In a letter to Stephen Willis, his workman at *Monticello,* he wrote:

Philadelphia Nov. 12. 1792.

Having long ago fixed on the ensuing spring for the time of my retiring to live at home, I did, when there the last fall, endeavor to put things into a train for resuming my buildings. this winter is employed in getting framing, limestone, & bringing up stone for the foundation of the new part to be first erected. the demolition of the walls wherein the present staircase is run up, & of the Antichamber (about 60,000 bricks) will, with about 20,000 new bricks which I possess, suffice I hope for the first summer's construction, building to the water table with those. I shall begin about the first of April to dig my cellars, & then do the stonework, and as far as I can judge I shall be in readiness after that to do the brick-work. but I cannot be certain of it, because I am not at home to make sure that the winter's preparations will be completed. I have thought it best to give you my prospect of asking your attendance, according to promise, merely that you may, if possible, so arrange your engagements as to come to Monticello, if I can get ready for you, & if I cannot be ready, that it may be no disappointment to you. I am extremely anxious to do the part of my house meditated this summer if possible. my operations of the subsequent years will be more certain. . . . (*Jefferson Papers,* M. H. S.)

Plans were also formulated for putting his farms on a paying basis. In order to carry out his plans Jefferson needed an overseer who could give all his labors to *Monticello*. To do this work he engaged Mr. Samuel Biddle, of Elkton, Maryland, who had been recommended to him by Mr. Jacob Hollingsworth, also of that town. The agreement was made between them toward the close of the year.

² Thomas Walker was born in King and Queen in 1715, was a student of William and Mary, and about 1741 married Mildred, the widow of Nicholas Meriwether. Through her he came into possession of Castle Hill [Albemarle County]. By profession he was a physician, but possessed too bold and energetic a nature to be contented with the ordinary routine of a country doctor. . . . He was Commissary of the Virginia troops under Braddock, and was at that general's defeat in 1755. More than once he was appointed to treat with the Indians in New York and Pennsylvania, and in 1778 was one of the Commission selected to fix the boundary between Virginia and North Carolina. Without any change of residence, he successively represented the counties of Hanover, Louisa, and Albemarle in the House of Burgesses, and in 1763 was the trustee of Albemarle to sell and convey the lots and outlots of Charlottesville, the new county seat. He died in 1794. (Woods, *Albemarle County:* 334–335.)

³ Probably Matthew Maury, son of the Reverend James Maury, to whose school Jefferson went as a boy. "Matthew was an Episcopal minister, and succeeded his father both at the homestead, and in the parish. He also taught school. He married Elizabeth, daughter of Dr. Thomas Walker. He died in 1808." (Woods, *Albemarle County:* 269.)

⁴ President James Madison's home *Montpelier,* Orange County, Virginia.

⁵ Cape Henry and Cape Charles, Virginia.

⁶ Jefferson was in Philadelphia on July 1. He did not reach *Monticello* until July 22, so that all of the entry relative to the weather was written after his return to *Monticello.*

⁷ Mr. George Divers lived at *Farmington,* Albemarle County, now the *Farmington Country Club.* He and Jefferson, both prominent men of the community, were warm friends and often visited each other to discuss agricultural matters and exchange plants and seeds. Mr. Divers married Martha Walker, daughter of Dr. Thomas Walker, of *Castle Hill.* (Mary Rawlings, *The Albemarle of Other Days* (Charlottesville, 1925): 122–123.)

⁸ The lower *Round-about* was also called the Fourth *Round-about.*

⁹ Jefferson bought this odometer on September 2, 1791, while in Philadelphia. See note 1, 1791.

¹⁰ Phaeton: a kind of light four-wheeled carriage (with or without a top) having no sidepieces in front of the seat or (two) seats.

¹¹ From the *Farm Book:* "1792, Sept. 18. the Orchard Roundabout, passing above the garden along the mulberry row, measured by the Odometer of the Phaeton $1473\frac{1}{3}$ yds. = .837 mile.

## LETTERS AND EXTRACTS OF LETTERS, 1792

(Jefferson to Thomas Mann Randolph.)

Philadelphia, Jan. 1, 1792.

. . . I thank you for your experiment on the Peach tree. It proves my speculation practicable, as it shews that 5. acres of peach trees at 21. feet apart will furnish dead wood enough to supply a fireplace through the winter, & may be kept up at the trouble of only planting about 70. peach stones a year. Suppose this extended to 10. fireplaces, it comes to 50. acres of ground, 5000 trees, and the replacing about 700 of them annually by planting so many stones. If it be disposed at some little distance, say in a circular annulus from 100. to 300 yards from the house, it would render a cart almost useless.—When I indulge myself in these speculations, I feel with redoubled ardor my desire to return home to the pursuit of them, & to the bosom of my family, in whose love alone I live or wish to live, & in that of my neighbors.—But I must yet a little while bear up against my weariness of public office. . . . (Ford, *Jefferson* 6: 359.)

(Jefferson to Martha (Jefferson) Randolph.)

Philadelphia, February 26, 1792.

. . . The season is now coming on when I shall envy you your occupations in the fields and garden, while I am shut up drudging within four walls. . . . (Randall, *Jefferson* 2: 76.)

(Jefferson to Thomas Mann Randolph.)

Philadelphia Mar. 30. 1792.

. . . I inclose you some seeds of the Acacia Farnesiana the most delicious flowering shrub in the world. it will require to be in boxes, and to be kept in the house in the winter. I formerly made use of the South bow room for the same kind of plant, & it was quite sufficient. if they come up and you will take charge of them next winter, I will take them off your hands afterwards. . . . in vegetation I have but little new for you. yesterday for the first time I discovered that the gooseberry, the lilac & weeping willow were leafing. they might have been so two or three days. the martins appeared here on the 21st of April the last year, & on the same day of the year before at New York. (*Jefferson Papers,* L. C.)

### (Jefferson to Martha (Jefferson) Randolph.)

Philadelphia, March 22d, 1792.

. . . The ensuing year will be the longest of my life, and the last of such hateful labors; the next we will sow our cabbages to-gether. . . . (Randolph, *Jefferson:* 209.)

### (Jefferson to Benjamin Hawkins.)

Philadelphia, April 1, 1792.

At Mrs. Trist's desire I forward to you about a dozen beans of three different kinds, having first taken toll of them as she had done before. They are of the scarlet flowering kind. This is all I know of them. The most beautiful bean in the world is the Caracalla bean which, though in England a green-house plant, will grow in the open air in Virginia and Carolina. I never could get one of these in my life. They are worth your enquiry. (Lipscomb and Bergh, *Jefferson* 19: 93–94.)

### (Jefferson to Martha (Jefferson) Randolph.)

Philadelphia April 6. 1792.

. . . I suppose you are busy in your garden. Shackleford promised me *on his honor* to cover it with manure. has he done it? if not, tell him I have written to enquire. . . . (*Jefferson Papers,* L. C.)

### (Jefferson to Nicholas Lewis.)

Philadelphia, Apr. 12, 1792.

. . . Unremitting business must be my apology, as it is really the true one, for my having been longer without writing to you than my affections dictated. I am never a day without wishing myself with you, and more and more as the fine sunshine comes on, which seems made for all the world but me. . . . (Ford, *Jefferson* 6: 475.)

### (Thomas Mann Randolph to Jefferson.)

Monticello April 16: 1792.

Your letter containing the seeds of the Acacia came safe to Monticello. Patsy and Miss Jane, who have become quite enthusiastic in gardening & Botany, are much pleased with the charge & promise themselves the satisfaction of presenting you the shrub reared by their own hands, in Sept^r. . . . (*Jefferson Papers,* M. H. S.)

(Jefferson to Thomas Mann Randolph.)

Philadelphia, April 19th. 1792.

. . . I am sorry to hear my sugar maples have failed.  I shall be able however to get here any number I may desire, as two nurserymen have promised to make provision for me.  It is too hopeful an object to be abandoned. . . .  (Ford, *Jefferson* 6: 480.)

(Mrs. Martha (Jefferson) Randolph to Jefferson.)

Monticello May 7, 1792.

. . . You will see that I am a much better gardener than last year tho in truth old George is so slow that I shall never shine in that way without your assistance.  Tom has been a man of honour with respect to the manure.  We have had some very high winds here lately one of which blew down 5 large trees, in and about the grove and did some other mischief.  it was accompanied with severe lightning.  the noise of the wind kept us from hearing any thing of the thunder except when it was extremely loud.  we have discovered a very beautiful tree near the lower round a bout a silver fir I believe.  it differs from the common pine in having a smooth green bark and the bottom of their leaves white and much finer than the other. . . .  (*Jefferson Papers*, M. H. S.)

(Jefferson to Elias Vanderhorst.)

Philadelphia May 11. 1792.

I have just received a letter from mr̄ Cathalan of Marseilles informing me [he] had sent by the same vessel to Baltimore 4. casks containing 100. olive trees, and a cask of caper plants, Mr. Sterrett, who happened to be then setting out for Baltimore promised to send them off immediately to Charleston.  I have taken the liberty of having them addressed to you as President of the Agricultural society.  these trees, as well as those sent before are of the best kind of Provence olive, and were intended to furnish slips for grafting.  I do not know how it happens that mr̄ Cathalan has not sent the olive berries for sowing in order to raise stocks, which he was desired to do this being the quickest way of getting into a large stock.

I cannot help taking the liberty of suggesting to the society the expediency of adopting some plan of employing a common labourer at Marseilles to raise plants, and to go annually with them himself through the canal of Languedoc to Bordeau to see them himself put on board a vessel for Charleston, with a quantity of the olive berries, then return to Marseilles to renew his operations.  the whole expense might be 50. guineas a year, & continued for 7. years would fill your state with this most valuable of the productions of the earth. . . .  (*Jefferson Papers*, M. H. S.)

(Jefferson to Doctor George Gilmer.)

Philadelphia May 11. 1792.

. . . I had rather be sick in bed there, than in health here. the next spring we will sow our cabbages together. . . . (*Jefferson Papers,* L. C.)

(Jefferson to George Washington.)

Philadelphia, May 16, 1792.

. . . I have 100 olive trees, and some caper plants, arrived here from Marseilles, which I am sending on to Charleston, where Mr. Pinckney tells me they have already that number living of those I had before sent them. (Ford, *Jefferson* 6: 487.)

(Jefferson to Martha (Jefferson) Randolph.)

Philadelphia, June 22$^d$, 1792.

. . . I suspect, by the account you give me of your garden, that you mean a surprise, as good singers always preface their performances by complaints of cold, hoarseness, etc. . . . (Randall, *Jefferson* 2: 76.)

(Thomas Mann Randolph to Jefferson.)

Monticello June 25. 1792.

. . . The weather for the last fortnight has been very seasonable and our prospects of Indian Corn are now great. Your harvest commenced three days ago: the grain is as fair & the crop as heavy as the land ever bore. . . . (*Jefferson Papers,* M. H. S.)

(Mrs. Martha (Jefferson) Randolph to Jefferson.)

Monticello July 2, 1792.

. . . What I told you of my garden is really true indeed if you see it at a distance it looks very green but it does not bear close examination, the weeds having taken possession of much the greater part of it. Old George is so slow that by the time he has got to the end of his labour he has it all to do over again. 2 of the acacia's are come up and are flourishing. . . . Dear papa the heat is incredible here. the thermometer has been at 96 in Richmond and even at this place we have not been able to sleep comfortably with every door and window open. I dont recolect ever to have suffered as much from heat as we have done this summer. . . . (*Jefferson Papers,* M. H. S.)

(Thomas Mann Randolph to Jefferson.)

Monticello, October 7, 1792.

. . . The frost has been severe on this mountain as high as the lower Roundabout-walk: a few leaves of the sweet-potatoe have felt it in the

Garden but it has been very slight as yet on the summit. . . . (*Jefferson Papers,* M. H. S.)

(Joseph Fay to Jefferson.)

Bennington, October 8, 1792.

I have taken the earliest I can to collect a few of the maple seeds which you will receive herewith by the post; Should the soil of Virginia prove friendly you will soon be able to furnish the State, as they produce very spontaneously. . . . The seeds must be committed to the Earth as soon as convenient this fall in some place where they will not be exposed to be damaged by fowls & squirrels. . . . (*Jefferson Papers,* M. H. S.)

(Jefferson to Charles Cotesworth Pinckney.)

Philadelphia, October 8, 1792.

I found on my return here three days ago, your favor of April 6th, and am happy to learn from it that the Agricultural Society has adopted the plan of employing a person at Marseilles to raise and send olive trees to them annually. Their success in South Carolina cannot be doubted, and their value is great. Olive grounds in France rent higher by the acre than those of any other growth in the Kingdom, which proves they yield the greatest nett produce. Marseilles is the proper place for your nurseryman to be fixed, because it is the neighborhood of the best olives; and Mr. Cathalan the properest person to whom we can commit the whole superintendence, because he is our consul, is concerned in our commerce, eager to extend it, is a good man, a wealthy one, and has offered his services repeatedly in this business. He was brought up in a counting-house in London, is connected there, and therefore I think that the most convenient place on which to enable him to draw for expenditures. This may be either by an annual letter of credit to him on some house there for any sum not exceeding fifty guineas, or a standing letter of credit for that annual sum till your further orders. . . . I am happy that while I was in the olive country I enquired for and procured the best book on the subject of the olive tree, which I now deliver to Mr. Smith for the use of the Society. I suspect that the excrescence on your olive trees, described in your letter, is what they call the leprosy, which prevails among these plants I believe in every country. (Lipscomb and Bergh, *Jefferson* 8: 412–414.)

(Charles C. Pinckney to Jefferson.)

Charleston Nov\(^r\). 13. 1792.

In consequence of your favour of the 8\(^{th}\) of October, the Agricultural Society have directed me to inform you that they will instantly take measures to lodge in the hands of the Mess\(^{rs}\). Bird, Savage, & Bird merchants in London by the first of January in every year for three years certain, & thence every year afterwards till countermanded by the Society the annual sum of Fifty Guineas, to be paid to the order of M[r]. Cathalan to procure Olive Plants for the Society in the mode pointed out by you. M[r]. Peter Smith their Treasurer will remitt by the first vessel a Bill to put Mess[rs]. Bird, Savage & Bird in cash for the ensuing January, & great care will be taken to prevent M[r]. Cathalan being even in advance for the Society. I beg the favour of you to forward the enclosed Letter to M[r]. Cathalan & to direct such a mode for conducting the enterprize as to you may seem best: but the Society would prefer, if possible, the transmitting the plants by ships immediately bound for this port, rather than by vessels destined to other ports of the Continent. The Society have directed me to return you their best thanks for your great attention to the objects of their institution, and for the polite present you have made them of the Traité de l'Olivier par M[r]. Couture which has arrived safe. . . . (*Jefferson Papers*, L. C.)

(Jefferson to Stephen Cathalan.)

Philadelphia, December 2, 1792.

The small essay which has been commenced under your kind assistance for colonizing the olive tree to South Carolina has induced some patriotic gentlemen of that country to turn their attention further toward its importance, and to give to their efforts a more steady and permanent form. I gave it as my opinion to them that the best plan which could be pursued at a moderate expense, would be to rent, near Marseilles, an acre of ground, or say your quarterelle, which is something less than an acre, to employ by the year a laboring man who understands engrafting, to make it his business to sow olives in this ground, to engraft on them cuttings from the best kinds, and to send to Carolina in the winter of every year all the plants he could have in readiness, together with a quantity of the olive berries to be sown in Carolina in order to be engrafted on them.

If before a given day in winter, say the first of January, any ship should be sailing from Marseilles to Charleston, it should be his business to pack properly his olive berries and young plants and put them on board; if no vessel should occur before that, or any more convenient day, it should be his business to proceed himself with his olive berries and plants, through the canal of Languedoc to Bordeaux, there to remain (under the patronage of Fenwick) till a vessel should sail from thence to Charleston, on board of which he should put his cargo and then return to Marseilles to recommence for the next year the same operation of sowing, engrafting, packing and dispatching in the same way to Charleston, the olive berries and plants which he could prepare for that year, and so to continue for a number of years. The first question occurring was to how small a sum can we reduce this expense annually, so as that it may be effected and yet not too sensible a burden on the gentlemen.

I recollect that the price of a quarterelle of the best lands close to Marseilles was one hundred louis, consequently its rent five louis a year. The hire of a laboring man six louis a year, his subsistence, considering he may have to move from Marseilles to Bordeaux, will be more than if he were always stationary, but still, if he uses economy which a man of his condition well understands, it need not exceed fourteen louis a year, and all together twenty-five louis. Therefore, to cover all errors of calculation, accidents and contingencies, I proposed double that sum, to wit: fifty louis. The gentlemen have accordingly appropriated that sum annually.

The second question arising was whom we should engage to manage this business at Marseilles? On this there could be but one opinion, your exertions heretofore, your goodness and your relations to this country marked you as the person whom we must engage to act there, and to their entreaties I must add mine in the most earnest degree. After you shall have put the business under way, that is to say, after you shall have engaged a proper laborer and piece of ground, I hope you will have no other trouble than to receive and pay the wages and rent, and to see the nursery now and then and that the person does his duty. Your reward will be the consciousness of doing good, our thanks, and those of a grateful posterity, nor can any objections arise from the circumstances of your own country, as that imports more oil than it exports, and consequently is interested to increase the quantity produced abroad as well as at home.

I will take it for granted, then, that you will become the father of our olive colony by superintending whatever is necessary to be done on that side the water. The plants will be received and their freight paid at their port of delivery here, which we must entreat to make, in every possible case, the port of Charleston. Great injury and loss happen in shipping and unshipping in warehouses, etc., but when a conveyance to Charleston direct cannot be had without danger of losing the season, then New York or Philadelphia are the next best ports. Baltimore is too uncertain and Norfolk still more so. I enclose you a letter from Charles Cotesworth Pinckney, Esquire, of Charleston, who is chairman of the agricultural society there, which will inform you of the arrangements taken to have the sum of money destined to this object, always under your order.

To his correspondence on the subject I must refer you for the future and to such alterations in my plan as he shall please to direct. It may not be amiss to add annually a few plants of the best figs for drying as also of the best grapes for making what we call "dried raisins", and you, I believe, "des panses;" only taking care that these be really few, so that they may in no wise abridge or interfere with the olives which are the main object. We will take care to procure the patronage of Mr. Fenwick at Bordeaux for so much of the business as must be transacted there.

I have the honor to be, with great and sincere esteem, dear Sir, your most obedient and humble servant. (Lipscomb and Bergh, *Jefferson* 19: 98–101.)

On November 22 Jefferson had written Mr. Jacob Hollings-worth, of Elkton, Maryland, to secure an overseer for *Monticello*. Jefferson received the following letter from Mr. Hollingsworth:

Elkton, 9 Decb[r]. 1792.

Yours of 22 Novb[r] I received and should have answered it sooner, but could not accommodate you with a young man which I thought would suit you until yesterday, when I think I have found one which I have every hopes will, a sartain M[r]. Samuel Biddle who was born with in five miles of me he was brought up to farming by his father who is as neat a farmer as Eny in our neighborhood, and as honest a old gentleman as Eny at all, from charactor, tho his Farm is not large nough to employ his sons as he has a moderat quantoty of negroes now by the industry of his sons, the young man has been an overseear for three years past and I expect nows well how to manage negros tho not in a very harsh manar he says he will undertake to manage them but not with[out] they are reasonably fed & clothed, his terms for a year is forty five pounds if your farm is not more than two hundred miles from this and if more you must pay his traveling expenses from there untill he reaches the farme, and he will be glad to come as soon as possible, if you and he can agree as he expects New years Day is the common time of entering the years business, as he expects to be ready then he desires you will commit your terms to wrighting, and your requests untill he see yous and a full informati of the situation and to know whether its a Quarter or a mentioned House or if the House is reasonably good, and your answer as soon as posable as he will attend here on Satterdy next for it. And I have every hopes from the caractor of his famaly, and knowing his father to have brought him up in the eact mode of farming you want that he will answer every purpose.

Remain your very Humb[l] Serv[t]
Jacob Hollingsworth

(*Jefferson Papers,* M. H. S.)

(Jefferson to Samuel Biddle.)

Philadelphia, Dec. 12, 1792.

Having asked the favor of Mr. Hollingsworth to look out for a person in his neighborhood who would be willing to go to Virginia and overlook a farm for me, he informs me that you will undertake it for a hundred and twenty dollars a year. He seems to have mistaken me in the circumstance of time, as he mentions that you would expect to go about the new year. I had observed to him that I should not want a person till after the next harvest. The person who now takes care of the place is engaged for the ensuing year, which finishes with us about November; but I should wish you to be there by seed time in order to prepare the crop of the following year. The wages are a good deal higher than I expected, as Mr. Hollingsworth mentioned that the usual wages in your neighborhood were from £25. to £30. Maryland currency. However I consent to give them, & the rather as there will be some matters under your care beyond the lines of the farm. I have a smith & some sawyers who will require to be seen once a day, and the first year of your being there I shall have some people employed in finishing a canal, who will also be to be attended to.

The place you are to overlook is that on which I live, & to which I shall return in March next. It is 70 miles above Richmond on the North branch of James River, exactly where it breaks through the first ridge of little mountains, near the village of Charlottesville, in Albemarle County. It is 225 miles from Elkton, a southwest course. From this description you may find it in any map of the country. The climate is very temperate both summer & winter, and as healthy as any part of America, without a single exception.

The farm is of about 5 or 600 acres of cleared land, very hilly, originally as rich as any highlands in the world, but much worried by Indian corn & tobacco. It is still however very strong, & remarkeably friendly to wheat & rye. These will be my first object. Next will be grasses, cattle, sheep, & the introduction of potatoes for the use of the farm, instead of Indian corn, in as great a degree as possible. You will have from 12 to 15 laborers under you. They will be well clothed, and as well fed as your management of the farm will enable us, for it is chiefly with a view to place them on the comfortable footing of the laborers of other countries, that I come into another country to seek an overlooker for them, as also to have my lands a little more taken care. For these purposes I have long banished tobacco, & wish to do the same by Indian corn in a great degree. The house wherein you will live will be about half a mile from my own. You will of course keep batchelor's house. It is usual with us to give a fixed allowance of pork; I shall much rather substitute beef & mutton, as I consider pork to be as destructive an article in a farm as Indian corn. On this head we shall not disagree, and as I shall pass Elkton in March, I will contrive to give you notice to meet me there, when we may descend to other details. But for the present I shall wish to receive your answer in writing, that I may know whether you consider yourself as engaged, so that I need not look out for another. I leave you free as to the time of going, from harvest till Christmas. If you will get yourself conveyed as far as Fredericksburg, which is as far as the stages go on that road, I will find means of conveying you from thence, which will be 70 miles. So far respects the farm over which I wish to place you.

Besides this I have on the opposite side of the little river running through my lands, 2000 acres of lands of the same quality, & which has been cultivated in the same way, which I wish to tenant out at a quarter of a dollar an acre, in farms of such sizes as the tenants would chuse. I would hire the labourers now employed on them from year to year to the same tenants, at about 50 dollars for a man & his wife, the tenant feeding & clothing them & paying their taxes & those of the land, which are very trifling. The lands to be leased for 7 years or more, the laborers only from year to year, to begin next November.  I would like the farms to be not less than 200 acres, because such a farmer would probably like to hire a man & his wife as labourers.  I have mentioned these circumstances to you, because I have understood that tenants might probably be got from Maryland, and perhaps it would be agreeable to you to engage some of your acquaintances to go & settle so near where you will be.  Perhaps you could inform me in what other part of Maryland or the neighboring States tenants might be more probably found, and I should willingly incur the expense of having them sought for.  Your assistance in this would particularly oblige me.  I would ease the rent of the first year, that the tenant might get himself under way with as few difficulties as possible, but I should propose restrictions against cultivating too great a quantity of Indian corn.

In expectation of hearing from you immediately I am, Sir,

Your humble sev<sup>t</sup>,
Th: Jefferson.

P. S.   There is a market for wheat, rye, &c, in two little towns on each side of my lands, neither more than two miles & half distant.  (Massachusetts Historical Collection, *The Jefferson Papers* (Boston, 1900), Seventh Series, 1: 43–46.  Hereafter cited as *Jefferson Papers*, M. H. C.)

The following agreement was drawn up between Jefferson and Mr. Biddle, probably towards the close of the month.  There was no date written in.  Mr. Biddle arrived at the stated time.

It is agreed between m$\overline{r}$ Samuel Biddle & myself that he shall overlook certain parts of my affairs in Virginia as explained in a letter to him Dec. 12, 1792. for which I am to pay him one hundred & twenty dollars a year.  his wages are to begin the 1<sup>st</sup> day of September next, & he is to proceed to Virginia about the middle of October.  he is to carry his bedding.  I promised to provide him half a dozen fly chairs, a table, pot etc.  the carpenters to fix up little conveniences for him, to find him a horse, 5 or 600 w<sup>t</sup>. of pork, or rather mutton etc. equivalent.  (*Jefferson Papers*, M. H. S.)

From the *Account Book 1791–1803:*

May 17.   Francis for earth for garden 8/2.
May 17.   drayage for olive trees 2/6.
May 17.   p<sup>d</sup> Morris for plants 1. D.
May 22.   p<sup>d</sup> drayage of Olive & Caper plants .25.
July   8.   p<sup>d</sup> at Grey's garden .195.

# 1793

Octob.    gave a greendressing of tob°. suckers to the three
          Westernmost squares of the garden, trenching
          them 10.I. deep & 2.f. wide at intervals of 2 feet,
          filling the trenches with green suckers and cover-
          ing them over with earth.

          covered the three terrasses of Asparagus under
          the garden wall with a thick coat of tobacco
          suckers, & on that a thick coat of well rotted dog.²

---

¹ *1793.* Jefferson continued in office as Secretary of State
until the end of this year.   President Washington had urged
him to remain in office longer, but Jefferson was unyielding in
his determination to resign.   He had planned to retire on
September 30, since this was the end of the quarterly accounts
of the Government, but Washington, feeling the need for
more time to select his successor, urged him to stay until December 31.   He agreed to do so, with the permission to go to
*Monticello* during the early fall to look after his private
affairs.   Jefferson and his daughter Maria arrived at *Monticello* on September 25 and remained until October 25.   This
was his only visit to *Monticello* during the year.

This year in many ways was a disagreeable one for Jefferson.   His enemies continued their abuses.   The war between
France and England confronted him with many vexatious
problems of neutrality, and he was involved in a long con-
troversy about Edmond C. Genet, the Minister Plenipotentiary
sent by the new French Republic to the United States.   And
towards the end of the year the fearful outbreak of yellow

fever in Philadelphia killed hundreds of its citizens and drove from the city a large majority of those spared. It was soon after the outbreak of fever that Jefferson and his daughter left Philadelphia for *Monticello*.

There was but one entry in the *Garden Book* for the year. Jefferson was not idle, however, for his letters show that he was making elaborate plans for the development of his farms. He wrote to Mrs. Randolph from Philadelphia on July 7: "My head has been so full of farming since I have found it necessary to prepare a plan for my manager that I could not resist the addressing my last weekly letters to Mr. Randolph and boring him with my plans." Jefferson was enthusiastic about a new model for a threshing machine which he was to receive from Mr. Thomas Pinckney, United States Minister to Great Britain, and showed considerable concern when it was delayed. There is no mention of olives and rice this year. Probably the war between France and England had delayed shipments to such an extent that a passage could not be found for plants.

Mr. Samuel Biddle, of Elkton, Maryland, came to *Monticello* as overseer, succeeding a Mr. Clarkson. After an interview with Mr. Biddle, Jefferson described him in a letter to Mr. Randolph on June 24: "This man is about 30. years of age, of not a very bright appearance, but seems to be docile, so that I hope to get my outlines followed by him." Mr. Biddle stayed at *Monticello* as overseer until November 1 of the succeeding year. The problem of hiring a successful overseer for his different estates was one which Jefferson never solved satisfactorily. On May 14, 1794, soon after his retirement to *Monticello,* he wrote to President Washington, "I find on a more minute examination of my lands than the short visits heretofore made to them permitted, that a ten years' abandonment of them to the ravages of overseers, has brought on them a degree of degradation far beyond what I had expected."

² Since relatively little tobacco is grown in Albemarle County today, this kind of greendressing is not used. This is the first mention that the vegetable garden was divided into squares.

## LETTERS AND EXTRACTS OF LETTERS, 1793

The following letters and extracts of letters show to what extent Jefferson's "head had been so full of farming."

### (Benjamin Hawkins to Jefferson.)

February 1, 1793.

I send you your share of the *bent grass,* so much valued by Mr. Bassett. I have sent the half of the remainder to the President. (*Jefferson Papers,* M. H. S.) [See *Garden Book,* "Objects for the farm, 1794," for mention of this grass.]

### (Jefferson to Thomas Mann Randolph.)

Philadelphia Mar. 3. 1793.

. . . I informed you in my last of a scheme I had of leasing my lands on the Shadwell side of the river. since that I have learned that about the same time two persons from the Head of Elk (the neighborhood where I was endeavoring to procure tenants) set out to examine my lands in order to decide for themselves & report to their neighbors. as they went without any letters from me, I am extremely afraid, as they may get into hands which may mislead them and on their return, throw cold water on an operation which bid fair to succeed to any extent I might have chosen to carry it. I wish my letter to you may have got to hand in time for their arrival. . . . (*Jefferson Papers,* L. C.)

### (Jefferson to Martha (Jefferson) Randolph.)

Philadelphia Mar. 24. 1793.

. . . how do my young chestnut trees? how comes on your garden? how fare the fruit blossoms etc. I sent to mr̄ Randolph, I think, some seed of the Bent-grass which is so much extolled. I now enclose you some seed which mr̄ Hawkins gave me, the name of which I have forgotten: but I dare say it is worth attention. I therefore turn it over to you, as I should hope not to reap what would be planted here. . . . (*Jefferson Papers,* M. H. S.)

### (Jefferson to James Madison.)

Philadelphia, Apr. 28, 1793.

Yours of the 12th inst is received and I will duly attend to your commission relative to the ploughs. We have had such constant deluges of rain & bad weather for some time past that I have not yet been able to go to Dr. Logan's to make the enquiries you desire, but I will do it soon. . . . (Ford, *Jefferson* 7: 301.)

(Jefferson to James Madison.)

Philadelphia, May 5. 93.

No letter from you since that of Apr. 12.—I received one from Mr. Pinckney yesterday informing me he expected to send me by the next ship a model of the Threshing mill. He had been out to see one work, which with 2. horses got out 8. bushels of *wheat* an hour. But he was assured that the mill from which my model was taken gets out 8 quarters (i.e. 64 bushels) of *oats* an hour with 4. horses. I have seen Dr. Logan. Your ploughs will be done in a week & shall be attended to. . . . (Ford, *Jefferson* 7: 307–308.)

(Jefferson to James Madison.)

Philadelphia, May 19, 1793.

. . . I expect every day to receive from Mr. Pinckney the model of the Scotch threshing machine. It was to have come in a ship which arrived three weeks ago, but the workman had not quite finished it. Mr. P. writes me word that the machine from which my model is taken, threshes eight quarters (sixty-four bushels) of oats *an hour,* with four horses and four men. I hope to get it in time to have one erected at Monticello to clean out the present crop. (Lipscomb and Bergh, *Jefferson* 9: 98.)

(Jefferson to Martha (Jefferson) Randolph.)

Philadelphia, May 26, 1793.

. . . We are in sight both of Bartram's & Gray's gardens, but have the river between them & us. . . . (Ford, *Jefferson* 7: 344.)

(Jefferson to James Madison.)

Philadelphia, June 2, 1793.

. . . Bartram is extremely anxious to get a large supply of seeds of the Kentucky Coffee tree. I told him I would use all my interest with you to obtain it, as I think I heard you say that some neighbors of yours had a large number of trees. Be so good as to take measures for bringing a good quantity, if possible, to Bartram when you come to Congress. . . . (Lipscomb and Bergh, *Jefferson* 9: 107.)

(Jefferson to Thomas Mann Randolph.)

Philadelphia, June 2, 1793.

. . . We have had here for a considerable time past true winter weather, quite cold enough for white frost. Though that accident has not happened, fires are still kept up, having been intermitted only for short intervals of very hot weather. I have not yet received my model of the threshing mill. I wish it may come in time for the present crop; after so mild a winter as the last we must expect weavil. . . . (Lipscomb and Bergh, *Jefferson* 9: 109.)

(Jefferson to James Madison.)

Philadelphia, June 9, 1793.

. . . Your ploughs shall be duly attended to. Have you ever taken notice of Tull's horse-houghing plough? I am persuaded that where you wish your work to be very exact, and our great plough where a less degree will suffice, leave us nothing to wish for from other countries as to ploughs, under our circumstances. I have not yet received my threshing machine. I fear the late, long, and heavy rains must have extended to us, and affected our wheat. (Lipscomb and Bergh, *Jefferson* 9: 121.)

(Jefferson to James Madison.)

June, 1793.

. . . The motion of my blood no longer keeps time with the tumult of the world. It leads me to seek happiness in the lap and love of my family, in the society of my neighbors and my books, in the wholesome occupations of my farms and my affairs, in an interest or affection in every bud that opens, in every breath that blows around me, in an entire freedom of rest, of motion, of thought—owing account to myself alone of my hours and actions. . . . (Randolph, *Jefferson:* 218–219.)

(Jefferson to Martha (Jefferson) Randolph.)

Philadelphia, June 10th, 1793.

. . . I sincerely congratulate you on the arrival of the mocking-bird. Learn all the children to venerate it as a superior being in the form of a bird, or as a being which will haunt them if any harm is done to itself or its eggs. I shall hope that the multiplication of the cedar in the neighborhood, and of trees and shrubs round the house, will attract more of them; for they like to be in the neighborhood of our habitations if they furnish cover. . . . (Randolph, *Jefferson:* 221.)

(Jefferson to Gouverneur Morris.)

Philadelphia, June 13, 1793.

. . . Though our spring has been cold and wet, yet the crops of small grain are as promising as they have ever been seen. The Hessian fly, however, to the north, and the weavil to the south of the Potomac, will probably abridge the quantity. . . . (Lipscomb and Bergh, *Jefferson* 9: 125.)

### (Thomas Mann Randolph to Jefferson.)

Monticello June 13: 1793.

You will observe by the abstract of my diary that we have had an uncommon proportion of rainy weather this spring; our fields of wheat and rye from this will give a smaller and a meaner product than we have hitherto expected from them. The plants, where they were late and stood close, have "lodged" as the farmers term it and of course cannot perfect the grain; where this has not happened many of the grains in every head appear to me to be of smaller size than usual, altho' the plants themselves are much larger than the same soil would produce in an ordinary year. There cannot, well, be too much rain for the Indian corn, but the weather has been so cold that it is but little advanced for the season; the last 8 or 10 days however have been so favorable, and it has improved so much in that time, that we expect an abundant *récolte*.

We have not prospered in our garden this year altho, for the first time, our exertions have been sufficiently great. Our young vegetables have been separated from the root under ground by grubs, or eaten in the seed-leaf by a very minute tribe of grasshopper, and two species of still more minute volatile insects, or devoured in whole squares when farther advanced by immence swarms of insects resembling a good deal the fire-fly tho wanting its phosphorus. Having once had some little technical knowledge in Entomology I felt a curiosity to ascertain the families to which these different insects belong but from the insufficiency of Linnaeuses descriptions and the smallness of the subjects I have not been able to satisfy it. The earth is alive with these creatures this summer owing I suppose to their being spared by the frost last winter. . . . (*Jefferson Papers,* M. H. S.)

### (Jefferson to Thomas Mann Randolph.)

Philadelphia June 24. 1793.

. . . The person engaged for me as a manager, came up from Elkton * to see me last week. He is not yet certain on the subject of tenants, his mother, who had decided to go as one, having met an advantageous situation at home, & his cousin, whom I formerly wrote you was gone to see the place, having been intercepted by another offer. He still thinks he shall get some, & is to let me know definitively by the last of August. The time of the tenant's removing in Maryland is not til March. This man is about 30. years of age, of not a very bright appearance, but seems to be docile, so that I hope to get my outlines followed by him. He agrees in condemning Indian corn & hogs, and in preferring the potatoe and clover to every other means of feeding all kinds of stock, even horses. If he does not get tenants for my lands on the East side of the river I shall perhaps propose to Clarkson to go there,

* June 18. p^d Samuel Biddle his expense from & to Elkton 5. D. (*Account Book 1791–1803.*)

unless I could find a person more kind to the labourers & with a smaller family. . . . I begin to be uneasy at not receiving my threshing machine. It cannot now be on time for this harvest.  My fear is that it may have been in some vessel which is captured.  I condole with you on the misfortunes of your garden.  From a feeling of self interest I would propose a great provision of Celery plants to be made.  (Ford, *Jefferson* 7: 409–410.)

(Jefferson to George Washington.)

Philadelphia, June 28, 1793.

I should have taken time ere this to have considered the observations of Mr. Young, could I at this place have done it in such a way as would satisfy either him or myself.  When I wrote the notes of the last year, I had never before thought of calculating what were the profits of a capital invested in Virginia agriculture.  Yet that appeared to be what Mr. Young most desired.  Lest therefore, no other of those, whom you consulted for him, should attempt such a calculation, I did it; but being at such a distance from the country of which I wrote, and having been absent from that and from the subject in consideration many years, I could only, for facts, recur to my own recollection, weakened by time and very different applications, and I had no means here of correcting my facts.  I, therefore, hazarded the calculation rather as an essay of the mode of calculating the profits of a Virginia estate, than as an operation which was to be ultimately relied on.  When I went last to Virginia I put the press-copy of those notes into the hands of the most skilful and successful farmer in the part of the country of which I wrote.  He omitted to return them to me, which adds another impediment to my resuming the subject here; but, indeed, if I had them, I could only present the same facts, with some corrections and some justifications of the principles of calculation.  This would not and ought not to satisfy Mr. Young.  When I return home I shall have time and opportunity of answering Mr. Young's enquiries fully.  I will first establish the facts as adapted to the present times, and not to those to which I was obliged to recur by recollection, and I will make the calculation on rigorous principles.  The delay necessary for this will I hope be compensated by giving something which no endeavors on my part shall be wanting to make it worthy of confidence.  In the meantime Mr. Young must not pronounce too hastily on the impossibility of an annual production of £750 worth of wheat coupled with a cattle product of £125.  My object was to state the produce of a *good* farm, under *good* husbandry as practiced in my part of the country.  Manure does not enter into this, because we can buy an acre of new land cheaper than we can manure an old acre.  Good husbandry with us consists in abandoning Indian corn and tobacco, tending small grain, some red clover following, and endeavoring to have, while the lands are at rest, a spontaneous cover of white clover.  I do not present this as a culture judicious in itself, but as *good* in comparison with what most people there pursue.  Mr. Young has never had an opportunity of seeing how slowly the fertility of the *original soil* is exhausted. With moderate management of it, I can affirm that the James river lowgrounds with the cultivation of small grain, will never be exhausted; because we know that under that cultivation we must now and then take them down with Indian corn, or they become, as they were originally, too rich to bring wheat. The highlands, where I live have been cultivated about sixty years. The culture was tobacco and Indian corn as long as they would bring enough to pay labor. Then they were turned out. After four or five years rest they would bring good corn again, and in double that time perhaps good tobacco. Then they would be exhausted by a second series of tobacco and corn. Latterly we have begun to cultivate small grain; and excluding Indian corn, and following, such of them as were originally good, soon rise up fifteen or twenty bushels the acre. We allow that every laborer will manage ten acres of wheat, except at harvest. I have no doubt but the coupling cattle and sheep with this would prodigiously improve the produce. This improvement Mr. Young will be better able to calculate than anybody else. I am well satisfied of it myself, that having engaged a good farmer from the head of Elk, (the style of farming there you know well,) I mean in a farm of about 500 acres of cleared land and with a dozen laborers to try the plan of wheat, rye, potatoes, clover, with a mixture of some Indian corn with the potatoes, and to push the number of sheep. This last hint I have taken from Mr. Young's letters which you have been so kind as to communicate to me. I have never before considered with due attention the profit from that animal. I shall not be able to put the farm into that form exactly the ensuing autumn, but against another I hope I shall, and I shall attend with precision to the measures of the ground and of the product, which may perhaps give you something to communicate to Mr. Young which may gratify him, but I will furnish the ensuing winter what was desired in Mr. Young's letter of Jan. 17, 1793. . . . (Lipscomb and Bergh, *Jefferson* 9: 139–143.)

(Jefferson to James Madison.)

June 29. 1793.

. . . As I must ere long put my general plan of farming into the hands of my Elkton manager, I have lately endeavored to establish a proper succession of crops for a farm of red highland of about 500. acres of open land fit for culture. in all successions of crops, the feilds must be supposed equal, each feild to go through the same succession, and each year's crop be the same. on these data the laws of combination pronounce that the number of feilds & number of years constituting a compleat rotation, must be always equal. if you cultivate three equal feilds only, your rotation will be of 3. years, 5. feilds. 5 years and I suppose 8 feilds of 60. acres each, & of course an 8. years rotation, in the following succession. $1^{st}$. year wheat & fall fallow. $2^{d}$. peas with $Ind^{n}$. corn thinly planted. $3^{rd}$. wheat & fall fallow. $4^{th}$. potatoes with $Ind^{n}$. corn thinly planted.   5th rye, & fall fallow.   6th. 7th. 8th. red clover.   the following diagram will show the system better, the initials of every article only being written in each square or feild.   to wit.

cl.  for clover
co.  corn
f.   fallow
pe.  peas
po.  potatoes
r.   rye
w.   wheat

|     | 1st. year | 2d. year | 3d. year | 4th. year | 5th. year | 6th. year | 7th. year | 8th. year |
|-----|-----------|----------|----------|-----------|-----------|-----------|-----------|-----------|
| A.  | w. f.     | pe. co.  | w. f.    | po. co.   | r. f.     | cl.       | cl.       | cl.       |
| B.  | pe. co.   | w. f.    | po. co.  | r. f.     | cl.       | cl.       | cl.       | w. f.     |
| C.  | w. f.     | po. co.  | r. f.    | cl.       | cl.       | cl.       | w. f.     | pe. co.   |
| D.  | po. co.   | r. f.    | cl.      | cl.       | cl.       | w. f.     | pe. co.   | w. f.     |
| E.  | r. f.     | cl.      | cl.      | cl.       | w. f.     | pe. co.   | w. f.     | po. co.   |
| F.  | cl.       | cl.      | cl.      | w. f.     | pe. co.   | w. f.     | po. co.   | r. f.     |
| G.  | cl.       | cl.      | w. f.    | pe. co.   | w. f.     | po. co.   | r. f.     | cl.       |
| H.  | cl.       | w. f.    | pe. co.  | w. f.     | po. co.   | r. f.     | cl.       | cl.       |

this gives 2. feilds of wheat                          120 acres
    1.          of rye                          60
    1.          of peas & corn                  60
    1.          of potatoes & corn              60
    1.          of the 1st year's clover        60
    1.                2d      do.               60
    1.                3d      do.               60
                                                              —
                                                             480

also 2. eighths of your farm are cleansing⎫
    3. eighths . . . . . . . . . . . . . fallowing⎬ every year
    3. eighths . . . . . . . . . . . . . resting⎭

    —
    8.

bye articles as follow

    oats & flax, a few acres only wanting.

    to be with the new sown clover.

    hemp, turneps, pumpkins, in the new clearings.

    artichokes in a perpetual feild.

    orchard grass in the hill sides too steep for the plough. qu?

    Lucerne, S$^t$. foin, cotton, in appropriate feilds.

    buckwheat to be ploughed into the washed lands.

As you are now immersed in farming & among farming people, pray consider this plan for me, well, and give me your observations fully & freely as soon as you can.  I mean to ask the same from the President, and also from my son in law.  cattle to be raised in proportion to the provision made for them.  also what number of labourers & horses will be necessary?  errors are so much more easy to avoid than to correct afterwards that I am anxious to be well advised before I begin. . . . (*Jefferson Papers,* L. C.)

## (Jefferson to Thomas Mann Randolph.)

Philadelphia June 30. 1793.

. . . My last letter to you was on the subject of my farm.  this will be so also.  the approach of the season of preparation for another year has rendered it necessary for me to consider for some time past what is to be the plan of farming I am to take up, and to give to my new manager for his government.  I will suppose my farm at Monticello to furnish 500. acres of land open, and capable of producing.  in all successions of crops, the fields must be supposed equal, each feild to go through the same succession, & each year's crop to be the same.  these fundamentals being laid down, the laws of combinations decide inflexibly that the number of feilds, & number of years constituting the compleat rotation must be always equal.  if your rotation is of 3. years, you must have 3. feilds, if of 5. years 5. feilds etc.  I propose to adopt the following rotation.  1$^{st}$. year, wheat & fall-fallow.  2$^d$. peas with Indian corn thinly interspersed.  3$^{rd}$. wheat & fall fallow.  4$^{th}$. potatoes with Indian corn thinly interspersed.  5$^{th}$. rye, or barley and a fall fallow.  6$^{th}$. 7$^{th}$. 8$^{th}$. red clover.  this occupying 8. years, will require 8. feilds, which of course will be of 60. acres each.  the following diagram will shew the system better.  the initials of every article only being written in each square or feild.  to wit.

    cl.  for clover

    co.  - - corn

    f.   - - fallow

    pe.  - - peas

    po.  - - potatoes

    r.   - - rye or barley

    w.  - - wheat

|   | 1st. year | 2d. year | 3d. year | 4th. year | 5th. year | 6th. year | 7th. year | 8th. year |
|---|---|---|---|---|---|---|---|---|
| A. | w. f. | pe. co. | w. f. | po. co. | r. f. | cl. | cl. | cl. |
| B. | pe. co. | w. f. | po. co. | r. f. | cl. | cl. | cl. | w. f. |
| C. | w. f. | po. co. | r. f. | cl. | cl. | cl. | w. f. | pe. co. |
| D. | po. co. | r. f. | cl. | cl. | cl. | w. f. | pe. co. | w. f. |
| E. | r. f. | cl. | cl. | cl. | w. f. | pe. co. | w. f. | po. co. |
| F. | cl. | cl. | cl. | w. f. | pe. co. | w. f. | po. co. | r. f. |
| G. | cl. | cl. | w. f. | pe. co. | w. f. | po. co. | r. f. | cl. |
| H. | cl. | w. f. | pe. co. | w. f. | po. co. | r. f. | cl. | cl. |

this gives 2. fields of wheat       120. acres
      1.       rye or barley       60.
      1.       peas & corn       60.
      1.       potatoes & corn       60.
      1.       of 1st. year's clover       60.
      1.       of 2d.    do. - -       60.
      1.       of 3d.    do. - -       60.

                                    480.

thus also
  2. eighths of the farm are cleansing⎫
  3. eighths ............. fallowing⎬ every year
  3. eighths ............ resting  ⎭
  ――
  8

the following bye-articles.
  oats & flax. a few acres only wanting. to be with the new sown
    clover.
  Hemp, turneps, pumpkins. in the new clearings.
  Artichokes in a perpetual feild.
  Orchard grass in the hill sides too steep for the plough. qu?
  Lucerne, St. foin in appropriate feilds.
  Buckwheat to be ploughed into worn lands.

When a 9th feild shall be added by new clearings, insert it in the rotation, as a feild of absolute rest, or pasture, or fallow. so of a 10th.

feild etc. such a farm will well maintain 150. cattle, which properly attended to will make manure enough for one feild every year. I suppose 5 ploughs & pair of horses, will do the business of such a farm, as in the throngest season, which is that of seeding & fallowing, there will be 6. feilds (say 360. acres) to plough. I have troubled you with these details with a view to trouble you further to give me your observations fully & freely on all the particulars. I am too little familiar with the practice of farming to rely with confidence on my own judgment, and in engaging in a plan of rotation it is material to set out right, as it is so much easier to correct a mis-combination before it is begun, than after one is embarked in it. I am asking the observations of 2. or 3. other friends in like manner and on receiving the whole, shall proceed to fix my rotation permanently, and put it into the hands of my manager. the produce of an acre of peas, *in drills,* (because it is to cleanse the ground) I am unacquainted with. also what number of constant hands will suffice for such a farm, supposing them men & women in equal numbers? I presume that each may be substituted for half the horses. I will ask as early an answer to this as you can give satisfactorily. . . . (*Jefferson Papers,* L. C.)

## (Jefferson to Dr. George Logan.)

July 1. 1793.

Th: Jefferson presents his friendly compliments to Dr. Logan. having engaged a good farmer to go and put one of his plantations in Virginia into a regular course of farming & being about to give him his plans, he takes the liberty of submitting it to Dr. Logan, in whose experience & judgment he has great confidence. he begs him to favor him with his observations on it, freely & as fully in writing as his leisure will permit. he is himself but a tyro in agriculture, and it being of great importance to set out right in plans *de longue haleine,* he hopes it will be his excuse with Dr. Logan for the trouble he gives him. what number of constant labourers (men & women in equal number) would not a farm require?—if sheep, instead of cattle should be made the principal object, what number of sheep are equivalent to a given number of cattle old & young, for making manure? Th: J. is desirous of substituting sheep for cattle to as great an extent as a true calculation of interest will admit. Mr. Young's writings are so voluminous one cannot think of buying the whole. which of them must one buy, in order to have every thing useful which he has written? for it is apprehended that many of his volumes are mere repetitions of that is to be found in the others. (*Jefferson Papers,* L. C.)

## (Jefferson to Martha (Jefferson) Randolph.)

Philadelphia, July 7th, 1873.

. . . My head has been so full of farming since I have found it necessary to prepare a place for my manager, that I could not resist the addressing my last weekly letters to Mr. Randolph and boring him with my plans. . . . I never before knew the full value of trees. My house is entirely embossomed in high plane-trees, with good grass below; and under them I breakfast, dine, write, read, and receive my company. What would I not give that the trees planted nearest round the house at Monticello were full-grown. (Randolph, *Jefferson:* 221–222.)

(Thomas Mann Randolph to Jefferson.)

Monticello July 11, 1793.

. . . I send you now the scheme of cultivation which I formed last year and am adopting at Edgehill. . . . You will observe that it differs from yours in four principal points. First there are two distinct systems intended to be coexistent. $2^d$. the years of rest are not successive. $3^{rd}$. white clover is substituted for red; (a consequence of the

| | $1^{st}$. | $2^d$. | $3^d$. | $4^{th}$. | $5^{th}$. | $6^{th}$. | $7^{th}$. | $8^{th}$. | Years |
|---|---|---|---|---|---|---|---|---|---|
| No. 1. | Corn & Peas | Wheat | Fallow | Wheat | Pasture | Corn & Potatoes | Rye | Pasture | |
| 2. | Wheat | Fallow | Wheat | Pasture | Corn & Potatoes | Rye | Past. | Corn & Peas | |
| 3. | Fallow | Wheat | Past. | Corn & Potatoes | Rye | Past. | Corn & Peas | Wheat | |
| 4. | Wheat | Pasture | Corn & Potatoes | Rye | Past. | Corn & Peas | Wheat | Fall. | Fields of 60 acres |
| 5. | Pasture | Corn & Potatoes | Rye | Past. | Corn & Peas | Wheat | Fall. | Wheat | |
| 6. | Corn & Potatoes | Rye | Past. | Corn & Peas | Wheat | Fall. | Wheat | Past. | |
| 7. | Rye | Past. | Corn & Peas | Wheat | Fall. | Wheat | Past. | Corn & Potatoes | |
| 8. | Pasture | Corn & Peas | Wheat | Fallow | Wheat | Past. | Corn & Potatoes | Rye | |

|       | 1st. | 2d. | 3d. | 4th. | 5th. | 6th. | Years |
|-------|------|-----|-----|------|------|------|-------|
| No. 1. | Pumpkins | Barley | Clover | Clover | Turnips | Oats | |
| 2. | Barley | Clover | Clover | Turnips | Oats | Pumpkins | |
| 3. | Clover | Clover | Turnips | Oats | Pumpkins | Barley | Fields of 10 acres |
| 4. | Clover | Turnips | Oats | Pumpkins | Barley | Clover | |
| 5. | Turnips | Oats | Pumpkins | Barley | Clover | Clover | |
| 6. | Oats | Pump. | Barley | Clover | Clover | Turnips | |

2ᵈ.) 4ᵗʰ. one field undergoes a summer fallow. I shall endeavor in my next to give my reasons for these. The system for small fields I think you will adopt. The other & yours I myself am ballancing. Besides the division of my farms which this scheme will require I have set aside a well-watered valley for a standing meadow. It is necessary to break up meadow grounds once in 5 or 6 years, & this 5ᵗʰ. or 6ᵗʰ. part of mine ruled[?] for hemp & flax which, with us, thrive no where so well as in the flat grounds on our little streams. You will see that they are not included in the rotation. Lucerne & St. Foin are too long-lived for it. The fields marked pasture I suppose to have nothing in them that is not spontaneous, but there I mean to introduce the white clover generally as soon as possible by sowing it in the autumn with the grain. The red clover you observe I prefer sowing with the Barley in Autumn. This may be necessary in every soil but in ours I am convinced it will do better than in the spring. I suppose it to be intended alltogether for the Scythe. . . .

*(Jefferson Papers,* M. H. S.)

### (Jefferson to Martha (Jefferson) Randolph.)

Philadelphia, July 21st, 1793.

. . . We had peaches and Indian corn on the 12th inst. When do they begin with you this year? Can you lay up a good stock of seed-peas for the ensuing summer? We will try this winter to cover our garden with a heavy coating of manure. When earth is rich it bids defiance to droughts, yields in abundance, and of the best quality. I suspect that the insects which have harassed you have been encouraged by the feebleness of your plants; and that has been produced by the lean state of the soil. We will attack them another year with joint efforts. (Randolph, *Jefferson:* 222.)

### (Jefferson to Thomas Mann Randolph.)

Philadelphia July 28. 1793.

. . . I am availing myself of the time I have to remain here, to satisfy myself by enquiring from the best farmers of all the circumstances which may decide on the best rotation of crops; for I take that to be the most important of all the questions a farmer has to decide. I get more information on this subject from Dr. Logan than from all the others put together. he is the best farmer in Pensylvᵃ. both in theory & practice, having pursued it many years experimentally & with great attention. he thinks that the whole improvement in the modern agriculture of England consists in the substitution of red clover instead of unproductive fallows. he says that a rotation which takes in 3 years of red clover instead of 3. years of fallow or rest, whether successive or interspersed leaves the land much heartier at the close of the rotation; that there is no doubt of this fact, the difference being palpable. he thinks it much best to sow it alone after harvest, for then it is in it's prime the next year, whereas if sown in the spring it can neither be cut nor pastured that year. he takes generally but the spring cutting, which yeilds him 2. tons to the acre, & pastures the rest of the year. it is the red clover alone which has enabled the English farmer to raise and maintain cattle enough to make a coat of dung a regular part of his rotation. I had at first declined the introduction of red clover into my rotation because it lengthens it so much: but I have determined now to take it in, because I see it the source of such wonderful richness around this place, and for a Virginia table it will certainly give unbounded plenty of meats, milk, butter, horse-food, instead of being eternally on the scramble for them as we are in Virginia for the want of winter & summer food. Dᵣ. Logan considers a green-dressing of buckwheat as equal to a coat of 10. loads of dung to the acre. (20 loads to the acre is what he thinks a good coat.) and as it is but 5. weeks from the sowing to it's being fit to plough in, it may be well introduced after a harvest of small grain, if your next crop is only to be put in in the spring. after a great deal of consultation therefore with him, we have arranged my rotation thus. 1ˢᵗ. year. a crop of Wheat. then a green dressing of buckwheat. 2ᵈ. peas & corn mixed. 3ᵈ. wheat, & after it a green dressing of buckwheat, and, in the succeeding winter put on what dung you have. 4ᵗʰ. potatoes & corn mixed. 5ᵗʰ. rye, & after it sow red clover. 6ᵗʰ. cut the 1ˢᵗ. crop of clover & pasture the 2ᵈ. 7ᵗʰ. pasture the 1ˢᵗ. crop, and cut the 2ᵈ. this change gives spring pasture and eases the mowing. 8ᵗʰ. pasture. or expressed more shortly

| 1. | 2. | 3. | 4. | 5. | 6. | 7. | 8. |
|---|---|---|---|---|---|---|---|
| w. bu. | pe. co. | w. bu. d. | po. co. | r. cl. | cl. pa. | pa. cl. | pa. |

he observes that if it were not for the want of the 8ᵗʰ. year's pasture, the rotation might close the 7ᵗʰ. year, and would then be clear of weeds & produce the heaviest crop of wheat possible: but he thinks the rotation will need the pasture of the 8ᵗʰ year, and that this will introduce so many weeds as to render an extra ploughing requisite. supposing the feilds of 60. acres each, this rotation gives you 9 times 60. acres, say 540. acres to plough between harvest and the end of seed-time, which I think may be done by 6. ploughs with a pair of oxen each, especially if 4. waggon horses are kept and called in to the aid of the ploughs a part of the fall. the President thinks that when corn & potatoes are mixed (in drills 8. f. apart, & the stalks of corn 8. f. apart in the drill) that as much is made from each as the same number of plants would yeild if alone. Logan reckons 300. bushels of potatoes to the acre an average crop, & 2. bushels of potatoes to yeild as much nutriment as one of corn. he allows a bushel of potatoes a day to a fattening ox, & a peck a day to a work horse, mixing a handful of bran, or rye-meal with each to give it flavor.—he considers the above rotation to be the best possible, where you are confined to the articles there mentioned, and that the land will improve very much under it. he has promised however to study it still more fully for me, so that something further may be yet done to it. the winter-spewing of our land may prevent sowing the clover in the fall of the 5$^{th}$. year. D$^r$. Logan is making some experiments to determine what number of sheep are equivalent to a given number of cattle as to the articles of dung, food etc. I am at loss what standing force will be sufficient for such a rotation. taking gangs of half men & half women, as with us, I guess we must allow a hand for every 5. acres constant of each feild, say 12. hands if the feilds are of 60. acres each.—you see how much my mind is gone over to the business of a farmer, for I never know when to finish, if once I begin on the subject. . . . (*Jefferson Papers,* L. C.)

### (Thomas Mann Randolph to Jefferson.)

Monticello July 31: 1793.

I prepare now to give you some reasons according to my promise for my preference of the plan of cultivation I transmitted you 3 weeks since to the one you did me the honor to consult me on.

The system of small fields in my plan is nothing more than an extension of method beyond what you thought requisite in farming. The crops of this rotation, although of small value comparatively are yet worth methodical treatment on the following principle, if on no other. From the diversity of constitution in plants, some are injured while others are benefited in the same stage of growth, by great heats or colds, by excessive moisture or droughts. The weather every day in the year, must be the most favorable that can be, for some particular crop. Again, there are few plants which have exactly the same length of life, or which flourish exactly in the same season: hence by a judicious arrangement the operations of sowing their seeds and gathering their fruits may be carried on without interference. The cultivation of a great variety of crops[?] will ensure a plenty. A perpetual seed time will make a perpetual harvest. Thus many plants are worthy of regular cultivation, which are of no value in the market, and cannot in consequence be introduced into the great system with propriety, as the equality of the fields is indispensable. Peas and Potatoes are of this Class, and ought not to keep their place among the corn if they are not greatly serviceable in preventing the working of the land. Your plan gives 3 successive years of rest in every 8, to each field, mine, the same number at intervals. For the preference I give the latter I have two or three reasons. Three years of rest successive to land full of the roots of trees must occasion considerable trouble in grubbing & clearing up to prepare for a crop at the end of that time. Our mountain land is so extremely prone to throw out the Tulip Tree, the Locust, the Hickory, and Sassafras, that after one year of rest, if it be not exhausted, a great deal of grubbing is requisite. After three, the labor of cleaning would be unsuccessful. The soil is so compact & so much the worse allways for being trodden, that a field after being grazed 3 years would probably yield a trifling crop at first if it did not get the very best tillage. These objections would be aleviated by sowing the land with Red Clover, and shutting it up for the Scythe, which would keep down the young trees, but I question whether this could be done readily to such an extent. Supposing it determined that the years of rest should be successive; I think it would be better to sow the white clover than the red, unless the force on the farm be sufficient to prepare 60 acres annually for the Scythe. The red clover is liable to be extirpated by the bite and treading of animals, the white bears grazing extremely well. The red clover would require to be sown annually in one of the fields of the farm; the white when once established would perpetuate itself; let it be eaten as closely as possible it perfects its seeds in so short a time, that it will allways keep the earth well stocked, and will spring again the moment the field is out of cultivation. The red clover indeed, affords a much greater quantity of food, and I believe will bear much better the want of rain, which is an immense advantage with us. This is the best on a small farm under exact management, the other does better for large fields and a loose agriculture.

With respect to the summer fallow, I know it is thought injudicious to expose bare, to the summer sun, but it will never be bare I think, there will allways be a coat of weeds to shelter it, and there is a considerable advantage in this, that it will divide the business of breaking up the ground, between Autumn and Spring. The field, which is to go from rest immediately into wheat in my plan, may receive the first ploughing in Spring. Those which are to bear corn with Peas & Potatoes, must be broken up as soon as the seed time is over. If I understand your system, one of the fields destined for wheat will be ploughed the first time, between harvest and seed-time, and will be sown immediately after. Would not this be inconvenient, as that season is rendered the busiest in the year by our apprehension of the weevil? Wheat after Red Clover would not succeed I fear, unless a fallow intervenes, to give the clover time to rot. This may be remedied at once, if a remedy be found requisite, by sowing the clover on the rye. Six months may be thought gained in the age of the clover, and in consequence a fallow of six months or seven may precede the wheat. If sown in the fall it will give one, perhaps two crops of hay the next summer; after the Rye is taken off, and 2 or 3 each summer following for 2 years; after which it will be worth little. I saw a field of clover seed ready for the Scythe a fortnight ago which had been sown upon barley last fall. When sown in the Spring, it never I believe, yields a tolerable crop of hay that summer. . . . (*Jefferson Papers*, M. H. S.)

## (Jefferson to Thomas Mann Randolph.)

Philadelphia Aug. 11. 1793.

. . . Biddle, my new manager, writes me from Elkton, that the persons who had it in contemplation to go & tenant my lands, will not engage till they go to see them which they will do in the fall. I must therefore take measures for going on with their culture myself the next year: & as I have engaged Biddle for Monticello, I must get you to announce it to Clarkson, and offer him the plantations over the river, on the terms given him for Monticello. this removal may be rendered palateable to him by being told it is the effect of my resolution to put Monticello into a farm on the plan of this country, with which he will know he is unacquainted. if he determines to quit altogether, and you can find any good overlooker for the plantations I must trouble you to engage one on any terms (not involving the payment of *money*) which you may think advisable. I must also trouble you to direct such sowings of small grain on both sides the river as you shall think best, & in good season, which overseers, about to remove, are apt to put off. if Clarkson goes to Shadwell, he will of course see to the sowings on that side himself. Biddle will be at Monticello about the middle of October.

Your reasons for a rotation of bye-articles in a set of small feilds are perfectly sound. nothing is more prudent than to vary articles of culture in order to have something to meet the varying seasons of the year. —my letter of the 28th. will have informed you of some alterations proposed in my rotation. the difference between your's and mine is the 3. years of clover (by which term I always meant *red* clover) instead of 3. years of rest or fallow; and this depends on the great problem of the clover husbandry. I did not at first propose to adopt it, because it lengthens the rotation so much. but further reflection, & observation here on it's great & palpable advantages, determined me to attempt it. my not explaining that by the term clover I always meant the *red,* left a just opening for the objection that three years of clover would produce a strong and troublesome growth of bushes. every year, in my rotation comes either the plough or the scythe through every feild; except the 8th. year, and I have considerable hopes I can lop off that year from the rotation altogether by other resources for pasture.—one difficulty you suggest is a very great one indeed, that I shall have too much ploughing in the fall, considering how busy a season our apprehensions of the weavil make that. I found considerable hopes on the threshing machine expected, as 4. horses suffice to work that, & I had proposed to work my ploughs with oxen. should that machine fail, more horses must be kept for treading wheat in the proper season, & to be employed in waggoning at other times. or the raising horses for sale must be gone into so as to derive assistance in treading a year or two before they are sold. still these are but conjectual remedies for the difficulty, which are by no means certain in their effect.—on revising my letter of the 28th. ult. I find I have illy expressed the President's method of mixing corn & potatoes. he puts them in alternate drills, 4 f. apart, so that the rows of corn are 8. f. apart, & a single stalk every 18. I. or 2. f. in the row. Judge Peters, an excellent farmer in this neighborhood, tells me he has taken this method from the President, and has generally made 40. bush. of corn & 120. bush. of potatoes to the acre, strictly measured. I propose the mixture because unless this or some other mode of cultivating corn can be found which may prevent it's ravages in our land, I should decline it's culture altogether. still our habits in favor of that plant render it eligible to try to reconcile the saving our lands with some degree of corn-culture. perhaps your idea of dressing our grounds absolutely flat, without hills or ridges, may be adopted for the corn, potatoes, & peas. mr D. Randolph discorages me as to the last article by the difficulty of gathering them. I receive encoragement from him in the article of manure, of which he tells me he makes from 7. to 10. loads for every head of cattle. this corroborates Dr. Logan's experiment according to which 150. cattle will manure 60. acres a year. however should we fall short in this, I rely on supplying it by green dressings of buckwheat. . . . (*Jefferson Papers, L. C.*)

(Thomas Mann Randolph to Jefferson.)

Monticello Aug: 14: 1793.

. . . We have had a very long drought, which has injured the Indian corn greatly. The crop will be less by a 4th. or perhaps a 3d. than was expected some weeks ago. It has probably been of service in checking the weevil, which appeared very early but has scarcely increased fast enough to give alarm.

One of the Italians whom Mazzei brought over, Giovannini, applied to me lately for a farm of 30 or 40 acres on Edgehill which he says he can cultivate and yet devote at least three days a week to a garden. He is an excellent gardener and one of the most sober, industrious men I ever knew. I mention this to you, thinking that you might perhaps be inclined to take him on those terms yourself. If you do not I shall take him without hesitation as I know he can cultivate a garden of considerable size & have half the week to spare. . . . (*Jefferson Papers, M. H. S.*)

(Jefferson to Samuel Biddle.)

Philadelphia August 30. 1793.

I duly received your letter of the 1st inst. I expect to leave this place on the 5th. or 6th. of October & to be on the afternoon of the next at mr Hollingsworth's, at Elkton, where I shall be glad to see you. I shall then proceed directly home, and with you to take measure for meeting me there as quickly after my arrival as possible, because, instead of remaining there as I expected, I find that after about three weeks stay I shall be obliged to come back to Philadelphia, and shall not be fixed at home again till the next year. it will be important for my own settlement as well as for arranging the crops of the ensuing year, that you should pass as much as possible of the three weeks stay I make at home. . . . (*Jefferson Papers, L. C.*)

(Jefferson to James Madison.)

Philadelphia, September 1, 1793.

. . . My threshing machine has arrived at New York. Mr. Pinckney writes me word that the original from which this model is copied, threshes 150 bushels of wheat in 8 hours, with 6 horses and 5 men. It may be moved either by water or horses. Fortunately the workman who made it (a millwright) is come in the same vessel to settle in America. I have written to persuade him to go on immediately to Richmond, offering him the use of my model to exhibit, and to give him letters to get him into immediate employ in making them. . . . I understand that the model is made mostly in brass, and in the simple form in which it was first ordered, to be worked by horses. It was to have cost 5. guineas, but Mr. Pinckney having afterwards directed it to be accommodated to water movement also, it has made it more complicated, and costs 13 guineas. It will thresh any grain from the Windsor bean down to the smallest. . . . (Lipscomb and Bergh, *Jefferson* 9: 214–215.)

(Jefferson to Thomas Mann Randolph.)

Philadelphia, September 2, 1793.

. . . My threshing machine is arrived at New York, and will be here this week. Mr. Pinckney writes me that the model from which my model is taken, gets out 150. bushels of wheat in 8. hours with 6. horses and 5. men. It will thresh any grain from the Windsor-bean to the milled, and may be moved by horses or water. . . . The character you give Giovannini is a just one. He is sober, industrious & honest. He lived with me as a gardener sometime before I went to Europe, however I shall find it necessary to have a gardener constantly at his business, and think to teach a negro at once. . . . (Ford, *Jefferson* 8: 17–18.)

(Jefferson to Thomas Mann Randolph.)

Germantown, Nov. 2. 93.

. . . Mr. Hollingsworth at the head of Elk thinks he can immediately send me on a good overseer in the place of Rogers. I authorized him to allow exactly the same as to Biddle. Consequently on his arrival I must get you to give him orders on Watson & Colo. Bell for the same necessaries which I have furnished to Biddle. . . . (Ford, *Jefferson* 8: 58.)

(Jefferson to David Howell.)

Germantown, Nov. 14, 1793.

. . . I sincerely wish you success, and shall be greeted with the tidings of it in the retirement into which I mean to withdraw at the close of the present year.   it will be the second time my bark will have put into port with a design not to venture out again; & I trust it will be the last.   my farm, my family & my books call me to them irresistably.   I do not know whether you are a farmer, but I know you love your family & your books, and will therefore bear witness to the strength of their attractions. . . . (Charles Francis Jenkins, *Jefferson's Germantown Letters* (Philadelphia, 1906): 84.   Hereafter cited as Jenkins, *Jefferson's Letters.*)

(Jefferson to Jacob Hollingsworth.)

Germantown, near Philadelphia, Nov. 22, 1793.

When I passed your home last, you told me you thought there would be to be bought there red clover seed, fresh and cheap.   I take the liberty to enclose you a twenty dollar bill * & to beg the favor of you to lay it out for me in as much fresh clover seed as it will buy, and to give the seed in charge to the overseer whom you shall be so good as to employ for me.   to be carried on with him.   Not having yet heard from you on that subject I am apprehensive you have found more difficulty than you expected, lest the terms should have escaped our memory I was to give Saml. Biddle 120. dollars a year, & 5 or 600 lbs. of fresh pork.   when he arrived there, as it had been too far to carry heavy things, & to save him the expense of buying, I had made for him a half dozen chairs, table, bedstead & such other things as my own workmen could make.   he carried his own bedding & small conveniences.   this is sufficient to serve as a guide with the person now to be employed. (Jenkins, *Jefferson's Letters:* 107.)

(Jefferson to Archibald Stuart.)

Germantown Nov. 24. 1793.

When I had the pleasure of seeing you at Monticello you mentioned to me that sheep could be procured at or about Staunton, good & cheap, and were kind enough to offer your aid in procuring them.   Reflecting on this subject, I find it will be much better to buy & drive them now, before they have young ones, & before the snow sets in, than to wait till spring.   I therefore take the liberty of enclosing you a 40. Doll. bank post note,† which I will beg the favor of you to lay out for me in sheep,

* ["Nov. 21. inclosed to Jacob Hollingsworth the bank bill for 20. D." (*Account Book 1791–1803.*)]

† ["Nov. 22.  gave order on bank of US. for 40. D. in a post bill to be remitted to A. Stewart [Stuart] to buy sheep."  "Nov. 24.  inclosed to A. Stewart [Stuart] a bank post note for 40. D. to buy sheep." (*Account Book 1791–1803.*)]

taking time between the purchase & delivery, to give notice to Mr. Randolph at Monticello to have them sent for, the letter to be directed to him, or in his absence to Samuel Biddle overseer at Monticello. . . . What apology must I make for so free a call on you?  And what thanks & apology for the use I made of your friendly offer as to the potatoes? But I am again a new beginner in the world, & it is usual for *old* settlers to help *young* ones. . . . (Ford, *Jefferson* **8**: 76–77.)

### (Jefferson to Thomas Mann Randolph.)

Germantown, Nov. 24, 1793.

. . . I am sorry you have so much trouble with my furniture.  However I shall soon be able to relieve you from any drudgery.  I enclose you a letter to Mr. Stewart, open, that you may see its contents, & give the necessary directions to Mr. Biddle to go or send for the sheep when notified that they are ready.  I think it important that they should be fetched before the snows.  (Jenkins, *Jefferson's Letters:* 118.)

### (Jefferson to Thomas Mann Randolph.)

Philadelphia Dec. 8. 1793.

. . . A person of the name of Eli Alexander is engaged for me at Elk, as overseer on the East side of the river.  he will set out this day week. I am to furnish him the same conveniences which I did to m̄r Biddle. be pleased therefore to desire the latter to have made immediately a bedstead & table, and to bespeak half a dozen chairs of Fitch.  also to have the house in which Rogers lived, put into habitable condition.  I mean as soon as I can to remove the Overseer's residence up to Hickman's. the other small utensils which were furnished to m̄r Biddle, may be got from the stores after Alexander's arrival, which will probably be but a few days before mine.  he had better employ his force at Shadwell as much as he can till I come, because I mean to reform the feilds at the upper place this winter. . . . (*Jefferson Papers,* L. C.)

### (Jacob Hollingsworth to Jefferson.)

Elkton 13 Decbʳ 1793.

Yours of 21 Novbʳ received [?] with twenty dollars for to buy Clover seed, and yours of 4 Decbʳ. with Direction for Mʳ Alexander who will go agreeable to appointment, and respecting the Clover seed I can supply you with and send it by Mʳ Alexander at Nine Dollars a Bushel and no less its of the Last years Seed which I think Equal to New, perhaps the New will be Cheaper but as it will not be thrashed until Janʸ or Febrʸ it will be too late for your purpose; if you chose I will forward two Bushels by Mʳ Alexander, your answer respecting it. . . . (*Jefferson Papers,* M. H. S.)

(Jefferson to Jacob Hollingsworth.)

Philadelphia, Dec. 17. 1793.

I received yesterday your favor of the 13th. & accept willingly the offer of the clover seed at the price you mention.  I hope mr̄ Alexander will be setting out by the time you receive this, as the place he is to overlook must be suffering much for want of him. . . . (*Jefferson Papers,* L. C.)

(Jacob Hollingsworth to Jefferson.)

Elkton 24 Decbr. 1793.

Yours received and agreeable to request have bought the Clover seeds two Bushels at Eighteen Dollars and this afternoon Mr Alexander is to set sail from Fricktown [= Fredericktown] with the seeds for Richmond.   he would have started sooner but was Disappointed by the post. . . . (*Jefferson Papers,* M. H. S.)

From the *Account Book 1781–1803:*

Apr.  28.    pd̄ ¼ of my subscription for Michaud's journey to Pacific sea 12.5.
Mar.  25.    12 lb. clover seed 2. D.
Dec.  20.    4 lb. lucerne seed 10/ and other seed 2/6 = 1.67.

# 1794

Objects for the garden this year.[2]

| Peas. Charlton | Lettuce.[10] cabbage | squashes [19] |
|---|---|---|
| Marrow-fat | Cos. | potato pumpk[n].[20] |
| green for soup. | longleaved | melons citron [21] |
| Beans. Windsor, brown | Endive.[11] curled | pineapple [22] |
| Lima [3] | winter | green |
| Mazareen [4] | radishes. | Venice |
| Alleghaney [5] | celery solid | Water |
| Snap. | parsley | strawberries |
| Cabbage | spinach | goose berries |
| Cauliflower | cresses mount[n].[12] | currans |
| Broccoli | nasturtium | vines Malesherb.[23] |
| turneps [6] | sorrel French [13] | artichokes |
| carrots | shalots [14] | pomegran[tes]. |
| parsneps | leeks.[15] | figs. |
| Jerusalem artichoke. | garlick [16] | hops.[24] |
| Indian potato [7] | onions | |
| beet. | white mustard [17] | |
| salsafia | cucumb[rs]. forw[d]. | |
| horse radish.[8] | long green [18] | |
| peendars [9] | | |

| Objects for the garden this year.[2] | | Objects for the farm. |
|---|---|---|
| sage [25] | Lilac. | Lucern [55] |
| balm [26] | jasmine white [40] | S[t]. foin [56] |
| mint [27] | yellow [41] | Burnet [57] |
| thyme.[28] | honeysuckle.[42] | red clover [58] |
| lavender [29] | althaea [43] | white clover [59] |
| marjoram [30] | gelder rose [44] | white bent grass.[60] |
| camomile [31] | dble bloss[d] almond [45] | corn. forw[d] yellow.[61] Mar.'s |
| tansey [32] | red maple | forw[d] white. |
| rue [33] | Lombardy poplar [46] | Indian peas. French. |
| wormwood [34] | Balsam poplar [47] | Wild pea |
| southernwood [35] | Weeping willow [48] | horsebean.[62] |
| rosemary [36] | Willow oak [49] | buckwheat [63] |
| hyssop [37] | Ground oak [50] | Irish potato |
| perywinkle | Kentuckey coffee [51] | Spring wheat [64] |
| marshmellow [38] | Missouri Laurus [52] | Dry rice [65] |
| beargrass.[39] | Paccan. | |
| | furze.[53] | |
| | Spanish broom [54] | |
| | Calycanthus | |
| | roses | |

208

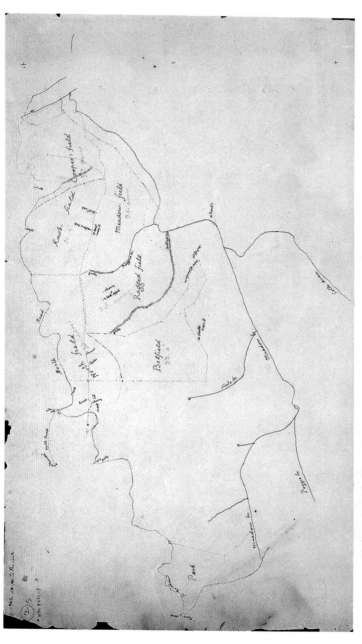

PLATE XIII.—Jefferson's survey of the fields on the side of *Monticello* Mountain, 1794. These fields are mentioned many times by Jefferson. Note the *Park* where Jefferson kept deer and other animals. (*Jefferson Papers*, Huntington Library and Art Gallery.)

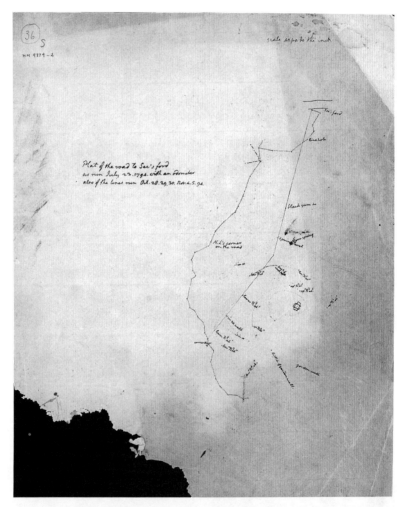

PLATE XIV.—Plat of the road to Secretary's Ford, 1794. See plate XXII.
(*Jefferson Papers*, Huntington Library and Art Gallery.)

Mar.  1.  sowed Charlton peas, lettuce & radishes.

     16.  peas up.

     17.  sowed a second patch of the same.

          Almonds blossom.

17.18.19.  planted 2400. cuttings of weeping willow.[66]
          a man plants 800. to 1000. a day. in the follow-
          ing places.

          lower roundabout [67]

          spring roundabout

          in the old Lucerne patch & the open spaces
          West of y$^t$ & between the same roundabout

          along the road from the gate to the overseer's
          house.[68]

          in the old feild within the park.

          along the road leading by the side of the Park
          to Colle.[69]

          along the road to the Thoroughfare.

          if 8. willows will yeild 1. cord at a lopping, &
          bear lopping every 3$^d$. year, then 800. of these
          may be lopped every year, & yield 100. cords
          of wood.

          grafted and planted in the nursery a variety
          of fruit trees.

          planted there also, balsam poplar,[70] Lombardy
          poplar, gelder roses, althaeas, yellow jasmine.
          grafted double blossomed almonds.   also 12.
          codlin [71] trees.

planted 200. paccan nuts.[72] and seeds of Kentuckey coffee.

20.   peaches blossom.

23.   cherries blossom.

27.   peas of Mar. 17. up.[73]

the first plant of asparagus up, & 5 I. high. under the shop.[74]

Apr.   2.   sowed a patch of latter peas.

7.   a great white frost last night off of the mountains.   the Blue ridge covered with snow Due North from hence and for about 10°. E. & W. of the North.

8.   our first dish of Asparagus.[75]

8.   another white frost off of the mountains.   the peaches killed [76]

19.   first dish of Spinach.[77]

*20.   there are 8. Sugar maples alive.[78]

on the 3[d]. inst. Davy & Phill made a path 4.f. wide in the orchard & 90.y[ds]. long in 2. hours it was set with briars & some grubbing.

on the 5th. they grubbed 76. yds 6 f. wide in 2. hours, in the thicket West of the orchard.

after it was grubbed Davy did 20. yards in an hour.

a man will grub an acre a week in winter of the worst wood lands and $1\frac{1}{4}$ in summer.   inclosed lands, in thicket, are worse.[79]

30.  planted Mazzei's corn in the S.W. angle of
the South orchard.  Derieux's [80] dº. (white)
in a horizontal slope of the North orchard.  a
few grains of another forward corn (yellow)
in the garden ground.  a few grains of Maryland forward corn (white) planted by mr
Biddle.

Sᵗ. foin & Succory [81] sowed in the North orchard on the 28ᵗʰ.

French blackeyed peas [82] sown this 30ᵗʰ. adjoining both patches of corn.

May. 19.  peas of Mar. 1. come to table. [83]

Aug. 12.  sowed forward peas from mr̄ Eppes's. [84]

Sep. 15.  they come to table [85]

Oct. 7.  65 hills of peendars [86] have yielded 16½ lb
weighed green out of the ground which is ¼ lb
each.  it was about 1½ peck

---

[1] *1794.* Jefferson left Philadelphia for *Monticello* on January 5, arriving home on the 16th.  His family circle at this
time included Mr. and Mrs. Randolph, their children, Thomas
Jefferson and Anne, and Jefferson's younger daughter, Maria.
Immediately Jefferson set about remedying the deplorable
condition into which his estate had fallen during the ten years
it had been left in charge of overseers.  With the aid of the
newly hired overseer he undertook to put into effect plans
which he had been formulating for some months.  One of his
first moves was to begin a plan for the rotation of crops.  In
order to improve the appearance of his estate he also divided
the arable lands into regular fields of forty acres each, and in
the place of unsightly rail fences, grown over with weeds,

vines, and trees, he substituted straight rows of peach trees. These rows of trees not only improved the appearance of the land, and served for dividing them off into definite fields, but also gave a superabundance of fruit. He planted eleven hundred and fifty-seven peach trees in December of this year.

Peach trees planted Dec. 1794                              trees
    Monticello.    in the North orchard, between the apples trees ... 263
                     dividing lines between the feilds ............. 537
                    dº.      between the Quarryfield & Longfield   70
    Lego.   dividing lines between the feilds .................... 287

*(Farm Book)*

During the year Jefferson began remodeling his house at *Monticello*. In the succeeding years, it was greatly enlarged and almost completely rebuilt.

Jefferson's correspondence meanwhile gives further insight into his garden and farm plans. He describes the new mouldboard for a plow he had perfected and further elaborates on his idea for the rotation of crops.

The *Garden Book,* after a lapse of several years, is alive again with plans and plantings. Among the most interesting of these jottings is the long list of plants under the headings of "Objects for the garden this year" and "Objects for the farm."

Samuel Biddle, his overseer for one year, proved unsatisfactory. He left *Monticello* on November 1 and was replaced on November 18 by Hugh Petit, who served as overseer until 1797.

The only cloud to pass over the happy family at *Monticello* during the year was the severe spell of rheumatism suffered by Jefferson in August and September. Evidently by December 11 he was completely recovered from his illness, for he wrote Colonel Blackden: "I should with more pleasure have received yourself. . . . You would have found me in my farmer's coat, immersed soul & body in the culture of my fields."

[2] This is the first year that Jefferson made a definite planting plan for his garden and farm. He probably made the list during the long winter evenings sitting in his "brick-kiln." See list of "Seeds saved 1794."

[3] *Phaseolus limensis* Macf., Lima bean.

[4] Probably Mazagan, a variety of *Vicia faba* L.

[5] No doubt a variety of bean some one had given him from the Allegheny Mountains.

[6] Turnip, *Brassica rapa* L.

[7] Indian potato, *Solanum tuberosum* L.

[8] Horse-radish, *Armoracia rusticana* Gaertn.

[9] Peendars, *Arachis hypogaea* L., peanuts.

[10] *Lactuca sativa* L. var. *capitata,* is the cabbage lettuce; var. *longifolia* Lam. is the Cos lettuce, of which there were the Black, the White, and the Upright White Cos. The long-leaved lettuce is var. *angustana* Irish.

[11] *Cichorium endivia* L.

[12] Probably *Barbarea vulgaris* R. Br. It is also called upland cress.

[13] *Rumex scutatus* L.

[14] Shallots, *Allium ascalonicum* L.

[15] *Allium porrum* L.

[16] *Allium sativum* L.

[17] *Brassica alba* Rabenh.

[18] A variety of *Cucumis sativus* L. with very long fruit.

[19] Probably a variety of *Cucurbita maxima* Duchesne.

[20] A variety of *Cucurbita moschata* Duchesne.

[21] *Cucumis melo.* L. This variety was extensively grown in the South.

[22] Another variety of *Cucumis melo.* L. "It is an excellent sort, easily grown and very productive" (L. Burr, *The Field and Garden Vegetables of America* (Boston, 1863) : 187. Hereafter cited as Burr, *Vegetables*).

[23] *Malesherbia,* a genus of South American herbs or under-shrubs constituting the family *Malesherbiaceae,* to which the passion flower is related. It is not known to which species Jefferson is referring here.

[24] *Humulus lupulus* L.

[25] *Salvia officinalis* L.

[26] *Melissa officinalis* L.

[27] *Mentha piperita* L.

[28] *Thymus vulgaris* L.

[29] *Lavandula spica* L.

[30] *Majorana hortensis* Moench.

[31] *Anthemis nobilis* L.

[32] *Tanacetum vulgare* L.

[33] *Ruta graveolens* L.
[34] *Artemisia absinthium* L.
[35] *Artemisia abrotanum* L.
[36] *Rosmarinus officinalis* L.
[37] *Hyssopus officinalis* L.
[38] *Althaea officinalis* L.
[39] *Yucca filamentosa* L.
[40] *Jasminum officinale* L.
[41] *Jasminum* sp.
[42] *Lonicera* sp.
[43] *Hibiscus syriacus* L.
[44] *Viburnum opulus* var. *sterile* DC.
[45] *Prunus triloba* Lindl.
[46] *Populus nigra* var. *italica* Du Roi.
[47] *Populus tacamahacca* Mill.
[48] *Salix babylonica* L.
[49] *Quercus phellos* L.
[50] *Quercus ilicifolia* Wangh.
[51] *Gymnocladus dioica* (L.) Koch.
[52] Probably *Laurus melissaefolium* Walt.
[53] *Ulex europaeus* L.
[54] *Spartium junceum* Lam.
[55] *Medicago sativa* L.
[56] *Onobrychis viciaefolia* Scop.
[57] *Sanguisorba minor* Scop.
[58] *Trifolium pratense* L.
[59] *Trifolium repens* L.
[60] *Agrostis capillaris* L.
[61] *Zea mays* L. (varieties).
[62] Variety of *Vicia faba* L.
[63] *Fagopyrum esculentum* Gaertn.
[64] *Triticum aestivum* L.
[65] A variety of *Oryza sativa* L.
[66] This was a phenomenal number of cuttings of weeping willows to set out. Jefferson never mentioned how many of the willows survived, or whether they yielded the number of cords of wood he calculated. He continued to plant willows for many years after this. See appendix III for Jefferson's description of the introduction of the weeping willow into America.

⁶⁷ See plate XXII for the location of these two *round-abouts*.

⁶⁸ See plate XXII for location of the overseer's house.

⁶⁹ *Colle* was the home of Phillip Mazzei.   See letter of Jefferson to Monroe, May 26, 1795.

⁷⁰ See list of "Objects for the garden this year."   This list of plants shows that Jefferson carried out part of his planting plan.

⁷¹ Codlin, also spelled codling, is a variety of apple.

⁷² Paccan, Indian name for the *Carya pecan*.   Jefferson, in his *Notes on the State of Virginia,* wrote:

Paccan, or Illinois nut.   Not described by Linnaeus, Millar, or Clayton.   Were I to venture to describe this, speaking of the fruit from memory, and of the leaf from plants of two years growth, I should specify it as the *Juglans alba, foliolis lanceolatis, acuminatis, serratis, tomentosis, fructu minore, ovato, compresso, vix insculpto, dulci, putamine tenerrimo.*   It grows on the Illinois, Wabash, Ohio, and Mississippi.   It is spoken of by Don Ulloa under the name of Pacanos, in his Noticias Americanas.   Entret. 6.

⁷³ These peas required ten days to come up, a long germination period.

⁷⁴ This shop is probably the present home of the superintendent of *Monticello.*

⁷⁵ See entry of October, 1793.

⁷⁶ See letter, Jefferson to Madison, May 15, 1794.

⁷⁷ *Spinacia oleracea* L.

⁷⁸ See letters, Jefferson to Prince, July 6, and Prince to Jefferson, November 8, 1791.

⁷⁹ Jefferson recorded this work in the *Farm Book* as follows:

1794. Apr.   Path of the Orchard Roundabout.   2 hands did 90. yards of it, 4 f. wide in 2. hours.   it was set with briars & some grubbing. they grubbed 76. yds 6. f. wide in 2 hours, in the thicket West of S. orchard.   after it was grubbed 1. hand did 20 yds in an hour.

⁸⁰ Comte de Rieux, who married Mrs. Mazzei's daughter. They were probably living at *Colle* at this time.

⁸¹ *Cichorium intybus* L.   See letter, Jefferson to John Taylor, May 1, 1794.

⁸² Probably a French variety of *Vigna sinensis* Endl.

[83] The peas planted on March 1 were above the ground on the 16th. They came to the table on May 19, 80 days from time of planting to time for eating.

[84] Francis Eppes of *Eppington,* Virginia.

[85] Mr. Eppes's peas, sowed on August 12, came to the table on September 15, a period of 35 days for forward peas from planting to eating, as compared to 80 days for the Charlton peas.

[86] Peanuts, *Arachis hypogaea* L. Peanuts are not planted to any extent in Albemarle County today.

LETTERS, EXTRACTS OF LETTERS, AND MEMORANDA, 1794

(Jefferson to Archibald Stuart.)

Monticello Jan. 26. 1794.

. . . My manager Mr. Biddle now sets out for the sheep, as the approach of the yeaning season leaves no time to spare as to them. I could have wished to have made one trip serve for them & the potatoes, but I am advised that the latter would be in danger of freezing on the road. I must therefore, as to them wait for milder weather. . . . Now settled at home as a farmer I shall hope you will never pass without calling, and that you will make this your headquarters when you visit the neighborhood. (Ford, *Jefferson* **8**: 137.)

(Jefferson to James Monroe.)

Monticello Mar. 11. 1794.

. . . Our winter was mild till the middle of January, but since the 22ᵈ. of that month (when my observations begun) it has been 23. mornings out of 49. below the freezing point, and once as low as 14°. It has also been very wet. Once a snow of 6. I. which lay 5. days, and lately a snow of 4. I. which laid on the plains 4. days. There have been very few ploughing days since the middle of January, so that the farmers were never backwarder in their preparations. (Ford, *Jefferson* **8**: 140.)

(Jefferson to James Madison.)

Monticello Apr. 3. 1794.

. . . I find my mind totally absorbed in my rural occupations. we are suffering much for want of rain, tho' now at the 3ᵈ of April, you cannot distinguish the wheat fields of the neighborhood yet from hence. fruit is hitherto safe. we have at this time some prospect of rain. asparagus is just come to table. the lilac in bloom, and the first whippoor-will heard last night. no martins yet. . . . (*Jefferson Papers,* L. C.)

## (Jefferson to George Washington.)

Monticello, April 25, 1794.

. . . The difference of my present and past situation is such as to leave me nothing to regret, but that my retirement has been postponed four years too long. The principles on which I calculated the value of life, are entirely in favor of my present course. I return to farming with an ardor which I scarcely knew in my youth, and which has got the better entirely of my love of study. Instead of writing ten or twelve letters a day, which I have been in the habit of doing as a thing in course, I put off answering my letters now, farmer-like, till a rainy day, and then find them sometimes postponed by other necessary occupations. . . . (Lipscomb and Bergh, *Jefferson* 9: 283–284.)

## (Jefferson to Ferdinando Fairfax.)

Monticello April 25. 1794.

. . . I have returned to farming with an ardour which I scarcely knew in my youth, and which has entirely taken the lead of my love of study. I indulge it because I think it will be more productive of health, profit, & the happiness depending on these, and perhaps of some utility to my neighbors, by taking on myself the risk of a first experiment of that sort of reformation in our system of farming, which surcharges the progressive depredation of our lands calls for imperiously. . . . (*Jefferson Papers,* L. C.)

## (Jefferson to Tench Coxe.)

Monticello, May 1, 1794.

. . . I am still warm whenever I think of these scoundrels, though I do it as seldom as I can, preferring infinitely to contemplate the tranquil growth of my lucerne and potatoes. . . . The prospect of wheat for the ensuing year is a bad one. This is all the sort of news you can expect from me. From you I shall be glad to hear all sort of news, and particularly any improvements in the arts applicable to husbandry or household manufacture. (Lipscomb and Bergh, *Jefferson* 9: 285–286.)

## (Jefferson to John Taylor.)

Monticello May 1, 1794.

In my new occupation of a farmer I find a good drilling machine indispensably necessary. I remember your recommendation of one invented by one of your neighbors; & your recommendation suffices to satisfy me with it. I must therefore beg of you to desire one to be made for me, & if you will give me some idea of it's bulk, & whether it could travel here on it's own legs, I will decide whether to send express for it, or get it sent around by Richmond. Mention at the same time the price of it & I will have it put in your hands.—I remember I showed you, for your advise, a plan of a rotation of crops which I had con-

templated to introduce into my own lands.   On a more minute examination of my lands than I had before been able to take since my return
from Europe, I find their degradation by ill-usage much beyond what I
had expected, & at the same time much more open land than I had calculated on.   One of these circumstances forces a milder course of cropping
on me, & the other enables me to adopt it.   I drop therefore two crops
in my rotation, & instead of 5. crops in 8 years take 3. in 6. years in the
following order.   1. wheat   2. corn & potatoes in the strongest moiety,
potatoes alone or peas alone in the other moiety according to it's strength.
3. wheat or rye.   4. clover.   5. clover.   6. folding & buckwheat dressing.   In such of my fields as are too much worn for clover, I propose to
try S$^t$ foin, which I know will grow in the poorest land, bring plentiful crops, & is a great ameliorator.   It is for this chiefly I want the
drilling machine as well as for Lucerne.   My neighbors to whom I had
distributed some seed of the *Succory intybus,* bro't from France by
Young, & sent to the President, are much pleased with it.   I am trying
a patch of it this year. . . .  (Ford, *Jefferson* 8: 145–146.)

## (Jefferson to George Washington.)

Monticello, May 14, 1794.

I am honored with your favor of April the 24th, and received, at the
same time, Mr. Bertrand's agricultural prospectus.   Though he mentions my having seen him at a particular place, yet I remember nothing
of it, and observing that he intimates an application for lands in America,
I conceive his letter meant for me as Secretary of State, & therefore I
now send it to the Secretary of State.   He has given only the heads of his
demonstrations, so that nothing can be conjectured of their details.   Lord
Kaims once proposed an essence of dung, one pint of which should manure an acre.   If he or Mr. Bertrand could have rendered it so portable,
I should have been one of those who would have been greatly obliged to
them.   I find on a more minute examination of my lands than the short
visits heretofore made to them permitted, that a ten years' abandonment
of them to the ravages of overseers, has brought on them a degree of degradation far beyond what I had expected.   As this obliges me to adopt
a milder course of cropping, so I find that they have enabled me to do it,
by having opened a great deal of lands during my absence.   I have
therefore determined on a division of my farm into six fields, to be put
under this rotation: first year, wheat; second, corn, potatoes, peas; third,
rye or wheat, according to circumstances; fourth & fifth, clover where
the fields will bring it, and buckwheat dressings where they will not;
sixth, folding, and buckwheat dressings.   But it will take me from three
to six years to get this plan underway.   I am not yet satisfied that my
acquisition of overseers from the head of Elk has been a happy one, or
that much will be done this year towards rescuing my plantations from
their wretched condition.   Time, patience & perseverance must be the
remedy; and the maxim of your letter, "slow and sure," is not less a
good one in agriculture than in politics. . . .  I do not forget that I owe

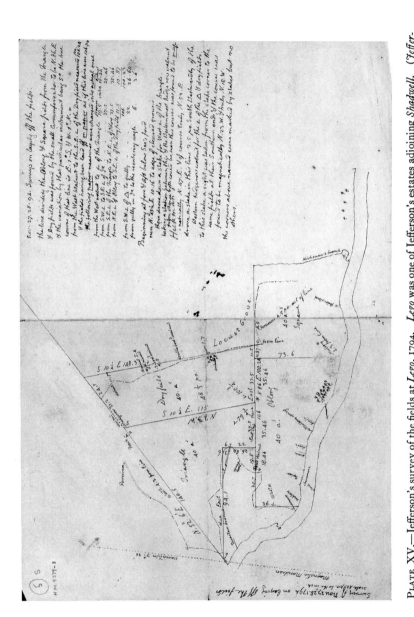

PLATE XV.—Jefferson's survey of the fields at *Lego*, 1794. *Lego* was one of Jefferson's estates adjoining *Shadwell*. (*Jefferson Papers*, Huntington Library and Art Gallery.)

Broomfield ab. [45]              low grounds, mill dam. 1½.
Longfield        37.25                    Sec's ford      12.
Slatefield       47.50           newlands thoro'-fare
Belfield         38.50
Elbowfield       {22.25
                 {18.
Crossfield       56.25
Riverfield       36.75

=43 /104/256    301.5

| | Wheat (bush) | Rye (bush) | Corn (bush) | Cowpea (bush) | Clover (bush) | Ravi pea (acres) | Potatoe (a.) | Pumpkins. | Turnips. |
|---|---|---|---|---|---|---|---|---|---|
| **4. fields of 80. a. each** | | | | | | | | | |
| 1. Patches. i.e. Cowpea 40.a. | | | | 500 | | | | | |
| Corn 40. | | | 500 | | | | | | |
| mix'd with corn. Ravi pea 10. | | | | | | 10 | | | |
| potat. 10. pumpk.10. turnip 10. | | | | | | | 10 | 10 | 10 |
| 2. Rye | | 1000 | | | | | | | |
| 3. } Clover | | | | | 160 | | | | |
| 4. } | | | | | | | | | |
| **5. fields of 64. a. each** | | | | | | | | | |
| 1. wheat | 800 | | | | | | | | |
| 2. Patches. | | | 400 | 400 | | | 8 | 8 | 8 | 8 |
| 3. Rye | | 800 | | | | | | | |
| 4. Clover } | | | | | 128 | | | | |
| 5. Clover } | | | | | | | | | |
| **6. fields of 53⅓ a. each** | | | | | | | | | |
| 1. wheat | 666⅔ | | | | | | | | |
| 2. Patches | | | | 666⅔ | | 13⅓ | 13⅓ | 13⅓ | 13⅓ |
| 3. Rye or Oats | | 666⅔ | | | | | | | |
| 4. Clover } | | | | | 106⅔ | | | | |
| 5. Clover } | | | | | | | | | |
| 6. Cowpea | | | | 666⅔ | | | | | |
| 14. mules @ 50. | 700 bush | 2500 lb | 35,000 fodder | | | | | | |
| 8. horses @ 100. | 800 | 5000 | 40,000 | | | | | | |
| | 1500 | | 75,000 dry hay, or green equival. | | | | | | |
| 3. cows | | | | | | | | | |

a better rotation for monticello.
6 fields of 25. or 30. a. each.
1. ~~~~ wheat.
2. clover ? oats
3. ~~~~ Barley
4. clover
5. millet
6. peas

you a letter for Mr. Young; but I am waiting to get full information.
. . . (Lipscomb and Bergh, *Jefferson* 9: 286–288.)

(Jefferson to James Madison.)

Monticello, May 15, 1794.

. . . It turns out that our fruit has not been as entirely killed as was
at first apprehended; some latter blossoms have yielded a small supply
of this precious refreshment.   I was so improvident as never to have
examined at Philadelphia whether negro cotton and oznabergs can be
had there; if you do not already possess the information, pray obtain it
before you come away.   Our spring has, on the whole, been seasonable;
and the wheat as much recovered as its thinness would permit; but the
crop must still be a miserable one.   There would not have been seed
made but for the extraordinary rains of last month.   Our highest heat
as yet had been 83°, this was on the 4th instant. . . . (Lipscomb and
Bergh, *Jefferson* 9: 289.)

(Jefferson to Thomas Mann Randolph.)

Monticello Aug. 7. 1794.

. . . We began to wish for rain to make our latter corn, & yesterday
there fell a very plentiful one, so that we shall scarcely need another.
the day before yesterday the mercury had got as high as 87°.   this morning it was down at 59°.   a fall of 28° in 36 hours. . . . (*Jefferson
Papers*, L. C.)

(Jefferson to Archibald Stuart.)

Monticello Oct 30. 1794.

. . . I have lodged with Colo. Bell two barrels of sweet potatoes for
you.   I think you told me they did not succeed well on your side the
mountain.   I hope therefore they may merit acceptance. . . . (*Jefferson Papers*, L. C.)

(Jefferson to Henry Remsen.)

Monticello Oct. 30. 1794.

. . . I am so much immersed in farming & nail-making (for I have
set up a Nailery) that politics are entirely banished from my mind. . . .
(*Jefferson Papers*, Franklin Collection, Yale University; photostat at
University of Virginia.   Hereafter cited, *Jefferson Papers*, Yale.)

(Jefferson to James Madison.)

Friday Morning, Dec. 12. 1794.

. . . We have nothing new for you; for it is not new that we have
fine weather.   it is, & has been delicious, with only too short intervals

of cold. in one of them (about the 22ᵈ of Nov.) it was extraordinarily cold, the mercury being at 19°. but it was only three mornings below freezing. in the other (Dec. 4.) it was one morning below the freezing point. but it has never once continued so thro the day. we have had five rains at proper intervals, which is the only interruption our ploughs have had. . . . (*Jefferson Papers, L. C.*)

## (Thomas Jefferson to John Taylor.)

Monticello, Dec. 29, 1794.

I have long owed you a letter, for which my conscience would not have let me rest in quiet but on the consideration that the paiment would not be worth your acceptance. The debt is not merely for a letter the common traffic of every day, but for valuable ideas, which instructed me, which I have adopted, & am acting on them. I am sensible of the truth of your observations that the atmosphere is the great storehouse of matter for recruiting our lands, that tho' efficacious, it is slow in it's operation, and we must therefore give them time instead of the loads of quicker manure given in other countries, that for this purpose we must avail ourselves of the great quantities of land we possess in proportion to our labour, and that while putting them to nurse with the atmosphere, we must protect them from the bite & tread of animals, which are nearly a counterpoise for the benefits of the atmosphere. As good things, as well as evil, go in a train, this relieves us from the labor & expence of cross-fences, now very sensibly felt on account of the scarcity & distance of timber. I am accordingly now engaged in applying my cross fences to the repair of the outer ones and substituting rows of peach trees to preserve the boundaries of the fields. And though I observe your strictures on rotations of crops, yet it appears that in this I differ from you only in words. You keep half your lands in culture, the other half at nurse; so I propose to do. Your scheme indeed requires only four years & mine six; but the proportion of labour & rest is the same. My years of rest, however, are employed, two of them in producing clover, yours in volunteer herbage. But I still understand it to be your opinion that clover is best where lands will produce them. Indeed I think that the important improvement for which the world is indebted to Young is the substitution of clover crops instead of unproductive fallows; & the demonstration that lands are more enriched by clover than by volunteer herbage or fallows; and the clover crops are highly valuable. That our red lands which are still in tolerable heart will produce fine clover I know from the experience of the last year; and indeed that of my neighbors had established the fact. And from observations on accidental plants in the feilds which have been considerably harrassed with corn, I believe that even these will produce clover fit for soiling of animals green. I think, therefore, I can count on the success of that improver. My third year of rest will be devoted to cowpenning, & to a trial of the buckwheat dressing. A further progress in surveying my open arable lands has shewn me that I can have 7 fields in each of my farms where I expected only six; consequently that I can add more to the portion of rest & ameliorating crops. I have doubted on a question on which I am sure you can advise me well, whether I had better give this newly acquired year as an addition to the continuance of my clover, or throw it with some improving crop between two of my crops of grain, as for instance between my corn & rye. I strongly incline to the latter, because I am not satisfied that one cleansing crop in seven years will be sufficient; and indeed I think it important to separate my exhausting crops by alternations of amelioraters. With this view I think to try an experiment of what Judge Parker informs me he practices. That is, to turn in my wheat stubble the instant the grain is off, and sow turneps to be fed out by the sheep. But whether this will answer in our fields which are harrassed, I do not know. We have been in the habit of sowing only our freshest lands in turneps, hence a presumption that wearied lands will not bring them. But Young's making turneps to be fed on by sheep the basis of his improvement of poor lands, affords evidence that tho they may not bring great crops, they will bring them in a sufficient degree to improve the lands. I will try that experiment, however, this year, as well as the one of buckwheat. I have also attended to another improver mentioned by you, the winter-vetch, & have taken measures to get the seed of it from England, as also of the Siberian Vetch which Millar greatly commends, & being a biennial might perhaps take the place of clover in lands which do not suit that. The winter vetch I suspect may be advantageously thrown in between crops, as it gives a choice to use it as green feed in the spring if fodder be run short, or to turn it in as a green-dressing. My rotation, with these amendments, is as follows:—

1. Wheat, followed the same year by turneps, to be fed on by the sheep.
2. Corn & potatoes mixed, & in autumn the vetch to be used as fodder in the spring if wanted, or to be turned in as a dressing.
3. Peas or potatoes, or both according to the quality of the field.
4. Rye and clover sown on it in the spring. Wheat may be substituted here for rye, when it shall be found that the 2$^d$., 3$^d$., 5$^{th}$., & 6$^{th}$. fields will subsist the farm.
5. Clover.
6. Clover, & in autumn turn it in & sow the vetch.
7. Turn in the vetch in the spring, then sow buckwheat & turn that in, having hurdled off the poorest spots for cowpenning. In autumn sow wheat to begin the circle again.

I am for throwing the whole force of my husbandry on the wheatfield, because it is the only one which is to go to market to produce money. Perhaps the clover may bring in something in the form of stock. The other fields are merely for the consumption of the farm. Melilot, mentioned by you, I never heard of. The horse bean I tried this last year. It turned out nothing. The President has tried it without success. An old English farmer of the name of Spuryear, settled in Delaware, has tried it there with good success; but he told me it would not do without being well shaded, and I think he planted it among his corn for that reason.    But he acknoleged our pea was as good an ameliorater & a more valuable pulse, as being food for man as well as horse.    The succory is what Young calls *Chicoria Intubus*.    He sent some seed to the President, who gave me some, & I gave it to my neighbors to keep up till I should come home.    One of them has cultivated it with great success, is very fond of it, and gave me some seed which I sowed last spring.    Tho' the summer was favorable it came on slowly at first, but by autumn became large & strong.    It did not seed that year, but will the next, & you shall be furnished with seed.    I suspect it requires rich ground, & then produces a heavy crop for green feed for horses & cattle. I had poor success with my potatoes last year, not having made more than 60 or 70 bushels to the acre.    But my neighbors having made good crops, I am not disheartened.    The first step towards the recovery of our lands is to find substitutes for corn & bacon.    I count on potatoes, clover, & sheep.    The two former to feed every animal on the farm except my negroes, & the latter to feed them, diversified with rations of salted fish & molasses, both of them wholesome, agreeable, & cheap articles of food.

For pasture I rely on the forests by day, & soiling in the evening. Why could we not have a moveable airy cow house, to be set up in the middle of the feild which is to be dunged, & soil our cattle in that thro' the summer as well as winter, keeping them constantly up & well littered? This, with me, would be in the clover feild of the 1st. year, because during the 2nd. year it would be rotting, and would be spread on it in fallow the beginning of the 3d., but such an effort would be far above the present tyro state of my farming.    The grosser barbarisms in culture which I have to encounter, are more than enough for all my attentions at present.    The dung-yard must be my last effort but one.    The last would be irrigation.    It might be thought at first view, that the interposition of these ameliorations or dressings between my crops will be too laborious, but observe that the turneps & two dressings of vetch do not cost a single ploughing.    The turning in the wheat-stubble for the turneps is the fallow for the corn of the succeeding year.    The 1st. sowing of vetches is on the corn (as is now practiced for wheat), and the turning it in is the flush-ploughing for the crop of potatoes & peas.    The 2d. sowing of the vetch is on the wheat fallow, & the turning it in is the ploughing necessary for sowing the buckwheat.    These three ameliorations, then, will cost but a harrowing each.    On the subject of the drilled husbandry, I think experience has established it's preference for some plants, as the turnep, pea, bean, cabbage, corn, &c., and that of the broadcast for other plants as all the bread grains & grasses, except perhaps lucerne & St. foin in soils & climates very productive of weeds.    In dry soils & climates the broadcast is better for lucerne & St. foin, as all the South of France can testify.

I have imagined and executed a mould-board which may be mathematically demonstrated to be perfect, as far as perfection depends on mathematical principles, and one great circumstance in it's favor is that it may be made by the most bungling carpenter, & cannot possibly vary a hair's breath in it's form, but by gross negligence. You have seen the musical instrument called a sticcado. Suppose all it's sticks of equal length, hold the fore-end horizontally on the floor to receive the turf which presents itself horizontally, and with the right hand twist the hind-end to the perpendicular, or rather as much beyond the perpendicular as will be necessary to cast over the turf completely. This gives an idea (tho not absolutely exact) of my mould-board. It is on the principle of two wedges combined at right angles, the first in the direct line of the furrow to raise the turf gradually, the other across the furrow to turn it over gradually. For both these purposes the wedge is the instrument of the least resistance. I will make a model of the mould-board & lodge it with Colº. Harvie in Richmond for you. This brings me to my thanks for the drill plough lodged with him for me, which I now expect every hour to receive, and the price of which I have deposited in his hands to be called for when you please. A good instrument of this kind is almost the greatest desideratum in husbandry. I am anxious to conjecture beforehand what may be expected from the sowing turneps in jaded ground, how much from the acre, & how large they will be? Will your experience enable you to give me a probable conjecture? Also what is the produce of potatoes, & what of peas in the same kind of ground? . . . (*Jefferson Papers,* M. H. C. 1: 49–55.)

## (Jefferson to Thomas Mann Randolph.)

Monticello Dec. 26. 1794.

. . . Before the receipt of your letter, we had taken up our asparagus bed & after replanting had given the spare roots to a neighbor. we have however done our best to send mṙs Fleming what more could be spared or collected. Patsy wrote for artichoke roots, but I presume she meant *Asparagus,* as our artichokes are but newly planted, and are most of them of so indifferent a kind that as soon as we can distinguish them, we mean to dig them up & throw them away. . . . (*Jefferson Papers,* L. C.)

## (Jefferson to James Madison.)

Monticello, December 28, 1794.

. . . If it [a letter from Mr. Jay] had been on the rotation of my crops, I would have answered myself, lengthily perhaps, but certainly *con gusto.* . . . (Lipscomb and Bergh, *Jefferson* 9: 293.)

## (Jefferson to George Wythe.)

1794.

. . . I ever wish to have opportunity of enjoying your society, knowing your fondness for figs, I have daily wished you could have partaken of ours this year. I never saw so great a crop, & they are still abundant.

of three kinds which I brought from France, there is one, of which I have a single bush, superior to any fig I ever tasted anywhere.—we are now living in a brick-kiln, for my house, in it's present state, is nothing better. I shall recommence my operations on it the next summer. (*Jefferson Papers, L. C.*)

### Seeds saved 1794

### (Bailey's Note, January 95)

*Pease*
Early Dwarf
Early Charlton
Hotspur
Pearl-eyed
Black eyed
White eyed
Small green
Black Indian

*Beans*
B. Windsor
Early Sesbon
White Carolina
White snap
Ground snap

Blue speckled Snap
Reid Speckled snap
Golden Dwarf
sugar bean

*Cabbage*
Scotch cabbage
York      "
Colesworts
Salsify
English cress
    Do.    Turnip
Carrot
Parsnips
Green Rape
Spinage

White mustard
onions
White Spanish
Corn Sallad
French Sorrel
Hanover Turnip
Leaf Lettice
Green      "
Garlick
Palm of Christi
Pumpeons, Kinds
Early cucumber
Water-melon
Musk-melon

### Wanting

½ colyflower
½ oz. green brocli
½ oz. white      "
1 oz. solid cellery
2 Broad leaved D°. endive
1 lb. English scarlet Radis
½ peck of more Broad Windsor Beans.

(*Jefferson Papers*, M. H. S.)

## From *Account Book 1791–1803:*

Jan.  31.  rec⁴. of Samˡ. Biddle 1.75 the remains of 5. D. he had borrowed of Col°. Bell on accᵗ for exp. to Stanton.

Feb.  11.  agreed with Bailey to serve me as gardener for £ 15 a year & 500 lb pork, with bread for his family. [Bailey served as gardener for many years. He lived in a house below the orchard and there was a walk near his house called *Bailey's walk.*]

Feb.  17.  Bailey commences his work.

Mar. 18.   pᵈ Biddle his expenses to Staunton for the Sheep 1.37.   [See letter January 26.]
June   3.   [Richmond] Collins for garden seeds 3/.
Oct. ˙11.   paid for 52 potatoe pumpkins 11/3.
Nov.   1.   on settlement with Samuel Biddle I owe him for 14.     D
            months service @ 10. D. ....................... 140
            travellˢ exp. from Elkton here .................   22.46
            on order of Davᵈ. Watson .....................      5
                                                            ─────────
                                                              167.46
            Biddle leaves my service this day.
Nov. 18.   Petit comes into my service as overseer @ £ 30. a year.

# 1795

Apr. 19.  two or three days of severe weather attended with frost have killed most of the fruit in the neighborhood.  here it is safe as yet, and I observed today that it is safe as low down as the old orchard where the 4. fields corner together.  about half the almonds however are killed.  it is safe to the river, but not at Tufton.[2]

May. 12.  for clearing the road along belfield & Slatefield,[3] where there was no digging, but every thing was grubbed up which could be grubbed, & the larger trees were cut down to a width of 1. pole, 4 men did 220. yds a day which was 10. square poles each.  I tried on that line the step of my horse, as a rough way of estimating distances without getting down to stride them off.  when pushed into a brisk a walk he stepped the 220. yds at 112 steps descending & 116. steps ascending.  110 steps would have been 2. yds at a step.  114 (the medium) is 5 f 9½ I. the step.

---

[1] *1795.* Jefferson remained at *Monticello* during the year, living quietly the life of a farmer.  Letters passed as usual between him and his friends on the problems of crop rotation and agriculture in general.  Political letters, however, were more numerous than in the preceding year.  The following from a letter to George Wythe, written on April 18, shows

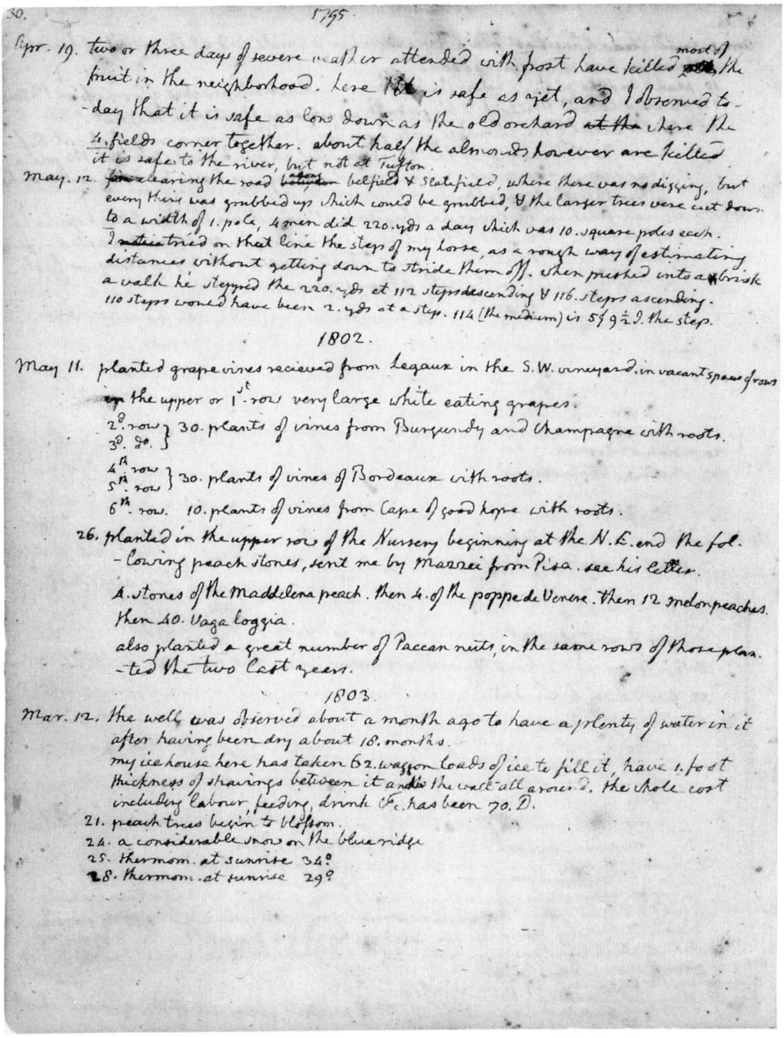

1795.

Apr. 19. two or three days of severe weather attended with frost have killed most of the fruit in the neighborhood. here it is safe as yet, and I observed to-day that it is safe as low down as the old orchard at the where the 4 fields corner together. about half the almonds however are killed it is safe to the river, but not at Tufton.

May. 12. for clearing the road between belfield & Scatsfield, where there was no digging, but every thing was grubbed up which could be grubbed, & the larger trees were cut down to a width of 1. pole, 4 men did 220 yds a day which was 10 square poles each. I tried on that line the steps of my horse as a rough way of estimating distances without getting down to stride them off. when pushed into a brisk walk he stepped the 220 yds at 112 steps descending & 116 steps ascending. 110 steps would have been 2 yds at a step. 114 (the medium) is 5 f 9½ I. the step.

1802.

May 11. planted grape vines recieved from Legaux in the S.W. vineyard in vacant spaces from up the upper or 1st row very large white eating grapes.

2d row
3d do. } 30. plants of vines from Burgundy and Champagne with roots.

4th row
5th row } 30. plants of vines of Bordeaux with roots.

6th row. 10. plants of vines from Cape of good hope with roots.

26. planted in the upper row of the Nursery beginning at the N.E. end the fol--lowing peach stones, sent me by Mazzei from Pisa. see his letter.

1. stones of the Maddelena peach. then 4. of the poppe de Venere. then 12 melon peaches then 40. Vaga loggia.

also planted a great number of Paccan nuts, in the same rows of those plan--ted the two last years.

1803.

Mar. 12. the well was observed about a month ago to have a plenty of water in it after having been dry about 18. months.
my ice house here has taken 62. waggon loads of ice to fill it, have 1 foot thickness of shavings between it and the wall all around. the whole cost including labour, feeding, drink &c. has been 70. D.
21. peach trees begin to blossom.
24. a considerable snow on the blue ridge
25. thermom. at sunrise 34°
28. thermom. at sunrise 29°

PLATE XVII.—Page 30 of the original *Garden Book*.

Dear Sir                    Washington Mar. 29. 1802.

This is merely to correct an error in my last. I mentioned that the brick pilasters should have their Capitals 3. courses of brick high & with 3. projections. but as the Capitel should be in height only half the diameter, & that is of a brick and a half, say 13. I. the height of the capi-tel must be of 2. courses only, each course projecting 1½ I. so as to make the upper one. 2. bricks square.

As I suppose mr Lilly is digging the North West offices, & Ice house I will now give further directions respecting them. the eves of those offices is to be of course exactly on the level of those on the South East side of the hill. but as the North West building is chiefly for coach houses, the floor must be sunk 9. feet deeps below the bottom of the plate to let a coach go under it. then the ice house is to be dug 16. feet deeper than that. the ice house is then to be walled, circular, to a height of 4. feet above the office floors, leaving a door 3½ feet wide on the N.W. side of it. on that height it is to be joisted with 2. I. plank, 9 I. wide & laid edge up & 9. I. apart from one another, these running across the building or N.W. & S.E. then to be covered with inch plank. by this means it will depend on the roof of the offices for shelter from rain, and there will be a space of about 2. or 3. f. (I do not remember exactly) between it's covering and the joists of the offices. thus.

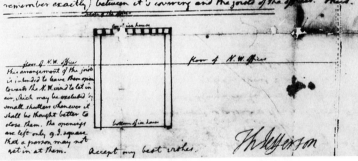

plan of ice house

floor of N.W. office
This arrangement of the joists is intended to leave them open towards the N.W. wind to let in air, which may be excluded by small shutters whenever it shall be thought better to close them. The openings are left only 9. I. square that a person may not get in at them.

floor of N.W. office

bottom of ice house

932                Accept my best wishes.        Th. Jefferson

how active Jefferson's life was during this brief retirement. "I live on my horse from an early breakfast to a late dinner & very often after that till dark." He was alone most of the winter because Mr. and Mrs. Randolph had spent their winter at *Varina,* Mr. Randolph's home. Jefferson mentioned in one of his letters a proposed visit to Bedford County in early May, but there is no indication that he made the trip. His new interest this year was the manufacture of nails, of which the account book shows a large sale. The nailery had been started the previous year. (See letter, Jefferson to Henry Remsen, October 30, 1794.) This business thrived for many years afterwards at *Monticello.* In February Jefferson carried on scientific experiments with seed germination, which put his knowledge of planting far in advance of that of his neighbors. (See letters, Jefferson to Randolph, February 12 and 19, 1795.)

The *Farm Book* recorded most of the agricultural affairs for the year. For some reason Jefferson placed only two entries in the *Garden Book,* and these did not concern planting either in the garden or on the farm. The following "Diary for 1795" is from the *Farm Book.*

### Diary for 1795.

The fall of 1794. had been fine, yet little ploughing was done, partly from the want of horses, partly neglect in the overseers, & a three months confinement by sickness in myself, viz from Sep. 1. to the latter end of Nov.

Petit came to Monticello about the middle of Nov. & soon after they began to plough on both sides, first with one plough, then 2. then 3. they did not get the 4$^{th}$. plough each till the 2$^d$. week in Mar. in the meantime 8. horses for each had been made up by purchasing 5.

Before Christmas, at Tufton the Highfield of about 35. acres, & at Monticello a part of the Riverfield, to wit about 20. acres, & about 15. acres for an Oatfield were ploughed, say about 70. a$^s$.

On the other side about 25. or 30. a$^s$. of the Squarefield were ploughed.

1795. Jan.⎱ Not a single ploughing day in either of these months.
     Feb.⎰ a degree of cold of extraordinary severity, with many little snows, prevailed through the whole of them. Petit cut down & grubbed about 8. acres between Franklin & Poggio fields, grubbed the S. Orchard cleaned part of the Hollow & Knob. f$^d$.

Alexander grubbed the patches in Squarefield employed his men in Mauling & cart in hauling rails to inclose Eastf$^d$. & repair the fences in general.

Mar. 9. at night.   John & his 4. companions have turned over the brick-earth.   have cut for fire wood 23. cords, & for coal 50. cords.

the mule carts have brought in 403½ hampers of coal.

12. loads of dung from Shadwell to the Lucerne.

19. P. M. John &c. have cut 86. cords of wood pine & 2 of hiccory, & 28½ of firewood.

Alexander has about 90. aˢ. ploughed.

Petit about 113 viz Highfield 30. & 8 aˢ. of Hollowfᵈ. for corn, 15 aˢ of the Riverfᵈ. 30. of Slatefᵈ.

for wheat, 20 for oats & about 10. aˢ. of S.

orchᵈ for peas.

Apr 4. began to plant corn at Lego.

finished bringing dung to the Lucerne with the mule carts.

peaches & cherries in blossom.

Martin's came to Charlottesville about the 24ᵗʰ. of March.

Apr 1. began to sow clover.   on trial with the box it took 11. gills to the acre.   Colᵒ. N. Lewis sowed an acre with 12. gills, but not so well done.   the sowings are Antientfᵈ. and an Oatfield at the head of Slatefᵈ. about 15. aˢ. also about 4. or 5. acres to compleat Poggio.

At Shadwell began to sow the Upper field about 30. aˢ.

6. the Oatfield has taken 135 gills of clover seed, so, at 11. gills to the acre, there must be about 12 ¼ acres.

20. finish sowing clover this day.   15. gallons have sowed Oatfield & Infield at Tufton.

May 6. the following is finished here to about 10. aˢ.

9. the clover at Poggio in general blossom.   begin now only to cut it for green food.   it has not been high enough till now.

10. the first lettuce comes to table.

14. strawberries come to table.

June 18. cut barley at Shadwell.

22. dᵒ.   at Tufton.

27. begin to cut wheat at Shadwell.   the force employed as follows

17. Cradlers, Ned. Toby. James. Val. Bagwell. Caesar. Jerry. Philip. Davy. John. Lewis. Johnny. George (Smith). Isaac. Isaac. Peter. Patrick.

5. reapers.   Frank. Martin. Tim. Austin. Phill Shoemaker

7. stackers &c.  Gr. George. Abram. Essex. Squire. Goliah. Tom. waggoner Phill.

36. gatherers.   Isabel. Ned's Jenny. Lewis's Jenny. Doll.
—            Rachael. Mary. Nanny. O. Betty. Molly.
65.          Sally. Amy. Minerva. Lucinda. Judy Hix. Thamar. Iris. Sulla. Bellinda. Phyllis. Moses. Shepherd. Joe. Wormly. Burwell.

Brown. Jamy. Barnby. Davy. Ben. Davy. John Kit Patty. Lucy. Lucy.

July 3. begun to cut wheat on this side the river.

3ᵈ. & 4ᵗʰ. these 2 days they cradled 73. aˢ. there were but 12. cradlers at work on an average, & they stopped cutting by an hour by sun the 4ᵗʰ. (Saturday) that all that was cut might be secured. they cut therefore fully 3. aˢ. a day each, & may be counted on for that.

the ox carts carry the sheaves of about 7. bushels of wheat at a load.

one of them with 3. loaders besides the driver loads in 15'. and to go ¼ of a mile & return took 22'. they would load, go & return ⅛ mile in 30'.

6ᵗʰ. finished cutting wheat.

7ᵗʰ. finished cutting rye.

8. began to tread at Monticello with 7. horses. Were the harvest to go over again with the same force, the following arrangement should take place the treading floor should be laid down before harvest.

½ a doz. spare scythes should be mounted, & fingers for ½ a dozen more ready formed, bent & mortised, & some posts should be provided.

1. great George with tools & a grindstone mounted in the single mule cart, should be constantly employed in mending cradles & grinding scythes. the same cart would carry about the liquor, moving from tree to tree as the work advanced.

18. cradlers should work constantly. Smith. George. John, Davy, Lewis. Johnny. Isaac. *Peter. Patrick. Isaac.* Ned. Toby James Val Bagwell Caesar Jerry Tim & Philip.

18. binders of the women & abler boys. Isabela. Jenny. Jenny. Doll. Molly. Amy. Minerva. Lucinda. Judy. Bellinda. York. Burwell. Jamy. Barnsby. Davy. Patty. Lucy. Lucy.

6. gatherers, to wit 5 small boys & 1. larger for a foreman. Wormly. Brown. Davy. John. Ben. Kit.

3. loaders. Moses, Shepherd & Joe, loading the carts successively with the drivers.

6. stackers. Squire. Abram. Shoemakʳ. Phill. *Essex.* Goliah. Austin.

2. cooks. O. Betty & Fanny.

4. carters. Tom. Phill. Frank. Martin.

———

58.

8. would remain to keep half the ploughs agoing.

66. Rachael. Mary. Nancy. Sally. Thamar. Iris. Scilla. Phyllis.

in this way the whole machine would move in exact equilibrio, no part of the force could be lessened without retarding the whole, nor increased without a waste of force.

this force would cut, bring in, & shock 54. aˢ. a day, and complete my harvest of 320. aˢ. in 6. days.

the proper allowance 4. gallons of whiskey, 2 quarts molasses, 1 midling besides fresh meat per day, with peas.

July 29.  began to lay fallow Slatefield.

Aug. 9.  the Knobfield was sown the last fall with wheat on the North side of the road, and rye on the South side. before harvest I laid off an acre on each side of the road where the ground appeared nearly equal. that of the wheat however was somewhat the best, but the wheat & the rye having been sown at the same time which was very late for the wheat & in good time for the rye. this circumstance was thought to make up for the difference in the quality of the ground. the wheat & rye being stacked separately, each stack measured exactly 4. 8 cubic yards: & the wheat yielded 3. bushels 3. pecks, & the rye 3½ bushels of clean grain.

the bulk of wheat in the stack then was to the bulk of grain as 129.6: 4.6875 :: 27.64: 1 that of rye. . . . . . . . .
. . . . . . . . . . . . as 129.6: 4.375 :: 29.62: 1

31.  one fallow field is sowed on each side the river.

Sep. 1.  begin to gather fodder. Colº. N. Lewis began a week ago. begin to gather peaches for mobby.

11.  the rains have been so constant that it has been impossible to tread out the wheat at Shadwell. 5. stacks of about 30. bushels each are still untrodden.

22.  finish treading wheat at Shadwell. no weavil yet to do injury. fodder got & stacked at Shadwell. at Monticello it took but 7. or 8. days.

Oct. 21.  began to gather corn & to dig potatoes.

Wheat sowed on each side of the river & the dates of sowing.

| Monticello | | acres | Shadwell | | acres |
|---|---|---|---|---|---|
| Aug. 20.–31. | Riverfield about . | 36 | Aug. 20–31. | Eastfield ... | 35 |
| Sep. | Highfield ....... | 36 | Sep. | Triangle 10. | |
| | New ground ..... | 8 | | Pantops .... | 10 |
| | Longfield ....... | 20 | | Road ...... | 60 |
| Oct. 10.–28. | Slatefield ....... | 35 | Oct. 18–26. | Triangle 20 . | 30 |
| | | —— | 27.–Nov. 21. | Middle- | |
| | | 135 | | field ....... | 35 |

170 = 305

Ploughing days this year have been as follow, viz.

Jan.⎱ not one.
Feb.⎰

Mar. 23. ⎤ during the Summer months of this year there were prob-
Apr. 24½. | ably twice as may wet days as in common years, for nothing
May. 20½. | like it has ever been seen within the memory of man.   yet
June 20.  | these 10. months, being 43. weeks & 5. days have given 220.
July 24.  | ploughing days, which average more than 5. a week.   the
Aug. 19.  | account stands thus.                                    days
Sep. 22.  ⎰ In these 10. months are ...................... 306
Oct. 24.  | of these there were Sundays & holidays .... 49
Nov. 23.  |             ploughing days ........ 220
Dec. 20.  |             wet, frozen &c. d°. .... 37       306.

    220. ⎦

² *Tufton,* one of Jefferson's estates adjoining *Monticello.*
It has passed through many hands since Jefferson's death.

³ See plate XIII for the location of Belfield and Slatefield.
This method of measuring distances with the step of his horse
shows again Jefferson's originality in doing things.

## LETTERS AND EXTRACTS OF LETTERS, 1795

(Jefferson to Thomas Mann Randolph.)

Monticello Jan. 29. 1795.

. . . We have had no ploughing weather since Christmas.   on the
24ᵗʰ we had snow 9. I. deep.   yesterday the South hill sides began to be
bare enough for work.   to-day we have a little rain & sleet which will
end in rain probably & carry off the remains of the snow. . . . could
you take the trouble of knowing whether, if I find we have lost the
method of making bricks without treading the mortar, I can have m͞r
Pleasant's man, & on what terms.   (*Jefferson Papers,* L. C.)

(Jefferson to James Madison.)

Monticello Feb. 5. 1795.

. . . Procure for me from some of the seedsmen some of the seed of
the winter vetch (it is the vicia sativa, senino alba of Miller).   as it is
cheap, you may be governed in the quantity. . . . convenience of bringing. . . . we have now had about 4 weeks of winter weather, rather
hard for our climate.   many little snows which did not lay 24. hours &
one 9. I. deep which remained several days.   we have had few thawing
days during the time.   (*Jefferson Papers,* L. C.)

### (Jefferson to Monsieur D'Ivernois.)

Monticello, in Virginia, Feb. 6, 1795.

. . . I have returned, with infinite appetite, to the enjoyment of my farm, my family & my books, and had determined to meddle in nothing beyond their limits. (Ford, *Jefferson* **8**: 163.)

### (Jefferson to Thomas Mann Randolph.)

Monticello Feb. 12. 1795.

Your favor of the 1ˢᵗ inst. came to hand on the 6ᵗʰ. we the next day strewed some clover seed on moistened cotton. this is the 6ᵗʰ day, & the plate has been set on the hearth every night. they have not sprouted, but I think they are swelled. by the next post we may probably decide whether they will sprout or not. the weather continues cold, snowy, & unfriendly to the labors of the field: no ploughing since Christmas. (*Jefferson Papers*, L. C.)

### (Jefferson to Thomas Mann Randolph.)

Monticello Feb. 19. 1795.

. . . James arrived yesterday with your favor of the 14ᵗʰ. the book & the Cole seed. your clover seed put on the moistened cotton has not yet sprouted. perhaps this is owing to the severity of the weather. this has indeed been very unusual, & I fear fatal to a great proportion of our wheat. the morning cold for these 10 days past has been from 11. to 33. the afternoon from 25. to 37°. no ploughing could be done, & very little of any other work: so those like my overseer, loss the fall, very little time will have been furnished by the winter to regain their loss. (*Jefferson Papers*, L. C.)

### (Jefferson to Thomas Mann Randolph.)

Monticello Mar. 5. 1795.

. . . we have now fine weather for work. as your clover seed did not sprout, I have advised the leaving it unsowed till you come. I shall not sow mine till the last week in March. I had your bags of clover seed emptied to search for the radish seed, but no such thing was in them. there was a paper of clover seed found in one of them, which I suppose has been put in by mistake for the other. if this finds you in Richmond, pray get me some of the scarlet radish seed, as it is not to be had in this neighborhood, & is I think the only kind worth cultivating. (*Jefferson Papers*, L. C.)

### (Jefferson to James Madison.)

Monticello Mar. 5. 95.

Your favor of Feb. 15. is duly received & I now enclose the letter for m͞r [illegible], which you will be so kind as to deliver to him open or sealed as you think best, & apologize to him for my availing myself of the opportunity of getting the vetch from England which you say is not to be had in Philadelphia.  the universal culture of this plant in Europe establishes it's value in a farm, & I find two intervals in my rotation where I can have crops of it without it's costing me a single ploughing. my main object is to turn it in as a green dressing in the spring of the year, having sowed it on the fall fallow.  in the meantime, should a short crop of fodder or hard winter call for it as fodder, it is a most abundant & valuable green fodder through the whole winter.— . . . (*Jefferson Papers*, L. C.)

(Jefferson to John Taylor.)

Monticello Apr. 13. 95.

This is not the long letter I intend to write in answer to yours of the 5ᵗʰ. ult.  that must await a rainy day, perhaps a rainy season.  but as the sowing of the succory will not wait I write a line for the present, merely to cover a little seed which I have procured from a neighbor for you.  it must be sown immediately in drills which will admit the plough, & very thin in the drill as the plant is a very tall & large one. it requires strong land, is perennial, and unquestionably valuable.—the mouldboard cannot come by post.  I have with very great satisfaction & saving, tried the seed box described in the New York agricultural trans-actions for sowing clover.  if you have not the pamphlet, the box is simply of half inch poplar (for lightness) 7. feet long, 6 inches broad 4 Inches deep, divided by partitions into seven equal compartments, or cells. a diagonal drawn in the bottom of each cell and 2 holes of $\frac{1}{2}$ I. diameter bored through the bottom on the diagonal equally distant from each other & from the corners: then a bit of strong paper is pasted over the holes, & a hole burnt thro' that with a wire of such size as on trial will be found to shed the seed exactly fast enough.  a neighbor of mine, Colᵒ. Lewis, the evenest seedsman we know came to try the box, in compari-son of his own sowing, and pronounced that the eveness of the work with the box exceeded anything possible from the human hand.  I have sowed an hundred acres of red clover with it within this fortnight, at 11. gills to the acre.  to have sowed it equally thick every where by hand would have taken 16. quᵗˢ, and consequently $\frac{5}{16}$ of the space would have been too thick.  consequently I have saved 13. gallons of seed, or 13. dollars.  I should have mentioned that 2. straps are nailed round the box for the seedsman to hold & shake it by, as he would a sifter.  he will sow a 9 foot land at a time.—I have received the drill.  several of it's parts got lost on the journey.  I can supply them all however, ex-cept the band & buckets for the seeds.  your letter mentions three of these for seed of different kinds, & there came only one, which I judge to be the one for turnep seed.  that for peas I shall particularly want. if you could forward the two deficient sizes to Colᵒ. Gamble at Rich-mond I shall soon get them; & if before pea-sowing so much the better. we were to have tried the drill to-day on a piece of Lucerne ground; but a glorious rain the last night has agreeably disappointed us.  could it not be made for drilling wheat in the broad-cast? that is to say, sow 8 rows, 9. I. apart at a time. the Jersey drill, (described in the N. Y. agric¹. transactions) sows in 13 I. rows, 4 rows at a time. I have tried the Jersey drill with small seeds, & it will not answer without some additional apparatus. we should save much seed & sow evener by sowing with machines in the broadcast. such a machine will be very desirable to me when I get my vetch. let me recommend to you to read Millar's gardener's dict. article *Vicia*. in my circle of crops I can have 2. or 3. fields of this every winter for either winter forage or spring green dressings, without their costing me a single ploughing more than I am to give without the vetch. . . . (*Jefferson Papers, L. C.*)

(Jefferson to John Taylor.)

Monticello Apr. 15. 95.

We have tried the drill with Lucerne seed, and found it shed a great deal too much, so that we were obliged to lay it aside. I presume therefore I was mistaken in saying the band & buckets which came were for turnep seed. we rather guess they were for peas or corn. I must correct therefore my petition for the two larger sizes, and in the uncertainty in which I am, I must rather pray for a complete set. . . . (*Jefferson Papers, L. C.*)

(Jefferson to James Madison.)

Monticello, April 27, 1795.

. . . My health is entirely broken down within the last eight months; my age requires that I should place my affairs in a clear state; these are sound if taken care of, but capable of considerable dangers if longer neglected; and above all things, the delights I feel in the society of my family, and in the agricultural pursuits in which I am so eagerly engaged. The little spice of ambition which I had in my younger days has long since evaporated, and I set still less store by posthumous than present name. . . . I am proceeding in my agricultural plans with a slow but sure step. To get under full way will require four or five years. But patience and perseverance will accomplish it. My little essay in red clover, the last year, has had the most encouraging success. I sowed then about forty acres. I have sowed this year about one hundred and twenty which the rain now falling comes very opportunely on. From one hundred and sixty to two hundred acres will be my yearly sowing. The seed-box described in the agricultural transactions of New York, reduces the expense of seeding from six shillings to two shillings and three pence the acre, and does the business better than is possible to be done by the human hand. May we hope a visit from you? If we may, let it be after the middle of May, by which time I hope to be returned from Bedford. I have had a proposition to meet Mr. Henry there this month, to confer on the subject of a convention, to the calling of which he is now become a convert. . . . (Lipscomb and Bergh, *Jefferson* 9: 302–304.)

(Jefferson to William B. Giles.)

Monticello, April 27, 1795.

. . . I believe I should be tempted to leave my clover for awhile, to go and hail the dawn of liberty & republicanism in that island. I shall be rendered very happy by the visit you promise me. The only thing wanting to make me completely so, is the more frequent society of my friends. It is the more wanting, as I am become more firmly fixed to the globe. If you visit me as a farmer, it must be as a condisciple: for I am but a learner; an eager one indeed, but yet desperate, being too old now to learn a new art. However, I am as much delighted and occupied with it, as if I was the greatest adept. I shall talk with you about it from morning till night, and put you on very short allowance as to political aliment. Now and then a pious ejaculation for the French and Dutch republicans, returning with due despatch to clover, potatoes, wheat, etc. . . . (Lipscomb and Bergh, *Jefferson* 9: 305.)

(Jefferson to M. De Meusnier.)

Monticello, Virginia, Apr. 29, 95.

. . . I am myself a nail-maker. On returning home after an absence of ten years, I found my farms so much deranged that I saw evidently they would be a burden to me instead of a support till I could regenerate them; & consequently that it was necessary for me to find some other resource in the meantime. I thought for a while of taking up the manufacture of pot-ash, which requires but small advances of money. I concluded at length however to begin a manufacture of nails, which needs little or no capital, & I now employ a dozen little boys from 10. to 16. years of age, overlooking all the details of their business myself & drawing from it a profit on which I can get along till I can put my farms into a course of yielding profit. My new trade of nail-making is to me in this country what an additional title of nobility or the ensigns of a new order are in Europe. . . . (Ford, *Jefferson* 8: 174–175.)

(Jefferson to James Monroe.)

Monticello May 26, 1795.

. . . If I can get the proper orders from him I will have the ground above mentioned [Monroe's new land he had bought near *Monticello*] planted in fruit trees from my own nursery, where I have made an extra provision on your account. . . . Collé is lately sold for £ 375. to a Mr. Catlet, a farmer, whom I do not know. . . . I have divided my farms into seven fields on this rotation. 1. wheat. 2. peas & potatoes. 3. corn & potatoes. 4. peas & potatoes till I can get the vetch from Europe. 5. rye. 6. clover. 7. clover. My lands were so worn that they required this gentle treatment to recover them. . . . There are two or three objects which you should endeavor to enrich our country with. 1. the Alpine strawberry. 2. The skylark. 3. The *red* legged Partridge.

I despair too much of the nightingale to add that.    (Ford, *Jefferson* 8: 178–181.)

### (Jefferson to Philip Mazzei.)

Monticello May 30. 1795.

. . . I send herein a few seeds of our cymlin (with running vines) & some squash (with upright stems) the last I got at New York, & are the best ever yet known. . . . I am returned home with an inflexible determination to leave it no more. . . . I am become the most ardent and active farmer in the state.    I live constantly on horseback, rarely taking a book & never a pen if I can avoid it.    this has had it's share in the tardiness of the present letter, for if I am ever in the house, it is in such a state of fatigue as prevents both thought & action.    I am just resuming my buildings. . . .    (*Jefferson Papers*, L. C.)

### (Jefferson to Tench Coxe.)

Monticello June 1, 1795.

. . . We are enjoying a most seasonable sowing after a winter which had greatly injured our small grain.    Nothing can give us a great crop. I doubt if it can be made even a good one.    Our first hay-cutting (clover) begins to-day.    This may mark to you the difference of your seasons & ours.    My clover in common upland fields which were never manured will yield 1500 lb. to the acre at this cutting, which I consider as an encouraging beginning.    (Ford, *Jefferson* 8: 183.)

### (Jefferson to General Henry Knox.)

Monticello June 1. 1795.

. . . have you become a farmer?    is it not pleasanter than to be shut up within 4. walls and delving eternally with the pen?    I am become the most ardent farmer in the state.    I live on my horse from morning to night almost.    intervals are filled up with attentions to a nailery I carry on.    I rarely look into a book, and more rarely take up a pen.    I have proscribed newspapers.    not taking a single one, nor scarcely ever looking into one.    my next reformation will be to allow neither pen, ink, nor paper to be kept on the farm.    when I have accomplished this I shall be in a fair way of indemnifying myself for the drudgery in which I have passed my life.    if you are half as much delighted with the farm as I am, you bless your stars at your riddance from public cares. . . . (*Jefferson Papers*, M. H. S.)

### (Jefferson to John Taylor.)

Monticello June 8. 1795.

I enclose you a few seed of the *Rutabaga*, or Swedish winter turnep. this is the plant which the English Government thought of value enough to be procured at public expense from Sweden, cultivated and dispersed. a mͬ Strickland, an English gentleman from Yorkshire, lately here, left a few seeds with me, of which I impart to you.   he tells me it has such advantage over the common turnep that it is spreading rapidly over England & will become their chief turnep.   it's principal excellence is it's remaining in the field unhurt even by the severities of the Swedish winter.   he suspects that in the seed he gave me, there is an accidental mixture of common turnep.   it may be easily distinguished when it comes up, as the leaf of the Ruta-bage resembles that of rape or cabbage & not at all that of turnep. . . . (*Jefferson Papers*, L. C.)

(John Breckenridge to Jefferson.)

Fayette, 25<sup>th</sup>. July, 1795.

Your note for the clover seed came to hand a week ago, and an opp°. which I think preferable to me by post now offers by Col°. Quarles, of sending you a few seeds.   It is not easily got in my neighborhood, having almost entirely disappeared.   Pray ought I not to send you a little of the *soil* also?   I fear the seed will not acknowledge that about Monticello.   I sincerely wish 1000 of the tens of thousand of acres of our fertile uncultivated land, could be spread around you.   You might then really farm with both pleasure & profit. . . . (*Jefferson Papers*, L. C.)

(Jefferson to Thomas Mann Randolph.)

Monticello Aug. 11. 95.

. . . we have had a terrible storm which has thrown our corn generally prostrate.   we shall be greatly at a loss in sowing wheat among it. Robertson set up as much of his as enabled him to sow 18. bushels of wheat.   in general we shall be obliged to put in our wheat with the houghs.   it will also much lessen the crop of corn.   Robertson has got out between 3. & 400 bushels of your wheat, & has about 260. to get out. he judges by having measured the produce of one stack, 20. bushels, & has 13. stacks still to get out.   he goes on constantly with 4. horses: but we have had such a quantity of wet weather as has greatly obstructed treading.   the weavil is very generally apprehended.—the result of my trial of the acre of wheat & rye was 4.8 cubic yards of each in the stack, and 14. pecks of rye & 15. of wheat, when cleaned.   this gives a cubic foot of wheat from every cubic yard of the stack, and of rye $\frac{1}{30}$ part of the stack.   the ground having been of the weakest kind, for it yeilded but $3\frac{1}{2}$ bushels to the acre, the experiment is decisively against the common opinion that it is better to put weak land into rye than wheat, and will change my rye after corn into wheat after corn. . . . (*Jefferson Papers*, L. C.)

(Jefferson to Thomas Mann Randolph.)

Monticello Aug. 18. 1795.

. . . Col° N. Lewis lies dangerously & almost desperately ill.   I mentioned in my last letter the ravages committed by the rains.   since that we have had still worse. I imagine we never lost more soil than this summer. it is moderately estimated at a year's rent. our crops of corn will be much shortened by the prostrate & drowned condition of the plants, particularly of the topsoil which can perform it's office of impregnation but partially & imperfectly. our peaches are getting into perfection. they are fine in quality & abundant. tobacco has fired excessively. many have cut their crops green. I fear to hear from Bedford. (*Jefferson Papers,* L. C.)

### (Jefferson to Mann Page.)

Monticello, August 30, 1795.

It was not in my power to attend at Fredericksburg. . . . The heat of the weather, the business of the farm, to which I have made myself necessary, forbade it; and to give one round reason for all, *mature sanus,* I have laid up my Rosinante in his stall, before his unfitness for the road shall expose him faultering to the world. But why did not I answer you in time? Because, in truth, I am encouraging myself to grow lazy, and I was sure you would ascribe the delay to anything sooner than a want of affection or respect to you, for this was not among the possible causes. (Lipscomb and Bergh, *Jefferson* 9: 306.)

### (Jefferson to George Washington.)

Monticello, Sept. 12. 1795.

. . . I must say a word to you about the Succory you received from m͞r Young, and were so kind as to give me some of the seed. I sowed about ¼ or ⅓ of an acre last year. it cut little figure that year, but this year it's growth has been most luxuriant indeed. I have not cut it, but kept the whole for seed, & to furnish young plants for transplanting which it does in very great abundance from what I see of it, and what m͞r Strickland told me (that he had known it cut 5. times a year in England) I consider it one of the greatest acquisitions a farmer can have. I sowed at the same time 2. acres of Lucerne, in exactly an equal soil, which in both instances had been originally rich, but was considerably exhausted. I gave the Lucerne this last year a good coat of dung, & due tillage; yet it is such poor dwindling stuff that I have abandoned it, while the Succory without dung or tillage is fine. . . . never had any reformer so barbarous a state of things to encounter as I have. it will be the work of years before the eye will find any satisfaction in my fields. . . . The field pea of Europe and their winter vetch I find to be great desiderata in the farm. . . . (*Jefferson Papers,* L. C.)

### (Jefferson to Monsieur Odit.)

Monticello, October 14, 1795.

. . . My books, my family, my friends, and my farm, furnish more than enough to occupy me the remainder of my life, and of that tranquil occupation most analogous to my physical and moral constitution. . . . (Lipscomb and Bergh, *Jefferson* 9: 312.)

### (Jefferson to James Madison.)

Monticello, Nov. 26, 95.

. . . Our autumn is fine. The weather mild & intermixed with moderate rains at proper intervals. No ice yet, & not much frost. . . . (Ford, *Jefferson* 8: 199.)

### (Jefferson to Edward Rutledge.)

Monticello, Nov. 30. 1795.

I received your favor of Oct. 12 by your son, who has been kind enough to visit me here, and from whose visit I have received all that pleasure which I do from whatever comes from you, and especially from a subject so deservedly dear to you. He found me in a retirement I doat on, living like an Antediluvian patriarch among my children & grandchildren, and tilling my soil. . . . I told your son I had long had it in contemplation to write you for half a dozen *sour* orange trees, of a proper size for small boxes, as they abound with you. The only trouble they would give would be the putting them into boxes long enough before sending them for them to take root, & when rooted to put them into some vessel coming *direct to Richmond* to the care of Mr Daniel Hylton there. . . . (Ford, *Jefferson* 8: 199–201.)

### From *Account Book 1795:*

Jan. 11. gave mͬ Petit to bear exp. to Augusta for sheep 12/.
Jan. 15. received from A. Stuart 20. sheep @ 6/7 - - 6–11–8.
                         23  dº. @ 7/6 - - 8–12–6.
June 1. pᵈ. for lamb 5/.
June 9. bought of Cornelius 7. old sheep & 1 young one for £ 3.
June 24. sent W. Gooch for a lamb 1. D.
Oct. 13. pᵈ. a negro (Will) for 12. quarts greensword seed 12/.
Oct. 25. pᵈ. for 12½ quarts greenswerd seed 12/6.
Nov. 24. Page comes into my service as overseer at Shadwell & Lego at £ 35 a year & 500 lb pork. [Page later became overseer at *Monticello*.]

### From *Farm Book:*

1795. Jan 8. the road which leads from the Grave yard gate, descending 1 foot in 10. into that leading to the Secretary's ford, being 250. yards took 21. days work, which is 12 yds each. there was some stone and grubs to dig, but ne'er a tree to take up. it may be estimated @ 1ᵈ ¼ a yard or 30. Dol. a mile.
it was 10. f. wide.

# 1796

*1796.** The most important happening to Jefferson this year was his election, on November 4, to the Vice Presidency of the United States. His election was a new active beginning into the political life of the nation which was to last until March, 1809. *Monticello* was again to be left to overseers. The systematic farming operations which he had put into effect during the past two years, and which were just beginning to show results, were soon to be only partially continued.

This year also saw the use at *Monticello* of his "mould-board of least resistence," which he had invented and perfected. He wrote to Jonathan Williams on July 3:

> You wish me to present to the Philosophical Society the result of my philosophical researches since my retirement. But, my good Sir, I have made researches into nothing but what is connected with agriculture. In this way I have a little matter to communicate, and will do it ere long. It is the form of a mould-board of least resistance. I had some time ago conceived the principles of it, and I explained them to Mr. Rittenhouse. I have since reduced the thing to practice and have reason to believe the theory fully confirmed. I only wish for one of those instruments used in England for measuring the force exerted in the drafts of different plows, etc., that I might compare the resistance of my mould-board with that of others. But these instruments are not to be had here. (Randall, *Jefferson* 2: 308.) (See appendix VI for Jefferson's description of his mould-board.)

The nailery continued to flourish. Jefferson wrote to Archibald Stuart on January 3: "My present works turn out a ton a month . . . & two additional fires which will be at work in a short time, will raise it to a ton and a half a month" (Ford, *Jefferson* 8: 212). He wrote to Mr. Randolph on January 11, about setting up stores of his own to sell nails at Milton, Charlottesville, and Staunton.

The remodeling of Jefferson's house was carried on through the spring, summer, and fall. In writing to James Madison on December 17, he mentioned that the weather was so severe,

* This year not represented in the *Garden Book.*

"It arrested my buildings very suddenly, when eight days more would have completed my walls, and permitted us to cover in."

One of the most pleasant experiences for Jefferson during the early summer was a visit from the Duke de la Roche-foucauld-Liancourt, of France. He reached *Monticello* on June 22 and remained until the 29th. In his *Travels through the United States of North America, in the Years 1795, 1796, 1797,* he gave an accurate picture of the life at *Monticello* during the time of his visit. He wrote at length on Jefferson's agricultural pursuits, an account of which is quoted here because of the faithful summary it gives of what Jefferson was undertaking and accomplishing. After describing the situation and the house, he wrote:

On this mountain, and in the surrounding valleys, on both banks of the Rivanna, are situated the five thousand acres of land which Mr. Jefferson possesses in this part of Virginia. Eleven hundred and twenty only are cultivated. The land left to the care of stewards has suffered as well as the buildings from the long absence of the master; according to the custom of the country, it has been exhausted by successive culture. Its situation on the declivities of hills and mountains renders a careful cultivation more necessary than is requisite in lands situated in a flat and even country; the common routine is more pernicious, and more judgment and mature thought are required, than in a different soil. This forms at present the chief employment of Mr. Jefferson. But little accustomed to agricultural pursuits, he has drawn the principles of culture either from works which treat on this subject or from conversation. Knowledge thus acquired often misleads, and is at all times insufficient in a country where agriculture is well understood; yet it is preferable to mere practical knowledge, and a country where a bad practice prevails, and where it is dangerous to follow the routine, from which it is so difficult to depart. Above all, much good may be expected, if a contemplative mind, like that of Mr. Jefferson, which takes the theory for its guide, watches its application with discernment, and rectifies it according to the peculiar circumstances and nature of the country, climate, and soil, and conformably to the experience which he daily acquires.

Pursuant to the ancient rotation, tobacco was cultivated four or five successive years; the land was then suffered to lie fallow, and then again succeeded crops of tobacco. The culture of tobacco being now almost entirely relinquished in this part of Virginia, the common rotation begins with wheat, followed by Indian corn, and then again wheat, until the exhausted soil loses every productive power; the field is then abandoned, and the cultivator proceeds to another, which he treats and abandons in the same manner, until he returns to the first, which has in the meantime recovered some of its productive faculties. The disproportion between the quantity of land which belongs to the planters and the hands they can employ in its culture, diminishes the inconveniences of this detestable method.   The land which never receives the least manure, supports a longer or shorter time this alternate cultivation of wheat and Indian corn, according to its nature and situation, and regains, according to the same circumstances, more or less speedily the power of producing new crops.   If in the interval it be covered with heath and weeds, it frequently is again fit for cultivation at the end of eight or ten years; if not, a space of twenty years is not sufficient to render it capable of production.   Planters who are not possessed of a sufficient quantity of land to let so much of it remain unproductive for such a length of time, fallow it in a year or two after it has borne wheat and Indian corn, during which time the fields serve as pasture, and are hereupon again cultivated in the same manner.   In either case the land produces from five to six bushels of wheat, or from ten to fifteen bushels of Indian corn, the acre.   To the produce of Indian corn must be added one hundred pounds of leaves to every five bushels, or each barrel, of grain.   These leaves are given as fodder to the cattle.   It was in this manner that Mr. Jefferson's land had always been cultivated, and it is this system which he has very wisely relinquished.   He has divided all his land under culture into four farms, and every farm into seven fields of forty acres.   Each farm consists, therefore, of two hundred and eighty acres.   His system of rotation embraces seven years, and this is the reason why each farm has been divided into seven fields.   In the first of these seven years wheat is cultivated; in the second, Indian corn; in the third, pease or potatoes; in the fourth, vetches; in the fifth, wheat; and in the sixth and seventh, clover.   Thus each of his fields yields some produce every year, and his rotation of successive culture, while it prepares the soil for the following crop, increases its produce.   The abundance of clover, potatoes, pease, etc., will enable him to keep sufficient cattle for manuring his land, which at present receives hardly any dung at all, independently of the greater profit which he will in future derive from the sale of his cattle.

Each farm, under the direction of a particular steward or bailiff, is cultivated by four negroes, four negresses, four oxen, and four horses. The bailiffs, who in general manage their farms separately, assist each other during the harvest, as well as at any other time when there is any pressing labor.   The great declivity of the fields, which would render it extremely troublesome and tedious to carry the produce, even of each farm, to one common central point, has induced Mr. Jefferson to construct on each field a barn, sufficiently capacious to hold its produce in grain; the produce in forage is also housed there, but this is generally so great, that it becomes necessary to make stacks near the barns.   The latter are constructed of trunks of trees, and the floors are boarded. The forests and slaves reduce the expense of these buildings to a mere trifle.

Mr. Jefferson possesses one of those excellent threshing machines which a few years since were invented in Scotland, and are already very common in England.   This machine, the whole of which does not weigh two thousand pounds, is conveyed from one farm to another in a wagon, and threshes from one hundred and twenty to one hundred and fifty bushels a day. A worm, whose eggs are almost constantly deposited in the ear of the grain, renders it necessary to thresh the corn a short time after the harvest; in this case the heat occasioned by the mixture of grain with its envelope, from which it is disengaged, but with which it continues mixed, destroys the vital principle of the egg, and protects the corn from the inconveniences of its being hatched. If the grain continued in the ears, without being speedily beaten, it would be destroyed by the worm, which would be excluded from the eggs. This scourge, however, spreads no further northwards than the Potomac, and is bounded to the west by the Blue Mountains. A few weeks after the corn has been beaten it is free from all danger, winnowed, and sent to market. The Virginia planters have generally their corn trodden out by horses; but this way is slow, and there is no country in the world where this operation requires more dispatch than this part of Virginia. Besides, the straw is bruised by the treading of horses. Mr. Jefferson hopes that his machine, which has already found some imitators among his neighbors, will be generally adopted in Virginia. In a country where all the inhabitants possess plenty of wood, this machine may be made at a very trifling expense.

Mr. Jefferson rates the average produce of an acre of land, in the present state of his farm, at eight bushels of wheat, eighteen bushels of Indian corn, and twenty hundred weight of clover. After the land has been duly manured, he may expect a produce twice, nay three times more considerable. But his land will never be dunged as much as in Europe. Black cattle and pigs, which in our country are either constantly kept on the farm, or at least return thither every evening, and whose dung is carefully gathered and preserved either separate or mixed, according to circumstances, are here left grazing in the woods the whole year round. Mr. Jefferson keeps no more sheep than are necessary for the consumption of his own table. He cuts his clover but twice each season, and does not suffer his cattle to graze in his fields. The quantity of his dung is therefore in proportion to the number of cattle which he can keep with his own fodder, and which he intends to buy at the beginning of winter to sell them again in spring; and the cattle kept in the vicinity of the barns where the forage is housed, will furnish manure only for the ajacent fields.

From an opinion entertained by Mr. Jefferson that the heat of the sun destroys or at least dries up in a great measure, the nutricious juices of the earth, he judges it necessary that it should be always covered. In order, therefore to preserve his fields, as well as to multiply their produce, they never lie fallow. On the same principle he cuts his clover but twice a season, does not let the cattle feed on the grass, nor incloses his fields, which are merely divided by a single row of peach trees.

A long experience would be required to form a correct judgment, whether the loss of dung, which this system occasions in his farms, and the known advantage of fields enclosed with ditches, especially in a declivitous situation, where the earth from the higher grounds is constantly washed down by the rain, are fully compensated by the vegetative powers which he means thus to preserve in his fields.  His system is entirely confined to himself; it is censured by some of his neighbors, who are also employed in improving their culture with ability and skill, but he adheres to it, and thinks it founded on just observations.

Wheat, as has already been observed, is the chief object of cultivation in this country.  The rise, which within these two years has taken place in the price of this article, has engaged the speculations of the planters, as well as the merchants.  The population of Virginia, which is so inconsiderable in proportion to its extent, and so little collected in towns, would offer but a very precarious market for large numbers of cattle. Every planter has as many of them in the woods as are required for the consumption of his family.  The negroes, who form a considerable part of the population, eat but little meat, and this little is pork.  Some farmers cultivate rye and oats, but they are few in number.  Corn is sold here to the merchants of Milton or Charlottesville, who ship it to Richmond, where it fetches a shilling more per bushel than in other places.  Speculation or a pressing want of money may at times occasion variations in this manner of sale, but it is certainly the most common way.  Money is very scarce in this district, and bank-notes being unknown, trade is chiefly carried on by barter; the merchant who receives the grain returns its value in such commodities as the vender stands in need of.

Mr. Jefferson sold his wheat last year for two dollars and a half per bushel.  He contends that in this district it is whiter than in the environs of Richmond, and all other low countries, and that the bushel which weighs there only from fifty-five to fifty-eight pounds, weighs on his farm from sixty to sixty-five.

In addition to the eleven hundred and twenty acres of land, divided into four farms, Mr. Jefferson sows a few acres with turnips, succory, and other seeds.

Before I leave his farm, I shall not forget to mention that I have seen here a drilling-machine, the name of which cannot be translated into French but by 'machine à semer en paquets.'  By Mr. Jefferson's account it has been invented in his neighborhood.  If this machine fully answers to the good opinion which he entertains of it, the invention is the more fortunate, as by Arthur Young's assertion not one good drilling-machine is to be found in England. . . .

In private life, Mr. Jefferson displays a mild, easy and oblidging temper, though he is somewhat cold and reserved.  His conversation is of the most agreeable kind, and he possesses a stock of information not inferior to that of any other man.  In Europe he would hold a distinguished rank among men of letters, and as such he has already appeared there; at present he is employed with activity and perseverance in the management of his farms and buildings; and he orders, directs and pursues in the minutest detail every branch of business relative to them.  I found him in the midst of the harvest, from which the scorching heat of the sun does not prevent his attendance.  His negroes are nourished, clothed, and treated as well as white servants could be.  As he cannot expect any assistance from the two small neighboring towns, every article is made on his farm; his negroes are cabinetmakers, carpenters, masons, bricklayers, smiths, etc.  The children he employs in a nail factory, which yields already a considerable profit.  The young and old negresses spin for the clothing of the rest.  He animates them by rewards and distinctions; in fine, his superior mind directs the management of his domestic concerns with the same abilities, activity, and regularity which he evinced in the conduct of public affairs, and which he is calculated to display in every situation of life.  In the superintendence of his household he is assisted by his two daughters, Mrs. Randolph and Miss Maria, who are handsome, modest, and amiable women.  They have been educated in France. . . .

The price of land is from four to five dollars per acre. . . . Meat— that is, mutton, veal, and lamb—fetches fourpence a pound; beef cannot be had but in winter.  The wages of white workmen, such as masons, carpenters, cabinet-makers, and smiths, amount to from one and a half dollars to two dollars a day. . . . There are not four stone masons in the whole county of Albemarle. . . . (Randall, *Jefferson* 2: 303–307.)

Mr. and Mrs. Randolph, and Maria, were away from *Monticello* for a part of the year.  Jefferson continued his correspondence with them, keeping them informed about the happenings on the mountaintop.

Jefferson placed no entries in the *Garden Book* during the year.  For some reason the *Garden Book* was not used again until 1802, the second year of his Presidency; rather the *Farm Book* was resorted to for jotting down the agricultural diary. Although the diary is not so complete as that for the preceding year, it does give a good picture of the agricultural pursuits.

He continued his letters to his friends, on a wide variety of subjects.  The *Account Book* recorded a few items of interest.

## Diary for 1796

### (From the *Farm Book*)

Jan.  1.  Petit ploughed the Knob field ab$^t$ 30. a$^s$.  Franklin's 26 a$^s$.  Page has ploughed the Chapel ridge 40. a$^s$. Mount$^n$. field 40. a$^s$.

Mar. 24.  [illegible] for cattle is out at Monticello this day.

Apr. 26.  there has been a most extraordinary, drought through the whole spring to this time.
the seeds sown for a long time past have not sprouted. copious rains now fall for 36. hours, gentle at first, heavy at last.

30.  the weather is become very cold.  a great frost in the neighborhood.

May   1.   the first blossom I see of red clover.
        5.   began to cut clover to feed.
        6.   Iris lays in with a boy Joyce.
       10.   began to sow peas.
June   1.   Lucy lies in with a boy.  Zachary.
        6.   Began to cut clover for hay.
       14.   finished cutting clover.
             Ned's Jenny lies in with a boy.  James.
       23.   the White pea beginning to blossom.

Diary of harvest.

| | | acres | stacks | | one oxcart of 4. or 6. oxen |
|---|---|---|---|---|---|
| June 23. | Eastfield | 35 | 100 | 3.6 | which did little. 2. carts |
| 25. | Riverfield | 40 | 65 | | of 3. mules each. |
| 28. | Poggio new | | | | |
| | ground | 8 | | 40.6 | 1. cart with 4. horses. |
| 29. { | Triangle | 30 | 63 | | a waggon aided 4. days |
| { | Pantops | 9 | | 95. | July 2. we stopped our ploughs; |
| 30. | Culpeper | 7 | 27 | 4.6 | the pickers up not keeping up |
| July 1. | Springfield | 16 | 48 | | with the cutters. tho. 18 |
| 2. | Smith's | 48 | 74 | | mowers had been fixed on & |
| 4. | Highfield | 32 | 72 | | furnished with 27. scythes. |
| 5. | Slatefield } | 55. | 70 | | yet the wheat was so heavy |
| | Longfield } | | | | for the most part that we had not |
| 7. | Middlefield abᵗ | 20 | 27 | | more than 13. or 14. mowers |
| | | | | | cutting on an average. 13. cutters |
| | | 300 | 546 | +135.6 | x 12 days = 156.  which gives |
| | | | | | near 2. aˢ. a day for each cutter, |
| | | | | | supposing 300. acres. |

        9.   sowed Buckwheat at Monticello.
Aug. 18.   Scilla has a child born.
       22.   Our Threshing machine begins to work at the River-
             field.
Nov. 23.   on this day a very severe spell of weather set in.   on the
             23ᵈ. it was at the freezing point.   24ᵗʰ. at 23°.   25ᵗʰ.
             at 21°.   26ᵗʰ. at 12°.   other indispensable work had
             prevented the digging our potatoes, & tho' the earth was
             remarkably dry (for it had not rained since the middle
             of Octob.)   the whole were lost by freezing.
       17.   we finished sowing our 3ᵈ. field of wheat over the river
             (Dryfield).
             May wheat.  the 4ᵗʰ. which should have been in wheat
             we thought better to put into rye.
Dec. 10.   we finish sowing our 3ᵈ. field of wheat on this side the
             river (Ridgefield).  May wheat.  our 4ᵗʰ. (Broken-
             field) which should have been in wheat is to be in rye.
             concluded with George that we will keep 12. breeding
             sows here.
             children born at Bedford this year.  Hanah (Dinah's)
             Aug.—a girl (Suck's) a girl (Abby's) Nace (Maria's)
             Aug.

ploughing days have been this year as follows.   Jan. 11.
Feb. 15. Mar. 20. Apr. 25. May 17. June 19. July 23.
Aug. 24. Sept. 20. Oct. 19. Nov. 24. Dec. 10 = 238.
List of tools at Monticello & Tufton.   given by Hugh
Petit Nov. 96.   18. hoes.   5. axes.   10. reaphooks.   6.
large ploughs.   8. small ploughs.   8. p\(^r\). chain traces.
3. oxchains.   1. toothed harrow.

'96. May 10.   in sowing with the drill plough a quart sowed 350.
yards of furrow, which at 4. feet rows would be 10½
quarts to the acre, or say 1¼ peck.   this was of the
white boiling pea of Europe, to wit their field pea, or
split pea.   sowing the same by hand, a quart sowed
only 310. yards which is 11.85 quarts per acre, say 3.
gallons.   the proportions are exactly as 31 : 35 : or
32 : 36. or 8 : 9.   so that the drill saves ⅛ of seed.   in
labor it saves the whole hand sowing, and the covering with a plough.   we find a great advantage in preceeding the drill by a harrow.   2 horses will harrow
15. a\(^s\). a day.

'96. Sept. 4.   m\(^r\) Eppes examines my North orchard and says it con-
sist of Clark's pear-mains.   Golden Wilding & red
Hughes.   he says the Golden Wilding must not be
mellowed before pressed ; it wild yeild nothing.   it must
be pressed as soon as gathered.   mixed with the red
Hughes they make the best cyder & yeild best.

Nov. 1796.   less than an acre of pumpkins have fed 9 horses at
Shadwell 5 weeks, as well as a gallon & a half of corn
a day would have done.   equal then to 35. days x 9.
horses, x 1½ gal\(^s\) of corn = 12 barrels of corn.   be-
sides this a great proportion of the pumpkins had rotted.
an acre of pumpkins then is equivalent to 5. acres of
corn.

## From the *Account Book 1796:*

Apr. 23.   gave Page to buy hemp seed 3. D.
Sept. 5.   agreed with Robert Chuning to serve me as overseer at
Monticello for £ 35. and 600 lb. pork.   he is to come Dec. 1.
Nov. 6.   p\(^d\) G. Divers's Will for 18. q\(^{ts}\) of greensword seed @ ⅓. 22/6.

## LETTERS AND EXTRACTS OF LETTERS, 1796

### (Jefferson to Thomas Mann Randolph.)

Monticello Feb. 29. 96.

. . . I have received some of the Albany peas from N. York which I
am told is the field pea of Europe.   I have enough to try a whole field.
spring is now opening on us.   the birds issuing from their state of torpor.
narcissus putting up. . . . (*Jefferson Papers,* L. C.)

(Jefferson to James Monroe.)

[Monticello] Mar. 2. 96.

. . . I have been desirous of planting some fruit trees for you that they may be growing during your absence. But Mr. Jones' visits to the neighborhood have been so rare & short that I have not had an opportunity of asking from him the inclosure & allotment of the piece of ground which seems proper for it. The season is now passing. Do not fail to send over the Apricot-peche. Bartram would receive & plant it, and then furnish new plants. . . . (Ford, *Jefferson* **8**: 223.)

(Jefferson to William Giles.)

Monticello, Mar. 19, 96.

. . . We have had a fine winter. Wheat looks well. Corn is scarce and dear. 22/ here, 30/ in Amherst. Our blossoms are but just opening. I have begun the demolition of my house, and hope to get through its re-edification in the course of the summer. But do not let this discourage you from calling on us if you wander this way in the summer. We shall have the eye of a brick-kiln to poke you into, or an Octagon to air you in. . . . (Ford, *Jefferson* **8**: 229.)

(Jefferson to Thomas Mann Randolph.)

Monticello Mar. 19. 96.

. . . We have had remarkable winds for 2 or 3. days past. this morning the mercury was at 26°. our peach blossoms are just opening. . . . (*Jefferson Papers*, L. C.)

(Jefferson to James Monroe.)

Monticello Mar. 21. 96.

. . . Mr. Jones happened fortunately to come into our neighborhood a few days after the date of my last, and ordered the proper ground to be inclosed & reserved for trees for you. My gardener is this day gone to plant such as we had, which will serve for a beginning. we shall engraft more for you this spring & plant them the next. (Ford, *Jefferson* **8**: 229–230.)

(Jefferson to Benjamin Hawkins.)

Monticello Mar. 22. 96.

. . . The vines you were so kind as to send me by mr̄ Chiles were delivered to me alive. every one budded after it was planted. yet every one died immediately after. it was certainly not for want of care. yours is unquestionably the most valuable collection in America, and I must keep it in view, & I pray you to do the same, to have a complete assortment of them, by the first opportunity which may occur. . . . I am now engaged in taking down the upper story of my house and building it on the ground, so as to spread all my rooms on the one floor. we shall this summer therefore live under the tent of heaven. the next summer however we shall be able to tent you better, and I shall hope you will think our part of the country worth a visit. if you will make it during the month of August & September, we have then a good deal of agreeable society who take refuge from the country below during the sickly season, among our hills, the most fertile soil, healthy and temperate climate in America. the mercury was never higher than 90°. here, and we abound in figs, which mark to you the limits of our heat & cold. a propos of figs. of three very fine kinds I brought from France, one is the most delicious I ever tasted in any country. I had one plant last year, but this spring have set out many cuttings. I have also a grape from Italy, of a brick dust color, coming about a fortnight later than the (sweet water) & lasting till frost, the most valuable I ever knew. . . . send me in a letter some seed of the Dionaea muscipulum Ad. (*Jefferson Papers*, L. C.)

(Jefferson to James Madison.)

[Monticello] Mar. 27, 96.

. . . Cold weather, mercury at 26. in the morning. Corn fallen at Richmond to 20/—stationary here. (Ford, *Jefferson* **8**: 232.)

(Jefferson to C. F. C. de Volney.)

Monticello April 10. 96.

. . . My house which had never been more than half finished had during a war of 8. years and my subsequent absence of 10. years gone into almost total decay. I am now engaged in repairing, altering & finishing it. (*Jefferson Papers*, L. C.)

(Jefferson to Thomas Mann Randolph.)

Monticello April 11. 96.

. . . we are in dreadful confusion with the demolition of our walls, which is more tedious than I expected. the walls are so solid that 7 men get down but between 3. & 4000 bricks a day. they would make new ones as fast. the tumbling of brick bats keeps us in constant danger. we have as yet had but one accident of a man knocked down. . . . (*Jefferson Papers*, L. C.)

(Jefferson to Phillip Mazzei.)

Monticello, Apr. 24, 1796.

. . . I enclosed in two of them [letters] some seeds of the squash as you desired. Send me in return some seeds of the winter vetch, I mean that kind which is sewn in autumn & stands thro the cold of winter, furnishing a crop of green fodder in March. Put a few seeds in every letter you may write to me. In England only the spring vetch can be had. Pray fail not in this. I have it greatly at heart. . . . (Ford, *Jefferson* **8**: 237.)

### (William Strickland to Jefferson.)

London, May 28, 1796.

As soon as it was in my power after my return to England I set about procuring the different kinds of Peas & Vetches which are cultivated in this country & which I promised to send you; as they were to be obtained from different & distant parts of the Kingdom they were not to be collected together at an earlier period than the present, which indeed is as early as is requisite, as they could not have been sown before the next season; a box marked T. J. Virginia, forming nearly a cube of fifteen or sixteen inches, containing those seeds, some others which I thought might be useful to you, and some recent publications, I put yesterday in the hands of Mr. Alexander Donald (Now residing at No. 5 Great Winchester Street, Broadstreet) who took the charge of them & said he would have them conveyed to you by the first eligible opportunity. . . . (Ford, *Jefferson Correspondence:* 64.)

### (Jefferson to George Washington.)

Monticello, June 19, 1796.

. . . I put away this disgusting dish of old fragments, and talk to you of my peas and clover. As to the latter article, I have great encouragement from the friendly nature of our soil. I think I have had, both the last and present year, as good clover from common grounds, which had brought several crops of wheat and corn without ever having been manured, as I ever saw on the lots around Philadelphia. I verily believe that a yield of thirty-four acres, sowed on wheat April was twelve-month, has given me a ton to the acre at its first cutting this spring. The stalks extended, measured three and a half feet long very commonly. Another field, a year older, and which yielded as well the last year, has sensibly fallen off this year. My exhausted fields bring a clover not high enough for hay, but I hope to make seed from it. Such as these, however, I shall hereafter put into peas in the broadcast, proposing that one of my sowings of wheat shall be after two years of clover, and the other after two years of peas. I am trying the white boiling pea of Europe (the Albany pea) this year, till I can get the hog pea of England, which is the most productive of all. But the true winter vetch is what we want extremely. I have tried this year the Carolina drill. It is absolutely perfect. Nothing can be more simple, nor perform its office more perfectly for a single row. I shall try to make one to sow four rows at a time of wheat or peas, at twelve inches distance. I have one of the Scotch threshing machines nearly finished. It is copied exactly from a model Mr. Pinckney sent me, only that I have put the whole works (except the horse wheel) into a single frame, moveable from one field to another on the two axles of a wagon. It will be ready in time for the harvest which is coming on, which will give it a full trial. Our wheat and rye are generally fine, and the prices talked of bid fair to indemnify us for the poor crops of the two last years. (Lipscomb and Bergh, *Jefferson* 9: 342–343.)

(Jefferson to Jonathan Williams.)

Monticello, July 3, 1796.

I take shame to myself for having so long left unanswered your valuable favor on the subject of the mountains.   But in truth, I am become lazy as to everything except agriculture.   The preparations for harvest, and the length of the harvest itself, which is not yet finished, would have excused the delay, however, at all times and under all dispositions. . . . (Lipscomb and Bergh, *Jefferson* 9: 346.)

(Jefferson to James Monroe.)

Monticello, July 10, 1796.

. . . We have had the finest harvest ever known in this part of the country.   Both the quantity and quality of wheat are extraordinary. We got fifteen shillings a bushel for the last crop, and hope two-thirds of that at least for the present one. . . .   (Lipscomb and Bergh, *Jefferson* 9: 349.)

(Jefferson to Francis Willis.)

Monticello July 15. 96.

. . . he found me absorbed in my farming, for I am become a monstrous farmer.   but my hills are too rough ever to please the eye. . . . P. S.   Doctor Willis promises to send me some of the cow-peas, a great desideratum in my [illegible] of farming.   I will solicit your attention as well as his to it.   (*Jefferson Papers*, L. C.)

(Philip Tabb to Jefferson.)

Toddsbury 30ᵗʰ Augᵗ. 1796.

I received your favor of the 6ᵗʰ. Inst. by post & begg leave to assure you that I shall have pleasure in giving every proof in my power of a disposition to comply with Mʳ. Jefferson's request.   I have for several years cultivated the pea you mention (the most general & perhaps proper name of which is the Cow Pea.)   I am induced to think the growth of this grain peculiarly calculated for the reduced Corn Lands of our lower Country, the soil of which has a great proportion of sand.   it is planted among the corn at the distance of abᵗ. 6 or 8 feet frequently in the same hill; & 'tho put in early as May or 1ˢᵗ. of June grows but slowly until the corn begins to decline then rapidly.   I think some fields near me has been much improved by this pea & is of considerable value by fatting different kinds of Stock both before & after the Corn crop is gathered, for rain does not spoil it in the pod when ripe as other Indian peas generally.   I doubt whether this pea would grow as kindly in Mʳ. Jefferson's Lands as it does here.   I think his has a redish soil & free from Sand but should he be disposed to make the experiment, I will endeavour to send a Bushell of Seed to any person he may think proper to appoint at Richmond & will then give any farther information in my power that may be wanted. . . . (*Jefferson Papers*, L. C.)

(Jefferson to Thomas Mann Randolph.)

Monticello, Nov. 28, '96.

It is so cold that the freezing of the ink on the point of my pen
renders it difficult to write. We have had the thermometer at 12°.
My works are arrested in a state entirely unfinished, & I fear we shall
not be able to resume them. Clark has sold our wheat in Bedford for
8/6 and the rise to the 1ˢᵗ of June, with some other modifications. It
appears to be a good sale. He preferred it to 10/6 certain, which was
offered him. I think he was right as there is little appearance of any
intermission of the war. . . . My new threshing machine will be tried
this week. (*Jefferson Papers,* M. H. C. 1: 55–56.)

(Jefferson to James Madison.)

Monticello, December 17, 1796.

. . . We have had the severest weather ever known in November.
The thermometer was at twelve degrees here and in Goochland, and I
suppose generally. It arrested my buildings very suddenly, when eight
days more would have completed my walls, and permitted us to cover in.
The drought is excessive. From the middle of October to the middle
of December, not rain enough to lay the dust. A few days ago there
fell a small rain, but the succeeding cold has probably prevented it from
sprouting the grain sown during the drought. . . . (Lipscomb and
Bergh, *Jefferson* 9: 352.)

(Jefferson to Edward Rutledge.)

Monticello, December 27, 1796.

. . . The newspapers will permit me to plant my corn, peas, etc., in
hills or drills as I please (and my oranges, by-the-by, when you send
them). . . . (Lipscomb and Bergh, *Jefferson* 9: 354.)

(Jefferson to Edward Rutledge.)

Monticello Dec. 27. 1796.

. . . I wish to obtain about 20 [illegible] a red field pea commonly
cultivated with you, and a principal article for the subsistence of your
farms, which we have not yet introduced. . . . (*Jefferson Papers,* L. C.)

# 1797

*1797.** Jefferson set out on February 20 for Philadelphia to assume the office of Vice President. A winter journey from *Monticello* to Philadelphia was a tremendous undertaking, and although he probably could have been sworn into office at home, he decided to make the trip as "a mark of respect to the public." He arrived in Philadelphia on March 2, and on March 4 he presided at the opening session of the Senate. He left Philadelphia on March 13, arriving at *Monticello* on the 20th. On March 10 he "p$^d$ seeing elephant .5," and on the day he left Philadelphia, "p$^d$ seeing elks .75." He was at home from March 20 to May 5, when he left again for Philadelphia. On July 11 he was back at *Monticello* and did not return to Philadelphia until December 4.

The happiest event of the year occurred on October 13, when his daughter, Maria, married her cousin, John Wayles Eppes, of *Eppington*. In a letter to Mrs. Randolph on June 8, who had written him about the approaching marriage, he wrote:

> I received with inexpressible pleasure the information your letter contained. After your happy establishment, which has given me an inestimable friend, to whom I can leave the care of everything I love, the only anxiety I had remaining was, to see Maria also so associated as to ensure her happiness. She could not have been more so to my wishes, if I had had the whole earth free to have chosen a partner for her. (Randall, *Jefferson* 2: 358.)

Although activities of all kinds went on at *Monticello* during the year, and although many of them were recorded in the *Account Book,* Jefferson failed to enter any item in the *Garden Book.* Letters, the *Account Book,* and a few entries in the *Farm Book,* are the only sources of information about Jefferson's agricultural interests. Nails were manufactured in abundance. The house was unroofed toward the end of the year preparatory to remodeling. He wrote to James Madison on August 3, inviting him and Mrs. Madison to come for

* This year not represented in the *Garden Book.*

253

a visit "before we uncover our house, which will yet be some weeks."

As in the preceding year, his family spent part of their time with him at *Monticello*. In the intervening periods the Randolphs were at their home, and after Maria's marriage she and Mr. Eppes were at *Eppington*.

A singular honor was bestowed on Jefferson on January 6 of this year. He was elected President of the American Philosophical Society, an office he was to hold until January 6, 1815.

## LETTERS AND EXTRACTS OF LETTERS, 1797

### (Jefferson to James Madison.)

[Monticello] Jan. 8 97.

. . . we apprehend our wheat is almost entirely killed: and many people are expecting to put something else in the ground. I have so little expectations from mine, that as much as I am an enemy to tobacco, I shall endeavor to make some for taxes and clothes. In the morning of the 23d of Dec. my thermometer was 5° below 0, & on the 24th it was at 0. The last day of Dec. we had snow 1½ I. deep & the 4th of this month one of 3. I. deep which is still on the ground. . . . (Ford, *Jefferson* 8: 268–269.)

### (Jefferson to James Madison.)

Monticello, January 30, 1797.

. . . We have now fine mild weather here. The thermometer is above the point which renders fires necessary. . . . (Lipscomb and Bergh, *Jefferson* 9: 376.)

### (Jefferson to Thomas Mann Randolph.)

Philadelphia Mar. 11. 97.

Yours has been duly received and the clover seed goes tomorrow in the schooner *Industry*, capt. Green bound for Richmond. it is addressed to Chaˢ. Johnston, and is in 3. casks containing 3⅛ bushels each, of which 4. bushels are for yourself & the rest for me. it will be desirable to have it forwarded immediately, & of preference by waggon. I shall be at home the 19ᵗʰ. or 20ᵗʰ. & consequently in time to receive it. . . . (*Jefferson Papers,* Huntington Library.)

### (Jefferson to Thomas Mann Randolph.)

Monticello Mar. 23. 1797.

I arrived at home on the 20ᵗʰ inst and found the cherry & peach trees in general blossom. they had begun about a week before that. this day our first dish of asparagus & spinach came to table.   this may enable you to compare climates. . . .

P. S.   I find on further enquiry that the first cherry and peach blossoms here appeared on the 19th inst.   I passed Fredericksburg on the 18th & the buds were not swelled. . . . (*Jefferson Papers, L. C.*)

## (Jefferson to Martha (Jefferson) Randolph.)

Monticello, March 27th, '97.

. . . I arrived in good health at home this day sennight.   The mountain had then been in bloom ten days.   I find that the natural productions of the spring are about a fortnight earlier here than at Fredericksburg; but where art and attention can do anything, some one in a large collection of inhabitants, as in a town, will be before ordinary individuals, whether of town or country. . . . The bloom of Monticello is chilled by my solitude.   It makes me wish the more that yourself and sister were here to enjoy it. . . . (Randall, *Jefferson* 2: 338.)

## (Jefferson to Peregrine Fitzhugh.)

Monticello, April 9, 1797.

. . . A nephew of mine, Mr. S., who married a daughter of Mr. Carr, near Georgetown, setting out this day for that place, I have sent him some of the peas you desired, which he will enclose under cover to you, and lodge in the care of Mr. Thompson Mason.   This letter goes separately by post, to notify you that you may call for them in time for the present season. . . . (Lipscomb and Bergh, *Jefferson* 9: 379.)

## (Jefferson to C. F. C. de Volney.)

Monticello Apr. 9. 1797.

. . . I have been in the enjoyment of our delicious spring.   the soft general temperature of the season, just above the want of fire, enlivened by the reanimation of birds, flowers, the fields, forests & gardens, has been truly delightful & continues to be so.   my peach & cherry trees blossomed on the 9th of March which was the day I had the pleasure of meeting you on the street of Philadelphia, as I returned from your lodging.   I passed Fredericksburg on the 18th of Mar. when not a blossom was opening.   I think we are a fortnight forwarder than Fredericksburg, and the fine temperate weather of spring continues here about two months.   indeed my experience of the different parts of America convinces me that these mountains are the Eden of the U. S. for soil, climate, navigation & health. . . . Today my workmen assemble & tomorrow begin their work, but they must suspend their work during my absence. . . . (*Jefferson Papers, L. C.*)

## (Edward Rutledge to Jefferson.)

Charleston May 19, 1797.

Two days ago, I shipt you Peas, & orange trees on board a vessel for Norfolk, and wrote by her to your merchant in Richmond. . . . The trees are small, & are packed in [moss] with a quantity of earth around them. . . . The Pea is usually planted between the Corn, but in the same row with it. It is not planted until the corn is at least two feet high. . . . (*Jefferson Papers, L. C.*)

(Jefferson to Mr. Giroud.)

Philadelphia, May 22, 1797.

I received at this place, from Mr. Bache, the letter of 20th Germinal, with the seeds of the bread-tree which you were so kind as to send me. I am happy that the casual circumstances respecting Oglethorpe's affairs, has led to this valuable present, and I shall take immediate measures to improve the opportunity it gives us of introducing so precious a plant into our Southern States. The successive supplies of the same seeds which you are kind enough to give me expectations of receiving from you, will, in like manner, be thankfully received, and distributed to those persons and places most likely to render the experiment successful. One service of this kind rendered to a nation, is worth more to them than all the victories of the most splendid pages of their history, and becomes a source of exalted pleasure to those who have been instrumental to it. May that pleasure be yours, and your name be pronounced with gratitude by those who will at some future time be tasting the sweets of the blessings you are now procuring them. . . . (Lipscomb and Bergh, *Jefferson* 9: 387–388.)

(Jefferson to Peregrine Fitzhugh.)

Philadelphia, June 4, 1797.

I am favored with yours of May 19, & thank you for your intentions as to the corn & the large white clover which if forwarded to mr. Archibald Stuart at Staunton will find daily means of conveyance from thence to me. . . . (Ford, *Jefferson* 8: 298.)

(Jefferson to Edward Rutledge.)

Philadelphia, June 24, 1797.

I have to acknowledge your two favors of May the 4th and 19th, and to thank you for your attentions to the commissions for the peas and oranges, which I learn have arrived in Virginia. Your draft I hope will soon follow on Mr. John Barnes, merchant, here; who, as I before advised you, is directed to answer it. . . . (Lipscomb and Bergh, *Jefferson* 9: 408.)

(Jefferson to James Madison.)

Monticello, July 24, 97.

. . . I am anxious to see you here soon, because in about three weeks we shall begin to unroof our house, when the family will be obliged to go elsewhere for shelter. . . . (Ford, *Jefferson* 8: 321.)

(Allen Jones to Jefferson.)

Mount Gallent Aug. 20th 1797.

By Mr. Macon I was honoured with your favor of May 23rd Phila. also a tin box containing the seeds of the bread tree mentioned in your letter, only that there were four instead of two Seeds. Accept my sincere thanks for this communication &. be assured no attention shall be wanting on my part to render your benevolent intentions successful. If they could be raised for two or three years in a greenhouse and then in the spring of the year turned into the full ground, I should make no doubts raising them, but I have no greenhouse and must therefore do the best I can without one. Whatever may be the issue, I am bound to acquaint you with the progress of this experiment to add this valuable plant to the list of our cultivated vegetables. . . . I have frequently asked the gentlemen from your State whether the Teffe or Ensette had been raised, or any attempt made to do it at Monticello? The answer has always been in the negative. This has surprised me as I knew you had correspondents both in France & England where I suppose these plants have been raised, as Mr. Bruce gave liberally of the seeds to both Kingdoms. Perhaps the Teffe is the most valuable acquisition that could be made for the lower parts of Virginia and the Southern States but as . . . & reaped like other small grain, there can be no doubt but it would grow any where in the Southern States and as the seed is probably a capsule I should hope it would escape the Weavil which renders the raising wheat so precarious. As to the Ensette I have not the same hopes, but think it might be cultivated probably as we do the Tannier, which I suppose the same plant that Capt. Cook found in the Islands of the South Sea, & called by the natives Taro. . . . it grows here in great vigour and is a valuable addition to our esculents. . . . (*Jefferson Papers*, Missouri Historical Society.)

(Jefferson to W. H. Van Hasselt.)

Monticello in Virginia Aug. 27. 97.

. . . My fortune is entirely agricultural, consisting in farms which are under the management of persons who have been long in my employ, have behaved well, & are therefore entitled to be continued as long as I continue to occupy my farms myself. but in fact I mean shortly to tenant them out, in order to relieve myself from the attention they require.—my family consists of only two daughters, the one married & just beginning an infant family, the other marriageable; and consequently the business of education is past.—the office to which I have been called takes me from home all the winter during which time my daughters also go into the lower country to pass their winter, so that our house is shut up one half the year. (*Jefferson Papers*, M. H. S.)

(Jefferson to John F. Mercer.)

Monticello Sept. 5. 1797.

I received safely your favor of Aug. 9, with the two packets of Smyrna & Sicilian wheat. the latter I shall value as well because it lengthens our fall sowing, as because it may be sown in the spring, and in a soil that does not suit oats (as is the case of ours) we want a good spring grain. the May wheat has been sufficiently tried to prove that it will not answer for general culture in this part of the country. in the lower country it does better. . . . (*Jefferson Papers, L. C.*)

(Jefferson to John Taylor.)

Monticello, Oct. 8, '97.

We have heard much here of an improvement made in the Scotch threshing machine by Mr. Martin, and that you have seen & approved it. Being myself well acquainted with the original *geered* machine & Booker's substitution of *whirls & bands* (as I have one of each kind), it will perhaps give you but a little trouble to give me so much of an explanation as will be necessary to make me understand Martin's, and let it apply, if you please, to the movements by horses or by hand. I must ask the favor of you to get me one of the same drills you sent me before, made in the best manner, with a compleat set of bands & buckets, and packed in a box, in pieces, in the most compact manner the workman can do it, & forwarded to me at Philadelphia as soon after the meeting of Congress as possible. It is for a friend, & to go still further, which renders this mode of packing necessary. For the amount when you will make it known, I will either inclose you a bank bill from Philadelphia, or send it you in fine tea or anything else you please to order. How did your turnep seed answer? I have received from England, & also, from Italy some seed of the winter vetch, a plant from which I expect a good deal. If it answers I will send you of the seed. I have also received all the good kinds of field pea from England, but I count a great deal more on our southern cow-pea. If you wish any of them, I will send you a part. . . . (*Jefferson Papers,* M. H. C. 1: 58.)

(Jefferson to Martha (Jefferson) Randolph.)

Philadelphia, December 27th, '97.

. . . Tell Mr. Randolph I shall be glad from time to time to exchange meteorological diaries with him; that we may have a comparative view of the climates of this place and ours. . . . (Randall, *Jefferson* 2: 379.)

# 1798

*1798.** Jefferson was in Philadelphia when the year opened, having reached there on December 12. He was concerned with political affairs, chiefly the furious attacks coming from many sides. On this subject he wrote to Peregrine Fitzhugh on February 23:

I have been for sometime used as the property of the newspapers, a fair mark for every man's dirt. Some, too, have indulged themselves in this exercise who would not have done it, had they known me otherwise than through these impure and injurious channels. It is hard treatment, and for a singular kind of offence, that of having obtained by the labors of a life the indulgent opinions of a part of one's fellow-citizens. However, these moral evils must be submitted to, like the physical scourges of tempest, fire, etc. (Lipscomb and Bergh, *Jefferson* 10: 1–2.)

He made only one trip to *Monticello* during the year. His stay, however, was a relatively long one, lasting from July 4 to December 18. On his return trip he reached Philadelphia on Christmas Day.

Although politics completely occupied his attention, *Monticello* was still uppermost in his thoughts. He wrote more interesting and lonely letters to his daughters. The job of roofing the house was still to be finished, and of that repair he wrote Mr. Randolph as late as May 3: "I am in hopes from Davenport's account that I shall find the house nearly covered, and that we shall not be long without a shelter to unite under. 'Oh! Welcome hour whenever!'" (*Jefferson Papers,* L. C.)

In March and April George Jefferson, his agent in Richmond, Virginia, sent plants and seeds for Jefferson to *Monticello* to be planted. The record shows that Mr. Randolph planted them on April 24. The plants had been forwarded to Richmond from Philadelphia by Jefferson. (See list of plants in a letter, Jefferson to Randolph, March 22, 1798.)

Because of the high price tobacco was bringing this year, Jefferson abandoned his previous system of rotation of crops at *Monticello,* a system in which he had great hopes, and began

* This year not represented in the *Garden Book.*

259

again growing tobacco.   He wrote to John Taylor on November 26:

We formerly had a debtor and creditor account of letters on farming; but the high price of tobacco, which is likely to continue for some short time, has tempted me to go entirely into that culture, and in the meantime, my farming schemes are in abeyance, and my farming fields at nurse against the time of my resuming them (Lipscomb and Bergh, *Jefferson* 10: 63).

In spite of the long visit to *Monticello* during the summer and fall, there are no entries in the *Garden Book,* and none in the *Farm Book,* dated this year, relative to gardening and farming.   The *Account Book* registers only a few items.   So again the correspondence gives us the only clue as to what was happening agriculturally at *Monticello.*

## LETTERS AND EXTRACTS OF LETTERS, 1798

### (Jefferson to Martha (Jefferson) Randolph.)

Philadelphia, Feb. 8th, '98.

. . . I am much concerned to hear the state of health of Mr. Randolph and the family, mentioned in your letters of Jan. 22d and 28th. Surely, my dear, it would be better for you to remove to Monticello. The south pavillion, the parlor, and study, will accomodate your family; and I should think Mr. Randolph would find less inconvenience in the riding it would occasion him, than in the loss of his own and his family's health.   Let me beseech you, then, to go there, and to use everything and everybody as if I were there. . . .   (Randall, *Jefferson* 2: 405.)

### (Jefferson to Thomas Mann Randolph.)

Philadelphia Feb. 15. 98.

. . . I write to Davenport by this post to inform me what he has done & is doing.   I expect that according to promise he has kept a strong force sawing sheeting plank, & getting & preparing shingles & that with the first open weather of the spring he would begin to cover the house, so that I may find that compleat on my return, & begin immediately to floor. . . .   It will immediately be time for John to be doing something in the garden.   on this head Martha can question him from my little Calendar of which she has a copy. . . .   (*Jefferson Papers,* L. C.)

### (Jefferson to Thomas Mann Randolph.)

Philadelphia Mar. 8. 98.

[On March 8 Jefferson sent Mr. Randolph, from Philadelphia, four bushels of clover seeds and also] a box just received from mr̄ Strickland,

containing a bag of true winter vetch & some hop-trefoil.  the vetch is
not to be sowed until autumn, the hop-tre-foil immediately.  (*Jefferson
Papers, L. C.*)

(Jefferson to Thomas Mann Randolph.)

Philadelphia, Mar. 22, 1798.

. . . I have just had put on board the sloop Sally, capt Potter for
Richmond, a harpsichord for Maria, and a box of plants, which I shall
desire mr. [George] Jefferson to forward up the river without delay.
The plants are distinguished by numbers as follows:

1. Rhododendron maximum, 3 plants to be planted in the Nursery.
2. Scotch pines 3 plants.
3. Norway firs 2 do.
4. Balm of Gilead 2 do.
6. Dwarf Ewe 3 do.  to be planted among the Kentuckey Coffee
    trees in an open space between the Pride of China trees & the
    grove, about S. W. & by W. from the house.  They may be
    planted within 20 feet of one another, therefore I suppose there
    will be space enough in the place I describe to receive them all,
    without disturbing the Coffee trees.
5. Juniper.  3 plants.  to be planted on the upper Roundabout be-
    tween or in continuation of the Arbor-vitaes & Cedars.
7. Aesculus virginica.  yellow Horse Chestnut 1.  plant on the
    Slope leading from the Pride of China trees down to the Shops,
    among the Catalpas, Crab apple trees & wherever there are vacant
    spaces.
8. . . . hybrida variegated. . . . 1. do.
9. . . . Pavia 1. . . . do.
10. . . . Alba white 1. . . . do.
11. Sugar maple 2. plants.
12. Balsam poplar.  3. do.
13. Viburnum opulifolium, bush cranberry.  3. plants.  in the cur-
    ran or gooseberry squares.
14. Alpine strawberries ⎫ in new & separate beds in the garden.
15. Chili strawberries   ⎬ both of these kinds are immensely valuable.
16. Antwarp raspberry.  twenty odd plants I expect.  in some new
    row by themselves.  It has the reputation of being among the
    finest fruits in the world.
    Peruvian winter grass.  Many roots of this are packed in among
    the plants, it is a most valuable grass for winter grazing.  John
    had better take some favorable place under trees to set it out.
    the cherry trees in the garden would be good places, if there is
    not danger of too much trampling.  Many nuts of the yellow
    and scarlet Horse chestnuts are stuck in among the moss.  John
    must set them out in the nursery instantly, & before they dry.

I must ask the favor of you, the moment these things arrive at Milton,
to send to James to go for them with his waggon, & to take a ride to

Monticello, as soon as they get there, & direct John where to plant them. he would do well perhaps to dig his holes beforehand, to mellow the earth. all the trees to be well staked, the numbers preserved. . . . (*Jefferson Papers,* L. C.) (Printed in *William and Mary College Quarterly,* n.s. **6**: 334–335, 1926.)

(Jefferson to [address lost].*)

Philadelphia, March 23, 1798.

I have to acknowledge the receipt of your favors of August 16th and 18th, together with the box of seed accompanying the former, which has just come to hand. The letter of the 4th of June, which you mention to have committed to Mr. King, has never been received. It has most likely been intercepted on the sea, now become a field of lawless and indiscriminate rapine and violence. The first box which came through Mr. Donald, arrived safely the last year, but being a little too late for that season, its contents have been divided between Mr. Randolph and myself, and will be committed to the earth now immediately. The peas and the vetch are most acceptable indeed. Since you were here, I have tried that species of your field pea which is cultivated in New York, and begin to fear that that plant will scarcely bear our sun and soil. A late acquisition too of a species of our country pea, called the cow pea, has pretty well supplied the place in my husbandry which I had destined for the European field pea. It is very productive, excellent food for man and beast, awaits without loss our leisure for gathering, and shades the ground very closely through the hottest months of the year. This with the loosening of the soil, I take to be the chief means by which the pea improves the soil. We know that the sun in our cloudless climate is the most powerful destroyer of fertility in naked ground, and therefore that the perpetual fallows will not do here, which are so beneficial in a cloudy climate. Still I shall with care try all the several kinds of pea you have been so good as to send me, and having tried all hold fast that which is good. Mr. Randolph is peculiarly happy in having the barleys committed to him, as he had been desirous of going considerably into that culture. I was able at the same time to put into his hands Siberian barley, sent me from France. I look forward with considerable anxiety to the success of the winter vetch, for it gives us a good winter crop, and helps the succeeding summer one. It is something like doubling the produce of the field. I know it does well in Italy, and therefore have the more hope here. My experience leaves me no fear as to the success of clover. I have never seen finer than in some of my fields which have never been manured. My rotation is triennial; to wit, one year of wheat and two of clover in the stronger fields, or two of peas in the weaker, with a crop of Indian corn and potatoes between every other rotation, that is to say once in seven years. Under this easy course of culture, aided with some manure, I hope my fields will recover their

* From the above letter of Jefferson to Randolph, March 8, the following letter was written to Mr. William Strickland.

pristine fertility, which had in some of them been completely exhausted by perpetual crops of Indian corn and wheat alternately. The atmosphere is certainly the great workshop of nature for elaborating the fertilizing principles and insinuating them into the soil. It has been relied on as the sole means of regenerating our soil by most of the landholders in the canton I inhabit, and where rest has been resorted to before a total exhaustion, the soil has never failed to recover. If, indeed, it be so run down as to be incapable of throwing weeds or herbage of any kind, to shade the soil from the sun, it either goes off in gullies, and is entirely lost, or remains exhausted till a growth springs up of such trees as will rise in the poorest soils. Under the shade of these and the cover soon formed of their deciduous leaves, and a commencing herbage, such fields sometimes recover in a long course of years; but this is too long to be taken into a course of husbandry. Not so, however, is the term within which the atmosphere alone will reintegrate a soil rested in due season. A year of wheat will be balanced by one, two, or three years of rest and atmospheric influence, according to the quality of the soil. It has been said that no rotation of crops will keep the earth in the same degree of fertility without the aid of manure. But it is well known here that a space of rest greater or less in spontaneous herbage, will restore the exhaustion of a single crop. This then is a rotation; and as it is not to be believed that spontaneous herbage is the only or best covering during rest, so may we expect that a substitute for it may be found which will yield profitable crops. Such perhaps are clover, peas, vetches, etc. A rotation then may be found, which by giving time for the slow influence of the atmosphere, will keep the soil in a constant and equal state of fertility. But the advantage of manuring, is that it will do more in one than the atmosphere would require several years to do, and consequently enables you so much the oftener to take exhausting crops from the soil, a circumstance of importance where there is more labor than land. . . . (Lipscomb and Bergh, *Jefferson* 10: 11–14.)

(Jefferson to Robert Patterson.)

Philadelphia, March 27, 1798.

In the lifetime of Mr. Rittenhouse, I communicated to him the description of a mouldboard of a plough which I had constructed, and supposed to be what we might term the *mould-board of least resistance.* I asked not only his opinion, but that he would submit it to you also. After he had considered it, he gave me his own opinion that it was demonstrably what I had supposed, and I think he said he had communicated it to you. Of that however I am not sure, and therefore now take the liberty of sending you a description of it and a model, which I have prepared for the Board of Agriculture of England at their request. Mr. Strickland, one of their members, had seen the model, and also the thing itself in use in my farms, and thinking favorably of it, had mentioned it to them. My purpose in troubling you with it, is to ask the favor of you to examine the description rigorously, and suggest to me any correc-

tions or alterations which you may think necessary, and would wish to
have the ideas go as correct as possible out of my hands.  I had sometimes thought of giving it into the Philosophical Society, but I doubted
whether it was worth their notice, and supposed it not exactly in the line
of their ordinary publications.  I had, therefore, contemplated the sending it to some of our agricultural societies, in whose way it was more
particularly, when I received the request of the English board.  The
papers I enclose you are the latter part of a letter to Sir John Sinclair,
their president.  It is to go off by the packet, wherefore I will ask the
favor of you to return them with the model in the course of the present
week, with any observations you will be so good as to favor me with.
. . . (Lipscomb and Bergh, *Jefferson* 10: 15–16.)  [See appendix VI.]

### (Jefferson to Martha (Jefferson) Randolph.)

Philadelphia, Apr. 5, '98.

. . . The advance of the season makes me long to get home.  The
first shad we had here was Mar. 16, and Mar. 28 was the first day we
could observe a greenish hue on the weeping-willow, from its young
leaves.  Not the smallest symptom of blossoming yet, on any species of
fruit tree.  All this proves that we have near two months in the year of
vegetable life, and of animal happiness so far as they are connected, more
in our canton than here. . . . (Randall, *Jefferson* 2: 407.)

### (Martha (Jefferson) Randolph to Jefferson.)

Belmont May 12 1798.

Nothing makes me feel your absence so sensibly as the beauty of the
season; when every object in nature invites one into the fields, the close
monotonous streets of a city which offers no charms of society within
doors to compensate for the dreariness of the scene without, must be
absolutely intolerable particularly to you who have such interesting employment at home.  Monticello shines with a transcendent luxury of
vegetation above the rest of the neighborhood as yet, we have been entirely supplied with vegetables from there having no sort of a garden
here nor any prospect of one this year.  I am glad to have it in my
power to give you a more favorable account of things than Mr Randolph
did in his last which was written immediately after a frost that blasted
every appearance of vegetation, but John informs me all the peaches,
cherries (except the Kentish) and figs which had been uncovered were
gone past recovery for *this* year, yet of strawberries, raspberries, currants
etc. there will be more than common.  I dined at Monticello a fortnight ago. . . . (*Jefferson Papers*, M. H. S.)

### (Jefferson to John Taylor.)

Philadelphia, June 4, '98.

. . . I promised you, long ago, a description of a mould board.  I
now send it; it is a press copy & therefore dim.  It will be less so by

putting a sheet of white paper behind the one you are reading. I would recommend to you first to have a model made of about 3 i. to the foot, or ¼ the real dimensions, and to have two blocks, the 1ˢᵗ of which, after taking out the pyramidal piece & sawing it crosswise above & below, should be preserved in that form to instruct workmen in making the large & real one. The 2ᵈ block may be carried through all the operations, so as to present the form of the mould board complete. If I had an opportunity of sending you a model I would do it. It has been greatly approved here, as it has been before by some very good judges at my house, where I have used it for 5 years with entire approbation. . . . (*Jefferson Papers,* M. H. C. 1: 61.)

(Jefferson to Stevens Thomson Mason.)

Monticello, Oct. 11, 98.

. . . You promised to endeavor to send me some tenants. I am waiting for them, having broken up two excellent farms with 12. fields in them of 40. acres each, some of which I have sowed with small grain. Tenants of any size may be accommodated with the number of fields suited to their force. Only send me good people, and write me what they are. (Ford, *Jefferson* 8: 450–451.)

From the *Account Book 1791–1803:*

Mar.  7.  pᵈ. annual subscription to [Charles Willson] Peale's Museum. **2.** D.
Mar. 16.  the first shad at this market to-day.
Mar. 28.  the weeping willow just shows the green leaf.
Apr.  9.  Asparagus comes to table.
Apr. 10.  Apricots blossom.

# 1799

*1799.** Jefferson was again in Philadelphia when January opened. He had been present on December 27 for the opening of the session of Congress and was now presiding over the Senate. A possible war with France was still brewing, so that political matters centered mainly on that unfortunate affair.

As in the preceding year, he made only one trip to *Monticello,* but this year his stay was longer, lasting over nine months, from March 8 to December 21.

On arriving home, he found that very little had been done toward covering his house. He wrote to Maria Eppes, on the day he arrived:

> I am this moment arrived here, and the post being about to depart, I sit down to inform you of it. Your sister came over with me from Belmont, where we left all well. The family will move over the day after to-morrow. They give up the house there about a week hence. We want nothing now to fill up our happiness but to have you and Mr. Eppes here. Scarcely a stroke has been done towards covering the house since I went away, so that it has remained open at the north end another winter. It seems as if I should never get it inhabitable. . . . (Randall, *Jefferson* 2: 506–507.)

Other affairs at *Monticello* also were not running so smoothly as they had previously. The nailery, which had been flourishing for the past two years, had slowed down. Jefferson wrote from *Monticello* on May 14 to Archibald Stuart: "A long illness of my foreman, occasions our work to go on so poorly that I am able to do little more than supply [nails to] this part of the country" (Ford, *Jefferson* 9: 66).

There is practically no record of the gardening and farming that was carried on during Jefferson's stay at *Monticello* this year. Even the letters were few, and those extant offer only the barest mention of what was happening agriculturally. But since the entire family was reunited, we may be sure that a considerable amount of agricultural work was both planned and carried out during this happy summer.

* This year not represented in the *Garden Book.*

## LETTERS AND EXTRACTS OF LETTERS, 1799

### (Jefferson to Maria (Jefferson) Eppes.)

Monticello, April 13, '99.

. . . Our spring has been remarkably backward. I presume we shall have asparagus to-morrow for the first time. The peach trees blossomed about a week ago. The cherries are just now (this day) blossoming. . . . (Randall, *Jefferson* 2: 507.)

### (Jefferson to John W. Eppes.)

Monticello June 7. 99.

. . . your prospect of a crop here has been as good as could be independant of the seasons, but there has been through the whole of this part of the country an extraordinary failure of plants. many have lost all; most the greater part. you are of the former number; mr̄ Randolph & myself of the latter. of three patches, I did not get a single plant from two of them. the 3ᵈ turned out well, but, as is the case generally the plants are so backward, that tho we have had fine seasons, we have been able to plant only 60. M. out of 150. M. as yet. we spared Page to-day 12. M. for he had not a single one: and I hope we shall be able to furnish him a considerable quantity more; but they are yet to grow to the necessary size. he shall share with us as favorably as possible. I have furnished him with corn for his people and horses till harvest. in order to make him frugal of it (for it costs me 30/ a barrel) I have said nothing to him of the prospect after that. however I shall now let him know that I always destined for your plantation the field of rye I sowed adjoining to it, so that he may prepare for harvesting it. I suppose it will yield a couple of hundred bushels. if corn is then to be had I will furnish him with enough to mix half & half with the rye for his people. . . . (*Jefferson Papers,* Alderman Memorial Library, University of Virginia. Hereafter cited as *Jefferson Papers,* U. Va.)

### (Jefferson to Stevens Thomson Mason.)

Monticello, Oct. 27, 1799.

. . . I find I am not fit to be a farmer with the kind of labor we have, & also subject to such long avocation. Mr. Craven had thought too much of the raspberry plains to be satisfied with our mountainous country; however, although we have not come to an absolute engagement, yet he departs under expectation of deciding to return, & to decide others to come. I have shewn him 800. acres of enclosed & cultivated lands, which I release in such parcels as the tenants desire. Before he arrived, I had leased 160. acres to a very good man, being afraid to lose the offer under the uncertainty whether I might get others. . . . (Ford, *Jefferson* 9: 85.)

(Daniel Clark, Jr., to Jefferson.)

New Orleans, Nov. 12, 1799.

[On November 12 Daniel Clark, Jr., wrote to Jefferson, saying that he had sent to him a barrel of oranges and a box of paccan nuts. He wrote of the paccan nuts:]

They grow everywhere on the Banks of the Mississippi River from the Ilinois River to the Sea, generally in the low grounds & even in Places occasionally overflowed by the annual size of the Waters, the Tree grows to the usual size of Forest Trees and affords a delightful shade in summer, it might be worth while to cultivate it in Virginia for use & ornament. . . . (*Jefferson Papers,* L. C.)

## From the *Farm Book:*

1799—Nov. 1.   70 bushels of the Robinson & red Hughes (about half of each) have made 120. gallons of cyder.   George says that when in a proper state (there was much rot among these) they ought to make 3. gall$^s$. to the bushel, as he knows from having often measured both.

# 1800

*1800.**  Jefferson wrote to Maria Eppes, from Philadelphia, on January 17: "I left home on the 21st, and arrived here on the 28th of December, after a pleasant journey of fine weather and good roads, and without having experienced any inconvenience" (Randall, *Jefferson* 2: 533).

This was Jefferson's last sojourn in Philadelphia.  He was never to visit again the city that had seen so much of his labors for the new Republic.  He was in Philadelphia presiding over the Senate, and coping with his ever-increasing political enemies, until May 14, when Congress adjourned.  He left Philadelphia May 15, and reached *Monticello* on the 29th. En route home he stopped at *Montblanco,* Maria's new home, *Eppington,* and *Edgehill,* the Randolph's new home.

In January Jefferson heard of the birth of Maria's first child, which unfortunately survived only a few weeks.  On February 12 he wrote to Maria:

Mr. Eppes's letter of January 17 had filled me with anxiety for your little one, and that of the 25th announced what I had feared.  How deeply I feel it in all its bearings I shall not say—nor attempt consolation when I know that time and silence are the only medicines.  (Randall, *Jefferson* 2: 535.)

Another sorrow that affected Jefferson keenly was the death of his body servant, Jupiter.  In the same letter referred to above, he wrote: "You have, perhaps, heard of the loss of Jupiter.  With all his defects, he leaves a void in my domestic arrangements which cannot be filled."

The Presidential canvass opened in the summer.  Jefferson and Aaron Burr were the two candidates on the Republican ticket.  Their opponents were John Adams and Charles C. Pinckney.  In June the capital was moved from Philadelphia to Washington, a change that greatly pleased Jefferson, for it brought him nearer to *Monticello* and his family.  When he returned to the Senate on November 27, it was meeting in Washington.

* This year not represented in the *Garden Book.*

Despite the political campaign that continued all summer, Jefferson remained in more or less retirement at *Monticello,* leaving his mountaintop only for a short trip to his Bedford estate, *Poplar Forest,* and a trip to another part of Albemarle County.   The family was together for a part of the summer. The garden and farming activities were more numerous than in the preceding year, but the *Garden Book* was completely neglected.   There were, however, a few entries in the *Farm Book.*

## LETTERS AND EXTRACTS OF LETTERS, 1800

### (Jefferson to Daniel Clark, Jr.)

Philadelphia Jan. 16. 1800.

Your favor of Nov. 12 has been duly received, as has also the parcel of Paccan nuts for which, as well as the oranges, be pleased to accept my acknowledgement. . . . the nuts I have immediately forwarded to Monticello, my residence in Virginia to be planted.   two young trees planted in that part of the country in 1780. and now flourishing, though not bearing, prove they may be raised there; and I shall set great value on the chance of having a grove of them. . . . (*Jefferson Papers,* L. C.)

### (Jefferson to Thomas Mann Randolph.)

[Philadelphia] Feb. 4, 1800.

. . . My anxiety to get my lands rented is extreme.   I readily agree therefore that Mr. Kerr shall take for 5 years, or say till Christmas, 1804, the oblong, square field, and the one on the river next below the square field, comprehending the orchard; only I should be very urgent that he should take a compleat field there; for I expect there is enough between the river and the road by old Hickman's settlement to make 2 fields of 40 a$^s$. each, by cleaning up and straightening the skirts, perhaps by cutting down some slips on the margin.   For so much as would be to clear I would take no rent the 1$^{st}$ year.   He would then have the 3 fields in a line on the river, and three other fields would remain along the road to the triangle inclusive for another tenant.   Observe I must have with him, as I have with Mr. Peyton, free passage along the roads; that is to say, along the road which used to be, & must be again, down the river side.   All the conditions to be the same as with Mr. Peyton.   I say I wish him to be pushed to the taking the 120 acres; yet, rather than lose a tenant, I would agree to the hundred acres, to wit, the oblong, square & half the lower field.   But you are sensible he would get by that means a great over-proportion of cream, & therefore I wish to force on him the other half field. . . . (*Jefferson Papers,* M. H. C. 1: 68.)

(Jefferson to Richard Richardson.)

Philadelphia Mar. 31. 1800.

In yours of the 21ˢᵗ you acknolege mine of Feb. 17. since that I wrote to you on the 16ᵗʰ. and 25ᵗʰ. inst: the last was merely to inform you of the departure of a box of plants. . . . (*Jefferson Papers,* Thomas Jefferson Memorial Foundation.)

(Jefferson to William Hamilton of *Woodlands.*)

Philadelphia, Apr. 22. 1800.

. . . Among the many botanical curiosities you were so good as to shew me the other day, I forgot to ask if you had the *Dionaea muscipula,* & whether it produces a seed with you. If it does, I should be very much disposed to trespass on your liberality so far as to ask a few seeds of that, as also of the *Acacia Nilotica,* or *Farnesiana,* whichever you have. . . . (Ford, *Jefferson* 9: 131.)

(Jefferson to Robert R. Livingston.)

Philadelphia, Apr. 30, 1800.

. . . I thank you for the volume of your agricultural transactions: & as I perceive you take a great interest in whatever relates to this first & most precious of all the arts, I have packed in a small box, a model of a mouldboard of a plough, of my invention, if that term may be used for a mere change of form. It is accompanied by a block, which will shew the form in which the block is to be got for making the mouldboard & the manner of making it. . . . (Ford, *Jefferson* 9: 133.)

(Daniel Clarke, Jr., to Jefferson.)

New Orleans May 29, 1800.

. . . I am happy to learn that the few Pacans I sent you are likely to turn to some good account, and sincerely wish your Grove of them may flourish, if there are any other Trees [illegible] or anything else which the country produces, & hitherto [illegible] not naturalized or neglected with you, I would take pleasure in procuring any you may desire, and forwarding them in safety to you. . . . (*Jefferson Papers,* L. C.)

(Jefferson to Dr. Benjamin Rush.)

Washington Dec. 14. 1800.

I have duly received your favor of the 2ᵈ. instant and the *melon seeds* accompanying them. I shall certainly cherish them, and try whether the climate of Monticello can preserve them without degeneracy. . . . (*Jefferson Papers,* L. C.)

(Jefferson to Andrew Ellicott.)

Washington, December 18, 1800.

. . . Attractive nature and the country employments are my apology to my friends for being a very unpunctual correspondent while at home; having no refuge here from my room and writing-table, it is here that I fetch the less easy of my correspondence. . . . (Lipscomb and Bergh, *Jefferson* 19: 121.)

From the *Farm Book:*

1800. Sep. 9.   on accurate trial 3. bush. of wheat in the chaff as it came from the threshing machine yielded 1. bush. of clean wheat.

From the *Account Book:*

Mar. 15.   p̄d portage to Bartram's .625.
Mar. 30.   weeping willow looks green.   frogs cry.
April  8.   peaches blossom.

## Plan for a Rotation of Crops Proposed by Thomas Jefferson to Craven Peyton

|          | 1800  | 1801  | 1802  | 1803  | 1804  |
|----------|-------|-------|-------|-------|-------|
| Nº. 1.   | wheat | corn  | rye   | *     | *     |
| 2.       | rest  | wheat | corn  | rye   | *     |
| 3.       | rest  | *     | wheat | corn  | rye   |
| 4.       | rye   | *     | *     | wheat | corn  |
| 5.       | corn  | rye   | *     | *     | wheat |

the │ above proposed by Th: J.

(*Jefferson Papers,* U. Va.)

# 1801

*1801.** Jefferson had arrived at the new capital, Washington, on November 27, 1800, so that he was still presiding over the Senate when the new year opened. He remained in Washington until April 1, on which day he left for *Monticello* for his spring vacation. During his stay in Washington he had been elected, on February 17, the third President of the United States, and on March 4 he was inaugurated.

He remained at *Monticello* during most of the month of April, returning to Washington on the 26th. He left a scant record of what happened in the garden during that month. In a letter to Maria, written on April 11, from *Monticello,* he wrote: "John being at work under Lilly [overseer at *Monticello*] Goliah is our gardener, and with his veteran aids will be directed to make what preparations he can for you." This would indicate that the usual garden preparations were being carried out. Rebuilding the house was still in progress, and since it had been covered, work was moving slowly on the interior.

Jefferson's new interest this year was the canal he was preparing on the Rivanna River. He had written Mr. Randolph on January 23: "When I come home I shall lay off the canal, if Lilly's gang can undertake it."

Jefferson's second visit to *Monticello* began on August 2. The family was together during his stay—Mr. and Mrs. Randolph with their four children, and Mr. and Mrs. Eppes with their one son. He returned to Washington on September 30, where he immediately became engrossed with problems of state. Two trips were made to *Mount Vernon* during the year, the purposes of which he did not state in his correspondence.

Another year passed unrecorded in either the *Garden Book* or the *Farm Book*. The *Account Book* has only one entry about farming: "Aug. 11. p^d R. J.'s [Randolph Jefferson's]

* This year not represented in the *Garden Book*.

273

Squire for 25¼ quarts of white clover seed @ 1/6 £ 1–17–10½."

## LETTERS AND EXTRACTS OF LETTERS, 1801

### (Jefferson to Thomas Mann Randolph.)

Washington, Jan. 23, 1801.

. . . P. S.   When I come home I shall lay off the canal, if Lilly's gang can undertake it.   I had directed Lilly to make a dividing fence between Craven's fields at Monticello & those I retain.   The object was to give me the benefit of the latter for pasture.   If I stay here, the yard will be pasture enough and may spare, or at least delay, this great & perishable work of the dividing fence.   At least it may lie for further consideration.   I hope Lilly keeps the small nailers engaged so as to supply our customers in the neighborhood, so that we may not lose them during this interregnum.   (*Jefferson Papers,* M. H. C. 1: 85.)

### (Jefferson to Thomas Mann Randolph.)

Washington, Jan. 29 [1801].

. . . Mr. Wilson Nicholas and myself have this day joined in ordering clover seed from New York, where it is to be had, it is said, at 12 dollars.   I have ordered 5 bushels for you.   I believe I have none to sow myself. . . .   My tender love to my ever dear Martha and to the little ones.   I believe I must ask her to give directions to Goliah & his senile corps to prepare what they can in the garden, as it is very possible I may want it.   (*Jefferson Papers,* M. H. C. 1: 87–88.)

### (Jefferson to Phillip Mazzei.)

Washington, Mar. 17, 1801.

. . . The vetches you were so good as to send by Baltimore came safely to hand; and being by that time withdrawn from my farm into public life again, I consigned them to a friend.   The seeds which I sent you were of the Cymbling (*Cucurbita vermeosa* [= *verrucosa*]) & squash (*cucurbita melopipo*) the latter grows with erect stems; the former trails on the ground altogether.   The squash is the best tasted.   But if you will plant the cymbling and pumpkin near together, you will produce the perfect equivalent of the squash, and I am persuaded the squash was originally so produced and that it is a hybridal plant.   (Ford, *Jefferson* 9: 210–211.)

### (Jefferson to Peter Legaux.)

Washington Mar. 24. 1801.

[On March 24 Jefferson wrote to M. Legaux, thanking him for his offer to send him some of his grape vines.   He also said:]

It is too late this season but will want them for next.   (*Jefferson Papers,* L. C.)   [See entry, May 11, 1802, in *Garden Book.*]

(Jefferson to John Bartram, Jr.)

Washington June 11. 1801.

. . . will you be so good as to plant for me [illegible] some plants of the Alpine, Hudson & Chile strawberries in a pot [of earth?]. in that way I can have them brought safely to this place and [illegible] them home from hence at my leisure. . . . (*Jefferson Papers,* L. C.)

(Julien Niemcewicz to Jefferson.)

16 June 1801.   Elizabeth Town New Jersey.

Amongst numerous petitions & applications which as the first Magistrate of the Commonwealth you daily receive Sir, you will not I hope reject the petition of an old Acquaintance. it is only for a Plant that grows in Virginia by the name of Seneca Root, Polygala Seneca of Lineus, being witness of its Efficacy in various diseases, & seeing the difficulty of procuring it here, I thought it would be of some utility for the Inhabitants to propagate it.   The Seed according the Directions of the Botanists must be sown as soon as it is ripe, I shall then be extremely obliged to you, if you have the Kindness to ask it from some of your friends in Virginia, & have it forwarded to me.   I am aware that to trouble the President of the U. S. amongst his Serious & Important occupations, for the sake of a Plant, is a bold Intrusion, but I know likewise, your Zeal & Eagerness, to promote & spread whatever may be useful & in the least beneficial to mankind.   A Single Child cured by your plant will, be sufficient reward for your trouble, & to me would be the highest pitch of ambition to which I aspire. . . . (*Jefferson Papers,* L. C.)

(Jefferson to Julien Niemcewicz.)

Washington June 29. 1801.

Your favor of the 16th is just received.   I shall be at Monticello during the months of Aug. & Sep. which I believe comprehends the seeding time of the Polygala Seneca, in which case I will endeavor to have some saved.   I know however it is become extremely rare. lest my efforts should fail, I may mention that in that want Bartram could furnish either the plants or seed. . . . (*Jefferson Papers,* L. C.)

(Daniel Clark, Jr., to Jefferson.)

New Orleans, July 20, 1801.

. . . In the last letter I had the honor of receiving from you, you mentioned that your Pacan Trees at Monticello tho' planted in 1780 had not hitherto borne fruit, this must be owing to their being planted in too elevated or too dry a soil as they bear in this country in ten or twelve years, and the trees in their natural state are I believe always found in the River Bottoms and in places occasionally overflowed at the annual rise of the river.   I have taken the liberty of mentioning this

Circumstance that you may try the experiment on some young Trees I
send herewith put up in a case as well as a few orange Trees which I
hope will get safe to hand. (*Jefferson Papers*, L. C.)

(William Maclure to Jefferson.)

Paris 20<sup>th</sup> Novem<sup>r</sup>. 1801.

I wrote you from England last summer and have since been thro'
Germany and on the Rhine. I thought both the soil and climate in
many places bore a greater resemblance to the soil and climate in the
back parts of Pennsylvania Maryland and Virginia than any part of
Europe I have yet been in and finding that the farmers from the want of
enclosures and pasture feed their cattle for some part of the year on roots
induced me to forward to you by this opportunity some of the Beets and
the Turnip Cabbage which they use principally as winter food for their
cattle and hope they will arrive in time for you to make the experiment.
Am rather induced to believe that sufficient attention has not been paid
in the choice of seeds to the previous habits of the vegetable depending
much on the nature of the Climate and perhaps something on the soil.
in many of the experiments to raise winter food for the Cattle in Virginia such as turnips etc. the seeds have been brought from England &
Holland where the climate is moist and not so variable in point of
temperature from their proximity to the sea and Insular situation for
the same reason perhaps the clover, lucern & other grasses which grow
in the upper parts of Germany might succeed with you where the English and Dutch seeds have failed and not improbably the vine from the
banks of the Rhine would thrive well on the Southwest Mountains as
the soil is much the same and the Climate equally warm. when I
passed that Country it was the Vintage and too early for the setts, or I
should have forced some from the different situations and exposures.—
They plant Tobacco very generally in Germany and have found it answers all the purposes of a Pulse crop in cleaning and envigorating the
soil. in June they plant and take it up in Septem<sup>r</sup> when they immediately sow wheat which experience has taught them yeilds a better crop
than if the land had lain fallow the price is from 15/ to 16/ lb [illegible]
which the farmer makes little or nothing but as a Pulse crop in the rotation they are induced to plant it every five years. Ive rather been of
oppinion that the common land in Virginia of the Tobacco being an im-
poverishing crop arose from allowing the soil to wash after having been
well pulverized and suffer the stalks to run to seed after they were cut.
In the Country round the Hartz Mountains they use pulverized Gypsum
as a top dressing for their Lucern & Clover tho this soil is calcarious and
frequently cut the lucern seven times and the clover five times by sowing about a bushel to the acre after every cutting.—both in Germany
and this Country they are turning their attention more to agriculture
than they used to do. the cheapest of labour facilitates this experiment
and is perhaps the only part of their improvements that can add to the
prosperity of America by addopting only those that have succeeded. . . .
(*Jefferson Papers*, L. C.)

# 1802

May 11.   planted grape vines recieved from Legaux[2] in the S.W. vineyard.[3]   in vacant spaces of rows in the upper or 1st. row very large white eating grapes.

2d. row  } 30. plants of vines from Burgundy[4]
3d. d°.  } and Champagne[5] with roots.

4th. row } 30. plants of vines of Bordeaux[6]
5th. row } with roots.

6th. row.   10. plants of vines from Cape of good hope[7] with roots.

26.   planted in the upper row of the Nursery beginning at the N.E. end the following peach stones, sent me by Mazzei from Pisa.[8]   see his letter.[9] 4. stones of the Maddelena peach.[10]   then 4. of the poppe de Venere.[11]   then 12 Melon peaches.   then 40. Vaga loggia.[12]

also planted a great number of Paccan nuts,[13] in the same rows of those planted the two last years.

———————————————— ✺ ————————————————

[1] *1802.* Jefferson was now entering his second year as President.   His time was taken up with the usual routine of the office.

He made a short spring visit to *Monticello* on May 5, returning to Washington on May 27.   During this visit he directed Anthony Giannini to plant grape vines sent to him by Mr. Legaux. (See entry in *Garden Book* and letter, Jefferson to Legaux, March 24, 1801.) The day before he returned to Washington he planted a variety of plants in the nursery.

Jefferson's second visit to *Monticello* took place on July 21. He was back in Washington on October 4. During this visit the family, which had been absent during the spring visit, was with him. There is no record as to what agricultural matters transpired during the visit.

Work on the house continued at a slow pace. Probably the most important addition to the house was the northwest offices, which contained the icehouse and the coach houses. Jefferson wrote to James Dinsmore, his carpenter at *Monticello,* on March 19:

As I suppose m͞r Lilly is digging the North West offices, & Ice house I will now give further directions respecting them. the eves of those offices is to be of course exactly on the level of those on the South East side of the hill. but as the North West building is chiefly for coach houses, the floor must be sunk 9. feet deep below the bottom of the plate to let a coach go under it. then the ice house is to be dug 16. feet deeper than that. the ice house is then to be sealed, circular, to a height of 4. feet above the office floors, leaving a door 3½ feet wide on the N. W. side of it. on that height it is to be joisted with 2. I. plank 9 I. wide & laid edge up & 9. I. clear apart from one another, running across the building, or N. W. & S. E. then to be covered with inch plank. . . . this arrangement of the joists is intended to leave them open towards the N. W. wind to let in air, which may be excluded by small shutters whenever it shall be thought better to close them. the openings are left only 9 I. square that a person may not get in at them. (*Jefferson Papers,* L. C.) (Pl. XVIII.)

Although the *Garden Book* had two entries for the year, there were none in the *Farm Book;* the letters again are the main source of agricultural information.

² Peter Legaux lived at Spring Mills, 13 miles northwest of Philadelphia. Bailey says of him: "Legaux appears to have been the most intelligent and public-spirited grape-grower which the country had known; and he was the person who introduced—though unknowingly—the grape which ushered in the distinctive American viticulture." (L. H. Bailey, *The Evolution of Our Native Fruits* (New York, 1911): 19. Hereafter cited as Bailey, *Fruits.*) See also letter, Jefferson

to Legaux, March 24, 1801.  In the *Account Book* for the
year is this entry: "May 11. p$^d$ Anthony Giannini for planting
grape vines from Legaux 1. D."

[3] See plates VII and XXXII for location of the vineyard.

[4] *Burgundy,* province of eastern France.

[5] *Champagne,* old province of northeastern France.

[6] *Bordeaux,* seaport city, capital of Department of Gironde,
France.

[7] Cape of Good Hope, province of Union of South Africa,
with Cape Town as the capital.  (See Bailey, *Fruits:* 42–45,
for a discussion of the grapes mentioned above.)

[8] Pisa, city of Tuscany, Italy, on Arno River.

[9] This letter has not been located.

[10] Maddelena, a variety of peach.

[11] Poppe de Venere, translated, "the breast of Venus," a
variety of peach.

[12] Vaga loggia, translated, "beautiful loggia," a variety of
peach.

[13] Jefferson probably received these paccan nuts from Daniel
Clark, Jr., of New Orleans.  See letter, Daniel Clark, Jr., to
Jefferson, July 20, 1801.

### LETTERS AND EXTRACTS OF LETTERS, 1802

(Jefferson to Robert Bailey.)

Washington Mar. 21. 1802.

. . . Would it be within the scope of m$\bar{r}$ Bailey's plan of gardening
for the common market, to make a provision of endive for the ensuing
winter, so as to be able to furnish Th: J. with a sallad of endive every
day through the winter till the spring sallading should commence, for
which Th: J. would send once a week, and preserve the week's provision
here by setting them in earth, to be drawn from day to day fresh. . . .
(*Jefferson Papers,* M. H. S.)

(Jefferson to John Bartram, Jr.)

Washington Apr. 5. 1802.

I am desired on the part of the Agricultural society of Paris to put the
inclosed list of seeds, which they want, into the hands of some person
who can be relied on to furnish them genuine and fresh.  I ask this
favor of you.  they would wish to receive them in autumn, or as early
in the next winter as possible.  as soon therefore as the season has admitted the whole to be [secured] or as many as can be got, I will thank

you to have them packed in a [strong] box, and to drop a line by post at this place informing me they are ready, and sending me your bill. I will immediately have that paid, and direct a person to call on you & receive the box. I will thank you to let me know whether you receive this letter and can undertake to execute it. . . . (*Jefferson Papers,* L. C.)

## (Jefferson to John Bartram, Jr.)

Wash. Dec. 2. 1802.

I received last night your favor of the 26th Nov. informing me that the seeds & plants are made up for which I had written to you some time ago. mr William Short sets out from this place tomorrow for Philadelphia & will call on you, receive & pay you for them. to him therefore be so good as to deliver them, & to accept assurances of my esteem & best wishes. (*Jefferson Papers,* L. C.)

## (Jefferson to Robert Bailey.)

Washington Dec. 9, 1802.

A friend of mine in France has asked me to procure the seeds and plants below mentioned, as this may not be out of your line, and the plants abound in this neighborhood, I will ask the favor of you to make the collection, and pack them well and properly for the sea, labelling each article so substantially as not to be erased. The sooner they are ready the better, should you not have the convenience of having the boxes made, and will send me a note of the sizes, they shall be made here. . . .

> black walnuts, half a bushel
> seeds of the Poplar half a bushel
> Cedar berries 1 lb.
> acorns of every kind, half a bushel to be packed in dry bran
> Sassafras seed 1 lb
> Swamp laurel 1 lb
> Dogwood ½ lb
> white ash seed ½ lb
> Catalpa seed ½ lb
> Wild roses of every kind, ½ bushel of each
> 12 plants of sassafras ⎫
> 12 do. of swamp laurel ⎬ to be packed in moss in a box
> 12 do. of Dogwood ⎭

(*Glimpses of the Past,* Missouri Historical Society: 89.)

## From the *Account Book 1791–1803:*

Apr.  2. the first martin appears.
May 12. note we had cherries ripe May 9. peas the 12th. strawberries the 14th.
Nov. 15. flower pots & trowel 1.36.

# 1803

Mar. 12.   the well² was observed about a month ago to have a plenty of water in it after having been dry about 18. months.

          my ice house³ here has taken 62. waggon loads of ice to fill it, have 1. foot thickness of shavings between it and the wall all around. the whole cost including labour, feeding, drink etc. has been 70.D.

    21.   peach trees begin to blossom.

    24.   a considerable snow on the blue ridge

    25.   thermom. at sunrise 34°.

    28.   thermom. at sunrise 29°.

---

¹ *1803.* There were two memorable events that occurred during Jefferson's third year as President, namely, the purchase of Louisiana from France, and the organization of the Lewis and Clark Expedition to explore the Missouri River to its source and to open a route to the Pacific Ocean. Both were to have profound influence on the future development of the United States.

An expedition to the west country had long been a dream of Jefferson. As far back as 1792, he had proposed to the American Philosophical Society to procure such an exploration, with funds raised by subscription; and it was under the auspices of this Society, and under instructions prepared by Jefferson, that Michaux, the celebrated French botanist and traveler, proceeded on his exploration westward, until recalled by the French Minister. (Randall, *Jefferson* 3: 36.)

Meriwether Lewis, Jefferson's private secretary, was selected to head the expedition. He was to be accompanied by William Clark and about ten woodsmen. Lewis's qualifications were set forth in an interesting letter to Benjamin Smith Barton, whom Jefferson asked to inform Mr. Lewis what natural objects he should especially observe on the expedition.

Washington, February 27, 1803.

. . . You know we have been many years wishing to have the Missouri explored, and whatever river, heading with that, runs into the western ocean. Congress, in some secret proceedings, have yielded to a proposition I made them for permitting me to have it done. It is to be undertaken immediately, with a party of about ten, and I have appointed Captain Lewis, my Secretary, to conduct it. It was impossible to find a character who, to a complete science in Botany, Natural History, Mineralogy and Astronomy, joined the firmness of constitution and character, prudence, habits adapted to the woods, and familiarity with the Indian manners and character, requisite for this undertaking. All the latter qualifications Captain Lewis has. Although no regular botanist, etc., he possesses a remarkable store of accurate observation on all the subjects of the three kingdoms, and will, therefore, readily single out whatever presents itself new to him in either; and he has qualified himself for taking the observations of longitude and latitude necessary to fix the geography of the line he passes through. In order to draw his attention at once to the objects most desirable, I must ask the favor of you to prepare for him a note of those in the lines of botany, zoology, or of Indian history, which you think most worthy of enquiry and observation. He will be with you in Philadelphia in two or three weeks, and will wait on you, and receive thankfully on paper, and any verbal communications which you may be so good as to make to him. I make no apology for this trouble, because I know that the same wish to promote science which has induced me to bring forward this proposition, will induce you to aid in promoting it. . . . (Lipscomb and Bergh, *Jefferson* 10: 366–368.)

Jefferson made two visits to *Monticello* during the year. The spring vacation lasted from March 7 to April 3, while the late summer visit extended from July 19 to September 25.

The *Garden Book* has five entries made during his spring vacation; only one, however, refers to the garden. In the

*Account Book 1791–1803* he jotted down: "Mar. 21. p^d Anthony Giannini for plants & trouble 2. D." Jefferson's note is vague.

Work on the house progressed slowly, as usual. One item in the same *Account Book* reads: "Sept. 22. paid Robert Hope for setting up columns. 20. D." The nailery, which was now in new quarters, made unusually high sales during the year. Another item in the *Account Book* says: "Mar. 1. the article of nails has been extraordinary this year."

Jefferson was a passionate lover of mockingbirds. He bought two mockingbirds and two cages during the year (*Account Book 1791–1803*). Mrs. Samuel Harrison Smith, a recorder of the first forty years of Washington society, left an interesting picture of Jefferson's interest in these birds.

In the window recesses [in his apartment in the White House], were stands for the flowers and plants which it was his delight to attend and among his roses and geraniums was suspended the cage of his favorite mocking-bird, which he cherished with peculiar fondness, not only for its melodious powers, but for its uncommon intelligence and affectionate disposition, of which qualities he gave surprising instances. It was the constant companion of his solitary and studious hours. Whenever he was alone he opened the cage and let the bird fly about the room. After flitting for awhile from one object to another, it would alight on his table and regale him with his sweetest notes, or perch on his shoulder and take its food from his lips. Often when he retired to his chamber it would hop up the stairs after him and while he took his siesta, would sit on his couch and pour forth its melodious strains. How he loved this bird! How he loved his flowers! He could not live without something to love, and in the absence of his darling grandchildren, his birds and his flowers became objects of tender care. (Margaret Bayard Smith, *The First Forty Years of Washington Society* (Gaillard Hunt, ed., New York, 1906): 385. Hereafter cited as Smith, *Washington*.)

No entries under 1803 appear in the *Farm Book*. Letters on agricultural subjects were more numerous than in the preceding years. They show a widening interest.

² The well, which was 65 feet deep, was dug in 1769 (*Weather Memorandum Book 1776–1820*). See appendix II.

³ The icehouse was built in 1802. This is the first mention of its being in use. From the *Account Book*: "Feb. 7. inclosed, to Gabriel Lilly for waggonage of ice 30. D." (See letter, Jefferson to Dinsmore, March 19, 1802 (quoted in note 1 for that year), and plate XVIII.)

LETTERS AND EXTRACTS OF LETTERS, 1803

(William Hamilton to Jefferson.)

Jan. 16, 1803.
The Woodlands [Philadelphia].

Mr. Hamilton presents his respectful compliments to the President, & with great pleasure sends him a few seeds of the *Mimosa farnesiana,* being all he saved during the last year. Lest these should not vegetate, Mr. H. will as soon as they ripen, forward some of the present years growth to the President, who will confer a favor on him, in naming any seeds or plants he may wish to have from the Woodlands collection. (*Jefferson Papers,* L. C.)

(Jefferson to Madame Noailles de Tessé.)

Washington Jan. 30. 1803.

M$^r$. Short delivered me your favor of the 1$^{st}$. Prairial an. 10. and gave me the welcome news of your good health. it has recalled to my mind recollections very dear to it. for the friendship with which you honoured me in Paris was among the circumstances which most contributed to my happiness there. When I left you at the close of 1790 I thought your situation in it's best possible state. at the end of 1791 I saw it was passed, and in the course of 1792. that all was desperate. in the gloomy years which then followed my anxieties attended my friends personally, and particularly yourself of whom I could seldom hear. after such a shipwreck it is fortunate indeed that you can resume the interest you take in planting trees. and I shall be very happy in contributing to aliment it. to this however my present situation is not favorable, partly from constant occupations but more from my geographical position. not a single person in this quarter has attended to botanical subjects beyond the ordinary produce of the kitchen garden: nor are there, scarcely ever, any means of conveyance from thence to France. I have therefore selected from the catalogue you put into m$\bar{r}$ Short's hands those articles only which the fruits of this neighborhood, or it's gardens can furnish. these are

> Liriodendron tulipifera.
> Juglans nigra.
> Juniperus Virginiana.
> des glands de plusieurs especes.
> Laurus Sassafras.
> Magnolia glauca.
> Magnolia tripetala (Umbrella)
> Cornus florida.
> fraxinus alba.  doubtful if here
> Catalpa.

these within my power. by undertaking more, I might have prevented

m̄ Short's engaging for them a more certain agent.   it was late in September when I received the catalogue.   I was then at Monticello.   the
Sassafras had already lost it's seeds, and those of the others were in a
milky unripe state.   on my return here I engaged an old Scotch gardener
of the neighborhood, who had formerly lived some years in my family,
to undertake this collection.   he called on me a few days ago and informed me that the means for collecting some of the articles had escaped
him, but that he had collected a part & would bring them in a few days.
my difficulty will then be to find a conveyance: but no exertions will be
spared to overcome this so that they may reach you in March.   they will
probably be addressed to m̄ la Motte, Vice Consul of the U.S. in
Havre.   I will continue to lay my shoulder to these articles annually till
you are fully supplied with them.

I own, my dear Madame, that I cannot but admire your courage in
undertaking now to plant trees.   it has always been my passion; insomuch that I rarely ever planted a flower in my life.   but when I return to live at Monticello, which may be in 1805. but will be in 1809.
at the latest (because then, at any rate, I am determined to draw the
curtain between the political world and myself.)   I believe I shall become a florist.   the labours of the year, in that line, are repaid within
the year, and death, which will be at my door, shall find me unembar-
rassed in long lived undertakings.   but I acknolege there is more of the
disinterested & magnanimous in your purpose.

This goes by mr. Monroe, my close, my best friend, & the honestest
man on earth, lately governor of Virginia, and now charged with a special mission to the governments of France and Spain.   he will be the
safest channel through which you can convey me any further orders.   be
so good as to present my respectful attachment to M. de Tessé, and accept yourself assurances of my constant & affectionate friendship & high
consideration.   (*Jefferson Papers*, L. C.)

(Jefferson to Benjamin Rush.)

Washington, Feb. 28, 1803.

. . . I wish to mention to you, in confidence that I have obtained authority from Congress to undertake the long desired object of exploring
the Missouri & whatever river, heading with that, leads into the western
ocean.   About 10. chosen woodsmen headed by Capt. Lewis my secretary will set out on it immediately & probably accomplish it in two
seasons.   Capt. Lewis is brave, prudent, habituated to the woods, & familiar with Indian manners and character.   He is not regularly educated, but he possesses a great mass of accurate observation on all the
subjects of nature which present themselves here, & will therefore
readily select those only in his new route which shall be new.   He has
qualified himself for those observations of longitude & latitude necessary
to fix the points of the line he will go over.   It would be very useful to
state for him those objects on which it is most desirable he should bring
us information.   For this purpose I ask the favor of you to prepare some
notes of such particulars as may occur in his journey & which you think

should draw his attention and enquiry.  He will be in Philadelphia about 2. or 3. weeks hence & will wait on you. . . . (Ford, *Jefferson* 9: 452–453.)

### (Jefferson to George Jefferson.)

Washington April 24. 1803.

Will you be so good as to procure from old mr Collins or any other faithful seedsman 1. gallon of earliest Frame peas and 2. gallons of Dwarf Marrowfats and send them addressed to Gabriel Lilly at Monticello. . . . (*Jefferson Papers*, M. H. S.)

### (Jefferson to John W. Eppes.)

Washington June 19. 1803.

. . . I have examined your Hessian flies & find them very genuine on which I condole with you. . . . the advantageous remedy is to sow no more wheat grounds than can be well manured & sowing the yellow bearded wheat, the surplus grounds put into rye and clover.  they attack barley more readily than wheat.  when they drive us to this, they are a great blessing. . . . I enclose you one of Binns's pamphlets on the use of plaister.  it is bunglingly composed, but it is generally said his facts may be relied on.  the important one is that from being poor he is become rich by it. . . . (*Jefferson Papers*, U. Va.)

### (Jefferson to Sir John Sinclair.)

Washington, June 30, 1803.

It is so long since I have had the pleasure of writing to you, that it would be vain to look back to dates to connect the old and the new. Yet I ought not to pass over my acknowledgments to you for various publications received from time to time, and with great satisfaction and thankfulness.  I send you a small one in return, the work of a very unlettered farmer, yet valuable, as it relates plain facts of importance to farmers.  You will discover that Mr. Binns is an enthusiast for the use of gypsum.  But there are two facts which prove he has a right to be so: 1. He began poor, and has made himself tolerably rich by his farming alone.  2. The county of Loudon, in which he lives, had been so exhausted and wasted by bad husbandry, that it began to depopulate, the inhabitants going southwardly in quest of better lands.  Binns' success has stopped that emigration.  It is now becoming one of the most productive counties of the State of Virginia, and the price given for the lands is multiplied manifold. . . .

I hope your agricultural institution goes on with success.  I consider you as the author of all the good it shall do.  A better idea has never been carried into practice.  Our agricultural society has at length formed itself.  Like our American Philosophical Society, it is voluntary, and unconnected with the public, and is precisely an execution of the plan I formerly sketched to you.  Some State societies have been formed heretofore; the others will do the same.  Each State society names two of its members of Congress to be their members in the Central society, which is of course together during the sessions of Congress. They are to select matter from the proceedings of the State societies, and to publish it; so that their publications may be called *l'esprit des sociétes d'agriculture,* etc. The Central society was formed the last winter only, so that it will be some time before they get under way. Mr. Madison, the Secretary of State, was elected their President. . . . (Lipscomb and Bergh, *Jefferson* 10: 396–398.)

### (Jefferson to Robert Bailey.)

Washington Oct. 10. '03.

I received lately from France a few grains of a wheat with a solid stem. as from this circumstance it will probably be proof against the Hessian fly, I am dividing it among those who I think will take care of it. I send you a few seeds, as also some seed of a cabbage said to grow 7. feet high, to put on several heads & reproduce them when cut off. this seems wonderful, but is worth seeing into. . . . (*Jefferson Papers,* M. H. S.)

### (Jefferson to Robert Bailey.)

Washington Oct. 19. 1803.

A gentleman here has given me 40. Balsam poplars to send to Monticello, and mr̄ Randolph's servant, who was to have returned tomorrow will be detained till the next day, to carry them. as I set much store by these trees which I have been a long time trying to get to Monticello, I wish them to be carefully taken up & packed in bundles for safe transportation. if it would suit you to come tomorrow morning & take them up & bundle them properly for the journey, it would oblige me, besides satisfactory compensation. I shall also be glad to receive the box for France, as the vessel will sail in a week. . . . (*Jefferson Papers,* M. H. S.)

### (Jefferson to Mde. Noailles de Tessé.)

Washington Oct. 31, 1803.

In my letter of Jan. 30, I informed you that the person whom I had employed in this neighborhood had provided such seeds of the list therein stated to you, as the lateness of the season had permitted. I had the mortification to see them remain here till summer without any opportunity occurring to forward them. our only commercial port is Alexandria, five miles distant. by casting your eye on a map you will perceive that to send a package from thence to Baltimore, Philadelphia, or New York to be reshipped to France, is as difficult as to send one from Havre to Marseilles for America. it would add much to the risk of miscarriage & more to the delay, which in the case of plants is fatal. It remains therefore that we depend solely on Alexandria, which has not a great intercourse with France. It happens fortunately at this moment that we are sending a ship on public account to the Mediterranean, but to touch at Lorient on her way. I have therefore required the gardener employed to make up his box of plants and seeds, which he has accordingly done; & delivered them to me. they will be put on board tomorrow, addressed to the care of Mr. Aaron Vale, Consul of the U. S. at Lorient, with directions to find the cheapest mode of conveying them to you; the box being very heavy, it's bulk is about 13 cubical feet. perhaps you can advise him the best method of sending it. I did not open it to see how it was packed, but the following is the list furnished by the gardener.

Plants No. 1 Magnolia glauca ⎫
        2 Laurus Sassafras ⎬ about 1½ dozen of plants
        3 Cornus florida   ⎭ of each of these

Seeds No. 1 Wild roses of various kinds.
        2 Quercus alba
        3 Quercus prinus, 2 kinds, castaneae foliis,
                          called Chestnut oak.
        4 Quercus Hispanica. a variety of the Rubra
        5 Quercus Rubra
    No. 6 acorns of the Box oak. I do not know this.
        7 Liriodendron
        8 Juglans nigra
          Magnolia glauca    ⎫ the names of these are
          Laurus Sassafras   ⎪ written on the bags
          Cornus florida     ⎬
          Juniperus Virginiana ⎭

I am sorry to find he has not put up any acorns of the Quercus Phellos (live oak) which abound here more than anywhere, nor the seeds of the Catalpa, which I presume is to be found in the gardens here, as the ship is not yet gone, perhaps I may be able to get them all. I will take care to renew this supply annually till you are sufficiently furnished with the articles composing it. I undertake it with the more satisfaction because it is within the limits of those attentions I may justifiably spare for it. They will sometimes fail for want of a conveyance from Alexandria to Havre, the only port I would have ventured to send to, had not the advantages of the present conveyance overbalanced the inconvenient distance of Lorient from Paris, perhaps our Vale will be able to send the box round to Havre & up the Seine, for which he will have plenty of time.

Altho' the times are big with political events, yet I shall say nothing on that or any subject but the innocent ones of botany & friendship. I shall be much gratified if I am able to contribute anything to your botanical pleasures & emploiments. I feel their importance to you the more, as they are congenial to my own mind. permit me to place here my friendly respects to M. de Tesse and M. & Mde. de la Fayette, and to assure yourself of my constant & affectionate esteem and respect. (*Glimpses of the Past,* Missouri Historical Society: 91–92.)

(Jefferson to Aaron Vale.)

Washington Nov. 4, 03.

The schooner Citizen, Capt. Lawson, being employed by our government to carry some gun carriages to the Emperor of Morocco, and to touch at Lorient in going, in order to deliver there the ratification of our late treaty with France, I take the benefit of your cover for a letter to Mr. Livingston, our Minister Plenipotentiary, accompanied by a small box of about 8 or 9 inches cube addressed to him; which I will pray you to put into the care of the French gentleman whom Mr. Pichon has entrusted with the ratification, if he can conveniently take charge of it, or otherwise to send it by the Diligence or such other conveyance as will be safe and not too costly for the value of the box which is but small. I avail myself of the same occasion to send a box of plants to my friend, Madame de Tessé (aunt of Marquis de la Fayette) at Paris. this is about three quarters of a ton in bulk (say 15 cubic feet) and is heavy; consequently requires the cheapest transportation possible to avoid its becoming a very burthensome present. if the state of the war will permit its going round by sea to Havre, & up the Seine to Paris, that is the best conveyance, but if that is blockaded, I must leave to you to choose the cheapest mode of conveyance to be depended on. if you could take the trouble to drop a line to Madame de Tessé (to the care of Mr. Livingston) suggesting to her the practicable modes of conveyance, she would probably say which she would prefer, but if they can go to Havre, that is so obviously the best, that she need only be informed you have sent them by that route. I pray you to excuse the trouble I give you, which is occasioned by the accident of the ship's touching at your port: & to accept my salutations & good wishes. (*Glimpses of the Past,* Missouri Historical Society: 92–93.)

(Jefferson to David Williams.)

Washington, November 14, 1803.

. . . The class principally defective is that of agriculture. It is the first in utility, and ought to be the first in respect. The same artificial means which have been used to produce a competition in learning, may be equally successful in restoring agriculture to its primary dignity in the eyes of men. It is a science of the very first order. It counts among its handmaids the most respectable sciences, such as Chemistry, Natural Philosophy, Mechanics, Mathematics generally, Natural History, Botany. In every College and University, a professorship of agriculture, and the class of its students, might be honored as the first. Young men closing their academical education with this, as the crown of all other sciences, fascinated with its solid charms, and at a time when they are to choose an occupation, instead of crowding the other classes, would return to the farms of their fathers, their own, or those of others, and replenish and invigorate a calling, now languishing under contempt and oppression. The charitable schools, instead of storing their pupils with a lore which the present state of society does not call for, converted into schools of agriculture, might restore them to that branch qualified to enrich and honor themselves, and to increase the productions of the nation instead of consuming them. . . . (Lipscomb and Bergh, *Jefferson* 10: 429–430.)

(Jefferson to Governor John Milledge.)

Washington Nov. 22. 1803.

. . . I thank you for the seeds & stones you have been so kind as to send me. I hope Congress will rise early enough to let me pass the month of March at home to superintend the planting them and some other things which may be growing & preparing enjoiment for me there when I retire from hence. . . . (*Jefferson Papers*, L. C.)

From the *Account Book 1791–1803*:

May 31.   gave Joseph Dougherty ord. on J. Barnes for 10. D to buy a mock$^g$ bird & cage.
Sept. 21.   paid Bezey in full 33. D. for gardening.
Oct. 21.   gave Davy Bowles to take care of trees.   2. D.
Nov. 17.   p$^d$ Steele for a mocking bird 15. D.
Dec.   8.   Bryan 15. D. for a bird-cage.

# 1804

Apr. 6. sowed seeds of the East India Asparagus in a small bed at the point of levelled triangle S.W. end of the garden.[2]

10. planted in the orchard below the garden black soft peaches of Georgia from W. Mer.[3]

12. planted 40. odd Hemlock [4] & Weymouth pines [5] near the Aspen thicket.

29. planted seeds of the Cherokee rose [6] from Gov'. Milledge [7] in a row of about 6.f. near the N.E. corner of the Nursery. Goliah [8] stuck sticks to mark the place.

this has been a remarkeably backward spring. we have had fires steadily thro' the whole month.

Apr. 22. a great fresh in the Rivanna this day. it was above the top of the hopper in my toll mill.[9] by marks at Henderson's distillery [10] in Milton [11] it wanted 6. feet of being as high as that in 1795.[12] which wanted but 3.f. of being as high as the great fresh on the 26th. of May 1771.[13]

---

[1] *1804.* Jefferson was reelected President in November by a tremendous majority. His first term ended on March 4 of the following year.

The Lewis and Clark Expedition, organized the previous year, finally reached the banks of the Mississippi and on May 14 began to travel up the Missouri River. Some of the seeds and plants collected by this expedition were later to find a place in Jefferson's gardens. Others were sent to interested gardeners and seedsmen in other parts of the country.

Jefferson suffered another of the tragic losses of his life when his daughter, Maria Eppes, died on April 17. Since she had given birth to a daughter a short time before, she was survived by two children. The son, Francis, grew to manhood; the daughter died in infancy. An extract from a letter written to his old friend, John Page, then Governor of Virginia, shows how poignantly Jefferson suffered over this loss.

> Your letter, my dear friend, of the 25th ultimo, is a new proof of the goodness of your heart, and the part you take in my loss marks an affectionate concern for the greatness of it. It is great indeed. Others may lose of their abundance, but I, of my want, have lost even the half of all I had. My evening prospects now hang on the slender thread of a single life. Perhaps I may be destined to see even this last cord of parental affection broken! The hope with which I had looked forward to the moment, when, resigning public cares to younger hands, I was to retire to that domestic comfort from which the last great step is taken, is fearfully blighted. (Randall, *Jefferson* 3: 103.)

Jefferson made his usual spring and late summer visits to *Monticello*. The first one lasted from April 4 to May 11; the second from July 26 to September 27. Entries in the *Garden Book* indicate that much planting was done during the spring visit. One planting of special interest was the forty hemlocks and white pines placed near the aspen thicket. No record has been found to show what work was undertaken in the garden during the summer visit.

About 1804 Jefferson again made elaborate plans for improving the grounds of *Monticello*. These plans he put down in a note book, which consisted of three folded sheets and one half-sheet laid in the center. (See Fiske Kimball, *Thomas Jefferson, Architect* (Boston, 1916): 168.) Two of these sheets are reproduced under the titles of "General Ideas for Improvement of Monticello," and "Garden or Pleasure Ground" (pls. XIX, XX).

There is no indication that the fruit trees sent by John Armstrong, of Cincinnati, and mentioned in his letter of February

Garden. Olitory. make the upper slope thus ⌐ᵈ⌐ at a plant
a hedge of hedgethorn, & at 6 one of privet, or Gleditsia, or cedar to
be trimmed down to 3.f. high. the whole appearance thus.
taking a border of 8.f. at the foot of the terras for
forward productions, the main beds must be reduced
from 50.f. to 42.f.

walk  beds
10.f   8.f

Garden or pleasure grounds.

The canvas at large must be Grove, of the largest trees (poplar,
oak, elm, maple, ash, hiccory, chesnut, linden, Weymouth pine sycamore) trimmed
very high, so as to give it the appearance of open ground, yet
not so far apart but that they may cover the ground with close
shade.

this must be broken by clumps of thicket, as the open
grounds of the English are broken by clumps of trees.
plants for thickets are broom, calycanthus, althaea, gelder rose,
magnolia glauca, azalea, fringe tree, dogwood, redbud, wild crab.
kalmia, mezereon, euonymus, halesia, quamoclid, rhododendron
oleander, service tree, lilac, honeysuckle, bramble,
The best way of forming thicket will be to plant it spirally, in labyrinth, putting the tallest plants in the center & lowering gradatim to the
external termination. a temple or seat may be in the center.
thus ⊙ leaving space enough between the rows to walk &
to trim up, replant &c the shrubs.

Vistas to very interesting objects may be permitted, but in gene-
ral it is better so to arrange thickets as that they may have
the effect of vista in various directions.
Dells or ravines should be close in trees & undergrowth,
Glens, or hollows should be opened downwards, being embraced by forest,
Glades opened on sloping hill sides, with clumps of trees within them
Temples or seats at those spots on the walks most interesting either for
prospect or the immediate scenery.
The Broom thicket on the South side to be improved for winter walking
or riding; conducting a variety of roads, through it, forming chambers
with seats, well sheltered from winds, & spread before the
sun. a temple with yellow glass panes would suit there, as it
would give the illusion of sunshine in cloudy weather.
a thicket may be of cedar, topped into a bush, for the center, surrounded by Kalmia.
or it may be of Scotch broom alone.

PLATE XIX.—Jefferson's plans for a garden or pleasure grounds, about 1804.
See plate XXI. (*Jefferson Papers*, M. H. S.)

General ideas for the improvement of Monticello.

all the houses on the Mulberry walk to be taken away, except
the stone house, and a ha! ha! instead of the paling along
it for an inclosure. this will of course be made when the
garden is levelled, and stone for the wall will be got out of the
garden itself, in digging, aided by that got out of the level in
front of the S.W. offices, the old stone fence below the stable, and
the lower wall of the garden, which is thicker than necessary.

the ground between the upper & lower roundabouts to be laid out
in lawns & clumps of trees, the lawns opening so as to give
advantageous catches of prospect to the upper roundabout.

from the lower roundabout to good portions of prospect.

Walks in this style, and △△△△ -ing up the mountain.

the spring on Montalto either to be brought to Monticello by pipes
or to fall over steps of stairs in cascade, made visible at Mon-
-ticello through a vista.

a fish pond to be visible from the house.

a level round-about from the Thoroughfare to circumscribe
the garden grounds.

the North side of Monticello below the Thoroughfare roundabout
quite down to the river, and all Montalto above the thoroughfare
to be converted into park & riding grounds, connected at the
Thoroughfare by a bridge, open, under which the public road
may be made to pass so as not to cut off the communication
between the lower & upper park grounds.

all the farm grounds of Monticello had better be turned into orchard
grounds of cyder apple & peach trees, & orchard grass cultivated
under them.

at the Rocks build a turning Tuscan temple 10.f. diam. 6. columns. proportions of Pantheon
at the Point build Demosthenes's lanthern.

over each angle of the offices the Chinese pavilion of Kew garden

along the lower edge of the garden have 4 little boxes arranged thus

No. 1. may be a Gothic. for designs see Meinert No. 8. 37. 38. 45.
through the whole line from 1. to 4. have the walk covered by an arbor, to wit
locust forks set in the ground crossed by poles at top, & laths on these

grape vines principally to cover the top, the sides quite
open. the boxes should be recesses from this walk
a gate, at the entrance of the garden, having a green house below.

No. 1. a specimen of Gothic.
    2. model of the Pantheon
    3. model of cubic architecture
    4. a specimen of Chinese.
but after all, the kitchen garden is not the place for ornaments
of this kind. bowers & treillages suit that better, & these temples
will be better disposed on the pleasure grounds.

PLATE XX.—Jefferson's general ideas for the improvement of *Monticello*, about
1804. (*Jefferson Papers*, M. H. S.)

20 to Jefferson, were planted. But, as has been seen before, there are many gaps of this kind. There were no entries in the *Farm Book* for the year.

[2] Jefferson began this year to re-level the garden, which had been laid out on March 31, 1774. The work was not completed until after he retired in 1809. (See letter, Jefferson to John W. Eppes, June 4, 1804; and *Garden Book,* March 31, 1774.)

[3] William Douglass Meriwether lived at *Clover Fields* on the east side of the South West Mountain, Albemarle County. He was a man of fine sense and great wealth. He was a magistrate of the county for 50 years, and the only one of the whole body of magistrates that filled the office of sheriff twice, in 1801 and 1828. His wife was Elizabeth, daughter of Nicholas Lewis, and through her he inherited the part of the *Farm* nearest Charlottesville, which in 1825 he sold to John A. G. Davis, who built on it the brick house now standing. He died in 1845. (See Woods, *Albemarle County:* 272.)

[4] *Tsuga canadensis* Carr.

[5] *Pinus strobus* L. More commonly called white pine. The late Dr. Rodney H. True, in his "Thomas Jefferson's Garden Book" (*Proc. Am. Philos. Soc.* 76: 944, 1936), wrote: "I know of no earlier planting of a nursery of forest trees in this country than that of Jefferson on April 12, 1804, when he planted hemlock and white pine 'near the aspen thicket'."

[6] *Rosa laevigata* Michx.

[7] John Milledge (1757 – February 9, 1818). Revolutionary patriot, Governor of Georgia, representative, senator, was associated with most of the noteworthy events in his state from the Revolutionary War to the War of 1812, but is remembered today chiefly because of his connection with the University of Georgia. (*Dict. Am. Biog.* 12: 617–618.)

[8] Goliah, slave and gardener of Jefferson at *Monticello.*

[9] This toll mill, on the Rivanna River, at *Shadwell,* was left to Jefferson by his father, Peter Jefferson. He was now engaged in building another mill, which cost him over $30,000. This mill became a constant source of worry to him.

[10] Probably the mill owned by the family of Bennett Henderson. He had been a magistrate of the county, and had

erected a large flouring mill and a tobacco warehouse. He died in 1793, and eventually (in 1811) his land came into Jefferson's hands. (Woods, *Albemarle County:* 227–228.)

[11] Milton, Albemarle County. This town dates from 1789. Up to the War of 1812 it was the chief commercial center of the county. Being at the head of navigation on the Rivanna, it became an important shipping port. Its business gradually declined as Charlottesville grew, and it quietly subsided into a straggling hamlet.

[12] Jefferson did not record a freshet in the Rivanna for 1795. (See his "Diary for 1795.")

[13] See entry in *Garden Book* for May 26, 1771.

## LETTERS AND EXTRACTS OF LETTERS, 1804

(Jefferson to Timothy Bloodworth.)

Washington, January 29, 1804.

I thank you for the seed of the fly trap. It is the first I have ever been able to obtain, and shall take great care of it. . . . (Lipscomb and Bergh, *Jefferson* 10: 443.)

(Jefferson to Maria (Jefferson) Eppes.)

Washington, Jan. 29, 1804.

. . . Since proposing to Anne the undertaking to raise bantams, I have received from Algiers two pair of beautiful fowls, something larger than our common fowls, with fine aigrettes. They are not so large nor valuable as the East India fowl, but both kinds, as well as the bantams, are well worthy of being raised. We must, therefore, distribute them among us, and raise them clear of mixture of any kind. All this we will settle together, in March, and soon after we will begin the levelling and establishment of your hen-house at Pantops. . . . (Randall, *Jefferson* 3: 97–98.)

(John Armstrong to Jefferson.)

Cincinnati February 20th. 1804.

Captain Lewis on his way to the Westward called on me and requested that I would at the proper season furnish you with some cuttings from my Nursery, which you will receive herewith, N°. 1. 2. 3. & 4 were sent me from Detroit two years since. N°. 5 & 6 are from bearing trees in my orchard.

N°. 1   Large White apple—tied with a white string
N°. 2   Large Red apple tied with a red string

Nº. 3  Pumgray an apple much admired and will keep the year round tied with a blue string

Nº. 4  Calvit apple which is without comparison the best apple that ever was Eaten—tied with a green string

Nº. 5  Ox Eye Striped Apple ripe in the fall, highly flavoured weighs from 16 to 20 Oz—tied with a yellow string

Nº. 6  Egg Plumb as large as a hens egg light colourd rich & Sweet with a small stone.   will succeed by Engrafting on a Damson, Wild Plumb or Peach Stock,   I generally cut my cions at this Season of the year, and place one end of the cuttings about two inches in the ground in a perpendicular position and there let them remain until the proper season for placing them into the stock—I practice Tonge Grafting, and seldom lose five trees out of one thousand,   have had trees to bear the second year after ingrafting them.

It would oblige me if thro some of your friends I could obtain a few cuttings of the Virginia Cyder apple, Generally called Hughes Crab, with a description of the fruit. . . . (*Jefferson Papers,* M. H. S.)

### (Jefferson to Maria (Jefferson) Eppes.)

Washington, Feb. 26, 1804.

. . . Will you desire your sister to send for Mr. Lilly, and to advise him what orders to give Goliah for providing those vegetables which may come into use for the months of April, August, and September— deliver her also my affectionate love. . . . (Randall, *Jefferson* 3: 98.)

### (Jefferson to Gibson & Jefferson.)

Monticello Mar. 13. 04.

[He wrote to his agents, Gibson & Jefferson, in Richmond, to secure from Mr. Collins, a seedsman there, the following seeds:]

3. gallons of dwarf marrow fat peas, if he has none of these send the best he has for common sowing.

3. oz. radish seed.   scarlet preferred.

3. oz. lettuce seed.   The Roman preferred.

1. oz. Endive seed (not the curled)

(*Jefferson Papers,* M. H. S.)

### (Jefferson to John W. Eppes.)

Washington, March 15, 1804.

. . . I will endeavor to forward to Mr. Benson, postmaster at Fredericksburg, a small parcel of the oats for you.   The only difficulty is to find some gentleman going on in the stage who will take charge of them by the way. . . . (Randall, *Jefferson* 3: 99.)

(Jefferson to Stephen Cathalan.)

Washington Mar. 22. 1804.

You remember how anxious I was, when with you at Marseilles, to get the admirable olive of your canton transferred to my own country, and how much trouble you were so kind as to take to effect it.  it did not happen that any one of those among whom the plants were distributed took up the plan with the enthusiasm necessary to give it success, and it has failed.  mr̄ John Cowper of St. Simon's island in Georgia now proposes to undertake it, & being led to it by inclination, and a gentleman of property, in the most favorable situation, he will give the culture a fair trial, and I trust it's favorable issue is beyond a doubt.  he has been informed of the superior excellence of the olive of Marseilles, and knowing your friendly dispositions to our country I have taken the liberty of advising him to address himself to you to put his commission into faithful & careful hands. . . . (*Jefferson Papers*, L. C.)

(Jefferson to Richard Gamble.)

Apr. 22. 04.

Heads of a lease to Richard Gamble

5. fields North of the road, of 40 acres each.  to wit 4. on the Shadwell tract now leased to J. Perry, and one on the Lego tract, adjoining to the Upper field of Shadwell, including the ground already open there & about Reynolds's house, & as much more to be opened adjacent as will make up 40. acres.

the lease to commence Oct. 15. 1804. (being John Perry's yearly day) and to continue 5. years.

each of the said 5. fields to be in Indian corn but once in the 5. years, & to rest from culture & pasture 2. of the 5. years unless it be well in clover, and neither of the years of rest to be next after a year of Indian corn.  the tenant to have free use of the woodlands North of the road for fire, fencing & repairs, and of all the uninclosed Woodlands for the range of stock.

to keep all houses built or to be built in repair, except against the gradual decays of time; and to keep fences & gates in constant repair.

the lease not to be assigned to any person to whom the landlord objects.

the rent 200. D. a year, payable at the end of the year towit Oct. 15. and if not paid by Christmas the landlord to have a right of reentry in aid of his right of distress.  in clearing the Lego field, the land-lord to cut down the trees & maul the rails, & the tenant to clean up, grub, and put up the fence; and this clearing to be done the next winter & the winter following.

the names of the fields are the Chapel ridge
                               Mountain field
                               Middle field
                               Upper field
                               Lego field

the course of their culture, according to these conditions will be as follows

|  | 1805 | 1806 | 1807 | 1808 | 1809 |
|---|---|---|---|---|---|
| Lego field | nothing | nothing | small grain | corn | small grain |
| Upper field | small grain | clover | clover | small grain | corn |
| Middle field | corn | small grain | clover | clover | small grain |
| Mountain field | small grain | corn | small grain | clover | clover |
| Chapel ridge | nothing | small grain | corn | small grain | clover |

by reading the column of each year downwards, it will be seen that the tenant has every year 2. fields of small grain, 1. of corn, & 2. of clover, and in which fields they are. by reading the lines horizontally, it will be seen how each field will be cultivated for 5. years successively, so as that each will rest or be in clover twice, not following corn, that each will be in small grain twice, and each in corn once. (*Jefferson Papers,* M. H. S.)

(Jefferson to John W. Eppes.)

Washington, June 4, 1804.

. . . After Lilly shall have done at the mill, which I suppose will be by the time of my return home, there are then three jobs for him, the levelling at Pantops, the road along the river, and the levelling of the garden at Monticello. (Randall, *Jefferson* 3: 99.)

(Jefferson to Robert Bailey.)

Monticello Sept. 9. '04.

I think I informed you that I should want such a box of plants & seeds put up every year as I first desired from you, for the same friend at Paris. I have only therefore to refer you to my former list, and call your attention to it at this time when the season for getting the seeds is commencing. when you come to pack the plants in autumn, they must have a great quantity of moss distributed among them. in this condition I received two boxes of plants from Italy this spring in such perfect vigor that not a single one I think was lost. . . . (*Jefferson Papers,* M. H. S.)

# 1805

*1805.** Jefferson began the second term of his Presidency on March 4. His inaugural address, in which he reviewed his previous term and suggested new improvements for the country during his present term of office, was well received.

Foreign affairs, as well as domestic ones, created troublesome problems. In his message to the ninth Congress, which met on December 2, he alluded to the dangers our commerce was meeting:

> Since our last meeting, the aspect of our foreign relations has considerably changed. Our coasts have been infested and our harbors watched by private armed vessels, some of them without commissions, some with illegal commissions, others with those of legal form, but committing piratical acts beyond the authority of their commissions. They have captured in the very entrance of our harbors, as well as on the high seas, not only the vessels of our friends coming to trade with us, but our own also. They have carried them off under pretence of legal adjudication, but not daring to approach a court of justice, they have plundered and sunk them by the way, or in obscure places where no evidence could arise against them; maltreated the crews, and abandoned them in boats in the open sea or on desert shores without food or covering. These enormities appearing to be unreached by any control of their sovereigns, I found it necessary to equip a force to cruise within our own seas, to arrest all vessels of these descriptions found hovering on our coast within the limits of the Gulf Stream, and to bring the offenders in for trial as pirates. (Randall, *Jefferson:* 150.)

Jefferson's two visits to *Monticello* took place from March 14 to April 17, and from July 15 to September 29. During the second he went to *Poplar Forest* on July 26, and returned home on August 2.

The house at *Monticello* was nearing completion. Much interior work was done; sheet iron was bought to cover the two offices, which connected the two pavilions with the main house; and a painter, Richard Barry, came to *Monticello*.

Jefferson settled with John Perry, on October 7, for completing work done on his manufacturing mill and two miller houses, located on the Rivanna River.

* This year not represented in the *Garden Book*.

298

On August 22 "J. Holmes Freeman commences as over-seer at £.60. a year." He replaced Gabriel Lilly, who had been overseer since 1800. (See letter, Jefferson to John Strode, June 5, 1805, and other letters about a new overseer.)

The year 1805 is not represented in the *Garden Book,* al-though Jefferson bought plants and trees from seedsmen in Washington, and received them from other sources. The *Farm Book* also does not mention any plantings for the year, but letters about plants are numerous, and the *Account Book* mentions several amounts paid for plants.

Of special interest this year was the introduction of live fences at *Monticello.* The first thorns for the hedges were sent there on March 22, by Mr. Dougherty, Jefferson's busi-ness manager in Washington. He wrote to Jefferson on that date: "I went immediately to Mr. Main [horticulturist and congenial friend of Jefferson in Washington] & brot. the 4000 thorns. On enquiring at the Stage Office I met a young man with whom I am well acquainted going from here to Richmond immediately in the stage." (*Jefferson Papers,* M. H. S.) The thorns were carried by this man to Richmond.

The extensive live fences planted at *Monticello* this year and for several years following were of considerable interest to Jefferson. Mr. Main called this particular thorn the American hedge thorn. It grew abundantly around Wash-ington. Linnaeus called the thorn *Crataegus cordata.* It is now known as *Crataegus phaenopyrum* Med., the Washing-ton thorn.

LETTERS AND EXTRACTS OF LETTERS, 1805

(Jefferson to Mrs. Martha (Jefferson) Randolph.)

Washington Jan. 7. 05.

. . . I send you a book of gardening which I believe has merit. it has at least that of being accomodated to our seasons. . . . (*Jefferson Papers,* M. H. S.)

(Jefferson to Madame de Tessé.)

Washington, Mar. 10, '05.

Your favors of April 10 & Aug. 17 were not received till autumn, that of Aug. 17 only the 1st of November. immediately on receipt of the former I wrote to a friend in Philadelphia to make the enquiries you desired respecting the affairs of M. de Noailles. I inclose you his answer on which much reliance may be placed. I detained this in expectation of sending it early in winter with another collection of plants & seeds which had been prepared for you, but early in December every harbour from this place northwardly blocked up with ice, and through the severest winter we have known for 20 years kept closed till within a few days past, so that no vessel could get out. now that our port (Alexandria) is open I find not a single vessel bound for any port of France except the Mediterranean. were the packages sent thither, they would cost you more for transportation than they are worth, & would besides be entirely after the season. indeed, for the same reason, the expence of transportation, I should be afraid to send you boxes to any port except Havre; & we know not when the blockade of that will cease. we are therefore compleatly defeated for this year in the new supply of plants; & must comfort ourselves with better hope for the next. your letters brought me information, always welcome, of your health continuing well. the flattering testimonies I receive of the good will of my fellow citizens would have been a source of great happiness to me were they not more than countervailed by domestic afflictions. I have had the inexpressible misfortune to lose my younger daughter, who has left me two grandchildren, & my elder one has such poor health, that I have little confidence in her life. she has 6 children. Determined as I am to retire at the end of 4 years, I know not if I shall have a family to retire to. I must learn philosophy from you & seek in a family of plants that occupation & delight which you have so fortunately found in them. it will be the greater with me as it will give me opportunities of communicating to you new objects. . . . (*Glimpses of the Past,* Missouri Historical Society: 95.)

## (Thomas Main to Jefferson.)

[Washington] Mar. 13th 1805.

Please pay to the bearer Mr. Robert Bunyie the sum of Thirty eight dollars as the full amount of my Accot. for trees and plants sold to the President and delivered on the 8th Inst. and oblige. . . .

Pd. in full Mar. 13. (*Jefferson Papers,* M. H. S.)

## (Jefferson to Egbert Benson.)

Monticello Mar. 23. 05.

Thos. Jefferson took the liberty of desiring that a box or package of plants should be sent by the stage from Washington to Fredericksburg addressed to the care of mr̄ Benson. he now asks the favor of mr̄ Benson to forward them by stage to Milton with a recommendation of them to the particular care of the driver. he expects they may arrive at Fredericksburg about the time this note does. . . . (*Jefferson Papers,* M. H. S.) [The plants were sent to Milton by Mr. Benson.]

(John Strode to Jefferson.)

Culpeper Mar. 25, 05.

My Son Tom has just sent me a Letter inclosing a few of the seed of the soft Simblin or Quash, which he humbly intreats the President to accept. . . . (*Jefferson Papers,* M. H. S.)

(Jefferson to James Madison.)

Monticello Apr. 11, 1805.

. . . We have had two very fine rains within the last fortnight.  the trees are all leaved here, but in the neighborhood generally only the poplar.  our first asparagus was Mar. 27, the 1st whippoorwill Apr. 2. the 1st tick & the Dogwood blossoms on the 4th.  (*Jefferson Papers,* L. C.)

(Jefferson to William Tunnicliff.)

Washington, Apr. 26. 05.

Th. Jefferson asks the favor of mr. Tunnicliff to add one other book to the list he sent him yesterday.  Knight on Culture of the Apple & Pear, Cider and Perry, 12 mo. printed in 1801. by Ludlow, Proctor, Longman and Rees, paternoster row, white Fleetstreet.  (Ford, *Jefferson Correspondence:* 114.)

(Jefferson to Benjamin Smith Barton.)

Washington May 2. '05.

Mr. Dunbar, during his excursion up the Washita, the last fall and winter, collected some dried specimens of plants which he has sent me in order to have them ascertained.  I know I cannot dispose of them better than by transmitting them to you, with a request of the result of your investigation.  he went as far as the hot springs on that river, 500 miles up it.  he found their temperature 150° of Farenheit.  his journal & Dr. Hunter's furnish us with the geography to it's natural history.  I shall put them into the hands of some one to reduce into a small compass the results divested of details too long for the common reader. I shall be happy to receive in time to incorporate into this, your information as to the plants now sent. . . . (*Jefferson Papers,* L. C.)

(Jefferson to Benjamin Smith Barton.)

Washington May 21. 05.

Th: Jefferson presents his friendly salutations to Doctr. Barton: when sending him the dried specimens of plants from mr Dunbar he omitted to send some moss which he had taken out of the hot-springs of the Washeta, in a temperature of 150°. in which he says are some of the animalculae, inhabitants of the moss.  Th: J. having no microscope here has been unable to see them: but he commits them now to the better hands of Doctr. Barton.  (*Jefferson Papers,* M. H. S.)

(Jefferson to Patrick Gibson.)

Washington May 29. 1805.

There was lately shipped for me from Philadelphia 1. box of grape vines, and 4. open boxes of monthly strawberries from Italy. altho' from the account I receive of the latter they seem irrecoverable yet if there be any hope of life I would ask the favor of you to give them to any careful gardener in Richmond who will hereafter furnish me with some roots from them if they live. their value is great, as in our climate they should bear 9. months in the year. the other box to be forwarded to Monticello by the first post. . . . (*Jefferson Papers*, M. H. S.)

(Jefferson to Thomas Mann Randolph.)

Washington June 2. 05.

. . . I have lately received a few grains of corn, originally from Italy, yielding 4. crops a year, at 40. days interval each; a winter muskmelon, eaten in Dec. Jan. Feb. pumpkins of 127. lb. cauliflowers of 25. to 30. lb. all of which I have put into the hands of gardeners here. . . . (*Jefferson Papers*, M. H. S.)

(Jefferson to Thomas Mann Randolph.)

Washington June 5. 1805.

. . . Lilly wishes to quit as manager unless he gets £100 per year. he has been getting £50 plus £10 additional for nailery. . . . (*Jefferson Papers*, L. C.)

(Jefferson to John Strode.)

Washington June 5. '05.

In a letter to me some years ago you recommended some person to me as a manager, should I want one at Monticello. not having the letter here I am not able to turn to it, nor to recollect the name. the person whom I have there at present is at the wages of £60 & the ordinary allowances of pork & corn for his family. he is as good a one as can be. but I yesterday received notice from him that unless I would raise his wages to £ 100. he could remain only this year. this is so great a jump, that if I can get another worthy of confidence, I think to do so. were I at home to have an eye to the manager myself it would be less important. but obliged as I am to abandon everything to him, it is all important to have one who may be confided in. my manager there has to provide for the maintainance of a family of about 40 negroes at all times, and for my own family about 3 months in the year; to hire annually, and overlook about 10. laboring men, employed in a little farming but mainly in other works about my mills, & grounds generally; to superintend the gristmill, and a nailery of 10. to 15. hands, provide their coal, sell nails etc. I love industry & abhor severity. would the person whom you formerly recommended answer these purposes, is he to be had, or do you know any other? it would render me the most essential service could I get one on whom I could repose myself entirely. indeed no event of this kind could have afflicted me more, as the conduct of the present man leaves me as perfectly satisfied absent as present. he has required an immediate answer from me, which however I shall endeavor to put off till I hear from you. I think I shall be with you about the middle of July I shall have the pleasure of calling. in the meantime be so good as to give me some comfort on the above subject with as little delay as possible. . . . (*Jefferson Papers*, L. C.)

## (Benjamin Smith Barton to Jefferson.)

[Philadelphia] June 12, 1805.

Of the plants with which you have forwarded me,

No.  1.  is a species of Dactylis.
No.  2.  Solidago glomerata of Bartram.
No.  3.  Solidago a new species.
No.  4.  a species of Aster.
No.  5.  Solidago suaveolens: The Sweet-scented or Anise-seed, golden rod of New Jersey.
No.  6.  Ascyrum multicaule of Michaux.
No.  7.  Liatris elegans of Michaux.
No.  8.
No.  9.  } Three new species of Aster.
No. 10.
No. 11.
No. 12.  } Two varieties of a species of Panicum.
No. 13.  A species of Cyperus.

(*Jefferson Papers*, L. C.)

## (Jefferson to Thomas Mann Randolph.)

Washington June 26. '05.

. . . I shall defer giving Lilly a final answer till I get home. (*Jefferson Papers*, L. C.)

## (Jefferson to Ellen Randolph.)

Washington July 10. 05.

To answer the question in your letter of the 4$^{th}$. I must observe that neither the *number* of the fine arts nor the particular arts entitled to that appellation have been fixed by general consent. many reckon but five Painting, sculpture, architecture, music & poetry. to these some have added Oratory, including within that Rhetoric which is the art of style & composition. others again, add Gardening as a 7$^{th}$. fine art. not horticulture, but the art of embellishing grounds by fancy.   I think L'. Kaims has justly proved this to be entitled to the appellation of a fine art.   it is nearly allied to landscape painting, & accordingly we generally find the landscape painter the best designer of a garden.   no perfect *definition* of what is a fine art has ever yet been given.   some say that as those are *mechanical* arts, which consist in manual operation unconnected with the understanding, those are *fine* arts which to manual operation join the exercise of the imagination or genius.   this would comprehend sculpture, painting, architecture & gardening, but neither music, poetry, nor oratory.   others say that the sciences are objects of the understanding, the fine arts of the senses.   this would add gardening, but neither poetry nor oratory.   a definition which should include Poetry & Oratory & no more would be very difficult to form. . . . the thermometer was yesterday 97½° here, and at 96°. the two preceding days.   I think it will be 96°. to-day.   should it be as hot when I am ready to depart, I shall certainly delay my departure. . . . (*Jefferson Papers,* M. H. S.)

(Jefferson to Mr. Barnes.)

Monticello Aug. 12. 05.

. . . We are all in good health here, & blest amidst luxuriant crops of every kind. . . . (*Jefferson Papers,* L. C.)

(Jefferson to James Madison.)

Monticello Aug. 17. 1805.

. . . We are extremely seasonable in this quarter.   better crops were never seen. . . . (*Jefferson Papers,* L. C.)

(Jefferson to James Madison.)

Monticello, August 25, 1805.

. . . We are now in want of rain, having had none in the last ten days. In your quarter I am afraid they have been much longer without it. We hear great complaints from F. Walker's, Lindsay's, Maury's, etc., of drought. . . . (Lipscomb and Bergh, *Jefferson* 11: 86.)

(Jefferson to Messrs. McDowell, Roger, Finley & Patterson.)

Monticello Aug 31. 05.

. . . I now enclose you a small parcel of the Jerusalem wheat I received from a gentleman in Ireland. . . . (*Jefferson Papers,* M. H. S.)

(Jefferson to W. A. Burwell.)

Monticello Sept. 20. 1805.

. . . I thank you for the vines & seeds which are all new and acceptable. . . . (*Jefferson Papers,* L. C.)

### (William Hamilton to Jefferson.)

The Woodlands Oct. 5, 1805.

. . . He [nephew of Hamilton] will at the same time, deliver to you, a small deciduous plant of the silk tree of Constantinople (Mimosa Julibrisin) which if well preserved for two or three years in a pot, will afterwards succeed in the open ground. I have trees of 20 feet height which for several years past have produced their beautiful & fragrant flowers & have shewn no marks whatever of suffering from the severity of the last winter. (*Jefferson Papers,* L. C.)

### (Jefferson to J. P. Reibelt.)

Washington Oct. 12. 05.

. . . [I] thank you for the magnet, for the Bengal sheep, and garden seeds. I enclose some seed of a vine growing only on the great Kannaway & answering the purpose of the Rattan. I never saw the plant growing, but the vine is curious. there is a garden plant in France which I have never been able to get, the Estragon. perhaps Mr. Labullage could furnish me a little of the seed. . . . (*Jefferson Papers,* L. C.)

### (Jefferson to Madame de Tessé.)

Washington, Oct. 26. 05.

The blockade of Havre still continuing and being likely to be of equal duration with the war, I had despaired almost of being able to send you any seeds this year. but it was lately suggested to me that a package sent to Nantes may go through the canal de Briare to Paris, and thus avoid a land carriage which would cost you more than the object is worth. I have therefore hastily made up a box of seeds, of such articles of those I propose to furnish you annually as the present season admits of being gathered. they are as follows. 1. Juglans nigra. 2. Liriodendron tulipifera. 3. Quercus alba. 4. Prinus. 5. Q. Phellos. 6. Q. Palustris. 7. Juniperus Virginica. 8. Cornus Florida. 9. Rosa sylvestris elatior foliis inodoris Clayton. 10. Bignonia Catalpa. 11. Magnolia acuminata. the preceding were in your catalogue, to which in order to fill vacant spaces I have added 12. Diospyros Virginiana. 13. Platanus occidentalis. 14. Cucurbita verrucosa Miller. 15. Arachis hypogaea. the season would have admitted procuring some other articles from a distance, but I was yesterday informed that the brig *Lucy* sails three days hence from Baltimore to Nantes. I therefore close the box to-day and send it off by stage tomorrow, the only means of getting to Baltimore in time. it is a box 4 feet long, and 1 foot wide and deep; will be addressed to you to the care of William Patterson, commercial agent of the U. S. at Nantes, with instructions first to ask your orders how to have them conveyed and to follow those orders. I shall make some observations on some of these articles. of the oaks I have selected the alba, because it is the finest of the whole family, it is the only tree with us which disputes for pre-eminence with the Liriodendron. it may be called the Jupiter while the latter is the Juno of our groves. the Prinos, or chestnut oak is also one of the fine and handsome species. the Phellos, or willow oak combines great irregularity with beauty, the Palustris of Michaux, which is the Quercus rubra dissecta R of La Marck Encyclop. Method. Botan. 1. 721. is nearly as singular by the deep indenture of it's leaves and their very narrow lobes, as the Phellos, and very handsome. it has also been called by some Quercus montanus, just as improperly as Palustris. it grows well in dry as well as moist lands. the acorns of the Q. Phellos are the smaller, we know. they fall early in the season, and I send you every individual acorn which multiplied researches could now procure. probably some of the minutest may not come up, but I trust a sufficient number will be found good. in each of the cells of the box are some leaves of the identical trees from which the acorns were gathered. Juniperus virgin. I presume some method is known and practiced with you to make the seeds come up. I have never known but one person succeed with them here. he crammed them down the throats of his poultry confined in the hen-yard and then sowed their dung, which has been completely effectual. Cornus Florida. we have a variety of this with a flesh coloured blossom, but it is so rare that I have seen it in but one place on my road from hence to Monticello, and could only be known at this season by marking the tree when in blossom. this research must be reserved for a situation more favorable than my present one. Magnolia acuminata. this plant is not of Virginia, except it's South Western angle, 250 miles from hence. I send you the only cone of it I ever saw, and which came to me accidentally not long since. the tree I have never seen. Platanus occidentalis, a most noble tree for shade, of fine form, its bark of a paper-white when old, and of very quick growth. cucurbita verrucosa, cymling. I recommend this merely for your garden. we consider it one of our finest and most innocent vegetables. I found the chicorée as dressed by your cooks in a pulpy form to resemble our cymling. Arachis hypogaea, a very sweet ground-nut. it grows well at this place where we can have neither figs nor artechokes without protection through the winter. it is hardier therefore than they are, and cannot be a mere-green house plant with you as Miller and Dumont Courset suppose. I write to you almost in despair that you will get either my letter or the box of seeds. such are the irregularities committed on the ocean by the armed vessels of all the belligerent powers that nothing is safe committed to that element. were it not for this, I would ask you to send me by some occasion some acorns of the Quercus rubre, some seeds of the Cedrus Lebani which you have in the Jardin des plantes, and perhaps some nuts of your Marronier: but I should only expose myself to the mortification of losing them. . . .

P. S. since writing the above I have been able to get some of the Pyrus coronaria, or malus sylvestris virginiana floribus odoratis of Clayton. both the blossom and apple are of the finest perfume, and the apple is the best of all possible burnishers for brass and steel furniture which has contracted rust. (Ford, *Jefferson Correspondence:* 118–120.)

(Thomas Main to Jefferson.)

Nursery near Geo: Town
Oct<sup>r</sup>. 29<sup>th</sup>. 1805.

Intending to set off for Richmond in a day or two, I have directed the bearer to wait for the Letter which you was so obliging as to offer me. . . . (*Jefferson Papers*, M. H. S.)

(Jefferson to Dr. James Currie.)

Washington Oct. 29. 05.

The bearer hereof is m͞r Thomas Main whom I have spoken of to you as the person who has been so successfully engaged here in raising the thorn hedge & whom you were so kind as to say you would patronize should he be willing to undertake the same business at Richmond.   indeed for his integrity, sobriety, industry & skill I can safely recommend him as worthy general patronage, and I am persuaded that in the present state of difficulty in fencing farms in that part of the country, he will be a valuable acquisition & will in a few years change the face of the country.   recommending him therefore, for no interests of mine but merely for those of the canton to which he goes, to your friendly offices & aid I offer you with sincerity affectionate salutations & assurances of respect. . . . (*Jefferson Papers,* M. H. S.)

(Jefferson to William Hamilton.)

Washington Nov. 6. 05.

Your nephew delivered safely to me the plant of the Chinese silk tree in perfect good order, and I shall nurse it with care until it shall be in condition to be planted at Monticello.   m͞r Madison mentioned to me you wish to receive any seeds which should be sent me by Capt. Lewis or from any other quarter of plants which are rare. . . . I happen to have two papers of seeds which Capt. Lewis inclosed to me in a letter, and which I gladly consign over to you, as I shall anything else which may fall into my hands and be worthy your acceptance.   one of these is the *Mandan tobacco,* a very singular species, uncommonly weak and probably suitable for segars. . . . I send also some seeds of the *winter melon* which I received from Malta.   some were planted here last season, but too early.   they were so ripe before the time of gathering (before the first frost) that all rotted but one which is still sound & firm & we hope will keep sometime, experience alone will fix the time of planting them in our climate.   I hope you will find it worthy a place in your kitchen garden. . . . (*Jefferson Papers,* L. C.)

(Jefferson to John Holmes Freeman.)

Washington, Nov. 14. '05.

. . . whenever the mill works shall be done the road and garden, and the engaging negroes for another year are pressing articles. . . . (Ford, *Jefferson Correspondence:* 124.)

(Thomas Main to Jefferson.)

Main's Nursery
[Georgetown] Nov$^r$. 18$^{th}$. 1805.

Immediately on my return from Richmond a sense of duty, with sentiments of the most unfeigned thankfulness for your benevolent intention to promote my interest through a benefit to the community, in an employment so congenial to my inclination, induces me to take the liberty to lay before you the result of my journey. It would have given me pleasure to have waited on the President for this purpose, had I not reflected that his time was at this period by far too precious to suffer such intrusion from my humble concerns.

Doctor Currie received me with great kindness, and was anxious to favour me with a place, though I found him unhappily afflicted with much grief for the loss of his only child: and he indeed nevertheless, honoured my errand with his whole attention. An obstacle of some magnitude however prevented an agreement. The house which was to be my dwelling stood contiguous, in the same yard with those of his overseer and labourers, which I found was permanently to be the case. This was a difficulty which I really durst not encounter, fearing that disagreeable collisions might eventually ensue from such an intermixture of authority, which would endanger that happy tranquility so dear to the quiet mind; one half of this dreaded evil being apprehended from a source over which I could have no control rendered it still more insuperable. These sentiments I respectfully submitted to the Doctor; and further added that it would be my anxious care and earnest desire to cultivate a good understanding with him and wished therefore that everything which might probably produce the seeds of discord should by anticipation be prevented. He allowed the observations to be reasonable but could not devise a remedy, as it was out of his power to dispense with the use of that place for the residence of his people. Finding this obstacle not to be overcome, he obligingly offered to introduce me to other landholders, gentlemen of his acquaintance, and to lay the Presidents letter before them, if I would tarry a day or two longer: but as I found I could not with propriety delay my return I was obliged to decline that offer. He then proposed for me to throw my ideas upon paper and write to him in Dec$^r$. I promised compliance and perceiving him very unwell took my leave: he requesting me to give his best respects to the President. Perhaps I ought to desist at this time from any further attempts to fix an establishment at Richmond. When I write to the Doctor I shall with permission, submit my letter to your correction, as it would distress me greatly should I inadvertently dictate anything that might seem to derogate in the least from the recommendation which you have been pleased to give me. Great part of the country through which I passed, and about Richmond appeared so far as I could observe highly susceptible of the improvement of Hedging and seemed also much to require it. Being treated with the greatest civility by every person with whom I had any intercourse in Virginia it could not fail of making a very favourable impression on my mind respecting its

inhabitants. I have only to add that your goodness, to me, so much un-
merited, shall ever be held in pleasing remembrance; and that with the
most affectionate attachment and sincere respect. . . . (*Jefferson Papers,*
L. C.)

### (Thomas Appleton to Jefferson.)

Leghorn Nov. 18, 1805.

. . . I have put on board ship a case of plants which are sent to you
by M^r. Mazzei. . . . (*Jefferson Papers,* L. C.)

### (Jacob Crowninshield to Jefferson.)

Washington, November 30, 1805.

I beg your acceptance of a head of Egyptian wheat, in high preservation, which was produced the last season at Portsmouth, New Hamp-
shire. It is said to be very prolific, & to produce whiter flour than our
common wheat. I am solicitous it should be distributed in the southern
states & particularly in Virginia & if none of it has already fallen into
your hands I am sure you will give it a fair trial. Should it answer my
expectations it will be a valuable acquisition to the U. States. . . . (*Jefferson Papers,* L. C.)

### (Jefferson to Benjamin S. Barton.)

Washington Dec. 22. 05.

Under another cover I send you drawings & specimens of the seed, cotton & leaf of the Cotton Tree of the Western Country, received from
Gen^l. Wilkinson at S^t. Louis. to these I must add that it appears from
the journals of Lewis & Clarke that the boughs of this tree are the sole
food of the horses up the Missouri during the winter. . . . (*Jefferson
Papers,* L. C.)

### (Benjamin Smith Barton to Jefferson.)

December 27, 1805.

I am greatly obliged to you for the drawing and specimen, which you
have forwarded to me. The cotton tree is, no doubt, the *Populus
deltoides* of Bartram and Marshall. I am not certain that it is noticed
in any of the Systematic books on Botany. . . . (*Jefferson Papers,*
L. C.)

### From the *Account Book 1805:*

Mar.  6.   p^d m̅r̅s Bailey for 80. trees 15. D.
Mar. 11.   gave Joseph to pay Hepburn 27.675 plants.
Mar. 11.   Gave Joseph to pay Maine 38. d°.
Aug. 22.   J. Holmes Freeman commences as overseer at £. 60. a year.
Oct. 21.   p^d Maine for thorns 12.

# 1806

Mar. 14.   the road from the Shadwell ford[2] to the top of the mountain, along the North side of the mountain, was begun & was finished May. 11. except some little blowing. it has taken 552. days work @ 2/[3] = 184. D.

The cherries & peaches are compleatly killed this year as well on the mountains as elsewhere. this was effected by cold freezing winds, mostly from the N.W. in the month of April, & of considerable continuance. the peaches & cherries (except Morellas) were then in bloom & killed. the Morella cherries & apples, not being then in bloom, escaped entirely.[4]

―――――――――――――

[1] *1806.* The letter to Mrs. Elizabeth Trist, quoted below, partly summarizes the political and family life of Jefferson during the early part of 1806:

Washington, Apr. 27, '06.

. . . my daughter & her family are here with me & well. They will set out for Albemarle in 2 or 3 days, whither I shall follow them to pass as many weeks in order to repose a little after the labors of the winter. Congress have had a squally session. some strange phaenomena disturbed that harmony which has been hitherto unbroken among the Republicans. however it furnished a comfortable proof of the steadiness & independence of the main body, which could not be led from its principles, and it has compleated my conviction that ours is the most stable government in the world. we are trying to lay the foundations of a long peace with Spain, in which your city is more interested than any other place. from Albemarle I can give you no news, having nobody there now who writes me. Mr. & Mrs. Gilmer go this spring to their lands in the southern part of the state, in which the title of the family is confirmed. we expect Colo. Monroe will return to us next autumn, and I am looking to my final return there with more desire than to any other object in this world. It is yet three years distant. this summer will entirely finish the house at Monticello & I am preparing an occasional retreat in Bedford, where I expect to settle some of my grandchildren. . . . (*Glimpses of the Past,* Missouri Historical Society: 97.)

Two observations are of special interest, "this summer will entirely finish the house at Monticello & I am preparing an occasional retreat in Bedford." The house at *Monticello,* although essentially finished this year, required many smaller alterations during the following years. In fact, Jefferson was constantly pulling down and rebuilding in a different and more convenient way.

The new house he was building at *Poplar Forest,* in Bedford County, was to be a summer haven for him. After he retired from the Presidency to *Monticello,* he made at least two visits there each year. In a letter to Mrs. Randolph, from Washington, on June 16, he wrote: "I find by a letter from Chisholm that I shall have to proceed to Bedford almost without stopping in Albemarle. I shall probably be kept there a week or 10 days laying the foundation of the house, which he is not equal to himself." (*Jefferson Papers,* M. H. S.)

In 1806 Burr's conspiracy took place. He was brought to trial the following year in Richmond. It was also in this year that the Lewis and Clark Expedition returned. The completion of this expedition brought as much happiness to Jefferson as the Burr conspiracy brought worry. The following letter to Meriwether Lewis was written on hearing the good news that the members of the expedition had arrived safely at St. Louis.

Washington, Oct. 20, 06.

I received, my dear sir, with unspeakable joy your letter of Sep. 23 announcing the return of yourself, Capt. Clarke & your party in good health to St. Louis. The unknown scenes in which you were engaged & the length of time without hearing of you had begun to be felt awfully. Your letter having been 31 [28?] days coming, this cannot find you at Louisville & I therefore think it safe to lodge it at Charlottesville. Its only object is to assure you of what you already know my constant affection for you & the joy with which all your friends here will receive you. Tell my friend of Mandane also that I have already opened my arms to receive him. Perhaps, while in our neighborhood it may be

gratifying to him, & not otherwise to yourself to take a ride to Monticello and see in what manner I have arranged the tokens of friendship I
have received from his country particularly, as well as from other Indian
friends: that I am in fact preparing a kind of Indian Hall.   Mr. Dinsmore, my principal workman, will shew you everything there. . . .
(Ford, *Jefferson* 10: 295–296.)

The spring visit to *Monticello* this year lasted from May 9
to June 4.   The summer vacation extended from July 24 to
October 1.   During the second visit he stayed at *Poplar
Forest* from August 17 to August 28, preparing the foundation for his house.

The toll mill was completed in the early part of the year.
(See letter, Jefferson to Mr. Cooch, February 23, 1806; and
other letters about the mill.)   On July 28 "John Gentry begins to assist & superintend the toll mill at 12. D. per month
(he went off in a few days)."   On August 1 or 2 "Bacon joins
Gentry in superintend^g toll mill."   (*Account Book 1804–
1808*.)   For some reason the toll mill failed to be as successful as Jefferson had planned.   Perhaps poor management was
one factor.

Edmund Bacon operated the mill with Gentry until September 29.   On that date he became the new overseer at
*Monticello*, succeeding John Freeman, who had been overseer
only one year.   Freeman had proven unsatisfactory.   Jefferson recorded in the *Account Book:* "Sept. 29. I am indebted
to Edmund Bacon for services to y^s day 20. D.   he agrees to
serve me as manager one year from this day for 100. D. 600.
lb. pork & half a beef."   Bacon continued as overseer at
*Monticello* for almost 20 years.

Although no record of planting occurs in the *Garden Book*
and the *Farm Book,* the *Account Book,* memoranda, and letters show the year to have been one of the busiest planting
years at *Monticello*.   Memoranda were left with, and sent to,
Mr. Freeman and Mr. Bacon.   Davy's cart was loaded with
trees and plants from the nurseries in Washington and carried
to *Monticello*.   To show where certain of the plants were to
be placed, Jefferson made a detailed diagram of the upper part
of the mountain.   (See plate XXI.)   This plan was sent to
Mr. Freeman, with planting instructions.   Mr. Bacon, re-
counting his reminiscences to the Reverend Hamilton W. Pierson, in 1862, said:

Mr. Jefferson sent home a great many kinds of trees and shrubbery from Washington. I used to send a servant there with a great many fine things from Monticello for his table, and he would send back the cart loaded with shrubbery from a nursery near Georgetown, that belonged to a man named Maine, and he would always send me directions what to do with it. He always knew all about every thing in every part of his grounds and garden. He knew the name of every tree, and just where one was dead or missing. (Reverend Hamilton W. Pierson, *Jefferson at Monticello* (New York, 1862): 38–39. Hereafter cited as Pierson, *Monticello*.)

In the early spring Bernard McMahon, seedsman and florist of Philadelphia, published *The American Gardener's Calendar*. On April 17 he sent Jefferson a copy and wrote the following letter to him:

Philadelphia, April 17, 1806.

I have much pleasure in requesting your acceptance of one of my publications on Horticulture which I forward you by this mail. Should my humble efforts, meet with your approbation, and render any service to my adopted and much beloved Country, I shall feel the happy consolation of having contributed my mite to the welfare of my fellow man, I am Sir,

With sincere esteem and best wishes yours,
Bernard McMahon.
(*Jefferson Papers*, M. H. S.)

Jefferson replied to this courtesy on April 25, in the following letter:

Washington Apr. 25. 06.

Th: Jefferson returns his thanks to mr Mc.Mahon for the book he has been so kind as to send him. from the rapid view he has taken of it & the original matter it appears to contain he has no doubt it will be found an useful aid to the friends of an art, too important to health & comfort & yet too much neglected in this country. the seeds which Th: J. received from the Missouri had been sent to the Philosophical society; but of some which had been received from the Mediterranean Th: J. sent a few of the most valuable kinds to mr Mc.Mahon by mr Duane; and will recollect him should he receive any thing in that way hereafter curious or valuable. Th: J. has been many years endeavoring to get some seed of the Tarragon, but without success. if mr Mc.Mahon has any, a little of it will be acceptable. (*Jefferson Papers*, L. C.)

Mr. McMahon's book made an especial appeal to Jefferson because it was among the first books to treat of American gardening and to take into consideration conditions in this country. From the publication of the book until 1815, several letters passed between the two men each year. Jefferson bought plants and seeds from McMahon which he planted at *Monticello*. Mr. McMahon and Mr. William Hamilton, of *The Woodlands,* received many of the plants and seeds sent or brought to Jefferson by the Lewis and Clark Expedition. (For additional information on McMahon, see p. 478, note 24.)

² Jefferson's ford over the Rivanna River at *Shadwell*. See letter, Jefferson to James Madison, September 2, 1806. Note the mention of this new road in several letters during the year. See plate XXII.

³ 2/ means 2 shillings.

⁴ See letter, Jefferson to Madison, May 11, 1806.

### LETTERS AND EXTRACTS OF LETTERS, 1806

(James Taylor to Jefferson.)

Belle Vue 3ᵈ. Febʸ. 1806.

I have thought proper to add a few more of the peach cutings supposing them a curiosity, never having seen any of the kind in Virginia. If Mr. Madison should wish any more of the peach The President will please to divide with him. I shall send on some of the Detroit apple as soon as I can procure them. Those I have were only grafted last season & will not furnish grafts this season. . . .

Jefferson wrote the following list at the bottom of the letter:

Monthly strawberry vines
Rose colᵈ. Nectarine grafts.  clearstone.
2. Magdalene peach cuttings.
a bundle of dº.

(*Jefferson Papers,* M. H. S.)

(Jefferson to John Freeman.)

Washington, Feb. 7. 06.

. . . I am sorry you have not yet attacked the road up the mountain. I suppose the extra work at the mill has prevented it. Jerry with the light cart & 2. mules had better set off for this place as speedily as you can get him ready. Fanny need not come. the purpose of his coming is to carry home a number of trees to be planted. for these the ground lying Westward from the garden pales to the young hedge must be entirely cleaned up. where peach or other fruit trees already exist there in the regular rows, they may be left; but all out of the rows must be taken up. the trees he will carry will fill the whole space between the pales & hedge from East to West, & up & down the hill from North to South from hedge to hedge. will you be so good as to see that the water is drawn out of the ice house, once or twice a week, or as often as necessary. . . . but really, these immence calls from Monticello distress me beyond measure. it renders it essential to get the nail house under steady way, to meet the money calls generally, and to begin our endeavors to prepare a farm which may furnish the pork, muttons, oats, peas & hay necessary for me while there & for the place at all times. to get this under way, the new road, & the fence described in the instructions I left with you are indispensable & should be undertaken as early as possible. whether you will be able to get ground ready to sow in oats & clover, & to plant cow peas, you alone can judge. I think we might have peas & potatoes in the ground you have to clean up for peach trees, and that oats & clover ought to be sown in that part from Bailey's house upwards which had corn last year. . . . (*Jefferson Papers*, U. Va.)

(Jefferson to C. F. Comte de Volney.)

Washington, Feb. 11, 1806.

. . . Our last news of Captn Lewis was that he had reached the upper part of the Missouri, & had taken horses to cross the Highlands to the Columbia River. He passed the last winter among the Manians [= Mandans] 1610 miles above the mouth of the river. So far he had delineated it with as great accuracy as will probably be ever applied to it, as his courses & distances by mensuration were corrected by almost daily observations of latitude and longitude. . . . He wintered in Lat. 47° 20' and found the maximum of cold 43° below the zero of Fahrenheit. We expect he has reached the Pacific, and is now wintering on the head of the Missouri, and will be here next autumn. . . . A newspaper paragraph tells me, with some details, that the society of agriculture of Paris had thought a mould-board of my construction worthy their notice & Mr. Dupont confirms it in a letter, but not specifying anything particular. I send him a model with an advantageous change in the form, in which however the principle is rigorously the same. (Ford, *Jefferson* 10: 227–228.)

(Jefferson to Mr. Cooch.)

Washington Feb. 23. 06

In answer to the enquiries in your letter of the 14th I have to observe that the mill I mentioned to you is on the Rivanna river at a place called Shadwell in the maps of Virginia 6 miles below Charlottesville, & ¾ mile above Milton. this last is the head of navigation; but from my mill boats go down a sheet of dead water to a short fall at Milton, where the load is transferred to the regular river craft which carry it to Richmond 80. miles by water. the river is regularly boatable about 7. or 8. months from the beginning of November (not obstructed by ice once in 2 years & then only a few days) and in the Summer months the boats always hold themselves in readiness to catch the accidental tides from showers of rain, so that a great deal is done that season: and there is rarely any accumulation of produce for want of a tide. I do not propose to occupy or be concerned in the mill in any way, but to rent her for 1200. D. she has two independent water wheels, single geered, one turning a pair of 5. f. Burr stones, the other a p͞r of 6. f. d°. she will be finished in the best manner with every modern convenience, is about 40. by 60. f. 3 floors in the body which is of stone, & 2. floors in the roof. one pair of stones will go July 1. the other Jan. 1. with a constant supply of water. there is an excellent miller's house of stone, 2 rooms below, & 2. garrets above, well finished. the merchants of Milton, who purchase most of the wheat of the neighborhood, will furnish the chief employ to be manufactured for a toll. . . .

P. S. a small gristmill near the other, retained by myself, will reserve the exclusive right to grind corn for consumption of the neighborhood for a toll. (*Jefferson Papers,* M. H. S.)

### (Thomas Main to Jefferson.)

[Washington] Feb^y 24^th 1806.

To accompany the President's Thorn plants. There are forty bundles, each containing 250 plants. Besides which there is one bundle of small plants containing 200. These last, to be planted in nursery to supply any accidental deficiencies that may happen in the hedges. If the weather should be dry and warm while the plants are on the road, they may be watered two [or] three times, according to directions, in the course of the journey. If the weather then should prove to freeze severely they ought not then to be watered at all during the continuance of the frost.

After the Hedges are planted the tops of the plants ought to be trimmed, or cut off with a pair of hedge shears just so low as to miss, untouched, the tops of the lower plants. This operation not only renders the hedge evenly and handsome to the eye but is also of essential benefit by tending to bring the plants to an equality of size and strength. (*Jefferson Papers,* M. H. S.)

### (Jefferson to John Freeman.)

Washington Feb. 26. 06.

Jerry arrived here the day before yesterday & sets off to-day. his cart is heavily laden with trees, thorns etc. I inclose you a plan of the grounds at Monticello where every thing is to be planted [see plate XXI], and a paper with full directions respecting the thorns & trees that nothing needs be added here, only to proceed to the planting with all your force the moment he arrives, as every hour the plants are out of the ground, some die. when a bundle is opened, do not leave the roots exposed to the air one moment unnecessarily. nothing is so fatal to them.

The garden seeds I send you are of the very best kind. if you sow a bed of each kind of peas immediately they will come to [table] before I leave Monticello. the sowings should be large as our daily consump-

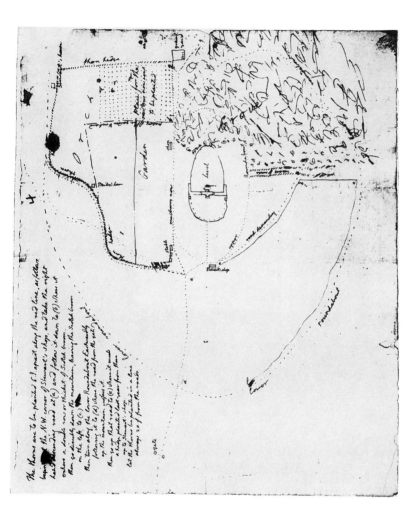

PLATE XXI.—Jefferson's plan of the top of *Monticello* Mountain, 1806.  Note the location of the garden, orchard, paling of the garden and orchard, mulberry row, grove, thorn hedges, roundabouts, and the graveyard.  (*Jefferson Papers*, M. H. S.)

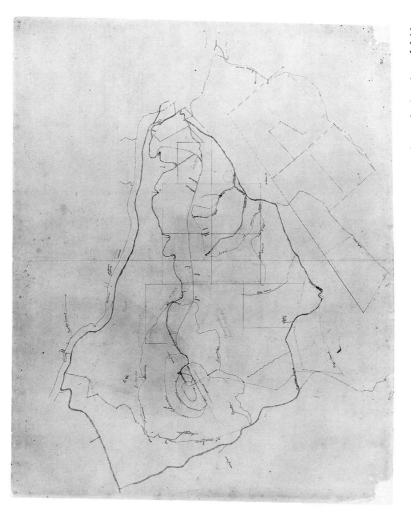

PLATE XXII.—Jefferson's plan of *Monticello* estate, 1806. This plan shows the location of fields, roads, round-abouts, springs, streams, fords, garden, and houses. (*Jefferson Papers*, M. H. S.)

tion of such things is great.   I send two pairs of hedge shears to be kept
for clipping the tops of the hedges every year. . . . (*Jefferson Papers,*
M. H. S.)

(Jefferson to Mr. Charles Clay.)

[Washington] Mar. 1. 06.

Th: Jefferson presents his compliments to mͬ Clay.  he was mistaken in believing he had a packet of seeds from Italy.  he was led into
the error by it's being entered as such at the Custom house, & no letter
of explanation came.  it turns out to be a packet containing 2. kinds of
the Peach-Apricot stones & a kind of plumb-stone.  the former are dis-
tinguishable from all others by a sheath in the side, through which you
may thrust a pin.  no other fruit stone has this peculiarity, so that there
is no doubt what this is.  but what kind of plumb-stone is that which
came, he has no means of knowing.  he will answer however for it's
being of distinguished merit.  altho' these may not be within the line of
the gardener on whose behalf mͬ Clay applied, yet the Apricots are so
valuable that they are well worth his attention.  this particular species
of Apricot is the finest fruit which grows in Europe.   Th: J. therefore
sends mͬ Clay some stones of each kind.   (*Jefferson Papers,* M. H. S.)

(Jefferson memorandum.)

Sent to Monticello.   Mar. 10. 06.

Cucurbita lagenaria.
2 bags peas.

(*Jefferson Papers,* M. H. S.)

(Sheffield to Jefferson.)

Board of Agriculture
Sackville Street
London
March 24ᵗʰ 1806.

Sir

On the receipt of a Box containing a small Model of a Mould Board
which in consequence of a long vacation, was not received till late in
January, it was referred to one of the Members, who has paid particular
attention to the Subject.   His report is extremely favorable & the Board
is very generally satisfied, that the Invention is important.   There is a
beautiful simplicity in the means of uniformly producing the same result; and the Theory of keeping a flat surface of the Mould Board, in
contact with the flat bottom of the Furrow Slice, is certainly just, and
entirely applicable to all Land that works, as the Farmers express it,
whole Furrow.   But there are some doubts whether the flatness in the
front of the Mould Board, while it rests in its own position, will not be

attended with inconvenience when turning a Furrow, consisting of loose Mould. As we are much interested in the complete success of this Invention, we shall be much obliged to you for the communication of any alterations, or improvements, which may hereafter be made. . . . (*Jefferson Papers,* United States Department of Agriculture.)

## (Jefferson to Edmund Bacon.)

Washington Apr. 21. '06.

. . . In the box No. 4. you will find some willow-oak acorns, peach stones, & a little more of the Quarentine corn which I had there.    this last you will add to our former stock & plant the whole as I have formerly directed.    put only a single grain in every hole that the seed may go as far as possible.    in this way I think you may have enough to plant 4. or 5. acres.    would it not be best to plant it in your new ground, which will leave your old ground for oats & clover.    the peach stones Wormly must plant in the nursery, as also the willow oak acorns.    the sooner they are put into the ground the better. (*Jefferson Papers,* M. H. S.)

## (Jefferson to William Charles Coles Claiborne.)

Washington, Ap. 27, 06.

. . . I thank you for a bag of peccans lately received from you.    If you could think of me in the autumn, when they are fresh, they will always be very acceptable, partly to plant, partly for table use. . . . (Ford, *Jefferson* 10: 256.)

## (Jefferson to Thomas Appleton.)

Washington April 29. 1806.

[Jefferson thanks Mr. Appleton for] the packages of trees, cuttings, plants & Seeds [that he had sent].    (*Jefferson Papers,* L. C.)

## (Bernard McMahon to Jefferson.)

Philadelphia 30ᵗʰ. [April] 1806

I have had the honor of receiving your friendly note, and likewise the seeds you were so good as to send me by Mʳ. Duane, for which I am extremely obliged to you, and my best endeavors shall be exerted to render these, as well as any other kinds that you will please to favour me with in future, useful to the country.

It gives me much pleasure to have it in my power to send you a few roots of the Artemisia Dracunculus, or Tarragon, these I forwarded by yesterday's mail and hope you will receive them in good condition; they propagate very freely and abundantly by the roots, and are perfectly hardy, requiring no additional care or protection in winter.    Should those forwarded miscarry I will send you a small box of them in a growing state, and you cannot confer a greater favour on me than to let me know of any seeds or plants which you would be desirous of obtaining, that I might have the pleasure of procuring them for you, if possible. . . . (*Jefferson Papers, L. C.*)

(Jefferson to James Madison.)

Monticello, May 11. 1806.

. . . The drought here is distressing, the crop of oats irrecoverably lost; the May wheat little better; common wheat tho' backward is healthy, and may yet do well.   peaches & cherries are almost wholly destroyed.  (*Jefferson Papers, L. C.*)

(Jefferson to James Madison.')

Monticello, May 23, 06.

. . . At length we have had a copious rain.   It continued with slight remissions two days (Wed & Thursday) falling moderately so that the earth is saturated without raising the streams.   It was from the N. E. and has cleared up cold, the wind at N. & thermometer 50°. . . . The above was written yesterday morning.   In the evening it recommenced raining, continued steadily tho' moderately thro' the night, and still continues this morning, with the wind at N. W.   The earth has enough, but more is wanting for the springs and streams.   May 24, 7 o'clock A. M. . . . (Ford, *Jefferson* 10: 268–269.)

(Alexander Hepburn to Jefferson.)

City of Washington June 12 1806.

Thomas Jefferson                     President of the United States

Debtor to A. Hepburn For Trees
Raised at his Garden

|  |  |  |
|---|---|---|
| 1. ............. | Apple Peach ................ | .12½ |
| 5. ............. | Alberges do do do ........... | .62½ |
| 34. ............. | vaga Lady Peach ........... | 4.25 |
| 12. ............. | Soft or Clear stone do ........ | 1.50 |
| 29. ............. | Teat Peach ................. | 3.62½ |
| 18. ............. | St. James Peach ............. | 2.25 |
| 20. ............. | Magdelene do do do do ....... | 2.50 |
| Apricots  8. Peach Apricots ........................... | | 1.00 |
| 1. Angelic ................................... | | .12½ |
| Plumbs  15. Mirrable Plumbs ....................... | | 1.87½ |
| 4. Queens Plumbs ........................... | | .50 |

$18.37½

Received the above amount.

(*Jefferson Papers,* M. H. S.)

(Jefferson to Christian Mayer.)

June 20. 06.

. . . The parcel of Quarentine corn, for which I return you many thanks. it is a present of real value, as this kind of corn is a timely successor to the garden pea, on our tables, where we esteem it as much as the pea: but its greater value is to furnish early subsistence after a year of scarcity. . . . (*Jefferson Papers,* M. H. S.)

(Jefferson to John H. Freeman.)

Washington June 28. '06.

. . . I remarked the day before I left home that the thorns on the North hillside were very foul. . . . (*Jefferson Papers,* M. H. S.)

(Jefferson to James Maury.)

Washington July 1. 06.

. . . We have been lately alarmed with the appearance of a caterpillar which at first threatened destruction to our small grain, Indian corn, tobacco & grasses. it has happily however disappeared after little injury. we are now gathering in one of the most plentiful harvests we have ever known. of tobacco there has not been plants enough to put in half a crop. this proceeded from the drought of the spring. . . . (*Jefferson Papers,* L. C.)

(John P. Van Ness to Jefferson.)

July 5, 1806

I take the liberty of sending you by the Bearer two worms which I took this afternoon on a lombardy poplar tree standing on dry ground, that answers, I think, very well (although the colour of the same worm is variegated and the shades of the two are different from each other) the description of the reptile, said to be poisenous, which infests these ornamental trees. As this subject has lately excited some speculation, I supposed it would be gratifying to you to observe the worm particularly; and therefore trouble you with this communication which I beg you will be so obliging as to excuse.

N. B. A description is enclosed. (*Jefferson Papers,* Missouri.)

(William Hamilton to Jefferson.)

[Philadelphia] The Woodlands, July 7, 1806

It was not until my return from an excursion of some days that I received your favor of the 20th ult. with the *quarantine corn* which accompanied it. will you be so good as to accept my best thanks for this mark of your kind attention. . . .

*N. B.* In the autumn I intend sending you if I live three kinds of trees which I think you will deem valuable additions to your garden viz—

*Gingko biloba* or China Maidenhair tree, *Broussenetia papyrifera* vulgarly called paper mulberry tree & *Mimosa julibrisin* or silk tree of Constantinople. The first is said by Kossmyler [?] to produce a good eatable nut—the 2nd in the bark as yields a valuable material for making paper to the inhabitants of China, Japan, & the East Indies, & for clothing to the people of Otaheite & other South Sea Islands—& the third is a beautiful flowering tree at this time in its highest perfection, the seeds of which were collected on the shore of the Caspian Sea. They are all hardy having for several years past borne our severest weather in the open ground without the smallest protection. . . . (*Jefferson Papers, L. C.*)

(John Vaughan to Jefferson.)

Philadelphia, July 8, 1806.

[Mr. Vaughan sends Jefferson from] F. A. Michaux his *Voyage* & a pamphlet relative to American Trees. (*Jefferson Papers, L. C.*)

(Jefferson to James Bowdoin.)

Washington, July 10, 1806.

. . . Our crops of wheat are greater than have ever been known, and are now nearly secured. A caterpillar gave for awhile great alarm, but did little injury. Of tobacco, not half a crop has been planted for want of rain; and even this half, with cotton and Indian corn, has yet many chances to run. . . . (Lipscomb and Bergh, *Jefferson* 11: 121.)

(Jefferson to F. André Michaux.)

Washington July 12. '06.

[He thanks him for his *Travels* and a pamphlet on trees. Mentions that he has his father's *Flora Boreali-Americana* and has seen his work on the American oaks,] both of which are valuable additions to our Botanical libraries. (*Jefferson Papers, L. C.*)

(Bernard McMahon to Jefferson.)

Philadelphia July 12th. 1806.

My being from home a few weeks in pursuit of plants and seeds was the cause of my not acknowledging sooner, the favour you were pleased to confer, in sending me the quarantine corn, which, I have no doubt, will become a valuable acquisition: it was sown in my absence, on the 25th. ult°. and is now about 20 inches high.

I take the liberty of requesting your acceptance of a few Tulip roots, the bloom of which I hope will give you satisfaction: they may remain in the state I send them till October, and be then planted as directed on page 528 of my book. I sincerely wish and solicit the favour of your pointing out to me how I can oblige you.

I am desirous to know if the Tarragon plants have succeeded, as, if necessary, I will send you a further supply.

Prefixed to the names of the Tulips you will find the following marks, significant of the Florist's divisions of the family; *Bz* signifies the flower to belong to the Bizards, *B,* to the Bybloemens, *I.* to the Incomparable Verports, *R,* to Baguet Rigauts. *r,* to the Rose coloured or Cherry, & *P.* to the Primo Baguets. . . . (*Jefferson Papers,* L. C.)

## (Jefferson to Bernard McMahon.)

Washington July 15. 06.

I received last night the tulip roots you were so kind as to send me, for which I return you my thanks. I shall go in a week to Monticello, whither I shall [take] them & have them planted in proper season. . . . about this time two years I shall begin to collect [plants] for that place because I shall be able to have them attended to. at that time I shall avail myself with pleasure of your obliging offer. but my situation there & taste, will lead me to ask for curious & hardy trees, than flowers. of the latter a few of those remarkeable either for beauty or fragrance will be the limits of my wishes. . . . (*Jefferson Papers,* L. C.)

## (Jefferson to James Madison.)

Monticello July 26. 1806.

. . . the drought in this quarter is successive . . . but there is a good deal of sickness generally, proceeding from the abundance of stagnant pools into which all the rivers, creeks, & branches are now converted. even the Rivanna, after taking out the water for my little toll mill, has not as much left as would turn another. the shallows in the river are all dry, & the deep parts covered with a green coat. all Charlottesville drinks out of one scanty spring which is constantly muddy, & more springs are failing daily. people come for bread from Amherst & Hanover to the three river mills we have in this neighborhood to wit, mine, Wood's 5 miles & Magruder's 10 miles below. we grind each about 40 barrels aday. (*Jefferson Papers,* L. C.)

## (Jefferson to William Hamilton.)

Washington July 1806.

Your favor of the 7th came duly to hand and the plant you are so good as to propose to send me will be thankfully recd. The little Mimosa Julibrisin you were so kind as to send me the last year is flourishing. I obtained from a gardener in this nbhd [neighborhood] 2 plants of the paper mulberry; but the parent plant being male, we are to expect no fruit from them, unless your [trees] should chance to be of the sex wanted. at a future day, say two years hence I shall ask from you some seeds of the Mimosa Farnesiana or Nilotica, of which you were kind enough before to furnish me some. but the plants have been lost during my absence from home. I remember seeing in your greenhouse a plant of a couple of feet height in a pot the fragrance of which (from it's gummy bud if I recollect rightly) was peculiarly agreeable to me and you were so kind as to remark that it required only a greenhouse, and that you would furnish me one when I should be in a situation to preserve it.  but it's name has entirely escaped me & I cannot suppose you can recollect or conjecture in your vast collection what particular plant this might be.  I must acquiese therefore in a privation which my own defect of memory has produced. . . .

Having decisively made up my mind for retirement at the end of my present term, my views and attentions are all turned homewards.  I have hitherto been engaged in my buildings which will be finished in the course of the present year.  The improvement of my grounds has been reserved for my occupation on my return home.  For this reason it is that I have put off to the fall of the year after next the collection of such curious trees as will bear our winters in the open air.

The grounds which I destine to improve in the style of the English gardens are in a form very difficult to be managed.  They compose the northern quadrant of a mountain for about $\frac{2}{3}$ of its height & then spread for the upper third over its whole crown.  They contain about three hundred acres, washed at the foot for about a mile, by a river of the size of the Schuylkill.  The hill is generally too steep for direct ascent, but we make level walks successively along it's side, which in it's upper part encircle the hill & intersect these again by others of easy ascent in various parts.  They are chiefly still in their native woods. which are majestic, and very generally a close undergrowth, which I have not suffered to be touched, knowing how much easier it is to cut away than to fill up.  The upper third is chiefly open, but to the South is covered with a dense thicket of Scotch broom (Spartium scoparium Lin.) which being favorably spread before the sun will admit of advantageous arrangement for winter enjoyment.  You are sensible that this disposition of the ground takes from me the first beauty in gardening, the variety of hill & dale, & leaves me as an awkward substitute a few hanging hollows & ridges, this subject is so unique and at the same time refractory, that to make a disposition analogous to its character would require much more of the genius of the landscape painter & gardener than I pretend to.  I had once hoped to get Parkins to go and give me some outlines, but I was disappointed.  Certainly I could never wish your health to be such as to render travelling necessary; but should a journey at any time promise improvement to it, there is no one on which you would be received with more pleasure than at Monticello.  Should I be there you will have an opportunity of indulging on a new field some of the taste which has made the Woodlands the only rival which I have known in America to what may be seen in England.

Thither without doubt we are to go for models in this art.  Their sunless climate has permitted them to adopt what is certainly a beauty of the very first order in landscape.  Their canvas is of open ground, variegated with clumps of trees distributed with taste.  They need no more of wood than will serve to embrace a lawn or a glade.  But under the beaming, constant and almost vertical sun of Virginia, shade is our Elysium.   In the absence of this no beauty of the eye can be enjoyed. This organ must yield it's gratification to that of the other senses; without the hope of any equivalent to the beauty relinquished.   The only substitute I have been able to imagine is this.   Let your ground be covered with trees of the loftiest stature.   Trim up their bodies as high as the constitution & form of the tree will bear, but so as that their tops shall still unite & yeild dense shade.   A wood, so open below, will have nearly the appearance of open grounds.   Then, when in the open ground you would plant a clump of trees, place a thicket of shrubs presenting a hemisphere the crown of which shall distinctly show itself under the branches of the trees.   This may be effected by a due selection & arrangement of the shrubs, & will I think offer a group not much inferior to that of trees.   The thickets may be varied too by making some of them of evergreens altogether, our red cedar made to grow in a bush, evergreen privet, pyrocanthus, Kalmia, Scotch broom.   Holly would be elegant but it does not grow in my part of the country.

Of prospect I have a rich profusion and offering itself at every point of the compass.   Mountains distant & near, smooth & shaggy, single & in ridges, a little river hiding itself among the hills so as to shew in lagoons only, cultivated grounds under the eye and two small villages.   To prevent a satiety of this is the principal difficulty.   It may be successively offered, & in different portions through vistas, or which will be better, between thickets so disposed as to serve as vistas, with the advantage of shifting the scenes as you advance on your way.

You will be sensible by this time of the truth of my information that my views are turned so steadfastly homeward that the subject runs away with me whenever I get on it.   I sat down to thank you for kindnesses received, & to bespeak permission to ask further contributions from your collection & I have written you a treatise on gardening generally, in which art lessons would come with more justice from you to me.   (*Jefferson Papers*, L. C.; and Fiske Kimball, *Jefferson's Grounds and Gardens at Monticello* (n. d.): 5–7.)

(Jefferson to Mrs. Mary Dangerfield.)

Monticello Aug. 10. 1806.

. . . They [negroes hired from her by Jefferson] have been engaged this year in some mill works, now nearly compleated.   the next year they would be engaged in levelling some garden grounds, making roads and other improvements of that nature. . . . (*Jefferson Papers*, M. H. S.)

(Jefferson to Oliver Evans.)

Monticello Sept. 1. 06.

. . . My mills will be going in October.   the situation is one of the best in the Union, without exception, and I am in want of a tenant for them.   perhaps it may lie in your way to fall in with some one, worthy

of being received, who would rent them, which would oblige me. . . .
(*Jefferson Papers,* L. C.)

### (Jefferson to James Madison.)

Monticello Sept. 2. '06.

. . . You had better not come through mr̄ Randolph's farm, but keep the public road till you get to his gate opposite Milton & there take the Charlottesville road, and half a mile further, at Johnson's, take the left hand by Shadwell mills.  the whole road after that is fine, and the ford made perfectly smooth.  the road by Milton is very hilly & doubles the distance.  the one by the mill is along the river bank to the foot of the mountain, where a new road gives an easy ascent.  we have had a divine rain yesterday afternoon & in the night. . . . (*Jefferson Papers,* L. C.)

### (Nicholas King to Jefferson.)

Washington, Sept. 11, 06.

The enclosed seeds were found, carefully folded up in a small bag of Chinese paper, & deposited among tea of the last importation. . . . I take the liberty of enclosing them to you, than whom no person has been more zealous to enrich the United States by the introduction of new and useful vegetables. . . . (*Jefferson Papers,* L. C.)

[Jefferson replied to the above letter, saying that he would take the seeds to Washington and place them in some one's hand.]

### (Jefferson to Thomas Moore.)

Monticello Sept. 16. 1806.

. . . I have been in the habit myself for a long time of noting the temperature of the air a little before sunrise & again between 3 & 4 P. M. these giving the maximum of cold & heat in a day where their progress is regular.  the points of time between these are uninteresting. I have noted at the same time the state of the weather the course of the wind & occasionally the access & recess of frost, flowering & leafing of plants, ripening of the cultivated fruits, arrival of birds & some insects, their hybernation etc.  the latter articles however have been omitted the last five years because my situation at Washington does not admit of their observation.  I now note only the temperature, weather & wind. any observations you make or procure to be made can always be compared with the cotemporary ones I made at Washington & Monticello. (*Jefferson Papers,* L. C.)

### (Jefferson to W. A. Burwell.)

Monticello, Sept. 17. 06.

. . . Can you send me some cones or seeds of the cucumber tree? (Ford, *Jefferson* 10: 291.)

(Jefferson to Étienne Lemaire.)

Monticello Sept. 25. '06.

. . . John Freeman is ill now for the 5ᵗʰ day of a fever, which has as yet shewn no signs of abatement. should he recover even quickly, he will be too weak to return with me. (*Jefferson Papers, L. C.*)

(Jefferson to Edmund Bacon.)

Washington Oct. 6. 06.

. . . When you have done the dam & pier-head before you go to digging at the mill, you should take a canoe & go down the canal, sounding everywhere to see if there is no place choaked with mud. I suspect there is from the circumstance of the canoe's grounding in it. it should be from 3. to 4. f. deep (I forget which) every where, & any obstruction found in it should be cleared out before it is too cold.

When you clean up the South orchard, you must do the same by the North orchard, that is to say, all the ground within the Thorn hedge on the North side of the mountain. I must have that cultivated the next year in the way in which I shall explain when I come home in March.

I must ask the favor of you to get a peck of the acorns of the ground oak, to make Wormely plant half of them in a nursery adjoining the present nursery, & send me the other half by Davy, to be forwarded to a friend in Europe. the oak I mean abounds in the poor lands about Hieron Gaines's. does not grow above 3. or 4. f. high, & is loaded with acorns shaped like chinquapins. be so good as to write to me once a fortnight informing me of the progress in our work. . . . (*Jefferson Papers, M. H. S.*)

(Jefferson to Edmund Bacon.)

Washington Oct. 19. .06.

. . . I should imagine that above & near the New road, and in the clearing you have to make in the river field you would find rail timber enough for the fence down the mountain. should you not however, you must get it where it is most convenient. when you proceed to mend up the fence which incloses the house & it's grounds, you will find a great deal of timber ready fallen in that inclosure, which I would wish you to use as far as it will go, before you cut down any more there, as I am unwilling to have a single tree fallen in that inclosure which can be done without. might not the lappings of the trees there be got up for coal wood, & made into a kiln where most convenient? . . . desire Stewart to send me immediately, by return of this post, the list of the iron wanting for the mill. two mules will be indispensably necessary for Davy's cart, when he comes here, as he will have a smart load back; & the cart should be made strong every where. I would not have you stop any property of mr̄ Freeman's. I do not believe him capable of taking away any thing of mine without accounting for it. the ill-will of the negroes to their overseer is always such, & their regard to truth so doubtful as not to justify our suspecting a man of honest character. if m͞r Freeman has taken anything of mine, I am sure I shall see it in his account. . . . will you be able to buy in the neighborhood as many Irish potatoes as will plant the whole of the North orchard, & what price must you pay? according to your answer I will determine whether it will be better to get them here. I wish you to keep an exact account of all the grain the mill gets that we may be able to know another year for how much we may depend on her. . . . (*Jefferson Papers,* Huntington.)

### (Jefferson to Martha (Jefferson) Randolph.)

Washington Nov. 27. 06.

. . . P. S. Mrs. Nourse has just sent a bundle of Wall flowers for you, with these there are some tussocks of Peruvian grass she sent me, & which I will ask Anne to take care of till March, when I will carry them to Monticello. . . . (*Jefferson Papers,* M. H. S.)

### (Jefferson to Edmund Bacon.)

Washington Dec. 8. 06.

I enclose you 700. Dollars, of which be pleased to pay to James Walker 100. D. John Perry 100. D. W͞m. Maddox 50. D. and there will remain 450. D. for your corn, fodder & pork, which you must pay out as you find most necessary, & let me know what will then remain due for these articles & it shall be remitted about this time next month. after getting all the coal wood you can on the Meadow branch I should think it most convenient to get the rest on the high mountain as near the Thoroughfare as you can. I think there is a great deal of fallen chestnut on that mountain which will make better coal than the green wood. there is a good deal also within the inclosure of the house at Monticello on the North side of the hill. we must use a good deal of economy in our wood, never cutting down new, where we can make the old do. I should think you might get the rails for the upper end of your long fence on the high mountain also. about 2. or 300. yds above the Thoroughfare gate there is a left hand roundabout road; pursuing that there is a 2ᵈ left hand going to the Secretary's ford, which is to be avoided, still pursuing the road on the level to a 3ᵈ left hand which descends to the Stone spring, and from that goes on to the new road, in this way rails may be carried from the high mountain. . . . (*Jefferson Papers,* Huntington.)

### (James Walker to Jefferson.)

Shadwell Decʳ. 12 1806

This comes to inform you of the present state of things about your Mills. in the first place Mr. Bacon has varied very much from your directions with regard to the diging and making safe every thing about the Mill and the waste in the side of the canal. the diging about the

Mill house is not near completed nor is the banks of the canal, and but little done to the waste, the stem is drawn off of the gate at the dam not being half pinned on by Mr. Perry. the wast and canal banks not being done and the water keeping up so high that we are affraid to take out the gate to adjust it as it could not be got in again before the water would overflow the bank at the mill. the weather at this time is too bad to do any thing towards it. Mr. Bacon had time enough to complete every thing about the mill before bad weather set in which I pressed to do but in vain, he took the negroes off to getting rails & wood the probability is that the Mill will not be completed this winter in consequence of these delays & others we are obliged to be very watchful to keep the dirting about the Mill from washing away. Maddox has done but little since you left home. I hardly suppose the addition to the Toal mill will be finished this winter. Perry has got timber for it but says he cant get it halled. Stewart has disappointed us very much in the balance of the Irons. I have taken many methods to get them done but all to no purpose. we have not got the spindle for the first pare of stones as yet also some other Irons for scales & packing Machine. but am in hopes of gettin them next Monday or Tuesday, the Mill on my part was ready all to the Irons above mentioned the 26 of Nov$^r$ and might have begun to grind the 29$^{th}$. I have done all that I can do towards the starting the other pare of stones untill I get Irons. am now at work about the alteration in toal mill and expect to be stopped for want of Irons as with the other mill. should Stewart disappoint us as he has done I think it will be better to get Isaac to do some of the work & let Stewart do the most difficult jobs. Mr. Shoemaker has been here sometime & seeing the prospect so gloomy is getting out of patience and unless the weather moderates so that the canal can be made safe enough to let in water he talks of returning back to Washington and not having anything to do with the Mill. he expects his Miller on every day and says he cannot afford to be on expenses here all winter & nothing coming in he seems anxious to be at business & if we can get the Mill in tolerable order will be satisfied for this season. . . . (*Jefferson Papers*, M. H. S.)

## (Bernard McMahon to Jefferson.)

Philadelphia Dec$^r$. 26$^{th}$. 1806

It is painful to me to trouble you at this period when you are so much occupied with the important affairs of the Nation; but your goodness I hope will excuse my anxiety to procure some seeds of the indigenous plants of the western parts of America, if you received such from Capt$^t$. Lewis on his return. A small portion of every kind you could conveniently spare would greatly oblige me and perhaps render me essential service; and it would be of some importance to get them as soon as you could make it convenient to have them forwarded, that each kind might be treated according to its apparent nature, and different methods tried to effect its successful propagation with the greater degree of certainty, especially the nondescripts, if any.

Of the Cucurbita you were so kind as to send me, some grew to the length of five feet five inches. I have one of them now in my shop window, perfectly dry, which is five feet one inch long, perfectly straight and in every part about four inches in diameter; they are excellent to use as squashes while young.

The quarantine Corn, was with me fit for the table, in fifty days after sowing; our last summer was colder than usual, or it probably would have been fit for use in forty days; however, it is a great acquisition and highly deserving of cultivation for the early part of the season. . . . (*Jefferson Papers*, L. C.)

## (Jefferson to Edmund Bacon.)

Washington Dec. 28. 1806.

. . . I pray you to arrange your work so as to spare your whole force to be at work in levelling the garden from the 10th of March to the last of April while I shall be at home. . . . (*Jefferson Papers*, L. C.)

## From the *Account Book 1804–1808*:

May 24.   recᵈ. by T. M. Randolph from Gabriel Lilly 1.375 the balance due me at his departure.
June 17.   pᵈ A. Hepburn for trees 18.375.
June 28.   pᵈ Holt garden seeds.   13.18.
June 28.   pᵈ Maine.   thorn plants 60.
Oct.   1.   left with John Freeman for his expenses to Washington 6. D.
Oct.   1.   left with Edmᵈ Bacon for expenses of Davy & Fanny to Washington 6. D.
Nov. 22.   gave Davy for expenses back to Monticello 6. D.

# 1807

*1807.** Jefferson, feeling the increasingly onerous responsibilities of his official position, again expressed his old desire to retire to the loveliness and quiet of *Monticello* and his family. On January 13 he wrote to his old friend, John Dickinson:

I have tired you, my friend, with a long letter. But your tedium will end in a few lines more. Mine has yet two years to endure. I am tired of an office where I can do no more good than many others, who would be glad to be employed in it. To myself, personally, it brings nothing but unceasing drudgery and daily loss of friends. Every office becoming vacant, every appointment made, *me donne un ingrat, et cent ennemis.* My only consolation is in the belief that my fellow citizens at large give me credit for good intentions. I will certainly endeavor to merit the continuance of that good-will which follows well-intended actions, and their approbation will be the dearest reward I can carry into retirement. (Lipscomb and Bergh, *Jefferson* 11: 137.)

The Aaron Burr trial, which opened on March 30, in Richmond, Virginia, certainly did not lessen the desire to retire from public office. The trial continued through the summer and was finally brought to a close on October 20. Burr was acquitted. The attack on the American ship, *Chesapeake,* off the Capes of Virginia, and the strained relations with England, were problems which also gave Jefferson much concern.

During the Burr trial Jefferson visited *Monticello* twice. The spring visit was made from April 11 to May 13. The summer visit lasted from August 4 to October 1.

The spring visit is of special interest because it was during Jefferson's stay at *Monticello* that he sketched, laid out, and planted the oval and round flower beds around the house. (See plate XXIII.) For some unaccountable reason Jefferson sketched the plan for the beds in a *Weather Memorandum Book,* which he had used partly for weather records since 1776, rather than in the *Garden Book.* In the same book he placed most of his planting diary for the year, again failing to

* This year not represented in the *Garden Book.*

enter anything in the *Garden Book* or in the *Farm Book*. The diary in the weather book, stray memoranda (chiefly to Bacon, the overseer), the account book for the year, and numerous letters, show this to have been the most active planting year since the early days of *Monticello*. It appears that he was working feverishly to get his mountaintop ready for his retirement.

The plan of the flower beds, referred to above, was the first one drawn which Jefferson actually laid out and planted with flowers. Jefferson had drawn a plan for formal beds near the house as early as 1772, but there is no indication that the plan was executed. (See plate III.) Jefferson, having decided definitely to retire at the end of his present term, evidently wished this part of his general landscaping plans to be well advanced.

On June 7 Jefferson wrote to his granddaughter Anne, describing the new winding walk and flower borders he proposed laying out on the broad lawn in the rear of the house. On the back of the letter he drew a sketch of his plans. The walk and borders were not laid out until 1808. (See letter, Jefferson to Anne Randolph, June 7, 1807; also plate XXIV.)

Minor work was done on the main house, and considerable work on the South Pavilion and Offices. The Indian Hall, which was the entrance hall to the house, was fast becoming filled with Indian relics, bones, rocks, and minerals. It was to become a show place for visitors in his retirement.

The mill presented its usual problem. It was still uncompleted, although James Walker, the builder, seems to have done his part in trying to finish it. Mr. Jonathan Shoemaker was the tenant.

During this period Jefferson carried on an interesting correspondence with his eldest grandchildren. Their letters are filled with talks about flowers and planting plans. Jefferson depended on Anne Randolph, his oldest grandchild, to attend to the flowers when she was at *Monticello*.

Two honors came to Jefferson this year which gave him much pleasure. The first was his reelection, once again, to the presidency of the American Philosophical Society; the other was his receiving a gold medal for his "mouldboard of least resistance" from the Agricultural Society of Paris. On receiving notice of his reelection to the presidency of the Philo-

sophical Society, he wrote to the Judges of Election, January
12:

I am again to return the tribute of my thanks for the continued proofs
of favor from the American Philosophical Society; and I ever do it with
sincere gratitude, sensible it is the effect of their good will, and not of
any services I have it in my power to render them. I pray you to convey
to them these expressions of my dutiful acknowledgments, and to accept
yourselves thanks for the favorable terms in which your letter of the 2d
instant announces the suffrage of the Society.

I am happy at the same time to greet them on the safe return of a
valuable member [Meriwether Lewis] of our fraternity, from a journey
of uncommon length and peril. He will ere long be with them, and
present them with the additions he brings to our knowledge of the geography and natural history of our country, from the Mississippi to the
Pacific. (Lipscomb and Bergh, *Jefferson* 11: 133–134.)

He wrote the following letter on May 29 to M. Silvestre,
Secretary of the Society of Agriculture of Paris, on receiving
the gold medal:

I have received, through the care of General Armstrong, the medal of
gold by which the society of agriculture of Paris have been pleased to
mark their approbation of the form of a mould-board which I had proposed; also the four first volumes of their memoirs, and the information that they had honored me with the title of foreign associate to their
society. I receive with great thankfulness these testimonies of their
favor, and should be happy to merit them by greater services. Attached
to agriculture by inclination, as well as by a conviction that it is the most
useful of the occupations of man, my course of life has not permitted me
to add to its theories the lessons of practice. I fear, therefore, I shall be
to them but an unprofitable member, and shall have little to offer of
myself worthy their acceptance. Should the labors of others, however,
on this side of the water, produce anything which may advance the objects of their institution, I shall with great pleasure become the instrument of its communication, and shall, moreover, execute with zeal any
orders of the society in this portion of the globe. I pray you to express
to them my sensibility for the distinctions they have been pleased to
confer on me, and to accept yourself the assurances of my high consideration and respect. (Lipscomb and Bergh, *Jefferson* 11: 212–213.)

From the *Weather Memorandum Book 1776–1820:*

Note the order of the terrasses below the garden wall is as follows.
the fig terras next to the wall.   then
the walk terras.
the strawberry terras.
1st. terras of the vineyard & so on to the 17th.
the 18th. terras of the vineyard is occupied chiefly by trees.
the 19th. is Bailey's ally.

Mar. 25.   S. W. vineyard.   at S. W. end of 1st. terras planted 2. Malaga grape vines.   Maine.

at N. E. end.   1st. terras 12 black Hamburg grape vines
2d. . . . . . .12. red d°.
3d. . . . . . .10. white Frontignac.
4th. . . . . . .20. Chasselas.
5th. . . . . . . 3. Muscadine.
6th. . . . . . .11. Brick coloured grapes.
7th. . . . . . .10. Black cluster grapes.

} from Main planted only in vacancies.

N. E. vineyard.   beginning at S. W. end of it, & planting only in vacancies

1st. terras.  6. plants of Seralamanna grapes 11. cuttings from them.
2d. . . . . . .15. cuttings of the same, or Piedmt Malmsy
3d. . . . . . .13. Piedmont Malmesy.  or Seralamana
4th. . . . . . . 1. Smyrna without seeds.
5th. . . . . . . 7. Galetlas.
6th. . . . . . . 7. Queen's grapes.
7th. . . . . . . 5. Great July grapes
8th. . . . . . . 6. Tokay
9th. . . . . . .13. Tokay.
10th. . . . . . .13. Trebbiano
11th. . . . . . .17. Lachrima Christi.
12th. . . . . . . 6. San Giovetto.
13th. . . . . . .15. Abrostine white
14th. . . . . . .21. d° . . . red or Aleaticos
15th. . . . . . .15. Aleatico.  or Abrostine red.
16th. . . . . . .13. Margiano.
17th. . . . . . .15. Mamsnole.

S. W. vineyard.   N. E. end.  9th. terras 4. Tokays, same as 9th. of N. E. Vineyard.
10th. . . . . . . 6. Trebbianos.  same as 10th. of N. E.
11th. . . . . . . 3. Lachrima Christi, same as 11th. of N. E.

Apr. 11.   Nursery.  begun in bed next the pales, on the lower side, where Genl. Jackson's peaches end to wit within 2. f. of the 4th. post from the S. E. corner.

N°. 1.   Quercus coccifera.   Prickly Kermes oak, 3. cross rows.
2.   Vitex Agnus castus.   Chaste-trees.  faux Poiorier.  9. rows.
3.   Cedrus Libani.   Cedar of Lebanon, 2. rows.
4.   Citisus Laburnum of the Alps.  2. rows.
5.   Lavathera Albia, the shrub Marshmallow. 2. rows.

} seeds recd. from Doctr Gouan at Montpelier.

1807. Apr. 15. 16. 18. 30.  planted & sowed flower beds as above [plate XXIII].

April 16.   planted as follows.

|  | N. E. clump | S. E. clump | S. W. clump | N. W. clump |
|---|---|---|---|---|
| 13. Paper mulberries | 2. | 2. | 5. | 4 |
| 6. Horse chestnuts | 3 | 3 | | |
| 2. Taccamahac poplars | 1 | 1 | | |
| 4. purple beach | | | 2 | 2 |
| 2. Robinia hispida | 1 | 1 | | |
| 2. Choak cherries | 1 | 1 | | |
| 3. Mountain ash. Sorbus Aucuparia | - - - - | - - - - | 1 | 2 |
| 2. Xanthoxylon | | | 1 | 1 |
| 1. Red bud | 1 | | | |

the above were from Maine except 5 horse chestnuts from
nursery & the Redbud

planted same day 1. Fraxinella in center of N. W. shrub
           circle                                                from
     *1. Gelder rose in d°. of N. E. d°.          Maine's
     1.  d°.     in d°. of S. E. d°.
     1. Laurodendron in margin of S. W. d°. from the
        nursery
planted also 10. willow oaks in N. W. brow of the slope, to wit from
    the N. Pavilion round to near the setting stones at S. W. end
    of level.
    and 12. Wild crabs from the S. to the N. pavilion near the
    brow of the slope.
    *Viburnum opulus rosea.
Apr. 17.  planted 2. Robinia hispida & 2. choak cherries on the S. W.
    slope.
         20. Weymouth pines on the slope by the Aspen thicket.
    In the Nursery.  began at the N. W. corner & extended rows
    from N. W. to NE. & planted
     1st. row abt. 2. f. from the pales ⎱ 100. paccans.
     2d. d°. 18 I. from that      ⎰
     3d. d°. . . . . . . . . . Gloucester hiccory nuts from Roanoke.
     4th. d°.      d°. from Roanoke. 79 in all. 6. d°. from
        Osages. 2. scarlet beans.
     5th. a bed of 4. f wide, 3 drills, globe artichoke. red.
     6th. a d°. . . . . d°. . . . . . . . . . . . . . . . . . . . . . . . . . . green
Apr. 18.     7th. a bed. Cooper's pale green asparagus. 5. rows [?]
        feet long, a seed every 6. I.
        at N. E. end of same bed 14. Ricara beans very for-
        ward.
     8th. a bed 26. f. long. 2. rows & about 8 f. of a 3d. say
        60 f. Missouri great Salsafia. 120 seeds 6. I. apart.†

† As stated elsewhere, the *Weather Memorandum Book* as a whole is
in the Library of Congress. However, the matter quoted down to this
point is from a detached sheet (comprising pages 51–52) now in the
Dreer Collection at the Historical Society of Pennsylvania.

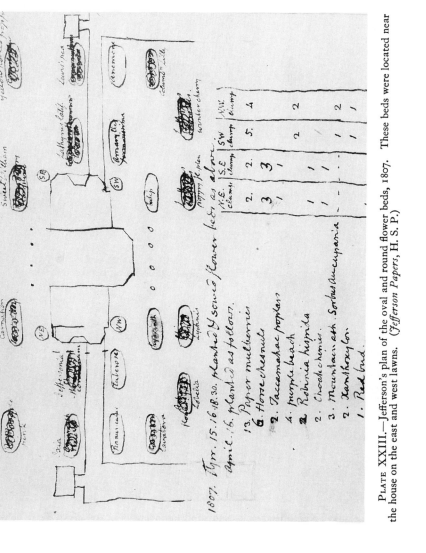

PLATE XXIII.—Jefferson's plan of the oval and round flower beds, 1807. These beds were located near the house on the east and west lawns. (*Jefferson Papers*, H. S. P.)

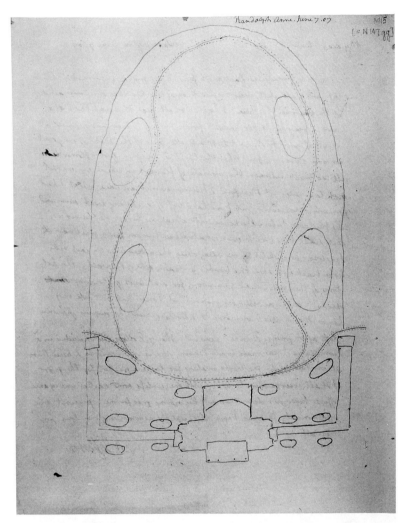

PLATE XXIV.—Jefferson's plan of the winding or *Round-about Walk,* flower borders, and beds, 1807. The flower beds were laid out and planted in April, 1807. The winding walk and flower borders were not laid out and planted until 1808. See plates XXIII, XXV, and letter, Jefferson to Anne Randolph, June 7, 1807. (*Jefferson Papers,* M. H. S.)

the following is the list of the flowers planted & sowed on the preceding page. [See Jefferson's Plan of the Round and Oval Flower Beds, 1807 (pl. XXIII), which is the page just referred to above.]

Dianthus Chinensis   China pink
        Caryophyllus Sweet William [Single carnation]
        barbatus Single carnation [Sweet William]
Glaucium   Yellow horned Poppy
Ixia Chinensis
Jeffersonia binata.
Lathyrus latifolius.   Everlasting pea
flowering pea of Arkansa.   from Capt. Lewis.
Lavatera Thuringica.
Lilly.   the yellow of the Columbia.   it's root a food of the natives.
Lobelia Cardinalis   Scarlet Cardinal's flower.
Lychnis Chalcedonica.   Scarlet Lychnis
Papaver Rhoeas flor. plen.   double Poppy
Physalis Alkekengi.   European winter cherry

50 Ranunculuses, double . . . . . . . . . .  ⎫
24. Polyanthus tuberosa.   double          ⎪
5. double pink hyacinths      ⎫              ⎪
10. double yellow d°.         ⎪              ⎬
6. double white d°.           ⎬  in one bed  ⎪  roots
6. double blue d°.            ⎪              ⎪
20. tulips                    ⎭              ⎪
6. Amaryllis formosissima                    ⎪
24. double anemones. . . . . . . . . . . . . ⎭

Apr. 19.   planted 9. Philadelphus coronarius, Mock orange in the 4. circular beds of shrubs at the 4. corners of the house.

    20.   planted among the old cherry trees in the 3d. & 4th. rows 4. cherry trees from Col°. Coles, to wit Carnations Maydukes.

    21.   planted the following trees from Timothy Matlack, see his list of Mar. 14. description. [See letter, Timothy Matlack to Jefferson, February 25, 1807.]

        h. (almond row) N. E. ⎧ N°. 1.   Carolina Canada peach.
           of Vineyard     ⎪        clingstone.
                          ⎨    2.   two Oldmixon peaches.
                          ⎪    3.   the Mammoth peach.
                          ⎪        clingstone.
                          ⎪    4.   the   Oldmixon   freestone
                          ⎩        peach (supposed Madeira)

        g. (Apricot row) d°.  ⎧   5.   the lady's favorite.   lately
                          ⎪        imported from France.
                          ⎨   6.   The Italian Redstone imported by Ro[bert] Morris.
                          ⎩   7.   the Moore park Apricot.

f. (Quince row) d°.            8.   the Italian white freestone.
                                     import^d. by Rob. Morris.

Note.   they were in the places of dead trees.   N°. 1. 2. 3.
4. run from S. W. to N. E.   7. 5. 6. d°. in this order.

m. (Pear row) Sickel's pear, no N°. blank.
        N°. 11. the Richmond pear.
        6. plants of Purple Syrian grape from Twickenham.
        upper row of S. W. vineyard at the N. E. end.

Apr. 24.   sowed liburnum in the 6. circular beds of shrubs.   also put
           into each 1. or 2. seeds of the honeysuckle of Lewis's river.

     27.   planted 11. Kentucky coffee seeds in the upper row of the
           nursery contin^d N. E. by 2. f. from pales, also some seeds
           of a tree from Kentucky, said to be handsome, but name for-
           gotten by n̄r̄s Lewis.   also Clematis or Virgin's bower seeds
           about the 3. springs on & near the road from the river up
           to the house & at the Stone spring.

     29.   planted a sod of Peruvian grass 15 I. square in the North
           corner of the Nursery.

     30.   planted 6. scarlet Alpine strawberry roots from M^c.Mahon
           on the lower side of the Peruvian tussock, within a few
           inches.   [See letter, McMahon to Jefferson, April 2, 1807.]

May  1.    planted 90. Antwerp raspberries from M^c.Mahon in the 6.
           upper raspberry terrasses.   [See letter, McMahon to Jeffer-
           son, April 2, 1807.]
           planted Pani corn in the orchard and Quarantine corn in the
           Riverfield.

Aug. 11.   my Quarentine corn planted May 1.   gave rosten ears in
           the last week of June.   being about 8. weeks.   it is now dry
           enough to grind, to wit 3⅓ months.
           my Pani corn planted the same day was a week or fortnight
           later.   but Shoemaker planted Pani corn about the 2^d. week
           of May, & had rosten ears the last week of June, 7 weeks
           exactly, he sais from planting, but by dates it seems less.
           m̄r̄ Randolph's Mandan corn planted 10 days before my
           Quarentine & Pani, yielded rosten ears the 4^th. of July.   it is
           now fit to grind.   an ear of Mandan corn which I gave him,
           planted May 15. gave rosten ears a few days only later than
           that planted Apr. 20.

Aug. 12.   Tuberoses blossom.

Sep. 29.   traced a road going level from the Thoroughfare towards
           Colle 3530. f. & then descending 1. foot in 10.   1600. feet to
           the branch at the foot of the stony hill on this side Colle,
           which branch proceeds from the Northernmost of the 2.
           springs corners between the Colle & Monticello tracts.

## LETTERS AND EXTRACTS OF LETTERS, 1807

### (Jefferson to Bernard McMahon.)

Washington Jan. 6. 07.

I received in due time your letter of Dec. 26. but it has been impossible for me to answer it sooner.   Cap$^t$ Lewis has brought a considerable number of seeds of plants peculiar to the countries he has visited. I have recommended to him to confide principal shares of them to m$\bar{r}$ Hamilton of the Woodlands & yourself, as the persons most likely to take care of them, which he will accordingly do.   he will carry them on to Philadelphia himself.

The tulip roots you were so kind as to send me, I planted at Monticello last autumn.   I intend to go there the first week in March in order to commence planting out some things to be in readiness for my kitchen & flour gardens two years hence.   a small cart will come here for such articles as I collect here, chiefly trees.   but there are several articles for the selection of which I would rather ask the assistance of your judgment than that of any other.   I note them at the foot of my letter, if you could be so good as to furnish me with them you would greatly oblige me.   seeds & bulbs can be so packed as to come with perfect safety by the stage, the best conveyance to this place because we can command it at all times.   whether tuberous & fibrous roots can come successfully in moss or any thing else not too bulky, you are the best judge. to give them the better chance they will be safest with you till about the 25$^{th}$. of February.   your bill for their amount shall be immediately provided for by remittance. . . .

| | |
|---|---|
| best Globe artichoke | Auricula |
| Antwerp raspberry | Ranunculus |
| Alpine strawberry | Hyacinths |
| Lillies of a few of the best kinds | Sweet William (Dianthus) |
| Tuberose | Wallflower |
| Crown Imperials | Marigold |
| Anemone | Saffron |

(*Jefferson Papers*, L. C.)

[Sent to Monticello by Jefferson] Jan. 7. 07.

Missouri hominy corn
soft corn
Pani 6. weeks corn.
9. nuts from Missouri
2. boxes d°. from Roanoke.

(*Jefferson Papers*, M. H. S.)

### (Jefferson to Charles Clay.)

Washington, January 11, 1807.

. . . I had hoped to keep the expenses of my office within the limits of its salary, so as to apply my private income entirely to the improve-

ment and enlargement of my estate; but I have not been able to do it.
. . . (Lipscomb and Bergh, *Jefferson* 11: 132.)

### (Jefferson to Edmund Bacon.)

Washington Jan. 11. 07.

. . . I wish you to keep a very exact account of all the toll the mill
recieves, for a whole year that we may know hereafter what yearly
dependance to place on her.   I remind you to have all pressing jobs done
before I come home that I may have all the hands during March &
April. . . . (*Jefferson Papers,* Huntington.)

### (James Walker to Jefferson.)

Shadwell Jan^y 16^th. 1807

I am sorry to inform you that the walls of the new addition to the
toal Mill has fallen down having been underminded by the water passing through the bank of the canal at the lower side of the long addition
the leak was occasioned by the frost & the bank not being high enough
together.   Mr. Bacon is now digging out the foundation deeper it appears that it will have to be dug as low as that of the old part to get a
foundation, as far as it is dug it appears to be quite miery.   Mr. Maddox says he will put up the wall again as soon as they are ready for him.
The part of the house passing over the canal is so low that there is not
sufficient room under it to make the canal bank high enough to hold the
water with safety besides the sills & joists will soon rot as it will have
to be dirted up to the top of them, and as a part is to be pulled down I
would have both new & old raised higher which may be easily done & I
think it will be better in every respect should you incline to do this you
will please let me know shortly.   the waist will be done in a few days
except bad weather.   we have done but little work for a few weeks past
towards the Mills having been disappointed by persons who ware at work
with me before christmas & promised to return in a few days after but
have not as yet.   I shall get the second pair of stones to work as soon as
possible.   The large Mill has not as yet begun to grind for want of a
Miller but was in readiness the eighth in^t.   perhaps their may be some
little alterations to make after it starts as is generally the case, which
will take up some time. . . . (*Jefferson Papers,* M. H. S.)

### (Jefferson to James Walker.)

Washington Jan. 26. 07.

I have received your letter of the 16^th. but I do not sufficiently understand the difficulty of containing the water within the banks of the
canal, under the toll-mill shed, to give directions about it.   I must
therefore leave it to your direction.

I receive with real grief the account of the tumbling down of the
new walls of the toll mill.   I had hoped that I had seen the end of my
expenses for that establishment.   I must pray that they may dig the

foundation now until it's sufficiency is beyond doubt, even if they must go down to the rock on which the house itself is built. I hope you will get the large mill finished off as soon as possible, so that she may begin by her rent to bring me in something. . . . (*Jefferson Papers,* M. H. S.)

### (Jefferson to Edmund Bacon.)

Washington Jan. 26. 07.

As I must carry thorn plants home in the spring to fill up the vacancies in my hedges, I must now get you to take the trouble of walking round the whole of the two thorn inclosures, and counting exactly how many are wanting. there should be one every 6. inches. then count how many plants are living in the thorn nursery, and send me the number, that I may be able to procure here the proper number. Davy will have to come on with the little cart & two mules about the 1st. of March. . . . I pray you to consider whatever relates to the mill as the most important of any thing under your care, and not to fail being there once every day. . . . (*Jefferson Papers,* Huntington.)

### (Jefferson to Madame de Tessé.)

Washington Feb. 21, 07.

On the 26th of October 1805 I had the pleasure of writing to you, and of informing you that I then made up for you a box of seeds acorns and nuts, which were to go by a vessel bound from Baltimore to Nantes. The box & my letter were addressed to Mr. Patterson our Consul at Nantes, not having heard from him in the course of the ensuing summer I began to apprehend all had miscarried, & in October last I wrote to Baltimore to have enquiry made from the owner of the ship, what had become of her. I inclose you the answers I received, which with a copy of my letter then sent, will give you the whole history of that attempt which I fear proved finally abortive.

I had made up another box for you, nearly similar to the former, this last autumn, & only waited for an article or two not yet dry enough, when our river blocked up with ice, a month sooner than usual, and has continued so till just now that it is again opened. I therefore, altho' late, send off the box to Baltimore to be forwarded to either Nantes or Bordeaux, to the address of our Consul Mr. Patterson of Nantes, or Mr. Lee of Bordeaux, who on receipt of it, will write and ask your directions concerning it. it is divided into 15 cells, numbered from I to XV & containing as follows Cell No. I Quercus Phellos II 2 Palestris or Rubra dissecta III 2 Prinos IV 2 Alba V VI IX Liriodendron tulipifera VII VIII Juniperus Virginiana X XI Bignonia Catalpa XII Cornus Florida XIII Juglans nigra, & in a bag some Lima beans for your garden. I never saw them in France. XIV Juglans Paccan & in a bag some Arachis hypogaea XV Diospyros Virginiana. to prevent every motive for suppressing this letter, I will only add my sincere & constant attachment and affections to yourself, M. de Tessé, M. & Mde. de la Fayette, & that you shall be remembered at the next season for a new supply. (*Glimpses of the Past,* Missouri 3: 99.)

## (Bernard McMahon to Jefferson.)

Philadelphia Feb^y 25^th. 1807

By this day's mail, I do myself the pleasure of sending you as many of the flower-roots you were pleased to write for, as I had at the time your kind letter came to hand; also some red and white Globe Artichokes, Early Cabbage and a small variety of Flower-seeds &c. which I solicit the favour of your accepting as a token of my best wishes.

Almost all my valuable hardy bulbs, I plant in October or in the early part of November, and previous to the planting season in the ensuing Autumn I shall do myself the pleasure of sending you a neat collection, and will then have no objection to charge a reasonable price for them. In a few days, when the weather becomes more mild I will send you some double Tuberose roots, but as they are extremely impatient of frost, it would be hazardous to send them at present.

Of Auriculas we have none here worth a cent, but I expect some good ones from London this spring; if they come safe, you shall have a division next season.

The Antwerp Raspberries cannot be had, as our ground is still bound by the frost. I shall forward them as soon as possible. The Alpine Strawberry is extremely scarce here; however, I think I shall be able to procure you some before the planting season in the ensuing autumn.

I am extremely obliged to you for your kindness in speaking to Cap^t. Lewis about the seeds; I anxiously wish for his arrival in this City, fearing to lose the advantage of early sowing for some articles which might require it. . . . (*Jefferson Papers*, L. C.)

## (Timothy Matlack to Jefferson.)

Lancaster [Pennsylvania] Feb. 25, 1807.

[He sends] a small bundle containing the nine cuttings which I had the honor of mentioning to you in the fall, the *Oldmaxon peach* tree and several other kinds of fruit in high esteem here, which I hope will prove acceptable to you. . . . I have sent some cuttings both of the pears and of the stone-fruits. . . . The cuttings of the Richmond pear are worth particular attention. . . .

### List of Fruit Trees

No. I. *Carolina Canada*—when fully ripe, the most juicy and highest flavoured of all the Clingstone peaches. For preserving it is the best of all the peaches, and being cut round lengthwise, and gently twisted, one half the peach comes from the stone as perfectly as from the freestone—the other half is taken out with the point of a knife. It retains more of the peach flavour in *brandy* than any other.

II. The much boasted *oldmixon* peach, which I fear will disappoint you in size.

III. The mammoth peach—large, perfectly beautiful and ripens tender—a clingstone.

IV. The Oldmixon freestone—a fine peach—I suppose the same as the Madeira peach.

V. The Lady's favourite—a small yellow peach of exquisite flavour —a late importation from France—ripens full of juice.

VI. The Italian red-freestone—imported by Robert Morris.

VIII. The Italian White-freestone—imported by R. M.

VII. The Moore Park Apricot—I presume the same as the *Anvon*.

The Purple Syrian Grape from Twitman { cuttings from each & also of the Purple Prune and of Coopers plum, a seedling from the Green Gage grafted on the Wild plum.

X. Sechell's pear—a small pear to be gathered about the 10th of October—They are red upon the tree & ripen in about two weeks to a beautiful lemon colour—They are juicy and tender as the best of the Burser pears, and much sweeter.

A small parcel of Coopers pale green Asparagus seed, which has long commanded the Philadelphia market. The head is large in proportion to its stem & very tender, the whole of this seed is gathered from *one* beautiful stalk in my garden.

The long crooked & warted Squash—a native of New Jersey, which the Cooper's family have preserved and cultivated for near a century. It is our best Squash.

(*Jefferson Papers*, L. C.)

(Jefferson to Ellen Randolph.)

Washington Mar. 1. 07.

. . . I shall write to Anne by the cart, because it will carry a box of flower roots which I shall consign to her care, but not to be opened till we get to Monticello & have every thing ready for planting them as soon as they are opened. . . . (*Jefferson Papers*, M. H. S.)

(Jefferson to Edmund Bacon.)

Washington Mar. 1, 1807.

I suppose Davy will set out tomorrow, and of course that he will hardly be back to Monticello before the 13th. in the meantime the season is advancing. I think therefore you had better take up the thorns in the Nursery, & plant them in the hedge of the South orchard as soon as the weather becomes favorable for it. the plants are to be every where 6. inches apart. a caution very strictly to be attended to is that when you take the plants out of the nursery, let the roots be exposed to the air as short a time & as little as possible. nothing is so fatal to a plant as the air getting at the root, and more than half the loss in transplanting is from that cause. mr̄ Perry was wrong in saying I had blamed you about the building the cooper's house & stable at the mill.

there is not such an idea in my letter. the blame was all for himself which I thought was for any body: however he has given me such an explanation since as satisfies me as to him also. I expect to be at home about the 12th. or 13th. . . . (*Jefferson Papers*, Huntington.)

## (John L. E. W. Shecut to Jefferson.)

Charleston, March 4, 1807.

[Mr. Shecut presents through Dr. Mitchill of New York a copy of his *Flora Carolinaeensis*.]   (*Jefferson Papers*, L. C.)

## (Thomas Main sold to Jefferson.)

[Georgetown] Mar. 7, 1807

| | | | | |
|---|---|---|---|---|
| 13 | Paper Mulberries | @ 50 | cent each | $6.00 |
| 4 | Ribinias [Robinias] | @ 25 | " " | 1.00 |
| 2 | Snowballs | @ Do. | " " | .50 |
| 3 | Mountain ash | @ 25 | " " | .75 |
| 2 | Tacamahac | @ Do. | " " | .50 |
| 2 | Prickly-ash-Xanthoxylon | @ 25 | " " | .50 |
| 4 | Choke cherry | @ 25 | " " | 1.00 |
| 1 | Fraxinella | | | 1.00 |
| 1 | Buckeye | | | |
| 4 | Purple Beeches | | | |
| 4 | Thousand American Hedge Thorns | @ | 6 Doll per M. | 24.00 |

$35.25

. . . Great care must be taken in unloosing this smallest bundle not to injure the buds of the plants particularly the purple Beeches and Fraxinella. The large buds of the Buckeye are trebly secured with the bandages.

### Directions to accompany the plants for the President

If the weather continues moist there will be little occasion to water the plants upon the road. But if it turns out dry and windy they may be watered once a day. They ought not to be watered if it should freeze while they are upon the journey.

When they arrive at Monticello, the thorns should be untied from the large bundles and continue an hour or two immersed in water; they may then be left with their roots only in the water all the night and then layed in a trench pretty deep so as entirely to cover their roots, where they may remain until the weather etc. is suitable to have them planted in the hedge.

If the weather should be frosty on their arrival they may be laid in a cellar unopened until the frost is over.

Thos. Main

March 10, 1807.                                (*Jefferson Papers*, L. C.)

(Jefferson to Timothy Matlack.)

Washington Mar. 12. 07.

You have very much gratified me by the collection of choice fruit trees you have been so good as to forward me.  it is gone on to Monticello to which place I shall follow it in a few days.  whither also I am withdrawing all my views as a place of rest from the labors & contentions of public life. . . . (*Jefferson Papers*, L. C.)

(Jefferson to Edmund Bacon.)

Washington Mar. 12. 1807.

Davy has been detained here until this day.  he now carries with him some bundles of trees, and 4,000 thorns.  as to the trees, the moment he arrives, dig a trench in the garden 18. I. deep and set them in it in their bundles, side by side, and fill in the earth again very close, so that the air may not possibly get to them, and let them remain so until I come home, only watering them every day that it does not rain.  with respect to the thorns, bury them in like manner in a trench in bundles, and press in the earth close.  then proceed to plant them, filling up all vacancies in the hedges at 6. inches distant.  take out of the group only one bundle at a time, and have a pail of water at hand while planting them, and dip the root of every plant into the water, before it is planted in its place. the most fatal thing to plants is the letting their roots be exposed to the air while planting.  these thorns should be planted as soon as the cart arrives.  Davy brings also some little boxes, etc. which may be put away in the house till my arrival.  I expect to get some clover seeds before he starts from here, but am not yet certain of it.  if he brings it, take care of it till I get home.  I shall set out for Monticello as soon as Mr. Randolph is strong enough to travel; but that will not be for a week or ten days to come. . . . (*Jefferson Papers*, M. H. S.)

(Jefferson to Albert Gallatin.)

[Washington] March 20, 1807.

. . . Indeed, I have but little moment in the morning in which I can either read, write, or think; being obliged to be shut up in a dark room from early in the forenoon till night, with a periodical headache. . . . (Lipscomb and Bergh, *Jefferson* 11: 165–166.)

(Jefferson to Bernard McMahon.)

Washington Mar. 20. 07.

I am in hopes I am more fortunate in the seeds I now send you than the effete roots before sent.  the enclosed seeds are given me by Cap$^t$ Lewis for my own garden:  but as I am not in a situation to do them justice, & am more anxious they should be saved in any way than merely to see them in my own possession, I forward them to you who can give them their best chance.  it will give you too an opportunity of committing them earlier to the ground than those you will receive from

Cap$^t$ Lewis for yourself, as it may yet be some time before he is with you. perhaps you may as well say nothing of your receiving this, lest it might lessen the portion he will be disposed to give you; and believing myself they will be best in your hands, I wish to increase the portion deposited with you. . . . (*Jefferson Papers*, L. C.)

## (Jefferson to Bernard McMahon.)

Washington Mar. 22. 07.

Governor Lewis's journey to Philadelphia being delayed longer than was expected, and the season advancing, we have thought it best to forward to you by post the packet of seeds destined for you. they are the fruits of his journey across the continent, & will I trust add some useful or agreeable varieties to what we now possess. I send a similar packet to m$\bar{r}$ Hamilton of the Woodlands. in making him & yourself the depositories of these public treasures, I am sure we take the best measures possible to ensure them from being lost. I sent you a small packet a few days ago which he had destined for myself: but I am in too indifferent a situation to take the care of them which they merit. . . . (*Jefferson Papers*, L. C.)

## (Jefferson to William Hamilton.)

Washington Mar. 22. '07.

It is with great pleasure that at the request of Governor Lewis, I send you the seeds now inclosed, being a part of the Botanical fruits of his journey across the continent. [He also mentions sending some of the seeds to McMahon. See letter above.] . . . (*Jefferson Papers*, L. C.)

## (John Threlkeld to Jefferson.)

[March 25, 1807.]

About two years ago I saw a peach apricot (at Hepburn's Garden in the City) belonging to you and requested Mr. Mason to ask your permission to take buds from it the Ensuing summer and that I would furnish you with as many as you wanted of the same kind from it, and that you risked loosing the kind by Removal having but one. this he omitted. the tree was removed and as I have been since inform'd Lost on the road. I was so fortunate as to get the twigs cut off to make it pack and from them got one to live by Grafting and last year raised a few from that Inoculation. they are small the bud not having grown more than 9 or 10 Inches last summer. will you please to accept 4 or 5 of them together with two very fine growing trees that derive their origin from the Bishop of Bourdeaux's Garden. the fruit is said to be large, fine and of the cling stone kind. the Peach Apricot can be moved now, next fall or next spring but after that would probably be too Large. if you remove them this spring they should be taken up directly to prevent their shooting which they will Do in a few days. . . . (Ford, *Jefferson Correspondence:* 141–142.)

### (Jefferson to John Threlkeld.)

Washington, Mar. 26. 07.

I thank you for the kind offer of the trees mentioned in your letter of yesterday. the Peach Apricot which you saw at Hepburn's was lost on the road, but I received with it from Italy at the same time a supply of the stones of the same fruit, which are planted at Monticello, and from which I hope to raise some trees, tho' as yet I do not know their success. should these fail I will avail myself of your kind offer the next fall or spring. the two peach trees you propose will be very acceptable at the same time. I am endeavoring to make a collection of the choicest kinds of peaches for Monticello. presuming you are attached to the culture of trees, I take the liberty of sending you some Paccan nuts, which being of the last years growth received from New Orleans, will probably grow. they are a very fine nut and succeed well in this climate. they require rich land. between the two lobes of the kernel there is a thin pellicle, excessively austere and bitter, which it is necessary to take out before eating the nut. . . . (Ford, *Jefferson Correspondence:* 142.)

### (Bernard McMahon to Jefferson.)

Philadelphia March 27th. 1807

I duly received the roots and seeds you were so good as to send me, for which I return you and Governor Lewis my hearty thanks. I have no doubt but I will be able to give a good account of the produce, for I never saw seeds in a better state of preservation, and their having reached me in good time will be a considerable advantage. I have already sowed several kinds, will treat the whole with very particular care, and have no doubt but I will be able to send you in due time, plants *of every kind* committed to my care.

I request the favour of your informing Governor Lewis that I wish him to accept from me, a collection of seeds of culinary & ornamental plants, to take with him when going to the territory over which he is to preside; they shall be ready for him whenever he pleases.

The dwarf Cedar of the plains of Missouri, I take, from the seed, to be a species of Juniperus; the *Shallan* of the Clatsops, a Vaccinium; and the flowering Pea of the plains of Arkansas, a Lupinus. I shall from time to time report to you or to Governor Lewis the progress of this precious collection, and of any other articles with which I may be favoured.

Mr. Duane intends to leave this City for Washington on Tuesday next; by him I will send the Antwerp Raspberries. . . . (*Jefferson Papers*, L. C.)

### (Jefferson to Monsieur Le Comte Diodati.)

Washington, March 29, 1807.

. . . At the end of my present term, of which two years are yet to come, I propose to retire from public life, and to close my days on my patrimony of Monticello, in the bosom of my family. I have hitherto enjoyed uniform health; but the weight of public business begins to be too heavy for me, and I long for the enjoyments of rural life, among my books, my farms and my family. Having performed my *quadragena stipendia,* I am entitled to my discharge, and should be sorry, indeed, that others should be sooner sensible than myself when I ought to ask it. I have, therefore, requested my fellow-citizens to think of a successor for me, to whom I shall deliver the public concerns with greater joy than I received them. I have the consolation too of having added nothing to my private fortune during my public service, and of retiring with hands as clean as they are empty. . . . (Lipscomb and Bergh, *Jefferson* 11: 182.)

### (Bernard McMahon to Jefferson.)

Philadelphia April 2nd. 1807

I do myself the pleasure of sending you per Mr. Duane who intends leaving this City for Washington tomorrow, 90 plants of the white Antwerp Raspberry, cut to the proper lengths for planting; and 8 plants of the true red Alpine Strawberry, being all I could procure of these kinds at present. They are packed in moss, in the larger of two boxes sent, so carefully, as not to suffer the least injury even if they should not be planted till the beginning of next month. In the small box I send you 24 roots Double Tuberoses and 6 roots of the Amaryllis formosissima; for the management of these, see pages 349 & 350 of my work on Gardening.

I have fine crops already up of the Aricara Tobacco, and perennial flax, and expect numbers of the others up in a few days. . . . (*Jefferson Papers,* L. C.)

### (Jefferson to Egbert Benson.)

Washington Apr. 7. 07.

With this will be forwarded by the stage for me at Monticello (to which place I am this moment setting out) two boxes containing plants, on which I set the greatest value. they are not yet arrived here from Philadelphia but are expected to-day. the object of this letter is to pray you to pay particular attention to the forwarding them by the first stage, that they may be out of the ground as short a time as possible. they are to be delivered to David Higginbothem at Milton who will pay the carriage. . . . (*Jefferson Papers,* M. H. S.)

### (Bernard McMahon to Jefferson.)

Philadelphia April 10th 1807

I was much surprised this day, to find that Mr. Duane did not proceed to Washington as he informed me he would when I had the pleasure of writing to you last, nor can he now for a few days; therefore, tomorrow I will forward the larger Box by the stage, and the smaller by the mail. I am very sorry that I did not take this method at first.

I have several sorts growing of the seeds you were pleased to send me, among which are four varieties of Currants, and I am confidant that I shall have plants from every kind I received. . . .

P. S. I am not at all apprehensive that the plants will suffer by this delay, as they are very carefully packed. (*Jefferson Papers, L. C.*)

(Jefferson to Jonathan Shoemaker.)

Monticello April 18. 07.

. . . tho' I have been here a week I have not had time to go to the mill, having a great deal of planting to do, & the season having burst out upon us very suddenly after my arrival. . . . (*Jefferson Papers, M. H. S.*)

(Jacob Crowninshield to Jefferson.)

Salem, Massachusetts, April 21, 1807.

Jacob Crowninshield has the pleasure to send Mr. Jefferson a sample of fresh *Guzerat* Wheat received by him from Bombay. he regrets that the package will not allow a greater quantity to be sent, but this may be of less consequence as the object will be merely to make a trial of the wheat & for the preservation of the seed in Virginia. . . . (*Jefferson Papers, L. C.*)

(Jefferson to James Madison.)

Monticello, Apr. 25, 07.

. . . We have had three great rains within the last 13. days. It is just now clearing off after 36. hours of rain, with little intermission. Yet it is thought not too much. . . . (Ford, *Jefferson* 10: 391.)

(Jefferson to James Madison.)

Monticello, May 1, 1807.

. . . Our weather continues extremely seasonable and favorable for vegetation. . . . (Lipscomb and Bergh, *Jefferson* 11: 199.)

(Jefferson to Edmund Bacon.)

May 13, 1807.

Directions for plantation affairs.

. . . Resume levelling of garden. . . .

. . . Use great economy in timber, never cutting down a tree for firewood or any other purpose as long as one can be found ready cut down & tolerably convenient. in our new way of fencing the shortest cuts & large branches and even hollow trees will come in for use. the loppings will do for firewood & coal wood. . . .

. . . Burwell paints & takes care of the house. . . .
. . . Keep the thorns constantly clean wed. . . .
. . . Wormly must be directed to weed the flower beds about the house,
the nursery, the vineyards, & raspberry beds, when they need it.  I wish
him to gather me a peck or two of clean broom seed, when ripe.  (*Jefferson Papers*, Yale.)

(Jefferson to George Divers.)

Washington May 24. '07.

. . . We had strawberries yesterday, when had you them?  no peas
here yet. . . . (*Jefferson Papers*, L. C.)

(Jefferson to the Marquis de Lafayette.)

Washington, May 26, 07.

. . . I wrote to Madame de Tesse on the 21st of Feb and at the same
time sent a box of seeds, nuts, acorns &c. to Baltimore, which were forwarded to Bordeaux for her, to the care of Mr. Lee our consul there.
I had done the same thing the preceding year.  That vessel was taken
by the English, detained, but got to France in April.  It is so difficult
in times of war to get anything carried safely across the Atlantic as to
be very discouraging.  I shall not fail, however, to repeat my endeavors
as to such objects as are in our neighborhood here, until she has a plenty
of them.  I am panting for retirement, but am as yet nearly two years
from that goal. . . . (Ford, *Jefferson* 10: 411.)

(Jefferson to Colonel James Monroe.)

Washington, May 29, 1807.

. . . I am not certain this letter will find you in England.  The sole
object in writing it, is to add another little commission to the one I had
formerly troubled you with.  It is to procure for me "a machine for
ascertaining the resistance of ploughs or carriages, invented and sold by
Winlaw, in Margaret street, Cavendish Square."  It will cost, I believe, four or five guineas, which shall be replaced here instanter on your
arrival. . . . (Lipscomb and Bergh, *Jefferson* 11: 211.)

(Jefferson to Edmund Bacon.)

Washington, [May] 31. 07.

. . . The Burr milstones for the toll mill are gone on.  the runner
weighs 1800 lbs, the bedstone 1400 lbs. . . . (*Jefferson Papers*, L. C.)

(George Divers to Jefferson.)

Farmington June 6, 1807.

We had peas on the 17th May 14 days later than last year, you had
strawberries 10 days before us. . . . (*Jefferson Papers*, M. H. S.)

(Jefferson to Anne Randolph.)

Washington June 7. 07.

I received last week from your papa information that you were all well except your Mama, who had still some remains of the pain in the face. I hope I shall hear this week that she is restored to her health. from yourself I may soon expect a report of your first visit to Monticello, and of the state of our joint concerns there. I find that the limited number of our flower beds will too much restrain the variety of flowers in which we might wish to indulge, & therefore I have resumed an idea, which I had formerly entertained, but had laid by, of a winding walk surrounding the lawn before the house, with a narrow border of flowers on each side. this would give us abundant room for a great variety. I enclose you a sketch of my idea, where the dotted lines on each side of the black line shew the border on each side of the walk. the hollows of the walk would give room for oval beds of flowering shrubs. . . . [See plate XXIV. Jefferson drew the plan on the back of this letter.] (*Jefferson Papers,* M. H. S.)

(Jefferson to Doctor Caspar Wistar.)

Washington, June 21, 1807.

I have a grandson, the son of Mr. Randolph, now about fifteen years of age, in whose education I take a lively interest. . . . I am not a friend to placing young men in populous cities, because they acquire there habits and partialities which do not contribute to the happiness of their after life. But there are particular branches of science, which are not so advantageously taught anywhere else in the United States as in Philadelphia. The garden at the Woodlands for Botany, Mr. Peale's Museum for Natural History, your Medical school for Anatomy, and the able professors in all of them, give advantages not to be found elsewhere. We propose, therefore, to send him to Philadelphia to attend the schools of Botany, Natural History, Anatomy, and perhaps surgery; but not Medicine. . . . (Lipscomb and Bergh, *Jefferson* 11: 242–243.)

(Wm. Lee to Jefferson.)

Bordeaux June 25, 07.

The box of seeds for Madame de Tessé I have received. . . . [See letter, Jefferson to Madame de Tessé, February 21, 1807.] (*Jefferson Papers,* L. C.)

(Jefferson to Stephen Cathalan.)

Washington June 29. 07.

. . . The articles by the Three friends, cap$^t$. Harvey came safely to hand, & I have since received by different conveyances the other articles desired in mine of Apr. 28. to wit the Artichoke bottoms, Mustard de Mailly, vinaigre d'estragon, Maccaroni, Parmesan & Smyrna raisins. . . . (*Jefferson Papers,* L. C.)

(Thomas Main to Jefferson.)

Mains Nursery
June 1807

Bo$^t$ of Thos Main

Thorn plants, Trees & shrubs—as per acco$^t$                          Amts
    rendered to the amount of .........................        35   25

The honorable Thomas Randolph Esq.
    for Thorn plants as p$^r$ acc$^t$ rendered                        24   00
                                                              _____
                                                                $59 . 25

Received the above in full.

                    Thos. Main.

                                        (*Jefferson Papers*, L. C.)

(Randolph Jefferson to Jefferson.)

July 9$^{th}$ 1807

Dear Brother,

I should have wrote to you on this business before but wished to be certain in seeing whether I could procure the quantity of seed that I agree$^d$ with the nigroes for which was a bushel of Green soard and as much of White Clover they are now delivering that quantity at Eight shillings pr Gallon I think the price high at that but I assure you that it was not in My power to get it cheaper if Convenient be pleased to inclose to Me as Much Money as will pay them of for these seed. . . . (*Carr-Cary Papers*, Alderman Memorial Library, University of Virginia. Hereafter cited as *Carr-Cary Papers*, U. Va. Also published in *Thomas Jefferson and His Unknown Brother*, by Bernard Mayo.)

(Jefferson to the Marquis de Lafayette.)

Washington, July 14, 1807.

. . . I am afraid I have been very unsuccessful in my endeavors to serve Madame de Tessé in her taste for planting. A box of seeds, etc., which I sent her in the close of 1805, was carried with the vessel into England, and discharged so late that I fear she lost their benefit for that season. Another box, which I prepared in the autumn of 1806, has, I fear, been equally delayed from other accidents. However, I will persevere in my endeavors. (Lipscomb and Bergh, *Jefferson* 11: 280.)

(Jefferson to J. P. Reibelt.)

Monticello Aug. 12. 07.

Your letter of Mar. 28. did not get to my hands at Washington till July 7, and as I had left Parkyn's designs of gardens at this place I was obliged to defer answering you till I came here. I now enclose it to you with many thanks for the use of it. I suspect you will find in the grounds you propose to improve on these models, in the highest degree an obstacle which we find considerable even here: that is that the luxuriance of the soil by it's constant reproduction of weeds of powerful growth & stature will bid defiance to the keeping your grounds in that clean state which the English gardens require. . . . (*Jefferson Papers,* L. C.)

(Jefferson to Randolph Jefferson.)

Monticello Aug. 12. 07.

Dear Brother,

I did not receive your letter of July 9 till the 8th inst. and now, by the first post inclose you 20. D. to pay for the clover & greenswerd seed; which goes by post to Warren. the greenswerd seed I wish to have here; but the white clover seed is to go to Bedford. . . . (*Carr-Cary Papers,* U. Va.)

(Charles Willson Peale to Jefferson.)

[Philadelphia] Museum Aug. 30. 1807.

. . . Agreeable to the request of Gov. Lewis I have prepaired one of the heads of the American Argali (big horns) to be placed in your Hall at Monticello. it will be put on board the Schooner Jane, Capt. Jackson on tomorrow. . . . (*Jefferson Papers,* L. C.)

(William Few to Jefferson.)

New York Sept$^r$ 26$^{th}$ 1807.

I take the liberty of sending to you by M$^r$. Gallatin a bottle of salad oil, the first perhaps that was ever made in the United States. It was pressed from the seed of a plant which grows in the southern States, and is known there by the name of Bene, and is cultivated in those States by the Negroes only for their own use, the pod which contains the seed before it is matured, I am told is the part which they use.

I have not learned the Botanic term of the plant nor under what class, or order it is arranged.

The seed was sent to me from Georgia by M$^r$. Milledge of the Senate of the United States whose Agricultural and scientific researches have rendered important services to that State.

Six Bushels of the seed produced about six gallons of cold drawn oil, of the quality I send, and about twelve gallons of warm drawn oil that is not quite so pure and well tasted, but it may be used as salad oil, or for painting, or lamps. . . . (*Jefferson Papers,* L. C.)

(Jefferson to George Divers.)

Monticello Sep. 29. 07.

I received the inclosed grass seed, & letter from a m̅r̅ Willis of whom, or whose place of residence I know nothing. the character he gives of the grass is such as to make it worthy an experiment. but my vagrant life renders it impracticable with me.   knowing nobody more likely to give it a fair trial than yourself I confide it to your care if you think it worthy of it. . . . (*Jefferson Papers,* M. H. S.)

(Jefferson to William Duane.)

Washington Oct. 14. 07.

[He asks him to procure the following books:]

McMahon's book of gardening
Barton's elements of botany, unbound because I
wish to have the two vols bound in one. . . .

(*Jefferson Papers,* L. C.)

(Jefferson to Timothy Matlack.)

Washington Oct. 19. 07.

I duly received your present of Sickel's pears, most of them in their highest point of perfection, two or three just past it.   they exceeded anything I have tasted since I left France, & equalled any pear I had seen there.   they renewed my regrets for the loss of the last spring.   the bundle of trees you so kindly sent me, were longer coming here than they should have been, but going hence to Monticello in a cart, they were out in the remarkable severe weather we had in the middle & latter part of March, and by the impassableness of the roads & breaking down of the cart were so long out that not a single one survived.   I will not trouble you with a new request until I go home myself to remain, which will be on the 4th of March after next.   but if in the February preceeding that (say Feb. 1809) you should have any plants to spare of what you deem *excellent* pears, peaches, or grapes, they will then be most acceptable indeed, and I shall be able to carry & plant them myself at Monticello where I shall then begin to occupy myself according to my own natural inclinations, which have been so long kept down by the history of our times; and shall bid a joyful adieu to politics and all the odious passions & vices of which they make us the object in public life.   I should be very much pleased to see you at Monticello & to prove to you that my heart has been always there, altho my body has been every where, except there, since our first acquaintance in 1775. . . . (*Jefferson Papers,* L. C.)

(Anne Cary Randolph to Jefferson.)

Edgehill November 9 1807

My Dear Grand Papa.

The tuberoses & Amaryllises are taken up we shall have a plenty of them for the next year.   the tulips & Hyacinths I had planted before I left Monticello they had increased so much as to fill the beds quite full. the Anemonies & Ranunculuses are also doing well, fourteen of Governor Lewis's Pea ripened which I have saved.   the pinks   Carnation's

Sweet Williams  Yellow horned Poppy  Ixia  Jeffersonia  everlasting Pea  Lavatera  Columbian Lilly  Lobelia  Lychnis  double blossomed Poppy & Physalis failed, indeed none of the seeds which you got from Mʳ Mᶜ Mahon came up.  Ellen & myself have a fine parcel of little Orange trees for the green house against your return.  Mʳˢ Lewis has promised me some seed of the Cypress vine. . . . (*Jefferson Papers,* M. H. S.)

(Thomas Main to Jefferson.)

Main's Nursery
The President                                                         Nov. 20, 1807
  Boᵗ of Thos. Main

| | |
|---|---|
| 2000 prime Transplants of the American Hedge Thorn @ 650 cents p. m. | 13.00 |
| 2 Portugal peach trees @ 25 cents each | .50 |
| 2 Black Georgia peach trees @ 25 cents each | .50 |
| 4 Purple Beeches | |
| 4 Robinias | |
| 4 Prickly Ash | |
| 6 Spitzenberg Apple trees | |
| 1 Blood peach, from the stone, had from W. Simmons and said to be very large & excellent | |
| 500 stones of the October peach | |
| A parcel of the roots of the Sweet scented grass | |
| Box & package | 2.00 |
| | 16.00 |

(*Jefferson Papers,* L. C.)

(Jefferson to James Maury.)

Washington, November 21, 1807.

. . . The crops of the present year have been great beyond example. The wheat sown for the ensuing year is in a great measure destroyed by the drought and the fly.  A favorable winter and spring sometimes do wonders towards recovering unpromising grain; but nothing can make the next crop of wheat a good one.  (Lipscomb and Bergh, *Jefferson* 11: 397.)

(John Threlkeld to Jefferson.)

[Georgetown,] Nov. 23, [1807.]

Mr. Threlkeld is much Obliged to Mr. Jefferson for the trees and seeds  he has the honor to send him six Peach Apricots from the tree Mr. Jefferson had at Hepburn Marked No. I  two Apricots fruit said to belonge (?) from the Bishop of Bourdeaux's Garden No. 2 and two Peach trees the fruit the finest Mr T. ever saw Peches not Paries, No 3

they are all he has fit to send.   Mr. T received from a Lady near Bourdeaux abt a month ago and they are now in the Ground 4 doz Peach
Apricot Stones the Lady says Eat by herself and put up so that I may be
sure of the kinds and to use her own words Plus de 8 pouces françois
dans sa plus Grande et 7½ dans sa plus Petit Circonference some prunes
De Reine Cloude.   The best kind she says in France and another kind
called Prunes de Dattes the most beautiful in appearance but not Equal
in taste if they should succeed Mr T begs Mr. Jefferson's Acceptance of
some of them.   (Ford, *Jefferson Correspondence:* 152.)

### (Jefferson to Martha (Jefferson) Randolph.)

Washington, Nov. 23. 07.

. . . Davy will set out on his return to-morrow.   He will carry an
earthen box of monthly strawberries, which I must put under Anne's
care till spring, when we will plant them at Monticello.   I have stuck
several sprigs of geranium in a pot which contained a plant supposed to
be orange, but not known to be so. . . . (*Jefferson Papers,* M. H. C.
1: 118.)

### (Jefferson to Captain William Meriwether.)

Washington Nov. 24. 07.

By the bearer Davy, I send you, according to our arrangement, the
following trees.

Nº. 1.   Six Peach Apricots engrafted from an engrafted tree, of Italy.
Nº. 2.   two Bourdeaux Apricots, large & fine in quality.
Nº. 3.   two Peach trees from France, soft, said to be the finest ever
seen.

also a small bag containing about 100. Paccan nuts, fresh, for planting.
wishing you all possible success with these fruits, which are of pre-
eminent value, I salute you with great friendship & respect.   (*Jefferson
Papers,* M. H. S.)

### (Jefferson to Edmund Bacon.)

Washington Nov. 24. 1807.

Davy has been detained till now, the earth having been so frozen that
the plants could not be dug up.   on the next leaf are directions what to
do with them, in addition to which I inclose mr Maine's directions as to
the thorns.   he brings a couple of Guinea pigs, which I wish you to
take great care of, as I propose to get this kind into the place of those we
have now, as I greatly prefer their size & form.   I think you had better
keep them in some inclosure near your house till spring.   I hope my
sheep are driven up every night & carefully attended to.   the finishing
every thing about the mill is what I wish always to have a preference to
every kind of work.   next to that my heart is most set on finishing the

garden. I have promised mͬ Craven that nothing shall run next year in the meadow inclosure where his clearing will be. this is necessary for ourselves that we may mow the clover & feed it green. I have hired the same negroes for another year, & am promised them as long as I want them. . . . P. S. I have forgot to mention that in the box of Paccans there are 3. papers of seeds, to wit, Cucumber tree, Mountain Laurel, & Pitch pine. the 2. former Wormley must plant in the Nursery, and he must plant the pitch pine in the woods along the new road leading from the house to the river, on both sides of the road. he is just to lay the seed on the ground & scratch half an inch of earth over it. (*Jefferson Papers,* Huntington.)

### Directions for Mr. Bacon

If the weather is not open and soft when Davy arrives, put the box of thorns into the cellar, where they may be entirely free from the influence of cold, until the weather becomes soft, when they must be planted in the places of those dead through the whole of the hedges which inclose the two orchards, so that the old and the new shall be complete, at 6 inches' distance from every plant. If any remain, plant them in the nursery of thorns. There are 2,000. I send Mr. Maine's written instructions about them, which must be followed most minutely. The other trees he brings are to be planted as follows:

4 Purple beaches. In the clumps which are in the southwest and northwest angles of the house, (which Wormley knows.) There were four of these trees planted last spring, 2 in each clump. They all died, but the places will be known by the remains of the trees, or by the sticks marked No. IV. in the places. I wish these now sent to be planted in the same places.

4 Robinias, or red locusts. In the clumps in the N.E. and S. E. angles of the house. There were 2 of these planted last spring, to wit, 1 in each. They are dead, and two of them are to be planted in the same places, which may be found by the remains of the trees, or by sticks marked V. The other 2 may be planted in any vacant places in the S.W. and N.W. angles.

4 Prickly ash. In the S.W. angle of the house there was planted one of these trees last spring, and in the N.W. angle 2 others. They are dead. 3 of those now sent are to be planted in their places, which may be found by the remains of the trees, or by sticks marked VII. The fourth may be planted in some vacant space of the S.W. angle.

6 Spitzenberg apple trees. Plant them in the S.E. orchard in any place where apples have been planted and are dead.

5 Peach trees. Plant in the S.E. orchard, wherever peach trees have died.

500 October peach stones; a box of Peccan nuts. The nursery must be enlarged, and these planted in the new parts, and Mr. Perry must immediately extend the paling so as to include these, and make the whole secure against hares.

Some turfs of a particular grass.  Wormley must plant them in some safe place of the orchard, where he will know them, and keep other grass from the place.  (Pierson, *Monticello:* 41–43.)

### (Fred H. Wollaston to Jefferson.)

Philada. 9. Decr. 1807

I have the honor to forward to you a letter from your estimabl friend Mr. Marrie [= Mazzei], whom I left at Pisa on the 19th Septr. recovering fast from his late dangerous illness. . . .

I hope in a few weeks to deliver to you in person a small phial of Strawberry Seeds from the above named respectable friend. . . . (*Glimpses of the Past,* Missouri **3**: 102.)

### (Jefferson to J. P. Reibelt.)

Washington Dec. 22. 07.

Your favor of Oct. 25 with the seed of the wild Estragon came to hand last night for which I now return you my thanks.  the inclosed duplicate of my letter of Aug. 12. written from Monticello, will explain to you why your letter of Mar. 12 could not be answered until I returned to Monticello where I had left Parkyn's designs of gardens, and that I then inclosed them to you with the letter. . . . (*Jefferson Papers*, L. C.)

### "MEMORANDUMS"

The following miscellaneous memoranda to Mr. Bacon are taken from *Jefferson at Monticello*, by Pierson.  They are undated except for the year:

The first work to be done, is to finish everything at the mill; to wit, the dam, the stone still wanting in the south abutment, the digging for the addition to the toll mill, the waste, the dressing off the banks and hollows about the mill-houses, making the banks of the canal secure everywhere.  In all these things Mr. Walker will direct what is to be done, and how.

The second job is the fence from near Nance's house to the river, the course of which will be shown.  Previous to this a change in the road is to be made, which will be shown also.

As this fence will completely separate the river field from the other grounds, that field is to be cleaned up; the spots in it still in wood are to be cut down where they are not too steep for culture; a part of the field is to be planted in Quarantine corn, which will be found in a tin canister in my closet.  This corn is to be in drills 5 feet apart, and the stalks 18 inches asunder in the drills.  The rest of the ground is to be sown in oats, and red clover sowed on the oats.  All ploughing is to be done horizontally, in the manner Mr. Randolph does his.

180 Cords of coal wood are next to be cut.  The wood cut in the river field will make a part, and let the rest be cut in the flat lands on

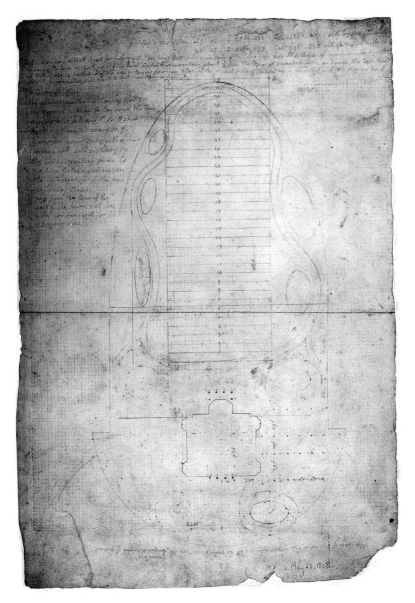

PLATE XXV.—Jefferson's plan of the winding or *Round-about Walk* on the western lawn. This walk was laid out in 1808. See plate XXIV and letter, Jefferson to Anne Randolph, June 7, 1807. (*Jefferson Papers*, M. H. S.)

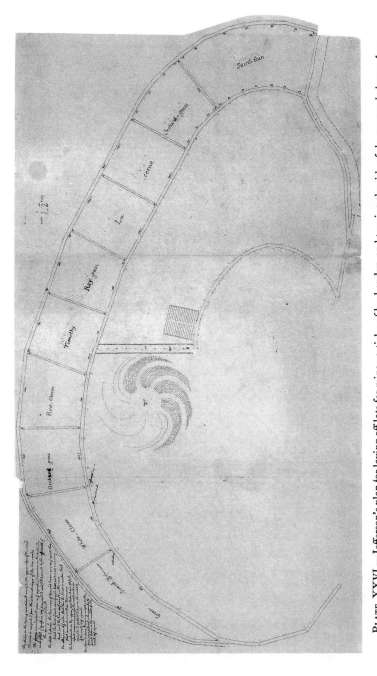

PLATE XXVI.—Jefferson's plan for laying off lots for minor articles of husbandry, and turning the side of the mountain into a *ferme ornée*, 1808. The pinwheel design is for a labyrinth of broom. See text, page 384, and plate XXVII. (*Jefferson Papers*, Huntington Library and Art Gallery.)

the meadow branch south of the overseer's house, which I intend for a
Timothy meadow. Let the wood be all corded, that there may be no
deception as to the quantity. A kiln will be wanting to be burnt before
Christmas; but the rest of the wood had better lie seasoning till spring,
when it will be better to burn it.

When these things are done, the levelling of the garden is to be resumed. The hands having already worked at this, they understand the
work. John best knows how to finish off the levelling.

I have hired all the hands belonging to Mrs. and Miss Dangerfield,
for the next year. They are nine in number. Moses the miller is to
be sent home when his year is up. With these will work in common,
Isaac, Charles, Ben, Shepherd, Abram, Davy, John, and Shoemaker
Phill; making a gang of 17 hands. Martin is the miller, and Jerry will
drive his wagon.

Those who work in the nailery, are Moses, Wormly, Jame Hubbard,
Barnaby, Isbel's Davy, Bedford John, Bedford Davy, Phill Hubbard,
Bartlet, and Lewis. They are sufficient for two fires, five at a fire. I
am desirous a single man, a smith should be hired to work with them, to
see that their nails are well made, and to superintend them generally; if
such an one can be found for $150 or $200 a year, though I would
rather give him a share in the nails made, say one-eighth of the price of
all the nails made, deducting the cost of the iron; if such a person can be
got, Isbel's Davy may be withdrawn to drive the mule wagon, and
Sampson join the laborers. There will then be nine nailers, besides the
manager, so that 10 may still work at two fires; the manager to have a
log house built, and to have 500 lbs. of pork. The nails are to be sold
by Mr. Bacon, and the accounts to be kept by him; and he is to direct
at all times what nails are to be made.

The toll of the mill is to be put away in the two garners made, which
are to have secure locks, and Mr. Bacon is to keep the keys. When
they are getting too full, the wagons should carry the grain to the overseer's house, to be carefully stowed away. In general, it will be better
to use all the bread corn from the mill from week to week, and only
bring away the surplus. Mr. Randolph is hopper-free and toll-free at
the mill. Mr. Eppes having leased his plantation and gang, they are to
pay toll hereafter.

. . . Davy and Abram may patch up the old garden pales when work
is going on from which they can best be spared.

The thorn hedges are to be kept clean wed at all times.

There is a spout across the canal near the head, which, if left as at
present, will do mischief. I will give verbal directions about it.

As soon as the Aspen trees lose their leaves, take up one or two hundred of the young trees, not more than 2 or 3 feet high; tie them in
bundles, with the roots well covered with straw. Young Davy being
to carry Fanny to Washington, he is to take the little cart, (which must
be put into the soundest order,) to take these trees on board. 3 Boxes
in my study, marked to go by him and Fanny and her things. She must
take corn for their meals, and provisions for themselves to Washington.

Fodder they can buy on the road.  I leave $6 with you, to give them to pay unavoidable expenses.  If he could have 2 mules, without stopping a wagon, it would be better.  They are to go as soon as the Aspen leaves fall.

The nailers are to work on the dam till finished, and then go to their shop.  The verbal directions which I gave Mr. Bacon respecting Carroll's farm, will be recollected and observed.

When the work at the mill is done, and the fence mended up on the top of the mountain, take as much time with your hands as will fill all the gullies in the field north of the overseer's house, (called Belfield,) with bushes, &c., so that they may be filling up by the time we are ready to clean it up.  The scalded places should also be covered with bushes.

The orchard below the garden must be entirely cultivated the next year; to wit, a part in Ravenscroft pea, which you will find in a canister in my closet; a part with Irish potatoes, and the rest with cow-pea, of which there is a patch at Mr. Freeman's, to save which, great attention must be paid, as they are the last in the neighborhood.

Get from Mr. Perry and Mr. Dinsmore, an estimate of all the nails we shall want for the house in Bedford; and when you have no orders to execute for others, let the boys be making them, and keep them separate from all others; and when the wagon goes up at Christmas, send what then shall be ready.

Mr. Higginbotham has all my transportation to and from Richmond under his care.  He settles with the watermen, and pays them.  I do not wish to have any accounts with them.

These rains have possibly spoiled the fodder you had agreed for.  You had better see it, and if injured, look out in time for more.

Mr. Dinsmore wants Allen's plank brought up immediately.  If you choose it, you can take your half beef now, killing one for that purpose, and sending the other half to the house, or to Mr. Randolph's.  (Pierson, *Monticello:* 45–52.)

A stray memorandum, probably to Bacon:

1807.  clean all the ground [illegible for one line] in autumn finish that Roundabout or rather finish the 4^th. Roundab^t in order—in winter to move the fence to the 4^th. Roundabout.  (*Jefferson Papers*, M. H. S.)

From the *Account Book 1807:*

Mar. 12.  gave Davy & Isaac for their expences home 10.D.
April 20.  gave Isaac .50 for bringing cider & trees from Col^o. Cole's yesterday.
July 30.  gave Tho^s Main ord. on bk. U.S. for 59.25 for trees &c.
Aug. 12.  inclosed to R. Jefferson 20. D. to pay for grass seeds.
Nov. 24.  gave Davy for expenses to Monticello 6. D.
Dec. 17.  p^d Maine for plants 16. D.

# 1808

*1808.** On December 27 of the preceding year Jefferson wrote to Mrs. Elizabeth Trist, "The ensuing year will be the longest year of my life." It was certainly a trying year.

The year saw not only repercussions of the Burr conspiracy in the action of the Senate expelling John Smith, an Ohio Senator, from membership in that body, but also the enforcement of the Embargo and the coming to a head of the New Orleans Batture Case. On November 7 Jefferson delivered his final message to the joint session of Congress. It was another election year. Jefferson refused to run for a third term. The Republicans again were victorious with James Madison elected President.

The usual two visits were made to *Monticello,* the first from May 11 to June 8, and the second from July 23 to September 28. A trip to *Poplar Forest,* where his new house was taking shape, occurred during the summer visit.

Plans, memoranda, and letters were as voluminous as in the preceding year. However, no entries were made in the *Garden Book* or in the *Farm Book.* Jefferson had only one year left to get *Monticello* in shape for his retirement, and as yet it was far from complete.

The two outstanding improvements made in the grounds were the leveling of the old vegetable garden (see letters, Jefferson to Bacon and Randolph, February 23, 1808), and the laying out of the winding walk and the flower borders, along each side of it, on the broad lawn back of the house. (See letters, Jefferson to Anne Cary Randolph, June 7, 1807, and February 16, 1808; also plates XXIV and XXV.) A paling fence was also planned to surround the garden. (See letter, Jefferson to Watkins, September 27, 1808.)

Jefferson's new agricultural interest this year was the benne oil and seed. The oil was sent to him by Mr. William Few, of New York, and Jefferson thought it equal to olive oil in its

---

* This year not represented in the *Garden Book.*

uses.   He was later to try growing benne seed at *Monticello*, but never with much success.

The house was still incomplete.   Floors were laid, the South Pavilion was remodeled, and work on the terraces over the offices went on.   More relics were added to the Indian Hall, especially those given to him by Meriwether Lewis. Mr. Clark presented bones of an animal he had excavated in Indiana.

The problem of the mill was still unsolved.   Mr. Shoemaker was proving to be an unsatisfactory tenant.   Added to these problems was the loss of the mill-dam by a freshet in the Rivanna River.

Interesting letters passed between Jefferson and his granddaughters on plants and the garden.   Letters also continued between Jefferson and McMahon, from whom he again bought seeds and plants.   The following letters and memoranda show the wide agricultural interest during the year.

A fish pond was built near the South Pavilion, mainly to conserve water, but also to serve as a decorative part of the flower garden.   Jefferson wrote in his *Weather Memorandum Book 1776–1820:* "The fish pond near the S. Pavilion is an Ellipses 5. yds. wide, 10. yds. long = 40. sq. yds., very nearly 1. yard deep = 40. cub. yds. contents."

On February 1 Jefferson made plans for an experimental garden.   He left with Mr. Bacon the following instructions:

1808.  Feb. 1.   in all the open grounds on both sides of the $3^d$. & $4^{th}$. Roundabouts, lay off lots for the minor articles of husbandry, and for experimental culture, disposing them into a ferme ornée by interspersing occasionally the attributes of a garden. [See plates XXVI and XXVII.]

the farming articles as follows

perennials

| | |
|---|---|
| Orchard grass | Pani Corn . . . . . followed by Pumpkins |
| Peruvian grass | Ravensworth pea . . . . . . round Potatoes |
| S$^t$. foin | Buckwheat . . . . . . . . . . . . . . . . carrots |
| Lucerne | Cherokee corn . . . . . . . . Miami melon |
| Succory | Albany pea . . . . . . . . . . . . . . . . . Beet |
| Burnet | Sesamum . . . . . . . . . . . . . . . Turneps |
| Vetch | Rape . . . . . . . . . . . . . . . . . . . . . Cotton |
| Sweet potatoes | |
| Jers. Artichoke | |

(*Jefferson Papers*, M. H. S.)

From the *Weather Memorandum Book 1776–1820:*

1808.  May 22.  Magnolia glauca blossoms.

May 31.  counted in the nursery as follows
artichokes.  red.  35. in upper bed.
green 140. in lower bed
Asparagus.  Cooper's pale green.  237
Salsafia.  Missouri.  13.

June  7.  sowed in Nursery (lower part) yew berries, and Furze.

Aug. 16.  plant<u>ed</u> 15. wild cherry stones brought from the Misipi by m̅r̅s̅ Trist, in the nursery.  Wormly was directed to plant them 6. I. apart & mark them particularly.  they are different from our wild cherry. m̅r̅ Randolph supposes it may be Padus avium.

## LETTERS AND EXTRACTS OF LETTERS, 1808

### (Jefferson to Robert R. Livingston, Esq.)

Washington, January 3, 1808.

. . . It is now among my most fervent longings to be on my farm, which, with a garden and fruitery, will constitute my principal occupation in retirement.  I have lately received the proceedings of the Agricultural Society of Paris.  They are proceeding with enthusiasm & understanding.  I have been surprised to find that the rotation of crops and substitution of some profitable growth preparatory for grain, instead of the useless and expensive fallow, is yet only dawning among them. . . . I lately received from Colonel Few in New York, a bottle of the oil of Beni, believed to be a sesamum.  I did not believe there existed so perfect a substitute for olive oil.  Like that of Florence, it has no taste, and is perhaps rather more limpid.  A bushel of seed yields three gallons of oil; and Governor Milledge, of Georgia, says the plant will grow wherever Palmi Christi will.  It is worth your attention, and you can probably get seed from Colonel Few.  (Lipscomb and Bergh, *Jefferson* 11: 411–412.)

### (Jefferson to William Few.)

Washington Jan. 3. 08.

I thank you for the specimen of Benni oil which you were so kind as to send me.  I did not believe before that there existed so perfect a substitute for olive oil.  I tried it at table with many companies & their guesses between two dishes of salad dressing, the one with olive oil, the other with that of Beni, shewed the quality of the latter in favor of which the greater number guessed.  certainly I would prefer to have it always fresh from my own fields to the other brought across the Atlantic and exposed in hot warehouses.  I am therefore determined to go into the culture of it for domestic use, and should be thankful to you for the process of expressing the oil from the seed in which you appear to have succeeded so perfectly. all the minutiae in new processes give aid towards perfecting them. D<sup>r</sup>. Mitchell supposes the Benni is a Sesamum. . . . (*Jefferson Papers, L. C.*)

(Jefferson to John Taylor.)

Washington Jan. 6. 08.

Your ingenious friend, m<sup>r</sup> Martin, formerly made for me a drill of very fine construction. I am now very desirous of sending one of them to the Agricultural society of Paris, with whom I am in correspondence, & who are sending me a plough, supposed to be of the best construction ever known. on trial with their best ploughs, by a dynamometer, it is drawn by from one half to ⅔ of the force requisite to their best former ploughs. will you be so good as to get m<sup>r</sup> Martin to make me one of his best drills, sparing no pains to make the workmanship worthy of the object, to pack it in a box and contrive it for me to Fredericksburg. the cost shall be remitted him as soon as known. I see by the agricultural transactions of the Paris society, they are cultivating the Jerusalem artichoke for feeding their animals. they make 10,000 lb to the acre, which they say is three times as much as they generally make of the potatoe. The African negroes brought over to Georgia a seed which they called Beni, & the botanists Sesamum. I lately received a bottle of the oil, which was eaten with sallad by various companies. all agree it is equal to the olive oil. a bushel of seed yields 3. gallons of oil. I propose to cultivate it for my own use at least. the embargo keeping at home our vessels, cargoes & seamen, saves us the necessity of making their capture the cause of immediate war: for if going to England, France had determined to take them, if to any other place, England was to take them. till they return to some sense of moral duty therefore, we keep within ourselves. this gives time. time may produce peace in Europe. peace in Europe removes all causes of differences till another European war; & by that time our debt may be paid, our revenues clear, & our strength increased. . . . (*Jefferson Papers,* M. H. S.)

(William Few to Jefferson.)

New York Jan. 11, 1808.

[Tells Jefferson how to extract oil from Beni seeds and the history of its introduction to America.] (*Jefferson Papers, L. C.*)

(Jefferson to Edmund Bacon.)

Washington Jan. 19. 08.

. . . I am very sorry indeed to hear how little the tollmill gets. however I hope you keep an exact account of all the toll she gets, as nothing but exact observations of that can enable us to know for how much we may depend on her as to our year's provisions. I am in hopes that from Saturday to this day you will have been able to fill my ice house. the lambs which fall in this weather will require vast care to be preserved from the cold.  I have some dropped here which require great attention. the chief difficulty is to have the ewes in such a sheltered situation that the lambs dropped may not perish before they are found. . . . I shall be glad to know from time to time how far you advance in finishing the garden, counting by the hundred feet from the South West end.  whenever you find that you dig so deep as to have to carry your earth too far, take a new level at the midway of the breadth of the garden. . . . (*Jefferson Papers*, Huntington.)

(Anne Cary Randolph to Jefferson.)

Edgehill January 22 1808

. . . I have not been to Monticello since we came from there but Jefferson was there the other day & says that the green house is not done, both your ice house & ours are filled.  I was at M^rs Lewis's on my way from the North Garden she told me she had saved some of the seed of the Cypress vine for you & some prickly ash trees.  the Alpine Strawberries are doing very well.  we were so unfortunate as to lose the Mignonett entirely although Mama divided it between M^rs Lewis Aunt Jane & herself but none of it seeded M^rs Lewis supposes that the climate is too cold for it for she has had it repeatedly before & it never would seed, we have a plenty of the two kinds of Marigolds that you gave us. . . . (*Jefferson Papers*, U. Va.)

(William Hamilton to Jefferson.)

The Woodlands, Feb. 5, 1808.

[He asks about the winter Haw which grows so beautifully around Washington.  See letter, Jefferson to Hamilton, March 1.] . . . Mr. Lewis's seeds have not yet vegetated freely, more however may come up with this coming spring.  I have nevertheless obtained plants of the yellow wood, or Osage apple, seven or eight of gooseberries & one of his kinds of Aricara tobacco, have flowered so well as to afford me an elegant drawing of it. . . . I have prepared for you plants of Broussonetia papyrifera or paper mulberry,—Sterculia platanifolia (wrongly called China varnish tree) & Mimosa julibrisin.  They were all designed to come last year, but no suitable opportunity offered.  I hope I will be more lucky this year. . . . (*Jefferson Papers*, L. C.)

(Jefferson to Anne Cary Randolph.)

Washington Feb. 16. 08.

The time at which Congress will adjourn is very uncertain; but certainly will not till April, and whether I shall be free to come home even then is doubtful.  under these prospects I shall not attempt to get any more flower roots & seeds from Philadelphia this season, and must rely entirely on you to preserve those we have by having them planted in proper time.  this you will see from M^c.Mahon's book, & m͞r Bacon will make Wormley prepare the beds whenever you let him know, so that they may be ready when you go over to set out the roots. the first time I come home I will lay out the projected flower borders around the level so that they shall be ready for the next fall; and in the spring of the next year I will bring home a full collection of roots & plants. we shall then have room enough for every thing. . . . (*Jefferson Papers,* M. H. S.)

### (Jefferson to Anthony G. Bettay.)

Washington, February 18, 1808.

. . . I shall be very glad to receive some seed of the silk nettle which you describe, with a view to have it raised, and its uses tried. I have not been able to find that any of your delegates here has received it. If you would be so good as to send me a small packet of it by post, it will come safely, and I will immediately commit it to a person who will try it with the utmost care. I salute you with respect. (Lipscomb and Bergh, *Jefferson* 11: 442–443.)

### (Jefferson to Edmund Bacon.)

Washington Feb. 23. 08.

I received last night your letter of the 19th. by which I learn you have done 250. f. of the garden. were we to go on, reducing the whole to the same level we have begun with, the labor would be immense. I therefore conclude to do it in 4. levels of 250. f. each, and taking such a level for each as that the earth to be dug away shall first fill up the part which is too low. in this way each quarter of 250. f. will do itself, and there will be no earth to carry out of it. I have this day written to mr̄ Randolph to request him to go and fix the level of the second quarter, in a way which I have described to him. this will shorten your work immensely. I am glad to hear you have lost no lambs. you must attend to the males being cut at a proper season in the spring: and at shearing time remember that the lambs are not to be shorn. I have here 18 ewes and shall have about the same number of lambs from them, by a many horned ram, all of which I shall propose to have driven to Monticello in the summer. this breed being very different from the big-tail we shall have to provide two separate ranges for them.

I am sorry to find the mill gets so little corn. however in the summer she will get more. . . . (*Jefferson Papers,* Huntington.)

### (Jefferson to Thomas Mann Randolph.)

Washington Feb. 23. '08.

. . . I received a letter from mr̄ Bacon last night which obliges me to ask you to take a ride to Monticello to advise him in his operations on the garden. he has done 250. feet. should he go on in the same level we assumed at first, the labour will be enormous on account of the prodigious mass of earth we should have to dig & the great distance to

carry it.  for that reason I propose to have the garden done in 4. different levels of 250. f. length, from East to West, each.  having done one
of these, a second should be measured off and a new level assumed for
that, so that the earth to be dug away from what is too high shall just
fill up the part which is too low, as nearly as can be guessed.  to do this
I should plant myself in such a point near the middle of the 250 f. piece,
as my eye would tell me would furnish as much to be dug away as to be
filled up.  the rafter level should then be run from that point to each
end of the 250 f. and sticks stuck.  this would enable the eye to form
a better guess than the first & to correct that by taking a new level
a little higher or a little lower, as the eye should judge, and making
the level line with sticks by the rafter level, and this would divide the
part to be dug from that to be filled.  I formerly wrote to him to do
this, but I doubt if he can, and therefore ask the favor of your assistance
to him, as it will save an immensity of work.  my affectionate love is
constantly with you all.  (*Jefferson Papers,* L. C.)

## (Jefferson to William Hamilton.)

Washington Mar. 1. 08.

I received in due time your friendly letter of Feb. 5. and was much
gratified by the opportunity it gave me of being useful to you even on
that small scale.  I was retarded in the execution of your request by the
necessity of riding myself to the only careful gardener on whom I have
found I could rely, & who lives 3. miles out of town.  it was several
days before I could find leisure enough for such a ride.  he has this day
brought me a box, in which are packed the plants stated in the enclosed
paper from him: that is to say 12. plants of what he calls the Winter
berry (Prinus verticillatus) which he does not doubt to be the plant
designated in your letter as the Winter haw.  in fact the swamps in this
neighborhood are now red with this berry.  Dᵣ. Ott however conceived
another plant to be that you meant, and delivered the gardener some
berries of it, which I now enclose you.  should these berries be of the
plant you meant, on your signifying it to me it may still be in time to
procure & forward it to you.  apprehending myself that neither of these
plants might be the one you wished, but a real *haw,* now full of beautiful
scarlet berries, and which I have never seen but in this neighborhood, I
directed mᵣ Maine (the gardener I mentioned) to put half a hundred
of them into the box.  even should they not be what you had in view
still you should know this plant, which is peculiar at least to America &
is a real treasure.  as a thorn for hedges nothing has ever been seen comparable to it certainly no thorn in England which I have ever seen makes
a hedge any more to be compared to this than a log hut to a wall of
freestone.  if you will plant these 6. I. apart you will be a judge of
their superiority soon.  he has put into the box 8. plants of the tree
haw you desired, taken from the very spot from which Dᵣ. Ott had
formerly got them for Doctᵣ. Muhlenberg.  you will find a nut from

them in the top of the box. these were all the small plants which he could get with any roots. to these I have added 9. plants of the Aspen from Monticello which I formerly mentioned & promised to you. it is a very sensible variety from any other I have seen in this country, superior in the straitness & paper whiteness of the body; & the leaf is longer in it's stem consequently more tremulous, and it is smooth (not downy) on it's underside. the box goes in the stage of this evening under the immediate care of mᵣ Sodershorn's servant.

I am very thankful to you for thinking of me in the destination of some of your fine collection. within one year from this time I shall be retired to occupations of my own choice, among which the farm & garden will be conspicuous parts. my green house is only a piazza adjoining my study, because I mean it for nothing more than some oranges, Mimosa Farnesiana & a very few things of that kind. I remember to have been much taken with a plant in your green house, extremely odoriferous, and not large, perhaps 12. or 15. I. high if I recollect rightly. you said you would furnish me a plant or two of it when I should signify that I was ready for them. perhaps you may remember it from this circumstance, tho' I have forgot the name. this I would ask for the next spring if we can find out what it was, and some seeds of the Mimosa Farnesiana or Nilotica. the Mimosa Julibrisin or silk tree you were so kind as to send me is now safe here, about 15. I. high. I shall carry it carefully to Monticello. I will not trouble you for the paper Mulberry mᵣ Maine having supplied me with 12. or 15. which are now growing at Monticello. your collection is really a noble one, & in making & attending to it you have deserved well of your country. when I become a man of leisure I may be troublesome to you. perhaps curiosity or health may lead you into the neighborhood of Monticello some day, where I shall be very happy to receive you & be instructed by you how to overcome some if it's difficulties. . . . (*Jefferson Papers,* L. C.)

## (Jefferson to Edmund Bacon.)

Washington Mar. 8. 08.

I received yesterday yours of the 4ᵗʰ. I would have you sow in oats the whole of the field we got of mᵣ Craven, and plant your last year's clearing in Pani corn, that is the kind of corn which was planted last year below the garden. the other kinds of corn I would not have planted at all, as the Pani is the best. I wish it were possible for you to get red clover seed to sow with your oats. Colº. Lewis used to raise seed for sale. in the open parts below the garden and in the South orchard I would plant Ravensworth peas, Cowpeas, and Irish potatoes, because in cultivating them we shall get rid of the briars, bushes, weeds &c. you mentioned in one of your late letters that you had not yet received your nailrod. two tons left Philadelphia January the 8ᵗʰ. . . . (*Jefferson Papers,* Huntington.)

(Anne Cary Randolph to Jefferson.)

Edgehill March 18 1808

. . . I am very anxious to go to Monticello to see how the flowers
come on but Papa has not a horse that can be riden by a lady with safety.
I hear however from them once or twice a week by Burwell for I never
fail to enquire after their health.   The last news was that they were all
coming up very well particularly the tulips of which he counted at least
forty flourishing ones.   you will be at home time enough to see them all
bloom.   the Strawberries I am sorry to say I cannot give so good an account of.   I put them when they came in a sheltered place but the cold
weather killed them.   2 have put out fresh leaves this spring & I hope
some more of them will.   the earth in which they were put was very
bad & 1 have been afraid to transplant them.   it is very poor clay & gets
baked as hard as a brick by the sun.   the winter has been so wet that
they have not required watering, but I have done it occasionally this
spring with water that had been standing in the sun, & used a watering
pot with such small holes, that it was exactly like a shower.   the embargo has set every body to making home spun.   Mama has made 157
yards since October.   you will see all the children clothed in it.   there
has been the greatest number of wild pigeons this spring that I ever saw.
Mr. Craven they say, by means of his net has caught nearly three thousand.   he kills some days 700 & seldom less than three or four hundred.
he salts & barrels them like fish for his people. . . . I enclose you some
white violets but fear they will lose their smell before they reach you.
(*Jefferson Papers,* M. H. S.)

(Jefferson to P. A. Guestier.)

Washington Mar. 20. 08.

Your letter of the 14th is received, and I have to return you my
thanks for the trouble you have been so good as to take in procuring the
seeds requested by mr Reibelt.   I remember that he was so kind as to
undertake through his friends to procure for me some maize of Italy, of
the kind called Quarentine, valuable for it's early coming to table, & I
presume what you have received is of that kind.   the rare a'l'huile I am
unacquainted with, but presume it is what we call rape. (*Jefferson*
Papers, L. C.)

(Jefferson to Edmund Bacon.)

Washington Mar. 22. 08.

The plants of Privet which you have received are from mr Gordon
and I intend them for a hedge in the garden which not being yet ready,
they must be set out in a nursery where you can find a convenient open
spot. . . . (*Jefferson Papers,* M. H. S.)

(Jefferson to Anne Cary Randolph.)

Washington Mar. 22. 08.

. . . I am sorry our strawberries are unpromising; however I trust
they will put out soon.  if some sand and stable manure were put on
the earth, the waterings would carry both down into the clay & loosen
& enrich it.  but we had better not transplant them till we get them to
Monticello, where we will take out the whole sod unbroken, and set it
in the ground without having disturbed the roots.  I ate strawberries
from these plants last October after my return to this place.  I inclose
you some seed of the Beny, or Oriental Sesamum.  this is among the
most valuable acquisitions our country has ever made.  it yields an oil
equal to the finest olive oil.  I received a bottle of it, and tried it with
a great deal of company for many days, having a dish of sallad dressed
with that & another with olive oil, and nobody could distinguish them.
an acre yields 10. bushels of seed, each bushel giving three gallons of oil.
an acre therefore, besides our sallad oil, would furnish all kitchen &
family uses, most of them better than with lard or butter.  you had
better direct Wormly to plant these seeds in some open place in the
nursery, by dropping two or three seeds every 10. or 12. I. along a row,
and his rows 2. feet apart.  the plant grows somewhat like hemp.  it
was brought to S. Carolina from Africa by the negroes, who alone have
hitherto cultivated it in the Carolinas & Georgia.  they bake it in their
bread, boil it with greens, enrich their broth &c.  it is not doubted it
will grow well as far North as Jersey, tho' Mᶜ.Mahon places it among
green house plants. . . . (Jefferson Papers, M. H. S.)

(Mrs. Samuel Harrison Smith to Jefferson.)

March. 26, 1808.

Mrs. H. Smith . . . sends to Mr. Jefferson some plants of the Antwerp raspberries which she has just received from Baltimore, with a
number of other shrubs.

The black-rose.  (Jefferson Papers, M. H. S.)

(Jefferson to John Strode.)

Washington Apr. 13. 1808.

[Jefferson had lost his mill-dam by a freshet in the Rivanna River.
After asking Mr. Strode's advice as to the best way to repair it, he gave
the following description of the dam.]

. . . Dam—It is 400. f. long, 15 ft. broad, 4 f. high on the upper
side & 5 f. on the lower, resting from one end to the other on a ridge of
solid rock, and made tight by a 10[?] f. dam of earth on the upper side.
the construction is of timber pens filled with loose irregular stones in
pretty large blocks. . . . (Jefferson Papers, L. C.)

(Ellen W. Randolph to Jefferson.)

Edgehill April 14, 1808.

. . . I wont say anything of the flower beds that is sister Anns part. the level is spoilt nearly.  Mr. Bacon has made a mistake (I presume) and covered it with charcoal, instead of manure, it looks rather dismal wherever the grass has not grown it is quite black, and is especially dirty to walk on, it is not near as bad as it was but it is still disagreeable and ugly.  They are finishing your terras now.  The sheep eat up 4 orange trees and bit half of the finest of besides, when we put them out, however I have 3 tolerably good [ones] though they are only 2 inches high. They are all mean little things except that which the sheep bit, but they are very young.  The third of April snow drops bloomed, you have none but I will give you mine if you want them, and have them set out in your garden when we go to Monticello.  (*Jefferson Papers,* M. H. S.)

(Anne Cary Randolph to Jefferson.)

Edgehill April 15 1808

. . . I have been twice to Monticello to see the sesamum & Governor Lewis's pea planted.  the hyacinths were in bloom, they are superb ones.  the Tulips are all buding.  neither the hyacinths nor Tulips grow as regularly this spring as they did the last.  Wormley in taking them up left some small roots in the ground which have come up about in the bed & not in the rows with the others.  the Strawberries Artichokes Salsafie Asparagus & Golden willow all look very well.  of the Alpine Strawberries that Davy brought 3 are flourishing.  but I am afraid the others are entirely dead. . . . (*Jefferson Papers,* M. H. S.)

(John Strode to Jefferson.)

April 18, 1808.

[Mr. Strode tells Jefferson how to construct his dam.]  (*Jefferson Papers,* L. C.)

(Ellen W. Randolph to Jefferson.)

Edgehill April 21, 1808.

. . . We have had blue & white lilac, blue and white flags and jonquils.  I found in the woods a great many mountain cowslips and wild Ranunculus besides other wild flowers.  I have got the seed of the Jerusalem Cherry which I am told is very beautiful. . . . (*Jefferson Papers,* M. H. S.)

(Jefferson to Marquis de Lafayette.)

Washington, April 28, 1808.

. . . Till the last autumn, I have every autumn written to Madame de Tessé and sent her a box of seeds.  I saw with infinite mortification that they were either carried into England or arrived so late as to answer no purpose to her.   The state of the ocean the last fall was, and continues to be, so desperate that it is vain to attempt anything again till that be changed.   By that time I shall be maker of my own time and can never employ it more in gratifying my own feelings than in doing what will be acceptable to her. . . . (Lipscomb and Bergh, *Jefferson* 19: 169–170.)

(Jefferson to A. Thoüin.)

Washington, Apr. 29. 08.

Your letter of the 11th of May last by mr. Godon came safely to hand together with your essay on the methodical division of rural economy, for which I return you my thanks.  the great views there presented of this interesting field of science are well worthy of one whose time and great talents for that science have been so much devoted to it's improvement.  you mention the having written to me a year and a half before on the subject of my description of a mould-board, by duplicate and triplicate, no one of which I assure you, ever came to my hands, nor a single line from you till that by mr. Godon.  my esteem for your virtues and talents, and the recollection of attentions received from you at the Jardin royale while I was in Paris, were pledges that I should have been incapable of omitting to acknolege the reciept of your letter.

With respect to my method of forming the mould-board so as to give the least resistance, the society of agriculture and yourself have given to it more importance that it had occupied in my own eye.  your translation and communication of it cannot but have been flattering to me. since the first form used, I have made a small alteration in the form of the toe of the Mould-board, which, while it preserves the principle untouched enables us to shorten the plough-share six or eight inches, which is preferred by the Agriculturists here to the first form.   I inclose you a description of this alteration; and, as the opportunity is favorable, I send you also a small box containing a model, which will be carried by the bearer of this letter to Paris.  proposing at the close of my present term (March, 1809) to retire altogether from public affairs, and to indulge myself in those pursuits more delightful to me, I may then perhaps become of some use to the Agricultural society who have conferred on me the honor of membership, pretending however, not to be an adept, but only a zealous Amateur in the objects of the society. . . . (Ford, *Jefferson Correspondence:* 162–163.)

(Jefferson to Dr. Gustavus Horner.)

Monticello May 15. 1808.

I found here a small remnant of the Benni seed I had sent on to be sown, which enables me to fulfil my promise to you.  open light furrows with a plough, 3½ or 4 f. apart, drop a very few seed every 12. inches along the furrow.  when up, thin them to a single plant at each 12. inches, and when advanced in growth draw a little earth to the roots.

they need little culture.  when the leaves fall from the stalk in autumn, cut off the top part bearing the pods, and tie them in small bundles. then leave them, with pods up, against a fence, or polls rested in forks driven in the ground.  when about half the pods are open, hold the bundle down over a sheet or close floor, and with a small stick, whip out the seed.  return the bundle to it's former position, & the remaining pods will open in 8. or 10. days, when the remaining seed is to be whipped out.

The seed is eaten parched, for a desert, or used in substance in soups, puddings etc.  but it's principal use is as an esculent oil.  one bushel of seed yielding about 3. gallons of oil.

The leaf is a specific in dysenteries & other visceral complaints.  two or three, without being bruised, being put into a pint of cold water, in a few minutes produce a mucilage equal to that of the white of an egg. 5. or 6. pints are taken in the course of the day.  the leaves dried under cover retain the property of producing mucilage.

The seed is usually planted as soon as the danger of frost is over, and covered with about an inch of earth.  it is the Sesamum trifoliatum of Miller's Gardener's dictionary, where a good account of it may be seen. . . . (*Jefferson Papers,* Yale.)

## (Jefferson to Edmund Bacon.)

June 7, 1808.

Consider as your first object the keeping a full supply of water to the mill, observing that whenever the water does not run over the waste, you should take your hands, and having put in a sufficiency of stone, then carry in earth and heighten till the water runs steadily over the waste. It ought to do this when both mills are running one pair of stones each. Take Mr. Randolph's advise on these occasions.

You will furnish Mr. Maddox, while working on the stable, with attendance, hauling, lime, and sand, so that I may only have to pay him for laying the stone.  I presume Mr. Dinsmore will let him be of his mess while here.  If objected to, however, do for him what you can best. . . .

Consider the garden as your main business, and push it with all your might when the interruptions permit.

Rake and sweep the charcoal on the level into little heaps, and carry them off.  Rather do this when the grass seed is ripe.  (Pierson, *Monticello:* 65–67.)

## (Jefferson to Edmund Bacon.)

June 7, 1808.

. . . The orchard below the garden must be entirely cultivated the next year; to wit a part in the Ravenscroft pea, which you will find in a cannister in my closet, a part with Irish potatoes, & the rest with cowpea, of which there is a patch at mr Freeman's, to save which great attention must be paid, as they are the last in the neighborhood.  (*Jefferson Papers,* Yale.)

(Jefferson to John Taylor.)

Washington June 23. 08.

The Agricultural society of Paris has had a plough presented to them which, performing equally good work requires but one half the force to draw it necessary for what had till then been deemed the best plough in France. in their zeal for improvement they sent one of them to England, and have sent me one, lately arrived at New York, & ordered round to Richmond where it will be open for inspection. the experiment being made with an instrument for the purpose (something I believe like a spring steel yard connecting the swingle tree to it's cross bar) it's accuracy may be relied on. they are collecting all the implements of agriculture of every country, good or bad, which of course will give them all the good. desiring to be useful to them in turn, I took the liberty, some time ago of asking the favor of you to procure for me one of Martin's drills. I have since heard he has retired from business which perhaps has produced a difficulty in getting one. should this have been got over, I shall be very much gratified by having one in time to send by a vessel which is to go in 3. or 4. weeks from this place to Havre & will afford the best possible opportunity of sending it. if it could be lodged at Fredericksburg & notified to me, I would have it either brought here or deposited some where on the Potomak where the vessel could take it in. all expenses shall be reimbursd as soon as known. I have gone into a detail of the motives for proposing this trouble to you, to shew that they are public in their object.

We have lately received from S. Carolina & Georgia the seeds of a plant brought from Africa many years ago by their negroes & by them called Benney. it is easy of culture, yields about as much seed to the acre as flax, and three gallons to the bushel of as fine salad oil as that of the olive. this I can affirm from an abundant sufficiency of trial. you will find a good account of it in Millar's Gardener's Dictionary under the head of Sesamum trifoliatum. many persons, from the account of this plant given by the members of the S. C. & G. at the last Congress, and the sample of the oil, have sown it this year. it bids fair to supply the place of olive oil, butter, lard & tallow in most cases. should you propose to try it, I could send you some seed from Monticello; tho' as it is now too late to sow it, & we shall have fresh seed this autumn, perhaps you would approve rather of waiting till then. (*Jefferson Papers,* M. H. S.)

(Bernard McMahon to Jefferson.)

Philadelphia June 28th. 1808

I do myself the pleasure of sending you by this mail a few gooseberries, as a sample of what we may have here, by first obtaining good kinds, and then judicious management. I fear that from the extreme heat of the present weather, they will undergo a fermentation and turn sour before they reach you; at all events, they will perspire and become much less in size than when pulled.

I am happy to inform you that I have fine plants of *all* the varieties of Currants (7) and Gooseberries (2) brought by Gov^r. Lewis, and of about 20 other *new species* of plants, as well as five or six new *genera;* this will add to natural history and the plants are forthcoming. I will not forget you in due time.

I would be very happy to know when Gov^r. Lewis may be expected here. . . . (*Jefferson Papers, L. C.*)

(Jefferson to Thomas Mann Randolph.)

Washington, June 28th, 08.

. . . I charged Bacon very strictly to keep the water of the canal always running over the waste, as Shoemaker has made the want of water the ground of insisting on a suspension of rent, and will probably continue to do it. . . . (Ford, *Jefferson* 11: 37.)

(Jefferson to Bernard McMahon.)

Washington July 6. 08.

I received duly your favor of June 28. with the gooseberries in good condition. they were certainly such as I had never seen before in any country, and will excite strenuous efforts in me to endeavor to raise such. for this purpose early in the next year I shall ask of you some cuttings of your bushes, and before that shall send a pretty copious list for a supply of the best kinds of garden seeds, and flowers. I shall be at home early in March for my permanent residence, and shall very much devote my [time] to my garden. I reserved very few of Gov^r. Lewis's articles, and have growing only his salsafia, Mandane corn, and a pea remarkeable for it's beautiful blossom & leaf. his forward bean is growing in my neighborhood. I have the tulips you sent me in great perfection, also the hyacinths, tuberoses, amaryllis, and the artichokes. I pray you to accept my thanks for the gooseberries and my respectful salutations. (*Jefferson Papers, L. C.*)

(Jefferson to Monsieur de la Cépède.)

Washington, July 14, 1808.

. . . [Governor Lewis's Journal] . . . the journal and geographical part of which may soon be expected from the press; but the parts relating to the plants and animals observed in his tour, will be delayed by the engravings. In the meantime, the plants of which he brought seeds, have been very successfully raised in the botanical garden of Mr. Hamilton of the Woodlands, and by Mr. McMahon, a gardener of Philadelphia; and on the whole, it is with pleasure I can assure you that the addition to our knowledge in every department, resulting from this tour of Messrs. Lewis and Clarke, has entirely fulfilled my expectations in setting it on foot, and that the world will find that those travellers have well earned its favor. . . . (Lipscomb and Bergh, *Jefferson* 12: 85.)

(Jefferson to A. F. Sylvestre.)

Washington, July 15, 1808.

I had received from you on a former occasion the four first volumes of the Memoirs of the Agricultural Society of the Seine, and since that, your letter of September 19th, with the 6th, 7th, 8th, and 9th volumes, being for the years 1804, '5, '6, with some separate memoirs. These I have read with great avidity and satisfaction, and now return you my thanks for them. But I owe particular acknowledgments for the valuable present of the Théâtre de Serres, which I consider as a prodigy for the age in which it was composed, and shows an advancement in the science of agriculture which I had never suspected to have belonged to that time. Brought down to the present day by the very valuable notes added, it is really such a treasure of agricultural knowledge, as has not before been offered to the world in a single work.

It is not merely for myself, but for my country, that I must do homage to the philanthropy of the Society, which has dictated their destination for me of their newly improved plough. I shall certainly so use it as to answer their liberal views, by making the opportunities of profiting by it as general as possible.

I have just received information that a plough addressed to me has arrived in New York, *from England,* but unaccompanied by any letter or other explanation. As I have had no intimation of such an article to be forwarded to me from that country, I presume it is the one sent by the Society of the Seine, that it has been carried into England under their orders of council, and permitted to come on from thence. This I shall know within a short time. I shall with great pleasure attend to the construction and transmission to the Society of a plough with my mould-board. This is the only part of that useful instrument to which I have paid any particular attention. But knowing how much the perfection of the plough must depend, 1st, on the line of traction; 2d, on the direction of the share; 3d, on the angle of the wing; 4th, on the form of the mould-board; and persuaded that I shall find the three first advantages eminently exemplified in that which the Society sends me, I am anxious to see combined with these a mould-board of my form, in the hope that it will still advance the perfection of that machine. But for this I must ask time till I am relieved from the cares which have now a right to all my time, that is to say, till the next spring. Then giving, in the leisure of retirement, all the time and attention this construction merits and requires, I will certainly render to the Society the result in a plough of the best form I shall be able to have executed. . . . (Lipscomb and Bergh, *Jefferson* 12: 88–90.)

(Jefferson to C. P. de Lasteyrie.)

Washington, July 15, 1808.

I have duly received your favor of March 28th, and with it your treatises on the culture of the sugar cane and cotton plant in France.

The introduction of new cultures, and especially of objects of leading importance to our comfort, is certainly worthy the attention of every government, and nothing short of the actual experiment should discourage an essay of which any hope can be entertained. Till that is made, the result is open to conjecture; and I should certainly conjecture that the sugar cane could never become an article of profitable culture in France. We have within the ancient limits of the United States, a great extent of country which brings the orange to advantage, but not a foot in which the sugar cane can be matured. France, within its former limits, has but two small spots, (Olivreles and Hieres) which brings the orange in open air, and *a fortiori,* therefore, none proper for the cane. I should think the maple-sugar more worthy of experiment. There is no part of France of which the climate would not admit this tree. I have never seen a reason why every farmer should not have a sugar orchard, as well as an apple orchard. The supply of sugar for his family would require as little ground, and the process of making it as easy as that of cider. Mr. Micheaux, your botanist here, could send you plants as well as seeds, in any quantity from the United States. I have no doubt the cotton plant will succeed in some of the southern parts of France. Whether its culture will be as advantageous as those they are now engaged in, remains to be tried. We could, in the United States, make as great a variety of wines as are made in Europe, not exactly of the same kinds, but doubtless as good. Yet I have ever observed to my countrymen, who think its introduction important, that a laborer cultivating wheat, rice, tobacco, or cotton here, will be able with the proceeds, to purchase double the quantity of the wine he could make. Possibly the same quantity of land and labor in France employed on the rich produce of your Southern counties, would purchase double the quantity of the cotton they would yield there. This however may prove otherwise on trial, and therefore it is worthy the trial. In general, it is a truth that if every nation will employ itself in what it is fittest to produce, a greater quantity will be raised of the things contributing to human happiness, than if every nation attempts to raise everything it wants within itself. The limits within which the cotton plant is worth cultivating in the United States, are the Rappahannock river to the north, and the first mountains to the west. And even from the Rappahannock to the Roanoke, we only cultivate for family use, as it cannot there be afforded at market in competition with that of the more Southern region. The Mississippi country, also within the same latitudes, admits the culture of cotton.

The superficial view I have yet had time to take of your treatise on the cotton plant, induces a belief that it is rich and correct in its matter, and contains a great fund of learning on that plant. When retired to rural occupations, as I shall be ere long, I shall profit of its contents practically, in the culture of that plant merely for the household manufacture. In that situation, too, I shall devote myself to occupations much more congenial with my inclinations than those to which I have been called by the character of the times into which my lot was cast.

About to be relieved from this *corvée* by age and the fulfilment of the *quadragena stipendia,* what remains to me of my physical activity will chiefly be employed in the amusements of agriculture. Having little practical skill, I count more on the pleasures than the profits of that occupation. They will give me, too, the leisure which my present situation nearly denies, of rendering such services as may be within my means, to the Institute, the Agricultural Society of the Seine, to yourself, and such other worthy individuals as may find any convenience in a correspondence here. I shall then be able particularly to fulfil the wishes expressed, of my sending to the Society of Agriculture a plough with my mould-board. Perhaps I may be able to add some other implements, peculiar to us, to the collection which I perceive the Society is making. . . . (Lipscomb and Bergh, *Jefferson* 12: 90–93.)

### (Jefferson to John Taylor.)

Monticello Aug. 20. 08.

Your favor of the 8ᵗʰ. came to hand only two days ago, & I hasten to say I shall be glad to receive m͞r Martin's drill whenever it can be ready. during the present interruption of commerce we send an Aviso every 6. weeks to France & England for the purposes of public & mercantile correspondence, and in any one of these I can send the drill.

I have received the plough from the Agricultural society of Paris. it is a wheel plough, as lightly made as we should have done it; and seeing no peculiar advantage in it's construction, I suspect it owes to it's lightness & shortness it's superiority over the ploughs with which it was tried; for the ploughs of Europe are barbarously heavy, & long, & therefore require great force. I believe Great Britain has lately begun to use lighter ploughs. I shall now not be afraid of sending to the society one of our best ploughs, according to their request, with my mouldboard to it. I shall previously try it's resistance to the draught, comparatively with theirs, by the same instrument they have used, which I expect to receive this fall. A m͞r Frazer, a gardener near London, whom I knew in Paris, & afterwards here, has lately sent me a very small parcel of seed of a new turnup, which he calls Frazer's new turnep. no letter nor explanation came, so that I know no more of it than it's name. I know I cannot have it tried more fairly than by yourself, and therefore I inclose you one half of what I received. I shall not sow my half till next year when I shall be at home to take care of it myself. I shall not fail in the winter to send you some fresh Sesamum seed. it is now growing luxuriantly in our neighborhood. . . . (*Jefferson Papers,* M. H. S.)

### (Jefferson to Governor Meriwether Lewis.)

Monticello, August 21, 1808.

. . . Your friends here are all well, except Colonel Lewis, who has declined very rapidly the last few months. He scarcely walks about now, and never beyond his yard. We can never lose a better man. . . . (Lipscomb and Bergh, *Jefferson* 12: 144.)

(Jefferson to Mr. Watkins.)

Monticello, Aug. 22. '08.

. . . [About hiring him as a carpenter] . . . The emploiment the first year will be as a carpenter, with 2 or 3 men under you for work to be done for myself. the paling a large inclosure of garden & orchard, building some granaries & other work of that kind would be the most wanted. . . . [See letter, Jefferson to Mr. Watkins, September 27, 1808, about the palings for the garden and orchard.] (*Jefferson Papers,* M. H. S.)

(Hugh Chisholm to Jefferson.)

Sept. 4, 1808.

. . . I have done both of the stairways & one of the nursery and in the course of this week I will have the other done. we have also run the collums for the South Portico & I think they will when finished be elegant, the west room is finished in the manner which you told me. . . . (*Jefferson Papers,* M. H. S.)

(Jefferson to Mr. Watkins.)

Sep. 27. 1808.

Directions for mr̄ Watkins when he comes.
Davy, Abram, & Shepherd are to work with him.
Phill Hubard & Bedford Davy are to saw for him when sawing is wanting. he is to live in Stewart's house.
His first work is to pale in the garden, with a paling 10. feet high. the posts are to be of locust, sufficiently stout, barked but not hewed, 12 f. long, of which 2½ f. are to go in the ground. it will take about 300: placing them 9. f. apart.
the rails are to be of heart poplar or pine. the stock is to be split into 4. quarters thus ⊟ then each quarter is to be split diagonally thus ◻ so as to make 2 three square rails out of each quarter. they are to be of the size usual in strong garden paling. I do not know what that is. there will be 3. to each pannel & consequently 900. in all.
The pales are to be of chestnut, riven, & strong, 5. f. 3. I long, to be dubbed on one another on the middle rail like clapboards, so that 1. nail shall do, & two lengths of pales will make the whole height. I suppose they will be generally from 5. to 7. I. wide, & should be so near as not to let even a young hare in. there will be about 7500. wanting. they are to be sharpened at the upper end thus ⊓ and not thus ⌂ as is usual.
they are not to be put up till I come home to shew the courses of the inclosure. the pine for the rails may be got either at Pouncy's or on my lands beyond Colle. the chestnut pales had better be got in the high mountain. (*Jefferson Papers,* M. H. S.)

### (William Brown to Jefferson.)

New Orleans 10ᵗʰ. October 1808

I have shipped a few Cumpeachy hammocks and a barrel of paccannes in a vessel for George Town to the care of the Collector of that port which I pray your acceptance of. . . . (*Jefferson Papers*, L. C.)

### (Jefferson to Edmund Bacon.)

Washington Oct. 17. 08.

. . . I expect mr̄ Madox is now about the stable, & the house laid off where an old loghouse stands, & of course that he draws off some of your force. I think it will be better to employ the rest on the garden & let us have that off of our hands. as the begining of Nov. is the best season for driving our sheep home, I would have you leave home for this place about the 30ᵗʰ. or 31ˢᵗ. of this month. . . . You will remember that our plan was to plant peas the next year in the field next your house, corn in the field elbowing round by Phill's house, and oats in those parts of our river field & that we had of Craven, as have not clover worth preserving. wherever the clover is well enough set, it will be worth more to us than oats. . . . (*Jefferson Papers*, Huntington.)

### (Jefferson to Martha (Jefferson) Randolph.)

Washington Oct. 18. 08.

. . . tell Anne that my old friend Thouin of the National garden at Paris has sent me 700 species of seeds. I suppose they will contain all the fine flowers of France, and fill all the space we have for them. . . . (*Jefferson Papers*, M. H. S.)

### (Jefferson to Mr. John Moody.)

Washington Oct. 26. 08.

I received two days ago your letter of the 20ᵗʰ. and readily consent to pay mr̄ Evans the usual compensation for his inventions employed in my mill, whenever you or he will be so good as to ascertain the amount. what these are I know not, having left to the millwright to do whatever he thought would be useful. she began to run in the autumn or winter of 1806. I make this paiment willingly as a voluntary tribute to a person whose talents are constantly employed in endeavors to be useful to mankind, and not as a legal obligation. my mill was erected after the expiration of mr̄ Evans's first patent & before the date of his second; and were there any doubt as to the proviso in the act covering those who adopted those machines when no law forbid it, the text of the constitution which declares that Congress shall have no power to pass an expost facto law, would annul any enactment of retrospective effect were there any such in the law in question. meaning however to claim nothing more than the justice of being considered as doing voluntarily what the law has not required, I shall receive with pleasure a specification of the amount. . . . (*Jefferson Papers*, M. H. S.)

### (William Bartram to Jefferson.)

Kingsess near Philadelphia
Oct. 29, 1808.

. . . Dr. Say will hand your excellency a small packet containing a few seeds of a beautiful flowering tree together with a Catalogue of our collection. The tree is the Mimosa julibrescens (silk tree) a native of Persia and Armenia; lately brought to us by the celebrated Michaux the elder. Its delicate sweet flowers grow in fascicles, composed of a number of slender silky threads, tipped with crimson anthers. The packet is tyed with a silky bark of a species of Asclepias, native to Pensylvania, which should it prove a useful substitute for flax or cotton, in linnen manufacture, it can be cultivated in any quantities and with less expense, as it is a perennial plant, and thrives in almost any soil.

I send you these articles, Sir, as a mark of my homage & respect, not knowing whether they are new to you or of any value. . . . (*Jefferson Papers*, L. C.)

### (Ellen W. Randolph to Jefferson.)

November 11, 1808.

. . . Your orange trees come on very well as to their looks but I never saw such little short things in my life they are near eighteen months old and they are not as high (any of them) as my hand is long. . . . (*Jefferson Papers*, M. H. S.)

### (Jefferson to Ellen W. Randolph.)

Washington Nov. 15. 08.

. . . It is the Anthoxanthum odoratum of the botanist. . . . I have 700 species of seeds sent me by Mr. Thouin from the National Garden of France. . . . (*Jefferson Papers*, M. H. S.)

### (Jefferson to Mr. James Lewis.)

Washington Nov. 22. 08.

I have received your letter of the 15ᵗʰ and by this post desire m͞r Bacon to let you take roots from the rose bush you mention as also to have you furnished with one pair of the East India fowls. our stock will not afford more and we have constant applications from other quarters. . . . (*Jefferson Papers*, M. H. S.)

### (Jefferson to Edmund Bacon.)

Washington Nov. 22. 08.

. . . James Lewis, [give him] also some roots of a rose bush which he says is in the yard on the East side of the house. . . . (*Jefferson Papers*, M. H. S.)

(Jefferson to Thomas Mann Randolph.)

Washington, Nov. 22, 08.

. . . For a scientific man in a town nothing can furnish so convenient an amusement as chemistry, because it may be pursued in his cabinet; but for a country gentleman I know no source of amusement & health equal to botany & natural history, & I should think it unfortunate for such an one to attach himself to chemistry, altho' the general principles of the science it is certainly well to understand. . . . (*Jefferson Papers*, M. H. C. 1: 125.)

(Jefferson to William Bartram.)

Washington Nov. 23. 08.

Th: Jefferson presents his compliments to his friend m͞r W. Bartram and his thanks for the seeds of the silk tree which he was so kind as to send him.   these he shall plant in March and cherish with care at Monticello.   the cares of the garden and culture of curious plants uniting either beauty or utility will there form one of his principal amusements. he has been prevented, by indisposition of some days, from having the pleasure of seeing Dr. Say. . . . (*Jefferson Papers*, L. C.)

(Anne Cary Randolph to Jefferson.)

Port Royal November 26 1808

. . . On coming from Edgehill I left all the flowers in Ellens care, however, I shall be with you early enough in march to assist about the border, which the old French Gentleman's present if you mean to plant them there, with the wild & bulbous rooted ones we have already, will compleatly fill. . . . I inclose you some Acacia flowers which M͞r Lomax sent me from the tree that you gave him I think he says in 76. (*Jefferson Papers*, M. H. S.)

(Jefferson to Doctor Benjamin Waterhouse.)

Washington, December 1, 1808.

In answer to the inquiries of the benevolent Dr. De Carro on the subject of the upland or mountain rice, *Oryza Mutica*, I will state to you what I know of it.   I first became informed of the existence of a rice which would grow in uplands without any more water than the common rains, by reading a book of Mr. De Porpre, who had been Governor of the Isle of France, who mentions it as growing there and all along the coast of Africa successfully, and as having been introduced from Cochin-China.   I was at that time (1784–89) in France, and there happening to be there a Prince of Cochin-China, on his travels, and then returning home, I obtained his promise to send me some.   I never re-

ceived it however, and mention it only as it may have been sent, and
furnished the ground for the inquiries of Dr. Carro, respecting my receiving it from China. When at Havre on my return from France, I
found there Captain Nathaniel Cutting, who was the ensuing spring to
go on a voyage along the coast of Africa. I engaged him to inquire for
this; he was there just after the harvest, procured and sent me a thirty-
gallon cask of it. It arrived in time the ensuing spring to be sown. I
divided it between the Agricultural Society of Charleston and some
private gentlemen of Georgia, recommending it to their care, in the
hope which had induced me to endeavor to obtain it, that if it answered
as well as the swamp rice, it might rid them of that source of their summer diseases. Nothing came of the trials in South Carolina, but being
carried into the upper hilly parts of Georgia, it succeeded there perfectly,
has spread over the country, and is now commonly cultivated; still however, for family use chiefly, as they cannot make it for sale in competition
with the rice of the swamps. The former part of these details is written from memory, the papers being at Monticello which would enable
me to particularize exactly the dates of times and places. The latter
part is from the late Mr. Baldwin, one of those whom I engaged in the
distribution of the seed in Georgia, and who in his annual attendance on
Congress, gave me from time to time the history of its progress. It has
got from Georgia into Kentucky, where it is cultivated by many individuals for family use. I cultivated it two or three years at Monticello,
and had good crops, as did my neighbors, but not having conveniences
for husking it, we declined it. I tried some of it in a pot, while I lived
in Philadelphia, and gave seed to Mr. Bartram. It produced luxuriant
plants with us both, but no seed; nor do I believe it will ripen in the
United States as far north as Philadelphia. . . . (Lipscomb and Bergh,
*Jefferson* 12: 204–205.)

## (Jefferson to Anne Cary (Randolph) Bankhead.)

Washington, Dec. 8, 08.

Your letter of Nov. 26 came safely to hand, and in it the delicious
flower of the Acacia, or rather Mimosa Nilotica, from Mr. Lomax.
The mother tree of full growth which I had when I gave him the small
one, perished from neglect the first winter I was from home. Does his
produce seed? If it does I will thank him for some, and you to take
care of them; altho' he will think it a vain thing at my time of life to be
planting a tree of as slow a growth. In fact the Mimosa Nilotica &
Orange are the only things I ever proposed to have in my green house.
. . . (*Jefferson Papers,* M. H. C. 1: 128.)

## (Ellen Randolph to Jefferson.)

December 15 1808

. . . there are at least a peck of Tuberoses and 12 or 14 Amaryllis
roots all packed in bran. . . . (*Jefferson Papers,* M. H. S.)

(Jefferson to Edmund Bacon.)

Washington Dec. 19. 08.

I received yesterday yours of the 15<sup>th</sup>. I am glad to learn your progress in the garden, which I wish to have pushed, because it will be inclosed in March, and it would be very inconvenient to have to do that work after it is paled in.    still we must not sacrifice the crop of the year for it.    for the work absolutely necessary to prepare for the crop, we must suspend the garden works, when it is necessary.    perhaps you might draw a little aid from your nail house at pinching times.    two tons of nailrod left Philā the 12<sup>th</sup>. of this month, & will probably be at Richmond about Christmas.    I have written to m͞r͞s Dangerfield to renew the hire of her negroes for the next year, except the runaway one, & I have no doubt she will do it.    When Davy comes with his cart, let him bring 200. young aspens, in bundles of 50. each, well wrapped round the roots with straw, tied on close. . . . (*Jefferson Papers,* Huntington.)

(Mrs. Anne (Randolph) Bankhead to Jefferson.)

Port Royal Dec. 19 1808

. . . I have not seen M<sup>r</sup> Lomax yet but make no doubt of getting the seed as I heard that he had some. . . . I would be much obliged to you if you will send me in a letter some of the ice plant seed    a Lady here has Lost it & is to give me a few roots of the Lily of the valley & a beautiful pink for it.    I know it is to be had in Washington.    M<sup>r</sup> Burwell got some there for Ellen. . . . (*Jefferson Papers,* M. H. S.)

(Jefferson to Charles Thomson.)

Washington, December 25, 1808.

[About retirement] . . . I am full of plans of employment when I get there, they chiefly respect the active functions of the body.    To the mind I shall administer amusement chiefly.    An only daughter and numerous family of grandchildren, will furnish me great resources of happiness. . . . (Lipscomb and Bergh, *Jefferson* 12: 217.)

Towards the end of the year Jefferson received the following note, written on a small piece of paper, from Mrs. Samuel Harrison Smith, wife of the founder and editor of the *National Intelligencer,* and a close friend of Jefferson.

(Mrs. Smith to Jefferson.)

I have seen in your cabinet a *Geranium,* which I understood you cultivated with your own hands.    If you do not take it home with you, I entreat you to leave it with me.    I cannot tell you how inexpressively precious it will be to my heart.    It shall be attended with the assiduity of affection and watered with tears of regret each day as I attend it, will I invoke the best blessings of Heaven, on the most venerated of human beings! (*Jefferson Papers,* M. H. S.)

(Jefferson's reply to Mrs. Smith.)

Washington, Mar. 6. 09.

Th: Jefferson presents his respectful salutations to mrs. Smith, and sends her the Geranium she expressed a willingness to receive. it is in very bad condition, having been neglected latterly, as not intended to be removed. he cannot give it his parting blessing more effectually than by consigning it to the nourishing hand of mrs. Smith. if plants have sensibility, as the analogy of their organisation with ours seems to indicate, it cannot but be proudly sensible of her fostering attentions. of his regrets at parting with the society of Washington, a very sensible portion attaches to mrs. Smith, whose friendship he has particularly valued. her promise to visit Monticello is some consolation; and he can assure her she will be received with open arms and hearts by the whole family. he prays her to accept the homage of his affectionate attachment and respect. (Ford, *Jefferson Correspondence:* 177.)

(Jefferson to Edmund Bacon.)

Washington Dec. 26. 08.

. . . you have little waggoning to do. it will be well therefore to have both waggons in order and proceed to waggoning dung to the garden. that from Milton should be first brought, and for this purpose it will be worth your while to put the road along the river side in order, I mean that on the South side. as this would be to be put into good order as soon as I come home, it will be better to do it now, that you may have the benefit of it in the job of bringing the dung from Milton. 6. waggon loads are first to be laid on the old asparagus bed below the wall, which Wormley must immediately spread even & then fork it in with the three pronged garden fork, taking care not to fork so deep as to reach the crown of the Asparagus roots. then begin at the S.W. end of the garden, and drop a good waggon load of dung every five yeards along a strait line through the middle of the garden from the S.W. to the N.E. end. this will take between 60. & 70. loads in the whole, which will do for the first year.

As it will be necessary that we make preparation for clothing our people another year, we must plant a large cotton patch, say two acres at the least. a light sandy soil is best. I suppose therefore it should be in the low grounds at the mill dam. seed can be procured from those who have cotton gins. the present method of cultivating cotton is very little laborious. it is done entirely with the plough. next, to secure wool enough, the negroes dogs must all be killed. do not spare a single one. if you keep a couple yourself it will be enough for the whole land. let this be carried into execution immediately. . . . (*Jefferson Papers,* Huntington.)

(Jefferson to Bernard McMahon.)

Washington Dec. 28. 08.

I lately received from my old friend M$^r$. Thouin superintendant of the National garden at Paris a package containing 700. different kinds of seeds of every country, except of the United States; they were gathered in 1807. and he says they will be good for sowing in the spring of 1809. on every paper is written the time for sowing it (according to the French calendar) and whether under frames, in open air & what sort of soil. satisfied I could not put them to so good an use as by presenting them to you, I got the favor of Cap^t Jones of Philadelphia to take charge of them by the mail.  they are in a small box addressed to you, and as he set out in the mail of this morning they will have arrived one day before you receive this.   Accept with them my salutations & assurances of esteem. . . . (*Jefferson Papers,* L. C.)

### From the *Account Book 1808:*

Mar.   2.   p^d Holt for 4 cones of Cedar of Lebanon 1. D.
Mar. 14.   gave Jonathan Shoemaker ord. on bk. US 21. D. for 2. bushels clover seed sent to Monticello.
May     4.   received from bank US, an order on d°. at Baltimore for 95.04 which I inclosed to P. A. Guestier for seeds.

### (Jefferson memorandum.)

[1808]

To describe on the ground the Labyrinth of broom.

go to the 5^th. beginning in the avenue of broom for the apple-tree-rows, viz. a.

measure off at right angles with that 165. f. to b.

describe round a circle of 55. f radius

where it crosses the line a. b. viz.   at c. stick a pin.

divide the circle into 8. parts, sticking pins, viz at 43.2 f distance measured on the periphery.

lay off a tangent from each point (with the theodolite)

take the radius (55 f.) on that tangent & describe a quadrant from the pin in the periphery

take for a new center the pin in the periphery which is a quadrant distant from the pin last ment^d. & with the semicircle (110 f.) for a radius describe from the end of the last quadrant a portion of a circle till it intersects the tangent.

on each side of this spiral, parallel to it, & at 9 f. distance from it describe lines

plant broom every 6 f. along these lines, and allowing the plants to put out branches 6. f. each way it will leave walks of 6. f. wide, without ever rend^g. necess^y to trim.

between walk & walk the whole interval must be filled with broom at 6. f. distance.   to bound which properly, a circle of 165 f. rad. must be circumscrib^d round the whole.

(note these walks will go off from the circle where the plats of broom were erroneously placed in the figure.)   [See plate XXVI.]

(*Jefferson Papers,* M. H. S.)

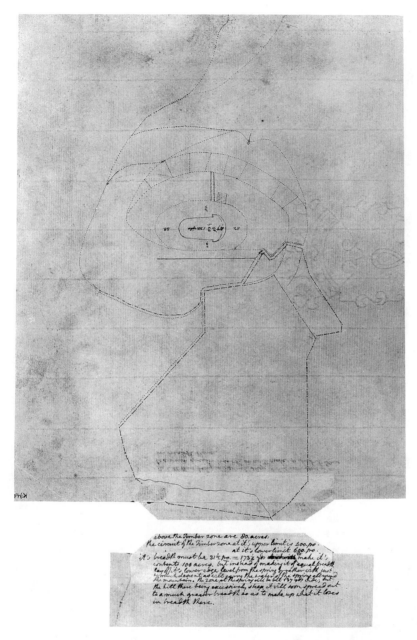

PLATE XXVII.—Jefferson's plan for laying off lots for the minor articles of husbandry, and for a *ferme ornée*, in relation to the other parts of the *Monticello* mountaintop.   See plate XXVI.   (*Jefferson Papers*, M. H. S.)

PLATE XXVIII.—The western or rear entrance to the *Monticello* house, with its broad lawn, flower borders, oval and round flower beds, and fish

# 1809

Apr. 10.   planted in the Nursery next below the little
grass terras, in a bed ranging with the upper
strawberry bed, 68. peach stones [W. Meriwether's [2] Georgia black.   unknown, but sup-
pos⁴ good because saved]

69. plumstones in the
row next below

68. apricot stones in the
next row & a half

these came from G.
Jefferson,[3]  probably
sent him from abroad,
directed to me in a
little bag.—they came
from m͞rs Hackley
Cadiz [4]

Apr. 13.   planted 32. seeds of the Mimosa Julibritzin [5]
in the earthen trough, in which were also
sowed on the 10ᵗʰ. inst. seeds of the Alpine
strawberry from Mazzei.[6]  sowed seeds of
Dionaea muscipula [7] in a pot.   they were several years old.

in square II.[8] beginning with the S.W. row
sowed

1. row of rheum undulatum,[9] esculent rhu-
barb.   the leaves excellent as Spinach.

1. d⁰. Long pod soup pea.  or Asparagus
bean.[10]   pods 3.f. long, to run on poles.
when green they are dressed as Asparagus, or as snaps, or boiled in soup.

385

1. d°. African early pea,[11] lately introduced from Africa into S. Carol[a]. where it gives 3. crops a year.   the two last articles from Gen[l]. Sumpter.[12]

1. d°. lentils.   Ervum lens.[13]

3. d°. Windsor beans.

14.   sowed oil radish [14] in the nursery in the former asparagus bed.

G. Divers finds the following sufficient for his family.

Celery 400.f. running measure.   to wit 10. rows of my squares 3.f. apart 4 f is better

Salsafy 320.f. = 8. rows of my squares of 40 f. at 6.I. every way

Carrots 320.f = 8. d°. 12.I. apart.

parsneps 200.f = 5. d°. 12.I. apart.

beet       200.f = 5. d°. 12.I. apart.[15]

26.   sowed Monthly strawberry seed from Col°. Worthington [16] in Nursery   E. corner.

April 29.   Squash from Maine.[17] / soft cymling.[18] / solid pumpkin from S. America. / long pumpkin from Malta. / 3. to 4.f. long. 2.f. circumference.   127. lb weight. / the seed look like gourd. / qu?   — in the terras next below the garden wall & in the order here named from   S.W.   to N.E. considerably distant from each other.

Benni.[19]   from Bailey's walk [20] to Stable yard.

May.   2.   Orange gourd in upper terras of N.E. vine-
            yard.

            long gourd.[21] in 15th. d°. of d°.

Sep.   5.   planted 8. figs from D[r]. Thorton [22] under S.W.
            end of wall, about 12.f. apart.

            m͞r Randolph's [23] onions have yielded at the
            rate of 240. bushels per acre. the largest
            squares [24] of my garden $\frac{1}{27}$ of an acre would
            yield 9. bush.

Oct.   5.   planted 14. Paulina Aurea, or Koelreuteria
            paniculata aurea [25] in 2 boxes & a pot, to wit 4.
II. III.    in the pot, 4. in the large box, N° 3. 2 in the
            small one. N°. 2. recieved the seeds from
            Mad°. de Tessé.[26]

Nov.   6.   planted from m͞r Lomax's [27]

       3.   Modesty shrubs,[28] viz 1. in N.E. circular
            bed,[29] 1. in N.W. & 1. in S.W. d°.

       5.   Jujubes,[30] viz 1. in S.E. clump 2. in S.W.
            d°. 2. in N.W. d°.

       21.  Star jasmines.[31]  2 in each of the oval beds

       24   Filberts [32] in the lowest terras below the
            old filbert bush.  & every other one above
            includ[g] 7. terrasses.

VII. VIII. IX.   2. Acacia Niloticas [33] box 7. 8. 1 or-
            ange,[34] 1. lime [35] in boxes in the Green-
            house.[36]  N°. IX

     N°. I.   a box. shell barks.[37]

       V.   is a sour orange brot from Washington.

Kalendar [38]  1809.

| | where | sowed | transplant$^d$ | come to table | gone | seed gather$^d$. | observations |
|---|---|---|---|---|---|---|---|
| frame peas | bord. I-IV. | Mar. 23. | | May 23. | June 8. | | 2 quarts sow$^d$ 440 f. @ ½ I. dist$^{ce}$. |
| Hotspurs | square I. | Mar. 27. | | June 5. | | | 40.f. gave 1. quart of seed. |
| Cabbage early York [39] | bord V.— | Mar. 25. | failed nearly | | | | 5. pints sow 440 @ ½ I. distance. |
| Lettuce Marseilles. [40] | stone house [41] | Mar. 25. | 245. May 19. W V 5$^{th}$. | | | | |
| Radishes | d$^o$. | Mar. 25. | | May 15. | | | |
| Spinach prickly | bord VI. | Mar. 29. | | May 20. | June 5. | | |
| Parsley double | bord. VI. | Mar. 29. | | | | | |
| Ledman's dwarf pea [42] | square III. | Apr. 10. | | July 1. | | | less than 2. q$^{ts}$. = 440.f |
| Alpine strawb$^y$ seed } from Mazzei | lowest bed Nursery } earthentrough | Apr. 10. | | | | | |
| Seakale [43] | 4$^{th}$. aspar. bed. | Apr. 10. | | | | | |
| Tarragon [44] | bord. VII. | 12. | failed. | | | | |
| cucumbers | bord. VII. | 12. | | | | | |
| Cabbage Early York | bord. V. | 12. | failed nearly. | | | | 9. plants transplanted July 10. to W. side sq. VI. |
| Windsor beans | square II. | 13. | killed by bug. | | | | |
| cucumbers early | Nursery. | 20. | | | | | |
| Cauliflower early | d$^o$. S.W. end of bed. | 20. | failed. | | | | |
| Roman Broccoli | d$^o$. N.E. end. | 20. | failed nearly. | | | | 54. plants of these transpl$^d$ June 30. Sq. XI of which some however were of May 3. |
| Ice lettuce | d$^o$. artichoke bed. | 20. | | | | | |
| radishes. E. scar | | | | | | | |
| lettuce. tennis ball | sq. IX.12.13. | 20. | failed. | | | | |
| radish E. scarlet | | | | | | | |
| lettuce. Marseilles | 3$^d$ Asp. bed N.E. | 21. | failed. | | | | |
| radish E. scarlet | | | | | | | |

Kalendar[38] 1809. (continued)

| | where | sowed | transplant[d] | come to table | gone | seed gather[d]. | observations |
|---|---|---|---|---|---|---|---|
| tree onion[45] | dº. S.W. | 21. | failed. | | | | of these seed bulbs, 111 fill a pint. to plant a square of 40.f in drill 12.I. apart & 4 I. in the drill will take 5½ gallons, say 3. pecks. |
| carrots. orange | 5th. & 6th. dº | 21. | | | | | |
| beets scarlet | 7th. dº | 21. | failed. | | | | |
| Snaps E. dwarf | V. SW. 5 rows | 21. | failed. | | | | |
| Ricara[46] | dº. NE. 5 dº | 21. | | | | | |
| Spinach. summʳ | IX. 1. | 22. | | | | | |
| Parsley | 2. | dº. | | | | | |
| Sorrel[47] | 3. | dº. | failed. | July 3. | | | |
| Okra | 4. 5. | dº. | failed. | July 1. | | | |
| Egg plant[48] | 6. | dº. | failed. | | | | |
| Chinese melon[49] | 7. | dº. | 4 plants | | | | |
| Spanish onion | nursery | 24. | | | | | |
| Squash. warted[50] | dº. | 24. | | | | | |
| parsneps | dº. | 24. | | | | | |
| giant Cabbage | dº. | 25. | failed. | | | | |
| early cucumbers | dº. | 26. | | | | | |
| Lima beans | sq. VIII. | 28. | | Aug. 19. | | | |
| celery solid.}  red | low grounds | May. 1. | failed. | | | | |
| dº.         red | | | | | | | |
| Broccoli Roman | bord. VIII. | May 3. | June. 30. XI | | | | |
| Ice lettuce }  E./S. | bord. IX. | dº. | | | | | |
| radishes | | | | | | | |
| Spinach. smooth | dº. | dº. | | | | | |
| parsley common | N.E. viney.ᵈ 1ˢᵗ | 4. | failed. | | | | |
| Lettuce tennis | | | | | | | |
| Radish. E.S. | 2ᵈ. terras | | | | | | |

Kalendar [38] 1809. (continued)

| | where | sowed | transplant$^d$ | come to table | gone | seed gather$^d$. | observations |
|---|---|---|---|---|---|---|---|
| Kale. Malta [51] | 3$^d$ | | Aug. 18. 2½ rows W. | | | | |
| Scotch | 4$^{th}$ | | 3. middle | | | | |
| Delaware | 5$^{th}$ | | X·bs | | | | |
| Cabbage Early York | 6$^{th}$ | | 3 E. rows | | | | |
| Peas Hotspur | SW } sq. IV. | 5. | | | | | |
| d°. Pruss$^n$. blue | NE } sq. IV. | | | July 10. | | | |
| Roman Watermelon | 1$^{st}$. terras of W. Vineyard } | 9. | | | | | |
| Salsafia | 2$^d$ & 3$^d$ d°. | | | | | | |
| frame peas | 4$^{th}$ d°. | 10. | | | | | |
| Potato pumpkin [52] | E. Appendix. | 13. | | | | | |
| Peas. Ravensworth [53] | orchard | 16. | | July 26. | | | |
| Cow | | | | Aug. 21. | | | from the 7$^{th}$. of Apr. to this day, excessive drought & cold. now a good rain. |
| Topinambours [54] | E. below B's walk | 19. | | | | | |
| Lettuce ice | bord. V. | May 19. | | | | | |
| Radish, summer | d°. | d°. | | | | | |
| Lettuce, tennis ball | d°. | d°. | failed. | | | | |
| Radish Summer | d°. | d°. | | | | | |
| Spinach | d°. | d°. | | | | | |
| Salsafia. Columbian. [55] | E. Viney$^d$. 7$^{th}$ T. | May 20. | | | | | |
| Peas. Hotspur | d°. 8.9.10.Ter. | d°. | | | | | |
| Erie corn | E. Viny$^d$. E. end.1.2. | | | | | | |
| Beet scarlet | d°. East end: 3.4. | d°. | failed. | | | | |
| Snaps. forward | d°. d° 5.6.7. | d°. | | | | | |
| Carrots orange | W. Viny$^d$ 6$^{th}$. Ter. | d°. | | | | | |
| potato solanum | below Nursery. | d°. | | | | | |
| Turnip Swedish | W. V. Terras. 7.8. | 23. | | | | | on the 22$^d$. good rain. |

Kalendar[38] 1809. (continued)

| | where | sowed | transplant | come to table | gone | seed gather. | observations |
|---|---|---|---|---|---|---|---|
| Peas Leadman's } Prussian blue } | Sq. VI. | 26. | | July 22. | | | from these & the remains of Ap. 20. May. 30 84. plants transpld. July 10. into sq. XI. making 135. in all. |
| Snaps dwarf | Sq. VII. W. side | Jun 2. | 40. plants. | | | | |
| Broccoli Roman | 3. aspar. bed. E. | June 3. | July 10. | | | | |
| Savoy cabbage | 5th. do | do. | a very few plants July 10. VI. | | | | |
| Ice lettuce } Summer radish } | 6th. do | do. | | | | | |
| Tomatas. from G. Divers. | 7th. do | | June 3. | | | | |
| Cabbage from TMR.[56] | Sq. VII. E. side. | | June 3. | | | | |
| Ice lettuce } Summer radish } | bord. X. | June 8. do. | | | | | |
| Scarlet beets | W. V. 11. | do. | June 6. | | | | |
| Oil radish | W. V. 9.10. | | | | | | |
| Tennis ball lettuce | bord. X. | June 10. | June 30. | | | | |
| Celery from Craven[57] | bord. XII. | | | | | | |
| lettuce loaf | bord. VII. | July 10. | | | | | |
| radish Summer | bord. VIII. | 15. | | | | | |
| cucumber early | bord. IV. | 15. | | | | | |
| melon winter | bord. I. | 15. | | | | | |
| lettuce Dutch brow[n] | bord. II. | Aug. 15. | | | | | |
| Endive green curled | bord. I. II. | do. | | | | | |
| Radish summer | bord. I. | do. | | | | | |
| Lettuce Dutch Brown | Stone H. E. end bord. IV. | | | | | | |
| Endive. green curled | Stone H. W. end | | | | | | |
| Summer r[a]dish | Stone H. bord. I. | | | | | | |

Kalendar [38] 1809. (continued)

| | where | sowed | transplant^d | come to table | gone | seed gather^d | observations |
|---|---|---|---|---|---|---|---|
| Lettuce D. brown | Stone house. X. | | | | | | |
| Endive green curled | bord XIII. XIV. | Octob. 6. | | | | | |
| Corn sallad | bord. | | | Feb. 26. | | | |
| Spinach | 3^d terras. | May. 7. | | | | | they occupy ground 2½ months. |
| warted squash | VIII. | May. 9. | | July 8. | | | 2928 = 1. pint. |
| yellow d^o | ib. | | | | | | 1^st. blossom. Aug. 8. |
| Asparagus bean | VII. | 12. | | | last dish Oct. 15. | | |
| African pea | | | | | | | |
| Summer. spinach | IX. 9. 10. | 14. | | | | | |
| Ice lettuce | 2. | | Jul. 14. XIII. 3. | | | | |
| Tennis ball lettuce | | | | | | | |
| Scarlet radish | 3^d. ter^s. | 15. | | | | | |
| Ricaras | lower level. | 17. | | | | | |
| White (or Cauliflower) broccoli | IX. 3. | | | | | | |
| Malta Kale | 4. | 31. | | | | | |
| Savoys green curled | 5. | June 1. | | | | | |
| Broccoli early purple | —XI. | | | | | | |
| cucumber early | IX. 6. | | June 12. | | | | |
| Egg plant | II. West side. | 12. | | | | | |
| Melon. Chinese | IX. 1. | | | | | | |
| Lettuce, tennis ball | | | | | | | |
| Radish Summer | V. intervals | June. 20. | | | | | came to nothing. |
| Snaps yellow | IX. 11. | 28. | | | | | |
| lettuce Tennis ball | IX. 12. | July 9. | | | | | |
| summer radishes | | | | | | | |

Kalendar [38] 1809. (continued)

| where | sowed | transplant^d | come to table | gone | seed gather^d. | observations |
|---|---|---|---|---|---|---|
| Melon. winter. 10. hills | Aspar. 7 | 9. | | Oct. 15. | | | killed by frost Oct. 23. |
| Swedish turneps | I. 11 | 19. | | | | |
| Snaps. yellow | IV | 21. | | | | |
| Swedish turneps | I. 11 | 28. | | | | |
| Lettuce Marseilles } | IX. 5. | | | | | |
| Radish | 10. | | | | | |
| Endive broad | 8. | | | | | |
| Broccoli. Roman | | | | | | |
| Hotspur peas | VI. | Aug. 1. | | | | killed by frost Oct. 23. |
| turneps. Swedish | XVIII. 6. 7 | Aug. 24. | | | | |
| Lettuce Dutch Brown | bord. I–V. | | | | | |
| Endive curled & smooth | high bord. | | | | | |
| Corn sallad | XIII. 5. S. end | | | | | |
| Hotspur peas | bord I–V. | 25. | | | | killed by frost Oct. 23. |
| Spinach prickly & smooth | bord I–V. | | | | | killed by frost Oct. 23. |
| Snaps red | sq. V. | | | | | |
| Endive curled & smooth | IX. 7. | | | | | |
| Corn sallad | IX. 7. | | | | | |
| Endive. both kinds | XIII. 1. | Sep. 1. | | | | |
| Lettuce D. Br. | 2. | | | | | |
| Corn sallad | 3. | | | | | |
| Spinach. both | 4. | | | | | |
| d° | XV. 1. N. end | | | | | |
| Lettuce D. Br. } | Stone house | | | | | |
| Endive | | | | | | |
| Corn sallad | | | | | | |
| Lettuce ice | Aspar. 6 | Sep. 15. | | | | |
| early scarlet radish | d°. | | | | | |
| Lettuce ice | IX. 1. 8. | | | | | |
| Cabbage Early York | 2. | | | | | |

¹ *1809.*   Jefferson retired from the Presidency on March 4. Three days before, he had signed the bill for the repeal of the Embargo.   As early as January 19, he was busy with "packing & breaking up my establishment."   On March 2 he wrote to his friend, Monsieur Dupont de Nemours:

Within a few days I retire to my family, my books and farms; and having gained the harbor myself, I shall look on my friends still buffeting the storm with anxiety indeed, but not with envy.   Never did a prisoner, released from his chains, feel such relief as I shall on shaking off the shackles of power.   Nature intended me for the tranquil pursuits of science, by rendering them my supreme delight.   But the enormities of the times in which I have lived, have forced me to take a part in resisting them, and to commit myself on the boisterous ocean of political passions.   (Lipscomb and Bergh, *Jefferson* **12**: 259–260.)

He left Washington on March 11, after seeing his devoted friend, James Madison, inaugurated President to succeed him. He arrived at *Monticello* on the 15th.   Probably no man ever returned to his home with more eagerness.   He had completed his public life and now was determined to live the happy and abundant life which his dear *Monticello* offered.   To help him enjoy his retirement were his daughter and son-in-law, Mr. and Mrs. Randolph; their children; and Francis Eppes, the only child of Maria (Jefferson) Eppes and Mr. Eppes. Mr. Eppes had remarried.

Jefferson was now in his sixty-seventh year.   Two days after he arrived home March 17, he wrote to President Madison:

I had a very fatiguing journey, having found the roads excessively bad, although I have seen them worse.   The last three days I found it better to be on horseback, and travelled eight hours through as disagreeable a snow storm as I was ever in.   Feeling no inconvenience from the expedition but fatigue, I have more confidence in my *vis vitae* than I had before entertained.   The spring is remarkably backward.   No oats sown, not much tobacco seed, and little done in the gardens.   Wheat has suffered considerably.   No vegetation visible yet but the red maple, weeping willow and lilac. . . . (Lipscomb and Bergh, *Jefferson* **12**: 266–267.)

When Jefferson retired, he did not find his estates in the condition they would have been had he been supervisor; still they were in a much better state than they had been after any other of his prolonged absences.   New roads and walks had been completed, the toll mill was now finished and running, and the orchard had been enlarged and planted with many new fruit trees and berries.   The house, too, had reached its final form, and was in appearance very much as it is today.

During his vice-presidency and presidency, Jefferson's expenditures had far exceeded his salary, so that he returned to *Monticello* in rather straitened financial circumstances.   Yet, despite this fact, many improvements were undertaken at his estates.

When he arrived home, he found the garden levelled, manured, and ready for the spring planting.   He divided it into at least eighteen beds or squares, of varying sizes, with an inner border next to the wall for certain vegetables, and a grass walk on the outer or opposite side.   The squares, by 1812, had been increased to twenty-four.   (See plate XXXIII.)

Mrs. Samuel Harrison Smith, of Washington, who visited *Monticello* during the summer of 1809, described the garden as follows:

When we rose from the table, a walk was proposed and he accompanied us.   He took us first to the garden he has commenced since his retirement.   It is on the south side of the mountain and commands a most noble view.   Little is as yet done.   A terrace of 70 or 80 feet long and about 40 wide is already made and in cultivation.   A broad grass walk leads along the outer edge; the inner part is laid off in beds for vegetables.   This terrace is to be extended in length and another to be made below it.   The view it commands, is at present its greatest beauty.   (Smith, *Washington Society:* 68.)

Jefferson filled the garden with an amazing number of vegetables, berries, and fruits.   In the *Garden Book* he made a *Kalendar* showing where the vegetables were planted; when sowed; if transplanted, when; and the time of coming to the table and when gone.   He also arranged columns for seeds gathered, and observations.

Three and one-half pages of the *Garden Book* were filled with plantings made in the garden and orchard.   Plants were discussed in numerous letters and memoranda.   The *Farm Book* has the following entry about the *Monticello* farm:

Monticello Farm

1809.   Divide it into 3. fields of 60 aˢ. each.   1. for half corn, half oats, peas, or millet.   one for wheat 60. aˢ. and one for clover 60 aˢ. and aim at a 4ᵗʰ. for clover also as soon as we can.

the North field, to wit the 60 aˢ. N. of the road leading through the farm will be one.

the Riverfield, to wit, the field on the River & up, between the road & Park branch to yᵉ. Ragged br.

Belfield, to wit the grounds South of the same road, & between that, the N. & S. fence & the perpetual pasture, for a 3ᵈ.

During the fall Jefferson visited Richmond, *Eppington, Carysbrook, Montpelier,* and *Poplar Forest.* He was at *Monticello* during the rest of the year, except for short trips to Charlottesville.

² See note 3, under 1804.

³ George Jefferson was a distant kinsman of Thomas Jefferson and his business correspondent and agent in Richmond, Virginia. There exists a voluminous correspondence between them, in various Jefferson collections.

⁴ Mrs. Harriet Hackley, wife of Richard S. Hackley. Mrs. Hackley was a sister of Thomas Mann Randolph. She was in Cadiz, Spain, when these fruit stones were sent to Jefferson.

⁵ *Albizzia julibrissin* Durazz. Mimosa or silk tree.

⁶ Philip Mazzei. See note 1, 1774.

⁷ See letter, Jefferson to Timothy Bloodworth, January 29, 1804. The seeds of *Dionaea muscipula* Ellis were over five years old. Small in his *Southeastern Flora* gives the range of *Dionaea muscipula* today, as Coastal Plain, Eastern South Carolina and North Carolina. See letter, Benjamin Hawkins to Jefferson, October 6, 1789.

⁸ This is the first mention that the vegetable garden was divided into *squares.*

⁹ Probably the same as *Rheum rhaponticum* L.

¹⁰ *Vigna sesquipedalis* W. F. Wright.

¹¹ Not identified.

¹² General Thomas Sumter was born in Orange County, Virginia, in 1734. He died at Camden, South Carolina, on June 1, 1832. His life was an active one. He served against the French in 1755 and was at Braddock's defeat. In March, 1776, he was made lieutenant colonel of the 3rd South Carolina Regiment, and was later raised to the rank of brigadier general. He was a member of the South Carolina Convention which ratified the Constitution. From 1801 to 1809 he was United States Senator from South Carolina, and in 1811 was sent as our Minister to Brazil. (Lippincott's *Pronounc-*

*ing Biographical Dictionary* (Philadelphia, 1930): 2267. Hereafter cited as Lippincott's *Biographical Dictionary.*)

[13] *Lens esculenta* Moench.

[14] Oil radish.  *Raphanus sativus* L.

A variety of the Common Radish, particularly adapted for the production of oil, and distinguished by the name *R. sativus olifer,* or Oil Radish. Its stems are dwarf, from a foot and a half to two feet in height, much branched, spreading, and produce more seed-pods than the Common Radish.  It is grown rather extensively in China for its oil; from whence it has been introduced into and cultivated in some parts of Europe; but it does not appear with any particular success, though much has been said and written in its favor.  (Burr, *Vegetables:* 613.)

[15] See letter, George Divers to Jefferson, April 22, 1809.

[16] Colonel Thomas Worthington was born July 16, 1773, near Charleston, Virginia, now West Virginia.  In 1798 he moved to Chillicothe, Ohio, where for the remainder of his life he had as an avocation the running of his large farm.  He represented the Territory of Ohio and later the State in several capacities.  He was twice Governor of the State.  He died June 20, 1827.  (*Dict. Am. Biog.* 20: 540–541.) There are two letters from Mr. Worthington to Jefferson in the *Jefferson Papers* of the Library of Congress, both about strawberries.  They are dated March 3 and September 3, 1805.  The seeds mentioned above were probably received in 1805.

[17] Thomas Main, seedsman and nurseryman of Georgetown, of whom Jefferson was a customer.  In a letter to Mr. Joel Barlow, written January 24, 1810, he said of Mr. Main: "You ask my opinion of Maine.  I think him a most excellent man.  Sober, industrious, intelligent and conscientious."  See letter, Jefferson to Madison, April 27, 1809.

[18] The botanical names of soft cymbling, solid pumpkin from South America, and long pumpkin from Malta have not been ascertained.

[19] Jefferson used various spellings for benne, *Sesamum orientale* L.  He wrote it "bene," "benny," and "benni." See various letters of 1808, 1809, 1810, about benne.

[20] See plate XXXII for location of Bailey's walk and the garden wall.

[21] Orange gourd and long gourd, varieties of *Lagenaria leucantha* Rusby.

[22] Dr. William Thornton was born in the West Indies on May 27, 1761, studied medicine at Edinburgh, and came to the United States and married in 1790. He is important as the first architect of the new Capitol in Washington. Jefferson and he were close friends. They often exchanged ideas on architecture, gardening, and other matters. He died March 27, 1828. (*Cyclopedia of American Biography* (Philadelphia, 1912) 2: 448.) See letter, Jefferson to Thornton, October 11, 1809, concerning these figs.

[23] Thomas Mann Randolph (October 1, 1768–June 20, 1828), son of Thomas Mann Randolph and Anne (Cary) Randolph, of *Tuckahoe*. He married Jefferson's daughter, Martha, on February 23, 1790, at *Monticello*. They lived at *Monticello, Varina,* and *Edgehill*. Randolph was a farmer, a member of Congress, and Governor of Virginia.

[24] This is one of the few times that Jefferson mentions the size of the squares of the garden. This would indicate that the squares were of different sizes.

[25] *Koelreuteria paniculata* Laxm. So far as I have been able to ascertain, Jefferson was the first one to plant this tree in Albemarle County. The tree is known as the Pride of India, China Tree, and Varnish Tree. See letter, Jefferson to Madame de Tessé, March 27, 1811.

[26] Madame Noailles de Tessé was an aunt of Lafayette. She was a connoisseur of gardening and the arts in general. A warm friendship grew up between her and Jefferson when he was in France, and it continued until her death. Many of their friendly letters on horticulture are extant. Jefferson sent her a collection of plants from Virginia almost yearly after his return from France. Both she and M. de Tessé died in 1814.

[27] Thomas Lomax was born at *Portobago,* in Caroline County, Virginia, in 1746. He married Anne Corbin Tayloe. He died in 1811.

[28] See letter, Thomas Lomax to Jefferson, October 30, 1809, and letter of Jefferson to Lomax, November 6, 1809. Modesty shrub, unidentified.

[29] See plate XXIII for the location of these flower beds.

[30] Jujubes. *Zizyphus jujuba* Mill.

[31] Star jasmine. Probably *Jasminum officinale* L.

[32] *Corylus avellana* L.

Kalendar.　　1809.

| | where | sowed | transplant | come to table | gone | seed gather | observations |
|---|---|---|---|---|---|---|---|
| frame peas | bord. I.—IV. | mar. 23 | | May 23 | June 8. | | 2 quarts sow'd 440 @ 5½ f. |
| Hotspurs | squan. I. | mar. 27 | | June 5. | | | 40 f. gave 1 quart of peas |
| Cabbage early york | bord V.— | mar. 25 | failed nearly | | | | 3 f. rents sow 440 @ 2 f. distant |
| Lettuce Marseilles | stonehouse | mar. 25 | 205. May 19. XII | | | | |
| Radishes. | do.— | mar. 25 | | May 15. | | | |
| Spinach prickly | bord VI. | mar. 29 | | May 20. | June 5. | | |
| Parsley double | bord VI | mar. 29 | | | | | |
| Ledman's dwarf peas | square III. | apr. 10. | | July 1. | | | less than 2. qt = 440. f |
| Alpine strawb'd seed | lewis beds nursery | apr. 10. | | | | | |
| from marzi | earthenborough | | | | | | |
| Seakale | 4.th aspar. bed | apr. 10 | | | | | |
| Terragon | bord. VII. | 12. | failed | | | | |
| cucumbers | bord. VII | 12 | | | | | |
| Cabbage Early York | bord. V. | 12 | failed nearly | | | | 9 plants transplanted |
| Windsor beans | squan. II | 13 | killed by bug | | | | July 10. to W. side sq. VI. |
| cucumbers each | nursery | 20 | | | | | |
| Cauliflower earl. | S.S.W. end f.d | 20 | failed. | | | | 54 plants of these transp. |
| Roman Broccoli | do. N.E. end | 20 | failed nearly | | | | June 30. sq. XI. of which |
| Ice lettuce | | | | | | | some however were of May 2 |
| radishes. E. scar. | do. artichokes | 20 | | | | | |
| lettuce tennis ball | | | failed | | | | |
| radish E. scarlet | sq. IX. 12. 13. | 20 | | | | | |
| Lettuce Marseilles | S. asp. bd NE | 21 | failed. | | | | of these seed balls, 311 fill a pint |
| radish E. scarlet | do. SW | 21 | failed — | | | | to plant a square of 50. f in drill |
| tree onion | do. SW | 21 | failed | | | | 12. 3 apart & 4 f in the drill |
| carrots. orange | 5.th & 6.th do. | 21 | failed | | | | will take 5½ gallons, say |
| beets scarlet | 7.th do. | 21 | failed | | | | 3. pecks. |
| Snaps E. dwarf | V. SW. 5 rows | 21 | | July 3. | | | |
| Ricara. | do. NE. 5 do | 21 | | July 1. | | | |
| Spinach summer | IX. 1. | 22 | | | | | |
| Parsley | 2. | do. | failed. | | | | |
| Sorrel | 3. | do. | failed | | | | |
| Okra | 4. 5 | do. | failed | | | | |
| Eggplant | 6. | do. | 2 plants | | | | |
| chinese melon | 7. | do. | | | | | |
| Spanish onion | nursery | 24. 24 | | | | | |
| squash warted | do | 24 | | | | | |
| barnejos | do | 25 | failed | | | | |
| giant Cabbage | do. | 26 | | | | | |
| early cucumbers | do. | 26 | | Aug. 19 | | | |
| lima beans | sq. VIII. | | | | | | |
| celery solid | low ground | may. 1. | failed | | | | |
| do. red | | may. 3. | June 30. XI | | | | |
| Broccoli Roman | bord. VIII | | | | | | |
| Ice lettuce | | do. | | | | | |
| radishes E. S. | bord. IX | do. | | | | | |
| Spinach smooth | do. | do. | | | | | |
| parsley common | NE wing 1. | | failed. | | | | |
| Lettuce tennis | 3. — 2 terraces | 4. | | | | | |
| Radish. E. S. | 2.d | | | Aug 18. 2⅔ rows W. | | | |
| Kale. Malta | 3.th | | | 3. middle | | | |
| Scotch | 4.th | | | 3 E. rows | | | |
| Delaware | 5.th | | | | | | |
| Cabbage Early York | 6. | | | | | | |
| Peas Hotspur | SW sq. IV | | 5. | July 10. | | | |
| do. Pruss.n blue | NE | | | | | | |
| Roman Watermelon | i. terrace | | | | | | |
| Salsafia | 1.st N. Virgin. | 9 | | | | | |
| frame peas | 2.nd & 3.d do | 10. | | | | | |
| Potato pumpkin | E. appendix | 13 | | | | | |
| Peas Ravensworth | orchard | 16. | | July 26. | | | from the 7.th of Apr. to this |
| Cow | | | | Aug. 21 | | | day, excessive drought & |
| Topinambours | E. below B.y walk | 19 | | | | | cold. now a good rain. |

PLATE XXIX.—Page 35 of the original *Garden Book*.　This page shows Jefferson's method for keeping the garden *Kalendar* for the year.

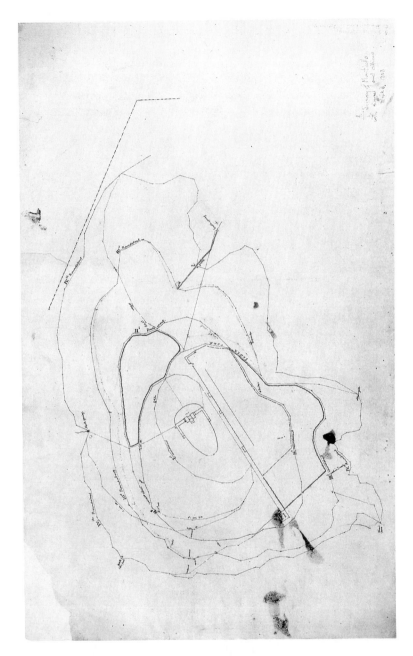

PLATE XXX.—Plan of the upper part of *Monticello* Mountain, 1809. See plate XXII. (*Jefferson Papers*, M. H. S.)

[33] "The species of acacia which produces gum-arabic, frank-incense, and the *fuccus accaciae* is the *mimosa nilotica,* and not the *mimosa senegal,* as was long imagined" (Colin Milne, *Botanical Dictionary* (London, 1805)). The acacia mentioned here is *Acacia farnesiana* Willd.

[34] *Citrus aurantium* L.

[35] *Citrus aurantifolia* Swingle.

[36] Jefferson's greenhouse was a glassed-in piazza on the southeastern end of his house. See letter, Jefferson to William Hamilton, March 1, 1808; and letter, Jefferson to McMahon, April 8, 1811.

[37] Shell barks. Probably *Carya laciniosa* Loud.

[38] The *Kalendar* was kept with varying completeness each year through 1824.

[39] According to Rogers, the Early York Cabbage was introduced into England from Flanders, more than a hundred years ago, by a private soldier named Telford, who was there many years in the reign of Queen Anne. On his return to England, he settled as a seedsman in Yorkshire; whence the name and celebrity of the variety. . . . In this country, it is one of the oldest, most familiar, and, as an early market sort, one of the most popular, of all the kinds now cultivated. (Burr, *Vegetables:* 257.)

[40] A variety of the so-called cabbage lettuce, *Lactuca sativa* L.

[41] One of the stone houses along the *Mulberry Row,* the *Round-about* just above the vegetable garden.

[42] Ledman's dwarf pea. See letters between Jefferson and McMahon of February 8 and February 28, 1809.

[43] *Crambe maritima* L. See letter, Jefferson to McMahon, February 8, 1809.

[44] *Artemisia dracunculus* L. See various letters about tarragon: Jefferson to McMahon, April 25, 1806 (p. 313); McMahon to Jefferson, April 30 and July 12, 1806, and January 17, 1809.

[45] Tree onion, *Allium cepa* var. *viviparum* Metz. The underground bulb is small and undeveloped, the bulbils being borne in flower-cluster, and used for propagation.

[46] See letter, Jefferson to Benjamin Smith Barton, October 6, 1810.

[47] *Rumex acetosa* L.

[48] *Solanum melongena* L.

[49] Probably *Benincasa hispida* Cogn.

[50] Probably a variety of *Cucurbita moschata* Duchesne.

[51] Malta, Scotch, and Delaware kales are different kinds of *Brassica oleracea* var. *acephala* DC.

[52] Probably the same pumpkin that is known today as the sweet potato pumpkin, *Cucurbita moschata* Duchesne.

[53] *Ravensworth* was the home of William Fitzhugh. It was about ten miles from Washington and hence a convenient first night stopping place for Jefferson on his trips to *Monticello* from Washington. These peas were, no doubt, given to Jefferson by Mr. Fitzhugh.

[54] Topinambour, another name for the Jerusalem artichoke, *Helianthus tuberosus* L.

[55] See letter, Jefferson to Benjamin S. Barton, October 6, 1810.

[56] TMR.   Thomas Mann Randolph.

[57] John H. Craven, who rented from Jefferson land adjoining *Monticello*.

## LETTERS, EXTRACTS OF LETTERS, AND MEMORANDA, 1809

(Jefferson to Edmund Bacon.)

Washington Jan. 3. 09.

My letter by Davy would lead you into an error as to the day of his departure, as I dated it Dec. 30. instead of 31. by mistake. if it is now as cold with you as it is here I am in hopes you will be able & ready to fill the ice house. it would be a real calamity should we not have ice to do it, as it would require double the quantity of fresh meat in summer had we not ice to keep it. I had really forgotten the article of flax, which is quite as necessary as cotton. but I am so much a stranger to the quantity an acre will bring, that I must leave it to you to fix. you know how much brown linen it will take to clothe all the people. . . . (*Jefferson Papers*, Huntington.)

(Bernard McMahon to Jefferson.)

Philadelphia Jan^y 3^rd. 1809.

With many thanks and obligations, I acknowledge the receipt of your kind letter of the 28^th. ult°. and also, the very valuable collection of seeds you were pleased to send me per favour of Cap^t Jones; and I hope the confidence you reposed in me on this, as well as on several other similar occasions, will not be disappointed.

I have pleasure and pride in the successful cultivation of plants; but in proportion to the actual or probable good I can render thereby to my fellow-men; and indeed I do not begrudge a share to such of the brute animals as can possibly be benefitted thereby.

Last month I purchased in the vicinity of this City 20 Acres of ground, well adapted for a Nursery & Botanic Garden, and hope that, in a few years, I shall enrich that spot, and through it, in some measure, the country in general, with as extensive and useful a collection of vegetable productions, as can reasonably be expected from the small means of which I am possessed; but perseverance and industry, even with trifling pecuniary resources, having so frequently surmounted what were considered great difficulties, leave me room to hope; therefore I do not despair. . . .

P. S.    M^r. Michaux informed me that there is a very large fruited kind of Hickory growing in Glocester County, V^a. which he takes to be a non described *species,* and at the same time M^r. Hamilton, of the Woodlands, shewed us some plants, which he said were produced from nuts, which you were so good as to send him, & as I wish for all the species of Juglans of the United States, that I can possibly procure, you would greatly oblige me by putting me in the way of obtaining some of the Glocester Nuts.    I have from time to time given M^r. Hamilton a great variety of plants, and altho' he is in every other respect a particular friend of mine, he never offered me one in return; and I did not think it prudent to ask him, lest it should terminate that friendship; as I well know his jealousy of any person's attempt to vie with him, in a collection of plants.    (*Jefferson Papers,* L. C.)

## (Jefferson to Bernard McMahon.)

Washington Jan. 8. 09.

The Gloucester hiccory nut, after which you enquire, has I think, formerly spread extensively over this continent from East to West, between the latitudes of 36°. & 38°. but only in the richest bottom lands on the river sides.    those lands being now almost entirely cleared, I know of no remains of these nuts but a very few trees specially preserved in Gloucester, and some on the Roanoke.    in Kentucky there are still a great many & West of the Missisipi it is, I believe, their only nut of the Juglans family.    the Osages brought me a parcel from their country which I distributed among the members of Congress & planted some myself.    having sent away my books, I have not Gronovius's (or rather Clayton's) Flora Virginica to turn to.    but he certainly must have described it, as he lived in Gloucester, & I know that it grew in his neighborhood.    a gentleman here happening to have two of these nuts lately brought from Kentucky, I have procured & now send them to you.    I have taken measures to have some sent me by post from Roanoke, and shall immediately write to Gloucester for some.    these may arrive in time to be planted. . . . (*Jefferson Papers,* L. C.)

(Bernard McMahon to Jefferson.)

Philadelphia Jan<sup>y</sup>. 17<sup>th</sup>. 1809.

I duly received the Gloucester nuts, and am extremely obliged to you for them; the more so as I have for two or three years past paid particular attention to the Juglans family, and have not been able to make out, to my satisfaction, more than 7 United States species, viz:

1. Juglans nigra, Lin.

2. Juglans cinerea Lin.
   oblonga Du Roi & Mill.
   cathartica, Michaux Jun<sup>r</sup>.

3. Juglans olivaformis Mich.
   pecan, Marsh. & Muhl.
   cylindrica Link

4. Juglans sulcata Willd.
   Mucronata Mich.
   amara, Muhl. & Mich j<sup>r</sup>
   alba minima, Marsh.

5. Juglans alba, Mich, nec Lin.
   alba ovata. Marsh.
   squamosa. Mich, j<sup>r</sup>.

6. Juglans tomentosa. Mich.
   alba Lin. & Gaertner

7. Juglans compressa. Gaert.
   alba odorata, Marsh.
   porcina, Mich. J<sup>r</sup>.

With the 7<sup>th</sup>. species, Willdenow has confounded the 5<sup>th</sup>. or alba of Michaux, our true Shell-bark; but I am inclined to believe that the J. glabra & J. obcordata, of Willdenow's edition of the Sp. Plan are but mere varieties of the above 7<sup>th</sup>. or compressa. I have seen and examined the trees of M<sup>r</sup>. Hamilton's from which these two species are said to have been made, by Doctor Muhlenberg, (the obcordata of Muhl. & Willd. M<sup>r</sup>. Hamilton calls ficiformis) but I really can find no difference, between either, & the compressa; except a trifling difference in the shape of the pericarpium, which is not at all uncommon in every species of the genus.

If the Glocester nut belongs to any of the above species, it must be to the 6<sup>th</sup>. the alba of Lin. & tomentosa of Mich. The latter name I would prefer, on account of its being descriptive. The alba of Mich. I never saw with more than five leaflets; consequently it cannot or ought not to be given as a synonym to compressa, which Willdenow describes, "J. foliolis septenis, &c." and which is just.

I wish to know if the Tarragon roots I sent you have succeeded as I can send you a supply in *due time* this season if they failed.

I am very anxious to learn when Governor Lewis may be expected here, as I have detained a man in my house upwards of twelve months, drawing & describing his plants, which he left with me for that purpose; this was accomplished in May last, as far as it could be done in the absence of Gov^r Lewis, and he told me on his leaving this City he expected to be here again in that month.   This man, who is completely adequate to the task, is becoming very uneasy, and I wish him not to leave the neighborhood till the arrival of M^r. Lewis, by whose particular instructions only, he can finish the drawings of some very important, but imperfect specimens. . . . (*Jefferson Papers,* L. C.)

### (Jefferson to Thomas Lomax.)

Washington Jan. 19. '09.

. . . I thank you for the plant of Acacia you have been so kind as to deliver m̅r̅s̅ Bankhead for me.   this is the only plant besides the Orange that I would take the trouble of nursing in a green house.   I rely on the garden & farm for a great portion of the enjoyment I promise myself in retirement. . . . (*Jefferson Papers,* L. C.)

### (Jefferson to Charles L. Bankhead.)

Washington, Jan. 19, 09.

I have waited till I could execute Anne's commission as to the seed of the ice-plant, before acknoleging the receipt of her letter of Dec. 19 and your's of the 20^th.   I now inclose the seed, in the envelope of a pamphlet for Doct^r. Bankhead's acceptance. . . . Mr. Lomax writes me he has given Anne a small plant of the Acacia for me, with which I hope I shall meet you both at Monticello in March. . . . (*Jefferson Papers,* M. H. C. 1: 132–133.)

### (General John Mason to Jefferson.)

Analoston Island Jan. 22, 1809.

. . . J. Mason presents his respects to the President, and with very great pleasure sends him the garden seeds asked in his note of the other day, in addition to which he begs his acceptance of a few of the *Buda-Kale*—an excellent kind of Cantaleup—Spanish tomato (very much larger than the common kinds)—and Estragon, from the plant the President was so good as to send J. M. a year or two ago, which has flourished well in the open air—and will in Spring afford plenty of slips—Should he find those convenient of carriage.
This Kale is a new vegetable lately introduced from Germany, it has been cultivated here for the last 3 years and found an acquisition particularly that it passes the winter without protection & is the first thing growing in spring, when it is a very early & grateful green boild as sprouts—it is said to be valuable for stock and particularly sheep in winter.

These seeds are all of J. M. own sowing and may be depended on.

That they may succeed at Monticello & furnish abundant crops—and that you Sir may live many years to enjoy your garden & your fields, in sweet repose from your long and inestimable labours will be the increasing prayer. . . . (*Jefferson Papers*, M. H. S.)

### (Williamson & Cowling to Jefferson.)

Savannah January 25th. 1809.

At the request of our friend the Honble John Milledge, we have shipped to your address, to the care of Messr. Fall & Brown Merchants, in Baltimore, Two tierces containing each ten Bushels Cotton Seed— the one of Green Seed, the other of the Sea Island black seed, which we hope will get Speedily & Safely to hand and, upon trial, equal your expectations.

The said seed is shipped on board the Schooner Mary Capt. Almeda, which vessel left this Port for Baltimore yesterday forenoon. . . . (*Jefferson Papers*, L. C.)    (See also letter, Jefferson to John Hollins, February 19, 1809.)

### (Jefferson to General John Mason.)

Jan. 26. 09.

Th: Jefferson has received the seeds which General Mason has been so kind as to send him, and returns him many thanks for them.    they will be a valuable acquisition to him.    he is very sensible of the kind sentiments expressed in his note and assures him he reciprocates them sincerely to mrs Mason & himself, and that at whatever distance withdrawn from them, the information of their welfare will always give him great pleasure.    should any circumstances ever draw them towards his part of the country it will give him real happiness to receive them at Monticello. . . . (*Jefferson Papers*, M. H. S.)

### (Ellen Randolph to Jefferson.)

Jan. 26 1809

. . . Although I have not much to say, unless I talk about plants; those in the large box were killed to the roots, but they are coming up all over the box, those in the small pot were killed also but are putting out small fresh buds, the evergreens have lost all their leaves, but one little branch on each which look lively enough.    The sweet scented grass looks very badly although Mama separated the roots and planted them with great care in a box of fine rich mould and the season in which it was done was warm and rainy. . . . (*Jefferson Papers*, M. H. S.)

### (Jefferson to Bernard McMahon.)

Washington Jan. 27. 09.

I received last night from my friend in Gloucester an answer to my letter requesting some Gloucester hiccory nuts.    he informs me that the few which are saved are generally consumed early in the season and that accident only has enabled him to send me 4. nuts, which are from the genuine trees. I now forward them to you, and expect soon to receive a better supply from Roanoke. by comparing the nuts now sent, with those sent before which were from Kentucky, you will be able to judge whether there is any difference. . . . (*Jefferson Papers,* L. C.)

### (Jefferson to Thomas Mann Randolph.)

Washington, Jan. 31, 09.

I received in due time your kind letter of the 20th. Certainly I shall be much pleased to receive your aid & councel in the management of my farms, which will become so essential. My whole life has been past in occupations which kept me from any minute attention to them, and finds me now with only very general ideas of the theory of agriculture, without actual experience; at a time of life too when the memory is not so retentive of observation as at an earlier period. The tracts of land which I propose to you to endeavor to sell are such as can be of little use to our family. I have acquired or kept them to furnish timber, but I am certain I never got an half per cent on their value in a year yet. A property yielding so little profit had better be sold and converted into more profitable form, and none can be more profitable, that is, yield so much happiness, as the paiment of debts, which are an unsufferable torment. Sharp and Crenshaw, who live near Pouncey's, told me they would rather undertake to crop on that land than on the best red land you or myself possessed. If you could find a purchaser, therefore, it might be at a price that might remove some more pressing calls. Perhaps the owner of Colle would buy the tract adjoining that. They can never be put to a better use, or one so pleasing to me, as in relieving your more valuable property from calls, and whether they go to pay your debts or mine is perfectly equal to me, as I consider our property as a common stock for our joint family. . . . (*Jefferson Papers,* M. H. C. 1: 134.)

### (Jefferson to Charles Willson Peale.)

Washington Feb. 6. 1809.

. . . I begin already to be much occupied in preparation for my departure to those scenes of rural retirement after which my soul is panting. . . . (*Jefferson Papers,* L. C.)

### (Jefferson to Ellen Randolph.)

Washington Feb. 6. 09.

[Jefferson's answer to Ellen's letter of January 26.]

Plants in pot & box:

*Savory*—a dead plant, it's leaves very aromatic. a little resembling thyme my dependance is that it's seed are shed on the earth in the box & will come up *arbor vitae*—a small evergreen tree, in a small pot.

*Ice-Plant*—a plant of some size. the leaves mostly dead.  I expect the seed is shattered & will come up.

*Geranium*—I think there was a plant of this but am not certain.

besides the above there was a box containing many sods of Sweet-scented grass packed one on another, & in the same box a bunch of monthly raspberry plants, which box Davy was directed to carry to Monticello.  (*Jefferson Papers,* M. H. S.)

### (Jefferson to Bernard McMahon.)

Washington Feb. 8. 09.

I have been daily expecting some of the large hiccory nuts from Roanoke which would possess you of what I believe is the same species from Gloucester, Kentucky & Roanoke.  but they are not yet arrived. I must now ask the favor of you to furnish me with the articles below mentioned for the garden, which will occupy much of my attention when at home.  I would wish the roots etc. to be so packed up as that they need not be opened till they get to Monticello.  if you will be so good as to send them by the Stage which leaves Philadelphia on the 1st. of March, addressed to me at this place, they will come in time for me to carry on to Monticello.  I will ask the favor of the bill at the same time, the amount of which shall be immediately remitted you. . . .

Chili strawberry
Hudson strawberry
some of the fine gooseberry plants of which you sent me the fruit last
    year.
some roots of Crown imperials
                lilium convallarium
Auricula
Sea kale, or Crambe maritima
1. gall^n. of Leadman's dwarf peas mentioned in your book page 310.

(*Jefferson Papers,* L. C.)

### (Jefferson to John Diffenderffer.)

Washington Feb. 10. 1809.

I have seen in a Baltimore paper an advertisement from you of Spring rye for sale.  I did not know that this grain was to be had in America, and am anxious to get a little for seed.  I enclose you a paper dollar, the only small remittance I can make in a letter and will pray you to do up a parcel in a bit of linen securely, of that value, and addressing it to me, send it by the stage, for which I will thank you.  (*Jefferson Papers,* M. H. S.)

### (Bernard McMahon to Jefferson.)

Philadelphia Feb^y. 13^th. 1809

I received your favour of the 8^th. ins^t. and such of the articles ordered as I have, or can procure, shall be forwarded in due time, provided the weather, in the interim, will admit of taking up the plants. The Chile Strawberry is not, to my knowledge, to be procured in this part of the Union; but that called the Hudson I think I can get. The Crown Imperial roots, as well as all my hardy bulbs, I planted in the fall, and taking them up before their bloom and subsequent decay of foliage, would ruin them. In July or August I can furnish you with a great variety.

The peas, sea-kale seed (for plants I have none) with some good ornamental flower seeds, I will send in good time, and the others if possible, but you will oblige me by letting me know, through what channel I can send you any articles after the 4$^{th}$. of March.

The nuts from Gloucester which you were so good as to send me, do not appear, as far as I can judge from the nut only, to be of the same species with the two you sent me of the Kentucky kind. I have planted them and will attend to the progress of their vegetation. I wish I could procure a few good specimens from the Gloucester trees *when in flower,* for the nuts of them appear to me to be very different from any I have yet seen. Does this species belong to the Walnut division, or is it a true Hickory?

I have taken the liberty of enquiring of you, in a letter sent by my friend Doctor Lieb, when Governor Lewis might be expected here; and for the reasons therein mentioned, I am anxious for the information. . . .
(*Jefferson Papers,* L. C.)

## (Jefferson to John Hollins.)

Washington, February 19, 1809.

A little transaction of mine, as innocent a one as I ever entered into, and where an improper construction was never less expected, is making some noise, I observe, in your city. I beg leave to explain it to you, because I mean to ask your agency in it. The last year, the Agricultural Society of Paris, of which I am a member, having had a plough presented to them, which, on trial with a graduated instrument, did equal work with half the force of their best ploughs, they thought it would be a benefit to mankind to communicate it. They accordingly sent one to me, with a view to its being made known here, and they sent one to the Duke of Bedford also, who is one of their members, to be made use of in England, although the two nations were then at war. By the Mentor, now going to France, I have given permission to two individuals in Delaware and New York, to import two parcels of Merino sheep from France, which they have procured there, and to some gentlemen in Boston, to import a very valuable machine which spins cotton, wool, and flax equally. The last spring, the Society informed me they were culti-vating cotton of the Levant and other parts of the Mediterranean, and wished to try also that of our southern States. I immediately got a friend to have two tierces of seed forwarded to me. They were consigned to Messrs. Falls and Brown of Baltimore, and notice of it being given me, I immediately wrote to them to re-ship them to New York, to be sent by the Mentor. Their first object was to make a show of my letter, as something very criminal, and to carry the subject into the news-papers. I had, on a like request, some time ago, (but before the em-bargo,) from the President of the Board of Agriculture of London, of which I am also a member, to send them some of the genuine May wheat of Virginia, forwarded to them two or three barrels of it. General Washington, in his time, received from the same Society the seed of the perennial succory, which Arthur Young had carried over from France to England, and I have since received from a member of it the seed of the famous turnip of Sweden, now so well known here. I mention these things, to show the nature of the correspondence which is carried on be-tween societies instituted for the benevolent purpose of communicating to all parts of the world whatever useful is discovered by any one of them. These societies are always in peace, however their nations may be at war. Like the republic of letters, they form a great fraternity spreading over the whole earth, and their correspondence is never inter-rupted by any civilized nation. Vaccination has been a late and remark-able instance of the liberal diffusion of a blessing newly discovered. It is really painful, it is mortifying, to be obliged to note these things, which are known to every one who knows anything, and felt with ap-probation by every one who has any feeling. But we have a faction, to whose hostile passions the torture even of right into wrong is a delicious gratification. Their malice I have long learned to disregard, their censure to deem praise. But I observe that some republicans are not satisfied (even when we are receiving liberally from others) that this small return should be made. They will think more justly at another day; but, in the meantime, I wish to avoid offence. My prayer to you, therefore, is, that you will be so good, under the enclosed order, as to receive these two tierces of seed from Falls and Brown, and pay them their disbursements for freight, etc., which I will immediately remit you on knowing the amount. Of the seed, when received, be so good as to make manure for your garden. When rotted with a due amount of stable manure or earth, it is the best in the world. I rely on your friendship to excuse this trouble, it being necessary I should not commit myself again to persons of whose honor, or the want of it, I know nothing.

Accept the assurances of my constant esteem and respect. (Lipscomb and Bergh, *Jefferson* 12: 252–254.) (See also letter, Williamson & Cowling to Jefferson, January 25, 1809.)

(Jefferson to Dr. James W. Wallace.)

Washington Feb. 28. 09.

You were so kind as to procure for me a pair of wild geese & a pair of Summer ducks, & to say you could give me some plants, to wit Balsam Poplar tree, Sunbriar, mammoth apple etc. . . . (*Jefferson Papers*, L. C.)

(Bernard McMahon to Jefferson.)

Philadelphia Feb^y. 28^th. 1809

I have the pleasure of sending you by the mail stage a collection of Flower seeds, some Early York & Sugarleaf Cabbage, red Celery, Long French Turnep (Navet de Freneuse) so much and I think so justly admired, for its flavour, in France; together with 8 Quarts of Leadman's Dwarf peas; they are contained in a small box addressed to you, and will reach you at the same time of this letter.

Price of the 8 Quarts peas .......................... $4.00
Paid freight at the Stage office ....................... .50
                                                        _____
                                                        $4.50

Our ground being yet covered with snow and bound by the frost, renders it impossible to get the Strawberry or Gooseberry plants up; but, as soon as possible, I shall send them, addressed to any place and person that you will please to point out to me.   I herewith enclose you one of my catalogues, and shall be happy to supply you with any articles therein mentioned, and in my power to furnish at the time. . . . (*Jefferson Papers,* L. C.)

(Jefferson to Baron Alexander von Humboldt.)

Washington, March 6, 1809.

. . . You have wisely located yourself in the focus of the science of Europe.   I am held by the cords of love to my family and country, or I should certainly join you.   Within a few days I shall bury myself in the groves of Monticello, and become a mere spectator of the passing events. . . . (Lipscomb and Bergh, *Jefferson* 12: 263.)

(Mr. Threlkeld to Jefferson.)

Wednesday Mar. 8, 1809.

Mr. Threlkeld sends Mr. Jefferson three English mulberrys, an American ones, & five Peach apricots he recommends great attention to be paid by the waggoner to them as the shoots are but small in some, & may tear off. . . . (*Jefferson Papers,* M. H. S.)

(Jefferson to George Jefferson.)

Monticello Mar. 25. 09.

. . . We are entirely unable to get cotton seed in this part of the country.   m͞r Bacon at my request wrote to you for some.   if you have or can procure it, it will be rendering me a great service. . . . (*Jefferson Papers,* M. H. S.)

### (Philip Tabb to Jefferson.)

Toddsburg 7th April 1809

Having just learnt from Captn Decatur who delivered a mole board I did myself the pleasure to send to you at Washington, that you had not received my letter pr post which left Gloster Ct. House about the 20th of Jany last—& which I expect was destroyed by a villainous rider who we now know was in the habit of robing the mail about that time, I trouble you with the copy, not willing that the appearance of neglect should pertain to one who will always feel himself honored by an oppy of rendering you any services in his power. . . .

### (Copy of the letter of January.)

I am sorry it is not in my power to send you as many of the large hickory nuts of this country as you wished to plant, very few of the best trees are now left & they produced less than usual the last year & were soon consumed five only were left by accident which I now forward. I have not been altogether inattentive to those nuts since apart of the lands producing them have been in my possession—I have planted some of the largest and best which are growing vigorously & I have little doubt but the trees raised properly from the nut will be more productive than those which grow in the woods, for on clearing the lands & exposing them suddenly after the tree has matured they become sickly & unproductive—

Having succeeded in getting moleboards cast in Pensylvania agreeable to a pattern which I shewed Mrs. (?) Thomas M. Randolph at Richmond sometimes since (& where the manager of the furnace failed in the attempt) I do myself the pleasure to present one of them to you, & have requested one of my sons who resides in Norfolk to forward it to Washington, they operate hansomely in our lands, much superior to any thing I have seen, after the board gets smooth but it requires some attention to get of the rough scale on the operating part of the board. . . . (*Jefferson Papers,* Missouri Historical Society.)

### (George Divers to Jefferson.)

Farmington Apr. 22, 1809.

I send you some parsnep seed which I think had better be sow'd pretty thick, they do not look very well and can easily be thin'ed if they come up better than I expect. I sow 200 feet each of parsnip and beet. 320 feet each salsafy and carrots and 400 feet cellery, all running measure in the rows, which is a very ample provision for my table and indeed more than sufficient. The small seed should be sown in drills 18 inches apart in the row. I send you a few of the early black eyed pea which you brought from France and can furnish you with some of the cow pea, and a large gray pea of the *Crouder kind,* which think very good one for the table, but fear I shall not be able to supply you with seed

potatoes they having been few away to my sheep nearer than I intended.
. . . (*Jefferson Papers*, M. H. S.)

### (Jefferson to Étienne Le Maire.)

Monticello Apr. 25. 09.

. . . my birds arrived here in safety, & are the delight of every hour.
. . . I am constantly in my garden or farms, as exclusively employed
out of doors as I was within doors when at Washington, and I find
myself infinitely happier in my new mode of life. . . . (*Jefferson Papers*,
M. H. S.)

### (Jefferson to James Madison.)

Monticello, April 27, 1809.

. . . Our spring continues cold and backward, rarely one growing
day without two or three cold ones following.   Wheat is of very various
complexions from very good to very bad.   Fruit has not suffered as much
as was expected, except in peculiar situations.   Gardens are nearly a
month behind their usual state.   I thank you for the squashes from
Maine; they shall be planted today. . . . (Lipscomb and Bergh, *Jefferson* 12: 277.)

### (Jefferson to Jefferson Randolph.)

Monticello May 6, '09.

. . . in what you say respecting the preservation of plants I suppose
you allude to mr Crowninshield's speciments which I showed you, but
I could not have promised to give you his method because I did not
know it myself.   all I know was from Genl. Dearborne, who told me
that mr Crowninshield's method was, by extreme pressure (with a
screw or weight) on the substance of the plants, but that he could never
make it adhere to the paper until he used garlick juice either alone or in
composition with something else. . . . I must also pray you to get for
me a gross of vial-corks of different sizes, & 4 dozen phials of 1. 2. 3 & 4
ounces, one dozen of each size.   The largest mouthed would be the best
as they are for holding garden seeds. . . . (*Jefferson Papers*, M. H. S.)

### (Jefferson to William Hamilton.)

Monticello May 7, 09.

. . . I have pressed upon him also [Jefferson Randolph] to study well
the style of your pleasure grounds, as the chastest model of gardening
which I have ever seen out of England. . . . I am the more tempted to
recommend them [Warm Springs for gout] to you, as it would lead you
near this place where I should be very happy to see you & to take from
you some of those lessons for the improvement of my grounds which
you have so happily practiced on your own. . . . (*Jefferson Papers*,
M. H. S.)

(Jefferson to Horatio G. Spafford.)

Monticello, May 14, 1809.

. . . In page 186 [General Geography, by Spafford,] you say the potato is a native of the United States. I presume you speak of the Irish potato. I have inquired much into the question, and think I can assure you that plant is not a native of North America. Zimmerman, in his "Geographical Zoology", says it is a native of Guiana; and Clavigero, that the Mexicans got it from South America, *its native country*. The most probable account I have been able to collect is, that a vessel of Sir Walter Raleigh's, returning from Guiana, put into the west of Ireland in distress, having on board some potatoes which they called earth-apples. That the season of the year, and circumstance of their being already sprouted, induced them to give them all out there, and they were no more heard or thought of, till they had been spread considerably into that island, whence they were carried over into England, and therefore called the Irish potato. From England they came to the United States, bringing their name with them. . . . I shall be happy to see you at Monticello, should you come this way as you propose. You will find me engaged entirely in rural occupations, looking into the field of science but occasionally and at vacant moments.

I sowed some of the Benni seed the last year, and distributed some among my neighbors; but the whole was killed by the September frost. I got a little again the last winter, but it was sowed before I received your letter. Colonel Few of New York receives quantities of it from Georgia, from whom you may probably get some through the Mayor of New York. But I little expect that it can succeed with you. It is about as hardy as the cotton plant, from which you may judge of the probability of raising it at Hudson. . . . (Lipscomb and Bergh, *Jefferson* 12: 278–282.)

(Jefferson to Philip Tabb.)

Monticello, June 1, '09.

Your favor of Apr. 7 has been duly received, with the copy of that of January. on reading the first paragraph of it respecting the nuts, I was confident I had received it, as I had forwarded the nuts on to a friend in Philadelphia. on searching my letter bundles, I accordingly found that of Jánuary received on the 27th of that month. yet when Capt. Decatur sent me the mould board, the part of your letter respecting that had as entirely escaped me as if I had never seen it. indeed I had found on other occasions that for the immence mass of matter which I was in the way of receiving, the memory was quite an insufficient storehouse. I thank you for the mould board. its form promises well, & I have no doubt of its good performance. it resembles extremely one which I made about 20 years ago which has been much approved by the agricultural societies of England and France, the latter of which sent me a gold medal as a premium. The form as I observed is very much that of yours, with the advantage of being made by so easy a rule, that the coarsest negro workman can do it.    I cannot possibly make it a hair's breath different from the true form.    if I can find a conveyance, I will send you a small model with its block which will shew you at once how to make it.    A description of it may be found in Maese's edition of Reese's domestic encyclopedia.    in agriculture I am only an amateur, having only that knolege which may be got from books.    in the field I am entirely ignorant, & am now too old to learn.    Still it amuses my hours of exercise, & tempts to the taking due exercise. . . . (*Glimpses of the Past,* Missouri **3**: 108–109.)

(Jefferson to Wilson C. Nicholas.)

Monticello, June 13, 1809.

. . . We have been seasonable since you left us.    Yesterday evening and this morning we have had refreshing showers, which will close and confirm the business of planting. . . . (Lipscomb and Bergh, *Jefferson* **12**: 290–291.)

(Jefferson to Henry Dearborn.)

Monticello, June 14, 1809.

So entirely are my habits changed from constant labor at my writing table, to constant active occupation without doors, that it is with difficulty I can resolve to take up my pen. . . . (Lipscomb and Bergh, *Jefferson* **12**: 291.)

(Jefferson to James Madison.)

Monticello, June 16, 09.

. . . For the last three days we have had fine & plentiful showers of rain, & were willing they should cease as appearances promised last night, but it commenced raining in the night & now continues with the wind at northeast.    This may become dangerous to the wheat which at best can only be a middling crop.    That of tobacco cannot become great if the observation of the planters is correct that there never was a great crop of tobacco which was not patched before the last of May.    This year not a plant was in the ground till June: but the rains have been so favorable since that the whole crop is now standing & growing. . . . (Ford, *Jefferson* **11**: 113–114.)

(Jefferson to Samuel H. Smith.)

Monticello Aug. 3. 1809.

[After expressing the hope that Mr. and Mrs. Smith would visit him again, Jefferson wrote:] and that I may be able to shew m͞rs Smith who is fond of gardening, the progress I shall have made the next year in the improvement of the grounds around me, as well those of pleasure as utility. . . . (*Jefferson Papers,* L. C.)

(Jefferson to Mess<sup>rs</sup>. Jones & Howell.)

Monticello Aug. 10. 09.

It is with real mortification that, instead of a remittance for the last supply of rod & iron, now due, I am obliged to send you this letter.  yet my feelings on the failure will not permit me to be merely silent.  I have now been for 13. or 14. years a customer of your house & of it's predecessors, and have never failed beyond a few days over the term of remittance, except on one occasion, I believe, where it had escaped attention.  my income is mainly from the produce or the rents of tobacco & wheat farms.  knowing that this came in but once a year, and owning a mill rented at 1200. D. a year, I reserved, when I leased it, quarterly paiments of the rent with the single view of meeting therewith your quarterly supplies of rod.  I had not pressed my tenant for two years past, not then wanting the money; but did so when I desired your last supply.  he made me fair promises, which I did not expect he would fail in, till within these few days.  he still renews his promises, but I cannot be certain that they are better than those he has broken.  we have no banks here to relieve disappointments, & little money circulation. all is barter.  my nails have never commanded money.  even the merchants, if cash were demanded, would prefer importing them, because they would then make paiment by remittances of produce.  under these circumstances I am obliged to throw myself on your indulgence, with the assurance it shall never be wilfully abused.  I am endeavoring to get rid of my present mill-tenant, in order to place that under arrangements which may ensure my paiments to you.  I have no other resource but agriculture, & that can supply deficiencies but once a year.  you must be so good as to indemnify yourselves by charging interest whenever I fail, for this may not be the only instance under present circumstances. formerly while I had this business under my own direction, it was very profitable, in as much as it employed boys, not otherwise useful.  during my absence it has not been so, but has been continued merely to preserve the custom.  I think to try it for a year or two, in my own hands, & if I find it is become unprofitable from causes which cannot be remedied I shall abandon it. . . . (*Jefferson Papers*, M. H. S.)

(Jefferson to J. Vaughan.)

Monticello Aug. 31. 09.

. . . P. S.  Can you inform me whether the instrument called the Distiller's syphon is to be had in Philadelphia, and what one sufficient to work in a cistern [Jefferson was then building his four cisterns] of 8. feet cube would cost?  I believe they are usually made of tin. . . . (*Jefferson Papers*, M. H. S.)   (See appendix II.)

(Judge William Johnson to Jefferson.)

Charleston, Sept. 20, 1809.

Judge Johnson having heard Mr. Jefferson express his admiration of the *Popinaque*, avails himself of the opportunity of Mr. Mitchell's visit to Monticello to transmit one of the *Pods* of that delicate little *Acacia*. The seeds may be put in the ground immediately about an inch deep but possibly they may not sprout till spring. The tree blossoms so late and is so wholly inacapable of withstanding the Frost that it is very seldom we are able to procure the seed. In the same packet, Mr. Jefferson will find a few seeds of the Grass which in Georgia is called Egyptian & the Benné. . . . (*Jefferson Papers*, L. C.)

(Jefferson to Robert Quarles.)

Monticello Oct. 4. '09.

. . . My mill has been established 52 years and although carried away in the meantime, & very long in the rebuilding, yet the right was always kept up by constant renewals of the order of courts. . . . (*Jefferson Papers*, M. H. S.)

(Jefferson to General John Smith.)

Monticello, Oct. 6, '09.

I am desirous of sowing largely the next spring a kind of grass called Tall Meadow oat, or Oat-grass, and sometimes, erroneously Peruvian grass, which I am told is much cultivated about Winchester, but cannot be had here. I have flatered myself I would so far make free with your friendship as to ask you to procure for me about a couple of bushels to be put into a tight barrel & forwarded to Staunton to the care of Judge Stewart. . . . I wish it to be of this year's seed, as I found it would not come up the second year, on a trial of some procured for me by Mr. Nourse which arrived too late in the first spring to be sowed. . . . if you have cultivated it, I should thank you for any instructions your experience may enable you to give, as to the soils it will delight in, or do in, the sowing & the care of it, the produce etc. for I am much a stranger to it. . . . (*Jefferson Papers*, Missouri Historical Society.)

(Jefferson to John Adlum.)

Monticello Oct. 7. 09.

. . . I think it would be well to push the culture of that grape [Fox Grape], without losing our time & efforts in search of foreign vines, which it will take centuries to adapt to our soil & climate. the object of the present letter is so far to trespass on your kindness, & your disposition to promote a culture so useful, as to request you at the proper season to send some cuttings of that vine. they should be taken off in February, with 5 buds to each cutting, and if done up first in strong linen & then covered with paper & addressed to me at Monticello near Milton, and committed to the post, they will come safely & so speedily as to render their success probable. Praying your pardon to a brother-amateur in these things. . . . (*Jefferson Papers*, L. C.)

(Jefferson to Governor John Milledge.)

Monticello Oct. 10. 1809

I have received from M. Thouin, Director of the National garden of France, a collection of many different species of rice. whether any of them possess, any properties which might render them preferable to those we possess, either generally or under particular circumstances of soil or climate I know not. but the scripture precept of 'prove all things & hold fast that which is good' is peculiarly wise in objects of agriculture. (*Jefferson Papers*, L. C.)

(Jefferson to Benjamin H. Latrobe.)

Monticello Oct. 10. 09.

. . . Your promised visit to Monticello, whenever it can be effected, will give me real pleasure, and I think could not fail of giving some to you. my essay in Architecture [house at *Monticello*] has been so much subordinated to the law of convenience, & affected also by the circumstance of change in the original design, that it is liable to some unfavorable & just criticisms. but what nature has done for us is sublime & beautiful and unique. . . . (*Jefferson Papers*, L. C.)

(Jefferson to William Thornton.)

Monticello Oct. 11. 1809.

. . . The tarragon you were so kind as to send me is now growing with the former bunch, but so extraordinary has been our drought that no efforts could save the figs. I think, in the spring, I must ask a few very small plants or cuttings to be done up in strong paper & addressed to me by post. I will take some occasion of sending you some cuttings of the Marseilles fig, which I brought from France with me, & is incomparably superior to any fig I have ever seen. (*Jefferson Papers*, L. C.)

(Thomas Lomax to Jefferson.)

Port Tobaco, Oct. 30ᵗʰ 1809.

By the carriage, which I now send up for my Daughter, you will receive some filbert cions, and Nuts, as well as the Juboli, and Acacia the latter I have been obliged to lay in a flat Box, as the weight of those, out of which they were taken, I was afraid would be too heavy, and dangerous to be put into the Carriage. They will I hope reach you in safety, to be placed in other Boxes. The Nuts, if you chuse to plant any of them, it ought to be done immediately; but I am doubtful whether they will Vegitate; as I always after they are put into Bags, expose them very much to the heat of the Sun; but you can try them, and should they come up in the Spring, they should, as well as the young trees, be watered whenever the weather becomes dry. The trees I think you had better set at 20 feet asunder; as mine are only fifteen, which I discover to be too near each other. I have also sent some of the Star-Jasmine, and a beautiful flowering shrub which I took from the Woods, and not knowing its real name, have given it that, of modesty, from its handsome delicate appearance, a quality which will disgrace no Garden. If you have any of the Paccan nut that you can conveniently spare, I will thank you for some by the return of the Carriage; as I expect they can now be moved with safety. . . . T. L. requests some of Mr. Jefferson's fine Lima-Beans, if he has any to spare. The Silk-Tree is very flourishing. There is an Orange and Lime Tree sent, the Orange has the broadest Leaf. (Ford, *Jefferson Correspondence:* 186–187.)

## (Jefferson to Thomas Lomax.)

Monticello, Nov. 6, '09.

Your carriage arrived here last night only, having been detained some days at Edgehill by the late rains and consequent rise of the river. all the donations which you have been so kind as to charge on it have arrived in perfect order, and being to set out tomorrow for Bedford, this day will be employed in setting out the plants. by the return of the carriage I shall send you three or four Paccans and some Lima beans. I propose to make me a large orchard of Paccan and Roanoke and Missouri scaly barks which I possess, and of Gloucester and common scaly barks of which I shall plant the nuts. to these I shall add the sugar maple if I can procure it. I do not see why we may not have our sugar orchards as well as our cyder orchards. . . . (Ford, *Jefferson Correspondence:* 190.)

## (Jefferson to Judge William Fleming.)

Monticello Nov. 28. '09.

I have received safely the extraordinary rattle of the rattle snake, as also the foliage of the Alleghany Martagon. a plant of so much beauty & fragrance will be a valuable addition to our flower gardens. should you find your roots of it I shall be very thankful to participate of them, & will carefully return you a new stock should my part succeed & yours fail. (*Jefferson Papers,* M. H. S.)

## (Bernard McMahon to Jefferson.)

Philadelphia Dec^r. 24^th. 1809

With many thanks I acknowledge the receipt of the fine collection of seeds you were pleased to send me some time ago, and would have done this much sooner, were I not in daily expectation of receiving from London a variety of esculent vegetable seeds, that I wished to send you some of, at the same time. Having received them by the Ship Coramandal which arrived here a few days ago, I do myself the pleasure of sending you by the same mail that conveys this letter, some early cabbage &

cauliflower seeds &c, and shall send you by subsequent mails several other seeds for your spring sowing.

I am extremely sorry for the death of that worthy and valuable man Gov$^r$. Lewis, and the more so, for the manner of it. I have, I believe, all his collection of dried specimens of plants, procured during his journey to the pacific ocean, and several kinds of *new* living plants, which I raised from the seeds of his collecting, which you and himself were pleased to give me. In consequence of a hint, to that effect, given me by Gov$^r$. Lewis on his leaving this City, I never yet parted with any of his plants raised from his seeds, nor with a single seed the produce of either of them, for fear they should make their way into the hands of any Botanist, either in America, or Europe, who might rob M$^r$. Lewis of the right he had to first describe and name his own discoveries, in his intended publication; and indeed I had strong reasons to believe that this opportunity was coveted by ————————— which made me still more careful of his plants.

On Governor Lewis's departure from here, for the seat of his Government, he requested me to employ M$^r$. Frederick Pursh, on his return from a collecting excursion he was then about to undertake for Doctor Barton to describe and make drawings of such of his collection as would appear to be new plants, and that himself would return to Philadelphia in the month of May following. About the first of the ensuing Nov$^r$. M$^r$. Pursh returned, took up his abode with me, began the work, progressed as far as he could without further explanation, in some cases, from M$^r$. Lewis, and was detained by me, in expectation of M$^r$. Lewis's arrival at my expense, without the least expectation of any future remuneration, from that time till April last; when not having received any reply to several letters I had written from time to time, to Gov$^r$. Lewis on the subject, nor being able to obtain any information when he probably might be expected here; I thought it a folly to keep Pursh longer idle, and recommended him as Gardener to Doctor Hosack of New York, with whom he has since lived.

The original specimens are all in my hands, but M$^r$. Pursh, had taken his drawings and descriptions with him, and will, no doubt, on the delivery of them expect a reasonable compensation for his trouble.

As it appears to me probable that you will interest yourself in having the discoveries of M$^r$. Lewis published, I think it a duty incumbent on me, to give you [illegible] preceding information, and to ask your advice as to the propriety of still keeping the living plants I have, from getting into other hands who would gladly describe and publish them without doing due honor to the memory and merit of the worthy discoverer. . . . (*Jefferson Papers, L. C.*)

## (Jefferson to Mrs. Anne (Randolph) Bankhead.)

Monticello, Dec. 29th, 1809.

Your mamma has given me a letter to inclose to you, but whether it contains any thing contraband I know not. Of that the responsibility must be on her; I therefore inclose it.    I suppose she gives you all the small news of the place—such as the race in writing between Virginia and Francis, that the wild geese are well after a flight of a mile and a half into the river, that the plants in the green-house prosper, etc., etc. *A propos* of plants, make a thousand acknowledgments to Mrs. Bankhead for the favor proposed of the Cape jessamine.    It will be cherished with all the possible attentions; and in return proffer her calycanthuses, pecans, silk-trees, Canada martagons, or anything else we have. . . . What is to become of our flowers?    I left them so entirely to yourself, that I never knew any thing about them, what they are, where they grow, what is to be done for them.    You must really make out a book of instructions for Ellen, who has fewer cares in her head than I have. Every thing shall be furnished on my part at her call. . . . (Randolph, *Jefferson:* 330–331.)

From the *Account Book 1809–1820:*

Feb.    1.    Theophilus Holt garden seeds 31.36.
Feb.    10.    inclosed to Baltimore for Spring rye 1. D.
               [see letter of Jefferson to John Diffenderffer, February 10.]
Mar.    31.    gave to Thos. J. Randolph 50. D. for his expenses to Philadelphia, out of which he is to pay 2. D. to J. Taggert whose bill is 72. D. and 6.50 to McMahon for seeds.
April    9.    paid for a plough 2. D.
Dec.    4.    Paid Price for 6 geese 2.50 (owe him for 12. muscovy ducks.)

# 1810

Mar. 17. — 20.   planted in the orchard as follows

a — 1.2 + 1.  
b. — 1.2 + 1  
c. — 1. + 1  
d. — 1.2  

} 10. Italian peaches from Mazzei. ante pa. 30. Maddelena. poppe de Venere. melon peaches & vaga loggia

d. 3.4.6.7.8. Nectarines from the Nursery.

g. 28.29.39. Peach Apricots  
38.42.43. Bordeaux Apricots  

} from Threlkeld.[2]

e. 27.31.32.35. 37.39.43.44.  
f. 29.41.43. . . .  

} fine soft peaches from T. Lomax.

d. — 3 . . . . . . . . . .  
f. 1.2.3.  
g. — 1.2.3. + 1.5.6.8.  
h. 27.30.33.35.38.43.  
i. 28.29.35.37.38.39. 40.41.42.  
j. 30.38.  
k. — 1.2. + 2.4.5.7.8. 9.14.18.19.21.26.30. 36.  
n. 9.   o.9   p.9 . . . . .  

} 46. select peaches from the Nursery.

General Arrangem[t]. of the Nursery

Terras. 1. almonds  
2. apples  
3. apricots  
4. cherries  
5. nuts  
6.  
7.  
} peaches  
8. pears  
9. plumbs  
10. etc  
} Miscellan[s].

i. — 2. + 2.3. Spitzenburg apple trees from m̄r Divers.[3]

New Nursery[4] Mar. 21.

420

1810.

Mar. 17.~20. planted in the orchard as follows

a.—1.2.   +1  ⎫
b.—1.2.   +1  ⎬ 10. Italian peaches from Mazzei. aisle pa. 30. Maddelena. poppede Venere melon peaches 4.
c.—1.    +1  ⎪ vaga loggia
d.—1.2.       ⎭                                          General arrangem.ᵗ of the nursery.

d. 3. 4. 6. 7. 8. Nectarines from the nursery.                    Terras. 1. almonds
g. 10. 29. 39. Peach apricots  } from Kirkfield.                         2. apples
   38. 42. 43. Bordeaux apricots                                         3. apricots
e. 27. 31. 32. 33. 37. 39. 43. 44 } fine soft peaches from T. Lomax      4. cherries
f. 29. 41. 43. . . . . .                                                 5. nuts
d.—3. . . . . . .                                                        6.⎫
f. 1. 23.                                                                7.⎬ peaches
g.—1.2.3.+ 1.5.6.8.                                                      8. pears
h.    27. 30. 33. 35. 38. 43.                                            9. plumbs
i.    28. 29. 33. 37. 38. 39. 40. 41. 42. } Abselect peaches from the nursery.
d.    30. 38.                                                           10.⎫ miscellan.ᵗ
k.—1.2.+ 2. 4. 5. 7. 8. 9. 14. 18. 19. 21. 26. 30. 36.                   &c.⎭
n. 9.  o. 9.  p. 9.
l. —2.+2.3. Spitzenburg apple trees from mr Divers.

New Nursery Mar. 21.
Terras. 1.ˢᵗ  1. to 8 feet. 52. hard shelled sweet almonds from Castle.
         2.    9. Spitzenburgs from mr Taylor. grafted
              13. Cauities & Red apples from Detroit. mr Taylor. grafted
              21. Spitzenburgs. cuttings from the 3 trees from mr Divers
              30. Newtown pippins. cuttings from my own trees. grafted
         3.ᵈ  70. Taliaferro apples. grafted from my own trees beginning them at E. end
         4.    1. to 5 f. planted. 21. Peach apricot stones, saved the last year from the tree f. 42. at W. end.
         5.ᵗʰ  1. to 11 f. planted 151. fellow nuts from T. Lomax.
         6.ᵗʰ  1. to 17 f. 18. soft peach trees from T. Lomax.  ⎫ 14. cuttings of the Magdalen peach. soft. grafted. Taylor
              18. to 20 f. 11. november soft peach stones.        ⎬ 5.
              20. to 21 f. 6. plumb peach stones gathered Oct. 5  ⎭ 9. cuttings of Kaskeskia soft nectarine. Taylor
         11.  21. to 27 f. 21. black plumb peach stones of Georgia
         10.ᵗʰ              1. root & 5. cuttings of the Mountain currant brought in my Gov.ᵗ house. from mr Taylor.
         11.ᵗʰ              1. row of Umbrella seeds, 1. ½ f. of Cucumber tree seeds.
         12.ᵗʰ  3. to 11 f.  seeds of the Magnolia glauca.
              1. to 13 f.  seeds of Kentucky locust.

Mar. 21. planted 7. Rhododendrons in 4. oval beds in each corner of the house.
N.ᵒ VI . . . 11 garden 36. Acacia Por: nagua (probably Karwinana) seeds from Judge Johnston, in a box.
         23. sowed Egyptian grass in the old nursery lowest bed West end.
              set out sprigs of sweet scented grass in lowest bed Eastward.
         24. Nursery. 8.ᵗʰ Terras. grafted 4. pear cuttings from Gallipolis. very large. eat. Dec. Jan. Taylor
                     9.ᵗʰ        grafted 6. plumb cuttings from d. 27. or d. 36. a large blue plumb.
         26.         3.ᵗ        grafted 12. codlings & 12. iron wildings. next to the Taliafers.
                     7.ᵗʰ       planted 13. stones of the Magdalen or White blossomed peach. soft. Taylor
Apr. 18. flower borders. sowed Larkspurs. poppies. balsam apple.
         11. oval bed on S.W. side. nutmeg plant.
          5. oval bed on S.W. side. American Columbo.
         20. planted in the 11. uppermost terraces of the E. vineyard 165. cuttings of a native vine grape rec.ᵈ from
             major Adlum of Maryland. this grape was first discovered by a garden of the Penn: & transplanted into his
             garden in or near Philadelphia. I have drunk of the wine. it resembles the Com. ess Burgundy 4.
         24. planted 3. yellow Jasmines from mr Cole? } in the oval beds next to the covered ways on both sides
         25.          5. d.ᵒ from mr Divers          } of each.
             planted in boxes. no. N.ᵒ IV. Acer Tartaricum. Joli petit arbre. propre au bosquets & 8. grains Poland spring wheat
                     X. hard shelled bitter almond. 10. kernels.
                    XI. . . . . . . . . . . . . . . . . To come up. 1. Chebeb. Mellimere. fescues
                   XII. . . . . . . . . . . . . . . . .
                  XIII. Brousonetia papyrifera. paper mulberry of China.

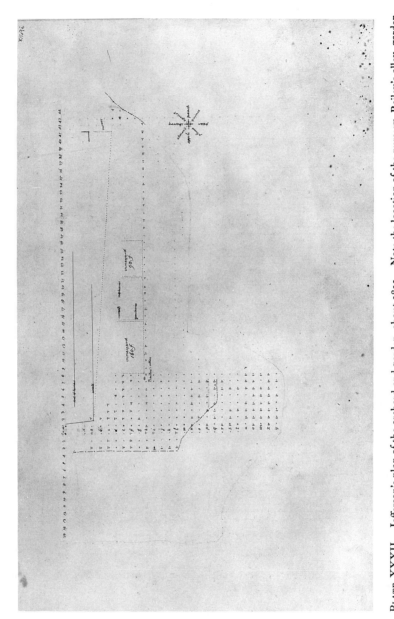

PLATE XXXII.—Jefferson's plan of the orchard and garden, about 1811.   Note the location of the nursery, Bailey's alley, garden wall, and Jefferson's scheme for location of fruit trees.   (*Jefferson Papers*, M. H. S.)

Terras. 1ˢᵗ. 1.to8.feet. 52. hardshelled sweet Almonds from Cadiz.[5]

2ᵈ.                    9. Spitzenburgs from m͞r Taylor.[6] grafted

                    13. Calvites & Red apples from Detroit. m͞r Taylor. grafted

                    21. Spitzenburgs. cuttings from the 3. trees from m͞r Divers

                    30. Newtown pippings. cuttings from my own trees. grafted.

3ᵈ. . . . . . . . . 70. Taliaferro apples. grafted from my own trees. beginning them at E. end.

3ᵈ. 1. to 5.f. planted 24. Peach apricot stones, saved the last year from the tree f.42. at W. end.

5ᵗʰ. 1. to 11.f. planted 141. filbert nuts from T. Lomax.[7]

6ᵗʰ. 1. to 17.f 48. soft peach trees. from T. Lomax.
18. to 20.f 11. November soft peach stones.
20. to 21.f 6. plumb peach stones gathered Oct. 5.
21. to 27.f. 41. black plumb peach stones of Georgia.[9]

14. cuttings of the Magdalen peach. soft. grafted. Taylor Terras 7ᵗʰ.
9. cuttings of Kaskaskia[8] soft nectarine. Taylor

10th.          1. root & 5. cuttings of the
              Mountain currant brought in
              by Gov[r]. Lewis.[10]  from m͞r
              Taylor.

11th.         1. row of Umbrella seeds.[11]  1.
              d°. of Cucumber tree seeds.[12]

      3. to 16.f.   seeds of the Magnolia glauca.[13]

12th. 1. to 13 f.  seeds of Kentucky locust.[14]

Mar. 21.  planted 7. Rhododendrons [15] in 4. oval beds [16]
          in each corner of the house.

N°. VI ..  planted 36. Acacia.  Popinaques [17] (prob-
           ably Farnesiana) seeds from Judge Johns-
           ton,[18] in a box.

    23.  sowed Egyptian grass [19] in the old nursery
         lowest bed, West end.

         set out sprigs of sweet scented grass [20] in low-
         est bed Eastwardly.

    24.  Nursery.  8th. Terras.  grafted 4. pear cut-
                                   tings  from  Galli-
                                   polis.[21]  very large.
                                   eaten Dec. Jan. Tay-
                                   lor

              9th.              grafted 6. plumb cut-
                                   tings from d.27. or
                                   e.36.  a large blue
                                   plumb.

    26.         3[d].             grafted 12. codlings
                                   & 12. iron wildings,
                                   next to the Taliafers.

7$^{th}$.        planted 13. stones of
the Magdalen or
White blossomed
peach. soft. Taylor

Apr. 18.   flower borders.[22] sowed larkspurs.[23] poppies.[24]
balsam apple.[25]

N. oval bed on S.W. side.  nutmeg plant.[26]

S. oval bed on S.W. side.  American Co-
lumbo.[27]

20.   planted in the 11. uppermost terrasses of the
E. vineyard 165. cuttings of a native winegrape
rec$^d$. from Major Adlum [28] of Maryland.  this
grape was first discovered by a gardener of
Governor John Penn's [29] & transplanted into
his garden in or near Philadelphia.  I have
drank of the wine.  it resembles the Comartin
Burgundy.

24.   planted 3. yellow Jas-┐ in the oval beds
mines [30] from m͞r │ next to the cov-
Coles [31] │ ered ways on
├ both sides of
25      5. d°. from m͞r │ each.
Divers . . . . . . . . ┘

planted in boxes.  viz. N°. IV. Acer Tartaricum.[32] joli petit arbre.  propre au bos-
quets.  & 8. grains Poland spring
wheat [33]

X. hard shelled bitter almond.  10. kernels.

XI. Mespilus Pyracanta.[34]  Prickly medlar.
2.y. to come up.  & Ghibeba Mellimeni.[35]  fescues

XII. Lonicera Alpigena.[36] red berried honey suckle

XIII. Broussonette papyrifera.[37] paper mulberry of China.

Apr. 26. sowed. Phaseolus rufus. Haricots roussatres.[38] West bed of XV. N.end.

Brassica sempervirens.[39] middle of same bed.

Valeriana vesicaria.[40] Candia corn sallad. S.end of same bed.

28. Pani corn [41] in the S.E.end of the Supplementary ground below Bailey's walk forward corn from Claxton in S.W.corner of d°.

Cherokee latter corn in the middle part.

Sweet or shriveled corn in the N.W.corner of d°. above Bailey's walk.

forward blackeyed peas of Georgia, 2. uppermost rows. ibidem.

forward French black eyes [42] in the rows next below.

Ravensworths in the next. 3563. of these = 1 pint

Cow peas in all the rest of the Supplement except as follows. *2587 = 1.pint.

Benni [43] in all the E. end above Bailey's walk.

May. 7. sowed upland rice [44] at the mouth of the Meadow branch.

8. sowed yellow jasmine seed in 2. boxes. XIV. XV.

14. planted 12. figs, just received from D$^r$. Thornton,[45] in the vacancies at the S.W. end of the wall.

beginning where those of Sep. 5. 1809. end. these of 1809. are all sprouting at the root.

June. 6. Note the following cluster of trees in the old nursery, to be suffered to remain there & be taken care of

1. in the row e. 15 f from the gate a May Duke cherry of the finest quality.

2. about 10 f below that a May cherry of very fine quality.

3. in a line with that, 12.f. eastwardly a plumb, supposed Magnum bonum.

4. a pear 2.f. from the 3$^d$.

5. due West from the May Duke 7.f.   a quince

6. due West nearly from the Quince 8.f.   a pear.

The cherry trees along the brow of the garden wall are as follows.

1$^{st}$. in the S.W. angle opposite the Asparagus beds a May cherry.

2$^d$. opposite walk A. a Carnation.

3$^d$.           square I. a May cherry.

4$^{th}$. . . . . . .       II. d$^o$.

XVI.⎫ a seedling black, but
in center of XVI.⎭   large & fine

in center of IX   not a May duke, yet like
it.   perhaps a black heart.

July.   2.   cucumber from mr̄s Lewis.[46]

3.   squashes from the Asparagus bed.

Sep.   14.   the ice in the ice house fails.

millet [47] is now fit for use.

* the largest cups of the drill [48] hold 5. cowpeas each, & 5 cups to a turn
of the wheel require 25. peas to a revolution of the wheel which is 6.f.
in circumference.   then 1. pint will sow 100. revolution = 200 yds,
and 18 pints or 1⅛ peck will drill an acre in rows 4.f. apart.   but it will
be better to use the cups which take up a single pea only each, with 6.
cups to the band, or 6. peas to the 6.f.   in this way 4¼ pints sow an
acre, and 1. bushel sows 15. acres.

———————————————————————

[1] *1810*.   Jefferson, at *Monticello* now for almost a year,
found that retirement, to which he had looked forward with
keen anticipation for so many years, resolving itself into a life
of financial worry.   However, his release from public affairs
and his many interests at home gave him much happiness.

A letter to his friend, General Thaddeus Kosciusko, written
from *Monticello* on February 26, gives a bright picture of how
his days were passing since his return home:

I am retired to Monticello, where, in the bosom of my family, and
surrounded by my books, I enjoy a repose to which I have been long a
stranger.   My mornings are devoted to correspondence.   From breakfast to dinner, I am in my shops, my garden, or on horseback among my
farms; from dinner to dark, I give to society and recreation with my
neighbors and friends; and from candle light to early bed-time, I read.
My health is perfect; and my strength considerably reinforced by the activity of the course I pursue; perhaps it is as great as usually falls to the
lot of near sixty-seven years of age.   I talk of ploughs and harrows, of
seeding and harvesting, with my neighbors, and of politics too, if they
choose, with as little reserve as the rest of my fellow citizens, and feel,
at length, the blessing of being free to say and do what I please, without
being responsible for it to any mortal.   A part of my occupation, and by
no means the least pleasing is the direction of the studies of such young
men as ask it.   They place themselves in the neighboring village, and

have the use of my library and counsel, and make a part of my society. In advising the course of their reading, I endeavor to keep their attention fixed on the main objects of all science, the freedom and happiness of man.   So that coming to bear a share in the councils and government of their country, they will keep ever in view the sole objects of all legitimate government.   (Lipscomb and Bergh, *Jefferson* **12**: 369–370.)

Improvements continued at *Monticello* and at the other estates, but they were more with an eye to utility than to ornament.   He makes this point in a letter written on August 6 to Mr. Samuel H. Smith, who had visited him at *Monticello* the year before: "I have made no progress this year in my works of ornament: having been obliged to attend first to the utile. my farms occupy me much, and require much to get them underway."   (*Jefferson Papers,* L. C.)

Although the spring had been "wonderfully backwards," the cold weather having done much damage to fruit trees and the "devastating rain" of the latter part of February having greatly injured the fields, a considerable amount of planting had been done throughout the spring and fall.   This was especially true of fruit trees, of which a large variety had been set out.

Toward the close of the year Jefferson completed four cisterns which he had been constructing during the preceding years.   Although they added to the supply of water which he had been getting from springs and the well, they were never satisfactory, and the water supply for his mountaintop continued to be a serious problem.

Trouble continued at the mill.   On November 9 the mill dam was almost completely destroyed, and the water stood on the floor of the mill, four feet deep.   The *Farm Book* states:

there fell in the course of 48. hours about 4¾ I. of rain.   it raised the river to the brim of the bank between the mill dam & ford on this side and carried away the middle of the dam, & tore very much to pieces the Eastern ⅓.   it barely entered the lowest part of the low grounds there & at Milton.   the water was about 4. f. deep in the lowest floor of the manufacturing mill.

The incompetent Shoemaker was still the manager of the mill. The nailery, however, was more prosperous, manufacturing six tons of nails during the year.

The *Garden Book* for this year contains numerous entries of planting, but no garden *Kalendar,* while the *Farm Book* includes observations on various agricultural improvements and plans. As usual, the letters are replete with discussions of agricultural and gardening subjects.

In addition to the Randolph family, Francis Eppes, Jefferson's grandson, spent most of the year with him, studying under his tutelage. Jefferson spent a greater part of the year at *Monticello;* however, he went to *Poplar Forest* in the spring, in August, and in December. No doubt he went there to hasten the work on his new house, which was nearing completion.

[2] See letter, Mr. Threlkeld to Jefferson, March 8, 1809.

[3] Mr. George Divers, of *Farmington,* Albemarle County.

[4] See entry of January 9, 1810, under *Farm Book.*

[5] Cadiz, Spain. The almonds were probably sent by Mrs. Harriet Hackley. See April 10, 1809, in *Garden Book.*

[6] Probably James Taylor, of Norfolk, Virginia. He was born December 14, 1771, and died June 7, 1826. He married his first cousin Sarah Newton, June 11, 1800; was clerk of the court, merchant, and importer of wine. (See *William and Mary College Quarterly* 3: 18, 1895; also letter, James Taylor to Jefferson, February 3, 1806.)

[7] See letter, Thomas Lomax to Jefferson, October 30, 1809.

[8] Probably named after the Kaskaskia River, in Illinois, or one of the several settlements on that river.

[9] See entry in *Garden Book* for April 10, 1809.

[10] Meriwether Lewis (1774–1809), private secretary to President Jefferson in 1801, and co-leader with Captain William Clark on the Northwest Expedition. After their return in 1806, Captain Lewis was appointed governor of the Missouri Territory. (Lippincott's *Biographical Dictionary:* 1543.)

[11] Seeds of *Magnolia tripetala* L.

[12] Seeds of *Magnolia acuminata* L.

[13] Now called *Magnolia virginiana* L. Common name, sweet bay.

[14] *Gymnocladus dioica* (L.) Koch. Commonly called Kentucky coffee tree.

[15] Probably either *Rhododendron maximum* L. or *R. catawbiense* Michx.

[16] See plate XXIII for location of these beds.

[17] *Acacia farnesiana* Willd.   See letters, Judge Johnson to Jefferson, September 20, 1809, and Jefferson to Judge Johnson, March 17, 1810.

[18] Judge William Johnson (1771–1834), born in Charleston, South Carolina, in 1771 and graduated from Princeton College in 1790 with high honors; became distinguished in law, and in 1801 was appointed by Jefferson to the Supreme Court of the United States.   (Lippincott's *Biographical Dictionary:* 1394.)

[19] Egyptian grass.   *Dactyloctenium aegyptium* (L.) Willd. See letters, Jefferson and Judge Johnson, mentioned in note 17.

[20] Sweet scented grass.   *Anthoxanthum odoratum* L.   See letter, Jefferson to Ellen Randolph, February 6, 1809.

[21] Gallipolis, Ohio.   A small manufacturing city on the Ohio River.

[22] This is the first mention of the flower borders in the *Garden Book*.   They were on each side of the winding or *Roundabout* Walk on the western lawn.   See plate XXIV.

[23] *Delphinium* sp.

[24] *Papaver* sp.

[25] *Momordica balsamina* L.

[26] Unidentified.

[27] *Frasera caroliniensis* Walt.

[28] Major John Adlum, of Maryland, collected and grew a large number of grape vines for commercial purposes, and owned one of the best vineyards in the United States.   He carried on some correspondence with his friend Jefferson, mainly on the subject of grapes and wines.   See letters, Jefferson and Adlum, March 13, 1810, and April 20, 1810.

[29] John Penn, the grandson of William Penn, was born in London on July 14, 1729, and died in Philadelphia on February 10, 1795.   He was educated at the University of Geneva and came to this country in 1753.   He was Lieutenant Governor and Governor of Pennsylvania.   (*Encyclopedia Americana* (*New York,* 1942) 21: 511.)

[30] May be either a species of *Jasminum* L. or *Gelsemium sempervirens* Juss.

[31] Probably Isaac A. Coles, who "was a member of the Albemarle bar, for a time President Jefferson's private secre-

tary, and a member of the House of Delegates. He lived at
Enniscorthy, married Mrs. Julia Stricker Rankin, widow of
Hon. Christopher Rankin, of Louisiana, and had two children, Isaetta and Stricker. He died in 1841, and his wife in
1876." (Woods, *Albemarle County:* 173.)

[32] *Acer tartaricum* L. Pretty, small tree, suitable for a
thicket (translated).

[33] *Triticum aestivum* var. *polonicum* Bailey.

[34] Now *Pyracanthus coccinea* Roem.

[35] Unidentified.

[36] *Lonicera alpigena* L.

[37] *Broussonetia papyrifera* Vent.

[38] Sowed red beans.

[39] *Brassica sempervirens.* See letter, Jefferson to Bernard
McMahon, February 16, 1812.

[40] *Valeriana vesicaria.* Unidentified.

[41] Pani corn. See letter, Jefferson to Edmund Bacon,
March 8, 1808. A corn brought back by Meriwether Lewis
from the West.

[42] French black-eye pea. See letter, George Divers to Jefferson, April 22, 1809.

[43] Benne. See letter, Jefferson to Judge Johnson, March
17, 1810, and various quoted letters about the benne plant.

[44] Upland rice. See letter, Jefferson to Benjamin Waterhouse, December 1, 1808.

[45] See letter, Jefferson to William Thornton, May 24, 1810.

[46] Probably the wife of Colonel Nicholas Lewis. Colonel
Lewis died in 1808.

[47] *Panicum miliaceum* L.

[48] A machine for sowing seeds.

## LETTERS AND EXTRACTS OF LETTERS, 1810

(Jefferson to Honoré Jullien.)

Monticello Jan. 8. 1810.

. . . the occupations of the garden, the workshops, & the farms fill
up the whole of T. Je.'s time. . . . (*Jefferson Papers*, L. C.)

(Jefferson to Bernard McMahon.)

Monticello Jan. 13. 10.

Your favor of Dec. 24. did not get to hand till the 3ᵈ inst. and I return you my thanks for the garden seeds which came safely. I am

curious to select only one or two of the *best* species or variety of every garden vegetable, and to reject all others from the garden to avoid the dangers of mixture & degeneracy. some plants of your gooseberry, of the Hudson & Chili strawberries, & some bulbs of Crown imperials, if they can be put into such moderate packages as may be put into the mail, would be very acceptable. the Cedar of Lebanon & Cork oak are two trees I have long wished to possess. but, even if you have them, they could only come by water, & in charge of a careful individual, of which opportunities rarely occur.

Before you receive this you will probably have seen Gen¹. Clarke, the companion of Governor Lewis in his journey, & now the executor of his will. the papers relating to the expedition had safely arrived at Washington, had been delivered to Gen¹. Clarke, & were to be carried on by him to Philadelphia, and measures to be taken for immediate publication. the prospect of this being now more at hand, I think it justice due to the merits of Govʳ. Lewis to keep up the publication of his plants till his work is out, that he may reap the well deserved fame of their first discovery. with respect to m͞r Pursh I have no doubt Gen¹. Clarke will do by him whatever is honorable, & whatever may be useful to the work. . . . (*Jefferson Papers,* L. C.)

## (Jefferson to John Barnes.)

Monticello Jan. 17. 10.

. . . I have 450 acres in wheat this year, all in excellent land, & the next year I shall be able to raise it to 600 acres, & to increase my tobacco crop from 40 to 60. in a couple of years more I shall be able to clear out all the difficulties I brought on myself in Washington. 11,000 D. (*Jefferson Papers,* L. C.)

## (Jefferson to Thomas Main.)

Monticello, Jan. 20, 1810.

Your favor of the 10th inst. has been duly received & I now return you the paper it inclosed with some subscriptions to it. I go rarely from home, & therefore have little opportunity of promoting subscriptions. these are of the friends who visit me, and if you will send their copies, when ready, to me, I will distribute them, and take on myself the immediate remittance of the price to you. I am anxious to learn the method of sprouting the haws the first year, which that work promises to teach us.

I visited always with great satisfaction your useful establishment and became entirely sensible of your own personal merit. I saw with regret your labours struggling against the disadvantages of your position. the farm is poor, the country around it poor, & the farmers not at all emulous of improving their agriculture. I was sensible that the James river lowgrounds were the field where your system of hedges would be peculiarly useful. it is the richest tract of country in the Atlantic states.

Its proprietors are all wealthy, and devoted to the improvement of their farms. timber for wooden inclosures is getting out of their reach and is liable to be swept away by floods. the hedge would quickly become an inclosure in such lands, & would withstand the floods. yet I was sensible of the difficulties of your removal. Nurseries are the work of years. they cannot be removed from place to place, nor all sold out at a moment's warning. to renew them in another place requires years before they begin again to yield profit. wishing you therefore all the success which your present situation admits & your own efforts, industry & good conduct merit I pray you to be assured of my entire esteem. (*Glimpses of the Past,* Missouri, **3**: 113.)

(Jefferson to Joel Barlow.)

Monticello, January 24, 1810.

. . . You ask my opinion of Maine. I think him a most excellent man. Sober, industrious, intelligent and conscientious. But, in the difficulty of changing a nursery establishment, I suspect you will find an insurmountable obstacle to his removal. . . .

P. S. The day before yesterday the mercury was at $5\frac{1}{2}°$ with us, a very uncommon degree of cold here. It gave us the first ice for the ice house. (Lipscomb and Bergh, *Jefferson* **12**: 351–352.)

(Jefferson to J. Garland Jefferson.)

Monticello, January 25, 1810.

. . . I am leading a life of considerable activity as a farmer, reading little and writing less. Something pursued with ardor is necessary to guard us from the *tedium-viatae,* and the active pursuits lessen most our sense of the infirmities of age. . . . (Lipscomb and Bergh, *Jefferson* **12**: 355.)

(Jefferson to William A. Burwell.)

Monticello, February 25, 1810.

. . . The present delightful weather has drawn us all into our farms and gardens; we have had the most devastating rain which has ever fallen within my knowledge. Three inches of water fell in the space of about an hour. Every hollow of every hill presented a torrent which swept everything before it. I have never seen the fields so much injured. Mr. Randolph's farm is the only one which has not suffered; his horizontal furrows arrested the water at every step till it was absorbed, or at least had deposited the soil it had taken up. Everybody in this neighborhood is adopting his method of ploughing, except tenants who have no interest in the preservation of the soil. . . . (Lipscomb and Bergh, *Jefferson* **12**: 364–365.)

(Jefferson to Mrs. Elizabeth Trist.)

Monticello Feb. 28. 10.

. . . Within ten days Monticello will begin to enrobe itself in all it's bloom. we are now all out in our gardens & fields. Since Christmas I have taken my farms into my own hands. . . . (*Jefferson Papers,* M. H. S.)

(James Ronaldson to Jefferson.)

Paris Mar. 4, 1810.

. . .

### List of seeds sent

| | |
|---|---|
| Canary seed | Alpiste |
| Oil poppy | oeillette |
| do.  do. | Pavot blaue |
| Dates | Datties |
| Olive | Olivies |
| Leigle de Mare | Spring Rye |
| Madder | |
| Teazel | Chardon a foulen |
| Wood | |
| Blue Wood | Pastel |
| Perrenial flax | lin vivace |
| Gold of Pleasure (Oil plant) | Cameline |
| Oil Raddish | Radis oleifer de la chine |

*Sainfoin* that gives two crops per annum

| | |
|---|---|
| Fall Cabbage | Chou Cavalier |
| Scarlet clover (an annual) | Trifle de Roussillon |
| Naked Barley | Orge nud |

(*Jefferson Papers,* L. C.)

(John Adlum to Jefferson.)

Wilton Farm Mar 13, 1810.

With this day's mail I send you a number of cuttings of the vines which I made the wine. . . . (*Jefferson Papers,* L. C.)

(I. A. Coles to Jefferson.)

Mar. 13th. 1810.

I. A. Coles presents his complem[ts] to M[r]. Jefferson & sends him a few scions of the Mountain Laurel. He hopes they will reach him without injury. (*Jefferson Papers,* L. C.)

(Jefferson to Captain W. D. Meriwether.)

Monticello Mar. 14. 1810.

The bearer now comes for the trees you have taken care of for me, that is to say my half of them. where there is only a single one of a kind do not risk the taking it up. a graft from it another year will do as well for me. be so good as to have the roots of those sent well wrapt in straw to keep the cold air from them. (*Jefferson Papers*, L. C.)

### (Jefferson to Judge William Johnson.)

Monticello Mar. 17. 1810.

I received by mr. Mitchell your letter of Sept. 20. and the favor of the Benne seed, Egyptian Grass and the Accacia seeds. a journey immediately succeeding took off my attention from the subject in the moment, and it was not till overhauling my seeds for the operations of the present season that I was reminded of the duty & pleasure of the acknolegement still due for your kind attention. all of these articles are highly acceptable. they bring nourishment to my hobby horse: for my occupations at present are neither in reading nor writing. the culture of the earth in the garden, orchard and farms engage my whole attention. two essays of the last year and year before with the Benni have failed. the first by the earliest frost ever known in this country, which killed the plants before maturity, and the last by as extraordinary a drought. I raised however the last year about as much as I sowed, and shall make another effort this year, and not without good hopes. I have provided myself with a press of cast iron, to wit, a cylinder holding half a bushel with an iron lid moving within it, and a screw to force that. it has not yet however been tried. I am very thankful for the Egyptian grass, having long heard of it & wished to try it. I have not been able to find the term Popinaque which distinguishes the species of Acacia you have been so kind as to send me, nor do I recollect the occasion of my mentioning it to you. being a great admirer of the two species Nilotica & Farnesiana, I suspect it must be one of these, & probably the latter which is a native of the W. India islands. I shall however cherish it. some two or three years ago, among other seeds I received from Malta, was that of the Wintermelon. I gave it to two or three gardeners near Washington. only one of them succeeded in raising it, on account of the criticalness of the time of planting. he raised a few, of which he sent me one on Christmas day. he planted on the 15th. of July. the fruit is gathered before the danger of frost. the planting must have been so timed that when gathered in autumn, and put away in a warm dry place, it will go on mellowing as an apple. it is eaten through the months of Dec. Jan. & February. it is a very fine melon. I inclose you a few seeds, as I think it will be more likely to do well with you than here, and shall be happy to administer to your taste for the care of plants in any way you can make me useful. . . . (*Jefferson Papers*, L. C.)

### (Jefferson to James Madison.)

Monticello Mar. 25. 1810.

. . . it is believed the fruit has been all killed in the bud by the late extraordinary cold weather. mine is untouched, tho I apprehend that a

very heavy white frost which reached the top of the hill last night may
have killed the blossoms of an Apricot which has been in bloom about a
week.   a very few peach blossoms are yet open. . . . (*Jefferson Papers,*
L. C.)

## (Jefferson to James Madison.)

Monticello Apr. 16. 10.

. . . our spring is wonderfully backward.  we have had asparagus
only two days.  the fruit has escaped better than was believed.  it is
killed only in low places. . . . (*Jefferson Papers,* L. C.)

## (Jefferson to Robert Fulton.)

Monticello, April 16, 1810.

. . . The object of this prompt reply to your letter, is the offer you
so kindly made of lending me your dynamometer.  It will be the greatest favor you can do me.

The Agricultural Society of the Seine sent me one of Guillaume's
famous ploughs, famous for taking but half the moving power of their
best ploughs before used.  They, at the same time, requested me to send
them one of our best, with my mould board to it.  I promised I would,
as soon as I retired home and could see to its construction myself.  In
the meantime I wrote to a friend at Paris to send me a dynamometer,
which he did.  Unfortunately this, with some other valued articles of
mine, were lost on its passage from Washington to Monticello.  I have
made the plough and am greatly deceived if it is not found to give less
resistance than theirs.  In fact I think it is the finest plough which has
ever been constructed in America.  But it is the actual experiment alone
which can decide this, and I was with great reluctance about to send off
the plough untried when I received your kind offer.  I will pray you to
send the instrument to Mr. Jefferson of Richmond by some careful passenger in the stage, who will see that it does not miscarry by the way;
or by some vessel bound from New York direct to Richmond, which is
the safest though slowest conveyance. . . . (Lipscomb and Bergh, *Jefferson* 19: 172–173.)

## (Jefferson to W. C. Nicholas.)

Monticello Apr. 16. 1810.

On enquiry of mr Randolph I find his process for rolling his seed corn
in plaister varies a little from what I told you.  he first dilutes the tar
with water stirred into it to such a consistency as will make the plaister
adhere.  corn is then put into a trough and diluted tar poured on it and
stirred till the whole of the grains are perfectly coated.  there must be
no surplus of the tar more than covers the grains.  then put the plaister
in and stir the whole until the corn will take up no more, and remains
dry enough to be handled.  he observed that if the corn was rolled in
pure tar and then plaistered, it would become as hard as marbles and
would be very late in coming up, and sometimes not come up at all.  he

takes this process from some Northern practice.   I wish you may receive this in time to correct my imperfect statement of it to you.   (*Jefferson Papers,* M. H. S.)

(Jefferson to Colonel Skipwith.)

Monticello Apr. 17. 10.

Overhauling my seeds reminded me that I was to send you some Millet seed. it is now inclosed. put it into drills 3. or 4. f. apart so that you may conveniently plough it, and the stalks at 6. I. distance in the drill. it is planted immediately after corn planting, say in May. it is to be used for the table as homony, boiled or fried, needs neither husking nor beating, & boils in about two hours. it is believed here it will yield 100 bushels to the acre. I shall have some acres of it this year. (*Jefferson Papers,* United States Department of Agriculture.)

(Jefferson to John Adlum.)

Monticello Apr. 20. 1810.

. . . On the 15th inst. I received yours of the 10th. & concluding the bundle of cuttings had been rejected at some post office as too large to pass thro' that line, I had yesterday, in despair, written my acknolege-ments to you for the kind service you had endeavored to render me but before I had sent off the letter, I received from the stage office of Milton the bundle of cuttings & bottle of wine safe. yesterday was employed in preparing ground for the cuttings, 165. in number, & this morning they will be planted. their long passage gives them a dry appearance, tho I hope that out of so many some will live and enable me to fill my ground. their chance will be lessened because living on the top of a mountain I have not yet the command of water, which I hope to obtain this year by *cisterns,* already prepared for saving rain water. . . . (*Jefferson Papers,* L. C.)

(Jefferson to Mr. Jonathan Shoemaker.)

Monticello Apr. 22. 10.

A little before my departure for Bedford I informed you that the pressures on me for money for corn & other objects would oblige me to rely on you for a very considerable sum of money, of which no delay could be admitted. on my return it was some days before I went to the mill to call on you, & then learned for the first time that you were gone to the Northward & would not be back till June, & no information left for me as to what I might expect. the urgency of my necessities there-fore oblige me to come to an immoveable determination, and so to state it to you candidly. your arrears of rent are at present about 600. D. & within 10 days after you receive this will be about 900. after giving every credit of which I have any knolege. not doubting but that this proceeds from difficulties of your own, I am willing to be accomodating as far as my own will permit: but my own necessities & my own credit must be attended to before those of others.   I would not demand this whole sum at once, if I could be assured of receiving 200. D. on the 1$^{st}$. day of every month for 3. months, & 100. D. a month on the 1$^{st}$. day of every month after, the first remittance to be made immediately on the receipt of this.   it would be with infinite reluctance that I should take any step which would destroy the credit of the mills, but necessity has no law, and I must yield to it unless you can engage the monthly paiments above mentioned and punctually fulfill the engagements.   in this case I might obtain indulgencies for myself until these monthly paiments should clear me; but I cannot get along unless I can count on the rents of the mill as a regular resource.   I pray you to let me hear from you immediately on the receipt of this letter, as after this painful explanation it would be as vain as inadmissible to admit the delay of writing another. be assured that it has cost me much to write this, and that I sincerely wish you well.   (*Jefferson Papers,* M. H. S.)

### (William Thornton to Jefferson.)

Farm. May 7, 1810.

. . . I shall take some young Fig trees down with me this Evening, but do not recollect the Post-Day, & consequently do not know whether I shall be in time for the Present Post.   I hope these will succeed, for I have taken them up *myself,* with good roots.   They ought to be planted in very light woodland mould, such as is generaaly obtained to put in Asparagus Beds, that the root may shoot freely in all directions, and run deep for a supply of moisture.   If placed toward the south they will also enjoy more sun, & be less subject to frosts. . . . (*Jefferson Papers,* M. H. S.)

### (Jefferson to James Madison.)

Monticello, May 13, 1810.

I thank you for your promised attention to my portion of the Merinos, and if there be any expenses of transportation, etc., and you will be so good as to advance my portion of them with yours and notify the amount, it shall be promptly remitted.   What shall we do with them?   I have been so disgusted with the scandalous extortions lately practiced in the sale of these animals, and with the description of patriotism and praise to the sellers, as if the thousands of dollars apiece they have not been ashamed to receive were not reward enough, that I am disposed to consider as right, whatever is the reverse of what they have done.   Since fortune has put the occasion upon us, is it not incumbent upon us so to dispense this benefit to the farmers of our country, as to put to shame those who, forgetting their own wealth and the honest simplicity of the farmers, have thought them fit objects of the shaving art, and to excite, by a better example the condemnation due to theirs?   No sentiment is more acknowledged in the family of Agriculturists than that the few who can afford it should incur the risk and expense of all new improvements, and give the benefit freely to the many of more restricted circumstances.   The question then recurs, What are we to do with them?   I shall be willing to concur with you in any plan you shall approve, and in order that we may have some proposition to begin upon, I will throw out a first idea, to be modified or postponed to whatever you shall think better.

Give all the full-blooded males we can raise to the different counties of our State, one to each, as fast as we can furnish them. And as there must be some rule of priority for the distribution, let us begin with our own counties which are contiguous and nearly central to the State, and proceed, circle after circle, till we have given a ram to every county. This will take about seven years, if we add to the full descendants those which will have passed to the fourth generation from common ewes. To make the benefit of a single male as general as practicable to the county, we may ask some known character in each county to have a small society formed which shall receive the animal and prescribe rules for his care and government. We should retain ourselves all the full-blooded ewes, that they may enable us the sooner to furnish a male to every county. When all shall have been provided with rams, we may, in a year or two more, be in a condition to give an ewe also to every county, if it be thought necessary. But I suppose it will not, as four generations from their full-blooded ram will give them the pure race from common ewes.

In the meantime we shall not be without a profit indemnifying our trouble and expense. For if of our present stock of common ewes, we place with the ram as many as he may be competent to, suppose fifty, we may sell the male lambs of every year for such reasonable price as, in addition to the wool, will pay for the maintenance of the flock. The first year they will be half-bloods, the second three-quarters, the third seven-eighths, and the fourth full-blooded; if we take care in selling annually half the ewes also, to keep those of highest blood, this will be a fund for kindnesses to our friends, as well as for indemnification to ourselves; and our whole State may thus, from this small stock, so dispersed, be filled in a very few years with this valuable race, and more satisfaction result to ourselves than money ever administered to the bosom of a shaver. There will be danger that what is here proposed, though but an act of ordinary duty, may be perverted into one of ostentation, but malice will always find bad motives for good actions. Shall we therefore never do good? It may also be used to commit us with those on whose example it will truly be a reproof. We may guard against this perhaps by a proper reserve, developing our purpose only by its execution.

Vive, vale, et siquid novisti rectius istis
Candidus imperti sinon, his ulere mecum.

(Lipscomb and Bergh, *Jefferson* 12: 389–391.)

(Jefferson to William Thornton.)

Monticello May 24. 10.

Your favors of May 7. & 10. are both received, and with them came the figs in perfect condition. on my proceeding to plant them in the same places where I had planted those you were so kind as to send me the last year, & reopening the holes, to my great astonishment I found a young bud putting out from the root of every one. they had been long on the road, were planted late, & this succeeded by the most calamitous drought which had been known for 55 years, so that not the smallest symptom of life had ever shown itself above ground. I covered them carefully & hope soon to see them rise from the dead. the others were planted elsewhere & I consider myself by your bounty as now in stock. I have this spring laid down some of the young branches of my Marseilles fig, to take root. this method being more secure than that of cuttings. I shall take care in due season to forward you some of them, when in a condition to be severed from the parent stock. . . . (*Jefferson Papers*, L. C.)

### (Jefferson to James Madison.)

Monticello May 25. 10.

. . . We are suffering under a most severe drought of now 3. weeks continuance. Late sown wheat is yellow but the oats suffer especially. . . . (Ford, *Jefferson* 11: 141.)

### (William Thornton to Jefferson.)

Washington, June 8, 1810.

I am very glad that the young Fig-trees arrived safe, and also that the former ones were still alive. I am much obliged by your kindness in reserving one of the sheep dogs for me. . . . (*Jefferson Papers*, M. H. S.)

### (Jefferson to General John Mason.)

Monticello June 22. 1810.

You were so kind, when I left Washington, as to give me some seed of the Swedish turnep. I sowed it carefully, but a drought from the middle of July till autumn, prevented a single plant from coming to perfection. can you give me a few seeds now, & inform me when you plant them. McMahon directs it in April or May. but this is so different from the season of sowing other turneps that I am in hopes this application is not yet too late. I lost by the same drought my egg plants but it is now too late to ask that seed. my garden & farms occupy me closely from breakfast to dinner, after which it is my habit to lounge, so that I read little. . . . I have the genuine Alpine Strawberry, which I received from Italy, but it bears so little that I think it would take acres to yield a dish. I propose therefore to remove it from the garden to the fields where alone we have acres to spare. . . . (*Jefferson Papers*, L. C.)

(Jefferson to David Warden.)

Monticello July 15. 10.

My distance from the seat of government and ignorance of safe conveyances to Paris have occasioned me to be late in acknoleging your
favor of Oct. 27. that of Jan. 19. is lately received. with the former
came the Memoires d'Agriculture, the map of M. Romarzewski, and
with the latter the seeds from the national garden. will you do me
the favor to make my just acknolegement to those to whom they are due
for these favors. . . . (*Jefferson Papers,* Maryland Historical Society.)

(Jefferson to William Lambert.)

Monticello, July 16, 1810.

. . . My occupations here are almost exclusively given to my farm
and affairs. They furnish me exercise, health and amusement, and with
the recreations of family and neighborly society, fill up most of my time,
and give a tranquility necessary to my time of life. . . . (Lipscomb and
Bergh, *Jefferson* 12: 398.)

(Charles Clay to Jefferson.)

[Bedford County] September 5, 1810.

My boy brings you some seed of the late invented *Hay-Rye,*—in its
wild state it is generally found on a light rich soil by the sides of Rivers,
Creeks etc. Yet from the single experiment I have made with it I apprehend it will thrive very well on any good clover soil.—This is the
fourth year it has stood where you saw it,—it has every year increased
in quantity, being at first sown very thin, in the month of March,—but
I am inclined to think the fall is the proper time for seeding it, & then it
would probably produce seed the next summer, which it does not when
sown in the spring. (*Jefferson Papers,* M. H. S.)

(Jefferson to Hugh Chisholm.)

Monticello Sept. 10. 1810.

. . . unless the Cistern be done in time to dry, it will give away again
in winter. (*Jefferson Papers,* M. H. S.)

(Jefferson to Benjamin S. Barton.)

Monticello Oct. 6. 1810.

. . . When we had the pleasure of possessing you here, you expressed
a wish to have some of the Ricara snap beans, and of the Columbian
Salsafia brought from the Western side of the continent by Gov$^r$. Lewis.
I now enclose you some seeds of each. the Ricara bean is one of the
most excellent we have had: I have cultivated them plentifully for the
table two years. I have found one kind only superior to them, but
being very sensibly so, I shall abandon the Ricaras. I have not yet
raised enough of the Salsafia to judge it. Gov$^r$. Lewis did not think it
as delicate as the kind we possess. (*Jefferson Papers,* L. C.)

## From the *Weather Memorandum Book 1776–1820:*

1810.  Jan. 21.   the thermometer in the Greenhouse is 4¾ Reamur =
21.3 Farenheit.   in my bedroom it was 37°   in the open air 9¾°.

Jan. 22.   bedroom 33°.   greenhouse 19½°.   outer air 5½°.
23.   bedroom 32½°.   greenhouse 20¾°.   outer air 11°.

1810.  Feb. 24.–Mar. 1.   in dressing the terras which forms the N. W.
side of the garden, digging turf below the garden wall, and
bringing & laying it on the terras. 3. men did 41. square yards
a day.

## From the *Farm Book:*

1810.  June 25.   began the wheat harvest at Monticello.

1810.  Jan. 9.   running the rafter level through a field to guide the
ploughs horizontally, Thruston makes a step of the level (10 f.)
every minute, which is 600. f. = 200. yds an hour.

Jan. 9.   in terrassing the new nursery in 4. f. terrasses 2 men
do 50. yds in length a day.

1810.  Nov.   the batteau with 8 hands collecting rock for the dam on
the mountain side about ½ a mile above the dam, bring about 6.
loads a day of 2. perch each. = 12. perch a day.   a waggon collecting stone in the plantation from the E. side of the meadow
branch bring 12 loads a day of ½ perch each = 6 perch a day.
having it's driver & 2. of the nail boys to load & unload.   12.
hands get the long logs (6 of 50 f. long) and tyers (21. of 16
to 20 f. long) for a pen 12. f. wide in the clear, 50. f. long &
3. f. high, bring them into place by water, and lay them down in
3. days.   the cost then of a pen 50. by 12. f. for the timber part

is                                                          18.  D.
the stone 70. perch @ 4/ =                                  48.67
                                                           ─────────
                                                            64.67

about 1.30 or 8/ a foot running measure
or 1. D. the cubic yard of the dam.

### Lego

#### plan for the crop of 1810

1810   clear the low grounds on the W. side of Secretary's ford (abᵗ 12
or 15 aˢ) for tobacco.

clean up the Square field for corn.   40 aˢ.

Triangle & Oblong, put into oats.   80. aˢ.

the belted grounds, not in wheat, put into oats.

# 1811

| Kalendar 1811[1] | where | when | transplant[d] | come to table | gone | Miscellaneous |
|---|---|---|---|---|---|---|
| Frame peas | bord. I-V | Mar. 1 | | May 11 | | in blossom Apr. 19. & in pod Apr. 27. to table May 11. |
| solid celery | plantbeds | Mar. 5 } | June 29. | | | |
| d[o] | Goodm's[5] | } | | | | |
| Frame peas | sq. I | Mar. 9. | | | | |
| mrs Cole's[2] forward | sq. I | | | May 23. | | |
| Sea Kale | IX. 6. | Mar. 22. | | | | |
| Peas Hotspur | III. | 25. | | June 4 | June 17 | blossoms May. 7. |
| Lettuce from Price[3] | IX. 3. | | | | | |
| Lettuce loaf | 9.10 | | Apr. 8. | | | |
| Malta Kale | I. | Apr. 8. | | | | |
| cabbage. many head | 2. | | June 29. | | | |
| early sugarloaf | 4. | | June 3.29. | | | |
| Savoy green curl? | 5. | | June 3.29. | | | |
| Broccoli. early purple | XIII. 3. North. | | | | | |
| Cauliflower early | 3. South. | | | | | |
| lettuce white loaf & Radish | I. | | | | | |
| Spinach Summer | 4. | | | | | |
| Onions hanging[4] | XVIII. | 9. | | | | |
| cucumber early | hhd. | 13. | | July 2 | | June 8. blossom. |
| long green | d[o] | | | July 2. | | |
| tomatas Span | bord VI. | 16. | | | | |
| early cucumbers | XI. E. | 18. | | | | |
| salsafia | XV. East. | 23. | | July 2 | | June 14. blossom |
| Leadman peas | IV. | | | | | |
| sorrel | IX. 7. | | | | | |
| grey snaps | XVI. | 24. | | | | |
| carrots | V. West half | 29. | | | | |
| red haricots. 4 rows | East half | 30. | | June 19. | | 750. fill a pint, & sow 355.f. June 9. blossom. |
| Windsor beans. 4 rows | II. | | | Aug. 4. | | 350 = $\frac{1}{6}$ pint sow 178 f. |
| grey Snaps 8. rows | | | | | | |
| Lima beans | X. | May 1. | | | | June 9. blossom 2. gills planted 72. hills |

1811. (continued)

| Kalendar 1811.[1] | where | when | trans-plant^d | come to table | gone | Miscellaneous |
|---|---|---|---|---|---|---|
| Asparagus beans. | VII. | 2. | | July. 16. | Oct. 24. | ⅔ pint sow a large square, rows 2½ f apart & 1 f. & 18.I. apart in the row, one half at each distance sow earlier hereafter |
| Lettuce. White loaf } | XV. 1 | 4. | | | | |
| Radish. early scarlet. } | | | | | | |
| Okra. | XV. middle. | | | | | |
| Peas Leadman's. | VI. | 7. | | | | June 17. blossom. |
| Cauliflower Leghorn [6] | XV. 2. S.end. | 10. | | | | from Mr. Reery [7]. |
| Broccoli Leghorn. | XV. 2. N.end. | 10. | | | | |
| Beet. | 3^d. terras. Raspb^y | 11. | | | | |
| Parsneps | d°. E. Vineyard. | | | | | |
| Rhubarb esculent. | Submural. | | | | | |
| Leadman's dwarfs. | VIII. | 20. | | | | July 1. blossom. |
| Lettuce. White loaf } | XV. | 23. | | | | |
| Radish. early scarlet. } | | | | | | |
| cucumber long green. | XI. W | | | | | |
| Miami melon. | N. border. | June 1. | | | | |
| Carrots. yellow. mrs. Lewis } | 3^d. terras W.V^d. | 4. | | | | |
| Lettuce Wh. loaf. Price } | XV. | | | | | |
| Radish early scarlet | | | | | | |
| Spinach Summer. | Submural. | 6. | | | | |
| double Parsley. | 3^d. terras. | 17. | | | | |
| Snaps. grey. | | 29. | | | | |
| Lettuce. Wh. loaf Price } | | | | | | |
| Radish. E. S. } | | | | | | |
| Lettuce White loaf } | | July 6. | | | | |
| Radish Summer } | | | | | | |
| Lettuce   Tennis } | | July 16. | | | | |
| radishes qu.[8] what. } | | | | | | |
| Lettuce. Tennis } | | 20. | | | | |
| radishes. Summer? } | | | | | | |
| Turnep. Swedish. } | 3^d. Terras. | 20. | | | | |
| Lettuce   Tennis } | | 22. | | | | |
| radish   qu. what. } | | | | | | |

1811. (continued)

| | where | when | transpl^d. | come to table | gone | Miscellaneous |
|---|---|---|---|---|---|---|
| Lettuce tennis  ⎫ | | | | | | |
| radishes   qu. what  ⎬ | | July 27. | | | | |
| turneps Summer | 3^d. terrace. | 29. | | | | |
| double parsley | submural. | | | | | |
| Lettuce White. | | Aug. 5. | | | | |
|     Dutch brown. | | ? | | | | |
| Endive curled. | | | | | | |
| radishes ?. | | | | | | |
| Spinach. winter. | | 12. | | | | |
| Lettuce White. | | | | | | |
|     Dutch brown. | | | | | | |
| Endive curled. | | | | | | |
| Spinach winter. | | 29. | | | | this sowing got exactly it's full growth by beginng. of winter. |
| lettuce, Dutch Brown. | | | | | | |
| Endive curled. | | | | | | |
| corn sallad. | | | | | | |
| Spinach winter. | Stone house. | Sep. 14. | | | | this sowing came tolerably well for winter use. |
| Lettuce Dutch brown. | 3^d terras. | .21. | | | | |
| Lettuce D. brown. | d°. | | | | | |
| Endive curled. | d°. | | | | | |
| Corn sallad. | d°. | | | | | |
| Spinach winter. | d°. | | | | | this sowing too late for winter. |

1811.

Mar. 16.   planted 5. Tuckahoe[9] gray cherries in the row
e–1–2 + 1.4.5 from Enniscorthy.[10]

   18.   planted 30 Monthly raspberries[11] in the 3 terrasses next below the common raspberry.

   planted Asparagus seed in beds 5.6.7. & replanted 3.4.

   22.   Mimosa pudica.[12] Sensitive plant. oval bed
in $\angle$ of N.W. Piazza & cov$^d$ way.

   Reseda odorata.[13] Mignonette         d°.
near N.W. cistern

   Delphinium exaltatum.[14] American larkspur.
outer flower border. N.W. quarter.[16]

   Pentapetes Phoenicia.[15] Scarlet Mallow.
Outer flower border. S.W. quarter.

   23.   Lathyrus odoratus.[17] sweet scented pea. oval
bed in S.W. $\angle$ of S.W. portico and d°. S.W.
$\angle$ of S. piazza & cov$^d$. way also Ximenesia
Encelioides. in the same belle grande plante
annuelle d'ornement. from Thouin

Apr. 3.   asparagus to table.

   8.   Anemone pulsatilla.[18]  belle plante vivace.[19]
oval in S.W. $\angle$ of S.W. portico & chamber

   Mirabilis tota varietas,[20] plante vivace d'ornement. oval in N.W. $\angle$ of S.W. portico &
Din$^g$. R.

   8.   New nursery. planted 5$^{th}$. Terras 15. Gloster
hiccory nuts.[21]

7th Peach stones.   fine soft from Pop. For.[22]

13th. Genista juncea.[23]   Span-⎤
ish broom                                    ⎬ from Thouin [30]
14. Cytisus Laburnum [24] . . . .⎦

15. 16. Thorn haws from Algiers [25]

13.    planted residue of the seeds of the Genista juncea on both sides of the Upper Round-about.[26]

9.    sowed Burnet [27] in the lower part of the W. end of the orchard ground.   rye grass [28] from m͞r Clay [29] next above that

—    planted Pani corn in the middle part of grounds below Bailey's alley.   come to table July 18.

Cherokee corn in the S.W. angle of those grounds.

13.    Quarantine corn from Thouin [30] in the old Nursery.

forward cucumbers.   in the h͞h͞d [31] by the middle gate of the garden

long green d°. in the same hogshead.

tomatas [32] in the high border VI.

16.    in drilling the Benni with the smallest cups 1. gill of seed drilled 12. rows of 153. yds on an average equal to 1836 yds.   consequently to drill an acre in 4.f. drills would take 2. gills of seed.

sowed seed of the silk plant [33] from mr̄ Erving [34] in oval bed near the S.E. cistern.

May. 15.   sowed in Old Nursery. d͞ble cropped Sͭ. foin.[35] considble square near S.E. corner.

madder [36] from France. in a bed below the former.

Span. Sͭ. foin. in a small bed above the d͞ble cropped.

Palma Christi.[37]   in a row round the Nursery.

16.   strawberries come to table.

28.   artichokes come to table.   the last dish is July 28.

---

[1] *1811.* The year passed quietly and interestingly for Jefferson. His financial affairs were improving, so that he was able to turn his mind to interests more to his liking.

A letter written on May 26, from *Monticello,* to his granddaughter, Mrs. Anne Cary Bankhead, shows the even tenor of the passing days on his mountain.

. . . Nothing new has happened in our neighborhood since you left us; the houses and the trees stand where they did; the flowers come forth like the belles of the day, have their short reign of beauty and splendor, and retire, like them, to the more interesting office of reproducing their like. The Hyacinths and Tulips are off the stage, the Irises are giving place to the Belladonnas, as these will to the Tuberoses, etc.; as your mamma has done to you, my dear Anne, as you will do to the sisters of little John, and as I shall soon and cheerfully do to you all in wishing you a long, long good-night. . . . (Randolph, *Jefferson:* 349.)

The two high points of this year were the birth of a son to Mr. and Mrs. Bankhead, making Jefferson a great-grandfather, and the beginning of a reconciliation between Jefferson and his old friend, John Adams.

While teaching mathematics to his young grandson, Francis Eppes, Jefferson became again deeply interested in its principles and spent much of his time studying it.   The eclipse of the sun on September 17 brought back his old interest in astronomy.   He sent his observations to William Lambert, and after receiving a reply from him, wrote the following letter, on December 29:

I am very thankful for your calculations on my observations of the late solar eclipse.   I have for some time past been rubbing off the rust of my mathematics contracted during 50 years engrossed by other pursuits, and have found in it a delight & a success beyond my expectations. I observed the eclipse of the sun with a view to calculate my longitude from it, but other occupations had prevented my undertaking it before my journey; and the calculations you have furnished me will shew it would have been more elaborate than I had expected, & that most probably I should have foundered by the way. . . . As soon as I have fitted up a little box for my instruments, I shall amuse myself with the further ascertainment of my longitude by the lunar observations, which have the advantage of being repeated *ad libitum,* and requiring less laborious calculations. . . . (*Jefferson Papers,* L. C.)

In the late summer Jefferson suffered another attack of rheumatism, which lowered his spirits considerably.   In September he was grief-stricken over the death of his sister, Mrs. Dabney Carr, a member of long standing in the household at *Monticello.*

As in the preceding years he made three visits to *Poplar Forest,* each visit lasting several weeks.   These visits gave him a relief from the constant flow of visitors at *Monticello,* and also a chance to pursue his own interests more freely.

The *Garden Book* again recorded the daily plantings and the names of the persons who had sent him plants.   Pertinent letters there were, but in a decreasing number.   Both the *Farm Book* and the *Account Book* contain several entries.

[2] Mrs. Isaac A. Coles, of *Enniscorthy,* Albemarle County.

[3] Probably Richard Price, who was one of the earliest inhabitants of Milton, Albemarle County.   He was twice married and died in 1827.   (Woods, *Albemarle County:* 298.)

[4] Probably *Allium cepa* var. *viviparum* Metz., which produces bulbils in the flower cluster.

[5] Jeremiah Goodman, who became overseer at *Poplar Forest* in 1811.   See letters and memoranda, Jefferson to Goodman, 1811, 1812, 1813, 1814.

[6] Leghorn, Italy.

[7] McReery, unidentified.

[8] *qu.* = query.

[9] Tuckahoe gray cherries, probably named after *Tuckahoe,* the home of Colonel William Randolph, a friend of Peter Jefferson, where Jefferson spent part of his childhood.   See letter, Coles to Jefferson, March 13, 1811.

[10] *Enniscorthy,* Albemarle County, home of Isaac A. Coles.

[11] Probably a variety of *Rubus idaeus* L.   See letter, George Divers to Jefferson, March 17, 1811.

[12] *Mimosa pudica* L.

[13] *Reseda odorata* L.

[14] *Delphinium exaltatum* Ait.

[15] *Pentapetes phoenicia* L.

[16] "Outer flower border.   N. W. quarter" and "Outer flower border.   S. W. quarter" refer to the flower borders along the round-about walk on the western lawn.   See plate XXIV.

[17] *Lathyrus odoratus* L.

[18] *Anemone pulsatilla* L.

[19] Translated: beautiful perennial plant.

[20] *Mirabilis* L.   Translated: all varieties, ornamental perennial plant.

[21] Gloster hiccory nut.   A special kind of hickory from Gloucester County, Virginia.   This nut has been mentioned frequently in Jefferson's correspondence.

[22] *Poplar Forest,* Bedford County.

[23] Now called *Spartium junceum* Lam.

[24] Now called *Laburnum anagyroides* Medic.   Golden Chain Tree.

[25] Capital of Algeria.

[26] The Upper *Round-about* was also known as the First *Round-about,* and included the *Mulberry Row.*

[27] *Sanguisorba minor* Scop.

[28] See letter, Charles Clay to Jefferson, September 5, 1810.

[29] The Reverend Charles Clay was a friendly neighbor of Jefferson at *Poplar Forest.*   They often exchanged plants.

Rev. Charles Clay, a cousin of Henry Clay, was an earnest minister, preaching not only in the churches, but also in private houses and at the Prison Barracks. . . . He finally settled in Bedford County, where he died, and by the directions of his will an immense heap of stones, twenty feet in diameter and twelve feet high, was piled up upon his grave. (Woods, *Albemarle County:* 126.)

[30] André Thoüin, a French botanist, was born in Paris in 1747. He was appointed chief gardener of the Jardin des Plantes about 1765. Jefferson formed a friendship with him when he was living in Paris, followed by a correspondence between them until Thoüin's death in 1824. . Thoüin sent Jefferson a large assortment of plants and seeds not native to the United States. Jefferson planted some of them at *Monticello;* but others were sent to botanical gardens and seedsmen, chiefly to Bernard McMahon and David Hosack. Thoüin wrote, besides others works, *Lectures on the Culture and Naturalization of Plants* (3 v., 1827). "Few men," says Cuvier, "exercise a more useful influence." (See Lippincott's *Biographical Dictionary:* 2314; also letter, Jefferson to Bernard McMahon, May 4, 1811.)

[31] hhd = hogshead.

[32] Tomatoes, *Lycopersicon esculentum* Mill.

[33] Probably *Boehmeria nivea* Gaud.

[34] George W. Erving.

Born in Boston, Massachusetts, 1771; went with his father's family to England in 1776; was educated at Oxford, England, and returning to his native country, was made Consul to London by Jefferson; was Secretary of Legation to Spain in 1804; Special Minister to Denmark in 1811, and Minister to Spain in 1814. Died in New York July, 1850. (Charles Lanman, *Biographical Annals of the Civil Government of the United States* (Washington, 1876): 138.)

[35] *Onobrychis viciaefolia* Scop. Jefferson first became acquainted with Saint-Foin grass when he was in Paris. It was one of the plants he wished to introduce into the United States. He was only partially successful. The grass has been mentioned frequently in his correspondence.

[36] Madder, *Galium mollugo* L.

[37] Palma Christi or castor-oil plant, *Ricinus communis* L.

## LETTERS AND EXTRACTS OF LETTERS, 1811

(William Coolidge to Jefferson.)

Boston 9 Jan[y]. 1811

. . . The Agriculture and Manufactures of our Country have considerably improved, and are rapidly progressing; and while we can make the one, in a measure dependant on the other, it will tend, not only to promote both, in a degree, render us independant of other nations, on whom we now depend for supplies.

The article of Madder, is of primary importance in Manufacturing: no ingredient yet discovered, for Dyeing, can have such *almost* universal application in the forming of different colors, and shades. Our climate & soil, are undoubtedly congenial to its cultivation; and considering the price we pay for that of foreign growth; it might be made an important article to our Agriculturalists: yet I do not find any attempt has been made in N. England, towards its cultivation, not even for experiment. But observing in one of our Newspapers, that a Lady in Virginia, had made a number of successful experiments in dyeing; and that in some of them she made use of Madder in its undried state; of course conclude that the article is then cultivated.

Not having the pleasure of a personal acquaintance with any Gentlemen of observation in that State, have taken the liberty to address to you for information in that subject viz.

1. In what part of the State is it cultivated? and when may application be made for the roots in a fit state for setting.
2. Presuming that experiments have been made, what is the soil best adapted to its growth?
3. What the most suitable season for planting?
4. Does it require artificial watering in a dry season?
5. How long before it comes to maturity?
6. What the most suitable season for gathering? or if any marks, what are they of its maturity?
7. The best mode of drying, whether in a kiln, as I understand is practiced in Holland, or in the open air. Any information you will afford me on these inquiries, or any of them, will confer an obligation. . . . (*Jefferson Papers, L. C.*)

## (Jefferson to D. B. Warden.)

Monticello Jan. 12. 11.

When I wrote my letter of the day before yesterday, I had not yet had time to look into the pamphlets you had been so kind as to send me. I have now entered on them, and find in the very entrance an article so interesting as to induce me to trouble you with a second letter. it is the first paper of the 1st. fasciculus published by the Belfast society in which mr. Richardson gives an account of a grass which he calls Fiorin, or *agrostis Stolonifera,* which from his character of it would be inestimable here to cover what we call our galled lands. these are lands which have been barbarously managed till they have all their vegetable mould washed off, after which we have no permanent grass which can be made to take on them. from the length of time which the fiorin is said to retain it's vegetative power after being severed from the earth, I am persuaded that if done up in moss under proper envelopes, it would come here with life still in it. perhaps your connections in Ireland might enable you to procure a little of it to be sent to me. if done up in a

packet not exceeding the size of a 12 <sup>mo</sup>. or 8 <sup>vo</sup>. volume and addressed
to me, it would come from any port of this country where it should be
landed, by post, with safety, & what is equally important, with speed.
you would render in this a great service to our agriculturists, for none
can be greater than the communication of the useful plants of one country to another. . . . (*Jefferson Papers*, L. C.)

### (Jefferson to William Coolidge.)

Monticello Jan. 24. 11.

Your letter of the 9<sup>th</sup>. has been duly received. I am able to give but
little information on the subject of Madder. I know it has been cultivated, ever since I can remember in this state for household use; and
before the revolution it was cultivated on a large scale by some. Col<sup>o</sup>.
Harrison, a member of the 1<sup>st</sup>. Congress, was one of these and told me
he did not believe it could be cultivated to better advantage in any
country than in this. I do not know why he discontinued it, but probably for the want of sale. there not being enough made to employ
merchants for that article only, and our merchants of that day being all
confined to the tobacco line. it is still cultivated over the whole of this
state, I believe, that is to say, by some one in every neighborhood, a little
being sufficient for a whole neighborhood: for altho with us, nearly
every family in the country make their own clothing, scarcely any is
made for sale. this answers your first quaere, and for all the rest I
must refer you to M<sup>c</sup> Mahon's book of gardening, published in Philadelphia where he resides, & carries on the business of a seedsman. he
gives the best account of it's culture, & can probably furnish the seed of
the best species. here it is preferred to use the root undried. in that
case it is washed, & after 12 hours beaten into a paste. the same quantity of root will go twice as far in that way as dried. we dry it in the
open air when necessary. it takes three years from the planting to be
fit for use. this is the sum of the information I have received on the
subject. . . . (*Jefferson Papers*, L. C.)

### (Jefferson to James Madison.)

Monticello, March 8, 1811.

. . . We have had a wretched winter for the farmer. Great consumption of food by the cattle, and little weather for preparing the ensuing crop. During my stay in Bedford we had seven snows, that of
February 22, which was 15 inches about Richmond, was 6 inches here,
and only 3½ in Bedford. . . . (Lipscomb and Bergh, *Jefferson* 13:
22–23.)

### (Bernard McMahon to Jefferson.)

Philadelphia March 10<sup>th</sup>. 1811.

I have it now in my power to send you some plants of the Hudson
Strawberry, and some good gooseberry plants, and anxiously wish to

know by what means or rout I can convey them to you, this being a very proper period for sending them. I earnestly request the favor of your sending me a list of any plants and seeds, which would be acceptable to you and add to your collection; but lest I should not have some particular kinds which you wish for, I pray you to enlarge the list, to afford me the better opportunity of furnishing you with some of them. Be so good as to inform me whether you have a Green House & a Hot House or only the former. As to fruit-trees my Nursery is of too recent an establishment to have as yet apple, pear, cherry, plum and peach trees, &c, and indeed, with the exception of a few superior sorts, these shall always be a minor consideration with me, as there are enough to devout their attention to them.

By this mail you will receive a small package of the Crambe maritima seeds from me, with a few other trifling seeds; the former you should sow immediately on the reception of them. In hopes of hearing from you shortly. . . . (*Jefferson Papers*, L. C.)

At the end of the above letter Jefferson wrote the following list of plants. Whether they were plants to be ordered from McMahon or some that McMahon had sent Jefferson is not stated.

        dble Anemone.  Auricula  dble. Carnation
        dble Ranunculuses.  Crown Imperial
            Mignonette.
        seakale              egg plant
        Chili                Hudson strawberries
        Gooseberries
        Cape Jasmine
        Cork tree.           Cedar of Lebanon
        Balm of Gilead fir.  Spanish Chestnut.   Mar.
seeds.  dble Anemone
        Auricula.
        dble Carnation
        Mignonette
        Sea Kale
        egg plant
bulbs.  dble Ranunculus
        Crown Imperial
plants. Hudson ⎫
        Chili  ⎬ Strawberries
        Gooseberries
        Cape Jasmine
        Cedar of Lebanon
        balm of Gilead Fir
        Cork tree
        Spanish Chestnut.  Maronnier.

### (I. A. Coles to Jefferson.)

Enniscorthy Mar: 13<sup>th</sup>. 1811.

I take the liberty of sending my servant for a few more Aspen trees, & for some cuttings of the Detroit Apple, and of the Spitsenburg. The season is I fear, almost too much advanced, but as I did not get back from the lower country until the day before yesterday, the evil has been unavoidable. I send a few of the Tuckahoe Cherry which may possibly succeed. Next Spring I will send others, with the Pears which I promised. but that I am so much occupied with planting, & sowing clover too, I had promised myself the pleasure of a visit to Monticello on tomorrow, & I still hope that it will be in my power to do it, in the course of a week. . . . (*Jefferson Papers,* L. C.)

### (Jefferson to George Divers.)

Monticello Mar. 16. 11.

I send the bearer for a bushel and a half of timothy seed, which I will replace in your hands as soon as it can be purchased the ensuing season. I send you a larger supply of Asparagus beans. . . . (*Jefferson Papers,* M. H. S.)

### (George Divers to Jefferson.)

Farmington 17<sup>th</sup> Mar. 1811

I send you a bushel & a half of Timothy seed which is all I have, it will not be wanted till September next. You expressed a wish some time ago for some of the *Monthly Rasp-berry* which I now send you. . . . Accept my thanks for Asparagus beans, and the box for sowing clover seed which I am told will be ready tomorrow. . . . (*Jefferson Papers,* M. H. S.)

### (Jefferson to George Divers.)

Monticello Mar. 18. '11.

The ground I have prepared for grass along a branch, is, in several spots too dry for timothy, and especially where we run a little up hill. it is moreover a red soil; thinking it will be better to put these spots into *oat-grass* if you can spare me a little seed of that, I shall be thankful for it. it will serve as a commencement to raise seed from as I wish to go a good deal into that kind of grass. [Jefferson sends the clover box.] (*Jefferson Papers,* M. H. S.)

### (Jefferson to Madame de Tessé.)

Monticello Mar. 27, 1811.

Since I had last the pleasure of writing to you, I have to acknolege the receipt of your favors of 1809 June 12, & Oct 9 & 1810 March 24. With the first came the seeds of the Paullinia or Koelreuteria, one of which has germinated, and is now growing. I cherish it with particular attentions, as it daily reminds me of the friendship with which you have honored me. yours of Octob. 9, mentions the having sent some Marrons d'Inde (Aesculus hippocastanea) perhaps however Marrons cultivees (castanea Sativa) which were what I requested. These however got into the hands of some English pirate. I regret it the more as that delicious nut has never yet been introduced into the United States, & altho' the nut itself, when planted, does not produce uniformly the same fruit, yet it is said to do it generally. I should have had also to regret the print of our illustrious & much valued friend Humboldt, had not your goodness supplied another by Count Pahlen, which came safe to hand. when shall I have the opportunity of returning these kindnesses? in other words when will the ocean be freed from the piracies which have so long shut it up? nothing would give me so much pleasure as to prepare annually here a box of what we have acceptable to you, but the several unsuccessful efforts which I made at Washington, one only of which reached you, & that in bad condition, have deterred me from the attempt. the time however will I hope return when the restoration of peace & safe intercourse may enable me to give you these proofs of my wishes to contribute to your happiness, which will, in that way, become a part of mine also. . . . (*Glimpses of the Past,* Missouri, 3: 114–115.)

(Jefferson to Bernard McMahon.)

Monticello Apr. 8. 11.

I have been long wishing for an opportunity, by someone going to Philadelphia in the stage, to take charge of a packet of seeds for you. it is too large to trespass on the post-mail. I received them from my old friend Thouin, director of the National garden of France. but the advance of the season obliges me to confide them to a gentleman going no further than Washington, there to look out for some one going on to Philadelphia. I have added to them a dozen genuine Glocester hiccory nuts of the last season sent me from the place of their growth. your favor of the 10th ul° came safe to hand with the seeds, for which accept my thanks. you enquire whether I have a hot house, greenhouse, or to what extent I pay attention to these things. I have only a green house, and have used that only for a very few articles. my frequent & long absences at a distant possession render my efforts even for the few greenhouse plants I aim at, abortive. during my last absence in the winter, every plant I had in it perished. I have an extensive flower border, in which I am fond of placing *handsome* plants or *fragrant*. those of mere curiosity I do not aim at, having too many other cares to bestow more than a moderate attention to them. in this I have placed the seeds you were so kind as to send me last. in it I have also growing the fine tulips, hyacinths, tuberoses & Amaryllis you formerly sent me. my wants there are Anemones, Auriculas, Ranunculus, Crown Imperials & Carnations: in the garden your fine gooseberries, Hudson & Chili strawberries: some handsome lillies. but the season is now too far advanced. during the next season they will be acceptable. small parcels of seed may come by post; but bulbs are too bulky.   We have always medical students in Philadelphia coming home by the stage when their lectures cease in the fall who would take charge of small packages, or they may come at any time by vessels bound to Richmond, addressed to the care of Mess^rs Gibson & Jefferson.   I have put into your packet some Benni seed.   we now raise it and make from it our own sallad oil preferable to such olive oil as is usually to be bought. . . . (*Jefferson Papers,* L. C.)

(Jefferson to F. A. Michaux.)

Monticello Apr. 15, 1811.

I have duly received your favor of Aug. 10 and, with it, your beautiful account of the pines & firs of our country, for which be pleased to accept my thanks.   I sincerely wish the work may be prosecuted, & that the citizens of the U. S. may not be wanting in due encouragement to it.   nothing should be spared which I could do to befriend it.   Accept my best wishes that you may enjoy health to continue your useful labors. . . . (*Glimpses of the Past,* Missouri, 3: 115–116.)

(John Dortie to Jefferson.)

New York, April 24, 1811.

[Mr. Dortie wrote Jefferson that he had some seeds sent him from Paris.   Jefferson later wrote him that they were from Thoüin, and for him to send them on to Bernard McMahon of Philadelphia.]   (*Jefferson Papers,* L. C.)

(Joel Barlow to Jefferson.)

May 2, 1811.

[Mr. Barlow sends the following seeds to Jefferson:]

Caspian wheat
Mammoth Rye
Persian Barley.

(*Jefferson Papers,* L. C.)

(Jefferson to Bernard McMahon.)

Monticello May. 4. 11.

My old friend Thouin, Director of the National garden of France has just sent me a fresh parcel of seeds which he thus describes.   'They consist of about 200. species, foreign to N. America, selected from among 1. the large trees, the wood of which is useful in the arts.   2. small trees & shrubs, ornamental for shrubberies.   3. plants vivacious & picturesque. 4. flowers for parterres.   5. plants of use in medicine & all the branches of rural & domestic economy.'   they left France in March & I presume therefore are of the last year's raising.   they are arrived (in a small

box) at N. York in the care of m̄ John Dortie. 121. William Street, who came passenger.  I have requested him to address them to you by one of the Philadelphia stages, on the assurance that you will pay the stage transportation, which I have no means of doing.  accept of them if you please with the assurance of my great esteem & respect. . . .
(*Jefferson Papers,* L. C.)

### (Jefferson to James Monroe.)

Monticello, May 5, 1811.

We are suffering here, both in the gathered and the growing crop. The lowness of the river, and great quantity of produce brought to Milton this year, render it almost impossible to get our crops to market. This is the case of mine as well as yours, and the Hessian fly appears alarmingly in our growing crops.  Everything is in distress for the want of rain. . . . (Lipscomb and Bergh, *Jefferson* 13: 60.)

### (John Dortie to Jefferson.)

New York May 11ᵗʰ. 1811.

Agreeably to your instruction respecting the Garden seed sent I forwarded it today to Philadelphia through the swift sure stage with the directions to Mr. Bernard McMahon.
The entry of that box was made with many other things and the value was estimated so low that the duty can not be calculated.  As for the freight, it is over paid by the pleasure I had to be agreeable to yourself.  I am sorry that the object was of so little consideration.  Whatever be the case you may depend upon my care as much as you may believe me very Respectfully. . . . (*Jefferson Papers,* L. C.)

### (Jefferson to Governor John Milledge.)

Monticello June 5. 11.

Our cultivation of Benni has not yet had entire success.  the 1ˢᵗ. year we sowed late & the frost caught it, so that we had scarcely seed the 2ᵈ. year to raise seed for the 3ᵈ.  we have at length made in the neighborhood two or three bushels.  I succeeded in expressing the oil in the iron press you saw at Foxall's.  but the iron giving a brown tinge to the oil, altho transparent & free from taste, I tried a wooden press, on the principle of that for flaxseed: which is a Mortise in a bench, into one end of which a small bag of seed is put, and the remaining space being filled with blocks, a wedge is forced between them by a sledge hammer & the oil drops from the bag, through a hole in the bottom of the mortise, into a vessel below.  we found this troublesome & embarrassing, and I then tried a conceit of my own.  it is a simple mortise in a block, 6. Inches square & deep, into which is inserted a stem of wood 2. feet long & pitted nicely to slide up & down in the mortise.  under this the bag of seed is placed in the mortise, & the whole put under the beam of a cyder or tobacco press.  this answered best of all.  I had but one bushel of seed, & having to try so many new projects before any one succeeded, I got from the whole but one gallon of oil.   I have mentioned these essays at presses on the possibility you might wish to make the oil at home. My greatest difficulty now is in separating the seed from the broken particles of the pod & leaf.   if we attempt to winnow, the seed is so light that it goes off with the refuse particles.   will you be so good as to inform me how you clear the seed from these particles.   the plant appears to me to be about as hardy as Cotton, & consequently our climate will barely permit us to make enough for family use. . . . I have written you quite a farmer's letter.   I am done with politics and have banished all it's passions, except the love of free government. . . . (*Jefferson Papers*, L. C.)

### (Jefferson to Isaac Coles.)

Monticello June 10. 11.

. . . P. S.   We were told by some one that m̄r̄s̄ Coles would be so kind as to spare us some bulbs of the Mourning bride.   altho the season is not naturally that of removing roots, yet they are so hardy a plant, that I have supposed it possible they might bear it.   m̄r̄s̄ Coles is a better judge; and if she thinks the removal would be safe I would ask a few: but if not safe, I would rather wait a more favorable season. . . . (*Jefferson Papers*, M. H. S.)

### (Isaac A. Coles to Jefferson.)

Enniscorthy June 10th 1811.

I have been intending for some days to visit Monticello, & have been prevented from doing so by indisposition which has confined me at Home & which I fear may still prevent me from executing my intention;—If however I am not worse I will be with you on Wednesday.

The Mourning Bride has not flourished well in our Garden, & I send 2 bulbs which were all that could be safely taken from the only remaining bunch of which we were certain—from another, which the Gardener believed to be Mourning bride, I have also sent a few roots, around which to distinguish them from the others, I directed him to fold a rag. As they are taken up with the hard earth adhering to them, I have no doubt but that they will succeed perfectly. . . . (*Jefferson Papers*, L. C.)

### (Jefferson to Charles Bankhead.)

Monticello June 10. 11.

. . . altho' we have lately had very seasonable rains, the wheat does not get over the injury of the fly.   the crop will be light except in the tobacco grounds & other very rich lands.   the Shoemakers deliver up the mill to morrow to m̄r̄ Randolph & Mᶜ.Kenny, who have bought them out at considerable sacrifices, and will carry on the business in partnership.   the Shoemakers, under all their bad management, have ground between 7. & 8000. barrels this year, on which they confess they have made a Dollar a barrel. I think their successors will receive at least 60,000. bushels of wheat a year, without buying a bushel. . . . (*Jefferson Papers,* Huntington.)

### (Jefferson to James Madison.)

Monticello, July 3, 1811.

. . . we are in the midst of a so-so harvest, probably one-third short of the last. We had a very fine rain on Saturday last. . . . (Lipscomb and Bergh, *Jefferson* **13**: 64.)

### (Jefferson to David B. Warden.)

Monticello July 8. 11.

. . . Arthur Young carried the Sichorium Intibus from France to England, & sent some seed to Gen¹. Washington who gave me a part. it has been growing here in abundance & perfection now 20. years without any cultivation after the first transplanting. I know no plant so valuable for green feeding, and m͞r Strickland told me they cut up the dry plant in England, & fed their horses with it. . . . (*Jefferson Papers,* Maryland Historical Society and L. C.)

### (Governor John Milledge to Jefferson.)

Near Augusta, Georgia,
12ᵗʰ. July 1811.

I have received your esteemed favor of the 5ᵗʰ of last month. I was apprehensive that Monticello and its neighborhood would be too cold for the bene so as to make it a profitable article of cultivation for market. If you can raise a sufficiency of seed for your own use, it will be in my opinion, as much as can be done. Accept my warmest thanks for communicating your different essays at presses for making of the oil. I have made oil for my own use and neighbors for two years past, it took me some time before I succeeded, and now with very little trouble, I can make about a gallon and a quart of pure cold drawn oil, to a bushel of seed. I took a block of sweet gum, 4 feet by 2½, a mortise in the centre, 12 inches long, 8 wide, and 9 inches deep, an inch Auger was passed obliquely through it, so as to hit the centre of one side of the mortise at the bottom, into which I introduced a piece of gun barrel as a tube at the bottom of the mortise, grooves were cut, with a chisel, in different directions, gradually made deeper as they inclined to the tube, strips of sheet iron about an inch wide, and nearly the length of the mortise, was placed over the grooves, about 3–8ᵗʰ of an inch apart. In my first essay I had no grooves, a considerable part of the oil was forced up, little ran out at the tube. I have the seed bruised in a mortar, then put into a bag, knitted of coarse yarn, the bag with the seed is placed in the mortise, a piece of sweet gum, about 3 inches thick, made exactly to occupy the mortise, is put on the bag, a block of the size of the mortise follows next.

A large wooden screw, which I have for compressing cotton into square cakes, is made to act on the block, the lever is of considerable length, and of course the power great.   Your method of the beam must answer equally as well as the screw, perhaps better, or the pressure is more gradual.   I was impressed with the belief, that the beam would answer, and recommended it last winter to Mr. Willis Alston of North Carolina.   The way I have hitherto taken to clear the seed of the refuse particles is by wenches riddling the seed in small baskets, in the same manner that is done with corn, to take the husk from it, after being beat for hommony.   I some times charge the seed by wind, putting a bench on a sheet for a person to stand on and lowering and raising the seed, according to the force of the wind.   I once used a wheat fanner, the only objection, the sieve was too coarse.   Col°. Few informs me, that a fanner has been invented for the bene seed, and is used at an oil mill on second river, New Jersey, which separates the seed remarkably well.   The rice which you sent me, I distributed among some of our best rice planters near Savannah, one of the aquatic kind, is said to be equal if not superior, to the rice now generally Cultivated.   The bearded rice grows well on high land, and requires only the usual seasons for bringing Indian Corn to perfection.   I will have the result of the experiments published.

I intend sending to our friend Gen¹. Smith of Baltimore, a nice barrel of bene seed for you, with a request that he send it to Richmond.   I think you will find a difference in the weight of the seed, raised in Georgia, and that with you.   I should like to know the method which is used in the Old Country to clarify oil.   I find a sediment after the oil remains some time bottled, and it retains a vegetable scent which ought to be remedied.   As we appear to have somewhat of an intercourse with France, would you be desirous of making a second attempt of cotton seed!   it is only to inform me, and it shall be sent to whatever port you may dictate. . . . (*Jefferson Papers*, L. C.)

(Jefferson to Archibald Stuart.)

Monticello, August 8, 1811.

I ask the favor of you to purchase for me as much fresh timothy seed as the enclosed bill will pay for, pack and forward, and that you will have the goodness to direct it to be lodged at Mr. Leitch's store in Charlottesville by the waggoner who brings it.   You see how bold your indulgencies make me in intruding on your kindness. . . . (Lipscomb and Bergh, *Jefferson* 13: 71.).   [See *Account Book,* August 8, 1811.]

(Jefferson to Benjamin Rush.)

Poplar Forest, August 17, 1811.

I write to you from a place ninety miles from Monticello, near the New London of this State, which I visit three or four times a year, and stay from a fortnight to a month at a time.   I have fixed myself comfortably, keep some books here, bring others occasionally, am in the solitude of a hermit, and quite at leisure to attend to my absent friends. . . . Having to conduct my grandson through his course in mathematics, I have resumed that study with great avidity. It was ever my favorite one. We have no theories there, no uncertainties remain on the mind; all is demonstration and satisfaction. . . . (Lipscomb and Bergh, *Jefferson* 13: 74–75.)

### (Jefferson to Charles W. Peale.)

Poplar Forest, August 20, 1811.

. . . I have heard that you have retired from the city to a farm, and that you give your whole time to that. Does not the museum suffer? And is the farm as interesting? Here, as you know, we are all farmers, but not in a pleasing style. We have so little labor in proportion to our land that, although perhaps we make more profit from the same labor, we cannot give to our grounds that style of beauty which satisfies the eye of the amateur. Our rotations are corn, wheat, and clover, or corn, wheat, clover and clover, or wheat, corn, wheat, clover and clover; preceding the clover by a plastering. But some, instead of clover, substitute mere rest, and all are slovenly enough. We are adding the care of Merino sheep. I have often thought that if heaven had given me choice of my position and calling, it should have been on a rich spot of earth, well watered, and near a good market for the productions of the garden. No occupation is so delightful to me as the culture of the earth, and no culture comparable to that of the garden. Such a variety of subjects, some one always coming to perfection, the failure of one thing repaired by the success of another, and instead of one harvest a continued one through the year. Under a total want of demand except for our family table, I am still devoted to the garden. But though an old man, I am but a young gardener. . . . But Sundays and rainy days are always days of writing for the farmer. . . . (Lipscomb and Bergh, *Jefferson* 13: 78–79.)

### (J. Chambers to Jefferson.)

New York, 16ᵗʰ. Sept. 1811

When my friend Mr. D. B. Warden was last here, he communicated to me a letter of yours on the subject of the Fiorin Grass mentioned in the Belfast Ag. Society's papers, & requested me to endeavor to procure some of it for you.

I have very great pleasure in now informing you, that in consequence of having written to a Botanical friend in Belfast, I have just received a small parcel in excellent preservation, & have put it into the care of Mr. Weightman, Bookseller, of Washington City who is now on his return, & expects to be in that City in about a week, & will then, search for the safest conveyance of it to you—but it is possible you may be able to point out one to him, upon which you may have more perfect reliance.

The parcel is too large to convey by Post, & I was unwilling to divide & put it into so small a compass, from a fear of injury.

This Grass has been chosen by a Gentleman of much Botanical knowledge, who has put it up in the manner directed by you in your letter to M^r. Warden; & I hope it will reach you in perfect safety, & fully answer the expectations you entertain of it.

Permit me to express the satisfaction I feel in having an opportunity of paying you even this small mark of attention. . . . (*Jefferson Papers, L. C.*)

### (Jefferson to J. Chambers.)

Monticello Sep. 30. 11.

Your favor of Sep. 16. has been duly received, and I pray you to accept my thanks for the trouble you have been so kind as to take in fulfilling my request to Mr. Warden. I had been impressed with the value of the fiorin grass described in the papers of the Belfast Agricultural society, and hoped it might answer good purposes here. I have ever considered the addition of an useful plant to the agriculture of a country as an essential service rendered to it, the merit of which in this case will be entirely yours. Mr. Weightman to whom you have been so kind as to confide the grass, will, I doubt not, forward it safely. the stage passing weekly between Washington & Charlottesville will furnish a safe conveyance. . . . (*Jefferson Papers, L. C.*)

### (Jefferson to John Dortie.)

Monticello Oct. 1. 11.

Your favor of Aug. 14. was received after an unusual delay of the post. I formerly believed it was best for every country to make what it could make to best advantage, and to exchange it with others for those articles which it could not so well make. I did not then suppose that a whole quarter of the globe could within the short space of a dozen years, from being the most civilized, become the most savage portion of the human race. I am come over therefore to your opinion that, abandoning to a certain degree those agricultural pursuits, which best suited our situation, we must endeavor to make every thing we want within ourselves, and have as little intercourse as possible with Europe in it's present demoralised state. wine being among the earliest luxuries in which we indulge ourselves, it is desirable it should be made here and we have every soil, aspect & climate of the best wine countries, and I have myself drank wines made in this state & in Maryland, of the quality of the best Burgundy. in answer to your enquiries respecting soils & their depth, in this state, I can only say in general that any character, & any depth of soil required may be found in the different parts of the state. I am best acquainted with James river, and may therefore affirm this fact more certainly as to that. the low grounds of that river are a deep vegetable mould, the same for 20. ft. depth. I live in a mountainous country, the vegetable mould of which is from 6. to 12. inches deep, &,

below that, many feet of fertile loam without any sand in it. but these soils are probably too rich to make fine wine. the Italian, Mazzei, who came here to make wine, fixed on these South West mountains, having a S. E. aspect, and abundance of lean & meagre spots of stony & red soil, without sand, resembling extremely the Cote of Burgundy from Chambertin to Monrachet where the famous wines of Burgundy are made. I am inclined to believe he was right in preferring the South Eastern face of this ridge of mountains. it is the first ridge, from the sea, begins on the North side of James river, & extends North Eastwardly, thro' the state under the different names, in different parts of it, of the Green Mountain, the Southwest Mountains, and Bull run mountains. doubtless however, other parts of the state furnish the proper soil & climate. beyond the blue ridge the climate becomes severe, & I should suppose less favorable. this, Sir, is as much as my scanty knolege of the subject will permit me to say. . . . (*Jefferson Papers, L. C.*)

## (R. C. Weightman to Jefferson.)

Washington, Oct. 12, 1811.

M<sup>r</sup>. Chambers of N. York put into my charge a parcel of Fiorin grass recently received from Ireland, with directions to take the earliest and safest mode of conveyance to Monticello. Since my return home I have had it boxed and directed to the care of the post master at Fredericksburg. M<sup>r</sup>. W<sup>m</sup>. B. Randolph did me the favor to take charge of the box and will deliver it safely into the hands of the post master. . . . (*Jefferson Papers, M. H. S.*)

## (Jefferson to Roger C. Weightman.)

Monticello, Oct. 19, '11.

I have duly received your favor of the 12th and also the parcel of fiorin grass of which you were so kind as to take charge and for your care of which I pray you to accept my thanks. It has been immediately planted, and every care will be taken to add it to the useful grasses of our country. . . . (*Glimpses of the Past, Missouri, 3: 116.*)

## (Jefferson to Archibald Stuart.)

Monticello, Nov. 14, 11.

We have safely received the cask of timothy seed, and also the very excellent parcel of butter which you have been so kind as to send us; for which be pleased to accept my thanks, or perhaps I should more properly request you to tender them with my respects to mrs. Stuart. (Ford, *Jefferson Correspondence: 201.*)

## From the *Farm Book 1811*:

1811. May. I think the road from the Pierhead up the riverside, about 60. or 70. yards which is now finished, has cost about 100. D.

it took 22. lbs. of powder, about 14. days work of 2. men & 2. boys blowing call then 42. days repair of augers, about 90. days work of common laborers last year, & about 15. days work, of common labourers now.

### Lego

1811. clear adjoining the Belted grounds for tob°.
clean up Hickman's field for corn.
Squarefield.   wheat.
Culpepper.   enlarge to 40 aˢ. & sow wheat.
[?] field wheat or oats & clover.
aim as soon as possible at getting 3. fields of 80. aˢ. each for this rotation, to wit:
1 field, half in corn, half in peas, oats or millet:
& in the next rotation change the halves.
1. in wheat 80. aˢ.
1. in clover 80. aˢ. and
a fourth field, as fast as we can, to be in clover also.
the △ and Dry field will be one.
the Oblong & ☐ field another.
Hickman's and the Belted field a third.
Culpeper etc. a 4ᵗʰ.

## From the *Account Book 1809–1820:*

July    2.    agreed this day with E. Bacon that his wages shall be £ 40.

Aug.    3.    bought of Wᵐ. D. Meriwether    26. ewes
                                            12. ewe lambs
                                            5. weather lambs
                                            ⎯
                                            43 @ 2 D. 86.

August 4.    agreed with Jeremiah Goodman to serve me next year as Overseer in Bedford over a plantation & 16. hands, for which I am to give him 200. D. a year, & all other articles to stand as by our original agreement.

Aug.    8.    inclosed to Judge Stewart [Stuart] 10. D. to buy timothy seed.   [See letter, Jefferson to Stuart, August 8.]

## Planting Memorandum for *Poplar Forest 1811:*

1811. Feb. 27.   planted 30. gooseberries.   W. end of the patch
                 11. grapes of one kind ⎱ S. side of d°. & E.
                 21. d°. of another        ⎰    end.
                 rose bushes ⎱ N. side of d°. at W. end.
                 bear grass  ⎰
                 pinks.   in locks of fence N. & W.

50  cutting of Athenian poplar.  Nursery next
N. fence between 2. stables.
prepared bed next Southwardly for tomatas
    next d°.                      lettuce
    next d°. 80. f. long for
            Asparagus.
planted 16. raspberries along side of the gooseberries
     25. cutting of Weep$^g$. willow along side of
        the Ath. poplars.
Memo$^m$. plant on each mound
        4. weeping willows on the top in a square
           20. f. apart.
        Golden willows in a circle round the
        middle.  15. f. apart.
        Aspens in a circle round the foot.   15. f.
        apart.
        plant 6. weeping willows round each
        Cloacinal.

Aug. 13.  I find growing in the truck patch 30. golden willows.
                                  20. weeping d°.
                                  10. Athenian poplars.
                                   3. Lombardy poplars.
                                   2. Aspens.

*(Jefferson Papers, U. Va.)*

## (Jefferson to Jeremiah A. Goodman.)

[Memorandum *Poplar Forest*] Dec. 1811.

The crop of the Tomahawk plantation for 1812.

corn, oats & peas.  The Shopfield, the best parts of it 64. acres
       the Eastern parts of M$^c$Daniel's field  36. acres
                                      100.

of the above, put about three fourths into corn, of the best parts, the
rest in oats & peas.   there will still remain about 16. a$^s$. of the Shopfield
for Burnet.

Wheat & oats.  the Ridgefield 130. a$^s$.  Early's 54.  Upper Tomahawk 25.  in all 209. acres.

tobacco.  half of the 2. year old ground 15. a$^s$.  the ground on the
road cleared & not tended last year 10. acres about 2. now cut down,
& perhaps some parts of the meadow ground.  as this is more than can
be tended, perhaps the 10. a$^s$. on the road, or part of them may go
into corn.

In general I would wish 4. a$^s$. of meadow ground to be prepared, to
be tended one year in tob°. and 8. or 10. a$^s$. of high ground to be tended
2. years in tob°. which will give from 20. to 24. a$^s$. of tob°. every year.
the high land for this year 1812. is to be cleared on the South side of
Tomahawk creek, between the upper & lower fields.  but as to the

meadow ground, I wish as much as possible to be prepared, of that which is easiest to prepare, & to be tended in tob°. pumpkins, peas or whatever will best suit it, & clean it, to be sown in timothy in the Fall. the parts already clean should be sown this spring.

All the ground which is in wheat, or which will be in oats, & turned out to rest, is to be sown in clover in February, and Burnet, if I can get seed, is to be sown in the old South hill side of the Shop field.

An acre of the best ground for hemp, is to be selected, & sown in hemp & to be kept for a permanent hemp patch.

The laborers for the Tomahawk plantation are to be the following:

Men.   Dick, Jesse, Gawen, Phill Hubard, Hercules, Manuel, Evans.
Women.   Betty, Dinah, Cate's Hanah, Gawen's Sal, Agg, Lucinda, Dinah's Hanah, Amy, Milly.

Nace, the former headman, and the best we have ever known, is to be entirely kept from labour until he recovers, which will probably be very long.  he may do any thing which he can do sitting in a warm room, such as shoemaking and making baskets.  he can shell corn in the corn house when it is quite warm, or in his own house at any time.

Will & Hal, when they have no work in the shop, are to get their coal wood, or assist in the crop.  they will make up for the loss of Hanah's work, who cooks & washes for me when I am here.  the smith's should make the plantation nails of the old bits of iron.

Edy is not named among the field workers, because either she or Aggy, whichever shall be thought most capable, is to be employed in weaving, and will be wanting to clean the house and assist here a part of the day when I am here.  until a loom can be got ready both may be in the ground.

Bess makes the butter during the season, to be sent to Monticello in the winter.  when not engaged in the dairy, she can spin coarse on the big wheel.  Abby has been a good spinner.  they may each of them take one of the young spinners, to spin with them in their own house, & under their care.  in that way one wheel will serve for two persons.  the spinners are to be Marie (Nanny's) Sally (Hanah's) Lucy (Dinah's) and Nisy (Maria's).  this last may spin at her grandmother Cate's & under her care; and so may Maria who is her niece, & whose mother will be there.  they had better spin on the small wheel.

2. cotton wheels will suffice for Abby & Bess and the 2. girls with them, & a flax wheel apiece for each of the other two girls.  hemp should be immediately prepared to set them at work, & a supply be kept up; and as there will be no wool to spin till May, mr̄s Goodman may employ the wool spinners for herself till then, if she chuses.  whatever terms have been settled between mr̄s Bacon & mr̄s Randolph, shall be the same with her.  (I do not know what they are) and as a compensation for teaching Aggy or Edy to weave, I propose to give her the usual price for all the weaving she may do for me, the first year, considering it as her apprenticeship: and that afterwards she shall have the same proportion of her time as she is to have of the spinners.

Several of the negro women complain that their houses want repair badly.  this should be attended to every winter.  for the present winter, repair, of preference those of the women who have no husbands to do it for them. the removal of so many negroes from this to the other place will require a good deal of work there to lodge them comfortably. this should be done at once, by the gangs of both places joined.

10. bushels of clover seed to be got early from Cofe, for the 2. plantations. fresh seed.

The ground laid off for my garden is to be inclosed with a picquet fence, 7. feet high, & so close that a hare cannot get into it. it is 80. yards square, & will take, I suppose about 2400. rails 8. f. long, besides the running rails & stakes. the sheep to be folded in it every night.

As soon as a boat load of tob°. is ready, it must be sent down to Gibson & Jefferson in Richmond, & an order given the boatman on them for the price of the carriage. good enquiry should be made before hand for responsible faithful boatmen. mr̄ Griffin knows them well; mr̄ Robinson also will advise.

If a physician should at any time be wanting for the negroes, let our neighbor Dʳ. Steptoe be called in. In pleurisies, or other highly inflammatory fevers, intermitting fevers, dysenteries, & Venereal cases, the doctors can give certain relief; and the sooner called to them the easier & more certain the cure. but in most other cases they oftener do harm than good. a dose of salts as soon as they are taken is salutary in almost all cases, & hurtful in none. I have generally found this, with a lighter diet and kind attention restore them soonest. the lancet should never be used without the advise of a physician, but in sudden accidents. a supply of sugar, molasses and salts should be got from mr̄ Robinson & kept in the house for the sick. there are 2. or 3. cases of ruptures among the children at the two plantations, to which the Doctor should be immediately called, & great attention paid to them, as if not cured now, they will be lost for ever.

The workhorses are to be equally divided between the 2. places, and one more apeice to be purchased if good ones can be got on good terms and on credit till the sale of our tob°. say April or May. a pair of well broke oxen, not above middle age is to be set apart for Monticello; & the rest equally divided. the cattle, sheep, & hogs to be equally divided as to numbers, ages, sexes &c but when the cows begin to give milk in the spring of the year, reserving at Bear creek enough for the overseer & negroes, the surplus milch cows must come to Tomahawk for the butter season, to make a supply for Monticello. the carts & tools equally divided.

Of the 28. hogs at Bear creek, the 39 in the pen at Tomahawk & 8. more expected at the same place, in all 75. 30 of the fattest must be sent to Monticello, 2 be given to the 2. hogkeepers Jame Hubᵈ. & Hal, 28. be kept for the negroes & harvest, & 15 to furnish the allowance to the 2 overseers, & what remains of the 15 after furnishing them, to be kept for my use while here. the offal of the 28. hogs for the negroes and of those for myself will serve them, it is expected, 6. weeks or 2. months before entering on the distribution of meat to them regularly.
(Courtesy of Dr. A. S. W. Rosenbach.)

Jefferson's plan for the Orchard, 1811:

| | almond | apples | Taliafers d°. | apricots | Cherries | Nectarines | peaches | pears | plumbs | quinces | vacancies |
|---|---|---|---|---|---|---|---|---|---|---|---|
| a. | | | | | 2. | | 2. | | | | |
| b. | | | | | 2. | | 3. | | | | |
| c. | | | | | 5. | | 2. | | | | |
| d. | | | | | 2. | 5. | 5. | | 1. | | |
| e. | | | | | 4. | | 17. | | 1. | | 7. |
| f. | | | | 1. | 10. | | 14. | | | 5. | |
| g. | | 6. | | 6. | | | 16. | | | | |
| h. | | 11. | | | 1. | | 19. | | | | 15. |
| i. | | 15. | | | 1. | | 22. | | | | 7. |
| j. | | 17. | | | 1. | | 15. | | | | 11. |
| k. | | 4. | | | 10. | | 26. | | | | 1. |
| l. | | 5. | | | 8. | | 11. | | | | 16. |
| m. | | 11. | | | 1. | | | 2. | | | 6. |
| n. | | | 6. | | | | 5. | | | | 1. |
| o. | | | 3. | | 1. | | 2. | | | | 3. |
| p. | | | 3. | | | | 1. | | | | 3. |
| q. | | | 3. | | | | | | | | 1. |
| Total 384 | | 69. | 15. | 7. | 48. | 5. | 160. | 2. | 2. | 5. | 71. |

the vacancies to be filled in 1811. as follows

e. 7. cherries.    viz. −1. 2. +1. 4. 6. 7. 8.
h. 15. pippins       −1. +2. 3. 5. 7. 13. 14. 16. 18. 19. 22. 23.
                               24. 25. 26.
i. 7. Spitzenbg̅s̅     +5. 8. 13. 16. 17. 24. 26.
j. 11. calvites      −1. 2. +2. 9. 12. 13. 16. 17. 24. 25. 26.
k. 1. qu? 16.
l. 16. paccans.     −2. +1. 2. 6. 8. 13. 16. 20. 23. 24. 25. 26. 27.
                               28. 31. 36.
m. 6 pears.        −1. +9. 11. 29. 33.
n. 1 +o. 3. +p. 3. +q. 1.=8.   Taliafers.

1811.    Mar. 16. in the row e. I found +5. d
        therefore planted e−1−2+1+4+5 with Tuckahoe grey
        hearts from m̅r̅ Coles [See *Garden Book*, March 16, 1811, and
        plate XXXII.]

                                         (*Jefferson Papers*, U. Va.)

# 1812

Arrangement of the Garden.[2] | N. W. Border

7. beds of Asparagus. at S.W. end

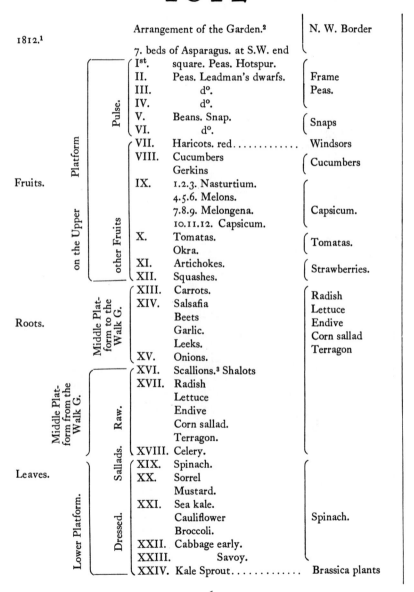

| | | | |
|---|---|---|---|
| Fruits. | Platform on the Upper | Pulse. | I[st]. square. Peas. Hotspur. |
| | | | II. Peas. Leadman's dwarfs. |
| | | | III. d°. |
| | | | IV. d°. |
| | | | V. Beans. Snap. |
| | | | VI. d°. |

Frame Peas.

Snaps

| | |
|---|---|
| other Fruits | VII. Haricots. red............ |
| | VIII. Cucumbers / Gerkins |
| | IX. 1.2.3. Nasturtium. / 4.5.6. Melons. / 7.8.9. Melongena. / 10.11.12. Capsicum. |
| | X. Tomatas. / Okra. |
| | XI. Artichokes. |
| | XII. Squashes. |

Windsors

Cucumbers

Capsicum.

Tomatas.

Strawberries.

| | |
|---|---|
| Roots. | Middle Platform to the Walk G. |

XIII. Carrots.
XIV. Salsafia
  Beets
  Garlic.
  Leeks.
XV. Onions.

Radish
Lettuce
Endive
Corn sallad
Terragon

| | | |
|---|---|---|
| Leaves. | Middle Platform from the Walk G. | Raw. |
| | Lower Platform. | Sallads. |
| | | Dressed. |

XVI. Scallions.[3] Shalots
XVII. Radish
  Lettuce
  Endive
  Corn sallad.
  Terragon.
XVIII. Celery.

XIX. Spinach.
XX. Sorrel
  Mustard.
XXI. Sea kale.
  Cauliflower
  Broccoli.
XXII. Cabbage early.
XXIII.     Savoy.
XXIV. Kale Sprout............

Spinach.

Brassica plants

469

1812.

| 1812. | where | when | transplant$^d$ | come to table | gone | Miscellanies. |
|---|---|---|---|---|---|---|
| Frame peas. | bord. I–V. | Feb. 15 | | *May 22. | | Mar. 6. up. Apr. 22. 1st. blossom. May. 1. pods. |
| Cucumbers. forward. | boxes I–III. | Feb. 22 | | | | Apr. 24. up. |
| Tomatas. | dᵒ. VII–XVIII. | 29 | June. 9.13. | | | |
| Lettuce. White loaf. | XIII.I. | | June. 13. | *May 22. | June 25. | June 12. in perfect loaf to wit. 104 days. |
| Radishes. scarlet. | XIII.I. | Mar. 2 | | | | |
| celery. | )plant bed Lego. | | June. 8. | | | |
| Savoys. | | | | | | |
| dᵒ. | dᵒ. Shadwell. | | | | | |
| Frame peas. | submural. | 6 | | *May 22 | | 1st. blossom. Apr. 25. May 4. pod. |
| Hotspurs. | II. | | | June. 5 | — | Mar. 23. up. Apr. 28. 1st. blossᵐ. |
| Ledmans. | I. | 8 | | June. 12 | | Mar. 25. up. |
| Cucumbers Early White. P.C. | boxes IV.V.VI. | | June. 9-13. | | | |
| Sprout Kale. | Nursery.17.W. | | | | | |
| Cabbage. many head. | dᵒ. 17.E. | | | | | |
| Savoy. | 18.W. | | | | | |
| | 18.E. | | | | | |
| Cauliflower. | 19. | | | | | |
| Broccoli. | | | | | | |
| Lettuce White loaf. | XVII.I.S.end. | Apr. 2. | | | | June 25. loafed. 12 weeks. |
| Radish. early scarlet. | ib. | 2. | | | | |
| Terragon. | XVII.I.N.end. | | Apr. 2. | | | |
| Sorrel transplanted. | 3ᵈ Terras.e.E. | | Apr. 3. | | | |
| Turnep. early Dutch. R. | ib. W. | 3. | | | | |
| Scallions. | XVI.I. | | 4. | | | |
| Shalots. | 2. | | 4. | | | |
| Carrots Early. R. | 3.T.c. East. | 11. | | | | |
| large R. | 3.T.c. middle. | | | | | |
| Orange. | 3.T.c. West. | | | | | |
| Tomatas. | Border VI. | 14. | | Aug. 14. | | |
| Ledman's peas. | III. | | | | | |
| Snaps. grey. | V. | 15. | | June 13 | | pod. June 8. |

* these articles might have been used some days sooner but I was from home.

1812. (continued)

| 1812. | where | when | transplant$^d$ | come to table | gone | Miscellanies. |
|---|---|---|---|---|---|---|
| Lettuce white. | XVII.2. | | | July. 1. | | 11. weeks. |
| Radish scarlet. | ib. S.end. | | | | | |
| Radish black. R. | ib. N.end. | | | | | |
| Benni. | int. 3$^d$ T. & Bailey. | | | | | |
| Malta Kale. | Nursery S. | 16. | | | | |
| Nasturtium. | IX. 1.2.3. | | | | | |
| Melon. Chinese. | 4. | | | | | |
| Melongena. white. | 7. | | | | | |
| purple | 8. | | | | | |
| prickly | 9. | | | | | |
| Leeks. common. | XIV.4.S. | | 17. | | | |
| flag. R. | N. | 17. | 18. | | | |
| Onions. | XV. | 21. | | | | |
| long haricots. ours. | Circ.T.6.E. | | | July. 15. | | |
| asparagus bean. Maryl$^d$ | W. | 22. | | July. 11. | | |
| Salsafia. | 3$^d$.T.d. | | | | | |
| Tomatas. | Submural. | | | | | |
| Lima beans. | Circ. T.7. | 23. | | Aug. 5. | | |
| Sea Kale. | Circ. T.3.E.end. | 24. | | | | |
| P.C. Cucumbers early white. | VIII.E. row. | | | | | |
| gerkins. | 2$^d$ row. | | | | | |
| Early green | 3$^d$ row. | 25. | | | | |
| Pani corn. | orchard. | | | Aug. 4. | | |
| Cherokee corn. | d$^o$. | 24. | | | | |
| Lettuce white. | XVII.3.S. | | | July 4.loaf$^d$ | | 10. weeks + 1. day. |
| radish. scarlet. | XVII.3.S. | 27. | | | | |
| Carrots. Orange. | XIII. | | | | | |
| Salsafia. Columbian. | XIV.1.N. | | | | | |
| d$^o$. common. | ib. S. | | | | | |
| beets. | ib. 2. | | | | | |
| Peas Leadmans. | IV. | 24. | | | last dish July. 17. | |
| cucumbers early. | hhd 1.2. | 30. | | | | |
| red haricots. | Circ. T.3.W. | May. 5. | | July. 7. | | 9. weeks + 1. day. |
| Lettuce white. | XVII.3.N. | May. 5. | | July. 8.loaf$^d$ | | |
| Radish black. R. | ib. | | | | | |

1812. (continued)

| | where | when | transpl^d | come to table | gone | Miscellanies. |
|---|---|---|---|---|---|---|
| Carrots | VII | May 6. | | | | 8. weeks – 1. day. |
| lettuce w radish.s | XVII 4.S. | 18. | | July 12. loaf | | |
| snaps | VI.S. | 18. | | July 9. | | failed. |
| lettuce w. radish scarlet | XVII.4.N. | 25. | | | | |
| red haricots | VI.W. | 26. | | | | |
| cucumbers early | VIII.W | 26. | | July 17. | | |
| tomatas | submur[1]. repl^d | | | | | |
| lettuce. wh. | XVII.5.S. | June 1. | | | | failed. |
| radish. | ib. | d°. | | | | |
| lettuce. wh. | XVII.2.N. | | | | | failed. |
| radish. summer | ib. | 8. | | | | |
|     ES | | | | | | |
| lettuce. wh. | XVII.5.N. | 15. | | Aug. 17. | | 9. weeks. |
| radish. | ib. | | | | | |
| lettuce wh. | XVII.6.N. | 22. | | Aug. 17. | | 8. weeks. |
| radish summer | ib. | | | | | |
| lettuce green loaf | XVII.4.N. | 25. | | | | failed. |
| radish Taragon | ib. | | | | | |
| lettuce. wh. | XVII.6.S. | 29. | | | | |
| lettuce wh. | XVII.7.N. | July 6. | | | | |
| lettuce white | XVII.7.S. | 13. | | | | |
| lettuce white | XVII.2.N. | 20. | | | | |
| d°. | XVII.6.S. | 27. | | | | |
| d°. | XVII.3.N. | Aug. 3. | | | | |
| Dutch brown | XVII.5.S. | 11. | | | | |
| Spinach prickly | XII.3^d from E. | 20. | | | | |
| Lettuce D. Brown | IX.4.& 6. | 28. | | | | |
| Spinach prickly | XII.1.2.4. from E. | | | | | |
| Swed. Turnep. Ronaldson[4] | IX. 4.5. | 25. | | | | |
| d°. — from France | VIII.E.half. | 25. | | | | |
| Spinach prickly | strait Terra. c. | Sep. 1. | | | | |
| Lettuce D. Brown | IX.7.8.9.10.11.12. / XVII. 1.2,3,S. half. / 4.N.half. / 7.entire. | Sep. 1. | | | | |

## 1812.

Calendar for this year.
Feb.  1.
        manure & make up hop-hills.
        Asparagus.  dress & replant.
   15.  Frame peas
        Radish & lettuces.  XIII
        Spinach.  XII
        Celery ⎫
        Savoys ⎭ plant beds.
        early Cabbage
        Savoys
Mar.  1.  Peas Frame, $1^{st}$. or submural terrace
            Hotspurs.  II.
            Ledmans   I.
        Potatoes.  early.  strait terras 1.f.
        Strawberries.  Hudson.  $3^{d}$. Ter. 1.a.
                Alpine.  Circular Terras.4.5.
   15.  Nasturtium.  IX.1.2.3.
        Tomatas.  X.
        Artichokes.  XI.
        Carrots XIII.
            $.3^{d}$. Ter. C.
        Beets XIV.2.
        Garlic.[5]  XIV.3.
        Leeks.  XIV.4.
        Onions.  XV.
        Chives.[6]  XVI.1.
        Shalots.  XVI.2.
        lettuce ⎫ XVII.1.
        radish ⎭
        Seakale.  Circ.T.3.
        Hops.[7]  $.3^{d}$.T.b.
        $Summ^{r}$ turneps $3^{d}$.T.e.
Apr.  1.  Peas Ledman's.  III.
        Snaps.  V.
        Capsicum Major.  IX.10.
                Bull nose.  IX.11.
                Cayenne.  IX.12
        Mustard Durham.  XII
        Salsafia.  XIV.  3.T.d.
        lettuce.  radishes.  XVII.1.
        terragon.  XVII.
        long haricots.  Circ.T.7.
        Lima beans.  Circ.T.8.a.
        Corn Pani.  Circ.T.8.6. & orchard.
        Ravensworths.  Circ.T.10.a.b. & orchard.
        cow peas.  Circ.Ter.II.a.b. & orchard.
   15.  Peas Ledmans.  IV.
        Snaps.  VI.
        Cucumbers.  Gerkins.  VIII.
        Melons.  IX.4.5.6.
        Melongena.  white IX.7.  purple 8.  prickly 9.
        Okra.  X.
        Squashes XII.
        lettuce.  radishes.  XVII.2.
        Sorrel.  .3.T.e.
May.  1.  red Haricots.  VII.
        lettuce.  radishes.  XVII.2.
        homony beans.  Circ.T.8.b.
        Swedish Turneps.  Circ.T.9.a.b.

May. June. July. take up flower bulbs. separate offsets. replant lillies.
Aug. 15. Spinach. Lettuce.
Sep. 1. sow spinach. Lettuce.
October. dress flower borders & set out bulbs.
Oct. ⎤ cover figs and tender plants. litter Asparagus beds.
Nov. ⎮ plant trees. privet. thorn
Dec. ⎬ trim trees, vines, rasp. gooseb. currants. turf. bring in manure
Jan. ⎦ and trench it into hills.

           E. Vineyard.  Mar. 26.
           Terras.  4$^{th}$. E. end.    Sweet scented grass seed
                  5.  d°.        a grass from Gen$^l$. Mason.[8]
                  6$^{th}$. W. end.  rye grass.[10] Ronaldson[9]
                  7.             yellow clover.[11]  R
                  8.
                  9.  ......    Oats Scotch.[12]  R.
                  10            *d°. red. Tuscany
                  11.           *barley[13] naked
                  12.           Tares.[14]  R
                  13.           Scarcity root[15]  R
                  14. ......   Parsneps R
                  15. ......   Scorzonera.[16]  R
                  16. ......   Cabbage. red.  R
                  17. ...........    Aberdeen R
                  18 .............    large Cattle R
                  19            Kale Russian.  R.
       the articles marked R. were sent me by m͞r Ronaldson from Edinb͞g.
Mar. 28.  sowed in Square XII. beg$^g$. on the West side in rows.
           row 1$^{st}$.  Cauliflower
               2$^d$    Broccoli white
               3$^d$    .......  green
               4$^{th}$.   .......  purple
               5$^{th}$.  Cabbage.  May
               6$^{th}$    .......  dwarf
               7$^{th}$    .......  sugar loaf
               8$^{th}$    .......  Savoy green
               9$^{th}$    ...........  yellow
            10$^{th}$. Sprouts Brussels.
         bed. 11. N. end Spinach prickly.⎱ S. end broad d°. R.
                           ⎰ 12. S. end. broad d°.
         flower borders.[17] Apr. 8. laid them off into compartm$^{ts}$. of 10.f.
         length each.
         in the N. borders are 43.⎱ comptm$^{ts}$.
         in the S. borders are 44½⎰
         the odd compartments are for bulbs requir$^d$. taking up
         the even ones for seeds & permanent bulbs.
         denote the inner borders .i. and the outer .o.
Apr.  8.  sowed Bellflower[18] in 28. on both sides ⎤ there was by mistake an in-
        African Marigold[19] 32$^d$. d°.          ⎬ terchange of place be-
        White poppy[20] 42$^d$. N. and 44$^{th}$. S.  ⎦ tween one of the parcels
                                    of bellflower & Poppy.
Apr.  8.  Asparagus comes to table.
    17.  Arbor beans[21] white, scarlet, crimson, purple. at the trees of the
         level on both sides of terrasses, and on long walk of garden.
June. 25.  E. Vineyard.
         terras 20. Polygonum Tartaricum.[22]  buckwheat
              21. Panicum Virgatum.[23]  Guinea millet.
July 23.  last dish of artichokes.
Mar. 12.  planted in the 12. I. boxes.  N°. IV.  red gooseberry
                             V.  Lewis' sweetscented Currant.
                             Odoratissima.

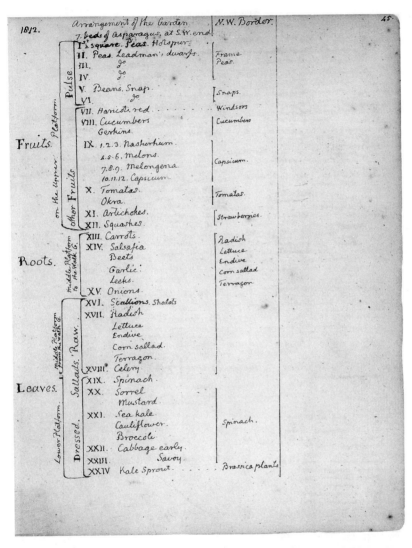

1812.    Arrangement of the Garden.    N.W. Border.    45.

7. beds of asparagus, at S.W. end

I. square. Peas. Hotspur.
II. Peas. Leadman', dwarfs.        Frame
III.        do                            Peas.
IV.        do
V. Beans. Snap.
VI.        do                            Snaps.
VII. Haricots. red . . . . . . . Windsors
VIII. Cucumbers                    Cucumbers
      Gerkins.
IX. 1.2.3. Nasturtium.
    4.5.6. melons.
    7.8.9. Melongena                Capsicum.
    10.11.12. Capsicum.
X. Tomatas.                         Tomatas.
   Okra.
XI. Artichokes.                     Strawberries.
XII. Squashes.

Fruits.  on the Upper Platform   other Fruits

XIII. Carrots.                      Radish
XIV. Salsafia                       Lettuce
     Beets                          Endive
     Garlic                         Corn sallad
     Leeks.                         Terragon
XV. Onions.

Roots.   middle Platform to the walk G.

XVI. Scallions. Shalots
XVII. Radish
      Lettuce
      Endive
      Corn sallad.
      Terragon.
XVIII. Celery
XIX. Spinach.
XX. Sorrel
    Mustard.
XXI. Sea kale.
     Cauliflower.                    Spinach.
     Broccoli
XXII. Cabbage early.
XXIII.        Savoy.
XXIV. Kale Sprout . . . . . Brassica plants

Leaves.   Sallads. Raw.  Dressed.  middle Platform from the walk G.  Lower Platform.

PLATE XXXIII.—Page 45 of the original *Garden Book:* "Arrangement of the Garden," 1812. This shows Jefferson's detailed arrangement and plantings in the vegetable garden. The garden was divided into three terraces, called platforms. The Roman numerals mark the numbers of the sres.qua

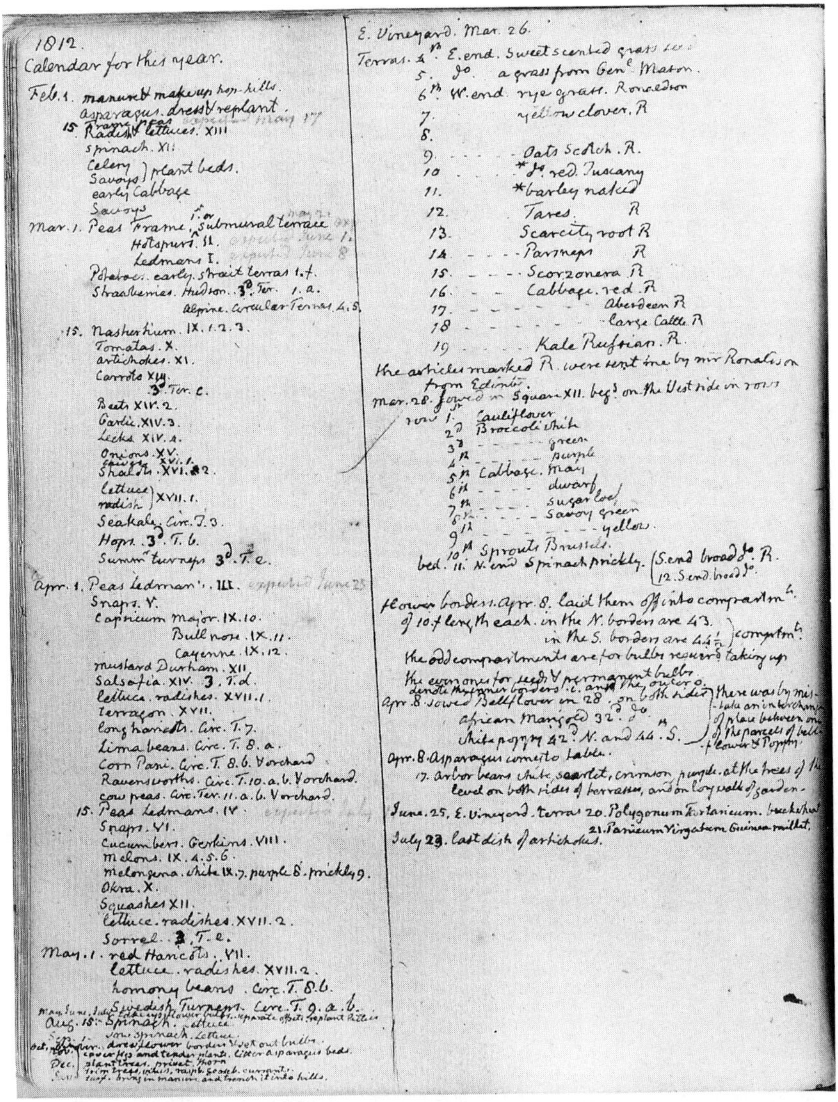

1812.
Calendar for this year.
Feb. 1. manure & make up hop-hills.
asparagus. dress & replant.
15. Frame peas. expected May 17
Radish & lettuce. XIII
spinach. XI.
Celery } plant beds.
Savoys }
early Cabbage
Savoys
Mar. 1. Peas Frame, for submural terrace
Hotspurs. II. expected June 1.
Ledmans I. expected June 8
Potatoes. early. strait terras 1. 4.
Strawberries. Hudson. 3d. Ter. 1. a.
Alpine. Circular Terras 4. 5.
15. Nasturtium. IX. 1. 2. 3.
Tomatas. X.
artichokes. XI.
Carrots XIII.
3d. Ter. c.
Beets XIV. 2.
Garlic. XIV. 3.
Leeks XIV. 4.
Onions. XV.
Chives. XVI. 1.
Shalots. XVI. 2.
Lettuce } XVII. 1.
radish }
Seakale. Circ. T. 3.
Hops. 3d. T. b.
Summer turneps 3d. T. e.
Apr. 1. Peas Ledman's. III. expected June 25
Snaps. V.
Capsicum major. IX. 10.
Bull nose. IX. 11.
Cayenne. IX. 12.
mustard Durham. XII
Salsafia. XIV. 3. T. d.
lettuce. radishes. XVII. 1.
Tarragon. XVII.
long haricots. Circ. T. 7.
Lima beans. Circ. T. 8. a.
Corn Pani. Circ. T. 8. b. & orchard.
Ravensworths. Circ. T. 10. a. b. & orchard.
cow peas. Circ. Ter. 11. a. b. & orchard.
15. Peas Ledmans. IV. expected July
Snaps. VI.
Cucumbers. Gerkins. VIII.
Melons. IX. 4. 5. 6.
Melongena. white IX. 7. purple 8. prickly 9.
Okra. X.
Squashes XII.
lettuce. radishes. XVII. 2.
Sorrel. 3. T. e.
May. 1. red Haricots. VII.
lettuce. radishes. XVII. 2.
homony beans. Circ. T. 8. b.
Swedish Turneps. Circ. T. 9. a. b.
May. June. July. take up flower bulbs. separate offsets. replant them
Aug. 15. Spinach. lettuce.
Sep. sow spinach. Lettuce.
Oct. dress flower borders & set out bulbs.
Nov. cover figs and tender plants. litter asparagus beds.
Dec. plant trees. privet. thorn
trim trees, vines, raspb. gooseb. currants.
turf. bring in manure and trench it into hills.

E. Vineyard. Mar. 26.
Terras. 4th. E. end. Sweet scented grass seed
5. do. a grass from Genl. Mason.
6th. W. end. rye grass. Ronaldson
7. yellow clover. R
8.
9. . . . Oats Scotch. R.
10. . . . *do. red. Tuscany
11. *barley naked
12. Tares. R
13. Scarcity root R
14. . . . Parsneps R
15. . . . Scorzonera R
16. . . Cabbage. red. R
17. . . . Aberdeen R
18. . . . Large Cattle R
19. . . Kale Ruffian. R.
the articles marked R. were sent me by mr Ronaldson from Edinbg.
Mar. 28. sowed in Square XII. begg. on the West side in rows
row 1st. Cauliflower
2d. Broccoli. white
3d. green
4th. purple
5th. Cabbage. May
6th. dwarf
7th. sugarloaf
8th. Savoy green
9th. yellow
10th. Sprouts Brussels.
bed. 11. N. end Spinach prickly. {S. end broad do. R.
12. S. end. broad do.
flower borders. Apr. 8. laid them off into compartmts. of 10. f. length each. in the N. borders are 43.
in the S. borders are 44½ } compartmts.
the odd compartments are for bulbs requiring taking up
the even ones for seeds & permanent bulbs
Apr. 8. sowed Bellflower in 28. on both sides
African Marigold 32. do.
white poppy 42. N. and 44. S.
there was by mistake an interchange of place between one of the parcels of bellflower & Poppy.
Apr. 8. Asparagus come to table.
17. Arbor beans white, scarlet, crimson, purple. at the trees of the level on both sides of terrasses, and on long walk of garden.
June. 25. E. Vineyard. terras 20. Polygonum Tartaricum. buckwheat
21. Panicum Virgatum Guinea millet.
July 23. last dish of artichokes.

Plate XXXIV.—Page 48 of the original *Garden Book*. Note: "flower borders. Apr. 8. laid them off into compartm$^{ts}$. of 10.f. length each."

VI. L's Snowberry bush.
VII. L's Yellow currant.

†also planted 3. plants of same gooseberry in the 2ᵈ. strait terras or upper Terras of Gooseberry Sq. at S.W. end.

11. currants. same. in the 3ᵈ. & 4ᵗʰ. strait terras or 2ᵈ. & 3ᵈ raspberry terrasses. S.W. end. ribes odoratissᵐᵃ

9. Yellow Currants in the 7ᵗʰ. and 8ᵗʰ terrasses or 1ˢᵗ. & 2ᵈ Currant terrasses. S.W. end.

8. Cape grapes for wine in the 2ᵈ terras or 1ˢᵗ. terras of E. Vineyard. S.W. end.

6. dᵒ. for wine or eating. 2ᵈ terras of dᵒ. S.W. end.

all the above were from Mᶜ. Mahon.[24]

planted 40. plants of Hudson strawberry from dᵒ. in the Strait Terras. a. + 3.

Mar. 17. & 18. planted as follows.

d. 28. to 36. 9 soft November peaches.

e. 4. a Carnation cherry.

27. 28. 31. 35. 39. 42. 43. 44. 8 plumb peaches of October.

f. 27. 29. 35. 40. ⎫ plumbs. supposᵈ.    f. 41. ⎫ 3 October plumb
g. 27. 30. 38. 39. ⎭ Cherokee from Bailey[25]   g. 42. 43. ⎭ peaches.

h. 2. 5. 6. 7. 12. 13. 14. 18. 19. 22. 23. 24. 25. 26. 28. 29. 30. 31. 32. 36. 39. 42. = 22. pippings

i. 5. 8. 9. 12. 13. 16. = 6. Spitzenb͞gs from m͞r Taylor.[26]
17. 18. 24. 25. 26. 27. = 6. Spitzenbgs from m͞r Divers.[27]

j. — 1. + 2. 8. 9. October, or November, or T. Lomax's[28] soft peaches, uncertain which.
12. 13. 16. 17. 23. 24. 25. 26. 39. = 9 soft peaches from T. Lomax.

k. 3. 6. 13. 17. 33. 35. Oct. or Nov. or T. Lomax's soft peaches.

l. 1. a Carnation cherry.    2. 6. Carnations or May Dukes.
8. pear from m͞r Divers[29]
13. 15. 16. 20. 23. 24. 25. = 7. choice pears from Walter Coles.[30]
26. 27. 28. 29. 31. 33. = 6 choice pears from m͞r Divers.[31]

m. 6. 27. 28. ⎫
n. 3.       ⎬ = 8. Taliaferro apples.
o. 3. 7.     ⎪
p. 4. 6.     ⎭

Allies of the Vineyards 25. paccans.

round the S.W. & N.E. ends of the garden pales, and about 12.f. from the pales 29, Roanoke hiccory nuts, and 6. Osage dᵒ. 25.f. apart.

Mar. 20. planted 9. Snowberry cuttings in the earthen trough.

21. Nursery. 1ˢᵗ. terras. planted 24. sweet almond ⎫
kernels from m͞r Diver's ⎪ & filled it up with
tree                ⎬ Larix seeds.[32]
1. plant hardshelled bitter ⎪ Ronaldson
Almond from box X. pa. ⎭
40

6ᵗʰ. begᵍ. at W. end. 16. Brock's soft peach stones. 33. fine soft peach stones. from P.R (yᵉ [33] kernels only)

10. W. end. English oak acorns.[34] ⎫
E. end. elm seed[35]            ⎪
11. Ash seed.[36] .......... Plane.[37] ⎪
12. something label lost. .... Crab ⎪
kernels                  ⎪
13. Scotch fir seed. ........ Silver ⎬ all these were sent
fir seed[38]             ⎪ me from Edinburg
14. Larix .... thro the whole .... ⎪ by mr Ronaldson.
15. Bladder Senna[39] ............. ⎪
Pyracanthus.           ⎪
16. Hawthorn ..... Broom[40] ..... ⎪
9ᵗʰ. Cedar of Lebanon[41]    thro ⎪
the whole. ......         ⎭

†Mar. 28. planted 6. plants of goose berries, continuing the same row. in the 4ᵗʰ. Terras. from Ronaldson Edinbḡ

  29. sowed fiorin grass seed [42] in the new 12.I. boxes N°. 1. to 7. & in the old boxes 1.2.4.6.10. and in the Meadow

Apr. 2. planted in the old boxes N°. 3. Silver fir. 7. Scotch fir. 12. Larix. 13. Cedar of Lebanon.

  3. sowed on the N.E. & N.W. sides of Aspen thicket seeds of Broom & Pyracanthus from Ed̄bg. Ronaldson.
in the grove,[43] Ash, elm, plane, Silver fir. Scotch fir. Larix

---

[1] *1812.* The year 1812 opened with the happy reconciliation between Jefferson and John Adams. The warmth of their former friendship returned, and they carried on a large correspondence until their deaths in 1826.

This was the first election year since Jefferson had retired from the Presidency. Certain groups urged him to become a candidate for the Presidency again, and others even suggested that he be appointed Secretary of State in Madison's cabinet. He disregarded all of these suggestions. Madison was re-elected President, and Elbridge Gerry, Jefferson's old friend, was chosen Vice President.

War was declared against England on June 18. Although Jefferson was in favor of the declaration under existing circumstances, it brought great hardships on the people, and placed pecuniary obstacles before him. Despite his straitened circumstances, Jefferson was obliged on account of the war to increase his household manufacture of linen, cotton, and woolens, in order to supply his household needs.

This was a flourishing year for the garden and farm. There are five pages in the *Garden Book* tabulating the plantings and other activities in the garden. For the first time Jefferson wrote down the exact plan and arrangement of the vegetable garden. It was divided into three long terraces or platforms, called the *Upper Platform,* the *Middle Platform,* and the *Lower Platfrom* (see pl. XXXIII).

In the early spring Jefferson completed a fish pond on the *Colle* Branch. He made several attempts to stock it with carp, but without much success. He later made several other fish ponds, a few of which were washed away by freshets in the branches. (See letters following about fish and fish ponds.)

The mill still continued unprofitable.   On account of this, Mr. Randolph became the sole tenant.   The change, however, did not increase the revenues.

In the early spring Jefferson made one important change in the flower borders along the winding or *Round-about* Walk on the west lawn.   He divided the borders into 10-foot compartments and planted them with groups of like flowers instead of a mixture in each compartment.   This change gave an interesting massed effect to the borders.   (Pl. XXXIV.)

Letters show that the exchange of plants and seeds continued between Jefferson and his neighbors and friends. Thoüin sent his yearly supply of seeds from France, and James Ronaldson, of Philadelphia, sent another large packet of them.   Bernard McMahon, as in previous years, sent roots, plants, and seeds.

Jefferson made his usual visits to *Poplar Forest,* where work on the house was progressing rapidly.   Extensive improvements were made in the grounds.   (See letters, Jefferson to John W. Eppes, April 18 and September 18, 1812; memoranda, Jefferson to Jeremiah Goodman, May 12 and December 13, 1812; and Planting Memorandum for *Poplar Forest,* 1812.)

[2] See plate XXI for location of the garden.

[3] *Allium ascalonicum* L.   Also called shallot.

[4] James Ronaldson was born in Scotland in 1780.   Emigrating to Pennsylvania, he settled in Philadelphia, and became identified with the industrial and educational interests of that city.   He was one of the largest type founders in the country and also an extensive horticulturist.   He was a friend of Jefferson and sent to him seeds and plants, which were planted at *Monticello.*   Mr. Ronaldson died in Philadelphia in 1841.   (*National Cyclopedia of American Biography* 12: 507–508.)   (See letter, Jefferson to Mr. McIntosh, March 15, 1812; and letter, Jefferson to Mr. Ronaldson, October 11, 1812.)

[5] *Allium sativum* L.   Garlic.

[6] *Allium schoenoprasum* L.   Chive.

[7] *Humulus lupulus* L.   Hop.

[8] John Thomson Mason was an American lawyer and statesman.   He was the son of Thomson Mason, the younger brother of George Mason.   He was born in Stafford County,

Virginia, in 1764, and died in 1824. He was a personal friend to Jefferson, who appointed him to several high offices. (Lippincott's *Biographical Dictionary:* 1676.)

[9] See letter, Jefferson to Ronaldson, October 11, 1812.

[10] *Lolium perenne* L.

[11] Probably *Trifolium agrarium* L.

[12] Probably a variety of *Avena sativa* L.

[13] A variety of *Hordeum vulgare* L.

[14] *Vicia sativa* L.     Tares.

[15] Mangel-wurzel, a large, coarse kind of beet, *Beta vulgaris macrorhiza,* extensively grown, especially in Europe, as food for cattle.

[16] *Scorsonera hispanica* L.     Black salsify.

[17] The flower borders of the western lawn were laid out in 1808.     (See pls. XXIV, XXV.)

[18] *Campanula* sp.

[19] *Tagetes erecta* L.

[20] *Papaver* sp.

[21] The *arbor bean* here is probably *Phaseolus coccineus* L. It is more frequently called scarlet runner.

[22] Buckwheat, now *Fagopyrum esculentum* Gaertn.

[23] *Panicum virgatum* L.     A native grass sometimes grown for ornament.

[24] Bernard McMahon was born in Ireland *circa* 1775.     He came to America in 1796 and soon after settled in Philadelphia, where he established a successful seed house and botanical garden.     He was one of the first successful gardeners in the United States.     In 1806 he published *The American Gardener's Calendar,* which went through several editions. Horticultural letters passed frequently between McMahon and Jefferson.     A large number of plants grown at *Monticello* came from McMahon's seed house.     McMahon died *circa* 1815.     (John W. Harshberger, *The Botanists of Philadelphia and Their Work* (Philadelphia, 1899): 117–119.) (See letters, McMahon to Jefferson, February 28, 1812; and Jefferson to McMahon, October 11, 1812.)

[25] Robert Bailey, a nurseryman, living in Washington, who often furnished Jefferson with plants.

[26] James Taylor.     See note 6, 1810.

[27] George Divers, of *Farmington,* Albemarle County.

[28] Thomas Lomax.     See note 27, 1809.

²⁹ See letter, George Divers to Jefferson, March 18, 1812.
³⁰ Walter Coles (1772–1854) was a son of John Coles and a brother of Isaac Coles.   His home was *Woodville*, Albemarle County, where he lived until his death.   (Woods, *Albemarle County:* 172.)
³¹ See letter, George Divers to Jefferson, March 18, 1812.
³² *Larix decidua* Mill.   Larch.
³³ Yᵉ means *the.*
³⁴ *Quercus robur* L.   English Oak.
³⁵ Probably *Ulmus campestris* L.   English elm.
³⁶ *Fraxinus* sp.   Ash.
³⁷ *Platanus* sp.   Plane tree.
³⁸ *Abies alba* Mill.   Silver fir.
³⁹ *Colutea arborescens* L.   Bladder senna.
⁴⁰ Probably Scotch broom, *Cytisus scoparius* Link.
⁴¹ *Cedrus libani* Loud.   Cedar of Lebanon.
⁴² *Agrostis palustris* Huds.   Fiorin grass.
⁴³ In the *Grove* Jefferson planted a larger assortment of native and exotic trees.   (See pl. XXI for the location of the grove.)

## LETTERS AND EXTRACTS OF LETTERS 1812

(Jefferson to John Adams.)

Monticello, January 21, 1812.

I thank you beforehand (for they are not yet arrived) for the specimens of homespun you have been so kind as to forward me by post.   I doubt not their excellence, knowing how far you are advanced in these things in your quarter.   Here we do little in the fine way, but in coarse and middling goods a great deal.   Every family in the country is a manufactory within itself, and is very generally able to make within itself all the stouter and middling stuffs for its own clothing and household use.   We consider a sheep for every person in the family as sufficient to clothe it, in addition to the cotton, hemp and flax which we raise ourselves.   For fine stuff we shall depend on your northern manufactories.   Of these, that is to say, of company establishments, we have none.   We use little machinery.   The spinning jenny, and loom with the flying shuttle, can be managed in a family; but nothing more complicated. . . .   (Lipscomb and Bergh, *Jefferson* 13: 122.)

(Jefferson to Bernard McMahon.)

Monticello Feb. 16. 12.

In your letter of March last, as on various other occasions, you were so kind as to offer to supply my wants in the article of plants, and in my

answer of April 8. I mentioned a few articles, as also the mode of conveyance, which could not occur till about this time. an opportunity now
presents itself of the most fortunate kind. mr̄ Harmer Gilmer, a student of medicine now in Philadelphia, and my neighbor, will be setting
out on his return to us very soon after you receive this. he will come in
the stage and will, I am sure, take charge of any small box you may be
so good as to put under his care. I write to him on this subject. never
expecting so good an opportunity again, & so seasonable a one, I will
still add a little to my former wants so as to put me in possession once
for all of every thing to which my views extend, & which I do not now
possess.

seeds.   Auricula. double Anemone. double Carnation. Mignon-
         nette. egg plant. Sea Kale.
bulbs.   Crown Imperial. double Ranunculus.
plants.  Hudson & Chili strawberries. fine gooseberries. Cape-jas-
         mine.
trees.   Cedar of Lebanon. balm of Gilead fir. Cork tree. Spanish-
         Chestnut or Maronnier of yᵉ French.

one plant of the Cape jessamine, & one or two of the trees will suffice.
the seeds may come in a letter packet by mail; the bulbs, plants & trees
(if the latter be chosen small) in a small and light box, packed in moss
which mr̄ Gilmer will take charge of: and if you will be so kind as to
inform me of the amount in the letter by mail, it shall be promptly remitted. mr̄. Gilmer will be so near his departure as to require immediate dispatch.

Among other plants I received from M. Thouin, was the Brassica
sempervirens, or Sprout Kale. one plant only vegetated, the 1ˢᵗ. year,
but this winter I have 20. or 30. turned out for seed. I consider it
among the most valuable garden plants. it stands our winter unprotected, furnishes a vast crop of sprouts from the beginning of December
through the whole winter, which are remarkably sweet and delicious.
I enclose you a few seeds, a part of what the original plant gave us; the
next year I hope to have a plenty. I send it because I do not perceive
by your catalogue that you have it. . . . (*Jefferson Papers*, L. C.)

(Jefferson to Jeremiah Goodman.)

Monticello Feb. 21. 12.

I have just received a letter from Majʳ. Flood informing me that his
neighbor mʳ. Duval will spare me from 6. to 8. bushels of Burnet seed.
you will therefore be pleased to send off two boys on horseback to bring
it. they should take bags which will hold 4. bushels each. the seed is
as light as chaff. it is sown half a bushel to the acre. Major Flood's
is 34. miles from Poplar Forest on the Great main road leading from
New London to Richmond. . . . (*Jefferson Papers*, M. H. S.)

(Bernard McMahon to Jefferson.)

Philadelphia Feb^y. 28^th. 1812.

I duly received your kind letter of the 16^th. ins^t. and am much obliged to you for the Brassica sempervirens. This morning I done myself the pleasure of sending you by M^r. Gilmer a box containing the following articles.

 2 Roots Amaryllis Belladonna
 6 pots of Auriculas, different kinds.
 1 d^o. of a beautiful polyanthus
32 Roots best Tulips of Various kind
32 d^o. Best double Hyacinths assorted.
40 plants of the Hudson Strawberry, the best kind we have here.

I have none nor have I seen any in America of the large Chili strawberry.

 4 roots Lillium superbum.    L.
 4 small plants Gooseberries, large red fruit & the best I have ever seen.
Some roots Amaryllis Atamasco L.

The labels are *laid in* with the above and the numbers attached to the following.

N^o. 1    Ribes odoratissimum (mihi).    this is one of Cap^t. Lewis's and an important shrub, the fruit very large, of a dark purple colour, the flowers yellow, showey, & *extremely fragrant.*

N^o. 2    Symphoricarpos leucocarpa (mihi).    This is a beautiful shrub brought by C. Lewis from the River Columbia, the flower is small but neat, the berries hang in large clusters and of a snow white colour and continue on the shrubs, retaining their beauty, all the winter; especially if kept in a Green House.   The shrub is perfectly hardy; I have given it the trival english name of Snowberry-bush.

N^o. 3    The yellow Currant of the river Jefferson; this is specifically different from the others, but I have not yet given it a specific botanical name.

N^o. 4    Cape of Good hope Grape Vine, according to M^r. Peter Legaux, who says he received it originally from thence.   This I am confident, from several years observation, is the variety of grape most to be depended on for giving wine to the United States, but particularly to be cultivated *for that purpose* in the middle and eastern states.

N^o. 5    An improved variety of the Cape grape, somewhat earlier and better *for the table,* and equally good for making wine.

I am very sorry that I *cannot* at present supply all your wants, but shall as soon as in my power; and that the opportunity which now offers does not admit of a conveyance for many articles which I wish to send you. I hope you will do me the favor of informing me whenever you hear of a favorable opportunity, for conveying them, other articles which I wish to send you. Excuse the confused manner in which I write, as there are several people in my store asking me questions every moment.

I would thank you to inform me whether you take the Glocester Nut to be a distinct species, as announced by Mich$^x$. f. (Juglans laciniosa) or whether, if only a variety, it is nearer allied to the Juglans tomentosa Mich$^x$. or to the J. squamosa Mich$^x$. fi. the J. alba of his father.

I send you a few seeds by this mail, and shall send some more in a few days. . . . P. S. You will please to excuse me for not making any charge for the new articles sent; such I could not think of. (*Jefferson Papers,* L. C.)

## (Jefferson to Patrick Gibson.)

Monticello Mar. 1. 12.

. . . I have usually got my stock of red clover seed from the other side of the Blue ridge, but am quite disappointed there this year, and am therefore obliged to apply for it at your market where I am told there is plenty but high in price as is general this year. I must pray you to procure & send me in tight barrels ten bushels, as it is an article of such necessity as to render the price but a secondary consideration. . . . (*Jefferson Papers,* M. H. S.)

## (Jefferson to Jeremiah A. Goodman.)

Monticello Mar. 1. [1812.]

Our distress on the article of hauling obliges me to send for the yoke of steers which were to come from Poplar Forest. you know our situation and will I hope send us a pair which will do solid service. of those which m$\bar{\text{r}}$ Griffin sent while you were here, we have never been able to make any thing. I have given Moses leave to stay a day with his friends. I suppose he can bring on the back of his steers as much corn as will bring them here, on your furnishing him a bag. I wrote to you on the 21$^{st}$. of February by post; but as I know that letters linger long on the road sometimes, I will repeat here one article of my letter which was pressing. Maj$^r$. Flood has informed me that m$\bar{\text{r}}$ Duval, his neighbor, can furnish me with 6. or 8. bushels of Burnet seed. two boys on horseback should therefore be sent off immediately with bags which will hold 4. bushels each. the seed is as light as chaff. it is sown half a bushel to the acre. Major Flood's is 34. miles from Poplar Forest on the great main road leading from New London to Richmond.

I inclose some lettuce seed, and shall be glad if you will sow about 8. or 10. feet of one of the beds behind the stable, and do the same on the 1$^{st}$. day of every month till the fall. . . . (Courtesy of Dr. A. S. W. Rosenbach.)

(Charles Willson Peale to Jefferson.)

Farm Persevere, Mar. 2ᵈ. 1812.

. . . Can you find no inducements to visit Philadelphia? It would give me a great deal of pleasure to see you at the Museum. Your garden must be a Museum to you. . . . (*Jefferson Papers*, L. C.)

(Larkin Smith to Jefferson.)

Norfolk 3d March 1812

A small package of garden seed was this day delivered to me, with your address, by a very safe conveyance to Richmond. I have committed it to the care of Mr. James Barbour, with a request that he would transmit it to you without loss of time, as the season for sowing the seeds has commenced. . . . (*Glimpses of the Past*, Missouri 3: 116.)

(James S. Barbour to Jefferson.)

Richmond March 10. 1812

The accompanying collection of garden seeds was forwarded to me by Colo Larkin Smith of Norfolk. He suggested to me the necessity of sending them as soon as possible as the time for sowing them had, probably, arrived. Supposing the Stage both the safest and most expeditious conveyance I avail myself of that opportunity. I hope you will receive them in the time. . . . N. B. Just as I had finished this note a waggon from Milton passed and I have confided the Seeds to him, R. Johnston. (*Jefferson Papers*, M. H. S.)

(Jefferson to George Divers.)

Monticello Mar. 10. 12.

I promised to stock you with the Alpine strawberry as soon as my beds would permit. I now send you a basket of plants and can spare you 10. baskets more if you desire it. their value, you know, is the giving strawberries 8. months in the year. but they require a large piece of ground and therefore I am moving them into the truck patch, as I cannot afford them room enough in the garden. I have received from McMahon some plants of the true Hudson strawberry. the last rains have brought them forward and ensured their living. I have been 20 years trying unsuccessfully to get them here. the next year I shall be able to stock you. I have received also from McMahon 4. plants of his wonderful gooseberry. I measured the fruit of them 3. I. round. by the next year I hope they will afford you cuttings. about 20. plants of the Sprout kale have given us sprouts from the 1ˢᵗ of December. their second growth now furnishes us a dish nearly every day, and they will enable me this year to stock my neighbors with the seed. we have now got the famous Irish grass, Fiorin, ensured and growing. they make hay from it in December, January, February. I received the plants from Ireland about a month ago. I am now engaged in planting a collection of pears.  I know you have several kinds of very fine.  if your nursery can spare 2. of each kind I will thank you for them: if not then some cuttings for engrafting, tying up each separately. . . . (*Jefferson Papers,* M. H. S.)

## (Jefferson to George McIntosh.)

Monticello Mar. 15. 12.

I am this moment favored with your's of the 4th inst. informing me you had received some plants for me from m[r] Ronaldson.  I had before received a letter from him notifying me that he had forwarded them. I will ask the favor of you to commit them to the Richmond stage addressed to Mess[rs]. Gibson & Jefferson of Richmond who will pay the portage & forward them to me.  they will come much safer if you can get some passenger to take them under his patronage by the way.  I presume they are properly packed; if not, a light box, and wet moss inveloping them, would be the best mode of preserving them, the expense of which will in like manner be reimbursed by Mess[rs] Gibson & Jefferson. Accept my thanks for your attention to this object. . . . (*Jefferson Papers,* M. H. S.)

## (George Divers to Jefferson.)

Farmington 18th Mar: 1812

I received the aspine [= alpine] strawberry plants sent by your servant, for which accept my thanks.  I send you seven pear cions.  they are small being ingrafted the last spring.  two of them is a very good forward pear.  the other five are of the best kinds that I have, would have sent you some slips, but I shall engraft some for myself and shall think of you when I set about it,

The Irish grass you speak of must be a great acquisition, I shall be thankful for a little of the seed of the Sprout Kale and a few cuttings of the large gooseberry when they can be spar'd. . . . (*Jefferson Papers,* M. H. S.)

## (Jefferson to Col. Larkin Smith.)

Monticello, Mar. 22, '12.

Your letter of the 3d. inst. with the packet of seeds you were so kind as to forward came safely to hand yesterday evening, and of course in good time for being committed to the earth.  accept my thanks for this kind attention and indeed I am afraid it may not be the last, as my foreign correspondents are much in the habit of directing packages for me to the Collector of the port to which the vessel is bound.  duties, or any other expenses which may have occurred, or may occur on such occasions, will always be immediately remitted by Messrs. Gibson & Jefferson, my established correspondents at Richmond, on notice of them; who will also receive such packages, pay charges & forward them to me. I mention this to lessen the inconveniences to which your friendship might expose you on any future similar occasion. . . . (*Glimpses of the Past,* Missouri 3: 117.)

### (Jefferson to Governor James Barbour.)

Monticello Mar. 22. 12.

Your favor of the 16th was safely delivered last night by the waggoner, together with the packet of seeds you were so kind as to receive and forward. I pray you to accept my thanks for this friendly care. my friends & correspondents Gibson & Jefferson, would have saved you the trouble of seeking a conveyance for the packet, & would do it on any future similar occasion, if simply sent to them; & would pay all charges. I mention this in the event of your being embarrassed again with such an address. the packet arrived in good time, exactly in the season for planting. . . . (*Jefferson Papers,* L. C.)

### (Jefferson to James Madison.)

Monticello, April 17, 1812.

. . . Our wheat had greatly suffered by the winter, but is as remarkably recovered by the favorable weather of the spring. . . . (Lipscomb and Berg, *Jefferson* 13: 140.)

### (Jefferson to John Wayles Eppes.)

Monticello Apr. 18. 12.

. . . I have already resumed the inside finishing [house at *Poplar Forest*], which I had not before intended. I have engaged a workman to build offices, have laid off a handsome curtilage connecting the house with the Tomahawk, have inclosed and divided it into suitable appendages to a Dwelling house, and have begun it's improvement by planting trees of use and ornament. . . . (*The Huntington Library Quarterly* 6 (3): 345, 1943.)

### (Jefferson to Mr. Ashlin.)

Monticello Apr. 20. 12.

I have just made me a fish pond and am desirous to get some carp fish to stock it. we used formerly when hauling the seyne for shad, to catch some carp also, and I presume therefore that some few are now caught at your place. I send the bearer therefore with a boat, with directions to stay a few days, and procure for me all the carp which shall be caught while he is there. I shall be obliged to you if you can aid him in getting them at as reasonable a price as you can. I presume they will not be higher than what is paid for shad, as they are by no means as good a fish. if through your interest he can be admitted to join in hauling the seyne & come in for a share of shad so as to bring us some, I will thank you, as well as for any other aid you may give him towards his object. . . . (*Jefferson Papers,* M. H. S.)

(Jefferson to James P. Cocke.)

Monticello Apr. 23. 12.

I have just finished a fish pond and wish to get some of the Roanoke chub to stock it. I am told you now possess the pond that was your relation & neighbor mr̄ Cocke's. Could you spare me a few to begin with? if you can, I will send tomorrow a light cart with a cask for water so that the cart may start the next morning and keep the fish out as short a time as possible. I propose so short a term, because I presume you have the means of commanding the fish at any time, and I am to set out for Bedford on Monday or Tuesday. . . . (*Jefferson Papers*, L. C.)

(James P. Cocke to Jefferson.)

Apˡ. 23. 1812.

I am sorry to observe that the geting [?] [a] supply of fish is most uncertain, not having made arrangᵗ. to command them. yet if you wish send and [?] the risque be assumed I will do my indeavors to procure them. I shall shortly set about some method in order to have them at command & would think the fall would be more proper to summons them as they are now spawning & would more certain to get them. . . . (*Jefferson Papers*, L. C.)

(Jefferson to James P. Cocke.)

Monticello Apr. 24. 12.

I am so anxious to save a year, by taking advantage of the present spawning season, not yet over, that I send the bearer to take the chance of your being able by some means to catch some chubs and the rather as his time is not very valuable insomuch that if a detention of 2. or 3. days could secure my object I should think it more than an equivalent for his time. I suppose that if taken with a hook & line and the hook carefully withdrawn from the mouth it would not hurt them, especially if the beard of the hook were filed off. I have therefore furnished the bearer with a line and hooks of different sizes, and altho' he knows nothing about angling, yet with a little of your kind direction he would immediately understand it, and may employ himself in collecting them until you think he has a sufficiency. I am sorry to give you so much trouble, and must rest for the apology on your friendship. . . . (*Jefferson Papers*, L. C.)

(Jefferson to James Maury.)

Monticello, April 25, 1812.

. . . I have withdrawn myself from all political intermeddlings, to indulge the evening of my life with what have been the passions of every portion of it, books, science, my farms, my family and friends. To these every hour of the day is now devoted. I retain a good activity of mind, not quite as much of body, but uninterrupted health. Still the hand of age is upon me. All my old friends are nearly gone. Of those in my neighborhood, Mr. Divers and Mr. Lindsay alone remain. If you could make it a *partie quarrée,* it would be a comfort indeed. We would beguile our lingering hours with talking over our youthful exploits, our hunts on Peter's mountain, with a long train of *et cetera,* in addition, and feel, by recollection at least, a momentary flash of youth. . . . (Lipscomb and Bergh, *Jefferson* 13: 148–149.)

(Jefferson to Captain Mathew Wills.)

Monticello, Apr. 26, '12.

I return you many thanks for the fish you have been so kind as to send me, and still more for your aid in procuring the carp, and you will further oblige me by presenting my thanks to Capt. Holman & Mr. Ashlin. I have found too late, on enquiry that the cask sent was an old and foul one, and I have no doubt that must have been the cause of the death of the fish. The carp, altho' it cannot live the shortest time out of water, yet is understood to bear transportation in water the best of any fish whatever. The obtaining breeders for my pond being too interesting to be abandoned, I have had a proper smack made, such as is regularly used for transporting fish, to be towed after the boat, and have dispatched the bearer with it without delay, as the season is passing away. I have therefore again to solicit your patronage, as well as Captain Holman's in obtaining a supply of carp. I think a dozen would be enough, and would therefore wish him to come away as soon as he can get that number. . . . (*Glimpses of the Past,* Missouri 3: 118.)

(James P. Cocke to Jefferson.)

Ap$^l$. 29$^{th}$ 1812.

I am concerned that every effort to procure fish for you have been ineffectual. two has been caught but so managed [?] that they are dead. So soon as I can command them I will advise you & then will endeavor to manage the thing better. . . . (*Jefferson Papers,* L. C.)

(Jefferson to Jeremiah A. Goodman.)

[Memorandum *Poplar Forest*] May 12. 1812.

[Memorandu]$^m$. for m$\bar{r}$ Goodman.

[as] soon as the green swerd seed is ripe, have [som]e gathered by the negro children and sowed on all the naked parts [of the] mound, and then cover those parts lightly [with s]traw first, & brush laid over that.

[if m]ore seed could be gathered by the children it might be sowed in the fall or spring in the square round the house where the greenswerd has not as yet taken.

have strong stakes 12. f. long stuck by such of the young trees as grow crooked, and tie them up to the stake in as many places as necessary.

I promised mr̄ Caruthers of Rockbridge to give him a ram & ewe lamb of this year, I believe if he should send, we must give him one of our rams, and a ewe lamb, and turn out another ram for ourselves the next year.
weed the gooseberries, raspberries, strawberries & rose bushes.
sow lettuce the 1st. of June.
bottle the beer.   (Courtesy of Dr. A. S. W. Rosenbach.)

(Jefferson to J. Peter Derieux.)

Monticello June 1. 1812.

Your favor of May 1st is just received, with the seed & root of the *Tarragon,* for which I return my thanks.   the root had become entirely dry and without any principle of vegetation left in it.   this was less important, as I had some years ago succeeded in obtaining the plant from N. Orleans where it grows wild. . . . (*Jefferson Papers*, L. C.)

(Jefferson to Elbridge Gerry.)

Monticello, June 11, 1812.

. . . Who knows but you may fill up some short recess of Congress with a visit to Monticello, where a numerous family will hail you with a hearty country welcome. . . . (Lipscomb and Bergh, *Jefferson* 13: 164.)

(Jefferson to Andrew Ellicott.)

Monticello, June 24, 1812.

. . . All this will be for a future race. . . . Yet I do not wish it less. On the same principle on which I am still planting trees, to yield their shade and ornament half a century hence.   (Lipscomb and Bergh, *Jefferson* 19: 185.)

(Bernard McMahon to Jefferson.)

Philadelphia 16th. Septr. 1812

I do myself the pleasure of sending you by this mail, in a small box, 3 roots of Crown Imperial which cary two tiers of flowers, *when in very luxuriant growth;* also 12 Roots of Gladiolus communis; both kinds hardy and fit for the open ground—please to have them planted as soon as possible.   I will send you other kinds of bulbs by subsequent mails. . . . (*Jefferson Papers*, L. C.)

(Jefferson to John Wayles Eppes.)

Monticello Sep. 18. 12.

. . . it [the house at *Poplar Forest*] is an Octagon of 50. f. diameter, of brick, well built, will be plaistered this fall, when nothing will be wanting to finish it compleatly but the cornices and some of the doors. when finished, it will be the best dwelling house in the state, except that of Monticello; perhaps preferable to that, as more proportioned to the faculties of a private citizen. I shall probably go on with the cornices and doors at my leisure at Monticello, and in planting & improving the grounds around it. I have just paid between 3. & 4000 Dollars cash for the building, besides doing all the planter's work, which is fully the half. so that it's cost may be very moderately rated at 6000. D. out of the lands South of Tomahawk, I should have to reserve 4. or 5. acres, from it's entrance into Blackwater down to my line for a canal & site for a mill & threshing machine I am about building there. the stream is very meagre, the head springs all rising in my own lands: but it may thro' a good part of the year grind for a family. there are on these lands about 100. acres cleared; 67. of them originally fine, but very old. they have now been at rest 4. or 5. years, & I am about taking them again into my rotation. the rest are fresh & of first quality, and I shall from time to time make clearings adjacent until the actual exchange of possession. . . . (*The Huntington Library Quarterly* **6** (3): 344, 1943.)

### (Bernard McMahon to Jefferson.)

Philadelphia 23rd. Septr. 1812

I herewith send you a small box containing 6 Dwarf Persian Iris, 12 Cloth of Gold Crocus 6 Iris Xiphium, 6 Iris Xiphium, *a new & fine variety,* 12 Double Persian Ranunculuses; with the seeds of some *very superior* Impatience Balsamina, Red Antwerp Raspberry & Centaurea macrocephala, as a part of a collection to be forwarded in a few days for your acceptance. . . . P. S. I am happy to inform you that my little business enables me to progress, in my line, in a ratio somewhat greater than I at first expected. (*Jefferson Papers,* L. C.)

### (Bernard McMahon to Jefferson.)

Philadelphia 24th. Septr. 1812

Herewith you will receive a small box containing

3 Roots of Antholyza aethiopica, a Green House bulb,
6 Feathered Hyacinth roots, Hyacinthus monstrosus L.
3 Double blue Hyacinths, named *Alamode* by the Dutch, remarkably early & proper for forcing.
6 Roots of a beautiful variety of Crocus vernus, of very early bloom; flower white inside & beautifully striped outside.
2 Roots Parrot Tulips, color of the flowers red, green and yellow mixed. Some seed of the Mirabilis longiflora, or Sweet-scented Marvel of Peru. . . . (*Jefferson Papers,* L. C.)

### (Samuel Brown to Jefferson.)

Natchez Oct. 1st. 1812.

Mr. Poindexter has obligingly offered to carry you a small package of Guinea Grass seed & a species of *Capsicum* indigenous in the provence of Taxas.   For all I know on the subject of Guinea Grass I take the liberty of referring you to a communication I have just made to the Editor of the Archives of Useful Knowledge.   It is highly probable, however, that you are much better acquainted with it than I am.   Of the Pepper I know little except that it grows in very great abundance in the prairies west of the Sabine & that it is with the Spaniards & Savages, an article in as great use as common Salt is among the inhabitants of the U. S.   As soon as I can obtain a more particular account of it I shall do myself the pleasure of communicating it to you.   The Roots are Perennial & in your climate would only require protection from the most severe frost. . . .  (*Jefferson Papers*, L. C.)

(Jefferson to James Ronaldson.)

Monticello Oct. 11. 1812.

. . . I had received in the spring the assortment of seeds you had been so kind as to address to me.   they were very long in their passage from Norfolk to this place, insomuch that the season was far advanced before they got to hand.   many have consequently failed, but several succeeded. the oats & barley particularly, the latter of which is valuable as being naked.   several of the cabbages and Kales succeeded, as also the spinach and a single plant of early turnep will give us seed.   three Scotch firs have vegetated, the fiorin grass seed came up well, but was soon checked by our own hot sun. . . .  (*Jefferson Papers*, L. C.)

(Jefferson to Bernard McMahon.)

Monticello Oct. 11. 12.

Your three boxes with flower roots are all safely arrived & carefully disposed of, for which accept my particular thanks.   the articles received in the spring by mr Gilmer have been remarkably successful, one only of the cuttings of the Snowberry failed.   the rest are now very flourishing and shew some of the most beautiful berries I have ever seen. the sweet scented currant, the yellow currant, the red gooseberries and the Hudson Strawberries are all flourishing.   I received from the National garden of France a box of seeds, which came too late for use this year; and no opportunity has occurred of a passenger going in the stage to Philadelphia to whom I could confide them.   but a medical student will be going from this neighborhood at the commencement of the next lectures by whom I will forward them to you: and as they are seeds of 1811. I presume they will generally succeed the next season. . . .  (*Jefferson Papers*, L. C.)

(Bernard McMahon to Jefferson.)

Philadelphia Oct[r]. 24th. 1812.

I had the pleasure of receiving yours of the 11th. ins[t]. and am happy that the articles sent to you last spring have succeeded to your satisfaction, and that you rec$^d$. the few roots I lately sent you in good condition. I am much obliged to you for your former favors and also for your intention of sending me the box of seeds you were pleased to mention.

With this letter I expect you will receive a small box containing,

6 Roots Watsonia Meriana.  (*Gawles*)
6 d°. Trittonia fenestrata ........ d°.
6 d°. Trittonia fenestrata ........ d°.
6 Morea flexuosa

All Cape of Good Hope bulbs and consequently, with you, belonging to the Green-House department.

1 Root silver striped Crown Imperial, *Hardy*
3 Roots *Amaryllis Belladonna* or Belladonna Lily:

they belong also to the Green-house; if their strong succulent fibers or roots retain their *freshness* on receipt of them, do not have them cut off, but let them be planted with the bulbs in pots of good rich mellow earth; the flowers are beautiful and fragrant; their season of flowering is Sept$^r$. & Oct$^r$. . . . (*Jefferson Papers, L. C.*)

## (James Ronaldson to Jefferson.)

Phila. Nov$^r$. 2 1812.

To remedy as far as possible the ill consequences arising out of the late arrival of the seeds I have sent you a few, by one of the last weeks mail. the quantity of each is very small, as my stock was about exhausted; they may be sufficient to shew which of 'em are adapted to the country and furnish the seed. I am sorry at not having it in my power to give you some of the European Ash, Scots fir, Silver fir, cedar of Lebanon etc. having handed all that class over to Mr. McMahon. with him however they will be in good keeping; and have the best chance of being introduced into the Nation. it was very unfortunate the Cork seeds I ordered from Bayonne were on board the *Amanda* taken and condemned last spring under the British orders of Council. this plant should be procured from Portugal, now that so much intercourse exists with that country. The Cork thrives on poor sandy land and I think is suited to all the coast land from Delaware to cape florida. it would be more profitable than pine trees. . . . (*Jefferson Papers, L. C.*)

## (Jefferson to E. I. Du Pont.)

Monticello, Nov. 8, 12.

. . . I am in hopes the Merino race of sheep is so well established among us as to leave you in no danger of wanting that article. I have been unlucky with them. I began with one ram & 3 ewes. One of the ewes died of the scab, and the others for two years have brought me only ram lambs, so that I remain still with only 2 ewes. But I have many half bloods. . . . (*Jefferson Papers, M. H. C.* 1: 177.)

(Bernard McMahon to Jefferson.)

Philadelphia 24<sup>th</sup>. Nov<sup>r</sup>. 1812

By this mail I send you a small box of Hyacinth roots, to be planted in the open ground, as soon as you shall have received them; they are of the *first rate* kinds, and nearly of as many varieties as roots: with due attention they will bring you into a stock of the best kinds. . . . (*Jefferson Papers*, L. C.)

(Bernard McMahon to Jefferson.)

Philadelphia 1<sup>st</sup>. Dec<sup>r</sup>. 1812

I enclose you a small paper of the Agrostis stolonifera or Fiorin-grass, which I rec<sup>d</sup>. from the Edenburg Botanic Garden.  This grass had been highly spoken of in that country, but I fear it will not prove equal to the report given of it, and I conceive that it grows wild about this City, whether indigenous or introduced I cannot say; however, next season I will have a fair comparison of the imported and aparently indigenous kinds, and I think both will turn out to be the same species.

I also do myself the pleasure of enclosing you some superior China Pink and Auricula seeds; the latter should be sown sometime in this month, as directed in page 646 of my work on Gardening. . . . (*Jefferson Papers*, L. C.)

(Jefferson to Jeremiah A. Goodman.)

[Memorandum *Poplar Forest*] Dec. 13. 1812.

. . . Supposing there are 40. bacon hogs at this place & 32. at Bear creek reserve 23. for the negroes, which allows a hog apiece for Hal & Jame Hubbard, and half a one for every grown & working negro, keep 6. for my use & Chisolm's then take out the Overseer's parts and send the rest to Monticello with the muttons.  send also Sally & Maria to learn to weave & spin.  if you can fix the time when the hogs will be ready, I will send up some of the young people from Monticello who want to visit their relations here and they will return with the waggon & drove & assist in driving them.  Billy is also to go, and can aid in driving.

The winter's work is to be 1. moving fences.  to wit, the fences for the curtilage of the house as laid off by Cap<sup>t</sup> Slaughter, that for the meadow by the still, and inclosing the Tomahawk field.

2. roads.  to wit, to change the road from the smith's shop down round the foot of the hill & across the meadow to where it will join m͞r Darnell's part on the Ridge branch; & to assist him in making the road down Bear branch, and up into the public road as Griffin marked it.  I have the establishment of this road extremely at heart, which will depend entirely on it's being done in an unexceptionable manner.

3. the negro houses all to be mended.

4. the meadow grounds which are cleared or nearly so, & only want cleaning, to be got in order for timothy. the meadow at Coleman's to be sowed with his leave.

all the rest of the winter to be employed in belting and clearing lands on the other side of the South branch of Tomahawk, to be prepared for a crop of tobacco, taking care of the wood for rails & for coalwood and stacking what remains, clearing & cleaning such meadow grounds as are adjacent to your clearing.

sow about half an acre of hemp.

Sow a bed of Carrots, & one of Salsafia, each about as large as the Asparagus bed; and sow a small bed of spinach. Long haricots to be planted as usual, & lettuce to be sown in the spring. if a thimblefull of seed could be sowed every other Monday, on a bed of 4. f. wide & 6. or 8. feet long it would be best, as I should then always find some fit for use when I come. (Courtesy of Dr. A. S. W. Rosenbach.)

(Jefferson to Charles Clay.)

Poplar Forest Dec. 14. 12.

I go certainly tomorrow, *wind* & weather permitting, and both have abated considerably. I promised you some sprout Kale seed, which I now send. I do not remember to have seen Salsafia in your garden, & yet it is one of the best roots for the winter. some call it oyster plant because fried in butter it can scarcely be distinguished from a fried oyster. I send you some seed. it is to be sowed and managed as carrots & to be taken up at the same time & put away for winter use. . . . (*Jefferson Papers,* L. C.)

From the *Farm Book 1774–1822:*

1812.  Sep. in making the Carlton path on the high mountain, thro' the woods & exceedingly steep, Wormly & Ned did about 50 yds a day, 4 f. wide. which is 25. yds apiece.

From the *Weather Memorandum Book 1776–1820:*

April.  1812. the two fish ponds on the Colle branch were 40. days work to grub, clean, & make the dams. (*Jefferson Papers,* L. C.)

From the *Account Book 1809–1820:*

Mar. 19. p^d. Giovanini for work in vineyard 1. D.
Mar. 21. a waggoner for bringing seeds 1. D.
April 20. gave James 5. D. to procure carp at Ashlin's for the pond.
April 26. gave James a 2^d time to buy live carp for the pond 5. D.

Planting Memorandum for *Poplar Forest,* 1812:

1812.   Jan.   planted Aspens from Monticello.  May 19. 5. living.
Calycanthuses.  May 19. 1. living.
Alpine strawberries.  living.
White strawberries.  living.

Nov.   plant a double row of paper mulberries from stairways to the Mounds.
Clump of Athenian & Balsam poplars at each corner of house.  intermix locusts, common and Kentucky, red-buds, dogwoods, calycanthus, liriodendron.

Nov. 20.   there are living 31. Golden willows, 19. Weeping willows.  10. Athenian Poplars, 3. Lombardy poplars, & 2 Mont°. Aspens.

Nov. 26.   the road & outer gate leading from the house to the Waterlick road bears S. 43½ W.  Magnetically 179. po. to the center of the house.

.25–27.   took from the Nursery & planted in the grounds round the house
20. weeping willows.  30. golden willows.  10. Athenian poplars.  3. Lombardy poplars.  2. Mont°. Aspens.  16. Calycanthuses.

27.   planted in the Nursery.  12. Mont°. Aspens. 16. paper mulberries.

Dec.   5.   planted Mont°. Aspens from mr Clay's.  viz.
12. round the Eastern mound & 4. round West d°. 6. still wanting.
planted also 2. European mulberries from mr Clay's as part of the double row from the Western Mound towards the house.
from the wall of the Western Stairway to the foot of the Western mound 91. feet.
Eastern d°. . . . . . . . . . . Eastern d°. 84. feet.
from the N. door along the circular road to the gate due South from the house is 270. yds.  Consq^ly. 540. yds round.  plant a row of paper mulberries on each side all around except the curve at the N. door; at 20 f. apart. will take about 160. trees.
plant on each bank, right & left, on the S. side of the house, a row of lilacs, Althaeas, Gelder roses, Roses, Calycanthus. (*Jefferson Papers,* U. Va.)

# 1813

| Kalendar. 1813.[1] | where | when | trans-pl[d]. | come to table | gone | Miscellaneous. |
|---|---|---|---|---|---|---|
| Frame peas | Bord. I.–V. | Mar. 1. | — | May 18. | June 9. | Mar. 16. up. |
| d° | Submur. D.E. | 2. | — | May 18. | June 10. | Apr. 21. blossom |
| lettuce radishes | Bord. VI | | | | | Mar. 16. up. |
| Savoy cabbages | ib. | 3. | | | | |
| Dwarf early Cabbage Ronaldson[2] | Asparagus bed | | | | | |
| York Cabbage. Ronaldson | Bord. VI. | | | | | |
| Sprout Kale | ib. | | | | | |
| Spinach. smooth or Summ[r] | Bord. XI | 6. | | Apr. 17. | | |
| d° | ib. | 15. | | | June 11. | |
| lettuce. radish | Bord. VI. | | | | | |
| lettuce. radish | XVII.1.N. | 22. | | | | |
| Celery | low grounds. | 23. | | | | |
| Savoys | | | | | | |
| Malta Kale | Sq. I | 29. | | June 5. | June 19. | |
| Hotspurs | Sq. II | | | 14. | | |
| Ledmans | XVII.1.S. | | | | | |
| Lettuce radishes | V | 31. | | | | |
| Snaps | XIII. | Apr. 3. | | June 5. | | |
| Carrots | | | | | | |
| Celery | low grounds. | | | | | |
| Savoys | | | | | | |
| Sprout Kale | | | | | | |
| Malta Kale | | | | | | |
| Lettuce. radish | XVII.2.S. | 6. | | | | |
| Dutch brown Lettuce (for seed) | | 7. | | run to | seed immediately | |
| Spinach | bord. IX | 9. | | July 29. | | |
| Tomatas | Sq. X. bord. X | | | | | |
| Okra | X. edging. | 10. | | | | |
| Lima beans | A. 3 | | | July 9. | | |
| long haricots | A. 4 | | | June 19. | | |
| Ledman's peas | Sq. III | 12. | | | | |
| Lima beans | A. 2 | 15. | | | | |

1813. (continued)

| Kalendar. 1813.[1] | where | when | trans-pl^d. | come to table | gone | Miscellaneous. |
|---|---|---|---|---|---|---|
| long haricots | A. 1. | | | | | |
| Benni | XIII. edging | 16. | | | | |
| Nasturtium | IX. | 17. | | | | |
| lettuce. rad | XVII. 3. N. | 20. | | | | |
| red Beet | XIV. 2. | | | June. 23 | | failed from drought & too late sowing. |
| red haricots | VI. | 22. | | | | |
| Salsafia | XIV. 1. | | | | | |
| Bess string bean. remarkably early | D. 3. | 23. | | June 17. | — | this is an early Snap. very dwarf |
| cucumbers | VIII | | | | | failed from drought |
| forward potatoes | D. 3. | 24. | | | | |
| warted cymlin | XII. 1. | | | | | |
| green Savoys. | XII. 3. N. | | | | | |
| cabbage Savoys.}Ronaldson | bord. VI. | | | | | |
| large cabbage | XII. 2. N. | | | | | |
| Lettuce. radishes | XVII. 6. N. | 26. | | June 29. | | failed from drought. |
| Ledman's peas | IV. | 27. | | | | |
| Carrots | A. 10. | 28. | | | | |
| Parsneps | A. 11. 12. | 29. | | | | failed. |
| Salsafia | | 30. | | June 28. | | |
| Snaps | VII. | May 4. | | | | |
| Lettuce | | 3. | | | | |
| d^o | | 10. | | | | |
| d^o | | 17. | | | | |
| Ravensworth peas.[3] | A. 15 | 22. | | | | |
| Arkansa peas | A. 14 | 24. | | | | |
| Fr. black eye d^o | am^g. Pani corn | 24. | | | | |
| Gerkins[4] | VIII. | July 24. | | | | |
| Swedish turneps[5] | A. 13. | | | | | |
| Lettuce | XVII. 7. | | | | | |
| Carrots | A. 11 | 29. | | | | |
| Summer turneps | A. 12. B. 4. G. 3. | Aug. 10. | | | | |
| Lettuce white | XVII. 6. | 10. | | | | |
| Spinach. Summer | E. 3. | 11. | | | | |

## 1813.

Mar. 22.  Guinea grass[6] from D[r]. Brown[7] Terras F. 7.
Apr.  2.  Fiorin roots.[8] in F. 8. 9.
      10.  planted in Nursery peach stones as follows
           Terras 1. W.   21. early soft peaches.. from m̄r̄ Clay[9]
                  1. E.   26. large yellow soft. ripe Sep. 1.  Clay
                  4. E.   26. fine white soft .............. Clay
                  4. W.   13. large white soft. Pop. for.[10]
                  5. W.   16. Malta peaches.
                  5. E.   108. fine soft peaches of Aug.        Clay
           Dates of Asparagus coming to table.[11]

| | | | | |
|---|---|---|---|---|
| 1794. | Apr. | 7 | 1814. | Apr. 13. |
| 1795 | ... | 12 | 1815 | Mar. 31. |
| 6. | ... | 3 | 1816. | Apr. 5. |
| 7. | Mar. | 23. | 17. | Apr. 11. |
| 9. | Apr. | 14 | 21. | Apr. 8. |
| 1804. | ... | 12 | | |
| 1810. | ... | 13. | | |
| 11. | ... | 3 | | |
| 12 | ... | 8 | | |
| 13. | ... | 11. | | |

May.  ab[t]. 5th. or 6th. put 2. chubs[12] from Cartersville[13] into the fish pond.
           lower one.
      23.  put 5. more from Ja[s]. P. Cocke[14] into d[o].
           Dates of Artichokes coming to table.

| | | | |
|---|---|---|---|
| 1794. | May 31. | 1818. | June 26. |
| 96. | June 6. | 1819. | June 14. |
| 99. | ... 12. | | |
| 1810. | July. 6* | | |
| 11. | May 28. | | |
| 13. | June 7. | | |
| 14. | | | |
| 15. | | | |
| 16. | June 11. | | |
| 17. | | | |

           * planted Mar. 22. preceding.
July   6.  cymlins   ⎫
       4.  cucumbers ⎬ from m̄r̄s Lewis.[15]
      11.  corn ..... ⎭
      14.  figs.
      29.  tomatas
Oct.   6.  Nursery. 5th. terras.
           W. end 4. fine Heath peach stones.  Carysbrook[16]
           next 22. fine soft white. like Brock's ⎫
                  33. very good soft            ⎬ from Poplar Forest
                  8.  d[o]. ...................... ⎭
Dec.  24.  filled the ice house with snow.
           1815. Mar. 2. the ice having sunk 5. or 6.f. was now replenished
           with ice from the river.[17]
           Method of distinguishing or designating the terrasses[18] below the
           garden wall, according to the squares of the garden to which they
           are opposite.
           A.  the curved terrases at the West end of the garden.
                1. 2. 3. 4.  vacant.
                5. 6.        Alpine strawberries.
                7.           Walk being a prolongation of 2. the Terras Walk,
                8. 9. 10. 11. 12. 13. 14. 15.  vacant,

B.   opposite to squares I. II. III.
     1$^{st}$. or Submural figs.   2$^d$. the Walk.
     3. 4. 5. 6. 7.   Hudson strawberries.
C.   IV. V. VI.   squares.   1$^{st}$. hops.
     next below is the old Nursery.
D.   VII. VIII. IX. X.
     Submural.   Frame peas.
     3$^d$. vacant for Fruits.
     below is the W. Vineyard.
E.   XI. XII.   submural.   Frame peas.   3. vacant for fruits.
     below are the squares of gooseberries, rasps, currans.
F.   XIII. XIV. XV.
     3$^d$. vacant for Roots.
     below is E. Vineyard.
G.   XVI. XVII. XVIII.   Submural Asparagus.
     3$^d$. vacant for Leaves.   Raw.
H.   XIX. etc.
     3$^d$. vacant for Leaves.   Dressed.

---

Location of each article.   1813.[19]

Peas.   Bord. I–V.   Sq. I. II. III. IV.   Terras. D. 1. 3.   E. 1.
Snaps.   Sq. V. VII.
Haricots red.   VI.
Harricots long.   Terras. A. 1. 4.
Limas                   2. 3.

Cucumbers.   Sq. VIII.
Gerkins.   XII. 2.
Nasturtium.      IX
Tomatas.      X.   Bord.   X.
Okra.      X.
Artichokes      XI.
Squashes.      XII.

Carrots.      XIII.   Terras.   A. 10. 11. 12.
Salsafia.      XIV. 1.          F. 3. G. 3.
Beets              2.
Garlic.   .......     3.
Leeks.          4.
Onions.      XV.
Scallions.      XVI. 1.
Shalots.      2.
Chives.            Terras. C. 1.

Lettuce      XVII.   Bord.   VI. VIII. IX
Terragon.           1. N.   Terras. H. 3.
Celery.      XVIII.
Spinach           Bord.   XI. XII.   Terras E. 3.
Sorrel.   ...................................   H. 3.
Cabbage.   early dwarf.
         York.
         Savoy.
Sprout Kale.
Pani corn.
Ravensworths. . . . A. 15.
Homony beans.
Arkansa peas. . . . A. 14.
Swedish turnep. Ter. A. .14.
Potatoes Early.
French black eyed pea.   among Pani corn

1813.

| Agenda 1813. | Ada | Agenda 1813. | Ada | Disposition of grounds. 1813. |
|---|---|---|---|---|
| Mar. 1. Frame peas Border I–V. | Mar. 1. | Apr. 26. grey Snaps Sq. VII............ | May 4. | Border I–V. Frame peas. |
| do. Submural VII. XII. | 1. | May 3. lettuce. rad. XVII. 4. N. | | VI. Lett. rad. Savoys. Mar. 2. 15. 22. |
| lettuce & radish. Bord. VI. | 2. | Salsafia. | | York cab. Sprout Kale Mar. 3. |
| Spinach. Bord. XI. | 6. | homony beans. | | VII. lettuce. Aug. 2. 9. 16. |
| dress Aspar. beds. | 4. | 6. Swed turneps. Ter. A. 13. | | VIII. lettuce Aug. 23. 30. Sep. 6. |
| hophills. | 13. | 10. lettuce ———— XVII. 4. S. 5. | | IX. Sep. 13. 20. 27. |
| Savoy..........Bord. VI. | 2. | 17. XVII. 5. N. | | X. Tomatas. Mar. 15. |
| York Cabage Ronaldson. ib. | 3. | 24. ..........5. S. | | XI. Spinach. Mar. 6. |
| Sprout Kale...........ib. | 3. | 31. .......... potatos. for winter crop | | XII. do. Mar. 15. |
| Celery. lowgrounds. | | May & June, transplant cabbages. | | Square I. Hotspurs. Mar. 1. |
| Hotspurs............Sq. I. | 29. | June 7. lettuce XVII. 6. S. | | II. Ledmans. 1. |
| Ledmans II. | 29. | 14. potatos for winter crop | | III. do. 15. |
| Potatoes early. | Ap. 24. | 21. 7. N. | | IV. do. Apr. 5. |
| Beet XIV. 2. | | .......... 7. S. | | Pulse. V. Snaps. Mar. 15. |
| Hudson strawberries. B. 5. 6. 7. | Ma. 3. | 28. ...........1. S. | | VI. red haricots Apr. 5. |
| Trees. | 12. | July 5. Cucumbers Gerkins Sq. XII. 2 Endive | | VII. Snaps. Apr. 26. |
| 15. lettuce radish. Bord. VI. | 15. | 15. carrots for autumn & winter. Endive | | VIII. Cucumbers. Apr. 19. July 5. |
| Spinach. Bord. XII. | 15. | Aug. 2. lettuce ⎱Bord. VII. for late | | other Fruits. IX. Nasturtium. Mar. 15. |
| Orach.[20] | | Endive ⎰fall & winter. | | X. Tomatas. Apr. 5. |
| Ledmans. Sq. III. | Ap. 12. | √ Spinach. E. 3. for Octob. | | XI. Artichokes. |
| Snaps. V. | Mar. 31. | Turneps for winter. from 1– to 15th. | | XII. Squashes. Apr. 19. |
| Savoy. Sprout Kale. | | 9. lettuce endive. Bord. VII. | | 2. Gerkins |
| Celery. low grounds ⎫low grds. | Ap. 3. | 16. lettuce endive.........VII. winter | | Roots. XIII. Carrots. Mar. 15. |
| Malta Kale.......... ⎭ | | Spinach. for winter. E. 3. | | XIV. 1. Salsafia. Apr. 5. |
| Tomatas. Bord. X. | 9. | 23. lettuce endive. corn sallad. Bord. VIII. | | 2. beets. Mar. 15. |
| Nasturtium. Sq. IX. | 17. | 30. lettuce. endive. corn sal. VIII. | | 3. garlic. 15. |
| early Turneps. | | Sep. 6. lettuce, endive, corn sal. Bord. VIII. | | 4. leeks. 15. |
| Carrots. Sq. XIII. | Ap. 3. | Spinach. E. 3. | | XV Onions. 15. |
| Le—— | 20. | 13. lettuce endive..........Bord IX. | | XVI. 1. Scallions. 15. |
| garlic.......... XIV. 3. | | Spinach E. 3. | | 2. Shalots. 15. |
| leeks......... 4. | | 20. lettuce endive.............IX. | | |
| Onions. Sq. XV. | | Spinach. E. 3. 6. | | |

1813. (continued)

| Agenda  1813. | Ada | Agenda  1813. | Ada | Disposition of grounds.  1813. |
|---|---|---|---|---|
| Scallions        XVI. 1. | | 27.  lettuce, endive............IX. | May 4. | XVII.  1. N.  lettuce.  Mar. 22. |
| Shalots..........2. | | Spinach  E. 3. | | lettuce. 2. S.  Mar. 29. 2. N. Apr. 5 |
| Chives.  Submural. C. 1. | | Oct.  3.  orach. | | 2. S.  Apr. 12.  5. S.  May 24. |
| 22. lettuce. radish Sq. XVII. 1. N. | | Nov.  cover figs, & tender plants. | | 3. N.    19.  6. N.    31. |
| 29. lettuce. rad.  Sq. XVII. 1. S. | M. 29. | litter Asparagus. | | 3. S.    26.  6. S.  June 7. |
| | | | | 4. N.  May 3.  7. N.    14. |
| Apr.  5.  lettuce rad...........2. S.. | Ap. 6. | Dec.  plant privet.  thorn.  trees. | | 4. S.    10.  7. S.    21. |
| & Spinach........Bord. IX. | 7. | trim trees.  vines.  raspberries | | 5. N.    17.  1. S.    28. |
| Ledmans.    IV. | | goose berries.  currans. | | Raw Sallads. |
| red Haricots    VI. | 22. | turf. | | XVIII.  Celery. |
| Haricots low.    Terras A. 4.... | 15. | Jan.  bring in manure & trench it. | | Terras. A. 2.  Limas.  Apr. 12. |
| - - - - - - | | | | 1.  long haricots.  Apr. 12. |
| Limas.............3. | 15. | | | 3.  Limas.  Apr. 5. |
| Early Bess bean.....D. 3. | 23. | | | 4.  long haricots.  Apr. 5. |
| Carrots.........A. 10 -- | 28. | | | 5. 6.  Alpine Strawb. |
| Parsnips.........A. 11. 12. | 29. | | | 7.  Walk. |
| Salsafia.        Sq. XIV. 1. | 22. | | | 8. 9.  Cabbages. |
| Terragon.  Terras H. 3. West | | | | 10.  Carrots. |
| Sorrel.......H. 3.  East | | | | 11. 12.  Parsneps  Apr. 15. |
| Tomatas.  Sq. X. | Ap. 9. | | | 13.-- Arkansa pea. |
| Pani corn. | | | | 14.  Swed turneps  May 3. |
| Ravensworths A. 15. | May 22. | | | 15.  Ravensworth peas |
| 12.  lettuce. rad.  Sq. XVII. 2. N. | Ap. 14. | | | B. 3. 4. 5. 6. 7.  Hudson strawb. |
| Haricots long.  Ter. A. 1. | | | | C. 1.  Chives.  3. Hops. |
| Limas.............2. | | | | D. 1.  Frame peas.  Mar. 1. |
| 19.  lettuce & rad.  Sq. XVII. 3. N. | 20. | | | 3.  Early.  Bess beans. |
| Ledmans.  Ter. D. 3. | | | | E. 1.  Frame peas.  Mar. 1. |
| Salsafia.    F. 3. G. 3. | 30. | | | 3.  Spinach.  Aug. 2. 16.  Sep. 6. 13. 20. 27. |
| Cucumbers.  Sq. VIII. | 23. | | | F. 3.  Salsafia.          Apr. 19. |
| - - - - - - | | | | G. 1.  Asparagus.  3.  Salsafia.  Apr. 18. |
| Okra.²¹  Sq. X. | 9. | | | H. 3.  Terragon.  Sorrel. |
| Squashes.  Sq. XII. 1. | 24. | | | |
| Melons. | | | | |
| 26.  lettuce. rad.  Sq. XVII. 3. S. | | | | |

¹ *1813.* The war with England was almost one year old. Although the United States had won victories, there had also been reverses. The Chesapeake Bay was closely blockaded; this prevented free shipping and caused much hardship in Virginia and the adjoining states. Jefferson, at *Monticello,* wrote letters to President Madison and others about the progress of the war, and in them offered suggestions which he thought would hasten the victory for the United States. The war was having a profound effect on his own finances.

He was removed, however, from the center of the activity of the war, so that he could still enjoy the peace of his *Monticello* and *Poplar Forest.* The following letter to his old friend, Mrs. Elizabeth Trist, gives us a glimpse of the life at the two estates.

Poplar Forest, May 10, '13.

I brought the inclosed book to this place, the last fall, intending to forward it to you; but having a neighbor here who loves to laugh, I lent it to him to read; he lent it to another, and so it went the rounds of the neighborhood and is returned to me at my Spring visit to this place. I now forward it, and if it diverts you for an hour or two, I shall be gratified by it. I was myself amused by its humor as much as its object would permit me to be; for that is evidently to deride the Republican branches of our government. I left all well at Monticello, except Benjamin whose health is very precarious. Lewis is become the favorite of all. his vivacity, his intelligence, & his beauty (for the mark on his forehead is disappearing) make him a perfect pet. you will perceive from these senile details of the nursery that I am becoming old. I wish I had no other proofs, but I am weakening very sensibly. I can walk no further than my garden. I ride, however, and in a carriage can come here without fatigue. I fear however this will not long be the case. your friends Mr. & Mrs. Divers, tho' they think themselves getting crazy are in better health than usual. I am hastening back to their first pea dinner, but I think I shall be too late. In your Southern situation I presume you have them now. Mr. Randolph has been seized with the military fever. He expects to be called to his regiment at Black Rock this month. He will be a great loss to his family, and no man in the world a greater one to his affairs. . . . (*Glimpses of the Past,* Missouri, **3**: 120.)

The friendship between Jefferson and John Adams grew more felicitous. Letters passed more frequently. Letters also renewed the friendship with Mrs. Adams, but Jefferson lost a close friend in the death of Dr. Benjamin Rush in April. He had been one of the signers of the Declaration of Inde-

pendence, and had been the avenue through which the friendship of Jefferson and Adams had been renewed.

A new friend came into Jefferson's life this year in the person of José Francisco Correa da Serra, a learned botanist,
Portuguese Minister Plenipotentiary at Washington, and a
man of wide interests, who visited him at *Monticello*. After
Mr. Correa's visit, Jefferson wrote to Mr. Du Pont:

I am indebted to you also for your letter by Mr. Correa, and the benefit it procured me of his acquaintance. He was so kind as to pay me a
visit at Monticello, which enabled me to see for myself that he was still
beyond all the eulogies with which yourself and other friends had pre-
conized him. Learned beyond any one I had before met with, good,
modest and of the simplest manners, the idea of losing him again filled
me with regret. . . . (Lipscomb and Bergh, *Jefferson* 19: 196.)

The following year William Short wrote to Jefferson from
Philadelphia: "Correa is here & has been for some time. He
was enchanted with Monticello & delighted with the owner, &
intends repeating his visit in the spring or summer." (*Jefferson Papers*, M. H. C., 1: 190.)

Jefferson was at *Poplar Forest* three times during the year.
The visits were made in the spring, late summer, and early
winter. His house there was nearing completion.

Extensive plantings were made at *Monticello* in the garden,
orchard, and fields, but the weather was unfavorable so that
poor crops were harvested. Jefferson wrote to James Madison from *Monticello*, on July 13:

We are at the close of the poorest harvest I have ever seen. I shall
not carry into my barn more than one-third of an ordinary crop. But
one rain to wet the ground since April. A remarkably drying wind
with great heat the first days of the harvest, dried up the skin of the
wheat so that it fell before the scythe instead of being cut. I have seen
harvests lost by wet, but never before saw one lost by dry weather. I
have suffered more by the drought than my neighbors. Most of them
will make half a crop, some two thirds. Much of the evil had been
prepared by the winter and the fly. It is not too late yet for the corn
to recover should there come rains shortly. It never was seen so low
before at this date. Our gardens are totally burnt up and the river so
low that you can almost jump over it in some places. (Lipscomb and
Bergh, *Jefferson* 19: 191–192.)

Details about the arrangement of the vegetable garden and
the calendar of plants and seeds to be planted were recorded
in the *Garden Book* as in 1812. More detailed accounts of

the terraces below the garden wall were added.   Letters continued to flow to and from Jefferson about agricultural matters, and the exchange of plants went on unabated.

² James Ronaldson, of Philadelphia.

³ See letters, Jefferson to Richard Fitzhugh, April 25, 1813;
Fitzhugh to Jefferson, May 9, 1813; and Jefferson to Fitzhugh, May 27, 1813.

⁴ *Cucumis anguria* L.   Gherkin.   (See letter, Jefferson to
Randolph Jefferson, June 20, 1813.)

⁵ See letter, Jefferson to John Taylor, June 8, 1795.

⁶ *Panicum maximum* Jacq.   Guinea-grass.   (See letter, Jefferson to Dr. Samuel Brown, April 17, 1813.)

⁷ Dr. Samuel Brown (1769–1830) was born in what is now
Rockbridge County.   He studied medicine with Dr. Benjamin
Rush, of Philadelphia, and spent two years at Edinburgh.
He practiced medicine at Bladensburg, Maryland; Lexington,
Kentucky; New Orleans; and Huntsville, Alabama.   About
1819 he accepted a chair at Transylvania College, at Lexing-
ton, Kentucky, where he stayed until 1825.   (*Dict. Am. Biog.*
3: 152.)

⁸ *Agrostis palustris* Huds.   Fiorin grass.   (See letters,
Jefferson to McMahon, January 11, 1813, and Jefferson to J.
Chambers, March 4, 1813.)

⁹ The Reverend Charles Clay, of Bedford County, Virginia.

¹⁰ *Poplar Forest,* Bedford County, Virginia.

¹¹ Jefferson often made summaries of this kind.   In the case
of vegetables the summary gave him a knowledge of the forwardness and lateness of the seasons, so that he knew at about
what time to expect certain articles for the table.   See below,
"Dates of Artichokes coming to table."

¹² Chub.   In America the word *chub* is used locally to mean
any of several very different fishes, as the Black Bass, etc.

¹³ See letters, James P. Cocke to Jefferson, May 18, 1813,
and Jefferson to James P. Cocke, May 22, 1813.

¹⁴ James Powell Cocke (1748–1829), life-long contemporary and friend of Thomas Jefferson, was the last of his line
to live at the ancestral home *Malvern Hills* in Henrico County
on James River.   Not long after the end of the Revolutionary
War he sold *Malvern Hills* to Robert Nelson, taking in exchange 1,600 acres of land in the North Garden of Albemarle
County.   In 1791 he purchased *Springhill* in Augusta County,

and two years later he moved from the Valley to Albemarle County, where he built his home called *Edgemont* on the south fork of the Hardware River, and where he lived all the rest of his days.   The house at *Edgemont* was built according to plans drawn by Thomas Jefferson.   (*Virginia Mag. Hist. and Biography* 43: 80–81, 1935, and 44: 129, 1936.   Courtesy of Professor James P. C. Southall.)

[15] Probably Mrs. Nicholas Lewis, of *The Farm*, Albemarle County.

[16] *Carysbrook*, Fluvanna County, Virginia, was the home of Wilson Miles Cary (1723–1817).

[17] Rivanna River.

[18] This was the first complete plan of the Terraces below the vegetable garden and wall.

[19] Compare with the "Arrangement of the Garden" for 1812, and the "Disposition of grounds, 1813."

[20] *Atriplex hortensis* L.   Orach.

[21] *Hibiscus esculentus* L.   Okra.


LETTERS AND EXTRACTS OF LETTERS, 1813

(Jefferson to Bernard McMahon.)

Monticello Jan. 11. 13.

I have too long delayed returning you thanks for your favors of Nov. 24. & Dec. 1. and the hyacinth roots with the seeds of the China pink, Auricula, & fiorin grass, which came safely to hand.   I had in a former letter mentioned that I should avail myself of the opportunity of a young medical student going on to Philadelphia to send you a box of seeds which I received from M. Thouin of the National garden of France.   they had arrived too late for spring sowing.   the gentleman I had in view, went off so suddenly that I missed the opportunity of getting the box into his hands.   I have been waiting since in the hope some other passenger might be going on; but none having occurred & the season beginning to approach, I have sent it to a friend in Richmond. between that place & Philadelphia there is a frequent intercourse by passengers, and my friend will find some one who will take care of the box by the way and deliver it safely to you.   on the subject of the Fiorin grass, I received 2. years ago some roots from Ireland, which we planted in moist ground, and took care of.   they flourished handsomely till the warm season, when the warmth of the sun & our cloudless climate proved too much for them.   the last spring I received some of the seed from Edinburg and sowed a part in a moist meadow, & a little in boxes.   the former failed, the latter came up well, but the sun destroyed it.   I will carefully repeat the experiment with what you have been so kind as to send me, but I fear it requires the protection of the clouds, fogs, & dripping climate of Ireland, of all of which our climate presents the reverse. (*Jefferson Papers,* L. C.)

### (Jefferson to James Ronaldson.)

Monticello, January 12, 1813.

Your favor of November 2d arrived a little before I set out on a journey on which I was absent between five and six weeks. I have still therefore to return you my thanks for the seeds accompanying it, which shall be duly taken care of, and a communication made to others of such as shall prove valuable. I have been long endeavoring to procure the Cork tree from Europe, but without success. A plant which I brought with me from Paris died after languishing some time, and of several parcels of acorns received from a correspondent at Marseilles, not one has ever vegetated. I shall continue my endeavors, although disheartened by the nonchalance of our Southern fellow citizens, with whom alone they can thrive. It is now twenty-five years since I sent them two shipments (about 500 plants) of the Olive tree of Aix, the finest Olives in the world. If any of them still exist, it is merely as a curiosity in their gardens; not a single orchard of them has been planted. I sent them also the celebrated species of Sainfoin, from Malta, which yields good crops without a drop of rain through the season. It was lost. The upland rice which I procured fresh from Africa and sent them, has been preserved and spread in the upper parts of Georgia, and I believe in Kentucky. But we must acknowledge their services in furnishing us an abundance of cotton, a substitute for silk, flax and hemp. The ease with which it is spun will occasion it to supplant the two last, and its cleanliness the first. Household manufacture is taking deep root with us. I have a carding machine, two spinning machines, and looms with the flying shuttle in full operation for clothing my own family; and I verily believe that by the next winter this State will not need a yard of imported coarse or middling clothing. I think we have already a sheep for every inhabitant, which will suffice for clothing, and one-third more, which a single year will add, will furnish blanketing. . . . (Lipscomb and Bergh, *Jefferson* 13: 204–205.)

### (Jefferson to James Madison.)

Monticello, February 8, 1813.

. . . The autumn and winter have been most unfriendly to the wheat in red lands, by continued cold and alternate frosts and thaws. The late snow of about ten inches now disappearing, has relieved it. . . . (Lipscomb and Bergh, *Jefferson* 13: 220.)

### (Randolph Jefferson to Jefferson.)

[Snowden] Feby 24; 1813

Dear Brother,

I have sent Squire over to you for the garden seeds you were so kind as to promise us. . . . (*Carr-Cary Papers,* U. Va.)

**(Bernard McMahon to Jefferson.)**

Philadelphia 27<sup>th</sup>. Feb<sup>y</sup>. 1813

I do myself the pleasure of sending you herewith a small packet of Oats raised by myself; it is the produce of the 5<sup>th</sup>. annual crop, after the original importation (by myself) from Ireland, where, as well as in England and Scotland, it is known by the trivial name of *Potatoe Oats.* The seed I imported 5 years ago weighed 40. lb. per Bushel, my crop this season of about 150 Bushels, the same as the sample I send you will average 42 or very near it per bushel; for which I am now able to command from our *neighbouring* farmers who have seen it growing, $2 per bushel, *for seed,* and a demmand for much more than I have this season.

I would advise you to sow the sample I send you, as soon as possible, that is to say, the very first day that the ground *will plough and harrow freely; the earlier in the season the better,* tomorrow if it was possible. By good seed, good ground, proper management, and *early sowing,* I am convinced that we can have as good Oats in the middle and eastern States, as in any part of Europe, and as productive and abundant crops.

I am extremely obliged to you for your effort to have the box of seeds forwarded to me as early in the season as possible, but I have not yet received it, nor heard from your friend in Richmond. . . . (*Jefferson Papers,* L. C.)

**(Jefferson to Randolph Jefferson.)**

[Monticello] Mar 2. 13.

Dear Brother,

Having been from home the last fall during most of the season for saving seeds, I find on examination that my gardener has made a very scanty provision. of that however I send enough to put you in stock: to wit Early Frame peas. Ledman's peas. long haricots. red haricots. grey snaps Lima beans. carrots. parsneps. salsafia. spinach. Sprout Kale. tomatas I have sent you none of the following because all your neighbors can furnish them, & my own stock is short. towit Lettuce radish. cucumbers. squashes cabbages. turneps. mrs. Randolph makes up some flower seeds for my sister. . . . (*Carr-Cary Papers,* U. Va.)

**(Jefferson to J. Chambers.)**

Monticello Mar. 4. 13.

The roots of the fiorin grass which you were so kind as to forward to me were received, with still enough of life in many of them to encourage the hope of their doing well. the hill on which I live being entirely dry & of a thirsty soil, I got my son in law, m<sup>r</sup> Randolph, to take them to his place, about 4. miles off, and set them out in a moist and favorable spot there. he inclosed them in a triangular pen. they recovered their life perfectly and gave the highest hopes of their success. but when our hot sun of July & August came on, it appeared to kill them completely; and I never doubted their being entirely lost, till, on the occasion of your letter, I enquired again into the subject, and was told the plants had recovered again in autumn, & had taken a new growth.   the ground being covered with snow at that time I deferred answering your letter till the snow should be gone, and I might go & examine the plants. this has not been till lately.   I found that in the autumn they had taken a luxuriant growth; had filled the pen compleatly, and now formed a mat of about 4. I. thick on the ground, but so killed by the winter as to be like other dry winter killed grass.   of course not convertible into hay.   I shall now make trial of it here on my hill to see if it will answer in a dry soil.   I suspect it to be a grass peculiarly adapted to the humid climate & the covered sky & mild winter of Ireland, but doubtful under our hot sun, cloudless skies & severe cold of winter, but yet it may possibly give us a good growth in spring before the summer heats set in, and another after they are over in autumn & before the severe cold comes on.   I will give a careful trial in the hope that sufficient experiments may point out the situations in which we also may participate of it's benefits. . . . (*Jefferson Papers,* L. C.)

### (Jefferson to John H. Cocke.)

Monticello Mar. 12. 13.

Th: Jefferson presents his compliments to mr̄ Cocke, whose servant is desired to take as many Broom plants as he pleases, but having never found them to succeed by transplantation, he sends him some seed, which generally succeeds, altho sometimes it does not come up till the second spring.   he sends him also a little seed of the *Sprout-Kale,* a plant he received from the National garden of France about 3 years ago, never before in this country.   it is to be sown & managed as the Cabbage, but to stand in it's place thro' the winter uncovered; it's only use is to furnish sprouts, of which it will yield 2. or 3. crops of 6. or 8 I. long, in a winter, beginning in December & continuing thro' the whole winter, till the plant goes to seed in the spring.   it is a tender & delicious winter vegetable. . . . (*Jefferson Papers,* U. Va.)

### (Jefferson to William Caruthers.)

Monticello Mar. 12. 13

Your letter of Feb. 3 has been received, and in answer to your enquiries respecting sheep, I will state that I have three distinct races which I keep at different places.   1. Merinos; of these I have but 2. ewes, and of course none to spare.   President Madison has been more successful, and sells some ram lambs, but not ewes.   the Merino is a diminutive tender sheep, yielding very little wool, but that of extraordinary fineness, fit only for the finest broadcloths, but not at all for country use. I do not know mr̄. Madison's prices, but in general the price of these rams is fallen to from 50. to 100. D. a piece.   the wool sells high to the Northward to the hatters, but our hatters do not know how to use it.

2. I have the bigtail, or Barbarry sheep.   I raise it chiefly for the table, the meat being higher flavored than that of any other sheep, and easily kept fat.   the tail is large.   I have seen one 12. I. square & weighing 14. lb.   they encumber the animal in getting out of the way of dogs, and are an obstacle to propagation without attentions which we do not pay to them.   they are well sized, & well fleeced but the wool is apt to be coarse & hairy.   3. I have a Spanish race, the ram of which I received from Spain in 1794.   I bred from him 7. years in and in, suffering no other ram on the place, and after his death I still selected the finest of his race to succeed him, so that the ram may now be considered as pure as the original.   they are above common size, finely formed, the hardiest race we have ever known, scarcely ever losing a lamb fully fleeced, the belly & legs down to the hoof covered with wool, & the wool of fine quality, some of it as fine as the half blood Merino.   we consider it the finest race of sheep ever known in this country.   having never cut or killed a ram lamb of them, but given them out to those who wished them.   this part of the country is well stocked with them, and they sell at the public sales 50. per cent higher than the country sheep.   I sent my flock of them to a place I have in Bedford, where they are beginning to be known & in great demand.   if you should wish to get into this breed, and will accept of a pair of lambs the ensuing summer, you shall be welcome to them. . . . I have no hesitation in pronouncing them the fittest sheep in the world for that country. . . . (*Jefferson Papers,* L. C.)

(Jefferson to Samuel Brown.)

Monticello Apr. 17. 1813

Your favor of Octob. 1. came to hand with a note from m̄r Poindexter, on the 20th. Ult. as also the Guinea grass seed, and Capsicum.   they were exactly in time for sowing and were immediately sowed.   they had got mixed by the way, and the capsicum seeds were difficult to find. not more than three or four could be discovered, & these rather doubtful.   I dibbled them however in a pot to give them their best chance. as being the production of a more Northern climate than those we cultivate I am in hopes they will be hardier, and if so, more valuable.   of the Guinea grass I know little.   the gentlemen of S. Carolina have told me of it's importance to them, and I have heard it yields a good growth in the West Indies in the driest seasons.   as we also are subject to long droughts, this grass may be useful to us when such occur.   I wish my interior situation admitted my getting, with more facility, useful articles of the growth of your region, and which would stand ours.   m̄rs. Trist has named to me several trees of use and ornament with you which would be desirable to us.   but the safe transportation of the plant itself I know from experience to be desperate.   should any more of the Capsicum seed fall into your hands, it will come safely by mail in a letter and will be thankfully received; it may ensure the success of the plant, should the three or four fail which I have planted.   planting is one of my great amusements, and even of those things which can only be for posterity,

for a Septuagenary has no right to count on any thing beyond annuals.
. . . (*Jefferson Papers, L. C.*)

(Jefferson to Charles W. Peale.)

Monticello, Apr. 17, 13.

I had long owed you a letter for your favor of Aug. 19, when I received eight days ago that of Mar. 2, 1812 [= 1813]. . . . Both your letters are on the subject of your agricultural operations, and both prove the ardor with which you are pursuing them. . . . Your position that a small farm well worked and well manned, will produce more than a larger one ill-tended, is undoubtedly true in a certain degree. There are extremes in this as in all other cases. The true medium may really be considered and stated as a mathematical problem: "Given the quantum of labor within our command, and land ad libitum offering it's spontaneous contributions: required the proportion in which these two elements should be employed to produce a maximum." It is a difficult problem, varying probably in every country according to the relative value of land and labor. The spontaneous energies of the earth are a gift of nature, but they require the labor of man to direct their operation. And the question is so to husband his labor as to turn the greatest quantity of this useful action of the earth to his benefit. Ploughing deep, your recipe for killing weeds, is also the recipe for almost every good thing in farming. The plough is to the farmer what the wand is to the sorcerer. It's effect is really like sorcery. In the country wherein I live we have discovered a new use for it, equal in value almost to it's services before known. Our country is hilly and we have been in the habit of ploughing in strait rows whether up and down hill, in oblique lines, or however they lead; and our soil was all rapidly running into the rivers. We now plough horizontally folowing the curvatures of the hills and hollows, on the dead level, however crooked the lines may be. Every furrow thus acts as a reservoir to receive and retain the waters, all of which go to the benefit of the growing plant, instead of running off into streams. In a farm horizontally and deeply ploughed, scarcely an ounce of soil is now carried off from it. In point of beauty nothing can exceed that of the waving lines & rows winding along the face of the hills & vallies. The horses draw much easier on the dead level, and it is in fact a conversion of hilly grounds into a plain. The improvement of our soil from this cause the last half dozen years, strikes every one with wonder. For this improvement we are indebted to my son-in-law, Mr. Randolph, the best farmer, I believe, in the United States, and who has taught us to make more than two blades of corn to grow where only one grew before. If your farm is hilly, let me beseech you to make a trial of this method. To direct the plough horizontally we take a rafter level of this form ◁△ . A boy of 13 or 14 is able to work it round the hill, a still smaller one with a little hough marking the points traced by the feet of the level. The plough follows running thro' these marks. The leveller having compleated one level line thro' the field, moves with his level 30 or 40 yards up or down the hill, and runs another which is marked in like manner & traced by the plough, and having thus run what may be called guide furrows every 30 or 40 yards thro the field, the ploughman runs the furrows of the intervals parallel to these. In proportion, however, as the declivitiy of the hill varies in different parts of the line, the guide furrows will approach or recede from each other in different parts, and the parallel furrows will at length touch in one part, when far asunder in others, leaving un-ploughed gores between them. These gores we plough separately. They occasion short rows & turnings which are a little inconvenient, but not materially so. I pray you try this recipe for hilly grounds. You will say with me, "Probatum est," and I shall have the happiness of being of some use to you, and thro' your example to your neighbors, and of adding something solid to the assurances of my great esteem & respect. (*Jefferson Papers*, M. H. C. 1: 178–180.)

### (Jefferson to Richard Fitzhugh.)

Monticello Apr. 25. 13.

I have unluckily got out of the Ravensworth pea, which I value so highly as to wish to recover it. I am in hopes you are able to supply me with a little. a few peas quilted into a piece of cloth, so as to lie flat, of the size and form of a letter, and inclosed in a paper cover and directed to me as a letter by mail will be sufficient to put me in seed by another year.

I inclose you the seeds of a very valuable garden vegetable which I received from France 2. or 3. years ago, it is called Sprout Kale. it is sowed and transplanted as other Kale or Cabbages, and about the beginning of December it begins to furnish sprouts, and will furnish 3. crops of them thro the winter; so abundantly that a few plants will give a dish every day. it stands our winter perfectly without cover. . . . (*Jefferson Papers*, M. H. S.)

### (Richard Fitzhugh to Jefferson.)

Ravensworth May 9th. 1813

I send you agreeable to your request a few of the Ravensworth pea, and am sorry that the mode of conveyance will not admit of my sending you a larger quantity—however perhaps it will be in my power to send by Mr. Eppes, when he returns from Congress about half bushel. if you think he can convey them to you, please to write to me. I have not the pleasure of a personal acquaintance with Mr. Eppes, therefore should thank you for a letter of introduction to him. my late ill health and my retirement from the world, prevented my regular inquiry at the post office, consequently your letter remained several days before I recd. it. It would give me singular pleasure to see you at my House once more— if not pray let me hear from you whenever it may be convenient for you to write. . . . (*Jefferson Papers*, M. H. S.)

(James Powell Cocke to Jefferson.)

May 18ᵗʰ 1813

Untill within a few days past we have not been able to procure the Chub fish.   If you will send on Thursday next a careful hand prepaired for there conveyance, I have little doubt but the necessary supply for your pond can be made which will give pleasure to your friend. . . . P. S.   Growth of the Chub at 1 year old 8 to 9 in. long, at 2–11 to 12—3–15 to 16—the weight not asertained but suppose the latter as 3 to 3½ lbs.   (*Jefferson Papers, L. C.*)

(Jefferson to James Madison.)

Monticello, May 21, 1813.

. . . We have never seen so unpromising a crop of wheat as that now growing.   The winter killed an unusual proportion of it, and the fly is destroying the remainder.   We may estimate the latter loss at one-third at present, and fast increasing from the effect of the extraordinary drought.   With such a prospect before us, the blockade is acting severely on our past labors. . . . (Lipscomb and Bergh, *Jefferson* **13**: 232.)

(Jefferson to Mr. Barnes.)

Monticello May 21. 13.

[Jefferson requests Mr. Barnes to get Mr. Milligan to buy for him Gardiner and Hepburn's book on gardening.]   (*Jefferson Papers, L. C.*)

(Jefferson to James P. Cocke.)

Monticello May 22. 13.

Your favor of Tuesday came to hand yesterday (Friday) afternoon, and expressing the expectation that you could furnish me with a supply of Chub fish for my pond if I should send on *Thursday* next, now past, I sent off a careful man with a cart and a cask this morning.   I am very thankful for this kindness having been very unsuccessful in my endeavors to get a stock for my pond.   I sent a boat & a couple of hands about three weeks ago to Cartersville, where mr̄ Harrison was so kind as to exert himself to get some.   he procured 9. but they were taken with a hook & line, and 7. of them died soon.   2 only got here alive, one of them much wounded, & both having the appearance of being the same sex; so that I had little expectation of a stock from them. . . . (*Jefferson Papers, L. C.*)

(Jefferson to Randolph Jefferson.)

Monticello May 25. 13.

Dear Brother,

Supposing the shad season not to be quite over, and that in hauling for them they catch some carp, I send the bearer with a cart and cask to procure for me as many living carp as he can to stock my fishpond. I should not regard his staying a day or two extra, if it would give a reasonable hope of furnishing a supply. he is furnished with money to pay for the carp, for which I have always given the same price as for shad. should he not be able to lay out the whole in carp he may bring us 3. or 4. shad if he can get them. . . .

Reflecting on the manner of managing your very valuable farm, I thought I would suggest the following which appears to me the best, & of which you will consider. to form your lowgrounds into two divisions, one of them to be in wheat, and the other to be half corn & half red clover, shifting them every year. then to form your highlands into three divisions, one to be in wheat & the other two in red clover, shifting them from year to year. in this way your low ground fields would be in corn but once in 4 years, in wheat every other year, and in clover every fourth year: and your highland in wheat once in every three years, and in clover two years in every three. they would improve wonderfully fast in this way, and increase your produce of wheat & corn every year. if it should be found that the low grounds should in this way become too rich for wheat, instead of putting them every fourth year into clover, you might put them that year into oats. your annual crop would then be half your low grounds in wheat, a fourth in corn, and a fourth in oats or clover: and one third of your highland in wheat, and two thirds in clover; and so on for ever, and for ever improving. I suggest this for your consideration. . . . (*Carr-Cary Papers,* U. Va.)

## (Samuel Brown to Jefferson.)

Natchez May 25th 1813.

Your letters of the 17th & 24th ult. arrived by the last mail & having just obtained a large supply of the Capsicum, it gives me great pleasure to transmit some of it, to you, in time for planting. That which I planted this spring is just coming up—the plants of last season are loaded with pods & will continue to bear both blossoms & fruit until December or January if protected from the severe frosts by a slight covering of straw. By the next mail I shall do myself the favor of sending you as much of the Capsicum as you can use until your own becomes productive. A tablespoonful of the pods will communicate to vinegar a fine aromatic flavor & that quantity is as much as would serve a northern family many months. In this warm climate our relish for Capsicum is greatly increased & I am much inclined to subscribe to the opinion of Mr Bruce that "nothing is so great a preservation of health in hot climates." I have even had thoughts of hinting to the Secretary of War the propriety of substituting Capsicum for a part of the Ration of Spirits which are allowed our troops & I am very confident that the effect of this change would soon be perceptible. I am informed by those who have lately returned from St. Antonio that the Inhabitants of that part of the Continent use this small indigenous Capsicum in almost every thing they eat & that they attribute to it medicinal qualities to which they acknowledge themselves indebted for the singular portion of health which they are said to enjoy.  In a few cases here, of disorders of the alimentary canal, I have had reason to think very highly of it but my experience has been too limited to permit me to say much of it at present.  The results of future observations I shall do myself the favor to communicate to you at another time. . . . I am more than ever pleased with the Guinea grass.  We have here a grass that will defy the heat of your "brown autumn."  I shall send it to you when the seed is ripe. (*Jefferson Papers*, L. C.)

### (Randolph Jefferson to Jefferson.)

May the 26: 1813

Dear Brother,

I received your friendly letter by the boy they catch no shad at all at this time so that I have sent James up to Warren to try and procure some carp for you and have wrote to Mr Brown about them if it is in his power to git any to fernish your boy With What you directed him to bring in the barril a live I have understood they catch a Number there every Night in the Mill race. . . . I am extreemly oblige to you for your advice as to Managing My farm but am a fraid it will be two great an undertakeng for Me   your Method I highly approve of I hope Mr Brown Will fernish you with the carp if they cetch any. . . . (*Carr-Cary Papers*, U. Va.)

### (Jefferson to Richard Fitzhugh.)

Monticello May 27. 13.

Your favor of the 9$^{th}$. has been safely received, together with the packet of Ravensworth peas.   these are now in the ground & will abundantly supply me with seed for the next year. . . . (*Jefferson Papers*, M. H. S.)

### (Jefferson to Bernard McMahon.)

Monticello May 30. 13.

I just now receive information from my old friend Thoüin of the national garden of Paris that he has sent me a box of seeds of 270. kinds of trees of every sort for either use or ornament.   this box, mr̄ Warden informs me, he sends by mr̄ Breuil of the schooner Bellona, bound to Philadelphia.   if you will be so good as to watch the arrival of this vessel, perhaps already arrived, this letter may suffice to authorize the delivery of it by M$^r$. Breuil to you, to whom I should send it were it to come here, as being the best mode of fulfilling the intentions of the benevolent giver.   if you could make up a collection of the seeds of the plants brought to us by Governor Lewis from beyond the Missisipi, it would be a just and grateful return which M. Thoüin merits at our hands.   he expresses to me 'a great desire for the plants of the region beyond the Missisipi.   if within the reasonable compass of the mail, it will come safest to me thro' that.   if larger, the stage is a good conveyance if a passenger can be found who will take charge of it.   such opportunities to Richmond must be almost daily with you, and if addressed to Messr. Gibson & Jefferson there it will come safely to me. . . . (*Jefferson Papers, L. C.*)

(Samuel Brown to Jefferson.)

Natchez June 13th. 1813

I hope that the small package of Capsicum, which I sent you, a few weeks ago, has arrived in safety.  You may even a month hence be very certain of obtaining Plants which, with a little care, can be preserved through the Winter & which will yeild fruit before the last of May.  I now send you as much as you will be able to use until that time.  The Spaniards generally use it in fine Powder & seldom eat anything without it.  The Americans who have learned to use it make a Pickle of the green Pods with Salt & Vinegar which they use with Lettuce, Rice, Fish, Beefstake and almost every other dish.  A single Tablespoonful will communicate to as much Vinegar as I can use in six months, as strong a taste of Capsicum as I find agreeable & I find this taste growing so fast that it will soon become as essential to my health as salt itself.  Many of my friends to whom I have recommended it, here ascribe to it Medicinal qualities for which I am not prepared to vouch. I do believe however that in cases of debility of the stomach & alimentary canal it may be employed with great advantage.  A Spanish officer with whom I conversed yesterday on the subject says that in Cuba it is called Achi & that the wealthy Inhabitants not only season almost every dish with it but place a cup of it beside every plate that each guest may use it ad libitum.  I have not yet been able to learn with certainty its "habitat".  It is abundant at St Antonio & some distance North of that Post.  I shall continue my enquiries & communicate the results.

This morning I recd from St Antonio a small package of seeds.  The gentleman who procured them for me has given me but a very imperfect account of them.

The Red Bean called Friholio has been often described to me by the Inhabitants of Taxas; & the Indians who inhabit the sources of the Red River seldom travel without it as it is their only means of Intoxication. They pulvarize it between two stones mix it with warm water & drink it through a cane until it produces violent vomiting & a most frantic kind of intoxication accompanied with an unstable disposition to violent bodily exercise.  The dose is often renewed & the debauch continued for three or four days.  Mr Davenport of Nacagdoches & a half Indian who lived several years with me often described these scenes.  But I never could procure the Bean before this day & have made no experiments of my own.  They are an article of commerce (as opium is in the east) among all the tribes west of Nacagdoches.  I suspect the plant which produces them is a species of the Erythryna— The Erythryna Corolladendron grows abundantly here & is a most beautiful Plant.  I send you some of the seeds.  I have often Planted them but they did not vegetate.  I have somewhere read an acct of a method of exposing such seeds to the action of the gastric juice of Turkeys in order to fit them vegetation.  But of this I have only an indirect recollection.

The round Black nut is said to be used at S$^t$ Antonio as a Poison for animals & insects & this is all the information that accompanies them.

The Gallavance Peas are the growth of S$^t$ Antonio & much esteemed. They are sometimes cultivated in Louisiana.

It is much to be regretted that no man of much knowledge of Botany or Natural History has been permitted to visit the Country surrounding the Gulf of Mexico.  I do not look for much from such men as compose the army of Patriots who are now marching towards Santa Fe. Their object must be rapine & Plunder. . . . (*Jefferson Papers, L. C.*)

## (Jefferson to Bernard McMahon.)

Monticello June 15. 13.

I have just received some Capsicum of the province of Techas, where it is indigenous as far Eastwardly as the Sabine river.  it's roots are perennial there, and it is believed it will stand our frosts with a little covering.  it grows in great abundance there and the inhabitants are in the habit of using it as a seasoning for everything as freely as salt, and ascribe much of their health to it.  the other kinds cultivated with us, coming from still warmer climates are difficult of cultivation.  my expectation is that this being indigenous so much nearer our latitudes, may be easier raised.  of what I received I send you a part.  altho' probably too late for the season, I have sowed a few seeds in a pot, and reserve others for the spring.  they will be more likely however to be preserved in your hands. . . . P. S.  I hope you have received the box of seed.  (*Jefferson Papers, L. C.*)

## (Jefferson to James Madison.)

Monticello, June 18, 1813.

. . . We are here laboring under the most extreme drought ever remembered at this season.  We have had but one rain to lay the dust in two months.  That was a good one, but was three weeks ago.  Corn is but a few inches high and dying.  Oats will not yield their seed.  Of wheat, the hard winter and fly leave us about two-thirds of an ordinary crop.  So that in the lotteries of human life you see that even farming is but gambling.  We have had three days of excessive heat. The thermometer on the 16th was at 92°, on the 17th 92$\frac{1}{2}$°, and yesterday at 93°.  It had never before exceeded 92$\frac{1}{2}$° at this place; at least within the periods of my observations. . . . (Lipscomb and Bergh, *Jefferson* 13: 260–261.)

## (Jefferson to Randolph Jefferson.)

Monticello June 20. 13.

Dear Brother,

. . . My sister desired that when I should send her seeds of any kind I would give her directions how to plant & cultivate them.  knowing that there was an excellent gardening book published at Washington [see letter, Jefferson to Barnes, May 21, 1813], I wrote for one for her, which I now inclose. she will there see what is to be done with every kind of plant every month in the year. I have written an index at the end that she may find any particular article more readily: and not to embarras her with such an immense number of articles which are not wanting in common gardens, I have added a paper with a list of those I tend in my garden, & the times when I plant them. the season being over for planting everything but the Gerkin, I send her a few seeds of them. she will not find the term Gerkin in the book. it is that by which we distinguish the very small pickling cucumber. . . . (*Carr-Cary Papers,* U. Va.)

(Randolph Jefferson to Jefferson.)

Snowden June 21: 1813.

Dear Brother,

I Received your letter by James and also the book Which you sent: . . . I wrote very pressingly to capt Brown by your boy in respect to the carp for you but found it was all in Vane from What James tell Me he got none. . . . (*Carr-Cary Papers,* U. Va.)

(Jefferson to N. G. Dufief.)

Monticello June 24. 13.

[He asked Mr. Dufief to purchase the following books for him:]

Tull's horseshoeing husbandry. an old book in 8*vo.*

Young's Experiments in Agriculture (I think in 3 vols.). (*Jefferson Papers,* L. C.)

(Jefferson to John L. E. W. Shecut.)

Monticello, June 29. 1813.

[Jefferson thanks Mr. Shecut for being elected to the Antiquarian Society of Charleston and comments on his botany for its alphabetical form and popular style &c.] . . . I avail myself of this occasion of enclosing you a little of the fruit of a *Capsicum* I have just received from the province of Texas, where it is indigenous and perennial, and is used as freely as salt by the inhabitants. It is new to me. It differs from your *Capsicum Minimum,* in being perennial and probably hardier; perhaps, too, in it's size, which would claim the term of *Minutissimum.* This stimulant being found salutary in a visceral complaint known on the seacoast, the introduction of a hardier variety may be of value. . . . (Lipscomb and Bergh, *Jefferson* 13: 295–296.)

(Jefferson to Dr. Samuel Brown.)

Monticello, July 14, 1813.

Your favors of May 25th and June 13th have been duly received, as also the first supply of Capsicum, and the second of the same article with

other seeds.   I shall set great store by the Capsicum, if it is hardy
enough for our climate, the species we have heretofore tried being too
tender.   The Galvance too, will be particularly attended to, as it appears very different from what we cultivate by that name.   I have so
many grandchildren and others who might be endangered by the poison
plant, that I think the risk overbalances the curiosity of trying it.   The
most elegant thing of that kind known is a preparation of the James-
town weed, Datura-Stramonium, invented by the French in the time of
Robespierre.   Every man of firmness carried it constantly in his pocket
to anticipate the guillotine.   It brings on the sleep of death as quietly
as fatigue does the ordinary sleep, without the least struggle or motion.
. . . (Lipscomb and Bergh, *Jefferson* 13: 310–311.)

(Jefferson to Samuel Harrison Smith.)

Monticello Aug. 15. 13.

. . . mrs. Smith would find I have made no progress in the improvement of my grounds.   all my spare labor having been in constant demand for the improvements of my farms, mills, canals, roads &c. having
given me constant occupation.   to these are added our establishment for
spinning & weaving, which occupy time, labor & persons.   (*Jefferson
Papers*, L. C.)

(Jefferson to Jeremiah A. Goodman.)

[Memorandum *Poplar Forest*] Sep. 8. 1813.

M^r. Goodman's crop for the next year 1814. will be as follows.

Corn in M^cDaniel's field; but as this turns out to be but 50. acres,
we must add other grounds to it; and there are none but what belong to some other field, except those over the S. Tomahawk, &
above the lower corn field.   we must of necessity then give the
tobacco ground & the stubble ground there to corn, and put the
upper corn grounds into oats to help out.   some of the strongest
spots in the Forkfield may be in corn.
Peas in the Forkfield.
Wheat in the Tomahawk Cornfield and in the Ridgefield.
tobacco, in such meadow grounds on S. Tomahawk as can be cleaned
up, and in a new clearing to be made on the S. side of the S. Tomahawk.   I should be glad to have 80. thousand tob°. hills tended.
the clearing to extend ¼ mile from the branch.
sow from half an acre to an acre in hemp.
sow timothy in the meadow ground ready for it, this month.
in all your fields of corn or small grain, reserve the galled & poor
spots and put peas into them.
let the ox-cart be employed in winter in carting out any manure you
may have, and straw.   generally speaking this ought to be put on

the galled & poor places of the field turned out to rest for 2. years, because that would give time for the straw to rot.  but as that would be for the present year, the Beltedfield which needs it least, I would give it to the galled & poor spots of the Ridgefield, which needs it most, and I would leave them without putting any thing into them.

take for your own use one eigth of the peach or apple brandy which will be made, & put the rest into the cellar of the house.

let the people have hereafter a fixed allowance of salt; to wit, give to their breadmaker a pint a month for each grown negro to put into their bread; and give besides to each grown negro a pint a month for their snaps, cymlins & other uses.  this will be a quart a month for every grown negro.

the people have asked for a little flour for their labors in harvest. give half a peck to each grown person.

I accept mͬ Mitchell's terms for grinding my flour this year.  let all the wheat be delivered to him in the course of this & the next month, and sent down in all October & November to Richmond. (Courtesy of Dr. A. S. W. Rosenbach.)

### (Jefferson to Isaac McPherson.)

Monticello, September 18, 1813.

. . . Your inquiry as to the date of Martin's invention of the drill-plough, with a leathern band and metal buckets, I cannot precisely answer; but I received one from him in 1794, and have used it ever since for sowing various seeds, chiefly peas, turnips, and benni.  I have always had in mind to use it for wheat; but sowing only a row at a time, I had proposed to him some years ago to change the construction so that it should sow four rows at a time, twelve inches apart, and I have been waiting for this to be done either by him or myself; and have not, therefore, commenced that use of it.  I procured mine at first through Colonel John Taylor of Caroline, who had been long in the use of it, and my impression was that it was not then a novel thing.  Mr. Martin is still living, I believe.  If not, Colonel Taylor, his neighbor, probably knows its date. . . . (Lipscomb and Bergh, *Jefferson* 13: 380.)

### (Jefferson to Dr. Samuel Brown.)

Monticello Nov. 13. 13.

. . . The Capsicum which accompanied your letters received in June, was of course too late for that season, but I shall give it a fair trial in the spring.  if it proves more equal to our climate than our former kinds it will be a valuable addition to our gardens.  I sent some to Dr. Shecut of S. C. author of Flora caroliniensis, and some to mͬ McMahon of Philadelphia that it might be tried in those places also. . . . (*Jefferson Papers*, L. C.)

## (Jefferson to Thomas Mann Randolph.)

Monticello Nov. 14. 13.

. . . we are just finishing our wheat sowing, as your people are also, and we are about to begin that of rye to feed us from harvest till the next corn season; for of corn I do not make a barrel to the acre. I believe it is expected you will make enough to serve till harvest at least. I buy largely at 20/ the price at which it starts. the manufacturing mill is just beginning to receive wheat and to do something. there have been some discouragements to the bringing it in. the want of a visible and responsible head is supplied to a certain degree of Jefferson's taking that post, which I dare say he will discharge satisfactorily. some flour for neighborhood use, perhaps too closely ground (to wit the barrel from 4 bush.—7 lb) has discredited the mill for a while. an assistant miller has been engaged by Jefferson on trial, and after a month's trial, the opinion of his skill & good conduct is favorable, and perhaps that he may understand grinding better than Gilmer. but he could not supply Gilmer's place as principal. I am still afraid it will be a losing concern to you as long as you are absent, unless you had a skilful and honest partner, not easy to be found. since our last operations on the dam, altho' the river is now very low indeed so that no boat can go down, we have the greatest abundance of water. I was at the mills yesterday. all were going with full heads, the locks leaking as usual, and a great deal of water running over the waste. I was disappointed in raising the breast of the dam a foot higher by the water becoming extremely cold just as we had got all our logs & stone in place ready to be laid down. this is therefore deferred to the spring, and will remove our difficulties from the dam to the Canal bank which will be in danger of overflowing. . . . (*Jefferson Papers*, L. C.)

## (Judith Lomax to Jefferson.)

Port-Tobago November 30, 1813.

I send you my dear Sir, the promised *Acacia* seed, together with a few of the Flowers, knowing you to be an admirer of the perfume. The Filbert scions you will get, whenever an opportunity shall occur at the proper season for removing them. . . . (*Jefferson Papers*, M. H. S.)

## (Jefferson to Madame de Tessé.)

Monticello, December 8, 1813.

. . . But let us drop these odious beings and pass to those of an higher order, the plants of the field. I am afraid I have given you a great deal more trouble than I intended by my inquiries for the Maronnier or Castanea Sativa, of which I wished to possess my own country, without knowing how rare its culture was even in yours. The two plants which your researches have placed in your own garden, it will be all but impossible to remove hither. The war renders their safe passage across the Atlantic extremely precarious, and, if landed anywhere but in the Chesapeake, the risk of the additional voyage along the coast to Virginia, is still greater. Under these circumstances it is better they should retain their present station, and compensate to you the trouble they have cost you.

I learn with great pleasure the success of your new gardens at Auenay. No occupation can be more delightful or useful. They will have the merit of inducing you to forget those of Chaville. With the botanical riches which you mention to have been derived to England from New Holland, we are as yet unacquainted. Lewis's journey across our continent to the Pacific has added a number of new plants to our former stock. Some of them are curious, some ornamental, some useful, and some may by culture be made acceptable on our tables. I have growing, which I destine for you, a very handsome little shrub of the size of a currant bush. Its beauty consists in a great produce of berries of the size of currants, and literally as white as snow, which remain on the bush through the winter, after its leaves have fallen, and make it an object as singular as it is beautiful. We call it the snow-berry bush, no botanical name being yet given to it, but I do not know why we might not call it Chionicoccos, or Kallicoccos. All Lewis's plants are growing in the garden of Mr. McMahon, a gardener of Philadelphia, to whom I consigned them, and from whom I shall have great pleasure, when peace is restored, in ordering for you any of these or of our other indigenous plants. The port of Philadelphia has great intercourse with Bordeaux and Nantes, and some little perhaps with Havre. I was mortified not long since by receiving a letter from a merchant in Bordeaux, apologizing for having suffered a box of plants addressed by me to you, to get accidentally covered in his warehouse by other objects, and to remain three years undiscovered, when everything in it was found to be rotten. I have learned occasionally that others rotted in the warehouses of the English pirates. . . . (Lipscomb and Bergh, *Jefferson* 14: 27–29.)

(Jefferson to André Thoüin.)

Monticello Dec. 14. 1813.

The perils of the ocean, my good and antient friend, are such that I almost despair of getting a letter to you. yet I cannot permit myself longer to withold the acknolegement of the reciept of your letters of Mar. 2. and Dec. 7. 11. and Mar. 11, 13. the boxes of seeds which you were so kind as to forward me in 1810. 1811. came safely to hand and were committed to our best seedsmen, in order that they might be preserved and distributed so as to become general. the box announced in yours of March 15. 13. has, I presume, been captured on the high seas; as I have never heard of it's arrival in any port. I thank you for the pamphlet sent me with the letter by M. Correa, as well as for having made me acquainted with that most excellent character. he favored me with a visit at Monticello, which gave me opportunities of judging of his great science, worth and amability. when he left me he meant to leave our continent immediately for Portugal. but I learn that he changed his mind afterwards and winters in Philadelphia. I learn with pleasure the success of several new cultures with you, and that you will by example teach us how to do without some of the tropical productions. the bette-rave, I am told, is likely really to furnish sugar at such a price as to rivalize that of the Cane. if you have any printed recipes of the process of manipulation, and could send me one, naming also the best species of beet, you would add a valuable item to the repeated services you have rendered us by a communication of the useful plants. if ever we should get the sea open again, I shall take great pleasure in repaying some of your kindnesses by sending you a collection of the seeds & new plants which were brought to us by Lewis & Clark from the other side of our Continent. they have been well taken care of by M<sup>r</sup>. Mc-Mahon, seedsman and botanist at Philadelphia from which port they can be readily shipped. at present we are blockaded by our enemies; as we were indeed for many years while they called themselves our friends. I know not therefore how the present letter is to get to you: but should it be so fortunate, let it be the bearer to you of sincere assurances of my great friendship and respect. (*Jefferson Papers*, L. C.)

### (Jefferson to David B. Warden.)

Monticello Dec. 29. 1813.

. . . and the box of seeds from M. Thouin came safely. the seeds were delivered to m<sup>r</sup> McMahon of Philadelphia, as the most likely person to preserve and distribute them. . . . the box of seeds therein mentioned from M. Thouin committed to the Bellona, I presume to have been captured, as I have never heard of it. . . . (*Jefferson Papers*, Maryland Historical Society.)

### From the *Account Book 1809–1820:*

May 25. gave Ned's James to buy fish 2. D.
Jan. 16. gave James for expenses to W. Champe Carter's 2. D. [for fish.]

### From the *Weather Memorandum Book 1776–1820:*

1813. Sep. 18. 19. 20. there fell 9. I. of rain. it did not raise the river out of it's banks at the low grounds adjacent to the saw mill. it fell very moderately, & the extraordinary drought of 5. months preceeding occasioned the earth to absorb a great deal of it.

# 1814

| Kalendar. 1814[1] | where | when | come to table | gone. | Miscellaneous |
|---|---|---|---|---|---|
| Frame peas | D. 1. E. 1. | Feb. 8. | May 9. | | Feb. 22. up. Apr. 13. blossom. Apr. 26. pod |
| Celery | low grounds | 16. | | | |
| Dutch brown } radishes | Bord. XVII | 17. | May 7. | | |
| Summer spinach | Bord. XII | 18. | | | |
| Frame peas | Bord. I–V. | 21. | May 13. | | Mar. 19. up. Apr. 22. blossom. 29. pod |
| Hotspurs | Sq. I. | 22. | | | 25. up. Apr. 29. blossom. May 15. pod |
| green curl'. Savoys. P.C. | low grounds | 23. | | | |
| Leadman's peas | Sq. II. | Mar. 2. | | | 26. up. |
| Tomatas | Bord X. | 7. | July 21. | | |
| Savoy cabbages | low grounds | 8. | | | |
| Brussels sprouts | d°. | | | | |
| Sprout Kale | low grounds | 12. | | | |
| Celery | d°. | | | | |
| Lettuce. white. | Sq. XVII. 7. | 14. | | | Mar. 30. up. May 10. blossom. |
| radishes | ib. | | | | |
| spinach. | Bord. XII. | | | | |
| Ledman's peas | Sq. III. | 16. | | | |
| Lettuce. white. | Sq. XVII. 7. | 23. | | | |
| radishes | ib. | | | | |
| beets | Sq. XIV. 2. | 25. | | | |
| Salsafia. | Sq. XIV. 1. | | | | |
| Capsicum Techas.[2] | Sq. XII. 3. | 26. | | | |
| Lettuce white | | 28. | | | peaches blossom. |
| radishes | | | | | |
| onions | Sq. XV. | Apr. 2. | | | |
| Bess snaps | Sq. V. | | | | Apr. 14. up. |
| Carrots | Sq. XIII. | | | | |
| Chives. submural. | C. 1. | | | | |
| Tarragon | H. 3. | | | | |

1814. (continued)

| Kalendar. 1814.[1] | where | when | come to table | gone. | Miscellaneous |
|---|---|---|---|---|---|
| Eggplant. | Sq. XII. 2. | 7. | | | May. 2. up. |
| Techas Garavance.[3] | Bord. XIII. | | | | Apr. 14. up. |
| Ledmans. | Sq. IV. | | | | |
| Pani corn. | isl[d]. | | | | |
| Parsley, double. | Submural. C. | 8. | | | |
| Long Haricots. | A. 1. 2. 3. 4. | 9. | July 13. | | Apr. 25. up. |
| potatoes. | D. E. | | | | |
| early cucumbers. | island. | | | | |
| long green d°. | d°. | | | | |
| lettuce. | Sq. XVII. | 12. | | | |
| radishes. | | | | | |
| Lima beans. | terras A. 5. 6. | 13. | Aug. 6. | | Apr. 29. up. |
| early cucumbers. | Sq. VIII. | 18. | July 3. | | May. 2. up. |
| long green d°. | ib. | | | | d°. |
| Lettuce. | Sq. XVII. | 19. | | | |
| radishes. | ib. | | | | |
| grey snaps. | Sq. VI | 26. | | | |
| warted cymlings. | island. | 22. | | | |
| Gerkins. | d°. | 28. | July 27. | | |
| d°. | Sq. IX. | 29. | | | May 10. up. |
| warted cymlings. | Sq. XII. | 28. | | | |
| carrots. | Sq. VII. | | | | |
| Gerkins. | Sq. IX. | 29. | | | May 8. up. |
| Lentils large & small. | Bord. XIII. | May 9. | | | |
| Miami cucurbita. | island. | | | | |
| Nasturtium. | Sq. IX. | | | | |
| French Kidney beans. | island. | | | | probably the Haricots secs. |
| Swedish turneps. | {Terras A} {Lego | Aug. 11. | | | |
| 7. Lopp[d]. turnep. | {Terras. 3D.} Lego. | d°. | | | |

1814.

Feb. 16.   planted 56 seeds of the Acacia Nilotica in the earthen trough, & the box N°. VI.   they were from mȓs Lomax's[4] which was from the plant at Greenspring.[5]

Mar. 19.   planted in vacant places in the Fruitery[6] as follows.

10. piῑpins from terras 2. of 1810.

14. Spitzenbergs.   from d°.

20. Taliaferro apples from terras 3. of 1810.

14. soft peaches, to wit 3. terras 6$^{th}$. suppos$^d$ Nov. from P.F. & 11. soft d°. from terras 7. from P.F.

8. black Georgia plumb peaches from terras 6. of 1810.

66

3. filberts from terras 5. of 1810.

26.   Almond in blossom.

28.   peaches d°.

Apr. 10.   planted in box N°. I. Liburnum[7] seeds in 16. holes, 2. in a hole.

16.   Nursery. 9$^{th}$. terras.   planted stones of the native Florida plumb,[8] said to yield fruit in 2. years from the stone.

box N°. IV.   planted Liburnum seeds in other 16. holes, 2. or 3. in a hole.

May 3.   put 6 living carp into the 2$^d$. fishpond.[9]

June   1.   a buck and a doe[10] from Enniscorthy were put into the Paddock inclosing the brick yard.

July   29.   in the course of 20. hours there fell $12\frac{1}{8}$ I. of rain, the earth being at the time extremely dry, it raised the river to the eves or upper floor of my toll mill.   or, more exactly half way up the joists.

at the saw mill[11] it was 10.I. deep on the barn floor, this seems to have been a rise of about 15.f. perpendicular from the surface of the river at the issue of the tail-race, or entrance of the ford.   Hardware[12] is said to have risen 30.f. perpendicular.   see page 31. for the freshes of 1771. 1795. 1804.

this fresh carried away the dam of my chub-pond.   see ante 1813. May 5. & 23.   and ran so deep over the dam of the carp pond that those ante May 3. probably went off.

Nov. 25.   carrots made this year 18. bushels

salsafia  —   —   —  11. bushels.

---

[1] *1814.*   The year 1814 saw the burning of the Capitol at Washington by the British, and the termination of the war. Jefferson was alert to all the events taking place in this important year, and he discussed them in a large number of letters.

Life at *Monticello* seems to have run the usual course. Jefferson was busy with his garden, farm, family, and neighbors and friends, who came to see him.   But the crops were not good, and prices paid for produce were low.   He wrote to Mr. Madison on March 10:

Our agriculture presents little interesting. Wheat looks badly, much having been killed by the late severe weather. Corn is scarce, but it's price kept down to 3. D. by the substitute of wheat as food both for laborers and horses, costing only 3/6 to 4/. . . . Tobacco is high, from it's scarcity, there having been not more than ⅓ of an ordinary crop planted the last year. This year there will probably be ⅔. . . . (Ford, *Jefferson* 11: 393.)

But by December 26 he was able to write Mrs. Elizabeth Trist, from *Monticello,* in more cheerful tones:

We are all well, little and big, young and old. Mr. and Mrs. Divers enjoy very so-so health, but keep about. Mr. Randolph had the command of a select corps during the summer; but that has been discharged some time. We are feeding our horses with our wheat, and looking at the taxes coming on us as an approaching wave in a storm; still I think we shall live as long, eat as much, and drink as much, as if the wave had already glided under our ship. Somehow or other these things find their way out as they come in, and so I suppose they will now. God bless you, and give you health, happiness, and hope, the real comforters of this nether world. (Randolph, *Jefferson:* 360.)

When the Capitol was burned, the books which had been collected for a library were destroyed. On September 21, in a letter to Mr. Samuel H. Smith, Jefferson offered to sell his extensive library to the Government. After much debate the offer was accepted, but the confirmation of it was not made until the following year. (See appendix VII.)

During the year Jefferson was elected to several American and foreign societies. These included the New York Historical Society, the American Antiquarian Society, and the Agronomic Society of Bavaria. In late November he resigned from the presidency of the American Philosophical Society, an office he had held since 1797.

He made only two visits to *Poplar Forest* during the year: one in May, and the other in October. Both visits lasted several weeks. During the summer most of the interior of the house at *Poplar Forest* was completed and a wing of offices, 110 feet long, in the manner of those at *Monticello,* was built. (See letter, Jefferson to John W. Eppes, July 16, 1814.) On his return from *Poplar Forest* in May, he spent a day at *Enniscorthy.*

The same variety of plants were used in the garden this year as in 1813. The *Garden Book* recorded the plantings and the progress in the garden. New fish ponds were made, but the dam of the chub pond was carried away, and most of the carp were lost by the freshet of July 20 (see *Garden Book, July 29*). However, Jefferson continued to buy carp and chub to stock the ponds.

Of the unusually large number of letters written this year, the most interesting relevant one was that directed on February 22 to Dr. John Manners, giving his reasons for adhering to the Linnaean classification as over against the newer theories (see letter, Jefferson to Dr. John Manners, February 22, 1814). Letters to and from Jefferson on agriculture were far less numerous than in the preceding years. Exchange of plants also slowed down, probably owing to the uncertainty of the war. There was only one observation made in the *Farm Book* for the year.

[2] *Capsicum* sp.   A pepper from Texas.   (See letter, Jefferson to Dr. Brown, April 28, 1814.)

[3] *Cicer arietinum* L.   Garavance, also called garbanzo and chick-pea.   (See letter, Jefferson to Dr. Brown, April 28, 1814.)

[4] Mrs. Lomax, the wife of Thomas Lomax.   (See letter, Judith Lomax to Jefferson, November 30, 1813.)

[5] *Greenspring*.   See entry in *Garden Book*, May, 1778.

[6] The Fruitery was located below and at both ends of the vegetable garden.

[7] Liburnum, probably *Laburnum* Griseb.

[8] The Florida Plum here mentioned may be *Prunus geniculata* Harper, which Small, in his *Southeastern Flora* (1933), says grows in the sandy pinelands of central Florida.

[9] See entry in *Account Book 1814*, under April 27.

[10] See letter, Isaac Coles to Jefferson, March 21, 1814.

[11] Jefferson had only recently completed his sawmill.   At this time he had three mills on the Rivanna River, a manufacturing mill, a small grist mill, and a sawmill.

[12] Hardware River, a small river in the southern part of Albemarle County.

### LETTERS AND EXTRACTS OF LETTERS, 1814

(Jefferson to Jeremiah A. Goodman.)

Monticello Feb. 3. 14.

. . . let the clover be sown about the 1st of March, and if the earth has no crust on the top, the first rain will cover it sufficiently, without drawing a bush over it.   clover sown at that time is pretty much out of danger of being injured by frost, and will get so strong before the heats set in as not to be hurt by them. . . . (*Jefferson Papers,* Thomas Jefferson Memorial Foundation.)

## (Jefferson to Dr. John Manners.)

Monticello, February 22, 1814.

The opinion which, in your letter of January 24, you are pleased to ask of me, on the comparative merits of the different methods of classification adopted by different writers on Natural History, is one which I could not have given satisfactorily, even at the earlier period at which the subject was more familiar; still less, after a life of continued occupation in civil concerns has so much withdrawn me from studies of that kind.   I can, therefore, answer but in a very general way.   And the text of this answer will be found in an observation in your letter, where, speaking of nosological systems, you say that disease has been found to be an unit.   Nature has, in truth, produced units only through all her works.   Classes, orders, genera, species, are not of her work.   Her creation is of individuals.   No two animals are exactly alike; no two plants, nor even two leaves or blades of grass; no two crystallizations. And if we may venture from what is within the cognizance of such organs as ours, to conclude on that beyond their powers, we must believe that no two particles of matter are of exact resemblance.   This infinitude of units or individuals being far beyond the capacity of our memory, we are obliged, in aid of that, to distribute them into masses, throwing into each of these all the individuals which have a certain degree of resemblance; to subdivide these again into smaller groups, according to certain points of dissimilitude observable in them, and so on until we have formed what we call a system of classes, orders, genera and species. In doing this, we fix arbitrarily on such characteristic resemblances and differences as seem to us most prominent and invariable in the several subjects, and most likely to take a strong hold in our memories.   Thus Ray formed one classification on such lines of division as struck him most favorably; Klein adopted another; Brisson a third, and other naturalists other designations, till Linnaeus appeared.   Fortunately for science, he conceived in the three kingdoms of nature, modes of classification which obtained the approbation of the learned of all nations.   His system was accordingly adopted by all, and united all in a general language.   It offered the three great desiderata: First, of aiding the memory to retain a knowledge of the productions of nature.   Secondly, of rallying all to the same names for the same objects, so that they could communicate understandingly on them.   And thirdly, of enabling them, when a subject was first presented, to trace it by its character up to the conventional name by which it was agreed to be called.   This classification was indeed liable to the imperfection of bringing into the same group individuals which, though resembling in the characteristics adopted by the author for his classification, yet have strong marks of dissimilitude in other respects. But to this objection every mode of classification must be liable, because the plan of creation is inscrutable to our limited faculties. Nature has not arranged her productions on a single and direct line. They branch at every step, and in every direction, and he who attempts to reduce them into departments, is left to do it by the lines of his own fancy. The objection of bringing together what are disparata in nature, lies against the classifications of Blumenbach and of Cuvier, as well as that of Linnaeus, and must forever lie against all. Perhaps not in equal degree; on this I do not pronounce. But neither is this so important a consideration as that of uniting all nations under one language in Natural History. This had been happily effected by Linnaeus, and can scarcely be hoped for a second time. Nothing indeed is so desperate as to make all mankind agree in giving up a language they possess, for one which they have to learn. The attempt leads directly to the confusion of the tongues of Babel. Disciples of Linnaeus, of Blumenbach, and of Cuvier, exclusively possessing their own nomenclatures, can no longer communicate intelligibly with one another. However much, therefore, we are indebted to both these naturalists, and to Cuvier especially, for the valuable additions they have made to the sciences of nature, I cannot say they have rendered her a service in this attempt to innovate in the settled nomenclature of her productions; on the contrary, I think it will be a check on the progress of science, greater or less, in proportion as their schemes shall more or less prevail. They would have rendered greater service by holding fast to the system on which we had once all agreed, and by inserting into that such new genera, orders, or even classes, as new discoveries should call for. Their systems, too, especially that of Blumenbach, are liable to the objection of giving too much into the province of anatomy. It may be said, indeed, that anatomy is a part of natural history. In the broad sense of the word, it certainly is. In that sense, however, it would comprehend all the natural sciences, every created thing being a subject of natural history in extenso. But in the subdivisions of general science, as has been observed in the particular one of natural history, it has been necessary to draw arbitrary lines, in order to accomodate our limited views. According to these, as soon as the structure of any natural production is destroyed by art, it ceases to be a subject of natural history, and enters into the domain ascribed to chemistry, to pharmacy, to anatomy, etc. Linnaeus' method was liable to this objection so far as it required the aid of anatomical dissection, as of the heart, for instance, to ascertain the place of any animal, or of a chemical process for that of a mineral substance. It would certainly be better to adopt as much as possible such exterior and visible characteristics as every traveller is competent to observe, to ascertain and to relate. But with this objection, lying but in a small degree, Linnaeus' method was received, understood, and conventionally settled among the learned, and was even getting into common use. To disturb it then was unfortunate. The new system attempted in botany, by Jussieu, in mineralogy, by Haüiy, are subjects of the same regret, and so also the no-system of Buffon, the great advocate of individualism in opposition to classification. He would carry us back to the days and to the confusion of Aristotle and Pliny, give up the improvements of twenty centuries, and co-operate with the neologists in rendering the science of one generation useless to the next by perpetual changes of its language. In botany, Wildenow and Persoon have incorporated into Linnaeus the new discovered plants. I do not know whether any one has rendered us the same service as to his natural history. It would be a very acceptable one. The materials furnished by Humboldt, and those from New Holland particularly, require to be digested into the catholic system. Among these the Ornithorhyncus mentioned by you, is an amusing example of the anomalies by which nature sports with our schemes of classification. Although without mammae, naturalists are obliged to place it in the class of mammiferae; and Blumenbach, particularly, arranges it in his order of Palmipeds and toothless genus, with the walrus and manatie. In Linnaeus' system, it might be inserted as a new genus between the anteater and manis, in the order of Bruta. It seems, in truth, to have stronger relations with that class than any other in the construction of the heart, its red and warm blood, hairy integuments, in being quadruped and viviparous, and may we not say, in its *tout ensemble,* which Buffon makes his sole principle of arrangement? The mandible, as you observe, would draw it towards the birds, were not this characteristic overbalanced by the weightier ones before mentioned. That of the Cloaca is equivocal, because although a character of birds, yet some mammalia, as the beaver and the sloth, have the rectum and urinary passage terminating at a common opening. Its ribs also, by their number and structure, are nearer those of the bird than of the mammalia. It is possible that further opportunities of examination may discover the mammae. Those of the Opossum are asserted, by the Chevalier d'Aboville, from his own observations on that animal, made while here with the French army, to be not discoverable until pregnancy, and to disappear as soon as the young are weaned. The Duckbill has many additional particularities which liken it to other genera, and some entirely peculiar. Its description and history need yet further information.

In what I have said on the method of classing, I have not at all meant to insinuate that that of Linnaeus is intrinsically preferable to those of Blumenbach and Cuvier. I adhere to the Linnaean because it is sufficient as a groundwork, admits of supplementary insertions as new productions are discovered, and mainly because it has got into so general use that it will not be easy to displace it, and still less to find another which shall have the same singular fortune of obtaining the general consent. During the attempt we shall become unintelligible to one another, and science will be really retarded by efforts to advance it made by its most favorite sons. I am not myself apt to be alarmed at innovations recommended by reason. That dread belongs to those whose interests or prejudices shrink from the advance of truth and science. My reluctance is to give up an universal language of which we are in possession, without an assurance of general consent to receive another. And the higher the character of the authors recommending it, and the more excellent what they offer, the greater the danger of producing schism.

I should seem to need apology for these long remarks to you who are so much more recent in these studies, but I find it in your particular request and my own respect for it, and with that be pleased to accept the assurance of my esteem and consideration. (Lipscomb and Bergh, *Jefferson* 14: 97–103.)

(Jefferson to Henry Muhlenberg.)

Monticello, Mar. 16. 14.

I thank you for your catalogue of North American plants. it is indeed very copious, and at the same time compendious in its form. I hardly know what you have left for your "Descriptio uberior". the discoveries of Govr. Lewis may perhaps furnish matter of value, if ever they can be brought forward. the mere journal of the voyage may be soon expected; but in what forwardness are the volumes of the botany, natural history, geography and meteorology of the journey I am uninformed. your pamphlet came during a long absence from home, and was mislaid, or this acknowledgement should have been sooner made. with my wishes for the continuance and success of your useful labors I embrace with pleasure this first occasion of assuring you that I have had long and much gratification in observing the distinguished part you have borne in making known to the literary world the treasures of our own country and I tender to you the sentiments of my high respect & etseem. . . . (Ford, *Jefferson Correspondence:* 211.)

(Isaac A. Coles to Jefferson.)

Enniscorthy. 21ˢᵗ Mar. 1814.

I have at length been able to steal a few days from my duty in Staunton to spend with my frⁿᵈˢ. here, & since my arrival have been examining the Deer & find there are three Does and a Buck that can very conveniently be spared. I have ordered a pen to be made in which they shall be fed, & in which it will hereafter be easy to secure them whenever it may be convenient for you to send for them. If the waggon cˡᵈ bring me a few small chub I shˡᵈ. consider it a great favor. . . . (*Jefferson Papers,* L. C.)

(Jefferson to David Gelston.)

Monticello Apr. 3. 14.

Th: J. presents his compliments to mr̄ Gelston and his thanks for the pumpkin seed he has been so kind as to send him. he will with pleasure give them a trial, the pumpkin being a plant of which he endeavors every year to raise so many as to maintain all the stock on his farms from the time they come till frost, which is from 2. to 3. months. besides feeding his workhorses, cattle and sheep on them entirely, they furnish the principal fattening for the pork, slaughtered. a more productive kind will therefore be of value. . . . (*Jefferson Papers,* M. H. S.)

### (George Divers to Jefferson.)

Farmington Apr. 11. 1814.

You will please to accept of a Bushel of the Mazzei pea which I send by your servant, which are all I have to spare. Plant them about the middle of next month. I am sorry they are so mixed with the cow pea, as you want them to put you in stock it will be well to have the latter picked from them. . . . (*Jefferson Papers*, M. H. S.)

### (Jefferson to J. Correa da Serra.)

Monticello, April 19, 1814.

. . . You will find the summer of Monticello much cooler than that of Philadelphia, equally so with that of the neighborhood of that place, and more healthy. The amusements it offers are such as you know which, to you, would be principally books and botany. Mr. Randolph's resignation of his military commission will enable him to be an associate in your botanical rambles. Come then, my dear Sir, and be one of our family as long as you can bear a separation from the science of the world. . . . (Lipscomb and Bergh, *Jefferson* 19: 209–210.)

### (David Gelston to Jefferson.)

New York 21st April 1814.

Perceiving by your note of the 3d instant, that, the seeds I sent you may be more useful than I had contemplated, and having plenty on hand, which are of the same species, but were taken from a pumpkin of a smaller growth, I do myself the pleasure to enclose a further supply.

I will just mention, that I have observed the greatest growth in a potatoe patch of strong new ground, and it appeared to me the moisture of the ground under the potatoe vines contributed greatly to the growth of the plant, a single seed in the situation here described, produced more than in any other way, without apparently injuring the crop of potatoes. . . . (*Jefferson Papers*, M. H. S.)

### (Jefferson to Samuel Brown.)

Monticello Apr. 28. 14.

. . . I have carefully committed to the earth the seeds you were so kind as to send me the last summer. the Capsicum I am anxious to see up; but it does not yet show itself. nor do the garavances appear. I do not yet however despair of them. I have just received from an European friend, M. Correa de Serra, a request to engage some friend on the Missisipi to send me a young branch or two of the Bow-wood, or bois d'arc of Louisiana pressed in brown paper with their leaves and both the male & female flowers. also some of the fruit, either dry, or in a mixture of $\frac{1}{3}$ whiskey & $\frac{2}{3}$ water. the dry no doubt can come most conveniently by mail, also in the proper season some ripe seeds. can I get the favor of you to execute the commission? Mr. Correa is now at

Philadelphia, setting out on a visit to Kentucky. he is perhaps the most learned man in the world, not merely in books, but in men & things. and a more amiable & interesting one I have never seen. altho' a stranger to no science, he is fondest of Botany. should you have gone to Kentucky as your last letter seemed to contemplate, take him to your bosom, and recommend all the attentions to him by which our brethren of Kentucky can honor themselves. . . . (*Jefferson Papers,* L. C.)

### (Jefferson to Martha (Jefferson) Randolph.)

Poplar Forest June 6. 14.

. . . there have not been more than 2. or 3. days without rain since I came here, and the last night the most tremendous storm of rain, wind & lightning I have ever witnessed. . . . I have not seen a pea since I left Albemarle, and have no vegetable but spinach and scrubby lettuce. . . . If Wormly & Ned should get through the ha! ha! and cleaning all the grounds within the upper roundabout, they should next widen the Carlton road, digging it level and extending it upwards from the corner of the grave yard up, as the path runs into the upper Roundabout, so as to make the approach to the house from that quarter on the northside instead of the South. . . . (*Jefferson Papers,* M. H. S.)

### (Jefferson to James Mease.)

Monticello June 29. 14.

On my return home after an absence of five weeks, I find here your letter of May 24. of the history of the Hughe's crab apple I can furnish nothing more than that I remember it well upwards of 60. years ago, & that it was then a common apple on James river. of the other apple after which you enquire I happen to know the origin. it is not a crab, but a seedling which grew alone in a large old field near Williamsburg where the seed had probably been dropped by some bird. Maj$^r$. Taliaferro of that neighborhood remarking it once to be very full of apples got permission of the owner of the ground to gather them. from these he made a cask of cyder which, in the estimation of every one who tasted it was the finest they had ever seen. he grafted an orchard from it, as did also his son in law our late Chancellor Wythe. the cyder they constantly made from this was perferred by every person to the Crab or any other cyder ever known in this state, and it still retains it's character in the different places to which it has been transferred. I am familiar with it, and have no hesitation in pronouncing it much superior to the Hughes's crab. it has more body, is less acid, and comes nearer to the silky Champaigne than any other. Maj$^r$. Taliaferro called it the Robertson apple from the name of the person owning the parent tree, but subsequently it has more justly and generally been distinguished by the name of the Taliaferro apple, after him to whom we are indebted for the discovery of it's valuable properties. it is the most juicy apple I have ever known, & is very refreshing as an eating apple. . . . (*Jefferson Papers,* L. C.)

(Jefferson to John Wayles Eppes.)

Monticello. July 16. 14.

. . . I had built a most excellent house [*Poplar Forest*] and, since our correspondence on the subject, have been doing much towards it's completion. the inside work is mostly done, and I have this summer built a wing of offices 110. feet long, in the manner of those at Monticello, with a flat roof in the level of the floor of the house. the whole, as it now stands, could not be valued at less than 10,000. D. and I am going on. I am also making such improvements of the grounds as require time to perfect themselves: and instead of clearing on the lands proposed for him [Francis Eppes] once in 5 years only as formerly mentioned, I clear on them every year. and by the time he comes of age, there will probably be 300. acres of open land. . . . (*The Huntington Library Quarterly* 6 (3): 348, 1943.)

(Jefferson to Dr. Thomas Cooper.)

Monticello, October 7, 1814.

. . . And Botany I rank with the most valuable sciences, whether we consider its subjects as furnishing the principal subsistence of life to man and beast, delicious varieties for our tables, refreshments from our orchards, the adornments of our flower-borders, shade and perfume of our groves, materials for our buildings, or medicaments for our bodies. To the gentleman it is certainly more interesting than Mineralogy (which I by no means, however, undervalue), and is more at hand for his amusement; and to a country family it constitutes a great portion of their social entertainment. No country gentleman should be without what amuses every step he takes into his fields. (Lipscomb and Bergh, *Jefferson* 14: 201.)

(Isaac Coles to Jefferson.)

Enniscorthy Oct: 11ᵗʰ. 1814.

I send you by the Bearer the *Wild Orange* of South Carolina. It grows in the middle upper parts of the State, is said to be a very hardy tree, some of the most beautiful in the world. I am induced to believe from the account I have received of it, that it will do well in our climate.

Mʳˢ. Singleton [?] from whom I received it, is very desirous of getting a few plants of the Marseilles Fig to carry back with her to Carolina, where it is not known at all, & where the climate will suit it so well. You will oblige me much by sending a few plants by the Servant. . . . (*Jefferson Papers*, L. C.)

(Jefferson to Jeremiah Goodman.)

Monticello Dec. 10. 1814.

. . . He [servant] brings some trees etc., [for *Poplar Forest*] which please have planted immediately in the nursery behind the stables 12. inches apart. (*Jefferson Papers*, L. C.)

(Jefferson to Jeremiah A. Goodman.)

Monticello Dec. 23. 14.

. . . I have a letter from mr̄ Radford desiring the road thro' his land may not be opened until the court establishes it, assuring me he will make no opposition. we must let that part lie then, & finish the rest. the account of your wheat crop is really disheartening. after taking out the seed sown, it does not give 2. for 1. the corn too is short. but it is sufficient if dealt out economically. by which I do not mean that any thing is to be under-fed. I know that neither people nor horses can work unless well fed, nor can hogs or sheep be raised. but full experience here has proved that 12. barrels for every laborer will carry the year through if kept under lock & key. we have tried this year the grinding the corn for the fattening hogs, & boiling the meal into mush. it is surprising how much sooner they have fattened. we think we have saved one half. the same saving might be made by grinding the corn for your horses and mixing the meal with chopped straw. the sending only 20. blankets was a mistake of mr̄s Randolph's. the other 2. shall go by the waggon. I hope you are hurrying the tobacco. Davy, Bartlet, Nace & Eve set out this morning for Poplar Forest. let them start on their return with the hogs the day after your holidays end, which I suppose will be on Wednesday night, so that they may set out Thursday morning. caution them against whipping the hogs. the last year there was one so bruised all over that not a single piece of it could be used, & several were so injured that many pieces of them were lost. I am very glad to learn that the negroes have received their clothes. . . . (Courtesy of Dr. A. S. W. Rosenbach.)

(Jefferson to Correa da Serra.)

Monticello, December 27, 1814.

Yours of the 9th has been duly received, and I thank you for the recipe for imitating purrolani, which I shall certainly try on my cisterns the ensuing summer. The making them impermeable to water is of great consequence to me. . . . (Lipscomb and Bergh, *Jefferson* 14: 221–222.)

From the *Farm Book 1814:*

1814. May 3.   the period for sowing wheat is from Oct. 10. to Nov. 10. what is sown either earlier or later is subject to the fly.

From the *Account Book 1809–1820:*

Apr. 27.   James (Isbel's) to procure some living carp for the pond 5. D.

# 1815

| Kalendar. 1815.[1] | where | when | come to table | gone. | Miscellaneous. |
|---|---|---|---|---|---|
| Frame peas. | Border I–V | Mar. 3. | May. 15. | | Mar. 11. up. blossom Apr. 19. pod. 27. |
| white lettuce. | | | | | |
| radish. | | Mar. 3. | | | |
| Frame peas. | Subm. | 8. | | | Mar. 21. up. Apr. 24. blossom. |
| Hotspurs. | Sq. I. | 13. | | June 12. | |
| Savoy green curled. | low grds | 14. | | | |
| Sprout Kale. | | | | | |
| Brussels sprouts. | | | | | |
| Ledmans. | Sq. II. | 18. | June 13. | | |
| Snaps. Bess. | V. | 25. | June 5. | | |
| early York cabbage. | | Apr. 1. | | | |
| Tomatas. | Sq. III. | | | | May 9. killed by frost. |
| Ledmans. | | 5. | | | May 9. killed by frost. |
| Okra. | | 8. | | | |
| White mustard. | | | | | |
| Salsafa. | | 12. | | | |
| Carrots. | | | | | |
| early cucumbers. | | | | | |
| Nasturtium. | | 17. | | | |
| long green Cucumber. | low ground. | | | | |
| Arkansa peas. | d°. | 20. | | | |
| French kidney beans. | d°. | 21. | | | |
| Lima beans. | Terras A. | 24. | July 16. | | |
| Long Haricots. | d°. | | | | |
| Salsafa. | Terras. | | | | |
| Carrots. | | 22. | | | |
| Benni. | Terras. | 28. | | | |
| Leadman's. | Sq. IV. | | | | |
| Snaps grey. | VI. | May 3. | | | |
| Long haricots. | | 16. | | | |
| grey snaps. | VII | | | | |

| | asparagus | | strawberries | | raspberries | | artichokes | | figs | | Sea Kale | |
|---|---|---|---|---|---|---|---|---|---|---|---|---|
| | come | gone | come | gone | come | gone | come | gone | come | gone | come | gone |
| 1816 | Apr. 5. | | May 25. | | | | June 11. | Jul. 20. | July 17. | | | |
| 17 | 11. | | | | | | | | | | | |
| 18 | 14. | | | | | | | | | | | |
| 19 | 10. | | | | | | | | | | | |
| 20 | 13. | | | | | | June. 9. | July 7. | {July 12. Aug. 25. | | | |
| 21 | 8. | | | | | | June 17. | July 22. | | | Apr. 1. | Apr. 28. |
| 22 | 1. | | | | | | June 20. | | | | Apr. 7. | May 11. |
| 23 | 16. | | | | | | 23. | July 3. | | | Apr. 6. | |
| 24 | 17. | | | | | | 1. | | | | 8. | |
| 25 | 8. | | | | | | | | | | | |

1815.[2] Apr. 30. m͞r Divers has a dish of peas.

¹ *1815.*   Early in January Congress passed a bill to purchase Jefferson's library.   On April 29 Jefferson wrote in his *Account Book 1809–1820:* "the sale of my library to Congress for 23,950 D."   The sale of his magnificent library no doubt gave Jefferson many sorrowful moments, but the money received came as a boon to his depleted finances.

Jefferson spent a happy year doing the things he most enjoyed.

His family remember that he was particularly active during the summer in both indoor and outdoor improvements, inventions, scientific investigations, etc.   He contrived a leather top for a carriage, which could be readily arranged to exclude rain, or leave the vehicle entirely uncovered—and which worked essentially on the plan of the modern extension-top carriage.   He invented a machine for breaking hemp, which he first had moved by the gate of his sawmill, and afterwards by a horse.   It answered its purpose completely, and produced a material saving in expense.   His fertile ingenuity also gave birth to many minor contrivances.   He measured the heights of Monticello and various contiguous hills—and of the peaks of Otter when he made his autumn visit to Poplar Forest.   Altogether he spent an active and agreeable year. (Randall, *Jefferson* 3: 425–426.)

The outdoor activity mentioned by Randall was not recorded in the *Garden Book,* where there is only one short page of notes on the plantings in the garden.   The *Farm Book* mentions only a few articles planted.

Varied letters continued from Jefferson's pen.   He was appealed to on almost every subject, and he usually had some answer for each correspondent.   Letters on agriculture were more numerous than in 1814.

There was a custom in Jefferson's neighborhood among the older gentlemen, that whoever first had peas in the spring should announce it by an invitation to the others to dine with him.   This custom stimulated a pleasant rivalry among them, each one planting his pea seed in early spring with the hope that his peas would be the first to come to the table.   Thomas Jefferson Randolph, writing to Mr. Randall, said:

A wealthy neighbor [Mr. George Divers], without children, and fond of horticulture, generally triumphed.   Mr. Jefferson, on one occasion had them first, and when his family reminded him that it was his right to invite the company, he replied, "No, say nothing about it, it will be more agreeable to our friend to think that he never fails."   (Randall, *Jefferson* 3: 674.)

PLATE XXXV.—The western lawn and house of *Monticello*. This photograph shows the graveled *Round-about Walk*, flower borders, and beds about the house, as restored by the Garden Club of Virginia (ca. 1944).

Jefferson wrote to Mrs. Elizabeth Trist on June 1:

Your friends m&#x0305;r & m&#x0305;rs Divers are in as good health as usual. I dined with them on peas the 29th. of April. here our first peas were the 29th of May, which shews the inattention here to the cheapest, pleasantest, & most wholesome part of comfortable living. (*Jefferson Papers,* M. H. S.)

See entry in *Garden Book,* April 30, and letter, George Divers to Jefferson, April 30, 1815.

Jefferson began this year to formulate outlines for the University of Virginia, a project which was to crown his later years.

Three visits were made to *Poplar Forest* during the year. During the autumn visit he made trips to the Peaks of Otter and to Natural Bridge. Joel Yancey was made overseer at *Poplar Forest,* succeeding Jeremiah Goodman. Edmund Bacon was still the efficient overseer at *Monticello.*

On August 7 Jefferson lost his only brother, Randolph Jefferson. This appears to have been the only sadness that came to *Monticello* during the year.

² This entry was removed from page 56 of the *Garden Book* to place it in its chronological order. See letter, George Divers to Jefferson, April 30, 1815.

## LETTERS AND EXTRACTS OF LETTERS, 1815

(Jefferson to Jeremiah Goodman.)

Monticello Jan. 6. 15.

Dick arrived here on the 4th. with the butter, salt, beef & hogs. one he said had been left at Lynchburg, one tired and was killed on the road, the other 13. have been killed here. their weights were 101. 99. 91. 91. 80. 76. 67. 67. 67. 61. 56. 55. 47. as they would not make bacon at all, being so small they would dry up to nothing, we shall try to make them up into salt pork, in which way they may do for the people. but such a supply of pork, and 14. bushels of wheat a hand carried to market are very damping circumstances. Dick carries with him a pair of the Guinea breed of hogs, of the same which I sent formerly, but which seem to have had no effect. we killed hogs of this breed here this year, not 18. months old weighing 200. lb. and a great part of them 150. & all under that age. yours average 73¾. I send by Dick 4. ploughs, which with the one sent by James, and a Peacock plough sent formerly, allows three for each place. he brings 2. barrels containing bottled beer, to be put into the cellar, and 2. barrels containing 40. lb of wool. we can very illy spare it, not having enough for our people here, but we will try a mixture of hemp & cotton for the negro children here, in order to

help out for your people. it is indispensably necessary that you take as
much care of the lambs & sheep as if they were children. we feel now
the misfortune of the loss of so many last year, as well as mr̄ Darnell's
trespass. the wool sent is half blooded Merino, and very difficult to
make any thing of for coarse cloth. you can do nothing with it with
wool-cards. it must either be carded with fine cotton cards, or carded
at some of the carding machines. it would be better indeed if you could
exchange it for common wool with some of the neighbors who want to
make fine cloth for their own use. I expected to have received by Dick
a list of the stock, and now send you blank lists for each place, which I
will be glad to have filled up and returned to me by the mail. I must
get you to speak to mr̄ Watkins and let him know I depend on his
promise to come and make a wheat machine for me. the stuff has been
all ready this twelvemonth. if he can make his arrangements to come
about the middle of April, it would be in time. I should have an opportunity of seeing him at Poplar Forest the 1st. week in April, when I
shall be there. Phill Hubard arrived here the 2d day after Christmas.
his subject of complaint is exactly what you supposed. he says that he
and Dick's Hanah had become husband & wife, but that you drove him
repeatedly from her father's house and would not let him go there,
punishing her, as he supposes, for receiving him. certainly there is
nothing I desire so much as that all the young people in the estate should
intermarry with one another and stay at home. they are worth a great
deal more in that case than when they have husbands and wives abroad.
Phill has been long petitioning me to let him go to Bearcreek to live with
his family. and Nanny has been as long at me to let her come to the
Poplar forest. we may therefore now gratify both, by sending Phill &
his wife to Bearcreek, and bringing Nanny and any one of the single
men from there, that is to say Reuben, Daniel, or Stephen. no new
house will be wanting because Phill can take the house Nanny leaves,
and Nanny may take the house which Cate's Hanah leaves. I would
wish you to give to Dick's Hanah a pot, and a bed, which I always
promise them when they take husbands at home, and I shall be very
glad to hear that others of the young people follow their example. a
crocus bed may be got from mr̄ Robertson. I would by no means have
Phill punished for what he has done; for altho I had let them all know
that their runnings away should be punished, yet Phill's character is not
that of a runaway. I have known him from a boy and that he has not
come off to sculk from his work. . . . Dick carries the two blankets
which were short of the number intended to have been sent by James.
let the beer be put into the cellar immediately, for fear of it's freezing,
setting the proper head of the barrels uppermost, that the bottles in them
may stand with the corks up. . . . (Courtesy of Dr. A. S. W. Rosenbach.)

(John Vaughan to Jefferson.)

Philad, Janʸ 9, 1815.

. . . P. S.   I do not know whether you possess any part of Michaux's
Amⁿ. Forest Trees. The 2d & 3d vol. are here. The first vol. consists

of the Pines & Noyers.  Some persons who had taken this being removed from the country, these two last vol. can be procured, but not, I
believe, the whole work.  It is much appreciated, & I could very readily
dispose of several complete copies if I had them.  (*Jefferson Papers,*
M. H. C., 1 : 224–225.)

### (Jefferson to William Thornton.)

Monticello Feb. 9. 15.

. . . I have endeavored to constitute a supply of water at Monticello
by cisterns for receiving and preserving the rain water falling on my
buildings.  these would furnish me 600 gallons of water a day, if I
could by cement or plaister make them hold water.  but this I have not
been able to do as yet.  they are of brick, 4 in number being cubes of
8. f. sunk in the ground. . . . my expectation is that my cistern water
may be made potable, which will add much to their value. . . . (*Jefferson Papers,* M. H. S.)  [See appendix II.]

### (Randolph Jefferson to Jefferson.)

Snowden February 13 : 1815

Dear Brother,

. . . I would be extreemly oblige to you for a few science, of your
good fruit, of apple & cherry.  if it should not be too late to moove
them Now, or any other fruit that you Would oblige Me With, that
you have to spare also a few cabbage seed and ice lettuce seed.  if it is
but one half spoon full provided you have as Many to spare Without
disfernishing yourself. . . . (*Carr-Cary Papers,* U. Va.)  [Note in
T. J.'s hand : Apples, cherries, cabbage, ice lettuce.]

### (Jefferson to Randolph Jefferson.)

Monticello Feb. 16. 15.

Dear Brother,

. . . I send you some green curled Savoy cabbage seed.  I have no
ice lettuce, but send you what I think better the white loaf lettuce.  the
ice lettuce does not do well in a dry season.  I send you also some sprout
kale, the finest winter vegetable we have.  sow it and plant it as cabbage, but let it stand out all winter.  it will give you sprouts from the
first of December to April. . . . (*Carr-Cary Papers,* U. Va.)

### (Jefferson to B. S. Barton.)

Monticello, February 26, 1815.

Congress having concluded to replace by my library the one they lost
by British vandalism, it is now become their property and of course my
duty to collect and put in place whatever stood in the catalogue by which
they purchased.  This renders it necessary for me to request the return
of Persoon's Botanical work of which you asked the use some time ago.

I am in hopes that you have been able to make it answer the purposes for which you wished its use. If well enveloped in strong paper it will come safely by mail. . . . (Lipscomb and Bergh, *Jefferson* **19**: 223.)

(Jefferson to Jean Baptiste Say.)

Monticello, March 2, 1815.

. . . I will proceed now to answer the inquiries which respect your views of removal; and I am glad that, in looking over our map, your eye has been attracted by the village of Charlottesville, because I am better acquainted with that than any other portion of the United States, being within three or four miles of the place of my birth and residence. It is a portion of the country which certainly possesses great advantages. Its soil is equal in natural fertility to any high lands I have ever seen; it is red and hilly, very like much of the country of Champagne and Burgundy, on the route of Sens, Vermanton, Vitteaux, Dijon, and along the Cote to Chagny, excellently adapted to wheat, maize, and clover; like all mountainous countries it is perfectly healthy, liable to no agues and fevers, or to any particular epidemic, as is evidenced by the robust constitution of its inhabitants, and their numerous families. As many instances of nonagenaires exist habitually in this neighborhood as in the same degree of population anywhere. Its temperature *French* may be considered as a medium of that of the United States. $=16°$ The extreme of cold in ordinary winters being about 7° of $=5°$ Reaumur below zero, and in the severest 12°, while the ordinary mornings are above zero. The maximum of heat in sum- $=96°$ mer is about 28°, of which we have one or two instances in a summer for a few hours. About ten or twelve days in July and August, the thermometer rises for two or three $=84°$ hours to about 23°, while the ordinary mid-day heat of those $=80°$ months is about 21°, the mercury continuing at that two or $=70°$ three hours, and falling in the evening to about 17°. White frosts commence about the middle of October, tender vegetables are in danger from them till nearly the middle of April. The mercury begins, about the middle of November, to be occasionally at the freezing point, and ceases to be so about the middle of March. We have of freezing nights about fifty in the course of the winter, but not more than ten days in which the mercury does not rise above the freezing point. Fire is desirable even in close apartments whenever the outward air is below 10°, ($= 55°$ Fahrenheit,) and that is the case with us through the day, one hundred and thirty-two days in the year, and on mornings and evenings sixty-eight days more. So that we have constant fires five months, and a little over two months more on mornings and evenings. Observations made at Yorktown in the lower country, show that they need seven days less of constant fires, and thirty-eight less of mornings and evenings. On an average of seven years I have found our snows amount in the whole to fifteen inches depth, and to cover the ground fifteen days; these, with the rains, give us four feet of water in the year. The garden pea, which we are now sowing, comes to the table about the 12th of May; strawberries and cherries about the same time; asparagus the 1st of April.   The artichoke stands the winter without cover; lettuce and endive with a slight one of bushes, and often without any; and the fig, protected by a little straw, begins to ripen in July; if unprotected, not till the 1st of September.   There is navigation for boats of six tons from Charlottesville to Richmond, the nearest tide-water, and principal market for our produce.   The country is what we call well inhabited, there being in our county, Albemarle, of about seven hundred and fifty square miles, about twenty thousand inhabitants, or twenty-seven to a square mile, of whom, however, one-half are people of color, either slaves or free.   The society is much better than is common in country situations; perhaps there is not a better *country* society in the United States.   But do not imagine this is a Parisian or an academical society.   It consists of plain, honest, and rational neighbors, some of them well informed and men of reading, all superintending their farms, hospitable and friendly, and speaking nothing but English. The manners of every nation are the standard of orthodoxy within itself. But these standards being arbitrary, reasonable people in all allow free toleration for the manners, as for the religion of others.   Our culture is of wheat for market, and of maize, oats, peas, and clover, for the support of the farm.   We reckon it a good distribution to divide a farm into three fields, putting one into wheat, half a one into maize, the other half into oats or peas, and the third into clover, and to tend the fields successively in this rotation.   Some woodland in addition, is always necessary to furnish fuel, fences, and timber for constructions.   Our best farmers (such as Mr. Randolph, my son-in-law) get from ten to twenty bushels of wheat to the acre; our worst (such as myself) from six to eighteen, with little or more manuring. . . . (Lipscomb and Bergh, *Jefferson* 14: 260–263.)

## (Jefferson to Charles Willson Peale.)

Monticello Mar. 21. 15.

. . . we have indeed had a hard winter.  our average of snow in a common winter is 15. I. which cover the ground 15. days in the whole. this winter we have had 29. I. of snow which covered the ground 39. days.  in general we have 4. ploughing days in the week, taking the winter through.   I do not think we have had 3. a week this winter; so that we have much ploughing still to do for our oats and corn.  but we have had a method of planting corn suggested by a m$\bar{r}$ Hall which dispenses with the plough entirely.  he marks the ground off in squares of 10 f. by a coulter, or an iron pin.  at each crossing of the lines he digs 2 f 3 I. square (equal nearly to 5. square feet) as deep as the mattock will go.  this little square is manured as you would have manured the whole ground, taking consequently but $\frac{1}{20}$ of the manure; a grain of corn is planted within 6. I. of each corner, so as to produce 4. stalks about 15. I. apart.  this is to be kept clean of weeds either by the hoe, or by covering it with straw so deep as to smother weeds, when the plant is 12. I. high.  he asks but 2. laborers to make 2500 bushels of corn.  he has taken a patent for his process, and has given me a right to use it, for I certainly should not have thought the right worth 50. D. the price of a licence.  I am about trying one acre.  I have lately had my mouldboard cast in iron, very thin, for a furrow of 9. I. wide & 6. I. deep, and fitted to a plough, so light that two small horses or mules draw it with less labor than I have ever before seen necessary.  it does beautiful work and is approved by every one.  I will have one made and send it to you now that the sea is open.  I think your farming friends will adopt it. . . . (*Jefferson Papers*, L. C.)

### (Jefferson to John C. Carter.)

Monticello Apr. 26. 15.

Th: Jefferson presents his compliments to mr̄ Carter and his thanks for the Copy of *Arator* which he has been so kind as to send him.  we are indebted to Col° Taylor for a great deal of valuable information given us in that volume on the subject of Agriculture. . . . (*Jefferson Papers*, L. C.)

### (George Divers to Jefferson.)

Farmington 30th. April 1815

We returned home yesterday from a visit of several days and I did not examine into the state of our peas till late in the evening, when I found them quite ready, they have suffered so much from the drought that they will last but a few days.  We should be glad you will come up and partake of our first dish today & that Mr. Maddison would come with you. . . . (*Jefferson Papers*, M. H. S.)

### (Jefferson to Archibald Robertson.)

Poplar Forest June 1. 15.

. . . Having found it necessary to make a change in the management of my affairs here, I have engaged mr̄ Joel Yancey to undertake the direction of them & superintendance of the overseers. . . . (*Jefferson Papers*, U. Va.)

### (Jefferson to Joel Yancey.)

Monticello June 7. 15.

I omitted among my memorandum to request you to have all the seed of the oat-grass at mr̄ Goodman's saved, in order to make lots near each of the overseer's houses.  it comes a month earlier than any other grass, and is therefore valuable for ewes and lambs, calves, yearlings, and poor cows.  there should also be good clover lots adjoining, independent of the larger clover fields.  I have inquired and got good information on the subject of clover sown in the husk.  it is to be cut as usual and laid up in hand-ricks of 3. or 4. feet high to rot to such a degree as to leave the husks separable from the stalk and from one another.  whenever it rains the ricks should be turned over to prevent its rotting too much or spoiling the seed at the bottom.  when it is sufficiently rotted it must either be beaten to pieces with flails on a plank floor, or passed thro' the threshing machine.  the object is not to separate the seed from the husk, but merely to separate at their bottom, where they grow together, the numerous husks of which a single clove blossom is composed.  7. bushels of this separated husk is necessary to an acre.  the time of sowing is from the middle of February to the 10th of March, and there is no better method than sowing it in snow.  the 2d cutting yields more seed than the 1$^{st}$. and is better, having been cut altogether it starts its 2$^{d}$. growth and ripens together.  everybody agrees that it comes up with much more certainty when sown in the husk. . . . (*Jefferson Papers,* M. H. S.)

(Jefferson to Charles Willson Peale.)

Monticello, June 13, 15.

. . . It will be yet some time (perhaps a month) before my workmen will be free to make the plough I shall send you.  You will be at perfect liberty to use the form of the mouldboard, as all the world is, having never thought of monopolizing by patent any useful idea which happens to offer itself to me; and the permission to do this is doing a great deal more harm than good.  There is a late instance in this State of a rascal going thro' every part of it, and swindling the mill-owners, under a patent of 2 years old only, out of 20,000 D. for the use of winged-gudgeons which they have had in their mills for 20 years, every one preferring to pay 10 D. unjustly rather than be dragged into a Federal court 1, 2, or 300 miles distant.

I think the cornsheller you describe, with two cylinders, is exactly the one made in a neighboring county, where they are sold at 20 D.  I propose to take some opportunity of seeing how it performs.  The reason of the derangement of machines with wooden cylinders of any length is the springing of the timber, to which white oak has a peculiar disposition.  For that reason we prefer pine as the least apt to spring.  You once told me of what wood you made the bars of the pen-frame in the polygraph, as springing less than any other wood; & I have often wished to recollect it, but cannot.  We give up here the cleaning of clover seed, because it comes up so much more certainly when sown in the husk; 7 bushels of which is more easily obtained for the acre than the 3 pints of clean seed which the sowing-box requires.  We use the machine you describe for crushing corn-cobs, & for which Oliver Evans has obtained a patent, altho' to my knolege the same machine has been made by a smith in George town these 16 years for crushing plaister, and he made one for me 12 years ago, long before Evan's patent.  The only difference is that he fixes his horizontally, and Evans vertically.  Yet I chose to pay Evans's patent price for one rather than be involved in a law suit of 2 or 300 D. cost.  We are now afraid to use our ploughs, every part of which has been patented, although used ever since the fabulous days of Ceres.   On the subject of the Spinning Jenny, which I so much prefer to the Arkwright machines, for simplicity, ease of repair, cheapness of material and work, your neighbor, Dʳ. Allison, of Burlington, has made a beautiful improvement by a very simple addition for the preparatory operation of roving.   These are much the best machines for family & country use.   For fulling in our families we use the simplest thing in the world.   We make a bench of the widest plank we can get, say half a yard wide at least, of thick & heavy stuff.   We cut notches cross wise of that 2 i. long. & 1 i. deep; the perpendicular side of the notch fronting the middle one from both ends; on that we lay a 4 i. board, 6 f. long, with a pin for a handle in each end, and notched as the under one. A board is nailed on each side of the under one, to keep the upper in place as it is shoved backwards & forwards, and the cloth, properly moistened, is laid between them.   2 hands full 20 yards in two hours. [Jefferson drew a picture of the machine he describes.]

Our threshing machines are universally in England fixed with Dutch fans for winnowing, but not with us, because we thresh immediately after harvest, to prevent weavil, and were our grain then laid up in bulk without the chaff in it, it would heat & rot. . . . (*Jefferson Papers, M. H. C.* 1: 233–235.)

### (Jefferson to William P. Newby.)

Monticello June 21. 15.

I have found it necessary to put my affairs under the direction of my grandson Jefferson Randolph, my activity being too much declined to take care of them myself. . . . (*Jefferson Papers,* L. C.)

### (Jefferson to Joel Yancey.)

Monticello July 18. 15.

. . . I am glad you approve my plan of culture, because it will be the more agreeable to you to pursue it.   it's general effect is this.   one third of the farm (2 fields out of 6.) is in wheat for market & profit.   one sixth (that is one field) is in corn for *bread* for the laborers.   the remaining half of the farm, that is to say, one field in peas or oats, one field in clover for cutting, and one in clover for pasture, is for the sustenance of the stock of the farm, aided by 8. acres of pumpkins at each place, which feeds every thing two months in the year & fattens the pork, and as much timothy as our meadow ground can be made to yield, which is very important when the clover crop fails from drought, a frequent occurrence.   on this plan I know it to be unnecessary that a single grain of corn should ever be given to any animal, unless a little perhaps to finish the fattening pork; but even for that peas are as good. of these you may certainly count on 10. bushels to the acre, which on 160. acres will be 1600. bushels, or 320. barrels, equal to that much corn, and all fall-fallowing will be saved.   to the produce for market my plan adds 80 M tobacco hills at each place, as much of it on the first year's land as can be cleared.  if this plan be fully executed, I will most gladly take all risk of the result to myself, and my own blame. . . . (*Jefferson Papers*, M. H. S.)

### (Jefferson to P. A. Guestier.)

Monticello July 23. 15.

I have to acknolege the receipt of your favor of the 12ᵗʰ and to thank you for your attention to the box of seeds.  this is an annual present from the National Garden of France.   I will pray you therefore to forward it to mr̅ Bernard Mᶜ.Mahon, gardener of Philadelphia. . . . (*Jefferson Papers*, L. C.)

### (Jefferson to Bernard McMahon.)

Monticello July 23. 1815.

With the return of peace, my old friend Thouin returns to a recollection of me in his annual presents of seeds.  a box of them is just arrived at Baltimore to the care of mr̅ P. A. Guestier merchant of that place.   I have desired him to forward it to you, and if possible by some stage passenger who will take charge of it to Philadelphia.   I have taken on myself all charges to Baltimore. . . . (*Jefferson Papers*, L. C.)

### (Jefferson to Captain Christopher Hudson.)

Monticello Aug. 9. 15.

. . . I am enabled to ask your acceptance of them [hedge shears]. you will perceive by their having never been used that I have no employment for them. . . . (*Jefferson Papers*, M. H. S.)

### (Jefferson to Martha (Jefferson) Randolph.)

Poplar Forest Aug. 31. 15.

. . . we are suffering from drought terribly at this place.  half a crop of wheat, and tobacco, and two thirds a crop of corn are the most we can expect.   Cate, with good aid, is busy drying peaches for you. we abound in the luxury of the peach, their being as fine here now as used to have in Albemarle 30 years ago, and indeed as fine as I ever saw anywhere. . . . (*Jefferson Papers*, M. H. S.)

### (Jefferson to Charles Clay.)

Poplar Forest Nov. 18. 15.

. . . and tomorrow, weather permitting, will pay you a morning visit. in the meantime I send you a note of the result of my ten days labor and some Otaheite or Paper Mulberries, valuable for the regularity of their form, velvet leaf & for being fruitless.  they are charming near a porch for densely shading it. . . . (*Jefferson Papers*, U. Va.)

(Charles Clay to Jefferson.)

[Bedford County, Virginia,] Dec. 5. 15.

As you appeared pleased with the sample of Potatoes the servant brought the Other Day M$^{rs}$. Clay by Bob sends you a few more for seed,   She says her mode of Cultivating them in the Garden, is to plant a fine large single pototoe, uncut in a hill, that by doing so, she has had the finest large potatoes & greatest in Number, of all the Modes she has tryed, that by cuting, she thinks the Vigor of the plant is lessened, the produce smaller in size & fewer in Number, that by planting the Small Ones the produce is similar to that from Cutings, & constantly decline from year to year if persisted in, until a fine potatoe is not to be expected. please accept our friendly Salutations. (*Jefferson Papers,* M. H. S.)

(Mrs. Henry Dearborn to Jefferson.)

Boston December 16, 1815.

Mrs. Dearborn's respectful compliments to Mr. Jefferson, recollecting his wish to have some of the seed of the *winter squash* She requested her son Brigadier General Dearborn to procure some for him.—he has put up some of several sorts which he says are very good.   Mrs. D. hopes Mr. Jefferson will be successful in raising them, and that they will be agreeable to him.   *The winter squash must not be gathered until they are ripe.* . . . (*Jefferson Papers,* M. H. S.)

(Jefferson to John David.)

Monticello Dec. 25. 15.

A long absence from home and but a late return to it must apologize for the delay in acknoleging the reciept of your letter of Nov. 26. on the subject of the vine & wine.   in the earlier part of my life I have been ardent for the introduction of new objects of culture suited to our climate.   but at the age of 72. it is too late.   I must leave it to younger persons who have enough of life left to pursue the object and enjoy it's attainment. . . . There is in our woods a native grape which of my own knolege produces a wine so nearly of the quality of the Caumartin of Burgundy, that I have seen at my own table a large company acknolege they could not distinguish between them.   I do not know myself how this particular grape could be known in our woods, altho' I believe it abounds: but there is a gentleman on Potomak who cultivates it.   this may be worth your attention.   should you think it worth while to examine the aptitude of this part of the country for the wine, I shall be very happy to receive you at Monticello. . . . (*Jefferson Papers,* L. C.)

From the *Farm Book 1815:*

1815.   7. bushels of cow peas plant 40. acres in drills 3½ f. apart.   Pop. For,

1815.  July.  1.  of the chain inclosing the semi-oval level in front of the house 182. f. weighs 90 lbs.

From the *Account Book 1809–1820:*

Aug. 2.  plants 2. D.

Planting Memorandum for *Poplar Forest*, 1815:

1815. Nov. 2.  planted 64. paper mulberries in the nursery.

25.  planted 5. Calycanthuses on each Mound.  4. Monticello aspens at the N. foot of the W. Mound & 3 d°. at the N. foot of the E. Mound.

19 paper mulberries in a clump between the W. Cloacina & fence & 19 d°. in a clump between the E. Cloacina and fence.  (*Jefferson Papers,* U. Va.)

# 1816

| Kalendar.  1816[1] | where | when | come to table | Miscellanies. |
|---|---|---|---|---|
| Frame peas | Celery beds. | Feb.  3. | May 22. | Mar. 1. up.  note, no rain from Apr. 6. to May 11.  6 weeks |
| lettuce ice | | }Feb.  3. | | |
| radishes. mrs Bankhead.[2] | | | | |
| spinach winter | | Feb.  3. | | |
| Celery solid | plant beds.. | Feb.  7. | | |
| Cabbage early York | d°. | .... 10. | | |
| Frame peas | submural | .... 16. | May 22. | Mar. 1. up. |
| lettuce white | } | | | |
| radish; scarlet. mrs B.[3] | } | | | |
| Spinach, summer | | .... 27. | | |
| Savoys | | .... 27. | | |
| Sprout kale | | | | |
| Brussels sprouts | | | | |
| Celery | plant beds | .... 29. | | |
| Sprout kale | d°. | | | |
| Frame peas | Border I–V. | Mar.  1. | May 23. | Mar. 16. up. |
| lettuce white | | | | |
| Radishes scarlet. mrs B.. | | | | |
| Salsafia | D.E.F.G.3 | .... 5. | | |
| Tomatas | Sq. X. | | | |
| Peas. Hotspur | Sq. I. | .... 6. | | May 8. blossom |
| Leadmans | Sq. II. | | June 12. | May 9. blossom / June 1. pod |
| Leadmans | III | .... 22. | | 19. blossom / June 5. pod. |
| Potatoes | | .... 23. | | |
| Bess snaps | V | .... 25. | June  9. | 26. blossom. |
| Nasturtium | IX | .... 26. | | |
| Carrots | XIII | | | |
| Beets | XIV. 2.. | .... 27. | | |
| Okra | XII. 2... | Apr.  4. | | |
| forwd. Cucumbers | VIII. | | | |
| Leadmans | IV | .... 8. | Ju...... | May 31. blossom / June 14. pod.  gone July 14. |
| Lima beans | | .... 9. | | |
| long Haricots | | | July 25. | Aug. 31. last dish of long haricots. |
| Benni | | | | |
| Jerusal. Artichoke | | | | |
| parsnips | | .... 10. | | |
| grey Snaps | VI | .... 13. | | |
| d° | VII | May 13. | | |
| d° | | Aug. 26. | | |
| Endive | | Sep. 7. | | |
| Dutch brown | | | | |
| Spinach winter | | | | |
| Bess snaps | | Sep.  9. | | |
| Dutch brown | | .... 16. | | |
| Spinach winter | | | | |
| Cabbage Battersea | | Aug. 13. | ........ | transplanted Sept. 16. |

1816.⁴  Mar. 18. replanted with Asparagus seed the Western half of the old Asparagus
          bed under the wall.
        May 10. peas at mr Divers.  they were sown Feb. 2.

---

¹ *1816.*  One may best get a glimpse into Jefferson's personal life and the happenings at *Monticello* and *Poplar Forest* from portions of three letters written during the year.  On January 9, Jefferson wrote from *Monticello* to his old friend Mr. Charles Thomson:

I retain good health, am rather feeble to walk much, but ride with ease, passing two or three hours a day on horseback, and every three or four months taking in a carriage a journey of ninety miles to a distant possession, where I pass a good deal of my time.  My eyes need the aid of glasses by night, and with small print in the day also; my hearing is not quite so sensible as it used to be; no tooth shaking yet, but shivering and shrinking in body from the cold we now experience, my thermometer having been as low as 12° this morning.  My greatest oppression is a correspondence afflictingly laborious, the extent of which I have been long endeavoring to curtail.  This keeps me at the drudgery of the writing-table all the prime hours of the day, leaving for the gratification of my appetite for reading, only what I can steal from the hours of sleep. (Lipscomb and Bergh, *Jefferson* 14: 386–387.)

Writing to his son-in-law, Mr. J. W. Eppes, on March 30, he showed again his great affection for Francis Eppes, his grandson, and expressed the desire to share in the expense of his education:

I am almost afraid to propose to you to yield to me the expense and direction of his education.  Yet I think I could have it conducted to his advantage.  Certainly no expense which could be useful to him, and no attention on my part would be spared; and he could visit you at such times as you should wish.  It you say yea to this proposition, he might come on to me at Poplar Forest, for which place I shall set out about the 6th of April, and shall be there about the 21st; and could I hear from you soon after my arrival there, I could be taking preparatory steps for his reception and the course to be pursued.  All this is submitted to your good pleasure.  Patsy, supposing Mrs. Eppes to have an attachment to flowers, sends her a collection of seeds. . . . Your servant asks for the large lima bean we got from Wᵐ. Hylton from Jamaica.  it has dwindled down to a very poor one, not worth sending if we had it to spare, which we have not.  (Randall, *Jefferson* 3: 433.)

Mr. Eppes consented to Jefferson's taking charge of Francis's education.  Jefferson then wrote to Mr. Eppes:

I am sensible, my dear sir, of the delicacy of your sentiments on the subject of expense. I am indeed an unskilful manager of my farms, and sensible of this from its effects, I have committed them to better hands [his grandson, Thomas Jefferson Randolph], of whose care and skill I have satisfactory knowledge, and to whom I have ceded the entire direction. This is all that is necessary to make them adequate to all my wants, and to place me at entire ease. (Randall, *Jefferson* 3: 433.)

His grandson continued to look after Jefferson's affairs until his death.

A portion of a letter from Jefferson to Mrs. Elizabeth Trist gives the gossipy news of the family. He wrote from *Poplar Forest* on April 28:

I am here, my dear Madam, alive and well, and, notwithstanding the murderous histories of the winter, I have not had an hour's sickness for a twelvemonth past. I feel myself indebted to the fable, however, for the friendly concern expressed in your letter, which I received in good health, by my fireside at Monticello. These stories will come true one of these days, and poor printer Davies need only reserve awhile the chapter of commiserations he had the labor to compose, and the mortification to recall, after striking off some sheets announcing to *his* readers the happy riddance. But, all joking apart I am well, and left all well a fortnight ago at Monticello, to which I shall return in two or three days. . . . Jefferson is gone to Richmond to bring home my new great-grand-daughter. Your friends, Mr. and Mrs. Divers, are habitually in poor health; well enough only to receive visits, but not to return them; and this, I think, is all our small news which can interest you. (Randolph, *Jefferson*: 362–363.)

The year 1816, in the United States, is known among meteorologists as the "year without a summer." (See appendix I.) The growing season throughout the States was so dry and cold that crops failed to mature, gardens were poor, and fruit was ruined. Jefferson wrote to Mr. Albert Gallatin on September 8:

We have had the most extraordinary year of drought and cold ever known in the history of America. In June, instead of $3\frac{3}{4}$ inches, our average of rain for that month, we only had $\frac{1}{3}$ of an inch; in August, instead of $9\frac{1}{8}$ inches our average, we had only $\frac{8}{10}$ of an inch; and still it continues. The summer, too, has been as cold as a moderate winter. In every State north of this there has been frost in every month of the year; in this State we have had none in June and July, but those of August killed much corn over the mountains. The crop of corn through the Atlantic States will probably be less than one-third of an ordinary one, that of tobacco still less, and of mean quality. The crop of wheat was middling in quantity, but excellent in quality. But every species of bread grain taken together will not be sufficient for the subsistence of the inhabitants, and the exportation of flour, already begun by the indebted and the improvident, to whatsoever degree it may be carried, will be exactly so much taken from the mouths of our citizens. . . . (Ford, *Jefferson* 12: 37–38.)

It has already been pointed out that Jefferson had turned over to his grandson the management of the farms and gardens. His "infirmities," as he called them, were gradually slowing up his activities in the fields. His supreme interest now lay in making plans for the new university which he hoped to induce the State to establish. And *Poplar Forest* was demanding much of his attention. The *Garden Book* for the year, as well as all the remaining years in which he kept a record in the *Garden Book,* shows chiefly the calendar of planting for the year. There were no new articles added to the long list of vegetables of the preceding years.

Jefferson was at *Poplar Forest* four times during the year. There appears to have been much activity in the flower gardens at that place, for on his late fall visit Jefferson wrote to Mrs. Randolph to send to him bulbs and other plants from the stock at *Monticello*. (See letters, Jefferson to Martha Randolph, November 10, and Martha Randolph to Jefferson, November 20, 1816.)

On March 19 Jefferson lost his old and devoted friend, Philip Mazzei. Through his gifts of plants and seeds *Monticello* had been abundantly enriched.

[2] Mrs. Ann Cary (Randolph) Bankhead was the eldest daughter of Mr. and Mrs. Thomas Mann Randolph, and Jefferson's granddaughter. She was born in January, 1791, and died in February, 1826. She was married to Charles L. Bankhead.

[3] Mrs. Bankhead.

[4] This entry was removed from page 56 of the *Garden Book* and placed here in proper chronological sequence.

### LETTERS AND EXTRACTS OF LETTERS, 1816

(Jefferson to J. Correa da Serra.)

Monticello, January 1, 1816.

. . . I am ashamed to ask whether your observations or information as to the cisterns of Charlestown can facilitate the perfecting of those I have constructed because by some accident which I cannot ascertain, I

lost the paper you were so kind as to give me at Dowthwaites. . . .
(Lipscomb and Bergh, *Jefferson* 19: 226.)

(David Gelston to Jefferson.)

New York, Jan. 8, 1816.

I have received a letter from Mr. Baker, consul at *Tarragona*, with
a box for you said to contain "flower garden seed"—since no use can be
made of them till spring, I shall wait your instructions. (*Jefferson
Papers,* M. H. S.)

[In a reply to the above letter Jefferson suggests that the seeds be
given to the Botanical Garden in New York.]

(Jefferson to John David.)

Monticello Jan. 13. 16.

Your favor of Jan. 1. is received.  you intimate in that a thought of
going to the Potomac to examine the vines I mentioned to you.  it was
a maj$^r$. Adlam [Adlum] near the mouth of that river who sent me the
wine, made from his own vineyard.  but this was 7. or 8. years ago,
and whether he still pursues the culture or is even still living I do not
know.  I should be sorry you should take such a journey on such an uncertainty.  I will write to him by the next mail, and will even ask him
to send me some cuttings of the vines.

I have heard with great pleasure that you have had some conversation with Gen$^l$. Cocke of the county adjoining this on the subject of his
undertaking a vineyard under your direction.  there is no person in the
U. S. in whose success I should have so much confidence.  he is rich,
liberal, patriotic, judicious & persevering.  I understand however that
all his arrangements for the present year being made, he cannot begin on
the vineyard till the next. . . . Col°. Monroe, our Secretary of State,
whose seat is within 2 or 3 miles of me, has a fine collection of vines
which he had selected & brought with him from France with a view to
the making wine.  perhaps that might furnish something for you.  you
will here too be within a few hours ride of Gen$^l$. Cocke, should any communications with him be desired. . . . (*Jefferson Papers,* L. C.)

(Jefferson to John Adlum.)

Monticello Jan. 13. 16.

While I lived in Washington you were so kind as to send me 2. bottles
of wine made by yourself, the one from currans, the other from a native
grape, called with you a fox-grape, discovered by m$\bar{r}$ Penn's gardener.
the wine of this was as good as the best Burgundy and resembling it.  in
1810. you added the great favor of sending me many cuttings.  these
were committed to the stage Mar. 13.  on the 27$^{th}$. of that month I set
out on a journey.  the cuttings arrived at our post office a day or two
after, & were detained there till my return.  they were received Apr.
19. and immediately planted, but having been 6. weeks in a dry situation not a single one lived.  disheartened by this failure and not having

any person skilled in the culture, I never troubled you again on the subject.   but I have now an opportunity of renewing the trial under a person brought up to the culture of the vine & making wine from his nativity.   am I too unreasonable in asking once more a few cuttings of the same vine?   I am so convinced that our first success will be from a native grape, that I would try no other.   a few cuttings, as short as you think will do, put into a light box, & mixed well with wet moss, if addressed to me by the stage to the care of m͞r William F. Gray in Fredericks^bg, will be forwarded by him to Milton without delay, where I shall be on the watch for them.   I must find my apology in this repeated trouble in your own patriotic dispositions to promote an useful culture. . . . (*Jefferson Papers, L. C.*)

(Jefferson to James Monroe.)

Monticello Jan. 16. 16.

. . . I have an opportunity of getting some vines planted next month under the direction of m͞r David, brought up to the business from his infancy.   will you permit me to take the trimmings of your vines such I mean as ought to be taken from them next month.   it shall be done by him so as to ensure no injury to them. . . . (*Jefferson Papers, L. C.*)

(Jefferson to Mrs. Henry Dearborn.)

Monticello Jan. 27. 16.

Th: Jefferson presents his compliments to m͞rs Dearborn and his thanks for the very acceptable seeds she has been so kind as to send him and which will occupy his care & attention in the season now beginning to invite the labors of the garden.   (*Jefferson Papers, M. H. S.*)

(Jefferson to Joel Yancy.)

Monticello Feb. 20. 16.

. . . I have some thought of sending up a waggon [to *Poplar Forest*] about the close of the month with some trees & necessaries for me. . . . (*Jefferson Papers, M. H. S.*)

(James Barbour to Jefferson.)

Barboursville, March 4, 1816.

[Mr. Barbour requests Jefferson to send him anything he can spare of plants.]   Being anxious to add to my new establishment whatever is rare or desirable of the fruit, shrub, or tree kind.   (*Jefferson Papers, M. H. S.*)

(Jefferson to James Barbour.)

Monticello Mar. 5. 16.

If I knew what you possessed, or what you particularly wished, my attention more especially applied to the latter might better have fulfilled them.  sending at random I fear I may add little to your actual possessions.  but I do the best I can by sending those things which are not absolutely possessed by every body.

for the garden.  Sprout Kale.  which no body in the U. S. has but those to whom I have given it.  sow & transplant as cabbage.  let it stand out all winter.  it needs no protection.  in the beginning of December it begins to furnish sprouts & will give 3 crops of them before spring.  a very delicate green.

long haricots a species of bean or snap brought me from Georgia by Gen¹. Sumpter.  plant in rows 3. f. apart, & 12 I. asunder in the row. stick the plants with flat prongy bushes, which will let you go between the rows.  early in July it gives beans from 2. to 6. f. long accdg to the ground, & continues till frost.  dress them as snaps or in all the ways of asparagus.  they are cut into lengths.

Trees & Shrubs.  2. pods of Kentucky locust.

> seeds of Spanish broom.  they come up best in cart-ruts and bottoms of gullies.
>
> lilac.
>
> Althaea.
>
> Balsam poplar, a branch for cuttings.
>
> Calycanthus.
>
> the Monticello Aspen, entirely peculiar & superior to all others.
>
> Paper mulberry from Otaheite.  the most beautiful & best shading tree to be near the house, entirely clean, bearing no fruit, scarcely yet known in America.

My collection of fruits went to entire decay in my absence and has not been renewed, so that it is in my power to send you but little in that way.  I send however cuttings of the Carnation cherry so superior to all others that no other deserves the name of cherry: and cuttings of the Taliafferro apple, the best cyder apple existing, discovered by old Majʳ. Taliaferro near Williamsburg.  wishing you good success with them I salute you with esteem & respect. . . . Mʳˢ. Randolph adds a collection of flower seeds for mrs Barber with her respects. (*Jefferson Papers*, M. H. S.)

(Isaac Coles to Jefferson.)

Enniscorthy Mar: 9ᵗʰ 1816.

Permit me to return you my best thanks for the Paper Mulberry, which you were kind enough to send me.  They have proven more acceptable to my friends than to myself, Mʳˢ. Randolph having been good enough to let me have a dozen or fifteen, which my servant brought me during your last visit to Bedford.

My brother Mʳ. Walter Coles sends eight Lemon Peaches, which will prove a great treasure if they can be defended against the attacks of the worms. . . . (*Jefferson Papers*, L. C.)

(Jefferson to Joel Yancey.)

Monticello Mar. 15. 16.

. . . I send also some plants which I pray you to have set out immediately in the nursery behind the old stable, in a rich part. . . . (*Jefferson Papers*, M. H. S.)

(Levin Gale to Jefferson.)

Chesapeake M^d. March 30^th. 1816.

I received sometime ago a letter from Major John Adlum near George Town D. C. requesting me to forward you some cuttings of a particular grape which was originally got from him. The same day this goes by the mail there will be put in the stage a box containing 150 cuttings of the kind mentioned Directed to you to the Care of M^r. W^m. F. Gray Fredericksburgh Virginia. I have to apologize for not complying sooner with his request but being from home at the time his letter reached this together with other circumstances prevented attending to his request with alacrity I could have wished. Should you wish more cuttings next year shall be happy to forward them and regret that our vines from neglect furnished so few. . . . (*Jefferson Papers*, M. H. S.)

(Jefferson to Levin Gale.)

Monticello May 7. 16.

Your favor of Mar. 30. came during an absence from home of considerable length, and the box of vine cuttings arrived soon after, in excellent order, and were immediately planted. I hope they will do well, as, judging from a sample of wine made from this grape and sent to me formerly by Maj^r. Adlam [Adlum], I expect to be gratified with the great desideratum of making at home a good wine. his was certainly equal to the best Burgundy I have ever seen, and they were tried together at the same time. the grape too, being native, is therefore preferable to anyone yet to be imported, acclimated, and tried with us. Accept my thanks for your kind attention to this object. . . . (*Jefferson Papers*, M. H. S.)

(Jefferson to David B. Warden.)

Monticello May 17. 16.

. . . the spring has been unusually dry and cold. our average morning cold for the month of May in other years has been 63°. of Farenheit. in the present month it has been to this day an average of 53°. and one morning as low as 43°. repeated frosts have killed the early fruits and the crops of tobacco and wheat will be poor. about the middle of April they had at Quebec snow a foot deep. . . . (*Jefferson Papers*, Maryland Historical Society.)

(Joseph C. Cabell to Jefferson.)

Warminster, July 4th, 1816.

I saw Gen. Cocke on his way to Norfolk, early in June, and had a conversation with him on the subject of hedges; in the course of which he informed me that you were under the impression that Maine's method of preparing haws, so as to make them vegetate quickly, had died with him. It affords me pleasure to furnish you with it, in an extract of a letter written by Maine to Mr. James Henderson of Williamsburg, at the time that the latter purchased of him about 10,000 of his thorns. I was making enquiries in the month of May, with the view of collecting information as to the practicability and expediency of introducing live fences into Virginia, when I accidentally got sight of Maine's letter to Mr. Henderson. It differs from all other methods I have yet heard of; and is more expeditious, by one winter, than that of McMahon, who follows the English and Scotch methods; and is the quickest of all the processes that have come to my knowledge, unless it be that of immersing the haws in fermenting bran, as recommended by Sir Isaac Newton. I have no where read of a successful experiment on a large scale, of the latter method; and have seen it merely suggested as recommended by Sir Isaac Newton. Maine's method is simple, quick, and well suited to common practice. I should be glad to know why Maine selected the maple leaf thorn in preference to all others. It does not appear to me to be as vigorous in its growth, or as strong in its appearance, as the laurel leaf thorn; nor do I know whether it is to be found in this part of the country. In crossing Willis' river, on my way up the country, I found a thorn in great abundance, which, from the shape of the leaf, appeared to be the maple leaf thorn. There may, however, be other varieties with a leaf of the same shape. You planted some years ago, a hedge around your house, of Maine's thorn. I should be happy, before I commence experiments in this line, to know your impression as to the practicability of making hedges of real use in this country where hogs are suffered to run at large; and as to the relative advantages of the holly, the cedar, and the thorn, for that purpose. I should also be much indebted to you, for a reference to such authors as treat best on the subject. I have consulted Dobson's Encyclopedia, Lord Kaimes, Maine's Pamphlet, and the articles in the ordinary books on agriculture. I have been informed by a young gentleman who attended the lectures of the Abbé Correa in Philadelphia, that the Abbé expressed the opinion, that hedges would not succeed in this country, because we have not the right kind of plant, and that the proper plant when imported, degenerates. The same person told me that the hedges about Wilmington, in Delaware, seemed to be declining. These are discouraging circumstances. Still I have a strong desire to go on. I had a cedar hedge of about two miles in length, planted on the Rappahannock low grounds, some years ago. It grew handsomely, and promised well. But during the war, it was neglected and beaten down by stock in many places. A part of it, about five hundred yards in length, is now entire and very beautiful. But whether it will be ultimately a secure fence, I am unable to say. As an object of ornament, I think it remunerates for the care and trouble it has cost; and it is of real use in breaking the force of the violent winds that often sweep those plains. I propose to renew it where it is defective, and to extend it to four miles in length. The holly is scarsely to be found in the woods of the upper country. Still I suppose it would succeed with the aid of cultivation, and I am about trying it as an enclosure for a yard and lots. . . . (*Early History of the University of Virginia as contained in the Letters of Thomas Jefferson and Joseph C. Cabell* (Richmond, 1856): 62–64. Hereafter cited as Jefferson and Cabbell, *Letters.*)

### (Jefferson to Joseph C. Cabell.)

Monticello, July 13, 1816.

I thank you for Maine's recipe for preparing the haw, inclosed in your favor of the 4th. I really thought it lost with him, and that the publication of it would be a public benefit. I do not know that his hedge thorn is to be found wild but in the neighborhood of Washington. He chose it, I think, for its beauty. I have extensive hedges of it, which I have too much neglected. The parts well grown appear rather weak against cattle; yet, when full grown, will probably be sufficient. He proposed to keep out hogs by a couple of rails passed along the bottom, and, I think, it will be sufficient: and that, should the upper part prove too weak for very strong cattle, a pole run horizontally through will bind them together, and make them sufficient. Col. Randolph thinks the cockspur hawthorn (our common one) would be preferable as being stronger. My grandson, Jefferson Randolph, found one common, about Willis's mountains, which he thinks eminently preferable to all others. The Pyracanthus which I got from Maine is a beautiful plant, but not fit for a hedge. He tried the honey locust, meaning to keep it down by the shears; but I thought it too straggling. The holly certainly will not do with us, because all but impossible to make live in our climate. I have one tree 44 years old, not yet taller than a hedge should be. Of the cedar I have no experience, but of the difficulty of either transplanting it or raising it from the berry. On the whole, I think nothing comparable with the thorn, and that they may be made to answer perfectly, with the aids I have mentioned. . . .

P. S. Col. Randolph tells me he has repeatedly heard Mr. Correa say that our cockspur hawthorn (crataegus crux galli) was the best for hedges he had ever met with. (Jefferson and Cabell, *Letters:* 65–66.)

### (Jefferson to Dr. David Hosack.)

Monticello July 13. 16.

Uninformed of the persons particularly connected with the Botanical garden of N. Y. I hope I shall be pardoned for this address to yourself. I have just received from my antient friend Thouin, director of the King's garden at Paris a packet of seeds selected by him as foreign to the U. S. they are of the last year's gathering, but he informs me that if

they arrive (as they have done) too late to be committed to the earth
this year, most of them will be still good for the ensuing year.  not believing I could make a better use of them than by presenting them to the
Botanical garden of N. York, I have taken the liberty of sending the
packet to your address by mail, and, altho' large, I have thought the
object justified my franking it.  I have not opened the packet knowing
I could not pack them so well again; but coming from Thouin I am sure
they are worthy the acceptance of the garden. . . . (*Jefferson Papers,*
L. C.)

(Jefferson to John Taylor.)

Monticello, July 16, 1816.

Yours of the 10th is received, and I have to acknowledge a copious
supply of the turnip seed requested.  Besides taking care myself, I shall
endeavor again to commit it to the depository of the neighborhood, generally found to be the best precaution against losing a good thing. . . .
(Lipscomb and Bergh, *Jefferson* 15: 44.)

(Joseph C. Cabell to Jefferson.)

Edgewood, 4th August, 1816.

I beg you to accept my sincere thanks for your favor of the 13th inst.
. . . The information you give me on the subject of hedges is very acceptable; it will exempt me from the mortification of failures in experiments that extend through so large a portion of human life.  I have
about half a bushel of holly seed now lying in my garden, undergoing
the process of preparation for the seedbed; but since the receipt of your
letter, I have determined to thrown them aside, or to make very small
use of them.  I shall direct my future attempts in this line towards the
thorn, and to the variety you recommend, unless I should be able to
procure that of which Mr. Jefferson Randolph speaks so highly, for
which purpose I have sent him the enclosed letter of enquiry.  I presume he alludes to a thorn in the old fields about Hendrick's tavern, the
strength and density of which have frequently been mentioned to me by
gentlemen who had been traveling that way.  It is not certain, although
it is probable, that Maine's recipe will succeed with all the different
thorns. . . . (Jefferson and Cabell, *Letters:* 67–68.)

(John Campbell White to Jefferson.)

Baltimore, 13th Augt. 1816.

Two of my sons travelling in England through the favour of Sir John
Sinclair, received some melon seed, of two species, brought from Persia
by Sir Gore Resely [?], it has a high character.  I have therefore much
pleasure in sending a portion of it, to the first character in the United
States. . . . (*Jefferson Papers,* United States Department of Agriculture.)

(Jefferson to Leroy & Bayard.)

Monticello Aug. 15. 16.

. . . my resources are those of a farmer, depending on the produce of my farm, which is usually sold in April or May. . . . (*Jefferson Papers,* L. C.)

(Jefferson to John Campbell White.)

Monticello, Aug. 24. 16.

Th: Jefferson presents his salutations and respects to M͞r. White with his thanks for the Persian melon seed he has been so kind as to send him. he will endeavor to do it justice by his attentions, and especially to disperse it among his most careful acquaintances. it is by multiplying the good things of life that the mass of human happiness is increased, and the greatest of consolations to have contributed to it. . . . (*Jefferson Papers,* United States Department of Agriculture.)

(Jethro Wood to Jefferson.)

Aurora 10 Mo 1st 1816

Friend Thomas Jefferson

The firm of which I am a partner requests thy acceptance of a plough, as a respectful tribute to thy Ingenuity in improving that important Instrument. We shall feel ourselves amply recompensed by thy approbation; or, additionally obliged by any suggestion which may tend to render it more Complete.

By an accident occasioned by the warping of the wooden patern the edges are raised ⅓ of an Inch to high. The plough is now gone for New york and will be forwarded to thee as soon as possible. . . . (*Jefferson Papers,* Missouri Historical Society.)

(Thomas Appleton to Jefferson.)

Oct. 20. 16.

*Lupinella-Grass seed*

The Lupinella grass is unquestionably, the most prolific & most nutritous known in Italy and preferred by horses, oxen, sheep &c. to every other species. It should be planted in grounds, not subject to inundations, or wet soils—it is commonly planted here, on small-elevations. It should be cut with a Sickle, as is grain, and bound in small bundles of about 7. [?] each, to prevent the flowers from wasting; and a short time before they are perfectly mature. The cattle fed on this hay require no oats or beans, indeed, it should be given with moderation to horses of luxury: to hard laboring horses, it may be freely given.—In addition to this qualities, the ground in which it has been planted, thru successive years, on the fourth, you may plant wheat, from which you will reap a most abundant harvest, without the aid of any species of manure.—the leanest grounds by this cultivation, becomes rich & fertile. It produces here about six thousand American pounds of hay, on a field which would require two bushels of wheat. (*Jefferson Papers, L. C.*)

### (Jefferson to Martha (Jefferson) Randolph.)

Poplar Forest Nov. 10. 16.

We are all well here my dear Martha, and thinking of our return home which will be about the 30th. or perhaps a day or two sooner. it is necessary therefore that the boys Johnny & Randall with the mules should set off from Monticello on the 19th. or 20th. to take the cart and baggage. I must pray you to desire mr̄ Bacon to let them have a good mule and geer in addition to Tulman and his. tell Wormley also to send some Calycanthus plants well done up in moss and straw, and about a bushel of Orchard grass-seed out of the large box in the Greenhouse. would it be possible for you to make up some of the hardy bulbous roots of flowers as to come safely on the mule. daffodils, jonquils, Narcissuses, flags & lillies of different kinds, refuse hyacinths &c. with some of the small bulbs of the hanging onion. I think if wrapped & sowed up tight in two balls, one to come in each end of a wallet with nothing else in it to bruise them, they would come safe. . . . (*Jefferson Papers,* M. H. S.)

### (Martha (Jefferson) Randolph to Jefferson.)

Monticello. Nov. 20, 1816.

We received your letter last night only, and the necessary preparations for the boy's Journey would take up so much of the day that we determined not to send them till tomorrow morning 21st. Wormley will see to every thing but the bulbous roots. the kinds you mention are all growing at present and could not be moved without destroying them but I have sent you a number of offsets of tulips and hyacinths some blooming roots and some that will not bloom till the ensuing year but I believe all of the finest kinds. they were intended to have been planted in the border last fall but were kept out waiting for a bed to be prepared for them. the others can be dug up at the proper season and planted next summer or fall. . . . the large crown imperial root is for Mrs Eppes, if you go that way. the smaller ones are not blooming roots yet, but will be in a year or 2. the tulips & hyacinths are mixed but Cornelia knows them all. . . . (*Jefferson Papers,* M. H. S.)

### From the *Account Book 1809–1820:*

Apr.  8.  gave Colo Monroe's gardener for vines 1. D. [See letter, Jefferson to Monroe, January 16, 1816.]

May 13.  pd. portage box of vines 1.

Planting Memorandum for *Poplar Forest,* 1816:

1816. Nov. 1.   planted large roses of difft. kinds in the oval bed in the N. front.

dwarf roses in the N. E. oval.   Robinia hispida in the N. W. dº.

Althaeas, Gelder roses, lilacs, calycanthus, in both mounds.   Privet round both Necessaries.

White Jessamine along N. W. of E. offices.

Azedaracs opp. 4 angles of the house.   Aug. 17.   5 livᵍ.

22.   planted 190. poplars in the grounds.   5 Athenian poplars.   2. Kentucky locusts near house.   European mulberries in the new garden.   (*Jefferson Papers,* U. Va.)

# 1817

| 1817.[1] | where | when | come to table | Miscellanies. |
|---|---|---|---|---|
| Frame peas............ | Border I–V.... | Feb. 19. | May 25. | Jan. 11.—Feb. 18. the whole of our winter lettuce & endive killed, tho' well covered. spinach stood tolerably. |
| lettuce ice, & radishes.... | Stone house E. | | | |
| spinach............... | | | | |
| Celery.................. | .................. | .... 21. | | |
| Frame peas............ | submural...... | Mar. 1. | May 25. | May 4. pod. these are forwarder yⁿ those of Feb. 19. |
| lettuce white & radish.... | .................. | ........ | June 1. | |
| Cabbage, Savoy......... | | | | |
| Sprout Kale........... | | | | |
| Brussels sprouts [2]....... | | | | |
| Hotspurs.............. | Sq. I............ | .... 10. | May 30. | |
| Ledmans............. | II. | | | |
| summer spinach........ | | | | |
| ice lettuce........... | | | | |
| violet radish. N. Y.[3].... | | | | |
| spinach. summer....... | .................. | .... 19. | | |
| lettuce white.......... | | | | |
| radish violet N. Y....... | | | | |
| Leadmans............. | III............ | .... 24. | | |
| lettuce white........... | | | | |
| radish scarlet.......... | | | | |
| beet.................. | XIV. 2. | | | |
| salsifia................ | XIV. 1. | | | |
| carrots................ | XIII. | | | |
| Bess snaps............ | V............ | .... 29. | June 7. | May 24. blossom. |
| Lettuce White......... | .................. | .... 31. | | |
| radish scarlet.......... | | | | |
| Tomatas. dwarf........ | Border X...... | ........ | July 28. | |
| Spanish....... | Sq. X.......... | Apr. 1. | July 28. | |
| Okra................. | XII. 2. | .... 2. | July 28. | |
| Nasturtium........... | IX. | | | |
| Lima beans........... | Terras A.5.6. | .... 3. | | |
| Long Haricots......... | Terras A.1.2.3.4. | ........ | July 16. | |
| Leadmans............. | Sq. IV.......... | .... 10. | | |
| Lettuce White......... | .................. | .... 8. | | |
| radishes............... | .................. | ........ | June 3. gone. |
| parsley............... | | | | |

| 1817.[1] | where | when | come to table | Miscellanies. |
|---|---|---|---|---|
| Jerus. Artichokes........ | ................ | .... 11. | | |
| Snaps grey............. | Sq. VI........ | .... 12. | | |
| lettuce white........... | ................ | .... 14. | | |
| cucumbers long green.... | Sq. VIII. | | | |
| Squashes. Winter........ | | | | |
|         Summer....... | ................ | June 29. | | |
| Fr. kidney beans......... | | | | |
| Grey snaps............ | VII........ | May 6. | June 28. | |
| winter cabbage.  Brussels | | | | |
|   sprouts?  Divers [4]..... | ................ | May 17. | | |
| Swedish turneps......... | ................ | Aug. 7. | | |
| Spinach winter......... | ................ | Sep. 23. | | |

1817.[5]   Jan. 20.   filled the Ice house [6] at the river with ice.
        Mar. 13.   filled the Snow house [7] here with snow.
        Apr.  4.   planted 15. Scuppernon vines [8] in lowest terras of Vineyard.
        May  4.   peas at mr Divers.  sown early in Jan[y].

[1] *1817.*   The cornerstone of Central College, later to become the University of Virginia, was laid on October 6.   This
was the outstanding event of the year for Jefferson.   From
this year until his death in 1826, this project was first in his
life.   He wrote to Joseph C. Cabell on October 24: "Our
Central College gives me more employment than I am equal
to.   The dilatoriness of the workmen gives me constant
trouble."   (Lipscomb and Bergh, *Jefferson* 19: 251.)   And
to George Ticknor he wrote on November 25 :

I am now entirely absorbed in endeavors to effect the establishment
of a general system of education in my native state. . . . In the meantime, and in the case of failure of the broader plan, we are establishing
a college of general science, at the same situation near Charlottesville,
the scale of which, of necessity will be much more moderate, as resting
on private donations only.   These amount at present to about 75,000
Dollars.   The buildings are begun, and by midsummer we hope to have
two or three professorships in operation.   (Ford, *Jefferson* 12: 77–79.)

The range of Jefferson's correspondence was the same as in
other years, and the number of letters written is surprising,
considering his age and the manifold projects he had under
way.   Although he was not so active in the garden and the
farm, agriculture, especially its theory, was still of great in-

terest to him.    His letters tell of the method of plowing sloping land and the kinds of plants to grow on it.

An   English   traveler,   Lieutenant   Francis   Hall,   visited
*Monticello* during the summer.    Later, in describing his visit,
he wrote in part:

> Having an introduction to Mr. Jefferson I ascended his little moun-
> tain, on a fine morning, which gave the situation its due effect.   The
> whole of the sides and base are covered with forest, through which roads
> have been cut circularly so that the winding may be shortened at pleas-
> ure: the summit is an open lawn, near to the south side of which the
> house is built, with its garden just descending the brow. . . . I walked
> with him round his grounds, to visit his pet trees and improvements of
> various kinds. . . . (Randall, *Jefferson* 3: 436.)

James Monroe was elected President of the United States
this year.    Monroe's election delighted Jefferson, and inaugurated for the nation what was called "The Era of Good Feeling."

Four visits were made to *Poplar Forest*.    The house there
was still uncompleted.    There were few changes at *Monticello*.    In the garden and the farms the usual kinds of plants
were set out.

² *Brassica   oleracea* var. *gemmifera* Zenker.    Brussels
sprouts.

³ New York.

⁴ George Divers.    See letter, George Divers to Jefferson,
March 27, 1817.

⁵ This entry has been removed from page 56 of the *Garden
Book* and inserted here in proper chronological order.

⁶ So far as I know, this is the only occasion on which Jefferson mentions an ice house at the river.    It was probably located near his mills.

⁷ Jefferson is referring here to his ice house at *Monticello*.

⁸ The scuppernong is a direct offspring of the curious muscadine grape (*Vitis rotundifolia*).    "It is said that the scuppernong was discovered on Roanoke Island, North Carolina,
by Sir Walter Raleigh's colony, and that the original vine is
still in existence."    (Bailey, *Our Native Fruits:* 83–84.)    A
delicious wine is made from the scuppernong grape.    It was
a favorite wine of Jefferson.    (See letter, Jefferson to Samuel
Maverick, May 12, 1822, in note 1, 1822.)

LETTERS AND EXTRACTS OF LETTERS, 1817

(Jefferson to George M. Jeffreys.)

Monticello Mar. 3. 17.

Your favor of Feb. 17. came to hand two days ago. I wish it were more in my power to fulfill the request of furnishing you with a full and compleat catalogue for an Agricultural library. for this first and most useful of all human arts and sciences I have had from earlier life the strongest partiality. yet such have been the circumstances of the times in which I have happened to live that it has never been in my power to indulge it. my reading in that line therefore has been necessarily restrained. and for practice I have had still less leisure and opportunity until age had deprived me of the activity it called for. the catalogue therefore now inclosed, is sent rather in proof of my readiness, than of my competence to serve your society. there is probably no better husbandry known at present than that of England. but that is for the climate & productions of England. their books lay for us a foundation of good general principles: but we ought, for their application, to look more than we have done into the practices of countries and climates more homogeneous with our own. I speak as a Southern man. the agriculture of France and Italy is good, and has been better than at this time; the former in the age of De Serres, the latter in the time of Cato, Varro &c. lessons useful to us may also be derived from Greece and Asia Minor, in the times of their eminence in science and population. I wish I could have been more copious in that part of my catalogue; but my acquaintance with their agricultural writings has not enabled me to be so.

The horizontal ploughing after which you enquire, has been practiced here by Col°. Randolph, my son in law, who first introduced it, about a dozen or fifteen years. it's advantages were so soon observed that it has already become very general, and has entirely changed & renovated the face of our country. every rain before that, while it did a temporary good, did greater permanent evil by carrying off our soil; and fields were no sooner cleared than wasted. at present we may say that we lose none of our soils, the rain not absorbed in the moment of it's fall being retained in the hollows of the beds until it can be absorbed. our practice is when we first enter on this process, with a rafter level of 10. f. span, to lay off guide-lines, conducted horizontally from one end to the other of the field, and about 30. yards apart. the steps of the level on the ground are marked by a stroke of a hoe, and immediately followed by a plough to preserve the trace. a man, or a boy of 12. or 15. years old, with the level, and two smaller boys to mark the steps, the one with sticks, the other with the hoe, will do an acre of this an hour, and when once done, it is forever done. we generally level a field the year it is put into corn, until all have been once levelled. the intermediate furrows are run by the eye of the ploughman, governed by these guide lines, and is so done as to lay the earth in horizontal beds of 6. f. wide with deep hollows or water furrows between them, to hold the superfluous

rain.  the inequalities of declivity in the hill will vary in places the distance of the guide lines, and occasion gores, which are thrown into short
beds.  As in ploughing very steep hillsides horizontally the common
plough can scarcely throw the furrows uphill, Col°. Randolph has contrived a very simple alteration of the share which throws the furrows
down hill both going and coming.  it is as if two shares were welded together at their strait side, and at a right angle with each other.  this
turns on it's bar as a pivot, so as to lay either share horizontal and the
other vertical, & is done by the ploughman in an instant by a single motion of the hand at the end of every furrow.  I enclose a bit of paper
cut into the form of the double share, which being opened, at the fold,
to a right angle, will give an idea of it's general principle.  I have transferred this method of ploughing to a possession I have near Lynchburg
90. miles to the S. W. from this place, where it is spreading rapidly, and
will be the salvation of that, as it confessedly has been of this part of
the country.  horizontal and deep ploughing, with the use of plaister &
clover which are but beginning to be used here, we believe will restore
this part of our country to it's original fertility which was exceeded by
no upland in the state.  This is the best account I am able to give you
of the horizontal ploughing.  poor as I am in the practice of agriculture,
and not rich in it's theory, I can do no more than prove my wishes to be
useful, adding those for the success of your institution. . . . [The list
inclosed in Jefferson's letter was of books included in his library.  See
appendix VII.]   (*Jefferson Papers, L. C.*)

(Thomas Appleton to Jefferson.)

Leghorn March 5, 1817.

[Mr. Appleton sends Jefferson a bag of Lupinella seeds.  See letter,
Thomas Appleton to Jefferson, October 20, 1816.]   (*Jefferson Papers,
L. C.*)

(Jefferson to Joel Yancey.)

Monticello Mar. 6. 17.

[Jefferson sends artichokes to be planted in the locks of the fence in
the big garden, and some] Pride of China plants which may be planted
somewhere near the mounds.  (*Jefferson Papers, M. H. S.*)

(Jefferson to John W. Eppes.)

Monticello Mar. 6. 17.

. . . Mrs. Eppes will receive herewith a box containing some calycanthuses, prickly locusts (Robinia hispida) a Snowberry bush and the
sweet-scented curran.  the two last were brought from the Pacific ocean
by Lewis and Clark.  the Snowberry is beautiful in autumn and winter
by it's bunches of snow white berries.  I send in a paper some sprout
kale to be sowed and transplanted as cabbage.  it is to remain in it's

place during winter and will give 2. or 3. successive crops of sprouts
from the beginning of December to April, and is a fine, tender, sweet
winter vegetable. . . . P. S.   a Halesia sent.   also purple & white figs.
(*Jefferson Papers*, Huntington.)

### (Jefferson to Archibald Thweatt.)

Monticello Mar. 16. 17.

. . . You ask the cost of a mill carrying 3 or 4 pair of stones.   mine
carries 2 p^r. of burrs, the one of 5. f. the other of 6. f. and a pair of
rubbers for cleaning the grain, with all the modern labor saving machinery, the house very roomly, & walls of stone.   it cost me 10,000. D.
but good judges say it ought to have cost but $8,000.   this is exclusive
of the canal which alone cost me 20.000 D. and of the dam. . . . (*Jefferson Papers*, L. C.)

### (Jefferson to Jethro Wood.)

Monticello Mar. 23. 17.

I received on the 7th of Nov. your favor of Oct. 1 and delayed its
acknolegement until the arrival, within this week past, of the plough
you have been so kind as to send me on the part of the firm of which
you are a member.   for this mark of their attention I pray them to accept my thanks.   I have examined it with care, and think it promises
well in all its parts; and shall exhibit it with pleasure to the notice of
our practical, as well as our theoretical farmers.   I have no doubt it
would produce many calls were there a deposit within the state from
which they could be furnished; as at Richmond, for example.   the water
communications from thence would place them within the reach of a
great part of the state.   with the tender of my great respect to your
firm, I pray you to accept the same for yourself personally.   (*Jefferson
Papers*, Missouri Historical Society.)

### (George Divers to Jefferson.)

Farmington Mar. 27, 1817.

. . . The large potatoes you gave me turned out very well,   I send
you in return seven that was produced from seed that came from the
eastward,   I also send you a few of a very forward kind that came from
Liverpool last spring,   I have divided with you a few peach stones &
some cabbage seed which I lately rec^d from Mr. Thomas Cropper which
I send by your servant. . . . (*Jefferson Papers*, M. H. S.)

### (James Barbour to Jefferson.)

Barboursville Mar. 29, 1817.

. . . If you have anything in the seed way which you would recommend & which is not common you will oblige me by sending it. . . .
(*Jefferson Papers*, M. H. S.)

(Joseph C. Cabell to Jefferson.)

Edgewood, 30th March, 1817.

I have had a good hunt among my papers for Maine's recipe for the preparation of haws; and at length, after almost despairing, have found it in the midst of a small volume of extracts from Brown's Rural Affairs. I now send it to you, agreeably to your desire. . . . (Jefferson and Cabell, *Letters:* 75.)

(Jefferson to Tristran Dalton.)

Monticello, May 2, '17.

I am indebted to you for your favor of Apr. 22, and for the copy of the Agricultural magazine it covered, which is indeed a very useful work. while I was an amateur in Agricultural science (for practical knolege my course of life never permitted me) I was very partial to the drilled husbandry of Tull, and thought still better of it when reformed by Young to 12 I. rows. but I had not time to try it while young, and now grown old I have not the requisite activity either of body or mind.

With respect to field culture of vegetables for cattle, instead of the carrot and potato recommended by yourself and the magazine, and the beet by others, we find the Jerusalem artichoke best for winter, & the Succory for Summer use. this last was brought over from France to England by Arthur Young, as you will see in his travels thro' France, & some of the seed sent by him to Gen$^l$. Washington, who spared me a part of it. it is as productive as the Lucerne, without its laborious culture, and indeed without any culture except the keeping it clean the first year. the Jerusalem artichoke far exceeds the potato in produce, and remains in the ground thro' the winter to be dug as wanted. A method of plowing over hill sides horizontally, introduced into this most hilly part of our country by Col°. T. M. Randolph, my son in law, may be worth mentioning to you. he has practiced it a dozen or 15 years, and it's advantages were so immediately observed that it has already become very general, and has entirely changed and renovated the face of our country. every rain, before that, while it gave a temporary refreshment, did permanent evil by carrying off our soil: and fields were no sooner cleared than wasted. at present we may say that we lose none of our soil, the rain not absorbed in the moment of it's fall being retained in the hollows between the beds until it can be absorbed. our practice is when we first enter on this process, with a rafter level of 10. f. span, to lay off guide lines conducted horizontally around the hill or valley from one end to the other of the field, and about 30 yards apart. the steps of the level on the ground are marked by a stroke of a hoe, and immediately followed by a plough to preserve the trace. a man or a lad, with the level, and two small boys, one with sticks, the other with the hoe, will do an acre of this in an hour, and when once done it is forever done. we generally level a field the year it is put into Indian corn laying it into beds of 6. f. wide with a large water furrow between the beds, until all the fields have been once leveled. the intermediate furrows are run by the eye of the ploughman governed by these guide lines. the inequalities of declivity in the hill will vary in places the distance of the guide lines, and occasion gores which are thrown into short beds. As in ploughing very steep hill sides horizontally the common plough can scarcely throw the furrow uphill, Col°. Randolph has contrived a very simple alteration of the share, which throws the furrow down hill both going and coming. it is as if two shares were welded together at their strait side, and at a right angle with each other. this turns on it's bar as on a pivot, so as to lay either share horizontal, when the other becoming vertical acts as a mould board. this is done by the ploughman in an instant by a single motion of the hand, at the end of every furrow. I enclose a bit of paper cut into the form of the double share, which being opened at the fold to a right angle, will give an idea of it's general principle. horizontal and deep ploughing, with the use of plaister and clover, which are but beginning to be used here will, as we believe, restore this part of our country to it's original fertility, which was exceeded by no upland in the state. Believing that some of these things might be acceptable to you I have hazarded them as testimonies of my great esteem and respect. (*Jefferson Papers,* L. C.)

### (Jefferson to Isaac Coles.)

Monticello May 7. 17.

Have you any orchard grass seed left? or have your brothers any? I want about a bushel to finish a grass lot now prepared for it, and should be very thankful for that much. I looked for you at court [to] invite you to come and see mr̄s Madison & mr̄ Madison, but could not find you. I thought too you ought not to need an invitation to come here or to see them. Appleton of Leghorn has sent me some grass seed (arrived at Boston) which he calls Lupinella, of which he gives a very high account as to produce. 6000 lb in the ground which requires 2. bushels of wheat when sown in wheat. when I receive it I shall wish to distribute it among careful farmers, in which number I count you. . . . (*Jefferson Papers,* M. H. S.)

### (Isaac Coles to Jefferson.)

Enniscorthy May 8th. 1817.

I have not an Orchard Grass seed left but as I think it possible that my Brother may still have some on hand I have directed your servant to go there. I fear however as it is now so much later than we are in the habit of sowing it, that you will be disappointed in getting any.

I only got a glimpse of you on Monday as you ascended to the Jury room, and was called off to dine before you came down again. I would have come up with Genl. Cocke in the evening to see you, & pay my respects to Mr. & Mrs. Madison, if I had not apprehended from the size of the party I heard were with you, that your House was entirely full.

I shall be very thankful for a few seed of the Lupinella when you receive it, & will certainly give it a fair experiment. . . . (*Jefferson Papers,* L. C.)

(Jefferson to William Johnson.)

Monticello May 10. 17.

. . . the pamphlet you were so kind as to send me manifests a zeal, which cannot be too much praised, for the interests of agriculture, the employment of our first parents in Eden, the happiest we can follow, and the most important to our country.   while it displays the happy capabilities of that portion of it which you inhabit, it shews how much is yet to be done to develop them fully.   I am not without hope that thro' your efforts and example, we shall yet see it a country abounding in wine and oil.   North Carolina has the merit of taking the lead in the former culture, of giving the first specimen of an exquisite wine, produced in quantity, and established in it's culture beyond the danger of being discontinued.   her Scuppernon wine, made on the Southside of the Sound, would be distinguished on the best tables of Europe, for it's fine aroma, and chrystalline transparence.   unhappily that aroma, in most of the samples I have seen, has been entirely submerged in brandy.   this coarse taste and practice is the peculiarity of Englishmen, and of their apes Americans.   I hope it will be discontinued, and that this fortunate example will encourage our country to go forward in this culture.   the olive, the Sesamus, the Cane & Coffee offer field enough for the efforts of your's and other states South & West of you.   we, of this state, must make bread, and be contented with so much of that as a miserable insect will leave us.   this remnant will scarcely feed us the present year, for such swarms of the Wheat-fly were never before seen in this country. . . . (*Jefferson Papers*, L. C.)

(Jefferson to Dr. Josephus B. Stuart.)

Monticello, May 10 1817.

. . . We all know that a farm, however large, is not more difficult to direct than a garden, and does not call for more attention or skill. . . . (Lipscomb and Bergh, *Jefferson* **15**: 112.)

(John Adams to Jefferson.)

Quincy, May 26, 1817.

. . . I congratulate you, and Madison and Monroe, on your noble employment in founding a university.   From such a noble triumvirate the world will expect something very great and very new; but if it contains anything quite original, and very excellent, I fear the prejudices are too deeply rooted to suffer it to last long, though it may be accepted at first.   It will not always have three such colossal reputations to support it. . . . (Lipscomb and Bergh, *Jefferson* **15**: 123.)

(Jefferson to Baron F. H. Alexander von Humboldt.)

Monticello, June 13, 1817.

The receipt of your *Distributio Geographica Plantarum,* with the duty of thanking you for a work which sheds so much new and valu-

able light on botanical science, excites the desire, also, of presenting myself to your recollection, and of expressing to you those sentiments of
high admiration and esteem, which although long silent, have never
slept. . . . (Ford, *Jefferson* **12**: 68.)

(Jefferson to Albert Gallatin.)

Monticello, June 16, 1817.

. . . We have had a remarkably cold winter. At Hallowell, in
Maine, the mercury was at thirty-four degrees below zero, Fahrenheit,
which is sixteen degrees lower than it was in Paris in 1788–9. Here it
was at six degrees above zero, which is our greatest degree of cold. . . .
(Lipscomb and Bergh, *Jefferson* **15**: 135.)

(John Love to Jefferson.)

Breckland, July 16th, 1817.

At an early period of the summer, the President passed on this road,
when I had the pleasure of seeing him. He was then satisfyed from
the different appearances of the common wheats, and the kind here called
the Lawler, that the latter was uninjured by the Hessian fly, and engaged from me 200 bush'ls for himself, and 200 for you, to whom he
mentioned his intention to write on the subject. I have still a considerable portion of my crop to dispose of, but orders for it have been received
to a considerable amount from different parts of the United States, and
will probably soon be equal to the quantity to be disposed of in this
neighborhood. It may, therefore, be proper that I should more certainly at this time be informed of your wishes on the subject, as I have
not had the honor of hearing from you. If more should be wished I
can supply it, or if less it will be a matter of no importance. I see small
parcels of it have been raised this year on James River. You have therefore probably seen the growth of it, or I would enclose a stalk, it is I
think much harder than that of any other kind. But as the cause of the
exemption of this wheat from the ravages of the fly could not be satisfactorily agreed on by the members of the committees of this neighborhood, it was not in our power to make any public statement on this part
of the subject.

The crops in this neighborhood of the Lawler wheat are of good
quality, not quite so heavy as the last year; the growth has been very
great as might be expected. My crop is entirely clear of disease, altho
I am told in the neighborhood of Fauquier C[ourt] h[ouse] the *smut*
has appeared in considerable quantity. My farm has not yet been visited
by this dreadfull disease, and I believe it has not found its way to James
river. I think from what I have seen in this neighborhood it is at-
tributable to bad seed, as it is very much the custom here to cut wheat in
a green state, and the seed does not mature so perfectly as when left to
the process of nature.

By the middle or 20th of August, I could be prepared to deliver wheat
for seed. . . . (Ford, *Jefferson Correspondence*: 231–232.)

(Jefferson to John Love.)

Monticello, August 3, '17.

Your favor of July 16, came to hand yesterday evening only, and I
feel much indebted to the President for having thought of me, and to
yourself for giving me an opportunity of procuring a supply of the
Lawler wheat for seed.  I have heard much of it's superior security
from the fly, and indeed know something of it from an example in my
neighborhood.  how it may stand in comparison with our red bearded
wheat in other important circumstances we do not know, and therefore
I have concluded to sow enough of it only to produce my stock of seed
for another year.   the little necessary for this I get in my own neighborhood and leave therefore the benefit you offer me for the supply of others
who will want, with abundant thanks for the preference you have been
so good as to offer me.  of smut we have had but one example here.   I
think with you it proceeds from bad or infected grain.  recollecting always with pleasure the scenes of our cooperation in the public councils I
pray you to accept assurances of my continued esteem and respect.
(Ford, *Jefferson Correspondence:* 232.)

(Francis W. Gilmer to Jefferson.)

Winchester, 18, Aug. 1817.

. . . I inclose for Mrs. Randolph a few seeds of the plant which has
been dedicated to you, under the name of Jeffersonia.  It is not very
beautiful but is curious, and its name will I am sure recommend it to her
piety.  It grows in deep, shady bottoms like the May apple (podophyllum peltatum).  The seeds came from Harpers Ferry where all the re-
gions of nature have conspired to do you honor. . . . (*Francis Gilmer
Letter Book,* Missouri Historical Society.)

(Jefferson to Martha (Jefferson) Randolph.)

Poplar Forest Aug. 31. 17.

. . . Ellen and Cornelia are the severest students I have ever met
with.  they never leave their room but to come to meals.  about twi-
light of the evening, we sally out with the owls & bats, and take our
evening exercise on the terras.  an alteration in that part of the house,
not yet finished, has deprived them the use of their room longer than I
had expected; but two or three days more will now restore it to them.
. . . (*Jefferson Papers,* M. H. S.)

(Jefferson to Edmund Bacon.)

[Monticello] Nov. 15. 17.

. . . We have saved red Hughes enough from the North orchard to
make a smart cask of cyder.  they are now mellow & beginning to rot.

I will pray you therefore to have them made into cyder immediately.
let them be made clean one by one, and all the rotten ones thrown away
or the rot cut out.   nothing else can ensure fine cyder. . . . (*Jefferson
Papers,* M. H. S.)

(Jefferson to J. Correa da Serra.)

Poplar Forest, November 25, 1817.

. . . I have taken measures to obtain the crested turkey, and will endeavor to perpetuate that beautiful and singular characteristic, and shall
be not less earnest in endeavors to raise the Moronnier. . . . (Lipscomb
and Bergh, *Jefferson* 15: 157.)

# 1818

| 1818 [1] | where | when. | to table | Miscellanies. |
|---|---|---|---|---|
| forward potatoes...... | .................. | Jan. | | |
| Hunter's peas........ | Border. I. 19yd.. | Feb. 27. | May 24. | Mar. 13. up. |
| Frame peas.......... | dº. E. end..... | .......... | .... 31. | Mar. 13. up. May 6. blossom.— |
| Hunter's............ | Submural W.... | .......... | May 24. | ....... dº. May 10. pod. |
| Frames............ | dº. E. ... | .......... | .... 31. | Mar. 13. up. May 6. blossom 15. pod. |
| Hotspur............ | I............ | Mar. 9. | June 5. | 24. up. May 21. pod. |
| Ledmans............ | II.................. | .......... | .... 14. | ..... 25. up. May 22. blossom. |
| Cabbage early York... | .................. | .......... | | |
| green Savoy.. | .................. | .......... | | |
| Savoy Leitch. | .................. | .......... | | |
| Sprout Kale.......... | .................. | .......... | | |
| Summer Spinach...... | .................. | .......... | | |
| Orache............ | .................. | .... 16. | | |
| cabbage early York.... | .................. | .... 20. | | |
| green Savoy... | .................. | .......... | | |
| Sprout Kale.......... | .................. | .......... | | |
| beets............ | .................. | .......... | | |
| carrots............ | .................. | .......... | | |
| salsafia............ | .................. | .......... | ........ | Mar. 24. almond blooms. |
| Ledmans............ | III............ | .... 24. | June 20. | Apr. 6. up. May 26. blossom. June 7. pod. |
| Snaps. grey.......... | .................. | .......... | June 11. | June 3. blossom. 7. pod. |
| Salsafia............ | .................. | .... 25. | | |
| Carrots............ | .................. | .......... | | |
| Span. tomatas....... | .................. | .... 26. | | |
| Nasturtium.......... | .................. | .......... | | |
| Summer Spinach...... | .................. | .......... | | |
| Okra............ | .................. | .... 30. | | |
| cucumbers frame...... | .................. | .......... | | |
| long haricots........ | Terras A.3.4.... | Apr. 2. | | |
| Lima beans.......... | 5.6.... | .... 3. | | |
| early frame cucumber.. | island [2]........ | .... 4. | | |
| Ledmans............ | .................. | .... 6. | ........ | June 5. blossom 13. pod. |
| squashes............ | .................. | .... 8. | | |
| grey snaps.......... | .................. | .... 11. | June 17. | June 10. pod. |
| frame cucumbers...... | island........ | .... 11. | | |
| long haricots........ | .................. | May 7. | | |
| Spinach............ | .................. | Sep. 18. | | |
| Dutch Brown........ | .................. | | | |

¹ *1818.*  Jefferson wrote to the Marquis de Lafayette on November 23:

> The hand of age, my dear friend, has been pressing heavily on me for the few last years and has rendered me unequal to the punctualities of correspondence.  My health, too, is lately very much broken down by an illness of three months from which I am but now on the recovery. If, therefore, I am slack in acknowledging the receipt of your much valued letters, goodness will ascribe it to its true causes, declining age and health.  (Lipscomb and Bergh, *Jefferson* 19: 268.)

In order to effect a cure for his illness, which he had suffered most of the summer, Jefferson spent the month of August at the Warm Springs of Virginia.

He made two trips to *Poplar Forest,* and as usual enjoyed the quiet surroundings and the absence of large numbers of visitors, which flowed to *Monticello.*

The Commissioners, who had been appointed to select a location for the State University of Virginia, decided that Charlottesville was the most central place and that Central College should be renamed the University of Virginia.  The final action for the change was not taken by the Legislature until the following year.  Jefferson was now busy with the plans for the enlarged school.

While Jefferson was absorbed in the new University of Virginia, his financial condition was growing more serious.  He wrote to Mr. Beckley, on April 16, "I have not at this moment more than 50. dollars in the world at my command" (*Jefferson Papers,* M. H. S.)   In spite of this, he endorsed two notes of ten thousand dollars each, for his old friend, Wilson C. Nicholas.  This favor was to cause Jefferson partial financial embarrassment for the remainder of his life.

Letters covering the same wide range of interests were written during the year.  They were less numerous, with relatively fewer on agriculture and related topics.

Edmund Bacon continued as overseer at *Monticello,* and Joel Yancey, at *Poplar Forest.*  His grandson, Thomas Jefferson Randolph, supervised the farm and garden affairs, as well as other concerns of Jefferson.  Jefferson recorded the routine calendar of the vegetable garden, letting others do most of the planning and planting.

² *Island* here probably referred to an isolated place in the garden.

## LETTERS AND EXTRACTS OF LETTERS, 1818

(Jefferson to David Hosack.)

Monticello Feb. 18. 18.

I received some time ago from M. Thouin, Director of the Botanical or King's garden at Paris, a box containing an assortment of seeds, Non-American, and therefore presumably acceptable to the American botanist, finding it more and more necessary to abridge the catalogue of my cares, this is among [those] which I have struck from it.  I have therefore this day sent the box to Richmond to the care of Cap^t Peyton of that place, to be forwarded to you for the use of the Botanical garden of N. York, to which I presume the assortment may be [acceptab]le, for I have not opened it nor do I know it's particular [conten]ts.  I am happy in this disposition of it to fulfill the good intentions of the donor, and to make it useful to your institution. . . . (*Jefferson Papers*, M. H. S.)

(Jefferson to Bernard Peyton.)

Monticello, Mar. 20, 18.

. . . The impossibility of buying raw cotton obliges [me] to recur to the cultivating it myself.  So much has it [got] out of practice that even the seed is lost in this part of the country.  Could you possibly buy me a sack or barrel of about 5 bushels?  It will be a great accommodation to me. . . . (*Jefferson Papers*, M. H. C. 1: 269.)

(Jefferson to Jacob Bigelow.)

Monticello, April 11, 1818

I thank you, Sir, for the comparative statement of the climates of the several States as deduced from observations on the flowering of trees in the same year.  It presents a valuable view and one which it is much to be desired could be extended through a longer period of years and embrace a greater number of those circumstances which indicate climate.

I closed the year before last a seven years' course of observations intended to characterize the climate of this State, which though very various in its various parts may be considered as reduced to a mean at this place nearly central to the whole.  In return for your favor I transcribe the heads of observation which I thought requisite and some of the general results with the assurance of my high respect and esteem.

1. The greatest and least height of the thermometer every day.
2. The greatest, least and mean height of the thermometer in every month, with the mean of each year and the mean of the seven years which last was $55\frac{1}{2}°$.
3. The minimum and maximum of the whole term, to wit: $5\frac{1}{2}°$ and $94\frac{1}{2}°$.
4. The number of freezing nights in a winter (50) and of freezing days (10).
5. How long fires are necessary in our apartments, to wit: 4 months constant, and on evening and morning of month before and after that time.

6.   The earliest frost in autumn Oct. 7–26, and the latest in spring Mar. 19–May 1.
7.   The earliest ice in autumn Oct. 24–Nov. 15, and latest in spring Mar. 8–Apr. 10.
8.   The quantity of water falling in a year, average 47.218.
9.   The number of rains in the year, 89.
10.  The number of fair days average 5 to the week.
11.  The number of snow 22½ inches average covers the ground 22 days.
12.  The number of days each wind prevailed through the year.
13.  The flowering of plants, ripening of their fruit and coming to table of the products of the garden, arrival of birds, insects, etc.
14.  The temperature of the springs 54½°, the winter air being at 75°.
15.  The latitude of the place of observation (Monticello) 37° 57' 51"–26".

> Extract from Number 13:
> The peach blossoms Mar. 9–Apr. 4.
> The tick appears Mar. 15–Apr. 2.
> The house martin Mar. 18–Apr. 9.
> Asparagus come to table Mar. 23–Apr. 14.
> The lilac blooms Apr. 1–Apr. 28.
> The red bud blooms Apr. 2–19.
> The whip-poor-will is heard Apr. 2–21.
> The dogwood blossoms Apr. 3–22.
> The locust blossoms Apr. 25–May 17.
> Garden pea comes to table (unforced) May 3–25.
> Strawberries ripe May 3–25.
> Fireflies appear May 8.
> Cherries ripe May 18–25.
> Wheat harvest begins June 21–29.
> Cucumbers at table (unforced) June 22–25.
> Peaches ripe July 7–21.
> Katydids or sawyers heard July 14–20.

| | Average of Every Month | | Prevalence of the several winds stated in days of year |
|---|---|---|---|
| | Therm. | Rain | |
| Jan. | 36 | 3.66 | |
| Feb. | 40 | 3.47 | N. 61 |
| Mar. | 46 | 2.92 | N. E. 29 |
| Apr. | 56½ | 3.59 | E. 15 |
| May | 61½ | 5.60 | S. E. 16 |
| June | 72 | 3.47 | S. 60 |
| July | 75 | 6.56 | S. W. 66 |
| Aug. | 73 | 4.06 | W. 47 |
| Sept. | 67 | 5.96 | N. W. 71 |
| Oct. | 57 | 3.40 | |
| Nov. | 45½ | 2.92 | 365 |
| Dec. | 37 | 1.56 | |

(Lipscomb and Bergh, *Jefferson* 19: 259–261.)

(Jefferson to Thomas Digges.)

Monticello June 15. 18.

. . . I thank you for thinking of me as to the spring wheat. my family will try it with pleasure. meddling little myself with the affairs of the farm. . . . (*Jefferson Papers, L. C.*)

(Jefferson to Honorê Jullien.)

Monticello Oct. 6. 18.

I thank you, my good friend, for the favors of the cheese & seeds mentioned in your letter of Sept. 11. to have been forwarded to me. if by water, they will probably still come safely to hand: but if by the stage, they have probably stopped at Fredericksburg or at some other stage house by the way. uncertain by what route they have been forwarded, I have been unable to enquire for them. but whether lost or safe, I receive it as a mark of your good will which is more acceptable to me than the objects themselves. I am recovering from a long indisposition, and not yet able to sit up to write but with pain. . . . (*Jefferson Papers, L. C.*)

(Jefferson to Nathaniel Bowditch.)

Monticello, October 26, 1818.

. . . The soil in this part of the country is as fertile as any upland soil in any of the maritime States, inhabited fully by substantial yeomanry of farmers (tobacco long since given up) and being at the first ridge of mountains there is not a healthier or more genial climate in the world. Our maximum of heat and that only of one or two days in summer is about 96, the minimum in winter is 5½, but the mean of the months of June, July, August is 72, 75, 73, and of December, January, February is 45, 36, 40. The thermometer is below 55 (the fire point) four months of the year and about a month before and after that we require fire in the mornings and evenings. Our average of snow is 22 inches, covering the ground as many days in the winter. . . . (Lipscomb and Bergh, *Jefferson* 19: 266.)

(Henry E. Watkins to Jefferson.)

Prince Edward
Nov. 6th 1818.

You were good enough to say, when I had the pleasure of seeing you in Stanton, that you would send me some of the seed of the succory, if I would remind you of it after your return home. It is therefore that I now take the liberty of requesting that you would forward me a parcel of the seed of this plant; and I do this with the less reluctance from a confidence that you think highly of its usefulness, and would be gratified in giving aid to its more extensive cultivation. I am desirous of trying it under favourable circumstances, and would be glad to be informed (if you have leisure) what kind of soil suits it best, what is the proper time and manner of sowing it, and how it should be worked. A package directed to me, and sent to the care of Ellis & Allan, of Richmond, would probably be safely received. . . . (*Jefferson Papers,* United States Department of Agriculture.)

(Jefferson to Henry E. Watkins.)

Monticello Nov. 27. 18.

Your favr. of the 6th did not get to hand till the 23d. and I now with pleasure send you as much of the Succory seed as can well go under the volume of a letter. as I mentioned to our colleagues at the Gap, I had forgotten which of them expressed a willingness to try this plant, and therefore I have waited for their application, having taken care to have a plenty of seed saved.

Sow the seed in rich beds, as you would tobacco seed, and take the advantage of good seasons in the spring to draw and transplant them. the ground should be well prepared by the plough. I have generally set the plants 18. I. or 2. f. apart every way, to give room for several weedings the 1st. summer, for during that they are too weak to contend with the weeds. after that they will not be in danger from weeds. do not cut the plants the 1st. year that they may shed their seed and fill up all the intervals. the grazing of sheep destroys the plant. it is perennial, and of immense produce, and is a tolerable sallad for the table in the spring, somewhat like the turnep tops but earlier. the warm spring bath proved extremely injurious to my health. I have been very poorly ever since, but within a week past have got on horseback, altho' not yet entirely well. . . . (*Jefferson Papers,* United States Department of **Agriculture.**)

# 1819

| 1819.[1] | where | when | come to table | Miscellenea. |
|---|---|---|---|---|
| Spinach............. | high bed..... | Jan. 26. | ........ | Mar. 3. up. |
| Orach................ | ............ | ........ | ........ | Mar. 3. up. failed afterwds |
| true early Frame peas called May peas....... | Submural.... | Jan. 27. | May 13. | these are Hunters. Mar. 3. up. Apr. 22. bloss[m]. 30. pod. May. 28. late gathering |
| Frames (former kind..... | Bord. I–V.... | ........... | .... 25. | Mar. 4. up. Apr. 30. blossom. May 9. pod. |
| Celery................ | low grounds .. | Feb. 5. | | |
| Early York............ | ........... | .... 11. | | |
| Savoys............... | | | | |
| Sprout Kale........... | | | | |
| Spinach.............. | | | | |
| Orach................ | | | | failed |
| Hotspurs............. | | Feb. 24. | June 4. | May 8. blossom. 14. pod. |
| Ledmans............. | | Mar. 3. | .... 13. | May 15. blossom. 26 pod. |
| Spinach. smooth....... | | | | |
| Orach................ | | | ........ | failed. |
| Lettuce ice⎫ radish. ⎭ | ........... | ........ | June 3. | |
| Spinach. Smooth........ | | .... 15. | | |
| Orach................ | | | June 2. | succeeded |
| Leadmans............. | | .... 18. | June 16. | May 21. blossom. pod June 2. |
| Chick peas from Julien[2]. | | | June 18. | try planting them 1st. week of April. say the 7th. |
| Snaps grey............ | | Apr. 1. | June 9. | May 25. blossom. June 2. pod. |
| Salsafia............... | | | | |
| Carrots............... | | | | |
| tomatas............... | | | | |
| okra................. | | | | |
| nasturtium............ | | | | |
| beets................ | | | | |
| cucumbers............ | | | | |
| orach................ | | ........... | ........ | succeeded |
| spinach smooth........ | | | | last dish. June 1. |
| lettuce. wh. & Ten. ball.. | | | | |

582

| 1819.[1] | where | when | come to table | Miscellénea. |
|---|---|---|---|---|
| radishes............... | | | | |
| Lima beans............. | ............... | .... 2. | | |
| Long Haricots.......... | ............... | ....... | July  9. | |
| lettuce ice & Tennis..... | ............... | .... 6. | | |
| wild goose bean   to wit.. | red bloss^d kidn|ey bean.. | July 13. | |
| French dry haricot. | | | | |
| Lange [3]............ | | | | |
| Marrow fats........... | IV............ | .... 9. | June 24. | May 27. blossom. |
| | | | | June 10. pod |
| Ledmans................ | ................ | ........ | June 21. | June 3. blossom. |
| | | | | June 10 pod^d some |
| | | | | day, |
| snaps.................. | ............... | ........ | ........ | June 4. blossom. |
| lentils................. | squitch spots [4] | .... 13. | | |
| Orach.................. | ............... | May  3. | | |
| green curled Savoys..... | | | | |
| snaps.................. | ............... | .... 12. | ........ | June 11. blossom |
| Silesia lettuce.......... | XVII.2.N..... | .... 17. | | |
| Orach.................. | ............... | .... 18. | | |
| Swed. turneps.  Vaughan [5] | A.13.terras... | .... 22. | | |
| snaps.................. | ............... | .... 26. | | |

1819.[6]   May   6. put 2 carp into the 2^d. fishpond and 4. chubs into the 3^d.   the 1^st. or
uppermost pond is for eels.[7]   the carp & chub came from Gen^l.
Cocke's [8]

May.   eels put into the 1^st. pond as we catch them are 4+2+2+7+3+1.

Oct.  19. planted Seakale [9] 6. rows 100 .f. long, 16 I. apart, & the seeds 16. I.
dist^t. in y^e row making 6. rows of 75. holes each = 600. holes or plants.   6 seeds in
each hole.

-----

[1] *1819.*  Jefferson suffered two severe spells of sickness during the autumn of the year.  The second one almost caused his death.  By the end of October, however, he was able to be on his horse again and was riding over his farms.

On April 9 the North Pavilion of Jefferson's house was burned.  Fortunately the fire was confined to the Pavilion and did not reach the main house.  He wrote to William Short on June 22: "The conflagration in which you are kind enough to take an interest was only of a detached pavilion, which is now again under repair" (*Jefferson Papers*, M. H. C. 1: 286).

The cisterns at *Monticello* were still leaking, causing the loss of a valuable supply of water that was so sorely needed on top of the mountain.  On May 15 Jefferson "inclosed to W. J. Coffee N. York 40. D. to procure Roman cement for my cisterns." It is doubtful if Jefferson's cisterns were ever wholly satisfactory.

Jefferson made only two visits to *Poplar Forest* this year; however, he remained there two months at the summer visit. While at *Poplar Forest,* he supervised the laying of a marble hearth and the plastering of the ceiling of the dining room.

The Calendar in the *Garden Book* is fuller this year, but the variety of vegetables is the same. There is no mention of fruit trees. Letters on agricultural matters dwindle markedly in number and in interest. The University of Virginia was taking the place of agriculture in Jefferson's thinking and writing. The work on the University buildings was progressing, but Jefferson had many problems to solve in order to carry on the building program.

[2] Mr. Jullien, one of Jefferson's favorite servants at the White House during his Presidency. See letter, Jefferson to Mr. Jullien, October 6, 1818.

[3] Abraham Lange. See letter, Jefferson to Abraham Lange [= Laage], January 24, 1819.

[4] Squitch spots (altered form of quitch), couch-grass (*Triticum repens*). It evidently means here that lentils were planted in spots where couch-grass formerly grew. (See *Oxford English Dictionary* 9: 751.)

[5] Benjamin Vaughan (1751–1835), diplomat, political economist, and agriculturist, the eldest son of Samuel Vaughan, a London merchant, and Sarah (Hallowell) Vaughan, of Boston, Massachusetts. He was graduated in medicine from Edinburgh in 1781. He was a friend of Franklin and Jefferson, and often corresponded with the latter. (*Dict. Am. Biog.* 19: 233–235.) See letter, Benjamin Vaughan to Mrs. Martha Randolph, June 23, 1819.

[6] This entry has been removed from page 56 of the *Garden Book* and inserted here in proper chronological order.

[7] *Anguilla bostoniensis,* the American eel, is often used for food.

[8] John Hartwell Cocke (September 19, 1780–July 1, 1866), planter, publicist, was born in Surry County, Virginia. He attended the College of William and Mary (1794–1799), and about 1803 settled at Bremo, his country estate, in Fluvanna County, Virginia. During the War of 1812 he rose

from a captain to a brigadier-general.    He was a progressive agriculturist and interested in varied public improvements. Jefferson and Mr. Cocke were friends and neighbors.    When Jefferson was founding the University of Virginia, Mr. Cocke played a conspicuous part in the building program.    (*Dict. Am. Biog.* 4: 253–254.)    (For Jefferson's estimate of General Cocke, see letter, Jefferson to John David, January 13, 1816.)

⁹ *Crambe maritima* L.    Sea kale.

## LETTERS AND EXTRACTS OF LETTERS, 1819

(Jefferson to Joel Yancey.)

Monticello Jan. 17. 19.

. . . I shall be very glad to receive the latter peas I liked so much the last year and hope *Nace* has saved me a full sowing of them. . . . I will ask the favor of you to send by Jerry the *Athenian poplars* in the nursery of the garden.    you will know them by the stem being ribbed, which distinguish them from the Lombardy poplars & aspens in the same place. . . .    (*Jefferson Papers*, M. H. S.)

(Jefferson to Abraham Lange [= Laage].)

Monticello Jan. 24. 19

Th: Jefferson presents his compliments to Mʳ. Lange and his thanks for the two parcels of beans he has been so kind as to send him.    they are safely received, and are quite sufficient in quantity to put him promptly into stock and with his acknolegements for the favor, he salutes M. Lange with esteem & respect.    (*Jefferson Papers*, L. C.)

(Fontaine Maury to Jefferson.)

Washington, Feby. 14, 1819.

I have lately imported from England a small quantity of Talevera wheat, which was procured by a particular Friend of my Brother from the Farm of Sir Watkins Williams Wynne of Wynnstay, Wales, who is estimated to be one of the most celebrated agriculturists in that Country, and as you, *at least,* have the reputation of being a zealous promoter of that Science, *in this,* I have taken the liberty to transmit to you *for trial* a small partition of what I have remaining.    You also have a description of its properties, to which I am told may be added the favorable circumstance of its maturing ten or fifteen days earlier than most other wheats.    My brother James in a late letter speaks of you with his usual interest, and has directed his son Matthew, to make you a call before he leaves this Country, which I have also desired him to do. . . .    (Ford, *Jefferson Correspondence:* 244–245.)

(Jefferson to Fontaine Maury.)

Monticello Feb. 21. 1819.

. . . the torpidity of age having detached me from all pursuits of that kind, I have put it [wheat] into the hands of my son in law, Colo. Randolph, and of my grandson, our best farmers in this neighborhood who will give it a fair and skilful trial. . . . be so kind as with my thanks for the wheat, to accept for yourself the assurance of my great esteem and respect. . . . (Ford, *Jefferson Correspondence:* 245.)

(Jefferson to James Madison.)

Monticello, Mar. 3. 19.

I promised your gardener some seeds which I put under a separate cover and address to you by mail. . . . (Ford, *Jefferson* 12: 116.)

Mar. 29, 1819

Notes on the Culture of the *Swedish Turnip,* as practised in Maine with success.

1. Rich loam, or black mould is found to suit it best.

2. The land should be new, (either from turning up the sod, or from burnt woods) ; or well manured with stable manure the year preceding; for if done the same year, you will be troubled with worms & other insects. Plaister of Paris may be applied to it, with great advantage;— both by rolling the seed in it, & as a top dressing.

3. When the ground is well ploughed & harrowed, & immediately after planting your corn; sow the turnip seed in drills, 3 or 3½ feet asunder; dropping at least one seed to every three inches; in order to admit of some being destroyed, and still having enough left for selection, when they are thinned at the second hoeing.

4. This crop must be kept clean by the hoe; and at the second hoing, the plants in the rows are to be left from 1 foot to 15 Inches from each other; always selecting the most vigorous.

The success of this crop depends much upon its being kept clean, & receiving frequent rains. Should both these circumstances concur, from 2 to 500 bushels may be expected on an acre; according to climate & soil.

In Maine, the Turnip must be housed early in the fall; tho' a slight frost does not affect it. Perhaps the whole crop would stand out during a Virginia Winter.

As food for cattle & sheep, it should be used with a proportion of hay or dry fodder; & not more than a peck, or half a bushel, per day, given to an ox weighing 800 lbs; & in like proportion to smaller animals. For horses & milch cows, the carrot is preferable. . . . (*Jefferson Papers,* L. C.)

(Jefferson to William J. Coffee.)

Monticello May 15. 19.

I have been long indebted to you for your letter of Nov. 7. explaining to me the nature & character of the Roman cement, and kindly offering your assistance in procuring it.   as the proper season is now arrived for using it, I wish to try it on one of my 4 cisterns, and if I find we can execute it effectually, I may then ask more for the other three.   I therefore now inclose 40. D. and ask the favor of you to send me as many barrels of the cement as that may procure to be forwarded by sea to Cap^t Bernard Peyton of Richmond.   I am particularly thankful for the exactness of your instructions as to the manipulation. . . . (*Jefferson Papers*, M. H. S.)

### (Benjamin Vaughan to Martha (Jefferson) Randolph.)

Hallowell, June 23, 1819.

. . . The packet of Swedish turnip seed was sent, as desired, with a letter from my eldest son, W^m. Oliver Vaughan. . . . (*Jefferson Papers*, M. H. C. 1: 283.)

### (Martha (Jefferson) Randolph to Jefferson.)

Monticello Aug. 7. 1819.

. . . We are still suffering from the drought here.   Jefferson thinks that not much of his corn is so far gone but what it might still recover if we have rain soon.   the thermometer in your window was many days at 94 the other one $15\frac{1}{2}$. . . . (*Jefferson Papers*, M. H. S.)

### From the *Account Book 1809–1820*:

Jan. 1.   m͞r. Eppes's Martin for Thorn haws.   50.

### Planting Memorandum for *Poplar Forest*, 1819:

1819. Apr. 23.   planted in the garden under the N. wall of the stable 20. cuttings of Balsam poplars from m͞r Radford (some may live).   (*Jefferson Papers*, U. Va.)

# 1820

| 1820.[1] | where | when | come to table. | |
|---|---|---|---|---|
| Celery | Th: J.R.[2] | Feb. 9. | | |
| May peas | below wall | Feb. 14. | May 9. | Feb. 25. up. Apr. 19. blossom {Mar. 31. to Apr. 30. thermom. |
| Frames (3. y. old) | Bord. I–V | | 19. | Feb. 28. up. Apr. 25. blossom {from 29. to 32. with snow, |
| white lettuce | high bed. | | | have prostrated these |
| Radish | | | May 9. | |
| Spinach. Summer | | 15. | | |
| Early York | | | | |
| Savoys | | | | |
| Sprout Kale | submural. III. IV. | 19. | | Mar. 16. up. Mar. 31. prostrated by cold |
| Frame peas. Lietch.[3] | | 23. | | |
| dwarf early Cabbage Coffee[4] | Sq. I. | Mar. 1. | May 25. | |
| Hotspurs | II. | | June 13. | |
| Marrow fats | III | 16. | | Mar. 28. appearing |
| d° | | | | |
| Spinach Summer | | | | |
| Orach | | 27. | | |
| carrots | | | | |
| salsafia | | | | |
| tomatas dwarf | | | | |
| Okra | | | | |
| Nasturtium | | | | |
| beet | | | | |
| snaps | | | June 8. | May 25. blossom. |

| 1820.[1] | where | when | come to table. | |
|---|---|---|---|---|
| Marrow fats. | IV. | Apr. 1. | | |
| purple broccoli. | | 5. | | |
| long haricots. | | 10. | July 13. | |
| Lima beans. | | 11. | | |
| Dry haricot. Lange. | terras. | | | |
| Scarlet beans. | terras. | 13. | June 20. | |
| Frame cucumbers from Coffee. | | | | |
| early d°. | | | | |
| Snaps. | | 15. | | |
| Roman   beans[5] | high terras. | 16. | June 19. | |
| Alexandr[n] | | | | |
| Tuscan | | | | |
| Italian | | | | |
| Tuscan beans | | May 25. | | |
| Pani corn. | | 3. | | |
| Benni. | | | | June 6. transplanted finally |
| Malta Broccoli. | | | | |
| Snaps. | | 5. | | |
| Chick peas. | | 15. | | |
| Broccoli. | | 16. | | June 6. transplanted finally. |
| Brussels sprouts. | | 29. | | |
| Chick peas. | | June 5. | | |
| borecole transpl[d] | Sq. I. | 12. | | |

1820.[6] May 26. planted the whole bed of sea kale with plants from mr̄ Divers.[7] about 400. plants in all.

May 27. put 3. carp into the carp pond. & 4. chub into the chub pond. from Gen[l] Cocke

¹ *1820.* Jefferson's health was far below normal during the year. He wrote to William Short on April 13:

You kindly inquire after my health. There is nothing in it immediately threatening, but swelled legs, which are kept down mechanically, by bandages from the toe to the knee. These I have worn for six months. But the tendency to turgidity may proceed from debility alone. I can walk the round of my garden; not more. But I ride six or eight miles a day without fatigue. I shall set out for Poplar Forest within three or four days; a journey from which my physician augurs much good. (Lipscomb and Bergh, *Jefferson* 15: 248.)

On September 30 he mentioned the same subject to his friend, Charles Pinckney, whom he had not seen for twenty years:

Twenty years added to fifty-seven make quite a different man. To threescore and seventeen add two years of prostrate health, and you have the old, infirm, and nerveless body I now am, unable to write but with pain, and unwilling to think without necessity. (Ford, *Jefferson* 12: 164.)

But Jefferson was not idle. In fact, he was far more active than these letters would indicate. He was spending all of his spare hours at the University, of which he wrote to Mr. Short, in another part of the letter quoted above:

Seven of the ten pavilions destined for the professors, and about thirty dormitories, will be completed this year; and three other, with six hotels for boarding, and seventy other dormitories, will be completed the next year, and the whole be in readiness then to receive those who are to occupy them.

That he was building the University with the same earnest zeal that characterized all of his labors is shown in a letter to Mr. Correa, written on October 24, in which he refers to "our University, the last of my mortal cares, and the last service I can render my country" (Lipscomb and Bergh, *Jefferson* 15: 285).

Jefferson again visited *Poplar Forest* twice during the year. He was usually accompanied on these trips by some of his granddaughters, whose presence took away much of the loneliness that he suffered when he was away from *Monticello*.

Jefferson's mills became more active during the fall of the year. He wrote in the *Account Book* for the year: "Sept. 7. the elevators of the mill are now ready for taking in wheat & we will grind next week." And on September 30 he wrote: "The merchant mill began to grind corn on the 25 inst."

In spite of his much stiffened wrist, Jefferson wrote more and more letters. The plants he received from others were usually passed on to his son-in-law, or to his grandson, Jefferson Randolph. A few new varieties of familiar species occur in the Calendar of the garden for the year.

Thomas Mann Randolph was now Governor of Virginia, so that most of his time was spent at Richmond. Mrs. Randolph divided her time between Richmond and *Monticello*.

[2] Thomas Jefferson Randolph (1792–1875), son of Thomas Mann Randolph and Martha (Jefferson) Randolph, and grandson of Jefferson.

[3] James Leitch was a prominent merchant of Charlottesville, with whom Jefferson traded for many years.

[4] William J. Coffee, of New York. See letters, Jefferson to William J. Coffee, May 15, 1819, and Jefferson to Richard Randolph, May 13, 1822.

[5] The Italian plants named here probably came from Thomas Appleton, of Leghorn, Italy.

[6] This entry has been removed from page 56 of the *Garden Book* and inserted here in proper chronological order.

[7] See letter, George Divers to Jefferson, May 3, 1820.

### LETTERS AND EXTRACT OF LETTERS, 1820

(Thomas Appleton to Jefferson.)

Leghorn 21st. January 1820.

. . . I have inclos'd in the bag of hemp seed, four little bundles of the white, gentilli wheat, and it is directed to the care of the Collector of the port of Alexandria. . . . (*Jefferson Papers,* L. C.)

(George Divers to Jefferson.)

Farmington Feb. 28, 1820.

I am sorry I cannot supply you with all the pot-herbs wanted, we have not the Sweet Marjoram, sweet basil, or summer savory. I send you some Marjoram, winter savory and Thyme. (*Jefferson Papers,* M. H. S.)

(Jefferson to Bernard Peyton.)

Monticello Apr. 11. 20.

I received in due time your favor of March 30. and on reconsideration of the subject, have changed my mind. while I lived in Washington I received sample of wheat from Chile, which I gave to mr Divers to take care of. it proves not so productive as our own but whiter than the whitest of the May wheat. at the next harvest I will get mr̄ Divers to prepare half a dozen barrels of that which sent as a rarity can be more delicately offered in that character as well as for its superior excellency. . . . (*Jefferson Papers,* M. H. S.)

(George Divers to Jefferson.)

Farmington May 3, 1820.

My sea kale plants are quite too small to transplant; they are however out of the way of the fly & if the worms don't destroy them I can supply you with as many plants as will make a pretty good bed in the course of 10 or 12 days. . . . (*Jefferson Papers,* M. H. S.)

(Jefferson to John S. Skinner.)

Monticello May 16. 20.

I am not able to give you any certain information of the Lupinella. mr̄ Appleton, our Consul at Leghorn sent me some of the seed. but, done at length with these things, and more disposed to retire from old cares than to undertake new ones, I put it into younger hands for trial. I saw, in one instance, the young plants, just up, and leafed, and thought them decisively the Saint foin, already known to us, and so generally cultivated on the borders of the Mediterranean. never having seen the term Lupinella in any book either of Italian or other husbandry nor even in a dictionary I supposed it to be the local, and especially the Tuscan name for S$^t$. foin. but this is conjecture only. there is a species of S$^t$. foin, called Sulla, raised abundantly in the island of Malta, where no rain falls from Spring to Autumn, and which still yields good crops. it is not so heavily leafed as the other, but is very valuable for countries subject to severe droughts. about the year 1785. or 6. I procured the seed of this from Malta, and sent it to the Agricultural society of South Carolina; but I believe they found it less advantageous than the Guinea grass and did not pursue it's culture. . . . (*Jefferson Papers,* M. H. S.)

# 1821

| 1821.[1] | where | when | come to table | Miscellaneous |
|---|---|---|---|---|
| May peas............ | .......... | Feb. 8. | .......... | Mar. 1. up. Mar. 19. compleatly killed. thermom. 20° |
| Lietch's peas........ | .......... | ........ | .......... | Mar. 19. compleatly killed. |
| Frame peas......... | .......... | .... 9. | June 2.... | Mar. 19. killed so as to make seed only. a few only came to table |
| Celery............. | | | | |
| lettuce wh. & Ice..... | .......... | .... 13. | loaf June 7. | |
| radishes............. | | | | |
| spinach summʳ........ | | | | |
| cabbage Early York.. | .......... | .... 15. | .......... | Feb. 21.[2] planted 7. mountain raspberries in the uppermost raspberry terras. |
| Spinach Sum........ | .......... | .... 27. | | |
| Carrots............. | .......... | ........ | | these run to seed. |
| Hotspur peas........ | .......... | Mar. 1. | June 2.... | Mar. 26. up. May 6. blossom. |
| Marrow fats......... | .......... | ........ | .......... | 21. up |
| Sprout Kale........ | | | | |
| spinach............. | .......... | .... 12. | | |
| Orach............. | | | | |
| Marrow fats......... | .......... | .... 15. | | |
| salsafia............ | | | | |
| beets............... | | | | |
| carrots............. | | | | |
| carrots............. | .......... | .... 22. | | |
| Salsafia............ | | | | |
| Sea Kale........... | .......... | .... 23. | | |
| Okra.............. | .......... | .... 24. | | |
| Sum. Spinach....... | .......... | .... 27. | | |
| Orach............. | | | | |
| Onions............. | .......... | .... 29. | | |
| Nasturtium......... | | | | |
| Tomatas. both....... | | | | |
| Marrow fats ⎫ Leitch's latter⎭...... | same bed | .... 30. | .......... | July 14. last dish. |
| Snaps............. | .......... | Apr. 3. | June 7.... | May 26. blossom. |
| squashes............ | .......... | .... 7. | .... 20. | |
| scarlet beans........ | .......... | .... 10. | June 23. | |
| white haricots....... | | | | |
| cucumbers.......... | .......... | ........ | .... 28. | |

| 1821.[1] | where | when | come to table | Miscellaneous |
|---|---|---|---|---|
| 2. kinds of peas. Lietch Marrow fats ⎫ Leitch's latter ⎭ | ...... | .... 16. | | |
| White haricots....... | ...... | .... 20. | | |
| long haricots....... | | | | |
| snaps.............. | | | | |
| squashes........... | | | | |
| scarlet beans........ | ...... | May 7. | | |
| Snaps.............. | ...... | .... 20. | | |
| Swedish turnep...... | ...... | June 21. | | |
| Sea Kale........... | | | | |
| Spinach winter....... ⎫ Lettuce Dutch B..... ⎭ | ....... | Sep. 17. | | |
| Sea kale........... | ...... | Sep. 26. | | |

[1] *1821.* Jefferson's health was greatly improved this year. His life, accordingly, became more active. He wrote to his old friend, Lafayette, on March 22: "My health is better, but not good, so weak as not to walk further than my garden. but I ride with little fatigue" (Ford, *Jefferson Correspondence:* 259). By November 24 he was writing to Mr. William Short in a much more buoyant spirit:

Your welcome favor of the 12th came to hand two days ago. I was just returned from Poplar Forest, which I have visited four times this year. I have an excellent house there, inferior only to Monticello, am comfortably fixed and attended, have a few good neighbors, and pass my time there in a tranquility and retirement much adapted to my age and indolence. You so kindly ask an explanation of the illness which held me so long that I feel it a duty to give it. Having been long subject to local and slight affections of rheumatism, and being at Staunton on other business, I thought I would go to the Warmsprings and eradicate the *seeds* of it, for I was then in perfect health. I used the bath moderately for three weeks. I was not quick enough, however, in observing the gradual debility it was bringing on me. At length it produced a general eruption and imposthume. After a painful journey I got home unable to walk without help, and the debility and indisposition rapidly increased and reduced me to death's door. Swelled legs began to threaten dropsy, aided by a prostration of the visceral powers. Abandoning medicine, however, and fortifying my legs by bandages continued 8 or 10 months, I am at length entirely recovered, and suppose myself as well as I ever shall be. I am very little able to walk, but ride freely without fatigue. No better proof than that on a late visit to the

Natural Bridge I was six days successively on horseback from breakfast to sunset. (*Jefferson Papers,* M. H. C. 1: 307–308.)

The renewed activity that Jefferson was enjoying was devoted mainly to the new University. Little time was alloted to the garden. The routine Calendar of the garden was set down in the *Garden Book,* with a few new varieties added. He did manage, however, to make four visits to *Poplar Forest.*

Repairs on the cisterns were made in the fall of the year. Jefferson received the Roman cement ordered from Mr. Coffee and paid on September 29 "Chisolm's Lewis gratuity for cistern 1. D."

Early in the year Jefferson wrote to Joel Yancey, his overseer at *Poplar Forest,* that he had now placed his grandson, Jefferson Randolph, in charge of all of his plantations. Before this year Jefferson had continued to supervise the plantation at *Poplar Forest,* while his grandson attended to those in Albemarle County.

Jefferson's letters generally were fewer this year, owing no doubt to his increased activity and the difficulty of writing with a stiffened wrist.

² See letter, Jefferson to Mrs. Trist, February 21, 1821.

## LETTERS AND EXTRACTS OF LETTERS, 1821

(Isaac A. Coles to Jefferson.)

> Clarksville, Pike County, Missouri.
> Feby 15ᵗʰ. 1821.

I send you enclosed a specimen of *Wild Hemp* which I find in great abundance on many parts of my Land. We have collected a sufficient quantity of it for all our purposes, and find that it makes a much stronger rope than the Hemp of Virginia. the stem is generally of the size of ones finger, and from 5 to 10 feet in height. it is a perennial Plant, delights in low, moist, rich land, and yields fully as well (I think) as the common hemp. The seeds are small, resembling very much the seed of the Yellow Jessamine but larger and more full, and are contained in pods on the top of the Plant. as these burst open in the early part of winter, I have not been able to procure any of the seed to send you. The specimen enclosed was [taken?] from a stalk which I yesterday cut in the woods and prepared as you see it, by merely rubbing it between my fingers & then combing it straight with my pocket comb. It has stood out exposed in the woods the whole winter. As there is now nothing remaining of this Plant, but the naked stem and the roots (which are exceedingly numerous) it will be difficult to class it, but it

does not appear to me to resemble at all either Hemp or flax. Whatever it may be, it must, I think, prove a Plant of great value. The
strength, delicacy, softness & whiteness of the fibre, will no doubt be
greatly improved by being cut at the proper time, & healed in a proper
manner, & being a perennial, when once sowed it will last for ages, and,
may be cut with as little trouble as a timothy meadow. I do not dispair
still of being able to procure a few of the seed, and if I succeed they shall
be forwarded to you. An inch or two of the top of the Plant, with two
pods are also inclosed. . . . (*Jefferson Papers,* L. C.)

### (Jefferson to Bernard Peyton.)

Monticello Feb. 20. 21.

. . . I am in want of some earthen pots for covering plants of Sea
Kale in the garden. I am told they are made at a Pottery, in or near
Richmond. will you get me ½ hundred. . . . I must also request you
to get from some of the seed-dealers 4. oz. green curled Savory seed and
forward it by mail in a letter. . . . (*Jefferson Papers,* M. H. S.)

### (Jefferson to Mrs. Elizabeth Trist.)

Monticello Feb. 21. 21.

I am very thankful my dear Madam for Miss Polly Mark's kind attention to my wishes for the Mountain raspberry, and I pray you give
her that assurance. I now send for them. . . . Mrs. Randolph is to
try the flowering bean. we were unlucky as to fail last year in saving
the seed of the green Curled Savory. if mr̄ Divers has any to spare I
shall be much obliged to him for a little. . . . (*Jefferson Papers,* M.
H. S.)

### (Jefferson to General John H. Cocke.)

Monticello Mar. 12. 1821.

Our last mail brought me a letter from mr̄ Rodney and the inclosed
seeds of pumpkin and asparagus for you. . . . if you have any Sea-Kale
seed to spare I will thank you for some to replenish my bed. they had
better come by mail dispatch. . . . (*Jefferson Papers,* L. C.)

### (Jefferson to John H. Cocke.)

Monticello Apr. 1. 21. Sunday Morn.

. . . I return you many thanks for the carp and for the Kale seed you
were so kind as to send and salute you with affectionate esteem and respect. . . . (*Jefferson Papers,* U. Va.)

### (Jefferson to Jonathan Thompson.)

Monticello, June 25, 21.

I am thankful to you for your notice of the 14th respecting a box of
seeds. This comes from the King's garden at Paris. They send me a

box annually, depending on my applying it for the public benefit. I have generally had them delivered for a public garden at Philadelphia or to Dr. Hosack for the Botanical Garden at N. York. I am inclined to believe that he now receives such an one from the same place. If he does not, be so good as to deliver it to him, but if of no use to him let it come to Richmond to the care of Capt Bernard Peyton my correspondent there, and your note of any expense attending it will be immediately replaced either by him or myself. . . . (*Jefferson Papers*, Missouri.)

### (Samuel Maverick to Jefferson.)

Montpelier, Pendleton Dist: So: Carolina, Augt. 11, 1821.

For many years past I have been in the habit of Cultivating the Grape Vine and with various Success, owing to some cause or other they verry generally Rotted, and which has allmost allways happened Just at the moment as it were when they have attained their full size, they then take a drab Coloured spot on one side which spreads in a few days over the Grape and has the appearance of being scalded and in that state they readily part from the Vine, that is they are easily shook of, this phenominon is most comon to the large Dark purple or Black Grape, the white Chasilas and several other Kinds of Grape are infested with the same Brown spot, drys a way flatning on one side, and the Branches fall off. I have a Valuable Grape now in Bearing, which is said to have been procured from you some years past it has made its appearance in this part of the Country or Rather I have procured it in two ways One from Col: Hawkins from the Creek Nation, and in another from a Mr. Booth from Virginia this has ripened well and is a good Bearer, I now have Inclosed two Leaves from that Vine in order that you may be better inabled to give me Information what grape it is, and where Imported from, for several reasons, One of which is to compair the similarity of Effect in perhaps different Latitudes, and for a further Importation of Vines, the Bunches on this Vine contain generally from 20 to 40 Grapes, and after attaining $\frac{1}{2}$ to $\frac{3}{4}$ Inch in Diameter, they turn light Coloured, then gradually assume the Colour of Madarah wine or light brick Colour, the Grape is nearly round, flattened a little at the ends, and rather most at the stem, the fruit is verry Excelent, but leaves a verry slight astringent tast in the skin.

I am in Latitude 34.20 the Land lays pleasantly Rolling, perhaps one of the Best watered Countrys in America, about 30 miles below the Table Mountain which forms part of the Great Chain running threw this Continant our soil is various, and in my particular neighbourhood and farm we have a mixture of sand and Black Loom from 4 to 12 Inches on a Greasy Red Retentive Clay, on which I have tryed various Methods to Cultivate the Vine, on Arbours, Aspilliers and frames $2\frac{1}{2}$ foot high training them Horisontally, but I find to train them on Poles about 10 foot high, running them up in single stems and Exposing them to the Sun and air, answers best with me and occasionally pulling off the Leaves, on a Gradual South Exposiour, I have Laid of Horisontal Beds 5 foot wide, with 10 foot space Between from which I have taken off all the Soil, I carted on Top soil, Cow manure and sand on the Beds and Incorporated them with a Portion of the Clay and soil from 2½ to 3 foot deep, and planted one Row of Vines about 6 to 8 foot apart on Each Bed, in this way alone I have been inabled to rase the Large Black Grape, which has allmost invariably rotted in every other way, the only appology I have to offer for this paper to you is the Emence Importance to this Country in the Introduction of a New and Valuable Article of Commerce, as well as a most delicious and agreeable fruit, the Introduction of which may perhaps ameliorate the awful effects of spiritual Liquor. I have in my Colection a Small Grape in Tolerable size Bunches say ¼ to ½ lb in weight which Ripens well, very sweet and delicious flavour, wild grapes are plenty and Consist of the Large Black Muscadine small thin Leaf groes on Rich Bottom Lands—Fox Grape Black Red and White—the summer Grape on high land the small winter Grape on water Coarses and a new kind I have just discovered, but some what similar to the summer Grape and I supose of that kind the Bunches and Berrys Larger ripens well, if there is any thing in this way, which strikes your fancy, you will please to order me to whom and where I shall send them by way of Charleston to you, to which place I will forward them by a waggon.

I shall consider it a great favour for any Information Relitive to the Grape Vine as to Soil, Manure, Climate, Exposier, prooning, Kinds, or any thing else, I once had the pleasure of speaking to you on the Road, my Uncle Wm. Turpin and myself met you in passing through Virginia on our way to Carolina about 13 years ago, since when he has settled himself at New Rotchell New York.

are they not Various other plants that might be Introduced for the great Convenience and Cumfort of the Inhabitance of this wide Extended Country, even Tea and other Luxerys to sasiate the avorice of Comerce, or at least to spair the Ne[ce]essity of the Millions yearly Expended in protecting the Introduction of scarce articles which we might have in great profusion at home, it appears to me that there is no Excuse Except to keep up a nursery of seamen and follow the old plan of those Nations of Europe differently situated from us, they from Ne[ce]ssity have become Amphibious, but we are Land Animals, and will perhaps indanger our political Existence by following them too far into the water. . . . (Ford, *Jefferson Correspondence*: 261–263.)

## From the *Account Book 1821–1826*:

Sept. 16.   pᵈ. Nace for bringing up pots for sea Kale 2. D.   [See letter, Jefferson to Bernard Peyton, February 20, 1821.]

Sept. 29.   Chisolm's Lewis gratuity for cistern 1. D.

# 1822

| 1822.[1] | where | when | come to table | |
|---|---|---|---|---|
| Lettuce wh. & Ice.... | .......... | Feb. 23. | ........ | March 2. potted [2] 30. plants of sea-kale 2y. old compleat. |
| Spinach Summer..... | | | | |
| May peas........... | }Submural | Feb. 25. | {...... | Mar. 9. up.  Apr. 22. blossom |
| peas from Leitch..... | | | {...... | Mar. 10. up   Apr. 25 blossom |
| Frames........... | submural | ........ | ........ | Mar. 11. up.   Apr. 26. blossom. |
| Hotspurs........... | bord. I–V | .... 26. | ........ | .......... Apr. 27. blossom |
| beet........ | | Mar. 6. | | |
| Savoys........ | | | | |
| Sprout Kale....... | | | | |
| Hotspurs........ | | .... 11. | | |
| Marrow fats...... | | | | |
| beets........ | | | | |
| carrots........ | | .... 16. | | |
| okra........ | | | | |
| orach........ | | | | |
| Spinach........ | | .... 25. | | |
| nasturtium........ | | | | |
| salsafy........ | | | | |
| snaps...... | ........ | ........ | ........ | partly killed by frost Apr. 22. |
| Span. tomatas...... | | | | |
| Marrow fats...... | | .... 29. | ........ | July 6. gone. |
| long haricots...... | | Apr. 11. | | |
| Lima beans........ | | ........ | July 15. | |
| scarlet beans....... | | | | |
| marrow fats...... | | .... 15. | | |
| snaps........ | | | | |
| Limas. G. D [3]...... | | .... 21. | | |
| squashes. Dearb [4]..... | | ........ | June 15. | |
| Cucumbers frame..... | | | | |
| d°. forward Bank.[5].... | ........ | ——— | | |
| white haricots...... | | .... 23. | | |
| cucumb. long green... | | .... 30. | | |
| Gerkins........ | | | | |
| snaps........ | | May 6. | | |
| lettuce. T.B. & D.B.[6] | .......... | Aug. 26. | ........ | sowed 3. beds |
| Spinach winter...... | | | | |
| mustard ? D. Hig [7]... | | | | |
| Dutch brown...... | | Sep. 2. | | |
| Spinach winter...... | | | | |
| Dutch brown...... | | Sep. 9. | | |
| Spinach winter...... | | | | |
| Dutch brown...... | | .... 30. | | |
| Spinach........... | | .... 30. | | |

¹ *1822*. A few extracts from letters written during the year give a pretty clear picture of Jefferson and what he was doing. His interests and complaints were the same as in the previous years. He wrote to Samuel Maverick, of South Carolina, on May 12:

Age, debility and decay of memory have for some time withdrawn me from attention to matters without doors. the grape you inquire after as having gone from this place is not now recollected by me. as some in my vineyard have died, others have been substituted without noting which, so that at present all are unknown. that as good wines will be made in America as in Europe the Scuppernon of North Carolina furnishes sufficient proof. the vine is congenial to every climate in Europe from Hungary to the Mediterranean, and will be bound to succeed in the same temperatures here wherever tried by intelligent vignerons. the culture however is more desirable for domestic use than profitable as an occupation for market. in countries which use ardent spirits drunkenness is the mortal vice; but in those which make wine for common use you never see a drunkard. (Ford, *Jefferson Correspondence:* 270-271.)

On October 29, in a letter addressed to Albert Gallatin, Jefferson wrote:

Our University of Virginia, my present hobby, has been at a stand for a twelve-month past for want of funds. . . . The institution is so far advanced that it will force itself through. So little is now wanting that the first liberal Legislature will give it its last lift. (Ford, *Jefferson* 12: 263.)

And to Mr. Henry Dearborn he wrote: "Our Virginia University is now my sole occupation" (Ford, *Jefferson* 12: 265). On October 28 he sent the following message to the Marquis de Lafayette:

On our affairs little can be expected from an Octogenary, retired within the recesses of the mountains, going nowhere, seeing nobody but his own house, & reading a single newspaper only, & that chiefly for the sake of the advertisements. . . . I learn with great pleasure that you enjoy good health. Mine is also good altho' I am very weak. I cannot walk further than my garden without fatigue. But I am still able to ride on horseback, and it is my only exercise. . . . (Ford, *Jefferson* 12: 259-261.)

In early spring Jefferson received six barrels of hydraulic cement from Richard Randolph, for further repairs on his cisterns. This cement proved to be useless, so Jefferson continued to use Roman cement. (See letters, Jefferson to

Richard Randolph, May 13, 1822, and Randolph to Jefferson, May 30, 1822.) On June 14 Jefferson wrote to William Coffee a more encouraging message about the cisterns:

Our 2ᵈ cistern answers well, having now 4. f. 3. I. water. the last (or 3ᵈ.) has but 2. ft. altho it has exactly the corresponding & equal area of roof to supply it. I think the fault may be in the gutters conveying the water, & shall have that examined. (*Jefferson Papers*, M. H. S.) [See Appendix II.]

In October Jefferson lost Edmund Bacon, the most efficient overseer who had served him in that capacity. After serving Jefferson as overseer since 1806 and before that working for him in various jobs, Bacon decided to settle in Kentucky. Jefferson highly esteemed Bacon, and when the latter had gone to Missouri in 1818, to search out a place to settle, Jefferson gave him the following recommendation:

The bearer, Mr. Edmund Bacon, has lived with me twelve years as manager of my farm at Monticello. He goes to the Missouri to look out for lands to which he means to remove. He is an honest, correct man in his conduct, and worthy of confidence in his engagements. Any information or instruction which any person may give him, will be worthily bestowed; and if he should apply particularly to Gov. Clarke on his way, the Governor will especially oblige me by imparting to him his information and advice. (Pierson, *Monticello:* 22–23.)

On November 12 Jefferson had the misfortune to fall down a flight of terrace steps, breaking his left arm near the wrist. Fortunately the bones knitted rapidly, but owing to excessive swelling, he was never able to use his arm again with perfect freedom. Both of his arms were now incapacitated.

Jefferson made only one trip to *Poplar Forest* during the year, the visit lasting from May 14 to May 28.

Nothing new appeared in the garden this year. The Calendar was kept as usual.

² See letter, Jefferson to Bernard Peyton, February 20, 1821.

³ George Divers, of *Farmington*, Albemarle County.

⁴ Mrs. Henry Dearborn, second wife of General Henry Dearborn. See her letter to Jefferson, December 16, 1815.

⁵ Mrs. Anne Cary (Randolph) Bankhead.

⁶ T. B., Tennis Ball; D. B., Dutch Brown lettuce.

⁷ David Higginbotham, of *Morven*, Albemarle County.

### LETTERS AND EXTRACTS OF LETTERS, 1822

(Jefferson to John W. Eppes.)

Monticello Jan. 17. 1822.

. . . I send mr̄s Eppes 2. trees of the most beautiful kinds known. The tallest is the *silk tree* from Asia. it will require housing about 2. years more and will then bear the open air safely. the mother tree growing here, about 15. years old and 25. f. high & still growing vigorously has stood winters which have killed my Azederacs & mulberries. the other is the celebrated *Bow wood* of Louisiana which may be planted in the spring where it is to stand as it bears our climate perfectly. it bears a fruit of the size and appearance of an orange, but not eatable. . . . (*Jefferson Papers,* U. Va.)

(Samuel Maverick to Jefferson.)

Montpelier, Pendleton District,
So: Carolina, March 4th, 1822.

I wrote you the inclosed Letter 11th Augt. last, but having in a few days after to go to Alabama, it was neglected until my return, and now take the Liberty to forward it, making enquiry respecting the Grape Vine. [See letter, Maverick to Jefferson, August 11, 1821.]

would not the Tea plant and the Bread fruit Tree be Valuable to those people who will indure the long tedious warm summers of Alabama, etc. there cotton grows so Luxuriantly as to produce 6 to 1200 lbs. and in some instances 1500 to 2000 lbs cotton in the Seed per Acre (Green Seed).

the Cultivation of the Vine has commenced on the Black warrior River by the Settlement of Frenchmen, but with what success I am unable to say, as I did not go so low by 70 miles, I saw several of the frenchmen. they appear confident of success of the Vine. in So. Ca. at Charleston the olive Tree looks helthy and well and some years produces fruit.

any Ideas respecting or on the Culture of the Vine, will be thankfully recd. . . . (Ford, *Jefferson Correspondence:* 269.)

(James W. Wallace to Jefferson.)

Washington April 5. 1822.

. . . In October 1811, I was at Monticello and well remember your account of a native grape like our common Fox grape. I have ever-since extended my enquiries and have only of late been able to procure some cuttings for you which I obtained in New York under the name of bland grape, carried there from Philadelphia which flourishes equally well in either City. To these I add some, given to me on the Delaware in the Steam boat, said to have been introduced by Joseph Bonaparte from France, called *Muscatel*—the account of their qualities so exactly resembles the one I heard you give that I am induced to believe tis a favorite grape with you, but, have no recollection of the name you gave it. These will be given to Mr. Nelson of Albemarle to whose politeness on this occasion their safe arrival will depend—they I expect will be well secured. (*Jefferson Papers*, L. C.)

(Jefferson to Richard Randolph.)

Monticello May 13. 1822.

Your favor of Apr. 10. was received in due time as had been some time before the 6. barrels of water proof cement from you. I had already laid in as much Roman cement as did my 2ᵈ. & 3ᵈ. Cisterns, with a barrel surplus towards the 4ᵗʰ and last. the 2ᵈ. and 3ᵈ. were done under the superintendance of mr Coffee, and with perfect success. we opened a barrel of yours and he tried several fair and careful experiments according to the directions you had given. in every instance this cement dissolved on being put into water, while we saw that the Roman became immediately set and hard on being put into water. I have still one cistern to finish, but after the unsuccessful trials by mr̄ Coffee who understood the manipulation of these things so much better than I do, I am afraid to risk it with yours. it would be giving up a finishing of the success of which we are certain for one which our experience teaches us to doubt at least. there is no call at the University for any thing of the kind nor could I recommend to that what I am afraid to try myself. in this state of things I will make any disposition of the 6. barrels you will direct. but seeing no probability of their being employed in this neighborhood, I think the best would be to send them down to you, which I will do if you think so also. I do not know whether you continue your pottery. if you do I will request of you 50. pots for the seakale such as you saw here, which indeed are made on the exact model of mr̄ Wickham's. if delivered packed in hogsheads to the order of Colᵒ. Peyton, he will, on sight of this letter, pay for them. . . . (*Jefferson Papers*, M. H. S.)

(Richard Randolph to Jefferson.)

Richmond 30ᵗʰ May 1822.

The six barrels of hydraulic cement were sent to you with a belief that they would answer the purpose for which it was intended, and be useful to you in the construction of your cisterns. I am sorry that you are afraid to hazard the success of it in the cistern, and request you to use them in any way that you may think proper. Perhaps you may have occasion to use it at the Mill. Majʳ Gibbon has a cistern laid, and lined, with that cement, which, after standing ten days, was filled, and is now getting quite hard, and holds water perfectly. I have given directions for your bleaching pots to be made, and as soon as they are done, shall be delivered to Colᵒ. Peyton. . . . (*Jefferson Papers*, M. H. S.)

(Jefferson to John Adlum.)

Monticello June 13. 22.

. . . I am very glad to learn that you are pushing that culture, and I hope you will particularly that of what I would call the Caumartin grape, as it's wine resembles so exactly that of the Caumartin Burgundy. I presume you know that a wine of remarkable merit is made in considerable quantities in a district of N. Carolina on the Scuppernon Creek. . . . (*Jefferson Papers*, L. C.)

(Bernard Peyton to Jefferson.)

Richmond, July 8, 1822.

I rec^d today a small Box of seeds from New York. Will send them the first opportunity. . . . (*Jefferson Papers*, M. H. S.)

(Jefferson to J. Peter Derieux.)

Monticello Sept. 25. 1822.

. . . I regret that it is not in my power to send you the Egyptian wheat which is the subject of your letter. I received it while I lived in Washington and having no means of taking care of such things there, I generally sent them to some careful neighbors. I do not recollect to whom of them I sent this particular article, but I remember that the result was that it was not of advantageous culture in our climate & was therefore abandoned. . . . (*Jefferson Papers*, L. C.)

(Virginia Randolph to Nicholas Trist.)

Monticello October 1, 1822.

. . . We have had constant rains, & on the 25^th of September a violent storm which strewed the whole mountain top with broken boughs of trees, & tore one of our willows completely asunder. . . . (*Nicholas Trist Papers*, L. C.)

(Jefferson to Constantine S. Rafinesque.)

Monticello Oct. 9. 22.

Your favor of Sep. 24. is received, and I thank you for the seeds it covered. too old to plant trees for my own gratification, I shall do it for my posterity. . . . (*Jefferson Papers*, M. H. S.) [The seeds mentioned above were from the tree *Virgilia fragrans* Raf.]

(Jefferson to N. Herbemont.)

Monticello Nov. 3. 22.

. . . I have long earnestly wished for the introduction of the Olive into S. Carolina & Georgia. while in France I procured for the Agricultural Society of Charleston a number of plants of the genuine olive of Aix, from which the finest oil in the world is made. this was 35 years ago, but I learn that some of these trees are still living in S. C. cuttings from them grafted on seedling stocks would soon yield a plentiful supply of trees. their culture is of little labor, as is that of silk also. . . . (*Jefferson Papers*, L. C.)

## From the *Account Book 1821–1826:*

July 18.   inclosed 5. D. to Jonathan Thompson Collector N. Y. to reimburse 2.47 for freight on a box of seeds from France.

Oct. 15.   had a final settlement with Edmund Bacon & paid him 41.90 the balance due him in ful.

Oct. 16.   p$^d$. Edm$^d$ Bacon 20.75 more to correct error in yesterday's settlement.

Nov. 10.   p$^d$. Israel for 100 cabbages 3. D.

Dec. 11.   p$^d$. Gill 53 cabbages 1.59.

# 1823

| 1823 [1] | where | when | to table | |
|---|---|---|---|---|
| May peas........ | ........ | Feb. 22. | May 11. | Apr. 19. blossom.    26. pod |
| Leitch's d°...... | ........ | ........ | .... 20. | .... 22. blossom.    28. pod |
| Frames.......... | ........ | ........ | .... 21. | .... 27. blossom    May 7. pod |
| lettuce.......... | | | | |
| Radish.......... | | | | |
| S. Spinach [2]...... | | | | |
| Hotspurs......... | ........ | Mar. 1. | June 1. | Apr. 28. blossom [bad peas and |
| | | | | to be discontin^d. |
| Marrow fats...... | ........... | .... 3. | .... 5. | May 2. blossom. |
| Dutch brown..... | | | | |
| Savoys........... | ........ | .... 5. | | |
| early York....... | | | | |
| Salsafia......... | ........ | .... 14. | | |
| Carrots.......... | | | | |
| Sprout Kale...... | | | | |
| Marrow fats...... | ........ | .... 15. | | |
| Spinach.......... | | | | |
| parsley.......... | | | | |
| Salsafia......... | ........ | .... 17. | | |
| parsneps......... | | | | |
| beet............. | ........ | .... 19. | | |
| orach............ | ........ | .... 20. | | |
| marrow fats...... | ........ | Apr. 1. | | |
| snaps............ | ........ | ........ | June 1. | |
| long haricots..... | ........ | .... 2. | | |
| tomatas.......... | | | | |
| okra............. | | | | |
| nasturtium....... | ........ | ........ | ........ | not a single seed produced.[3] |
| Limas........... | | | | |
| Scarlets.......... | ........ | .... 3. | | |
| white haricots..... | ........ | .... 4. | | |
| Marrow fats...... | ........ | .... 14. | | |
| forw^d Cucumbers.. | ........... | .... 17. | ........ | May 10. up |
| Benni........... | | | | |
| squashes......... | | | | |
| gerkins.......... | | | | |
| Snaps............ | ........ | .... 26. | | |
| Snaps............ | ........ | May 10. | | |
| Dutch brown..... | ........ | Sep. 2. | ........ | }abundance for winter & spring. |
| winter Spinach.... | ........ | Sep. 3. | ........ | |

Compend of a Calendar [4]

Jan. last week.   plant forward potatoes.

Feb.  1.   lettuce. radish. spinach. carrots. from this
           time to Sep. 30. sow lettuce every Monday
           morning and radishes with yᵉ early sowings

      15.  May peas. and Frame peas. spinach. celery.

Mar.  1.   Hotspurs. Marrow fats. spinach. parsley.
           cabbage. onions. celery.

      15.  Marrow fats. carrots. salsafia. beet. orach

Apr.  1.   Marrow fats. snaps. Lima beans. long hari-
           cots. white dᵒ. scarlet beans. tomatas. okra.
           nasturtium. orach. parsneps. cucumbers

      15.  Marrow fats. snaps. squashes. Jerus. arti-
           chokes

May.  1.   melons. Gerkins. Benni. snaps

      15.  snaps.

Aug.  1.   may peas for autumn. turneps.

      15.  carrots for the spring. Spinach for winter.
           snaps. lettuce for winter

Sep.  1.   sow Spinach, a full crop for winter use. let-
           tuce weekly to Sep. 30

---

[1] *1823*.  Jefferson was now eighty years old.  His finances were in a deplorable state.  Both of his arms were so crippled that they were almost useless to him.  His disposition was to carry on, and he did it with a brave spirit.  His grand-

daughters wrote many of his letters, which continued to cover a wide range of interests. Little attention, however, was given to agricultural matters in them.

His first interest, the University of Virginia, was nearing its completion. Needless to say, it still presented problems.

Jefferson's health was discouraging in the spring. He wrote to William Short on March 28:

> The bone of my arm is well knitted and strong, but the carpal bones, having been disturbed, maintain an oedematous swelling of the hand and fingers, keeping them entirely helpless and holding up no definite term for the recovery of their usefulness. I am now in the 5th months of this disability. (Ford, *Jefferson* 12: 283.)

By November he was better and on the fourth wrote to Lafayette:

> After much sickness, and the accident of a broken and disabled arm, I am again in tolerable health, but extremely debilitated, so as to be scarcely able to walk in my garden. (Lipscomb and Bergh, *Jefferson* 15: 494.)

Jefferson made a month's visit to *Poplar Forest* in the spring. It was his last visit to the estate where he had spent many quiet and happy months. In letters written to Francis Eppes on May 1, 1824, and April 6, 1825 (*q. v.*), he intimated proposed trips to *Poplar Forest,* but there is no indication that he made them. In his will *Poplar Forest* was left to Francis Eppes, his grandson. In October visits were made to James Barbour at *Barboursville,* and to Mr. Madison at *Montpelier.*

In a letter of May 31 to Thomas Leiper, after thanking him for millet seed, he wrote:

> I shall turn it over to my grandson T. J. Randolph, to whom I have committed the management of the whole of my agricultural concerns, in which I was never skilful and am now entirely unequal from age and debility. He had recd. some seed of the same kind from another quarter and had sowed an acre & a half by way of experiment. To this he will add what you are so kind as to send if it comes in time. (Ford, *Jefferson* 12: 286–287.)

Keeping the Calendar of the garden was again Jefferson's chief agricultural pursuit.

² Summer spinach.

PLATE XXXVI.—East view of *Poplar Forest*, showing the main house, kitchen, and smokehouse (ca. 1944). At the left is a portion of one of the two mounds. See Jefferson's planting plans for *Poplar Forest* (pp. 464, 465, 494, 549, 563). (Courtesy of Mr. C. S. Hutter, Jr.)

³ See letters, Jefferson to Bernard Peyton, May 6, 1824, and Peyton to Jefferson, May 10, 1824.

⁴ Jefferson's summary of the planting dates for vegetables in his garden.

## LETTERS AND EXTRACTS OF LETTERS, 1823

(André Thoüin to Jefferson.)

Paris February 5, 1823.

[Mr. Thouin sends Jefferson a collection of 107 species of grains, cereals, trees, and legumes. Letter in French.]      (*Jefferson Papers,* L. C.)

(Frank Carr to Jefferson.)

Red Hill, Sept. 26ᵗʰ. 1823.

Instead of the seed, I send you three potatoe pumpkins. The two smallest, I should think from their form, are the most genuine. The fourth is a cushaw, (my ear directs the orthography as I have only heard the name,) not inferior, when thoroughly ripe, in their edible qualities to the potatoe pumpkin. Both delight in a light, moist soil. fresh land is very propitious to their growth. You would seldom fail, I think to grow them successfully in a situation selected with reference to the above description. . . . (*Carr-Cary Papers,* U. Va.)

# 1824

| 1824 [1] | where | when | to table | | |
|---|---|---|---|---|---|
| May peas.......... | submur!.. | Feb. 19. | May 24. | Apr. 25. 1st. blossom. | May 2. pod. |
| Frames............ | und[r] shop | .... 20. | May 28. | .................. | May 9. pod |
| lettuc. wh. & Br, ice[2]. | } ......... | .... 21. | | | |
| radish, leather coal... | } | | | | |
| winter spinach....... | | .... 25. | | | |
| d[o]................. | | Mar. 1. | | | |
| lettuce wh. & Brown.. | | | | | |
| Frame peas........ | Sq. I..... | | | | |
| Marrow fats G. & L.. | II.... | .... 3. | | | |
| Green Savoys........ | | .... 5. | | | |
| Sprout Kale........ | | | | | |
| Marrow fats {Richm[d 3] S. Car.[4] | ......... | .... 20. | | | |
| Salsafia........... | | | | | |
| Carrots........... | | | | | |
| Beets........... | | | | | |
| Orach........... | | | May 15. | | |
| Spinach......... | | | | | |
| green Savoy........ | | .... 25. | | | |
| Marrow fats. Richn[d] | | Apr. 1. | | | |
| d[o]. small parcel S.C.[5] | | | | | |
| snaps............. | | .... 3. | June 5. | May. 26. blossom. | |
| Lima beans....... | | | | | |
| long haricots..... | | .... 6. | | | |
| scarlet beans..... | | | June 16. | | |
| Chick peas........ | | | | | |
| dwarf Tomatas.... | | .... 12. | | | |
| Benni........... | | | | | |
| early Cucumbers.... | | | .... 27. | | |
| Marrow fats...... | | .... 15. | | | |
| Snaps........... | | .... 21. | | | |
| squashes......... | | | | | |
| Snaps........... | | May 3. | | | |
| Gerkins......... | | | | | |
| Nasturtium[6]...... | | .... 13. | ........ | from Richmond. very late | |
| Guinea grass...... | | .... 17. | | | |
| snaps........... | | .... 31. | | | |
| W. Spinach........ | | Sep. 9. | | | |
| D. Brown let...... | | | | | |
| W. Spinach........ | | .... 15. | | | |
| D. Brown let...... | | | | | |

[1] *1824.* Jefferson brought the *Garden Book* to its close in the fall of 1824. The culture of the earth had been one of his constant joys. The theory of this culture had fascinated him, even though he had never been able to apply it profitably. For the remaining two years of his life, declining health even deprived him of tabulating the garden Calendar.

Lafayette visited *Monticello* in November. This renewal of friendship gave Jefferson much happiness. Building the University of Virginia and employing professors to instruct in it, still came first in Jefferson's life. The University opened its doors for instruction on March 5, 1825. On April 3 following, Jefferson wrote to Judge Augustus B. Woodward:

> Withdrawn by age from all other public services and attentions to public things, I am closing the last scenes of life by fashioning and fostering an establishment for the instruction of those who are to come after us. I hope its influence on their virtue, freedom, fame and happiness, will be salutary and permanent. The form and distributions of its structure are original and unique, the architecture chaste and classical, and the whole well worthy of attracting the curiosity of a visit. (Lipscomb and Bergh, *Jefferson* 16: 117.)

Plants and seeds came from Jefferson's friends and there were also letters about them. The year 1825 was the last one in which he ordered seeds.

Among Jefferson's last botanical interests was the establishment of a botanical garden at the University of Virginia. He wrote to the Proctor, A. S. Brockenbrough, on August 3, 1825: "The botanical garden, after being laid off under the direction of Dr. Emmett, to be pursued at all spare time" (*Jefferson Papers,* L. C.). And on April 26, 1826, he wrote to Dr. John P. Emmet, professor of natural history at the University, about the introduction of a School of Botany and the details for establishing a botanical garden in the University (see letter, Jefferson to Dr. John P. Emmet, April 27, 1826). The botanical garden was never established.

Jefferson's pecuniary problems gradually grew worse. None of his plans for relieving them suceeded. The worry over these and his growing debility brought his life to a close on July 4, 1826.

[2] Lettuce, white, & Brown, ice.

[3] Richmond. See letter, Bernard Peyton to Jefferson, March 22, 1824.

4, 5 South Carolina.

6 See letter, Jefferson to Bernard Peyton, May 6, 1824; and letter, Peyton to Jefferson, May 10, 1824.

### From the *Account Book 1821–1826:*

July   4. 1824.   drew on dº. [Raphael] for 11. D. my s[u]bscript[io]n to Albemarle Agricultl. society. payable to Peter Minor.

Sept. 29. 1824.   desired him [B. Peyton] also to deposite in some bank of Richmd to the credit of Edmund Bacon 33. D. which finally closes my account with Bacon, principal & all interest.   See ante.   Aug. 1823.

### From the *Farm Book:*

1824. Apr.   Genl Cocke says the Peach tree worm is hatching all July, Aug. Sep. and lays it's egg immediately on being hatched. it may be seen & taken out from Mar. to June.   it should always be done before harvest.

### LETTERS AND EXTRACTS OF LETTERS, 1824, 1825, 1826

### (William Mewburn to Jefferson.)

South East, 8 Feby. 1824.

William Mewburn has the honour of presenting to Mr. Jefferson his highest respects, & hopes for his excuse in the liberty taken by sending the enclosed to his care.

The inclosure contains a few seeds of the cowslip & primrose, recd by WM in a letter from England, it is believed there are none in the United States & hoped they will be acceptable to Mrs. Randolph.

They are enclosed to Mr. Jefferson, because it is expected the letter to him will receive more care & attention than by any other mode WM has been able to devise. . . . WM has been lately in correspondence with Mr. Willis of Maryland for fruit trees, in raising of which, the Editor of the American Farmer, states that Gentleman to have been emminently successful.   Mr. Willis in his letter, mentions his high obligations to Mr. Jefferson, for which he expresses great gratitude. (*Jefferson Papers,* Missouri.)

### (James Wilkinson to Jefferson.)

City of Mexico
March 21st. 24.

It is rather to gratify curiosity than from the expectation of utility, that I send you by Mr. McAndrews of Phila samples of a few of the

Seeds of this Country, to amuse your Agricultural avocations; and therefore should they be turned either to pleasure or profit under your fostering direction, I shall experience unexpected complacency.—Should Col. Randolph be near you; I will thank you to furnish Him specimens, for experiment, from the small stock I send you, which must be ascribed to the entire destitution of Seeds-man or Shop, in this filthy monstrous City. Before I leave the Country (I would even it were Tomorrow & forever) I will take measures to have you supplied with some seed Wheat, from the ensuing Crop, which begins to invite the sickle in the Province of Puebla the next month. . . . (*Jefferson Papers*, L. C.)

Mexico, March 21st, 1824.

Seed & Grain committed to the care of W. [Mc]Andrews For Mr. Jefferson.

*Chirmolla,* Avocate, Zapote, J Mamae arborous, tropical Fruits.
*Beans* in great variety, called Frijol; & composing the chief aliment of the natives.
*Two kinds of early corn,* 1 red, 1 white. Flour & 2 white of wheat.
*Cantilope* from tierra Galunte [= Caliente].
*Large Pepper,* a good salad the seeds being removed.
*Carrots* 12 inches in circumference—Lentilles to be drilled 2 ft apart.
*Garravances,* a favorite vegetable of the Potagé.
*Small white* Table Pea.
*Chilikiote* a kind of Pumpkin used as Cucumber for Ragouts when Young & tender. When ripe the Entrails cleansed of the seed & stewed with Syrup makes a sweet [mash] of this Country.
*Large white Cabbage,* white onion, Tomata, Beets, Lettuce, Artichoke, Radish, Parsly, Turnips. (*Jefferson Papers*, L. C.)

(Bernard Peyton to Jefferson.)

Richmond, March 22, 1824.

On Friday last I sent you by a waggon, to Charlottesville—one and an half Gallons best Marrow Fat Peas, which I hope will reach you in time for your purposes. By a waggon a few days prior to the one above referred to, sent you a Box of Grape cuttings, sent to my Counting House, by Dr. Norton of this City, without directions, he tells me they were intended for Jefferson Randolph. Please acquaint him with it. . . . (*Jefferson Papers*, M. H. S.)

(Jefferson to Francis Eppes.)

Mont[icell]o May 1. 24.

. . . I am engaged in a piece of work here which will probably detain me till the next month, when I hope I may be able to pay you a short visit. . . . (*Huntington Library Quarterly* 6 (3): 355, 1943.)

(Jefferson to Bernard Peyton.)

Monticello May 6. 1824.

. . . I missed raising Nasturtium seed the last year and it is not to be had in this neighborhood.  can your seedsmen furnish it?  the quantity sufficient to sow a bed of 10 yd & 19.  the seed may come by mail as the season is passing by. . . . (*Jefferson Papers*, M. H. S.)

(Bernard Peyton to Jefferson.)

Richmond May 10, 1824.

. . . The seed you write for, I have procured & just put them in the hands of Col. Randolph, now on his way to Monticello, for you. . . . (*Jefferson Papers*, M. H. S.)

(Jefferson to Bernard Peyton.)

Monticello May 16. 24.

A neighborhood debt obliges me to draw on you in favor of John Winn for 64.85 which I do with reluctance until we get tob°. down, or receive monies due.  M$^r$. Thompson Collector of N. York has sent to your care for me a box of seeds from France for which he has paid charges 1. D. 90 c.  can you remit so small a sum . . . ? (*Jefferson Papers*, M. H. S.)

(Jefferson to J. Barnes.)

Monticello June 3. 24.

. . . I am quite in good health not able to walk further than my garden. . . . (*Jefferson Papers*, M. H. S.)

(Jefferson to the Marquis de Lafayette.)

Monticello, Sept. 3. 24.

. . . I see you are to visit our Yorktown on the 19th of Oct.  My spirit will be there, my body cannot.  I am too much enfeebled by age for such a journey.  I cannot walk further than my garden, with infirmities too which can only be nursed at home. . . . (Ford, *Jefferson* 12: 376.)

(Jefferson to David Gelston.)

Mont°. Sep. 10. 24.

I have duly received your favor of the 4$^{th}$. covering a specimen of wheat, for which be pleased to accept my thanks.  withdrawn by age from all agricultural attentions I have made the most advantageous disposition of it by consigning it to the Agricultural society of my county, who will give it a fair trial. . . . (*Jefferson Papers,* M. H. S.)

## (Thomas Appleton to Jefferson.)

Leghorn October 8, 1824.

. . . As the vessel has delayed her Departure, I am enabled to send you a small collection of garden seeds of Naples, which though I wrote for six months ago, I received, only yesterday, as they are all of this year. The herbage of Naples, is the finest, I have seen in any part of Europe. Their numerous qualities of Broccoli, is not, anywhere equalled. Their Cauli-flowers which I have seen at Naples, would not enter, into a peck-measure. The Fennel, is beyond, every other vegetable, Delicious. It greatly resembles in appearance the largest size Sellery, perfectly white, and there is no vegetable, equals it in flavour. It is eaten at Dessert, crude, and, with, or without Dry Salt, indeed, I preferred it to every other vegetable, or to any fruit. I think they will all thrive in your climate; the experiment may compensate the Labour. . . . No. 22. is the genuine flax seed of Cremona which invariably sells for Double of all other flax of Europe or Africa. It will be a valuable acquisition, if it should thrive in your climate: of which, I have little, or no Doubt. The Seeds I have perfectly well packed, thus there can be no mixture.

No. 1.   Curled cabbage.
"    2.   Curled Schiane cabbage.
"    3.   Curled Cabbage of Paisinetta.
"    4.   Early cabbage.
"    5.   Curled cabbage, Different quality from 3.
"    6.   Broccoli of Palermo, in January.
"    7.   "    "    "    , in February.
"    8.   "    "    "    , Feb. 7, different quality.
"    9.   "    of March, Naples.
"    10.   "    of Palermo, March.
"    11.   "    of Palermo, March, 2. diff. quality.
"    12.   "    of Romani, March.
"    13.   "    of October.
"    14.   "    of December.
"    15.   "    Black.
"    16.   "    of Florence.
"    17. Cauliflower of February.
"    18.   "    of March.
"    19.   "    of December.
"    20. Fennel of April.
"    21.   "    of December.
"    22. Cremona flax-seed.

(*Jefferson Papers,* L. C.)

(Jefferson to Edward Livingston.)

Monticello, March 25, 1825.

. . . Worn down by time in bodily strength, unable to walk even into my garden without too much fatigue. . . . (Lipscomb and Bergh, *Jefferson* 16: 112.)

(Jefferson to Francis Eppes.)

Mont[icell]o Apr. [6, 1825]

The difficulty with which I write, my aversion to it, and the satiating dose which is forced upon me by an overwhelming correspondence have occasioned me to be thus late in acknoleging the rec[eip]t of your letter of Feb. 24.    I was glad to learn the damage to your house by fire was less considerable than I had supposed.    John Heming and his two aids have been engaged in covering this house with tin which is not yet finished.    they shall repair to your assistance as soon as I can accompany them, which shall be as soon as the roads become practicable.    I would rather you should do nothing more than shelter by slabs or other temporary coverings the uncovered parts of the house, any want of sawing which you can foresee had better be obtained while Cap[tai]n Martin's sawmill has water.    for the terras, joists of the length and breadth of the former will be needed but they may be 3. I. thick only as we can make the gutters in a different way which will for ever protect the joists from decay.    pine would be the best timber—heart poplar will do, oak is too springey.    I will desire Colo[nel] Peyton to send up tin for covering the dwelling house.

I will bring with me a plat of the land as you desire, but mr Yancey knows so well the line between Cobb[s] and myself; that I am sure he can point it out.    so also can the surveyor who run the lines. . . . (*Huntington Library Quarterly* 6 (3): 355–356, 1943.)

(Jefferson to Thomas Worthington.)

Monticello, Nov. 29. 25.

You will startle at the receipt of this letter as if it were from the dead; and indeed the ordinary term of man's life says I ought to have been so sometime.    however, here I am as yet, not in very good health indeed, but as good perhaps as I ought to expect; and avail myself of a little circumstance to take occasion to recall myself to your recollection. I have pasted the text of my letter at it's head.    but texts cut out of a newspaper are not like those of holy writ, articles of faith.    and the object of my letter is to ask you if this text is really true?    and if it is to request further that you will procure for me and send in a letter by mail half a dozen seeds of these mammoth cucumbers.    one of 4 f. 6 i long, and another of 4 f. 5¾ should afford so many seeds as to spare a few to a beggar.    altho giants do not always beget giants, yet I should count on their improving the breed, and this vegetable being a great favorite of mine, I wish to take the chance of an improvement.    but whether suc-

cessful or not I shall find my reward in the occasion it furnishes of re-
calling myself to your recollection and of assuring you of my constant
esteem and respect. (Ford, *Jefferson Correspondence:* 298.)

### (Thomas Worthington to Jefferson.)

Adena (near Chillicothe), 7 Jany. 1826.

I did not receive your letter of the 29th Nov. until yesterday. You
had directed it to Cincinnati, from whence it was returned to me here
which has occasioned the delay. I cannot very well express the pleasure
its receipt has given me. I believe, sir, you were sensible of the sincere
respect and affection I entertained for you whilst you were in office.
My continuation in the Senate under the administration of others I can
say with truth encreased both, which to this moment remain unabated.
I have often in my rambles determined to call on you, but have been
deterred by the consideration that you were too much troubled in that
way, and from the same causes contrary to my inclination have not
written to you. I rejoice to hear you enjoy as much health as you do,
and hope it will be better and long continued to you with the faculties
of your mind to enable you to see your most sanguine expectations exceeded in the extraordinary strides of a nation which under providence
you have had so great a share in the establishment of its independence
towards physical strength, wealth, and rational happiness beyond any
thing history gives us knowledge. What was Ohio in 1821, when as
the agent of the people I presented myself before the national Legislature requesting their admission as a state. A population less than
40,000. What is she now. Her forests changed to cultivated fields
and her population at this time at least 1,000,000 and most probably at
the next census 11 or 12,000,000. Pardon me, my good sir, for troubling you with what you already know. I could not help noticing
hastily what I have done, under the belief that you have great pleasure
in seeing the rising greatness of the nation. I had noticed the extraordinary growth of cucumbers of which [you] refer, but paid no attention to it. I am much gratified to have it in my power to ascertain
the truth, and, if true, to get some of the seed. Our Legislature are in
session and a member with whom I am well acquainted and can relie
[upon], and who lives in Cleveland will give me the whole truth and
get some of the seed, if true. As soon as this is done, I will do myself
the pleasure to write again.[1] . . . (Ford, *Jefferson Correspondence:*
299–300.)

[1] Governor Worthington later sent a letter received from Leonard Case,
of Columbus, Ohio, dated January 13, 1826, in which he said:

The story of the cucumbers as published in the Cleveland Herald I have not
the least doubt is correct; I did not go to see them myself but heard them spoken
of at the time by Gentleman of the strictest veracity who said they had seen the
measurement. Dr. Long is himself a Gentleman who would not have suffered
a statement of that kind to go uncontradicted if it had not been true. When I
return home I will endeavor to procure some of the seed and forward to you as
you request. (Ford, *Jefferson Correspondence:* 300.)

(Jefferson to James Monroe.)

Monticello, Feb. 22. 26.

. . . A Virginia estate managed rigorously well yields comfortable subsistence to it's owner living on it, but nothing more. But it runs him in debt annually if at a distance from him, if he is absent, if he is unskilful as I am, if short crops reduce him to deal on credit, and most assuredly if thunder struck from the hand of a friend as I was. . . . (Ford, *Jefferson* **12**: 460–461.)

(Ellen (Randolph) Coolidge to Jefferson.)

Boston, March 8, 26.

. . . I know not whether my sisters mentioned to you the wish of M^r John Gray, son of the late Lieutenant Governor Gray, to procure some slips of a cider apple which he understands you have, & consider one of the best in the State. I presume it to be not the Crab, for that is common in other parts of Virginia, but a red apple, which I remember you prized for its cider, and Horace Gray, who visited you some years ago, was the person who spoke of it to his brother in such a way as makes him anxious to obtain & propagate it here. . . . (*Jefferson Papers,* M. H. C. **1**: 373.)

(Jefferson to Ellen (Randolph) Coolidge.)

Monticello, Mar. 19, 26.

Your letter of the 8^th was received the day before yesterday, and as the season for engrafting is passing rapidly by I will not detain the apple-cuttings for Mr Gray (until I may have other matter for writing a *big* letter to you), but I send a dozen cuttings, as much as a letter can protect, by our 1^st mail, and wish they may retain their vitality until they reach him. They are called the Taliaferro apple, being from a seedling tree discovered by a gentleman of that name near Williamsburg, and yield unquestionably the finest cyder we have ever known, and more like wine than any liquor I have ever tasted which was not wine. If it is worth reminding me of the ensuing winter, I may send a larger supply, and in better time, through Col. Peyton. . . . (*Jefferson Papers,* M. H. C. **1**: 373–374.)

(Jefferson to Leonard Case.)

Monticello Apr. 8. 26.

The seeds of the Serpentine cucumber which you have been so kind as to send me at the request of my friend m͞r Worthington are safely come to hand. how much of their extraordinary size may be ascribed to the exuberant soil and the climate of Ohio cannot be foreseen, but that a good portion of it may be retained we are permitted to hope. with my thanks for this friendly and acceptable present be pleased to receive the assurance of my great esteem and respect. (*Jefferson Papers*, M. H. S.)

### (A. B. Woodward to Jefferson.)

Tallahassee, Apr. 21, 1826.

. . . I transmit twelve seeds of the indigenous orange of Florida. . . . (*Jefferson Papers*, L. C.)

### (Jefferson to George Divers.)

Monticello Apr. 22. 26.

You perhaps noted in the newspapers some 3. or 4. months ago the mention of cucumbers in a particular garden in Ohio which measured 2½ f. and 3. f. in length.   having a friend in that quarter I wrote and requested him to procure and send me some seed from one of the identical cucumbers.   he has sent it, and to multiply chances of securing it, I send you 9. seeds, assured that nobody will be more likely to succeed than yourself. . . . (*Jefferson Papers*, M. H. S.)

### (Jefferson to Dr. John P. Emmet.)

Monticello, April 27, 1826.

It is time to think of the introduction of the school of Botany into our institution.   Not that I suppose the lectures can be begun in the present year, but that we may this year make the preparations necessary for commencing them the next.   For that branch, I presume, can be taught advantageously only during the short season while nature is in general bloom, say during a certain portion of the months of April and May, when, suspending the other branches of your department, that of Botany may claim your exclusive attention.   Of this, however, you are to be the judge, as well as of what I may now propose on the subject of preparation.   I will do this in writing, while sitting at my table, and at ease, because I can rally there, for your consideration, with more composure than in extempore conversation, my thoughts on what we have to do in the present season.

I suppose you were well acquainted, by character, if not personally, with the late Abbé Correa, who passed some time among us, first as a distinguished savant of Europe, and afterwards as ambassador of Portugal, resident with our government.   Profoundly learned in several other branches of science, he was so, above all others in that of Botany; in which he preferred an amalgamation of the methods of Linnaeus and of Jussieu, to either of them exclusively.   Our institution being then on hand, in which that was of course to be one of the subjects of instruction, I availed myself of his presence and friendship to obtain from him a general idea of the extent of ground we should employ, and the number and character of the plants we should introduce into it.   He accordingly sketched for me a mere outline of the scale he would recommend, restrained altogether to objects of use, and indulging not at all in things of mere curiosity, and especially not yet thinking of a hot-house, or even of a green house. I enclose you a copy of his paper, which was the more satisfactory to me, as it coincided with the moderate views to which our endowments as yet confine us. I am still the more satisfied, as it seemed to be confirmed by your own way of thinking, as I understood it in our conversation of the other day. To your judgment altogether his ideas will be submitted, as well as my own, now to be suggested as to the operations of the present year, preparatory to the commencement of the school in the next.

1. Our first operation must be the selection of a piece of ground of proper soil and site, suppose of about six acres, as M. Correa proposes. In choosing this we are to regard the circumstances of soil, water, and distance. I have diligently examined all our grounds with this view, and think that that on the public road, at the upper corner of our possessions, where the stream issues from them, has more of the requisite qualities than any other spot we possess.

To wit, 19,360 square yards = 4 acres for the garden of plants.
　　　 9,680 　"　　　"　 = 2 acres for the plants of trees.
　　　29,040 square yards = 6 acres in the whole.

170 yards square, taken at that angle, would make the six acres we want. But the angle at the road is acute, and the form of the ground will be trapezoid, not square. I would take, therefore, for its breath all the ground between the road and the dam of the brick ponds extending eastwardly up the hill, as far and as wide as our quantity would require. The bottom ground would suit for the garden plants; the hillsides for the trees.

2. Operation. Enclose the ground with a serpentine brick wall seven feet high. This would take about 80,000 bricks, and cost $800, and it must depend on our finances whether they will afford that immediately, or allow us, for awhile, but enclosure of posts and rails.

3. Operation. Form all the hillsides into level terrasses of convenient breadth, curving with the hill, and the level ground into beds and alleys.

4. Operation. Make out a list of the plants thought necessary and sufficient for botanical purposes, and of the trees we propose to introduce and take measures in time for procuring them.

As to the seeds of plants, much may be obtained from the gardeners of our own country. I have moreover, a special resource. For three-and-twenty years of the last twenty-five, my good old friend Thouin, superintendent of the garden of plants at Paris, has regularly sent me a box of seeds, of such exotics, as to us, as would suit our climate, and containing nothing indigenous to our country. These I regularly sent to the public and private gardens of the other States, having as yet no employment for them here. But during the last two years this envoi has been intermitted, I know not why. I will immediately write and request a re-commencement of that kind office, on the ground that we can now employ them ourselves. They can be here in early spring.

The trees I should propose would be exotics of distinguished useful-ness, and accommodated to our climate; such as the Larch, Cedar of Libanus, Cork Oak, the Marronnier, Mahogany, the Catachu or Indian rubber tree of Napul, (30°) Teak tree, or Indian oak of Burman, (23°) the various woods of Brazil, etc.

The seed of the Larch can be obtained from a tree at Monticello. Cones of the Cedar of Libanus are in most of our seed shops, but may be had fresh from the trees in the English gardens. The Marronnier and Cork Oak, I can obtain from France. There is a Marronnier at Mount Vernon, but it is a seedling, and not therefore select. The others may be got through the means of our ministers and consuls in the countries where they grow, or from the seed shops of England, where they may very possibly be found. Lastly, a gardener of sufficient skill must be obtained.

This, dear Sir, is the sum of what occurs to me at present; think of it, and let us at once enter on the operations. . . . (Lipscomb and Bergh, *Jefferson* 16: 163–167.)

(Jefferson to John P. Emmet.)

Monticello May 12. 26

By a letter from mr Madison I now learn that Thouin has been dead some time, that his successor sends the box annually to him as Presi-dent of the Agricultural society of Albemarle, that such a box is now arrived at N. York, of which he has notified Secretary Barbour, his suc-cessor. to him I have written requesting it's consignment to us, and the sooner the better as the Season is fast advancing. it may by pos-sibility reach us in 3. or 4. weeks. . . . (*Jefferson Papers,* L. C.)

# APPENDIX I

## Jefferson's Summary of His Meteorological Journal for the Years 1810 through 1816 at Monticello

1817, January.   Having been stationary at home since 1809, with opportunity and leisure to keep a meteorological diary, with a good degree of exactness, this had been done: and, extracting from it a term of seven years complete, to wit from January 1, 1810, to December 31, 1816, I proceed to analyze it in the various ways, and to deduce the general results, which are of principal effect in the estimate of climate. The observations, three thousand nine hundred and five, in the whole, were taken before sunrise of every day; and again between three and four o'clock P. M.   On some days of occasional absence they were necessarily omitted.   In these cases the averages were taken from the days of the same denomination in the other years only, and in such way as not sensibly to affect the average of the month, still less that of the year, and to be quite evanescent in their effect on the whole tenor of seven years.

The table of thermometrical observations, shews the particular temperature of the different years from 1810 to 1816 inclusive.   The most interesting results, however, are that the range of temperature with us may be considered as within the limits of $5\frac{1}{2}°$ and $94°$ of Fahrenheit's thermometer; and that $55\frac{1}{2}°$ degrees as its mean and characteristic measure.   These degrees fix the laws of the animal and vegetable races which may exist with us; and the comfort also of the human inhabitant, so far as depends on his sensations of heat and cold.   Still it must be kept in mind that this is but the temperature of Monticello; that in the northern and western parts of the State, the mean and extremes are probably something lower, and in the southern and eastern, higher.   But this place is so nearly central to the whole State, that it may fairly be considered as the mean of the whole.

It is a common opinion that the climates of the several States, of our Union, have undergone a sensible change since the dates of their first settlements; that the degrees both of cold and heat are moderated.   The same opinion prevails as to Europe; and facts gleaned from history give reason to believe that, since the time of Augustus Caesar, the climate of Italy, for example, has changed regularly, at the rate of $1°$ of Fahrenheit's thermometer for every century.   May we not hope that the methods invented in later times for measuring with accuracy the degrees of heat and cold, and the observations which have been and will be made

622

A TABLE OF THERMOMETRICAL OBSERVATIONS, MADE AT MONTICELLO, FROM JANUARY 1, 1810, TO DECEMBER 31, 1816.

| | 1810. | | | 1811. | | | 1812. | | | 1813. | | | 1814. | | | 1815. | | | 1816. | | | Mean of each Month |
|---|---|---|---|---|---|---|---|---|---|---|---|---|---|---|---|---|---|---|---|---|---|---|
| | Min. | Mean. | Max. | Min. | Mean. | Max. | Min. | Mean. | Max. | Min. | Mean. | Max. | Min. | Mean. | Max. | Min. | Mean. | Max. | Min. | Mean. | Max. | |
| Jan. | 5½ | 38 | 66 | 20 | 39 | 68 | 5½ | 34 | 53 | 13 | 35 | 59 | 16½ | 36 | 55 | 8½ | 35 | 60 | 16 | 34 | 51 | 36 |
| Feb. | 12 | 43 | 73 | | | | 21 | 40 | 75 | 19 | 38 | 65 | 14 | 42 | 65 | 16 | 36 | 57 | 15½ | 41 | 62 | 40 |
| Mar. | 20 | 41 | 61 | 28 | 44 | 78 | 31½ | 46 | 70 | 28 | 48 | 71 | 13½ | 43 | 73 | 31 | 54 | 80 | 25 | 48 | 75 | 46 |
| April | 42 | 55 | 81 | 36 | 58 | 86 | 31 | 56 | 86 | 40 | 59 | 80 | 35 | 59 | 82 | 41 | 60 | 82 | 30 | 49 | 71 | 56½ |
| May | 43 | 64 | 88 | 46 | 62 | 79 | 39 | 60 | 86 | 46 | 62 | 81 | 47 | 65 | 91 | 37 | 58 | 77 | 43 | 60 | 79 | 61½ |
| June | 53 | 70 | 87 | 58 | 73 | 89 | 58 | 74 | 92½ | 54 | 75 | 93 | 57 | 69 | 87 | 54 | 71 | 88 | 51 | 70 | 86 | 72 |
| July | 60 | 75 | 88 | 60 | 76 | 89½ | 57 | 75 | 91 | 61 | 75 | 94½ | 60 | 74 | 89 | 63 | 77 | 89 | 51 | 71 | 86 | 75 |
| Aug. | 55 | 71 | 90 | 59 | 75 | 85 | 61 | 71 | 87 | 62 | 74 | 92 | 56 | 75 | 88 | 58 | 72 | 84 | 51 | 73 | 90 | 73 |
| Sept. | 50 | 70 | 81 | 50 | 67 | 81 | 47 | 68 | 75 | 54 | 69 | 83 | 52 | 70 | 89 | 45 | 61 | 82 | 54 | 63 | 90½ | 67 |
| Oct. | 32 | 57 | 82 | 35 | 62 | 85 | 39 | 55 | 80 | 32 | 53 | 70 | 37 | 58 | 83 | 38½ | 59 | 76 | 37 | 57 | 73 | 57 |
| Nov. | 27 | 44 | 69 | 32 | 45 | 62 | 18 | 43 | 76 | 20 | 48 | 71 | 23 | 47 | 71 | 20 | 46 | 70 | 24 | 46 | 71 | 45½ |
| Dec. | 14 | 32 | 62 | 20 | 38 | 49 | 13 | 35 | 63 | 18 | 37 | 53 | 18 | 38 | 59 | 12 | 36 | 57 | 23 | 43 | 69 | 37 |
| Mean of clear weather | | 55 | | | 58 | | | 55 | | | 56 | | | 56⅓ | | | 55½ | | | 54½ | | 55½ |

and preserved, will at length ascertain this curious fact in physical history?

Within the same period of time, about fifty morning observations, on an average of every winter, were below the freezing point, and ten freezing days for the average of our winters.

It is generally observed that when the thermometer is below 55°, we have need of fire in our apartments to be comfortable. In the course of these seven years, the number of observations below 55°, was as follows:

|  |  |  |  |  |
|---|---|---|---|---|
| In 1810— | 195 | mornings and | 124 | afternoons |
| '11 | 176 | | 102 | |
| '12 | 209 | | 137 | |
| '13 | 197 | | 123 | |
| '14 | 190 | | 127 | |
| '15 | 189 | | 116 | |
| '16 | 172 | | 116 | |
| Average | 190 | | 120 | |

Whence we conclude that we need constant fires four months in the year, and in the mornings and evenings a little more than a month preceding and following that time.

The first white frost in

|  |  |  |  |  |  |
|---|---|---|---|---|---|
| 1809–10 | was October | 25, | the last | April | 11 |
| '10–11 | | 18, | | Mar. | 19 |
| '11–12 | | 21, | | April | 14 |
| '12–13 | | 9, | | | |
| '13–14 | | 22, | | April | 13 |
| '14–15 | | 24, | | May | 15 |
| '15–16 | | 26, | | April | 3 |
| '16–17 | | 7, | | " | 12 |

But we have seen in another period a destructive white frost as early as September.

Our first ice in

|  |  |  |  |  |  |
|---|---|---|---|---|---|
| 1809–10 | was in Nov. | 7, | the last | April | 10 |
| '10–11 | " Oct. | 24, | " | Mar. | 8 |
| '11–12 | " Nov. | 15, | " | April | 12 |
| '12–13 | " " | 13, | " | Mar. | 25 |
| '13–14 | " " | 14, | " | " | 17 |
| '14–15 | " " | 9, | " | " | 22 |
| '15–16 | " " | 13, | " | " | 19 |
| '16–17 | " " | 7, | " | " | 20 |

The quantity of water (including that of snow) which fell in every month and year of the term was as follows.

|  | 1810. | 1811. | 1812. | 1813. | 1814. | 1815. | 1816. | Average of every month |
|---|---|---|---|---|---|---|---|---|
| Jan. | 1.873 | 3.694 | 3.300 | 1.735 | 4.179 | 6.025 | 4.86 | 3.656 |
| Feb. | 4.275 | 2.351 | 4.060 | 1.763 | 3.760 | 5.90 | 2.205 | 3.473 |
| Mar. | 3.173 | 2.295 | 3.090 | 1.750 | 4.386 | 2.96 | 2.825 | 2.926 |
| Apr. | 4.570 | 4.342 | 2.228 | 3.685 | 5.471 | 1.35 | 3.52 | 3.595 |
| May | 2.124 | 3.779 | 14.761 | 2.670 | 7.134 | 2.57 | 6.19 | 5.604 |
| June | 5.693 | 5.574 | 5.565 | 0.799 | 3.450 | 2.94 | 0.33 | 3.470 |
| July | 5.729 | 8.206 | 2.025 | 3.319 | 13.654 | 7.59 | 4.63 | 6.565 |
| Aug. | 1.883 | 5.969 | 8.963 | 3.920 | 3.370 | 3.48 | 0.85 | 4.062 |
| Sept. | 4.908 | 2.923 | 0.630 | 14.224 | 6.834 | 2.32 | 9.91 | 5.964 |
| Oct. | 0.731 | 7.037 | 5.184 | 4.264 | 2.632 | 0.73 | 3.23 | 3.401 |
| Nov. | 6.741 | 0.781 | 1.187 | 3.932 | 4.794 | 2.09 | 0.96 | 2.926 |
| Dec. | 0.333 | 0.5 | 1.232 | 6.658 | 1.259 | 3.55 | 0.36 | 1.556 |
| Average of a year | 42.033 | 47.451 | 53.025 | 45.719 | 60.923 | 41.505 | 39.87 | 47.218 |

From this table we observe that the average of the water which falls in a year is 47¼ inches, the minimum 41½, and the maximum 61 inches, from tables kept by the late Col. James Madison, father of the President of the United States, at his seat about [?] miles from Monticello, from the year 1794 to 1801 inclusive, the average was 43¼ inches, the minimum 35¾ inches, and the maximum 52 inches.

During the same seven years there fell six hundred and twenty two rains, which gives eighty nine rains every year, or one for every four days; and the average of the water falling in the year being 47½ inches, gives fifty three cents of an inch for each rain, or ninety three cents for a week. Were this to fall regularly, or nearly so, through the summer season, it would render our agriculture most prosperous, as experience has sometimes proved.

Of the three thousand nine hundred and five observations made in the course of seven years, two thousand seven hundred and seventy six were fair; by which I mean that the quarter part of the sky was unclouded. This shows our proportion of fair weather to be as two thousand seven hundred and seventy six to one thousand one hundred and twenty nine, or as five to two, equivalent to five fair days to the week. Of the other two, one may be more than half clouded, the other wholly so. We have then five of what observing astronomers call "observing days" in the week; and of course a chance of five to two of observing any astronomical phenomenon which is to happen at any fixed period of time.

The snows of Monticello amounted to the depth in

1809–10 of 16¼ in. and covered the ground 19 days
'10–11 " 31¾ " 31 "
'11–12 " " 11 "
'12–13 " 35 " 22 "
'13–14 " 13¼ " 16 "
'14–15 " 29¾ " 39 "
'15–16 " 23 " 29 "
'16–17 " 19¼ " 19 "
Average—22½ 22

Which gives an average of 22½ inches in a year, covering the ground twenty two days, and a minimum of eleven inches, and eleven days, and a maximum of thirty five inches and thirty nine days. According to Mr. Madison's tables, the average of snow, at his seat, in the winters from 1793 to 1801–2 inclusive, was 23½ the minimum, 10⅛ and maximum, 33½ inches, but I once (in 1772) saw a snow here three feet deep.

The course of the wind having been one of the circumstances regularly observed, I have thought it better, from the observations of the seven years, to deduce an average for a single year and for every month of the year. This table accordingly exhibits the number of days in the year, and in every month of it, during which each particular wind, according to these observations may be expected to prevail. It will be for physicians to observe the coincidences of the diseases of each season, with the particular winds then prevalent, the quantities of heat and rain, &c.

| | N. | N.E. | E. | S.E. | S. | S.W. | W. | N.W. | Total |
|---|---|---|---|---|---|---|---|---|---|
| Jan. | 4 | 1 | 1 | 1 | 5 | 7 | 5 | 7 | 31 |
| Feb. | 3 | 3 | 1 | 1 | 4 | 6 | 4 | 6 | 28 |
| Mar. | 5 | 3 | 2 | 2 | 6 | 5 | 3 | 5 | 31 |
| Apr. | 4 | 2 | 3 | 2 | 7 | 6 | 2 | 4 | 30 |
| May | 5 | 2 | 1 | 1 | 6 | 6 | 4 | 6 | 31 |
| June | 5 | 2 | 1 | 1 | 4 | 6 | 5 | 6 | 30 |
| July | 6 | 2 | 1 | 1 | 6 | 5 | 5 | 5 | 31 |
| Aug. | 6 | 3 | 1 | 2 | 3 | 6 | 4 | 6 | 31 |
| Sept. | 6 | 5 | 1 | 2 | 4 | 4 | 3 | 5 | 30 |
| Oct. | 5 | 2 | 1 | 1 | 5 | 5 | 5 | 7 | 31 |
| Nov. | 7 | 2 | 1 | 1 | 5 | 5 | 5 | 7 | 30 |
| Dec. | 5 | 2 | 1 | 1 | 5 | 5 | 5 | 7 | 31 |
| Total | 61 | 29 | 15 | 16 | 60 | 66 | 47 | 71 | 365 |

|  | Dry | Wet |
|---|---|---|
| N. | 4 | 1 |
| N.E. | 3 | 1 |
| E. | 3 | 1 |
| S.E. | 3½ | 1 |
| S. | 4 | 1 |
| S.W. | 6 | 1 |
| W. | 9⅓ | 1 |
| N.W. | 10¼ | 1 |

In this separate table I state the relation which each particular wind appeared to have with rain or snow: for example, of every five north winds, one was either accompanied with rain or snow, or followed by it before the next observation, and four were dry. Of every four north-easters, one was wet and three, dry. The table consequently shows the degree in which any particular wind enters as an element into the generation of rain, in combination with the temperature of the air, state of clouds, &c.

An estimate of climate may be otherwise made from the advance of the spring, as manifested by animal and vegetable subjects. Their first appearance has been observed as follows.

| | | | | |
|---|---|---|---|---|
| The Red Maple comes into blossom, | from Feb. | 18 | to March | 27 |
| The Almond | " Mar. | 6 | to Apr. | 5 |
| The Peach | " " | 9 | " | 4 |
| The Cherry | " " | 9 | " | 13 |
| The Tick appears | " " | 15 | " | 2 |
| The house Martin | " " | 18 | " | 9 |
| Asparagus comes first to table | " " | 23 | " | 14 |
| The Shad arrives | " " | 28 | " | 18 |
| The Lilac blossoms | " April | 1 | " | 28 |
| The Red bud | " " | 2 | " | 19 |
| The whip-poor-will is heard | " " | 2 | " | 21 |
| The Dogwood blossoms | " " | 3 | " | 22 |
| The wood Robin is heard | " " | 20 | to May | 1 |
| The Locust blooms | " " | 25 | " | 17 |
| The Fringe tree blooms | " " | 27 | " | 5 |
| The red clover first blossoms | " May | 1 | to | |
| The garden pea first at table | " " | 3 | " | 25 |
| Strawberries first ripe | " " | 3 | " | 25 |
| Fire flies appear | " " | 8 | to | |
| Cherries first ripe | " " | 18 | " | 25 |
| Artichokes first at table | " " | 28 | to June | 12 |

| Wheat harvest begins | " | June | 21 | " | 29 |
|---|---|---|---|---|---|
| Cucumbers first at table | " | " | 22 to July | | 5 |
| Indian corn first at table | " | July | 4 to | | |
| Peaches first ripe | " | " | 7 | " | 21 |
| The Sawyer first heard | " | " | 14 | " | 20 |

The natural season of the vegetable is here noted, and not the artificial one produced by glasses, hot-beds &c. which, combining art with nature, would not be a test of the latter separately.

Another index of climate may be sought in the temperature of the waters issuing from fountains. If the deepest of the reservoirs feeding may be supposed at like distances from the surface, in every part of the globe, then the lowest temperature of water, flowing from them, would indicate that of the earth from and through which it flows. This will probably be found highest under the equator, and lower as you recede towards either pole. On an examination of 15 springs in the body of the hill of Monticello, the water of the coolest was $54\frac{1}{2}$, the outer air being then at 75°. A friend assures me that in an open well of 28 feet depth in Maine, lat. 44° 22', and in the month of August, the water in it being then 4 feet deep, its temperature was 52° of Farenheit's thermometer, that of the water of Kenebec river being at the same time $72\frac{1}{2}$.

Lastly, to close the items which designate climate, the latitude of Monticello is to be added, which by numerous observations lately made with a Borda's circle of 5 inches radius, with nonius divisions of 1'. I have found, by averaging the whole, to be 37° 57' 51". (*Virginia Literary Museum, and Journal of Belles Lettres, Arts, Sciences, &c.* (Charlottesville, June 24, 1829) 1 (2): 26–29.)

# APPENDIX II

## THE WATER SUPPLY AT MONTICELLO

### THE WELL

1778. Feb. 23. the water is returned into the well at Monticello, having been now dry for 13 months. it was dug in 1769. it failed once before, to wit, in the fall of 1773. but came to the spring following, when it failed the second time as mentioned above, to wit January 1777, the succeeding spring happened to be remarkeably dry, insomuch that the river did not afford water to carry down tobacco etc. so that the well not being replenished in the spring, had no water all the summer of 1777. 1789 it failed again from beginn^g Oct. to beginn^g Dec. 1796. again in the fall & winter till Feb.

dug in 1769
   failed 1773
       1777
       1789
       1791
       1796
       1797.

1791. the well has failed this year. it has been the dryest summer since 1755.

1797. the well has failed this summer. the spring & summer remarkeably dry till July. then dry again from August.

1799. Sept. 11. the well had got very low this summer (which was dry) so as not always to furnish clear water for drinking, nor water for washing. from the 20^th to the 22^d were 3. days of heavy rain. again from Sept. 2. to 10. were the most constant & heavy rains in this neighborhood which were ever known in the memory of man. at the end of that time there were 28. feet depth of water in the well. the wells in the neighborhood were raised nearly as much. the water perfectly clear and fine.

1803. Mar. 12. The well was observed about a month ago to have a plenty of water in it after having been dry about 18. months.

1818. May. the well is found to have in it a plenty of water, and very fine. it has been several years out of use. (*Weather Memorandum Book 1776–1820, L. C.*)

629

## The Springs on Monticello Mountain

1817. June 15. the circuit of the base of Monticello is 5¼ miles; the area of the base about 890. acres. within the limits of that base I this day tried the temperature of 15. springs, 10 on the South & 5. on the N. side of the mountain, the outward air being generally about 75°. of Farenheit. the springs were as follows.

| South side | | North side | |
|---|---|---|---|
| 10. Bailey's spring | 58½° | 3. Rock spring | 55½° |
| 11. South stone spring | 59 | 9. North road. left | 58½ |
| 5. Ned's | 56½ | 7. d°. right hand | 57½ |
| 14. Abram's | 63½ | 4. falling spring | 56 |
| 15. Lewis's | 66 | 2. N. stone spring | 55 |
| 12. Nailery | 60 | | |
| 1. Overseer's | 54½ | | |
| 8. ragged branch | 58 | | |
| 13. Goodman's | 61 | | |
| 6. mouth of Meadow br. | 57½ | | |

## The Cisterns at Monticello

August 16. 1808.

Supposing 4. f. of rain water to fall in the year, the following calculation shews how much the area of my whole buildings would furnish to cisterns.

| | square feet |
|---|---|
| area of the Dwelling house | 6096 |
| the 2. pavilions 484 × 2 | 968 |
| 2. covered ways, each 90. f. ¾ I. by 10. f. 8. I. | 1922 |
| 2. ranges of offices, each 120. f. 5. I. by 22. f. 10. I. | 5497 |
| the whole buildings ...................... | 14483 = 1609. sq. yds. |
| rain falling in one year .................. | 4 |
| cub. feet falling on them in one year | 57,932 |

$\frac{57,932}{365}$ gives for every day an average of 158.72 cub. feet which at 1.48 gall$^s$ of 231 cub. I. pr. cub. foot gives daily 1187.22 gall$^s$.

& at 126. gall$^s$. per butt. or pipe gives daily 9.42 pipes or butts. (Note a rain of 1. I. gives 11.62 butts of 16.84 cub. f. each or 1201. cub feet = 9028 gall$^s$. (9028.36).

Make 4. cisterns of 8. f. cube each, or 3830. gallons to wit. one on each side of each covered way, near it's angle with the offices and allot to them the water gutters as follows.

| | area sq. f. | Yearly fall | | daily |
| --- | --- | --- | --- | --- |
| | | cub. f. | galls. | galls. |
| to the kitchen the South Western quarter to wit | | | | |
| S.W. spout of S.W. portico | 1041 | 4164 | 31,147 | 85. 33 |
| S.W. dº. of S. piazza | 483 | 1932 | 14,451 | 39.59 |
| internal moiety of S. covered way | 450 | 1800 | 13,464 | 36.88 |
| | 1974 | 7896 | 59,062 | 162. |
| to the Garden the S. Eastern quarter, viz. | | | | |
| S.E. spout of N.E. portico | 1041 | 4164 | 31,147 | 85.33 |
| S.E. dº. of S. piazza | 483 | 1932 | 14,451 | 39.59 |
| external moiety of S. covered way | 511 | 2044 | 15,289 | 41.88 |
| | 2035 | 8140 | 60,887 | 166.80 |
| to the bathing room the N.W. quarter, viz. | | | | |
| N.W. spout of S.W. portico | 1041 | 4164 | 31,147 | 85.33 |
| N.W. spout of N. piazza | 483 | 1932 | 14,451 | 39.59 |
| internal moiety of N. covered way | 450 | 1800 | 13,464 | 36.88 |
| | 1974 | 7896 | 59,062 | 162 |
| to the house & slope the N.E. quarter, viz. | | | | |
| N.E. spout of N.E. portico | 1041 | 4164 | 31,147 | 83.33 |
| N.E. spout of N. piazza | 483 | 1932 | 14,451 | 39.59 |
| external moiety of N. covered way | 511 | 2044 | 15,289 | 41.88 |
| | 2035 | 8140 | 60,887 | 166.80 |
| to the South pond | | | | |
| internal moiety of S. Offices | 1344 | 5375 | 40,205 | 110.15 |
| N. side of S. pavilion | 242 | 968 | 7,240 | 19.83 |
| | 1586 | 6343 | 47,445 | 130. |
| to the North pond | | | | |
| internal moiety of N. offices | 1344 | 5375 | 40,205 | 110.15 |
| S. side of N. pavilion | 242 | 968 | 7,240 | 19.83 |
| | 1586 | 6343 | 47,445 | 130. |
| for irrigating the slopes & for the garden | | | | |
| External moiety of N. offices | 1405 | 5620 | 42,030 | 115.15 |
| dº. of S. offices | 1405 | 5620 | 42,030 | 115.15 |
| N. side of N. pavilion | 242 | 968 | 7,240 | 19.83 |
| S. side of S. dº. | 242 | 968 | 7,240 | 19.83 |
| | 3294 | 13176 | 98,540 | 270. |

The fish pond near the S. pavilion is an Ellipses 5. yds. wide, 10. yds. long = 40. sq. yds, very nearly 1. yard deep = 40. cub. yds. contents. (*Weather Memorandum Book 1776–1820,* L. C.)

# APPENDIX III

Paris Feb. 5. 1786

. . . I wrote to m͞r Lewis soon after I arrived in France to get you to graft me a good number of the fine white, red, & yellow plumb peaches from Balyal's, taking the grafts from the old trees remaining at Balyal's, to plant these in the room of all those which die in my orchard, and in the room of all such as are found to bear indifferent peaches. I hope this has been done & if not, that you will do it the first season. I depend also that you will fill up my apple orchard on the North side of the mountain with the kinds of trees I directed, and winding the rows on a level round the hill as was begun before I came away: and always as soon as any fruit tree dies, replant another of the same kind in it's place, except the peach trees which are always to be replaced with grafted ones from Balyal's. I hope my trees of every kind are taken good care of, and also the grass grounds, & that they go on sowing grass seed where I described. how does my vineyard come on? have there been grapes enough to make a trial of wine? if there should be, I should be glad to receive here a few bottles of the wine. I trust much to you for the replacing my trees which die, and extending them, and that George takes care of them thro' the year so that nothing may hurt them.

I send you inclosed a list of seeds which I wish you to gather for me. they are intended for friends here whom I very much desire to oblige, and I write to you yourself for them that I may be sure to get them. do not let time nor trouble prevent your getting them, I pray you, but go yourself in quest of them at the proper season. I depend much on your skill and care in packing them so that they may neither get too dry, nor yet too moist. I believe that the nuts & acorns had better be packed in sand. besides the seeds &c. send me a leaf or two of every article. the way to do this will be to make a little book of paper of about 30 leaves, a little larger than the largest leaf you are to send. then put one or two leaves of the plants between every two leaves of the book writing the name of the plant in the page of the book where it is placed. do not put leaves of different kinds in the same page. wrap up the book very well that they may not drop out. send all these things to Doctor Currie who will forward them to me. and write me at the same time in Italian a full account of what you send. I shall be glad also if you will write me a very full state of the condition in which my trees, grasses and other matters of that kind are. but put these things into a separate letter from that in which you give me an account of what you send.

* This letter was found too late to be placed in its chronological order. See year, 1786.

there are some of these things which you might send me immediately,
such as persimmons, locusts, walnuts, Cedar, Pride of china, laurel,
Umbrella, acorns of the last year, by which means they would arrive in
time to plant the ensuing fall. besides this I would have you send the
same things again in the fall when you send the others. if you are at a
loss to know any of these plants, I think mr̄s Lewis will be very able to
tell you how to know them. as to the time which you may employ in
doing this business now & whenever I send you the like commissions
hereafter, mr̄ Lewis I am sure will satisfy you, either in the same way
you were always paid by me or in any other more agreeable to you. but
do not let any difficulties of this kind prevent your doing this business,
but rely on me that you shall be satisfied as I rely on you that you will
not let me be disappointed in receiving them, which would be a great
mortification to me. I hope on my return, which will not be very distant I shall find that you & George have kept up my plans well in my
absence. tell him & my other servants that I have their welfare much
at heart: I have left them under the protection of so good a man mr
Lewis, that my mind is tolerably quiet. . . .

[Inclosure]

a list of seeds which Anthony Giannini is desired to send me.

Wild honeysuckle. a gill of the seed.
Haw tree. both black & red. a gill of each.
Persimmon. a pint of the seeds.
Honey locust. a pint of the seeds.
Common locust. two pints of the seeds.
Black walnuts. half a bushel.
White walnuts. a gallon. this is the kind which grows along the
river side from the Secretary's ford down to the old
mill. a gallon.
Hiccory nut.⎱ I am not certain whether these are of different kinds, or
Pignut - - -⎰ whether they are the same. a gallon of each if different.
Scaly barks. a gallon.
Cedar. half a bushel.
Lilly of Canada. this is the lilly which George found for me in the
woods near the stone spring. I think that before I
left home we took up some roots and planted them
in the flower borders near the house. send all the
seed you can get, & some roots.
Pride of China. a pint.
Swamp laurel. 20. cones. the nearest place where these are to be had
is about the Byrd ordinary. waggoner Phill knows
the spot.
Umbrella. 20. cones.
Wild cherry. a gill of the stones.
Wild plumbs. a gill.
Poke. a gill.

Willow oak.  half a bushel of acorns.
Ground oak.  half a bushel of acorns.  this grows in the barrons about
     Hieron Gaines's.  it is a bush not more than 4. feet high.
     George once got me a peck of the acorns, which I be-
     lieve we planted in the park.
Sumach.  2. pints.  if there are two kinds of Sumach, send of both.
Scarlet flowering maple.   ⎫ I do not know the size of the seed
Maple with a leaf like an Ash.⎪ of these trees; but send about the
Fringe tree        ⎪ same proportion with those before
Ash.           ⎬ directed, according to the size of the
Green ivy.  the broad leaved ⎪ seed.
    the narrow leaved. ⎪
Sweet gum         ⎭
Poplar. ⎱ I do not know the size of these seeds; but send a very great
Sassafras.⎰ quantity.
the sweet potatoe.  I mean that kind which the negroes tend so gen-
     erally.  the roots will not keep during the voiage,
     therefore send a quantity of the seeds, which doubt-
     less may be got as I remember it bears a quantity
     of blossoms.

                (*Jefferson Papers*, L. C.)

## A LIST OF PLANTS SENT BY JEFFERSON FROM PARIS
### ABOUT 1786 TO FRANCIS EPPES

Pois Marly, hatif.  forward peas of Marly.
Pois carré.  tardif.  latter peas.
Pois micheau.  hatif.  forward peas.
Pois nain d'hollande hatif, a chassis.  dwarf peas of Holland.  for
  frames.
Haricots.  nain d'hollande.  dwarf beans of Holland.
Haricots gris de Suisse.  en Mars.  Grey beans of Switzerland.  sow
  in March.
Haricots flajolet.  little beans.  said to be very good.
Feves de Marais    Marsh beans.
Feves Julienne.  hatif.  Julian beans.  forward.
Laitue, coquille d'hyver.  shell-winter-lettuce.
Laitue feuille de chicorée    Endive-leaved lettuce.
Laitue golle hative.  forward lettuce.
Laitue gorge d'eté    summer lettuce
Laitue Berlin.  Berlin lettuce.
Chicoré frize.  semé en Mai et en Septembre.  curled endive.  sow in
  March & September
Chicoré de Meaux.  Endive of Meaux.
Radis rose, rond, hatif.  Rose radish.  round & forward.
Radis blanc, rond, hatif.  White radish.  round & forward
Raves hatives.  forward turneps
Raves conteur de rose    rose turneps.

Choux de Milan. en Mars. Milan cabbage. in March.
Choux de York  York cabbage.
Choux, coeur de boeuf. hatif. Ox-heart cabbage. forward.
Coux, pommé. bon á semes en Septembre. loaf-cabbage. sow in Sep-
     tember.
Choux-fleurs de la Meilleure espece. semé en Mai et 7^{bre}. cauliflowers
     of y^e best kind. May & Septemb.
Choux-fleurs dur d'Angleterre. English hard Cauliflowers.
bon Choux-fleur marecher. bon entout temps. Cauliflowers good for
     all seasons
Choux-fleur dur d'Hollande. Dutch hard Cauliflowers.
Peach-apricots.
Giroffle royal. Gilly flowers, royal. to be sown in March. very fine
     & very rare.
Heliotrope. to be sowed in the spring. a delicious flower, but I sus-
     pect it must be planted in boxes & kept in the house in the winter.
     the smell rewards the care.
Balsamine. sow in the spring
Reseda. qu. if this is woad (for dying)
4. especes d'oeillet. 4. kinds of pink. sow in beginning of summer.
Amaranthe tricolor. three-coloured Amaranth.
Amaranthe. passe velour. Velvet amaranth.
Amaranthe toydenne. Amaranth.
Roses of various kinds.
Anemoné double. double Anemone
Tulipes doubles. double Tulips
Jacinthe bleu, roy grand bretagne. blue hyacinths
Jacinthe rouge. roy grand bretagne. red hyacinths
Couronne Imperial. Crown imperial.
Ranoncle rouge. red Ranunculus.
Martagon.

(Jefferson Papers, U. Va.)

### A Memorandum, Probably Left to Edmund Bacon, about 1808 or 1809

In the roundabout there are 23 Honeylocust living. plant 8 arbor vitaes
     and 8 cedars in those places nearest to the grove, and fill up the other
     vacancies with golden willows. it will require 22 to reach to the
     Wild cherries.
on the S. side are 3 Umbrellas living. plant the vacancies with golden
     willows, about 9. plant horn beams & Elms. plant weeping willows
     in the semi-circle in N. E. front one half way between each two shrubs.
     plant a hedge of them round the graveyard exactly in the line of the
     old paling and a dble row of them on a line with the dble row of
     mulberries from where the mulberries end at the saw pit, down to
     the graveyard. the forest trees in the way are to be left.
take up the young aspens & plant a dble row of them on the road lead-
     ing from the gate down towards the landing. Where they fail, plant

locusts, walnuts, wild cherries, elms. lindens, maples, & cedars, just as you can get them.
plant figs from the bearing bush along under the garden wall.

(Fiske Kimball, *Jefferson's Grounds and Gardens at Monticello,* [n. d] : 17.)   (Original among *Jefferson Papers,* M. H. S.)

EXTRACT OF A LETTER WRITTEN TO HENRY S. RANDALL BY JEF-
FERSON'S GRANDDAUGHTER, ELLEN RANDOLPH COOLIDGE

. . . He [Jefferson] loved farming and gardening, the fields, the orchards, and his asparagus beds.  Every day he rode through his plantation and walked in his garden.  In the cultivation of the last he took great pleasure.  Of flowers, too, he was very fond.  One of my early recollections is of the attention which he paid to his flower-beds.  He kept up a correspondence with persons in the large cities, particularly, I think, in Philadelphia, for the purpose of receiving supplies of roots and seeds both for his kitchen and flower garden.  I remember well when he first returned to Monticello, how immediately he began to prepare new beds for his flowers.  He had these beds laid off on the lawn, under the windows, and many a time I have run after him when he went out to direct the work, accompanied by one of his gardners, generally Wormley, armed with spade and hoe, whilst he himself carried the measuring-line.  I was too young to aid him, except in a small way, but my sister, Mrs. Bankhead, then a young and beautiful woman, . . . was his active and useful assistant.  I remember the planting of the first hyacinths and tulips, and their subsequent growth.  The roots arrived, labelled each one with a fancy name.  There was Marcus Aurelius, and the King of the Gold Mine, the Roman Empress, and the Queen of the Amazons, Psyche, the God of Love, etc., etc., etc.  Eagerly, and with childish delight, I studied this brilliant nomenclature, and wondered what strange and surprisingly beautiful creations I should see rising from the ground when spring returned, and these precious roots were committed to the earth under my grandfather's own eye, with his beautiful grand-daughter Anne standing by his side, and a crowd of happy young faces, of younger grandchildren, clustering round to see the progress, and inquire anxiously the name of each separate deposit.  Then, when spring returned, how eagerly we watched the first appearance of the shoots above ground.  Each root was marked with its own name written on a bit of stick by its side, and what joy it was for one of us to discover the tender green breaking through the mould, and run to granpapa to announce, that we really believed Marcus Aurelius was coming up, or the Queen of the Amazons was above ground!  With how much pleasure compounded of our pleasure and his own, on the new birth, he would immediately go out to verify the fact, and praise us for our diligent watchfulness.  Then when the flowers were in bloom, and we were in ecstacies over the rich purple and crimson, or pure white, or delicate lilac, or pale yellow of the blossoms, how he would sympathize in our admiration, or discuss with my mother and elder sister new groupings and combinations and contrasts. Oh, these were happy moments for us and for him!

It was in the morning, immediately after our early breakfast, that he used to visit his flower-beds and his garden. . . . (Randall, *Jefferson* 3: 346–347.)

EXTRACTS FROM THE DIARY OF GENERAL JOHN HARTWELL COCKE, OF BREMO, FLUVANNA COUNTY, VIRGINIA

March 27, 1817.

. . . Sent to Monticello for some Marseilles figs and Paper Mulberry, and at the same time sent M$^r$. Jefferson some wine made from the Scuppernong grape of North Carolina, a fruit which must be well worthy to be cultivated. The wine is of delicious flavour, resembling Frontinac. . . .

March 28, 1817.

Jesse returned from Monticello with plants of the Marseilles fig, the Otaheit or Paper Mulberry, some cuttings of a peculiar species of lombardy poplar which M$^r$. Jefferson brought from France, "being a tree of some shade", two plants of the prickly locust (Robinia hispida) & two plants of the snowberry bro$^t$ by the late Capt Lewis from the Pacific. . . .

July 26, 1817.

M$^r$. Jefferson gave us the following history of the introduction of the Cedar into Albemarle: M$^r$. Hukman the fourth settler in that County carried up the first tree. M$^r$. Bolling the Brother in law of M$^r$. J, planted two near the grave of one of his children at Shadwell about the year 1755 from which all in that neighborhood came.

M$^r$. Madison gave us the following acc$^{nt}$. of the first introduction of the Cedar into Orange County. His Father who married his mother in y$^e$. neighborhood of Port Royal made various attempts to transplant the young trees from that part of the county without success. At length, being advised to try to succeed with the berries, he accordingly brought up a quantity and buried them in a corner of the yard where after a lapse of seven years two only were found to have vegetated. This he says from the best recollection of his mother, who is still living, was about 60 years ago. . . .

From M$^r$. Jefferson we got the following history of the Lombardy Poplar and Weeping Willow.

M$^r$. Thomas Willing, of Phil$^a$. receiving a basket of fruit from the Island of Madeira, having used the fruit, threw the Basket into a sink in his yard. After some time it was found that a part of the basket had taken root and was growing and became the first Weeping Willow tree ever known in America. M$^r$. J— saw it first in the year 1775 when he supposes from its size at that time it must have been four or five years old.

The Lombardy Poplar was first introduced into Philadelphia by M$^r$. W$^m$ Hamilton in the year 1785. In the year 1789 M$^r$. J. brought from

Europe with him a species of this tree somewhat different from the common tall and slim lombardy, M$^r$. J's being a tree of some shade

The Catalpa first introduced from North Carolina when M$^r$. Jefferson was a boy.

Received from M$^r$. Jefferson when last with him this acc$^{nt}$ of the Pear known in Albemarle by the name of the Meriweather Pear:

On a visit he once made to M$^r$. Nick Meriweather, he informed that he had once put up a parcel of these pears packed in tow in a trunk. Twelve months after supposing the pears were all used in getting some tow to wash his gun he found one of the fruit and that it was in a candied state like a preserve. The following year M$^r$. Jefferson put up some of this fruit in the like manner packed it in tow and in the course of the following winter went on to Congress then sitting at Annapolis, from whence he was sent on a mission to France where he remained seven years. Upon his return to Monticello to his great astonishment he found his pears in the state of candied preserve. (Courtesy of Miss Betty Cocke.)

A STATEMENT OF THE VEGETABLE MARKET OF WASHINGTON, DURING A PERIOD OF 8. YEARS, WHEREIN THE EARLIEST & LATEST APPEARANCE OF EACH ARTICLE WITHIN THE WHOLE 8. YEARS IS NOTED.

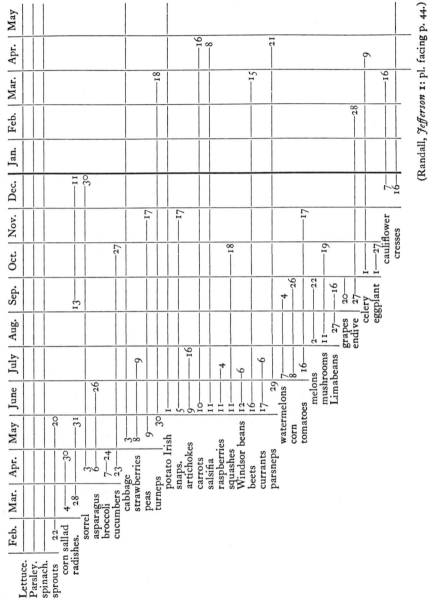

(Randall, *Jefferson* I: pl. facing p. 44.)

# APPENDIX IV

## Jefferson's
### Scheme for a System of Agricultural Societies
### March, 1811

Several persons, farmers and planters of the county of Albemarle, having, during their visits and occasional meetings together, in conversations on the subjects of their agricultural pursuits, received considerable benefits from an intercommunication of their plans and processes in husbandry, they have imagined that these benefits might be usefully extended by enlarging the field of communication so as to embrace the whole dimensions of the State. Were practical and observing husbandmen in each county to form themselves into a society, commit to writing themselves, or state in conversations at their meetings to be written down by others, their practices and observations, their experiences and ideas, selections from these might be made from time to time by every one for his own use, or by the society or a committee of it, for more general purposes. By an interchange of these selections among the societies of the different counties, each might thus become possessed of the useful ideas and processes of the whole; and every one adopt such of them as he should deem suitable to his own situation. Or to abridge the labor of such multiplied correspondences, a central society might be agreed on to which, as a common deposit, all the others should send their communications. The society thus honored by the general confidence, would doubtless feel and fulfil the duty of selecting such papers as should be worthy of entire communication, of extracting and digesting from others whatever might be useful, and of condensing their matter within such compass as might reconcile it to the reading, as well as to the purchase of the great mass of practical men. Many circumstances would recommend, for the central society, that which should be established in the county of the seat of government. The necessary relations of every county with that would afford facilities for all the transmissions which should take place between them. The annual meeting of the legislature at that place, the individuals of which would most frequently be members of their county societies, would give opportunities of informal conferences which might promote a general and useful understanding among all the societies; and presses established there offer conveniences entirely peculiar to that situation.

In a country, of whose interests agriculture forms the basis, wherein the sum of productions is limited by the quantity of the labor it possesses, and not of its lands, a more judicious employment of that labor would be a clear addition of gain to individuals as well as to the nation, now lost to both by a want of skill and information in its direction. Every one must have seen farms otherwise equal, the one producing the double of the other by the superior culture and management of its possessor; and every one must have under his eye numerous examples of persons setting out in life with no other possession than skill in agriculture, and speedily, by its sole exercise, acquire wealth and independence. To promote, therefore, the diffusion of this skill, and thereby to procure, with the same labor now employed, greater means of subsistence and of happiness to our fellow citizens, is the ultimate object of this association; and towards effecting it, we consider the following particulars among those most worthy of the attention of the societies proposed.

1st. And principally the cultivation of our primary staples of wheat, tobacco, and hemp, for market.

2d. All subsidiary articles for the support of the farm, the food, the clothing and the comfort of the household, as Indian corn, rye, oats, barley, buckwheat, millet, the family of peas and beans, the whole family of grasses, turnips, potatoes, Jerusalem artichokes, and other useful roots, cotton and flax, the garden and orchard.

3d. The care and services of useful animals for the saddle or draught, for food or clothing, and the destruction of noxious quadrupeds, fowls, insects, and reptiles.

4th. Rotations of crops, and the circumstances which should govern or vary them, according to the varieties of soil, climate, and markets, of our different counties.

5th. Implements of husbandry and operations with them, among which the plough and all its kindred instruments for dividing the soil, holds the first place, and the threshing machine an important one, the simplification of which is a great desideratum. Successful examples, too, of improvement in the operations of these instruments would be an excitement to correct the slovenly and unproductive practices too generally prevalent.

6th. Farm buildings and conveniences, inclosures, roads, fuel, timber.

7th. Manures, plaster, green-dressings, fallows, and other means of ameliorating the soil.

8th. Calendars of works, showing how a given number of laborers and a draught of animals are to be employed every day in the year so as to perform within themselves, and in their due time, according to the usual course of seasons, all the operations of a farm of given size. This being essential to the proportioning the labor to the size of the farm.

9th. A succinct report of the different practices of husbandry in the county, including the bad as well as the good, that those who follow the former may read and see their own condemnation in the same page which offers better examples for their adoption. It is believed that a judicious execution of this article alone, might nearly supersede every other duty of the society, inasmuch as it would present every good practice which has occurred to the mind of any cultivator of the State for imitation, and every bad one for avoidance. And the choicest processes culled from every farm, would compose a course probably near perfection.

10th. The county communications being first digested in their respective societies, a methodical and compact digest and publication of these would be the duty of the central society; and on the judicious performance of this, would in a great degree depend the utility of the institutions, and extent of improvement flowing from them.

11th. That we may not deter from becoming members, those practical and observing husbandmen whose knowledge is the most valuable, and who are mostly to be found in that portion of citizens with whom the observance of economy is necessary, all duties of every kind should be performed gratis; and to defray the expenses of the central publication alone, each member should pay at the first stated meeting of his society in every year, —————— dollars, for which he should be entitled to receive a copy of the publication bound in boards.

12th. The first association of —————— persons in any county notifying themselves as constituted to the central society, should be received as the society of the county making a part of the general establishment here proposed; but every county society should be free to adopt associate members, although residents of other counties, and to receive and avail the institution of communications from persons not members, whether in or out of their county.

We are far from presuming to offer this organization and these principles of constitution as complete, and worthy the implicit adoption of other societies. They are suggested only as propositions for consideration and amendment, and we shall readily accede to any others more likely to effect the purposes we have in view. We know that agricultural societies are already established in some counties; but we are not informed of their particular constitutions. We request these to be admitted into their brotherhood, and to make with them parts of one great whole. We have learned that such a society is formed or forming at the seat of our government. We ask their affiliation, and give them our suffrage for the station of central society. We promise to all our zealous co-operation in promoting the objects of the institution, and to contribute our mite in exchange for the more abundant information we shall receive from others.

For these purposes we now constitute ourselves an agricultural society of the county of Albemarle, and adopt as rules for present observance, the principles before stated.

Our further organization shall be a president, secretary and treasurer, to be chosen at the first stated meeting to be held in every year, by a majority of the members present, provided those present be a majority of the existing members, and to continue in office until another election shall be made.

There shall be four stated meetings in every year, to wit: on the first Mondays in January, April, July and October.

The place of meeting, and rules of the society, shall be established, revoked or altered, and new members admitted, at any of the stated meetings, by a majority of the attending members, if they be a majority of those present, not being less than one-fourth of the whole. And, lest the powers given to the greater quorum of a majority of the whole, should at any time remain unexercised from insufficient attendance, the same may be exercised by a resolution of the lesser quorum of one-fourth, passed at a stated meeting: provided it be confirmed at the next stated meeting, by either a greater or lesser quorum, and in the meantime have no force.

Those who for two whole years shall not have attended any stated meeting shall, *ipso facto,* cease to be members. And to ascertain at all times who are the existing members, the names of those attending every meeting shall be regularly entered in the journals of the society.

The president shall preside at all meetings when present, and when absent a president *pro tempore* may be appointed for that purpose *by those present.* (Lipscomb and Bergh, *Jefferson* 17: 404–410.)

[The Albemarle Agricultural Society was founded October, 1817, with James Madison as its first President.]

# APPENDIX V

## JEFFERSON'S *Notes on the State of Virginia*

### PLANTS

Jefferson's *Notes on the State of Virginia* was written in the year 1781 in answer to a series of questions from M. de Marbois, of the French Legation in Philadelphia, who had requested some statistical accounts of the State of Virginia for the use of his Government. At the request of his friends for copies of the *Notes,* Jefferson had it published in France in 1784–1785. This edition of two hundred copies, which is dated 1782, was followed by an unauthorized French edition, and in 1787 by an authorized English one. Since that date other English editions, a French and a German translation, and numerous American editions have been published.

Under *Query VI, A Notice of the Mines and other Subterraneous riches; its trees, plants, fruits, &c,* Jefferson answered the query on plants as follows:

A complete catalogue of the trees, plants, fruits &c. is probably not desired. I will sketch out those which would principally attract notice, as being 1. Medicinal, 2. Esculent, 3. Ornamental, or 4. Useful for fabrication; adding the Linnaean to the popular names, as the latter might not convey precise information to a foreigner. I shall confine myself too to native plants.

1. Senna. Cassia ligustrina.
   Arsmart. Polygonum Sagittatum.
   Clivers, or goose-grass. Galium spurium.
   Lobelia of several species.
   Palma christi. Ricinus.
   (3.) James-town weed. Datura Stramonium.
   Mallow. Malva rotundifolia.
   Syrian mallow. Hibiscus moschentos.
                 Hibiscus Virginicus.
   Indian mallow. Sida rhombifolia.
                 Sida abutilon.
   Virginia Marshmallow. Napaea hermaphrodita.
                 Napaea dioica.
   Indian physic. Spiraea trifoliata.
   Euphorbia Ipecacuanhae.

Pleurisy root. Asclepias decumbens.
Virginia snake-root. Aristolochia serpentaria.
Black snake-root. Actaea racemosa.
Seneca rattlesnake-root. Polygala senega.
Valerian. Valeriana locusta radiata.
Gentian. Saponaria villosa & centaurium.
Ginseng. Panax quinquefolium.
Angelica. Angelica sylvestris.
Cassava. Jatropha urens.
2. Tuckahoe. Lycoperdon tuber.
Jerusalem artichoke. Helianthus tuberosus.
Long potatoes. Convolvulas batatas.
Granadillas. Maycocks. Maracocks. Passiflora incarnata.
Panic. Panicum of many species.
Indian millet. Holcus laxus.
Holcus striosus.
Wild oat. Zizania aquatica.
Wild pea. Dolichos of Clayton.
Lupine. Lupinus perennis.
Wild hop. Humulus lupulus.
Wild cherry. Prunus virginiana.
Cherokee plumb. Prunus sylvestris fructu majori.⎱ Clayton.
Wild plumb. Prunus sylvestris fructu minori. ⎰
Wild crab apple. Pyrus coronaria.
Red mulberry. Morus rubra.
Persimmon. Diospyros virginiana.
Sugar maple. Acer saccharinum.
Scaly bark hiccory. Juglans alba cortice squamoso. Clayton.
Common hiccory. Juglans alba, fructu minore rancido. Clayton.
Paccan, or Illinois nut. Not described by Linnaeus, Miller, or
    Clayton. Were I to venture to describe this, speaking of the
    fruit from memory, and of the leaf from plants of two years
    growth, I should specify it as the Juglans alba, foliolis lanceolatis,
    acuminatis, serratis, tomentosis, fructu minore, ovato, compresso,
    vix insculpto, dulci, putamine tenerrimo. It grows on the Illinois,
    Wabash, Ohio, and Missisipi. It is spoken of by Don Ulloa
    under the name of pacanos, in his Noticias Americanas. Entret. 6.
Black walnut. Juglans nigra.
White walnut. Juglans alba.
Chesnut. Fagus castanea.
Chinquapin. Fagus pumila.
Hazelnut. Corylus avellana.
Grapes. Vitis. Various kinds, though only three described by
    Clayton.
Scarlet Strawberries. Fragaria virginiana of Millar.
Whortleberries. Vaccinium uliginosum?
Wild gooseberries. Ribes grossularia.
Cranberries. Vaccinium oxycoccos.

Black raspberries.   Rubus occidentalis.
Blackberries.   Rubus fruticosus.
Dewberries.   Rubus caesius.
Cloudberries.   Rubus chamaemorus.
3. Plane-tree.   Platanus occidentalis.
Poplar.   Liriodendron tulipifera.
            Populus heterophylla.
Black poplar.   Populus nigra.
Aspen.   Populus tremula.
Linden, or lime.   Tilia Americana.
Red flowering maple.   Acer rubrum.
Horse-chestnut or Buck's-eye.   Aesculus pavia.
Catalpa.   Bignonia catalpa.
Umbrella.   Magnolia tripetala.
Swamp laurel.   Magnolia glauca.
Cucumber-tree.   Magnolia acuminata.
Portugal bay.   Laurus indica.
Red bay.   Laurus borbonia.
Dwarf-rose bay.   Rhododendron maximum.
Laurel of the western country.   Qu. species?
Wild pimento.   Laurus benzoin.
Sassafras.   Laurus sassafras.
Locust.   Robinia pseudo-acacia.
Honey-locust.   Gleditsia.   1.
Dogwood.   Cornus florida.
Fringe or snowdrop-tree.   Chionanthus virginica.
Barberry.   Barberis vulgaris.
Redbud or Judas-tree.   Cercis canadensis.
Holly.   Ilex aquifolium.
Cockspur hawthorn.   Crataegus coccinea.
Spindle-tree.   Euonymus Europaeus.
Evergreen spindle-tree.   Euonymus Americanus.
Itea Virginica.
Elder.   Sambucus nigra.
Papaw.   Annona triloba.
Candleberry myrtle.   Myrica cerifera.
Dwarflaurel.   Kalmia angustifolia.} called ivy with us.
                     Kalmia latifolia.
Ivy.   Hedera quinquefolia.
Trumpet honeysuckle.   Lonicera sempervirens.
Upright honeysuckle.   Azalea nudiflora.
Yellow jasmine.   Bignonia sempervirens.
Calycanthus floridus.
American aloe.   Agave virginica.
Sumach.   Rhus.   Qu. species?
Poke.   Phytolacca decandra.
Long moss.   Tillandsia Usneoides.

4. Reed.   Arundo phragmitis.
   Virginia hemp.   Acnida cannabina.
   Flax.   Linum Virginianum.
   Black or pitch-pine.   Pinus taeda.
   White pine.   Pinus strobus.
   Yellow pine.   Pinus virginica.
   Spruce pine.   Pinus foliis singularibus.   Clayton.
   Hemlock spruce fir.   Pinus Canadensis.
   Abor vitae.   Thuya occidentalis.
   Juniper.   Juniperus virginica.   (Called cedar with us.)
   Cypress.   Cupressus disticha.
   Black oak.   Quercus nigra.
   White oak.   Quercus alba.
   Red oak.   Quercus rubra.
   Willow oak.   Quercus phellos.
   Chesnut oak.   Quercus prinus.
   Black jack oak.   Quercus aquatica.   Clayton.   Query?
   Ground oak.   Quercus pumila.   Clayton.
   Live oak.   Quercus virginiana.   Millar.
   Black birch.   Betula nigra.
   White birch.   Betula alba.
   Beach.   Fagus sylvatica.
   Ash.   Fraxinus americana.
       Fraxinus novae angliae.   Millar.
   Elm.   Ulmus americana.
   Willow.   Salix.   Query species?
   Sweet gum.   Liquidambar styraciflua.

The following were found in Virginia when first visited by the English; but it is not said whether of spontaneous growth, or by cultivation only. Most probably they were natives of more southern climates, and handed along the continent from one nation to another of the savages.

Tobacco.   Nicotiana.
Maize.   Zea mays.
Round potatoes.   Solanum tuberosum.
Pumpkins.   Cucurbita pepo.
Cymlings.   Cucurbita verrucosa.
Squashes.   Cucurbita melopepo.

There is an infinitude of other plants and flowers, for an enumeration and scientific description of which I must refer to the Flora Virginica of our great botanist, Dr. Clayton, published by Gronovius at Leyden, in 1762. This accurate observer was a native and resident of this state, passed a long life in exploring and describing it's plants, and is supposed to have enlarged the botanical catalogue as much as almost any man who has lived.

Besides these plants, which are native, our *Farms* produce wheat, rye, barley, oats, buck wheat, broom corn, and Indian corn. The climate suits rice well enough, wherever the lands do. Tobacco, hemp, flax, and cotton, are staple commodities. Indigo yields two cuttings. The silk-worm is a native, and the mulberry, proper for its food, grows kindly.

We cultivate also potatoes, both the long and the round, turneps, carrots, parsneps, pumpkins, and ground nuts (Arachis). Our grasses are Lucerne, St. Foin, Burnet, Timothy, ray and orchard grass, red, white, and yellow clover, greenswerd, blue grass, and crab grass.

The *gardens* yield musk melons, water melons, tomatas, okra, pomegranates, figs, and the esculent plants of Europe.

The *orchards* produce apples, pears, cherries, quinces, peaches, nectarines, apricots, almonds, and plumbs. (Thomas Jefferson, *Notes on the State of Virginia* (Paris, 1782 [1784–1785]: 61–69.)

# APPENDIX VI

## JEFFERSON'S DESCRIPTION OF HIS MOULDBOARD OF LEAST RESISTANCE IN A LETTER TO SIR JOHN SINCLAIR

Philadelphia, March 23, 1798.

Dear Sir,

I have to acknowledge the receipt of your two favors of June 21, and July 15, and of several separate parcels containing the agricultural reports. These now form a great mass of information on a subject, of all in the world, the most interesting to man: for none but the husbandman makes anything for him to eat; and he who can double his food, as your exertions bid fair to do, deserves to rank, among his benefactors, next after his Creator. Among so many reports of transcendent merit, one is unwilling to distinguish particulars. Yet the application of the new chemistry, to the subject of manures, the discussion of the question on the size of farms, the treatise on the potatoe, from their universality have an advantage in other countries, over those which are topographical. The work which shall be formed, as the result of the whole, we shall expect with impatience.

Permit me, through you, to make here my acknowledgments to the board of agriculture for the honour they have been pleased to confer on me by, associating me to their institution. In love for the art, I am truly their associate: but events have controuled my predelection for its practice, and denied to me that uninterrupted attention, which alone can enable us to advance in it with a sure step. Perhaps I may find opportunities of being useful to you as a centinel at an outpost, by conveying intelligence of whatever may occur here new and interesting to agriculture. This duty I shall perform with pleasure, as well in respectful return for the notice of the board, as from a zeal for improving the condition of human life, by an interchange of its comforts, and of the information which may increase them. . . .

In a former letter to you, I mentioned the construction of the mouldboard of a plough which had occurred to me, as advantageous in its form, as certain and invariable in the method of obtaining it with precision. I remember that Mr. Strickland of York, a member of your board, was so well satisfield with the principles on which it was formed that he took some drawings of it; and some others have considered it with the same approbation. An experience of five years has enabled me to say, it answers in practice to what it promises in theory.

The Mouldboard should be a continuation of the wing of the ploughshare, beginning at it's hinder edge, & in the same plane. it's first office is to receive the sod horizontally from the wing, to raise it to a proper height for being turned over, & to make, in it's progress, the

649

*least resistance possible;* & consequently to require a minimum in the moving power. were this it's only office, the wedge would offer itself as the most * eligible form in practice. but the sod is to be turned over also. to do this, the one edge of it is not to be raised at all: for to raise this would be a waste of labour. the other edge is to be raised till it passes the perpendicular, that it may fall over with its own weight. and that this may be done so as to give also the least resistance, it must be made to rise gradually from the moment the sod is received. the mould-board then in this second office, operates as a transverse, or rising wedge, the point of which sliding back horizontally on the ground, the other end continues rising till it passes the perpendicular, or, to vary the point of view, place on the ground a wedge of the breadth of the ploughshare, of it's length from the wing backwards, & as high at the heel as it is wide. draw a diagonal on it's upperface from the left angle at the point to the right upper angle of the heel. bevil the face from the diagonal to the right-bottom-edge which lies on the ground. that half is then evidently in the best form for performing the two offices of raising and turning the sod gradually, & with the least effort: and if you will suppose the same bevil continued across the left side of the diagonal, that is, if you will suppose a strait line, whose length is at least equal to the breadth of the wedge, applied on the face of the first bevil, & moved backwards on it parallel with itself & with the ends of the wedge, the lower end of the line moving along the right-bottom-edge, a curved plane will be generated whose characteristic will be a combination of the principle of the wedge in cross directions, & will give what we seek, *the mould board of least resistance.* it offers too this great advantage that it may be made by the coarsest workman, by a process so exact, that its form shall never be varied by a single hair's breadth. one fault of all other mould-boards is that, being copied by the eye, no two will be alike. in truth it is easier to form the mouldboard I speak of with precision, when the method has been once seen, than to describe that method either by words or figures. I will attempt however to describe it. whatever may not be intelligible from the description may be supplied from the model I send you.

Let the breadth & depth of the furrow the farmer usually opens, as also the length of his plough-bar, from where it joins the wing to the hinder end, be given; as these fix the dimensions of the block of which the mouldboard is to be made. suppose the furrow 9. Inches wide, 6. Inches deep, & the ploubhbar 2. feet long. then the

---

* I am aware that were the turf only *to be raised* to a given height in a given length of mouldboard, & not to be turned over, the form of least resistance would not be rigorously a wedge with both faces strait, but with the upper one curved according to the laws of the solid of least resistance described by the mathematicians. but the difference between the effect of the curved, & of the plain wedge, in the case of a mouldboard, is so minute, and the difficulty in the execution which the former would superinduce on common workmen is so great, that the plain wedge is the most eligible to be assumed in practice for the first element of our construction.

block Fig. 1. must be 9. I. wide at bottom (b. c.) 13½ I. wide at top (a. d.) because if it were merely of the same width with the bottom, as a. e., the sod, only raised to the perpendicular, would fall back into the furrow by it's own elasticity. I find from experience that, in my soil, the top of the mouldboard should over-jet the perpendicular 4½ I. in a height of 12. I. to ensure that the weight of the sod shall preponderate

FIG. 1

over it's elasticity. this is an angle of nearly 22°. the block must be 12. I. high, because, unless the mouldboard be in height double the depth of the furrow, in ploughing friable earth, it will be thrown in waves over the mouldboard; and it must be 3 feet long; one foot of which is

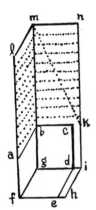

FIG. 2

added to form a tailpiece, by which it may be made fast to the plough handle. the first operation is to give the first form to this tailpiece, by sawing the block Fig. 2. across from a. b. on it's left side (which is 12. I. from it's hinder end) along the line b. c. to c. within 1½ I. of the right side, & to the corresponding point in the bottom, 1½ I. also from the side. then saw in again at the hinder end from d. e. (1½ I. from the right side) along the line d. c. the block a. b. c. d. e. f. g. drops out & leaves the tailpiece c. d. e. h. i. k. 1½ I. thick. the fore part of the block a. b. c. k. l. m. n. is what is to form the real mouldboard. with a carpenter's square make a scribe all around the block at every inch. there will of course be 23. of them. then from the point k. Fig. 2. and 3. draw the diagonals k. m. on the top, & k. o. Fig. 3. on the right side. enter a saw at the point m. being the left-fore-upper corner, & saw in, guiding the hinder part of the saw along the diagonal m. k. (Fig. 2. 3.) & the forepart down the left edge of the block at the fore-end m. l. (Fig. 2.) till it reaches k. and l. in a strait line. it will then have reached the true central diagonal of the block k. l. Fig. 5. then enter the saw at the point o. being the right-fore-bottom corner, & saw in, guiding the hinder part of the saw along the diagonal o. k. (Fig. 3.) & the forepart along the bottom edge of the fore-end o. l. till it again reaches k. l. Fig. 5. the same central diagonal to which you had cut in the other direction. consequently the pyramid k. m. n. o. l. Fig. 4. drops out, & leaves the block in the form Fig. 5. you will now observe that if, in the last operation, instead of stopping the saw at the central diagonal k. l. we had cut through the block in the same plane, we should have taken off a wedge l. m. n. o. k. b. Fig. 3. and left the block in the form of a wedge also. l. o. k. b. a. p. k. which, when speaking of the principle of the mouldboard, I observed would be the most perfect form, if it had only to raise the sod.

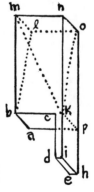

FIG. 3

but as it is to be turned over also, the left half of the upper wedge is preserved to furnish, on the left side, the continuation of the bevil which

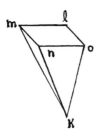

FIG. 4

was proposed to be made on the right half of the bottom wedge. We are now to proceed to the bevil, for which purpose the scribes round the block were formed before the pyramidal piece was taken out; & attention must be used not to mismatch or mistake them now that they are disjoined by the withdrawing of that piece. enter the saw on the two points of the 1st. scribe, where it has been disjoined, which is exactly where it intersected the two superficial diagonals, & saw across the hollow of the block, guiding the saw, both before & behind, along the same scribe, till the forepart of the saw reaches the bottom edge of the right side, & the middle of the saw reaches the central diagonal: the hinder part will of course continue the same strait line, which will issue somewhere on the top of the block. then enter the saw in like manner on the two projecting points of the 2d. scribe, and saw in, along the scribe, before and behind, till it reaches the same bottom edge of the right side, & the central diagonal. then the 3d. 4th. 5th. etc. scribes successively. after cutting in several of the earlier scribes, the hinder part of the saw will issue at the left side of the block, & all the scribes being cut, the saw will have left strait lines from the bottom edge of the right side of the block, across the central diagonal. with an adze dub off all the sawed parts to the bottoms of the sawmarks, just leaving the traces visible, & the face of the mouldboard is finished. these traces will show how the cross wedge rises gradually on the face of the direct wedge, which is preserved in the trace of the central diagonal. a person may represent to himself sensibly and easily the manner in which

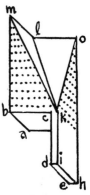

FIG. 5

the sod is raised on this mouldboard by describing on the ground a parallelogram 2 feet long, & 9. I. broad, as a. b. c. d. Fig. 6. then rest one end of a stick $27\frac{1}{2}$ I. long on the ground at b. & raise the other 12. I. high at e. which is $4\frac{1}{2}$ I. from d. & represents the overhanging of that

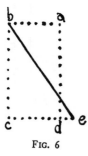

FIG. 6

side of the mouldboard. then present another stick 12. I. long from a. to b. and move it backwards parallel with itself from a. b. to d. c. keeping one end of it always on the line a. d. & letting the other rise as it recedes along the diagonal stick b. e. which represents our central diagonal. the motion of the cross stick will be that of our rising wedge, & will shew how every transverse line of the sod is conducted from it's first horizontal position, till it is raised so far beyond the perpendicular as to fall reversed by it's own weight. But, to return to our work, we have still to form the underside of our mouldboard. turn the block bottom up. enter the saw on the 1st. scribe, at what was the bottom edge of the left side, & cut in, guiding the instrument at both ends by the scribe, till it has approached within an inch, or any other distance according to the thickness you chuse, of the face. then cut in like manner all the other scribes, & with the adze dub out the sawed parts, & the mouldboard is done.

It is to be made fast to the plough, by resting the toe in the hinder edge of the wing, which must be made double like a comb-case, to receive & protect the fore-end of the mouldboard. then pass a screw through the mouldboard & helve the ploughshare where they touch each other, & two others through the tailpiece of the mouldboard & right handle of the plough, & cut off so much of the tailpiece as projects behind the handle, diagonally, & the whole is done.

I have described this operation in it's simplest mode, that it might be the more easily understood. but, in practice, I have found some other modifications of it advantageous. thus instead of first forming my block as a. b. c. d. Fig. 7. where a. b. is 12. I. and the angle at b. a right one, I cut a wedge-like piece b. c. e. off of the bottom, through the whole length of the block, b. e. being equal to the thickness of the bar of the share (suppose 1½ I.) because, the face of the wing declining from the top of the bar to the ground, were the block laid on the share without an equivalent

FIG. 7

bevil at it's bottom, the side a. b. would decline from the perpendicular, and a. d. from it's horizontal position. Again, instead of leaving the top of the block 13½ I. wide from m. to n. Fig 8. I cut a wedge from the right side n. k. i. c. p. n. 1½ I. thick at top, & tapering to nothing at

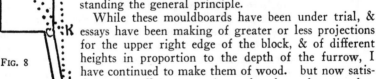

bottom; because I find that the tailpiece, being by this means made oblique, as c. i. instead of k. i. is brought more advantageously to the side of the handle. the first superficial diagonal is consequently brought from m. to c. and not from m. to k. as in the first directions. these variations will be easy to any one after understanding the general principle.

While these mouldboards have been under trial, & essays have been making of greater or less projections for the upper right edge of the block, & of different heights in proportion to the depth of the furrow, I have continued to make them of wood. but now satisfied by a sufficient experience that for a furrow of 9.

FIG. 8

by 6. I. the dimensions I have stated are the best, I propose to have the mouldboard made of cast iron.

I am sensible that this description may be thought too lengthy and elaborate for a subject which has hardly been deemed worthy the application of science. but if the plough be in truth the most useful of the instruments known to man, it's perfection cannot be an idle speculation. and, in any case whatever, the combination of a *theory* which may satisfy the learned, with a practice intelligible to the most unlettered laborer, will be acceptable to the two most useful classes of society.

Be this as it may, from the widow her mite only was expected. I have contributed according to my poverty; others will from their abundance.—None so much as yourself, who have been the animating principle of the institution from its first germ. When I contemplate the extensive good which the proceedings under your direction are calculated to produce, I cannot but deplore every possibility of their interruption. . . . (Original letter in the Jefferson Papers, M. H. S.; also printed in *Trans. Am. Philos. Soc.* 4: 313–320, 1799.)

*A Supplementary* note on the mould board described in a letter to Sir John Sinclair, of March 23, 1798, inserted in the American Philosophical transactions, vol. 4, and in Maese's [= Mease's] Domestic Encyclopaedia voce Plough.*

The chief object in that description was to establish the true principle on which the mould board of a plough should be constructed, and to point out a mechanical method of making it's curved surfaces. The mould board there described, by way of example, was made with a square toe, to receive the sod at the hinder edge of the fin of the ploughshare; but neither the principle nor the method is restrained to that single form. If it be desired for instance to give to the mould board a pointed toe, adapted to the fine of the plough-share, which may begin to raise the sod from the point, a small variation in the process effects it, and the principle of the curved surface is still the same. Having formed your block of the length, breadth, and height suited to the nature of

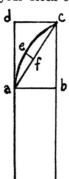

your soil, to the breadth and depth of your furrow, having scribed it, and taken out the pyramidal block as directed, lay it bottom upwards and draw a line a. b. across it, distant from the fore end about once and a half the breadth of the bottom; then draw the diagonal a. f. c. and if you wish to make the toe with the cutting edge oblique and straight, chip off the corner d. to the diagonal line a. f. c. or if you wish to make the cutting edge curved as that of the fin generally is, lay off the curvature you desire from f. to e. and either mark the curve by the eye, or with a pair of compasses, and chip off the corner d. to the curved line a. e. c. then saw in on your scribes and finish as directed, in the letter. It is hardly necessary to observe that the block being here represented bottom upwards, the cutting edge of the mould board appears on the left, though it will really be on the right side when turned up.

Th: Jefferson.

* This "supplementary note" is from some printed but unidentified source.—Ed.

# APPENDIX VII

## Books and Pamphlets on
## Agriculture, Gardening, and Botany in the
## Library of Thomas Jefferson

The following list of books and pamphlets in Jefferson's library was taken from the *Catalogue of the Library of Congress,* December, 1830; *Catalogue, President Jefferson's Library,* to be sold at auction, at the Long Room, Pennsylvania Avenue, Washington City, by Nathaniel P. Poor, February, 1829; miscellaneous letters; and Jefferson's manuscript of his library, 1783 (original in the Massachusetts Historical Society; photostatic copy at the University of Virginia Library).

ABERCROMBIE, JOHN. 1786. The gardener's pocket dictionary, 3 v. London.

ADLUM, JOHN. 1823. A memoir on the cultivation of the vine in America, and the best mode of making wine. Washington.

Address and rules of the South Carolina Society for promoting and improving Agriculture and other Rural Concerns. 1785. Charleston.

AGRICOLA, G. A. 1726. A philosophical treatise of husbandry and gardening, tr. from the German, with remarks and an appendix, by R. Bradley. London.

AUBER, M. JOURNU. 1804. Mémoir sur l'amélioration des races de bêtes à laine dans le Department de la Gironde. Bordeaux.

BAIRD, THOMAS. 1793. General views of agriculture in the county of Middlesex. Board of Agriculture, London.

BAKEWELL, ROBERT. 1808. Observations on the influence of soil and climate upon wool. London.

BARTON, BENJAMIN SMITH. 1803. Elements of Botany. Philadelphia.

BASSO, CASIANO. 1781. Geoponica, 4 v. in 2. Lipsiae.

BEAUMONT, SIR HARRY (JOSEPH SPENCE). 1761. A particular account of the Emperor of China's gardens near Pekin, translated from the French of Frère Attiret, in Dodsley's Fugitive Pieces, Vol. 1. London.

BELSCHES, R. 1796. General view of the agriculture of the county of Stirling. Board of Agriculture, London.

BIDET, NICOLAS. 1759. Traité sur la nature et sur la culture de la vigne; revue par M. du Hamel du Monceau, 2 v. Paris.

BILLINGSLEY, JOHN. 1794. General views of agriculture in the county of Somerset. Board of Agriculture, London.

BINNS, JOHN A. 1803. Treatise on practical farming. Fredericktown.

BOERHAAVE, H.   1731.   Historia plantarum.   Londini.
BONNETERIE, SABOUREUX DE LA.   1783.   Traduction d'anciens ouv-
    rages latins relatifs à l'agriculture, et à la médicine vétérinaire,
    avec des notes, 6 v.   Paris.
BORDLEY, J. B.   1796.   Sketches on rotations of crops and other rural
    matters.   Philadelphia.
——— 1799.   Essays and notes on husbandry and rural affairs.
    Philadelphia.
——— 1799.   Hemp.   Philadelphia.
——— 1800.   Husbandry dependant on live stock.   Philadelphia.
BOSWELL, GEORGE.   1792.   A treatise on watering meadows.   London.
BRADLEY, RICHARD.   1724.   A general treatise of husbandry and gar-
    dening, 3 v.   London.
——— 1726.   New improvements of planting and gardening.   Lon-
    don.
——— 1728.   Dictionarium botanicum: or, a botanical dictionary for
    the use of the curious in husbandry and gardening.   London.
——— 1733.   Ten practical discourses concerning the four elements,
    as they relate to the growth of plants.   London.
BROUSSE, M. DE LA.   1724.   Traité de la culture du figuier.   Amster-
    dam.
BROWN, ROBERT.   1811.   A treatise on agriculture and rural affairs.
    Edinburgh.
CADET DE VAUX, A. A.   [1800].   Instruction sur l'art de faire le vin.
    Paris.
CAREY, MATTHEW.   1820.   The new olive branch: or an attempt to
    establish an identity of interest between agriculture, manufac-
    ture, and commerce.   Philadelphia.
CATO, VARRO, COLUMELLA, et PALLADIUS.   1595.   De re rustica.
    Heidelberg.
Catalogue of the Botanic Garden at Liverpool.   1808.   Liverpool.
Catalogue of the plants of New York.   [n. d.]
CHAMBERS, WILLIAM.   1763.   Plans, elevations, sections, and per-
    spective views of the gardens and buildings at Kew.   London.
——— 1772.   A dissertation on oriental gardening.   London.
CHAPTAL, ROSIER, PARMENTIER, ET DUSSIEUX.   1801.   Traité sur la
    culture de la vigne, 2 v.   Paris.
COINTERAUX, ———.   1803.   Nouveau traité d'economie rurale.   Paris.
Country Habitations.   [n. d.]   On the culture of Lucerne.   Richmond.
CROWNINSHIELD, ———.   MS, 1807.   Hortus Siccus.
CUSTIS, G. W. P.   1808.   Address to the people of the United States,
    on the importance of encouraging agriculture and domestic
    manufactures.   Alexandria.
DARWIN, ERASMUS.   1798.   The botanic garden.   New York.
DAUBENTON, LOUIS JEAN MARIE.   1810.   Advice to shepherds and
    owners of flocks, on the care and management of sheep; tr. from
    the original French.   Boston,

Description of Stowe. [1797.] A description of the house and gardens of the most notable and puissant prince, George-Grenville-Nugent-Temple, Marquis of Buckingham. London.

DICKSON, ADAM. 1788. Husbandry of the ancients, 2 v. Edinburgh.

DIOSCORIDE. 1573. Traduzione é discorsi di Matthioli. Venice.

DIOSCORIDES. 1549. (Gr. et Lat.) Paris.

DONALDSON, JAMES. 1794. General views of the agriculture in the county of Northampton. Board of Agriculture, London.

DOUETTE-RICHARDOT, NICHOLAS. 1806. Pratique de l'agriculture. Paris.

DUHAMEL DU MONCEAU, H. L. 1754. Traité de la conservation des grains. Paris.

———— 1759. A practical treatise of husbandry. London.

DUHAMEL DU MONCEAU ET TILLET. 1762. Histoire d'un insecte qui devore les grains de l'angoumois. Paris.

DUMÉRIL, ANDRÉ MARIE CONSTANT. 1807. Traité élémentaire d'histoire naturelle, 2 v. Paris.

DUMONT-COURSET. 1802. Le botaniste-cultivateur, 4 v. Paris.

ERSKINE, J. F. 1795. General view of the agriculture of the county Clackmannan, etc. Board of Agriculture, London.

EVELYN, JOHN. 1664. Sylva, pomona, and kalendarium hortense. London.

———— 1787. Terra; with notes, by A. Hunter. New York.

FABBRONI, A. 1785. Dissertazione sopra il quesito indicare le vere teorie con le quali devono eseguirsi le stime dei terreni, stabilite le quali abbiano i pratici stimatori delle vere guide, che gli conducono a determinarne il valore. Firenze.

———— 1786. Istruzione elementari di agricoltura. Perugia.

FILLASSIER, M. 1783. Culture de la grosse asperge, dite de Hollande. Amsterdam.

FORDYCE, GEORGE. 1771. Elements of agriculture and vegetation. London.

FORSYTH, WILLIAM. 1802. A treatise on the culture and management of fruit-trees. Philadelphia.

FRANÇOIS (DE NEUFCHÂTEAU), CITOYEN. 1801. Rapport sur le perfectionnement des charrues. Paris.

FRANÇOIS (DE NEUFCHÂTEAU), N. 1806. Voyages agronomiques dans la Senatorerie de Dijon. Paris.

GARDINER, JOHN, and DAVID HEPBURN. 1818. The American gardener. Georgetown.

GENTIL, FRANÇOIS. 1723. Le jardinier solitaire. Paris.

GINANNI, FRANCESCO. 1759. Delle malattie del grano in erba. Pesaro.

GOUAN, M. 1787. Explication du systême botanique du Chevalier von Linné. Montpellier.

GRONOVIUS, JOH. FRED. 1762. Flora Virginica. Leiden.

HALE, THOMAS. 1758–59. A compleat body of husbandry, 4 v. London.

HALES, STEPHEN. 1738. Statical essays, 2 v. London.
HEELY, JOSEPH. 1777. Letters on the beauties of Hagley, Envil, and Leasowes. With critical remarks: and observations on the modern taste in gardening. London.
HEPBURN, GEORGE BUCHAN. 1794. General view of the agriculture and rural economy of East Lothian. Board of Agriculture, London.
HILL, JOHN. 1758. The gardener's new kalendar; divided according to the twelve months of the year—containing the whole practice of gardening. London.
HILLHOUSE, AUGUSTUS LUCAS. 1820. An essay on the history and cultivataion of the European olive-tree. Paris.
HIRZEL, HANS KASPAR. 1800. The rural Socrates. Hallowell (District of Maine).
HOME, FRANCIS. 1762. The principles of agriculture and vegetation. London.
HOME, HENRY. 1779. The gentleman farmer. Edinburgh.
HUZARD, J. B. 1802. Instruction sur l'amélioration des chevaux en France. Paris.
JACOB, GILES. 1717. The country gentleman's vade mecum. London.
JAMES, JOHN. [1712]. The theory and practice of gardening, from the French of J. B. Alexandre le Blond. [Paris.]
JUTAIS, F. DE LA. 1805. L'abondance, ou la véritable pierre philosophale. Philadelphia.
KENNEDY and LEE. 1784. Catalogue of plants and seeds, sold at the Vineyard, Hammersmith. London.
KIRWAN, R. 1796. The manures most advantageously applicable to the various sorts of soils. London.
KNIGHT, THOMAS ANDREW. 1802. A treatise on the culture of the apple & pear, and on the manufacture of cider & perry. Ludlow.
LANGLEY, BATTY. 1729. Pomona: or the fruit garden illustrated. London.
LASTEYRIE, C. P. DE. 1799. Traité sur les bêtes-à-laine d'Espagne. Paris.
———— 1808. Du cotonnier et de sa culture. Paris.
LASTRI, MARCO ANTONIO. 1801. Corso di agricoltura, 5 v. Firenze.
L'economie rurale, 6 v. [n. d.]
Lettres du Lord Somerville, du Duc de Bedford, de M. Arthur Young, au C. François (de Neufchâteau) sur la charrue. 1803. Paris.
LINNAEUS, CAROLUS (or CAROLUS A LINNÉ). 1737. Critica botanica. Lugduni-Batavorum.
———— 1737. Flora lapponica. Amstelaedami.
———— 1756. Systema naturae. Lugduni-Batavorum.
———— 1762. Species plantarum, 2 v. Holmiae.
———— 1763. Philosophia botanica. Viennae Austriae.
———— 1764. Genera plantarum, ed. 6. Holmiae.

———— 1782.  A system of vegetables.  Litchfield.

———— 1786–1787.  Fundamenta botanica, edente Gilibert, 3 v. Coloniae-Allobrogum.

LIVINGSTON, ROBERT.  1809.  Essay on sheep.  New York.

LOGAN, GEORGE.  1797.  Agricultural experiments on gypsum; and experiments to ascertain the best rotation of crops.  Philadelphia.

———— 1800.  On the necessity of promoting agriculture, manufactures, and the useful arts.  Philadelphia.

MCMAHON, BERNARD.  1806.  The American gardener's calendar. Philadelphia.

MAIN, THOMAS.  1807.  Directions for the transplantation, etc., of young thorn or other hedge plants.  Washington.

MALLET, ————.  1795.  Le parfait jardinier.  Paris.

MARSHALL, HUMPHRY.  1785.  Arbustrum Americanum: the American grove.  Philadelphia.

MARTYN, T.  1785.  Rousseau's botany.  London.

MAUPIN, M.  1779.  L'art de faire le vin.  Paris.

———— 1782.  Nouvelle méthode pour cultiver la vigne.  Paris.

MAWE, THOMAS.  1794.  Every man his own gardener.  London.

Médailles d'encouragement données par la Société d'Agriculture du Département de la Seine.  1803.  Paris.

Mémoires de la Société d'Agriculture du Departement de la Seine, 11 v. 1801–1808.  Paris.

Mémoires de la Société Royale et Centrale d'Agriculture.  1815–1816.

Memoirs of the Philadelphia Society for Promoting Agriculture, vols. 1–2.  1808–1811.  Philadelphia.

MICHAUX, ANDRÉ.  1801.  Histoire des chênes de l'Amerique.  Paris.

———— 1803.  Flora Boreali-Americana, 2 v.  Paris.

MICHAUX, F. A.  1805.  Mémoire sur la naturalisation des arbres forestiers de l'Amerique septentrionale.  Paris.

———— 1811.  Histoire des arbres forestiers de l'Amerique septentrionale.  Paris.

———— 1819.  The North American sylva, 3 v. in 2.  Paris.

MILLER, PHILIP.  1765.  The gardener's calendar.  London.

———— 1768.  The gardener's dictionary.  London.

———— 1785.  Dictionnaire des jardiniers; tr. de l'Anglois, par M. de Chazelles, avec notes, etc., par M. Hollandre, 5 v.  Paris.

MILLS, JOHN.  1762.  Practical treatise of husbandry.  London.

———— 1770.  Natural and chemical elements of agriculture.  London.

MOORE, THOMAS.  1801.  The great error of American agriculture exposed.  Baltimore.

MORTIMER, JOHN.  1721.  The whole art of husbandry, 2 v.  London.

MUHLENBERG, H.  1813.  Catalogus plantarum Americae septentrionalis.  Lancaster.

NAISMYTH, JOHN.  1795.  Tour through the sheep pastures in the southern parts of Scotland.  Board of Agriculture, London.

Nomenclator botanicus (Lat. Gal. Ang. Germ. Suec. et Dan.).  1769. Copenhagen.

Notice sur l'agriculture des Celtes et des Gaulois. 1806. Paris.

Outlines of a plan for establishing a state society of agriculture in Pennsylvania. 1794. Philadelphia.

OWEN, T. 1805. Geoponica, 2 v. in 1. London.

PALLUEL, CRETTÉ. 1802. Mémoire sur l'utilité qu'on peut tirer des marais desséchés, en général, et particulièrement de ceux du Laonois. Paris.

Papers on agriculture, published by the Massachusetts Society for Promoting Agriculture. 1803–1804. Boston.

PARKINSON, JOHN. 1640. Theatrum botanicum: the theater of plants. Or, an herball of a large extent. . . . London.

PARKINSON, RICHARD. 1799. The experienced farmer, 2 v. Philadelphia.

PARMENTIER, M. 1781. Recherches sur les végétaux nourissans. Paris.

———— 1784. Méthode facile de conserver a peu de frais les grains et les farines. Londres.

Particulars of the breeding stock, late the property of Robert Fowler, of the county of Oxford, England. 1791. London.

PEARCE, WILLIAM. 1794. General views of agriculture in Berkshire. Board of Agriculture, London.

PERSOON, C. H. 1805–1807. Synopsis plantarum, 2 v. Paris.

PETERS, RICHARD. 1797. Agricultural enquiries on plaster of Paris. Philadelphia.

PITT, W. 1794. General views of agriculture in the county of Stafford. Board of Agriculture, London.

Plan of the re-printed reports of the Board of Agriculture. 1806. London.

Proceedings of the British Privy Council, in relation to the insect called the Hessian Fly. 1789. London.

RAFINESQUE, C. S. 1817. A flora of the state of Louisiana. New York.

RANDOLPH, JOHN. 1793. A treatise on gardening. Richmond.

Rapport, et médailles d'encouragement données par la Société d'Agriculture du Département de la Seine. 1808. Paris.

ROBERTSON, THOMAS. 1796. General report upon the size of farms. Board of Agriculture, London.

ROCCA, L'ABBÉ DELLA. 1790. Traité complet sur les abeilles, 3 v. Paris.

RONCONI, IGNAZIO. 1783. Dizionario d'agricoltura, 2 v. Venezia.

ROSCOE, WILLIAM. 1802. Address on opening the Botanic Garden of Liverpool. Liverpool.

ROZIER, FRANÇOIS, ed. 1785–1800. Cours complet d'agriculture théorique, pratique, économique . . . ou dictionnaire universel d'agriculture, 10 v. Paris.

SAINT-GERMAIN, J. J. DE. 1784. Manuel des végétaux (Lat. et Fr.). Paris.

SERRES, OLIVIER DE. 1804. Le théâtre d'agriculture, 2 v. Paris.

SHECUT, JOHN L. E. W. 1806. Flora Carolinaeensis. Charleston.

SINCLAIR, JOHN. 1791–1793. Statistical reports. London.

———— 1793. Plan of the Board. Board of Agriculture, London.

———— 1795. General view of the agriculture of the northern counties and islands of Scotland. Board of Agriculture, London.

———— 1795. Plan of an agreement among the powers of Europe, and the United States of America, for the purpose of rewarding discoveries of general benefit to the Society. Board of Agriculture, London.

———— 1795. Substance of Sir John Sinclair's addresses to the Board, 20th of June, and 14th of July. Board of Agriculture, London.

SOMERVILLE, ROBERT. 1795. Report on the cultures and use of potatoes. London.

———— 1795. Report on the subject of manures, with appendix. Board of Agriculture, London.

SMITH, ————. 1786. Linnaeus on the sexes of plants, and study of nature. London.

SPURRIER, JOHN. 1793. The practical farmer. Wilmington.

STACKHOUSE, J. 1816. Nereis Britannica. Oxonii.

STONE, THOMAS. 1793. General views of agriculture in the county of Huntingdon. Board of Agriculture, London.

———— 1800. Letter to Lord Somerville, late President of the Board of Agriculture, with a view to show the inutility of the plans and researches of that institution. London.

STRICKLAND, WILLIAM. 1801. Observations on the agriculture of the United States of America. London.

SURFLET, RICHARD. 1600. Maison rustique, or the countrie farme; tr. from the French of Charles Stephens and John Liebault. London.

SYLVESTRE, A. F. 1801. Essai sur les moyens de perfectionner les arts economiques en France. Paris.

TAYLOR, JOHN. 1813. Arator, or agricultural essays. Georgetown.

THEOPHRASTI ERISII. 1644. De historia plantarum (Gr. et Lat.) Gazae, commentariis Bodaevs à stapel, Jul. Caes. Scaligeri et Constantini. Amstellodami.

THOÜIN, ANDRÉ. [n. d.] Monographie des greffes. Paris.

TOURNEFORT, J. P. 1719. Institutiones rei herbariae, 2 v. Paris.

Transactions of the Society, instituted in the State of New York, for the Promotion of Agriculture, Arts, and Manufactures, part 1. 1792. New York.

Transactions of the Society for Promoting Agriculture in Connecticut. 1802. New Haven.

TRINCI, COSIMO. 1796. L'agricoltore sperimentato, 2 v. Venezia.

TUKE, ————, JR. General views of agriculture in the North Riding of Yorkshire: first report from the select committee on the cultivation and improvement of the waste, uninclosed, and unproductive lands of the Kingdom. 1795. Board of Agriculture, London.

TULL, JETHRO. 1762. The horse-hoeing husbandry. London.

Tupputi, Dominique. 1807. Réflexions succinctes sur l'état de l'agriculture, et de quelques autres parties de l'administration, dans le royaume de Naples. Paris.

Ure, David. 1797. General view of the agriculture of the county of Kinross. Board of Agriculture, London.

Valentin, L. 1807. Coup-d'oeil sur la culture de quelques végétaux exotiques, dans les départemens méridionaux de la France. Paris.

Vancouver, C. 1795. General views of agriculture in the county of Essex. Board of Agriculture, London.

Vettori, Piero. 1762. Trattato della coltivazione degli ulivi. Firenze.

Walpole, Horace. 1798. Aedes Walpolianae. Collected Works, ed. by Mary Berry. London.

Walter, Thomas. 1788. Flora Caroliniana. Londini.

Waterhouse, Benjamin. 1811. The botanist. Boston.

Watts, William. 1779. The seats of the nobility and gentry. Chelsea.

Whately, Thomas. 1770. Observations on modern gardening. London.

Young, Arthur. 1771. A course of experimental agriculture, 4 v. Dublin

———— 1771. The farmer's guide, in hiring and stocking farms, 2 v. Dublin.

———— 1773. Rural economy. London.

———— 1793. Travels in France, 1787–1789, 2 v. Dublin.

# BIBLIOGRAPHY

## MANUSCRIPTS

### Original Sources

*Carr-Cary Papers,* Alderman Memorial Library, University of Virginia. (Cited as *Carr-Cary Papers,* U. Va.)

*Jefferson Papers,* Alderman Memorial Library, University of Virginia. (Cited as *Jefferson Papers,* U. Va.)

*Jefferson Papers,* Henry E. Huntington Library and Art Gallery, San Marino, California. (Cited as *Jefferson Papers,* Huntington.)

*Jefferson Papers,* Historical Society of Pennsylvania. (Cited as *Jefferson Papers,* H. S. P.)

*Jefferson Papers,* Library of Congress. (Cited as *Jefferson Papers,* L. C.)

*Jefferson Papers,* Maryland Historical Society, Baltimore, Maryland. (Cited as *Jefferson Papers,* Maryland.)

*Jefferson Papers,* Massachusetts Historical Society. (Cited as *Jefferson Papers,* M. H. S.)

*Jefferson Papers,* Missouri Historical Society, St. Louis, Missouri. (Cited as *Jefferson Papers,* Missouri.)

*Jefferson Papers,* New York Public Library, New York City, New York.

*Jefferson Papers,* The Rosenbach Company, Philadelphia.

*Jefferson Papers,* Thomas Jefferson Memorial Foundation, *Monticello.*

*Jefferson Papers,* United States Department of Agriculture.

*Jefferson Papers,* Yale University, New Haven, Connecticut. (Cited as *Jefferson Papers,* Yale.)

The *Account Books* of Thomas Jefferson are located at the following institutions. There is a photostatic set of the entire group at the Alderman Memorial Library, University of Virginia.

Library of Congress:

1767–1770 (deposited by Brigadier General Jefferson R. Kean)
1773
1779–1782

Massachusetts Historical Society:

1771
1772
1774
1776–1778
1783–1790
1804–1808
1809–1820
1821–1826

Henry E. Huntington Library and Art Gallery:
1775

New York Public Library:
1791–1803

### LITERATURE

BAILEY, L. H. 1911. Sketch of the evolution of our native fruits. New York. (Cited as Bailey, *Fruits.*)
—— 1925. Manual of cultivated plants. New York.
—— 1927. The standard cyclopedia of horticulture, 3 v. New York.
—— and E. Z. BAILEY. 1930. Hortus. New York.
BETTS, EDWIN M., and HAZLEHURST B. PERKINS. 1941. Thomas Jefferson's flower garden at Monticello. Richmond.
BRITTON, NATHANIEL L., and ADDISON BROWN. 1896. An illustrated flora of the northern United States, Canada and the British possessions, 3 v. New York.
BULLOCK, HELEN DUPREY. 1941. The papers of Thomas Jefferson. *Am. Archivist* 4 (4).
BURR, FEARING, JR. 1863. The field and garden vegetables of America. Boston. (Cited as Burr, *Vegetables.*)
Calendar of the correspondence of Thomas Jefferson, part I, letters from Jefferson. 1894. Bureau of Rolls and Library, Department of State, no. 6. Washington.
Calendar of the correspondence of Thomas Jefferson, part II, letters to Jefferson. 1895. Bureau of Rolls and Library, Department of State, no. 8. Washington.
Calendar of the correspondence of Thomas Jefferson, part III, supplementary. 1903. Bureau of Rolls and Library, Department of State, no. 10. Washington.
Calendar of papers of Thomas Jefferson at the University of Virginia Library (2 typescript vols., University of Virginia Library).
CHASTELLUX, FRANÇOIS JEAN, MARQUIS DE. 1787. Travels in North-America in the years 1780, 1781, and 1782, 2 v. London.
CHINARD, GILBERT. 1924. Les amitiés américaines de Madame d'Houdetot. Paris.
—— 1927. Trois amitiés françaises de Jefferson. Paris.
—— 1939. Thomas Jefferson, the apostle of Americanism. Boston.
DARLINGTON, WILLIAM. 1865. American weeds and useful plants. New York.
Dictionary of national biography (63 v., with supplements). 1885–1930. New York.
DOWNING, A. J. 1846. The fruits and fruit trees of America. New York and Boston. (Cited as Downing, *Fruits.*)
Early history of the University of Virginia as contained in the letters of Thomas Jefferson and Joseph C. Cabell. 1856. Richmond. (Cited as *Jefferson and Cabell Letters.*)

FESSENDEN, THOMAS G. 1839. The new American gardener. Boston and Philadelphia.

FOLEY, JOHN P. 1900. The Jeffersonia cyclopedia. New York and London.

FORD, PAUL LEICESTER, ed. 1904–1905. The works of Thomas Jefferson, 12 v. New York. (Cited as Ford, *Jefferson.*)

FORD, WORTHINGTON CHAUNCEY, ed. 1916. Thomas Jefferson correspondence. Printed from the originals in the collection of William K. Bixby, Missouri Historical Society. Boston. (Cited as Ford, *Jefferson Correspondence.*)

GARLICK, RICHARD CECIL, JR. 1933. Philip Mazzei, friend of Jefferson, his life and letters. Baltimore. (Cited as Garlick, *Philip Mazzei.*)

HAMBIDGE, GOVE, ed. 1941. Climate and men, 1941 yearbook of agriculture. Washington.

HARSHBERGER, JOHN W. 1899. The botanists of Philadelphia and their work. Philadelphia.

HEDRICK, U. P. 1928. Peas of New York, part 1. Albany. (Cited as Hedrick, *Peas.*)

HENDERSON, PETER. 1881. Handbook of plants. New York.

HITT, THOMAS. 1754. A treatise of fruit trees. London.

HOVEY, C. M. 1853. The fruits of America. New York.

JEFFERSON, THOMAS. 1784. Notes on the State of Virginia. Paris.

——— 1787. Notes on the State of Virginia. London.

JENKINS, CHARLES FRANCIS. 1906. Jefferson's Germantown letters. Philadelphia. (Cited as Jenkins, *Jefferson's Letters.*)

JOHNSON, CUTHBERT. 1855. The farmer's and planter's encyclopedia. New York. (Cited as Johnson's *Farmer's Encylopedia.*)

KENDRICK, WILIAM. 1835. The new American orchardist. Boston.

KIMBALL, FISKE. [n. d.] Jefferson's grounds and gardens at Monticello. (Reprinted from *Landscape Architecture* for the Thomas Jefferson Memorial Foundation.)

——— 1916. Thomas Jefferson, architect. Boston.

KIMBALL, MARIE. 1943. Jefferson, the road to glory. New York.

LANMAN, CHARLES. 1876. Biographical annals of the civil government of the United States during its first century. Washington. (Cited as Lanman, *Biography.*)

LIPSCOMB, ANDREW A., and ALBERT ELLERY BERGH, eds. 1903. The writings of Thomas Jefferson, 20 v. (Cited as Lipscomb and Bergh, *Jefferson.*)

Massachusetts Historical Collection. 1900. The Jefferson Papers, Seventh series. Boston. (Cited as *Jefferson Papers,* M. H. C.)

MAYO, BERNARD. 1942. Thomas Jefferson and his unknown brother. Charlottesville.

McMAHON, BERNARD. 1806. The American gardener's calendar. Philadelphia.

MILLER, PHILIP. 1759. The gardener's dictionary. London.

MILNE, COLIN. 1805. Botanical dictionary. London.

Missouri Historical Society. 1936. Glimpses of the past, III, nos.

4–6, April–June.   Saint Louis.   (Cited as *Glimpses of the Past, Missouri.*)

PHILLIPS, HENRY.   1823.   Sylva florifera: the shrubbery.   London.

PIERSON, HAMILTON W.   1862.   Jefferson at Monticello.   New York.   (Cited as Pierson, *Monticello.*)

RAGAN, W. H.   1905.   Nomenclature of the apple.   Washington.

———   1908.   Nomenclature of the pear.   Washington.

RANDALL, HENRY S.   1858.   The life of Thomas Jefferson, 3 v.   New York.   (Cited as Randall, *Jefferson.*)

RANDOLPH, JOHN, JR.   1924.   A treatise on gardening (Marjorie F. Warner, ed.).   Richmond.   (Cited as Randolph, *Gardening.*)

RANDOLPH, SARAH N.   1871.   The domestic life of Thomas Jefferson.   New York.   (Cited as Randolph, *Jefferson.*)

RANDOLPH, THOMAS JEFFERSON.   1829.   Memoirs, correspondence, and private papers of Thomas Jefferson, 4 v.   London.

RAWLINGS, MARY.   1925.   The Albemarle of other days.   Charlottesville.

REED, C. A.   1926.   Nut-tree propagation.   *U. S. Dep. Agric., Farmer's Bull.* 1501.   Washington.

REHDER, ALFRED.   1927.   Manual of cultivated trees and shrubs.   New York.

ROBINSON, BENJAMIN L., and MERRITT L. FERNALD.   1908.   Gray's new manual of botany.   New York.

SADLER, ELIZABETH HATCHER.   1926.   The bloom of Monticello.   Richmond.

SMALL, JOHN K.   1933.   Manual of the Southeastern flora.   New York.

SMITH, MARGARET BAYARD.   1906.   The first forty years of Washington society.   (Gaillard Hunt, ed.)   New York.

STEVENSON, ———.   1764.   The gentlemen gardener.   London.

SWEM, E. G.   1934.   Virginia historical index, 2 v.   Roanoke.

THOMAS, JOSEPH.   1930.   Universal pronouncing dictionary of biography and mythology.   Philadelphia.   (Cited as Lippincott's *Pronouncing Dictionary.*)

TUCKER, GEORGE.   1837.   The life of Thomas Jefferson, 2 v.   London.

TYLER, LYON G.   1915.   Encyclopedia of Virginia biography, 3 v.   New York.   (Cited as Tyler, *Virginia Biography.*)

WARD, JAMES EDWARD, JR.   Thomas Jefferson's contribution to American agriculture (a dissertation presented to the Graduate Faculty of the University of Virginia in candidacy for the degree of Doctor of Philosophy).

WASHINGTON, HENRY A., ed.   1853–1854.   The writings of Thomas Jefferson, 9 v.   New York and Washington.

WATSON, ALEXANDER.   1865.   The American home garden.   New York.   (Cited as Watson, *Garden.*)

WHATELY, THOMAS.   1770.   Observations on modern gardening.   London.

WOODS, EDGAR.   1901.   History of Albemarle County in Virginia.   Charlottesville.   (Cited as Woods, *Albemarle County.*)

# INDEX

Carriages, 538

Carro, Dr., 381

*Carrossa* (ship), 133

Carrot, 48, 49, 55, 59, 75, 208, 224, 360, 386, 410, 442, 469, 472, 473, 493, 495, 496, 498, 500, 506, 522, 523, 525, 536, 550, 564, 570, 576, 582, 588, 593, 599, 606, 607, 610, 613, 639, 648; early, 470; large, 470; orange, 389, 390, 470, 471; yellow, 443

Carter, Charles, 159–160

Carter, John C., letter from Jefferson, 544

Carter, W. Champe, 521

Carter's Mountain, Va., 81, 160

Carters, 229

Cartersville, Va., 497

Caruthers, William, 488; letter from Jefferson, 507

Cary, Anne (Edwards), 59

Cary, Col. Archibald, 48–49, 59

Cary, Henry, 57

Cary, Richard, 121; letters from Jefferson, 115, 116, 129

Cary, Wilson Miles, 504

*Carya laciniosa,* 399; *pecan,* 215

*Carysbrook,* Fluvanna County, Va., 396, 497, 504

Cascades, 113

Case, Leonard, 617; letter from Jefferson, 618

Caspian Sea, 321

Cassava, 645

*Cassia ligustrina,* 644

Cassine, 23, 27

Cassioberry, 23, 27

*Castanea dentata,* 43; *pumila,* 30; *sativa,* 43, 455, 519

*Castle Hill,* Albemarle County, Va., 174

Castles, 113

Castor-oil plant, 450

Catachu, 621

Catalogues, agricultural, 567; Jefferson's library, 541, 655–662; plant, 167, 531; seed, 285, 379

Catalpa, 638, 646

*Catalpa,* 23, 27, 261, 280, 284, 288; *bignonioides,* 31

Catchfly, 9

Caterpillars, 320–321

Catesby, Mark, 140

Cathalan, Stephen, 138, 143, 147, 162, 177, 179; letters from Jefferson, 132, 140, 152, 180, 296, 349; letter to Jefferson, 135

Cathalan, Stephen, Jr., letter from Jefferson, 160

Catlet, Mr., 235

Cato, Marcus Porcius, 567

Cattle, 194, 242–245, 467, 531, 544, 559, 561, 562, 586

Cauliflower, 5, 117, 208, 224, 302, 418, 443, 469, 470, 474, 615, 639; Dutch hard, 635; early, 388, 442; English hard, 635

*Caversham,* England, 112

*Cawsons,* Prince George County, Va., 59

Ceanothus, flowering, 23

*Ceanothus,* 27; *americanus,* 30, 110, 116

Cedar, 25, 189, 261, 558, 559, 633, 635–637, 647; dwarf, 345; red, 31, 280, 637

Cedar of Lebanon, 333, 384, 431, 453, 475, 476, 479, 480, 491, 621

*Cedrus libani,* 306, 333, 479

Celery, 4, 5, 8, 24, 33, 36, 49, 60, 191, 386, 391, 410, 469, 470, 473, 495, 498–500, 522, 550, 564, 588, 593, 607, 615, 639; red, 389, 409; solid, 49, 208, 224, 389, 442, 550

Cellars, 16

*Celosia argentea,* 8

Cement, 541; hydraulic, 600, 603; Roman, 583, 586–587, 595, 603

Cemetery. *See* Burying ground

*Centaurea macrocephala,* 489

Central College. *See* Virginia, University of

*Cerasus,* 23, 27

*Cercis canadensis,* 31, 646

Cereals, 609

*Ceres* (ship), 104

Cevennes Mountains, France, 128

Chain, 549

Chair, one-horse, 3

Chambers, J., 463, 503; letters from Jefferson, 462, 506; letter to Jefferson, 461

Champagne, France, 277, 279

Chapel Branch, Va., 79

Charcoal, 326, 327, 347, 356, 369, 371, 466

Charles City County, Va., 22, 28, 35

Charles City Court House, Va., 20

Charleston, S. C., 107, 108, 177, 180

Charleston, W. Va., 390

Charlottesville, Va., 60, 68, 84, 102, 159–160, 174, 183, 240, 244, 248, 294, 325, 542–543, 565

Chastellux, François Jean, Marquis de, 96

Chaste-tree, 333

Chatham, William Pitt, Earl of, 114

*Chelsea,* King William County, Va., 10, 12, 20

Chemistry, 289, 380

Cherokee Indians, 130

Furnaces, iron, 410
Furniture, 184, 205, 206
Furze, 208, 361

Gaines, Hieron, 326
Gaines, Humphrey, 71, 74
Gaines, Richard, 93
Gale, Levin, letter from Jefferson, 557; letter to Jefferson, 557
*Galium mollugo,* 450; *spurium,* 644
Gallatin, Albert, 351; letters from Jefferson, 63, 343, 552, 573, 600
Gallipolis, Ohio, 429
Gamble, Col. Richard (Jefferson's mistake for Robert), 233; letter from Jefferson, 296
Game refuge, 27
Garavances, 527, 532, 613; Texas, 523
Garbanzo, 527
Garden books, Jefferson's, 19, 110
Garden calendars, Jefferson's, 388–393, 399, 420–426, 442–444, 470–476, 495–500, 522–525, 536–537, 550–551, 564–565, 576, 582–583, 588–589, 593–594, 599, 606, 610; Jefferson's notes for, 515–516
Gardeners, 25, 144, 177, 273, 288, 290, 365, 376, 418, 423, 506; French, 138; Italian, 203, 204; Scotch, 285
*Gardener's Dictionary, The,* 19, 58, 140, 234, 371, 372
*Gardenia,* 139, 140
Gardening, books on, 303, 352, 636, 655–662
Garden plans, 25, 208, 212, 335
Gardens, 2, 50, 57, 60, 61, 73, 83, 98, 104, 110, 132, 293, 297, 307, 329, 347, 350, 356, 357, 363–365, 396, 411, 426, 469–472; botanical, 60, 401, 450, 478, 492, 520, 547, 554, 559, 578; English, 110–114, 323–324; of King of France, 105; kitchen, 112, 114, 284, 307, 337; National Garden of France, 378–379, 383, 440, 455, 456, 490, 504, 507, 513, 547, 559, 578; prisoners', 87–88
Garland, James, 88
Garlic, 47, 58, 208, 224, 469, 473, 477, 498, 499
Garth, Thomas, 71, 74, 88, 149
Gates, 78, 635
Geese, 46, 94, 408, 419
*Gelsemium sempervirens,* 31, 429
Gelston, David, letters from Jefferson, 531, 614; letters to Jefferson, 532, 554
Genet, Edmond Charles, 185
Geneva, Switzerland, 429
*Genista juncea,* 446
Genoa, Italy, 124, 128
Gentian, 645

Gentry, John, 312
Geography, 301, 332, 412, 531
Georgetown, Md., 255, 313, 545
Georgia, 117–118, 120–121, 123, 134, 143–144, 381, 412, 505, 556, 604; University of, 293
Geranium, 283, 354, 382–383, 406
*Geranium gibbosum,* 109, 116; *maculatum,* 109, 116
Germany, 139, 403
Gerry, Elbridge, 3, 476; letter from Jefferson, 488
Gherkin, 469, 471, 473, 496, 498, 499, 503, 516, 523, 599, 606, 607, 610
*Ghibeba mellimeni,* 423
Giannini, Anthony, 81, 278, 279, 283; letter from Jefferson, 632
Gibbon, Major, 603
Gibson, Patrick, letters from Jefferson, 302, 482
Gibson & Jefferson, 456, 467, 484, 514; letter from Jefferson, 295
Giles, William B., letters from Jefferson, 235, 248
Gilliam (Gillam, Gillum), William, 34, 38, 235, 248
Gilliflower, 24, 27; royal, 635
Gilmer, Mr., 310, 519
Gilmer, Mrs., 310
Gilmer, Francis Walker, letter to Jefferson, 574
Gilmer, Dr. George, 57; letter from Jefferson, 178
Gilmer, Harmer, 480, 490
Gilmore, Robert, & Co., letter from Jefferson, 162
*Ginkgo biloba,* 321
Ginseng, 645
Giovannini, 203, 204, 493
Giroud, Mr., letter from Jefferson, 256
*Gladiolus communis,* 488
Glasgow, Scotland, 25
*Glaucium,* 335
*Gleditsia,* 146, 646; *triacanthos,* 110, 115, 150
Gloucester County, Va., 401, 406, 445
Gloucester Court House, Va., 410
Godon, Mr., 370
Gold of pleasure, 433
Golden chain tree, 449
Goldenrod, anise-seed, 303; sweet-scented, 303
Goldy-lock, 24, 27
*Gomphrena globosa,* 8
Gooch, W., 239
Goochland County, Va., 27, 37, 252
Goodman, Charles, 81
Goodman, Mrs. J. A., 466
Goodman, Jeremiah, 442, 448, 464–467, 477, 487–488, 492–493, 517–518, 539–

686 INDEX

Lentil, 386, 583, 584, 613; green, 49, 60; large, 523; small, 49, 60, 523
Leontodon taraxacum, 162
Lepidium sativum, 58, 74
Leroy & Bayard, letter from Jefferson, 561
Leslie, Robert, 158
Lettuce, 4, 5, 47, 48, 56, 65, 70, 71, 77, 83, 209, 228, 442, 465 469, 473, 474, 482, 488, 493, 495, 496, 498, 500, 506, 514, 523, 533, 543, 606, 607, 613, 639; Berlin, 634; brown, 610, 611; cabbage, 208, 213, 399; cos, 64, 208, 213; Dutch brown, 391, 393, 444, 472, 495, 522, 550, 576, 594, 599, 601, 606, 610; endive-leaved, 634; forward, 634; green, 224; ice, 55, 64, 388–393, 541, 550, 564, 582, 583, 593, 599, 610, 611; loaf, 224, 391, 442, 443, 470, 472, 541; long-leaved, 208, 213; Marseilles, 388, 393; radish, 442; Roman, 295; Silesia, 583; summer, 634; tennis ball, 388–392, 443, 444, 582, 583, 599, 601; white, 444, 471, 472, 496, 522, 536, 550, 564, 565, 582, 588, 593, 599, 610, 611; winter, 564, 634
Levantine Empire, 118
Lewis, Mrs., 336, 353
Lewis, James, letter from Jefferson, 379
Lewis, Jane (Meriwether), 19
Lewis, Mary (Walker), 19, 363, 426, 443, 497
Lewis, Meriwether, 281–282, 285, 292, 294, 307, 309, 315, 328, 332, 335–337, 340, 343–345, 360, 363, 369, 373, 403, 407, 418, 422, 428, 430, 440, 481, 513, 520, 531, 637; letters from Jefferson, 311, 376
Lewis, Nicholas, 16, 19, 22, 57, 74, 87, 88, 89, 103, 136, 149, 155, 166, 169, 220, 230, 233, 237, 293, 366, 376, 430, 632, 633; letters from Jefferson, 118, 124, 130, 137, 151, 152, 176
Lewis, Robert, 19
Lewis and Clark expedition, 311, 314, 373, 418, 428, 431, 520, 521, 531, 568, 637
Lewis's Ferry, Va., 30
Lewis's River, Idaho, 336
Lexington, Ky., 503
Liatris elegans, 303
Libraries, agricultural, 567
Library of Congress, 526, 538, 541
Liburnum. See Laburnum
Lieb, Dr., 407
Lilac, 4, 23, 27, 161, 165, 176, 208, 216, 394, 494, 556, 563, 579, 627; blue, 369; Persian, 31; white, 369

Lilium, 31; canadense, 109, 115; candidum, 99; chalcedonicum, 99; convallarium, 406; superbum, 481
Lilly, Gabriel, 274, 278, 283, 286, 295, 299, 302, 303, 329
Lily, 5, 24, 27, 31, 337, 455, 474, 562; belladonna, 117, 447, 491; Canada, 633; Columbian, 335, 353; fiery, 94; madonna, 99; scarlet, 99; white, 94
Lily-of-the-valley, 24, 27, 382
Lime, 34, 36, 371, 646
Limestone, 23, 29, 34, 36, 173
Lime tree, 417
Limozin, Andrew, 132, 137, 140; letters from Jefferson, 121, 130, 133, 135, 136
Linden, 636, 646
Lindsay, Mr., 304, 487
Linnaeus, Carolus, 19, 109, 110, 115, 117, 172, 275, 527–530, 619, 645
Linnaeus, Carolus, fils, 109, 115
Linum usitatissimum, 89; virginianum, 647
Lions, 170
Liquidambar styraciflua, 110, 115, 647
Liquor, 46, 229
Liriodendron, 150, 494; tulipifera, 110, 139, 140, 147, 284, 288, 305, 339, 646
Liverpool, England, 569
Livingston, Edward, letter from Jefferson, 616
Livingston, Robert R., 289; letters from Jefferson, 271, 361
Livorno, Italy. See Leghorn
Lobelia, 353, 644; cardinalis, 335
Locust (tree), 23, 27, 201, 377, 579, 623, 627, 636, 646; common, 494, 633; honey, 559, 633, 635, 646; Kentucky, 422, 494, 556, 563; prickly, 568, 637; red, 355; yellow-flowered, 118
Locusts (insects), 68
Logan, Dr. George, 187, 188, 199, 200; letter from Jefferson, 196
Log houses, 357, 378
Lolium perenne, 478
Lomax, Mrs. Judith, 524, 527; letter to Jefferson, 519
Lomax, Thomas, 380, 382, 387, 398, 421, 428, 475, 478, 527; letters from Jefferson, 403, 417; letter to Jefferson, 416
Lombardy, Italy, 123–126
Long, Dr., 617
Lonicera, 146, 214; alpigena, 424, 430; sempervirens, 31, 646
Looming, 85
Looms, 479, 505
L'Orient, France, 109, 121, 288, 289
Loudoun County, Va., 286